PSYCHOTHERAPY RESEARCH

An International Review
of Programmatic Studies

Edited by

Larry E. Beutler
Marjorie Crago

American Psychological Association
Washington, DC

Published by
The American Psychological Association
1200 Seventeenth Street, NW
Washington, DC 20036

Copies may be ordered from
APA Order Department
P.O. Box 2710
Hyattsville, MD 20784.

This book was typeset in Century Schoolbook by BG Composition, Baltimore, MD.

Printer: Patterson Printing, Benton Harbor, MI
Cover designer: Debra E. Riffe
Copy editor: Lisa McCullough
Production coordinator: Christine P. Landry

Library of Congress Cataloging-in-Publication Data
Psychotherapy research : an international review of programmatic
    studies / edited by Larry E. Beutler and Marjorie Crago.
        p.   cm.
    Includes bibliographical references.
    ISBN 1-55798-090-X
    1. Psychotherapy—Research.   I. Beutler, Larry E.   II. Crago,
Marjorie.
    [DNLM: 1. Psychotherapy. 2. Research—Europe. 3. Research—
United States.   WM 420 P975825]
RC337.P768   1991
616.89′14′072—dc20
DNLM/DLC
for Library of Congress   91-4544
                                                                CIP

Printed in the United States of America.
First edition

Contents

Section III   Small-Scale and Developing Programs   261

Preface

Psychotherapy research has traditionally been a "cottage industry" because the lack of tangible and marketable technology arising from it has led the field to be neglected by private funding agencies. At the same time, because its concepts seem elusive, many varieties of psychotherapy that are of interest to the practitioner have been identified for government funding purposes under one specific label, *psychosocial interventions.* In the midst of this uncertain attention, psychotherapy research has strangely flourished. This proliferation reveals the intrigue that the processes and theories of psychotherapy hold for both the research scientist and the public.

In 1968, such interest among a small group of researchers stimulated the organization of the Society for Psychotherapy Research (SPR). In the ensuing years, the organization has expanded to 26 countries, representing more than 1,000 members. This membership has been divided into three formal geographic areas: continental Europe, the United Kingdom, and North America.

The visibility provided by a large and active organization has brought increased recognition for psychotherapy research among government funding agencies in many countries. There has been an active sharing of research findings, and many fledgling and struggling research programs have benefited from becoming acquainted with the methods and findings of larger programs. In many cases, this has resulted in the sharing of research instruments, data, and resources. In turn, through the growth of collaboration among sites and countries, research has benefited from this cross-fertilization by becoming increasingly sophisticated.

This book is designed to further the movement toward research collaboration and enhanced communication among research centers and to communicate the diverse nature of psychotherapy research. It was published under the auspices of the SPR and represents the work of many members of that organization. The reader of these chapters will see that a great deal of diversity exists among centers in both the nature of the questions addressed and the methods used to explore these questions. We believe that this diversity is healthy if it serves to stimulate debate and sharing.

We have chosen to present a wide range of research programs that we believe samples the variety represented internationally. We have also chosen to present these descriptions without substantial comment or criticism in the hope that doing so will stimulate wider discussion, debate, and (ultimately) collaboration. We hope that the book will serve to stimulate research interest among students in the mental health sciences and will portray the variety and intensity of interest in this area of research worldwide. In addition, we hope that this portrayal will provide some incentive for the development of new sources of funding and foster new directions of investigation.

We have specifically elected against the usual convention of arranging chapters by subject population or topical focus. We believe that imposing such structure would not do justice to the cross-cutting nature of the research objectives in most programs. Rather, we chose to organize the book first by the size of the program and second by broad regional boundaries (North America and Europe). This latter division is especially arbitrary and underlines the omission of research in the Far East, in Central and South America, in the Middle East, and in Africa. It should be stated, however, that efforts were made to learn of and to invite contributors who are doing psychotherapy research around the world. Our failure to do so may represent the relative absence of research in these regions or simply the lack of cross-cultural sharing that currently exists. Certainly it is interesting that neither we nor our colleagues were able to gain much knowledge of research in these regions.

In recruiting contributors to this book, we invited two types of submissions: large-scale programs and small-scale and developing programs. We defined large-scale programs as those in which there is

• an organized structure for coordination of the research program in the institution,

• a minimum of three doctoral-level faculty or staff members (not students) who are integrally involved in the research program,

• a record of previously published research from the program in refereed journals of at least 5 years' duration,

• a commitment by the institution for continuous financial support of the program.

In imposing these restrictions, we hoped to portray those programs that do not depend exclusively on a single researcher and are likely to remain active for the foreseeable future. Small-scale and developing programs were defined as those that met three of these four criteria. The programs described under this label tend to have smaller research staffs or to lack the organizing structure that is present in the larger programs. Although we allowed more space for large-scale programs, we asked that all submissions contain the following information:

• aims and history of the program,

• major research methods employed,

• major research contributions and accomplishments,

• a description of research in progress,

• a description of probable future directions,

• an outline of the research organization,

• current efforts at interprogram collaboration.

We have included an introductory chapter to acquaint the reader with the many issues that confront the psychotherapy researcher. We have also provided a concluding chapter to discuss commonalities and shared findings among programs, to highlight some of the methodological differences, and to reaffirm the advantages of programmatic research.

In compiling this book, we are indebted to many individuals. Most notably, the contributors kindly elected to forego honoraria in recognition of the supportive affiliations within SPR and so that the SPR could direct a share of revenues to support student research and student travel. We are also grateful to all of our colleagues in SPR; to Carol Fathera, who provided secretarial assistance; to Paulo P. P. Machado, who helped with editing; and to our colleagues at the University of California, Santa Barbara, and at the University of Arizona. During a portion of this work, Larry E. Beutler served as a visiting scholar in the Department of Psychology at Memphis State University, where the faculty and environment were very supportive. Finally, portions of this work were made possible by National Institute of Mental Health Grant MH-39859 to Larry E. Beutler.

Contributors

Frans A. Albersnagel, Klinische Psychologie, Academisch Ziekenhuis, Oestersingel 59, 9713 EZ Groningen, the Netherlands.

Jon E. Allen, PhD, C. F. Menninger Memorial Hospital, Department of Psychology, Box 829, Topeka, KS 66601.

Timothy M. Anderson, Department of Psychology, Miami University, Oxford, OH 45026.

Bengt Å. Armelius, PhD, Applied Psychology, University of Umeå, 901 87 Umeå, Sweden.

Hassan F. A. Azim, MB, Department of Psychiatry, Faculty of Medicine 1 E 1.01 Mackenzie Centre, University of Alberta, Edmonton, Alberta, Canada T6G 2B7.

Anthony Badalamenti, PhD, Nathan S. Kline Institute for Psychiatric Research, Building 37, Orangeburg Road, Orangeburg, NY 10962.

Elizabeth Bankoff, PhD, Department of Psychology, Northwestern University, Evanston, IL 60201.

Jacques Barber, PhD, University of Pennsylvania, Hospital of the University of Pennsylvania, 309 Piersol Building, 3400 Spruce Street, Philadelphia, PA 19104-4283.

Michael Barkham, PhD, University of Sheffield, MRC/ESRC Social & Applied Psychology, Sheffield S102TN England.

David Barlow, PhD, Department of Psychology, State University of New York, Albany, NY 12203

B. Berckhan, Universität Hamburg, Fachbereich Erziehungswissenschaften (06), Von-Melle-Park 8, W-2000 Hamburg 13, Federal Republic of Germany.

Jeffrey S. Berman, PhD, Department of Psychology, Memphis State University, Memphis, TN 38152.

Edward M. Bernat, 2808 N. Fontana, Tucson, AZ 85705.

Larry E. Beutler, PhD, ABPP, Graduate School of Education, University of California, Santa Barbara, CA 93106.

Susan Blumberg, MA, University of Denver, 2460 S. Vine Street, Denver, CO 80202.

Simon H. Budman, PhD, Harvard Community Health Plan, Management Office, One Fenway Plaza, Boston, MA 02215.

Roseann Cardella, PsyD, Illinois School of Professional Psychology, One Quincy Court, 220 South State Street, Chicago, IL 60604.

John E. Carr, PhD, University of Washington, School of Medicine, Department of Psychiatry and Behavioral Sciences, RP-10, Seattle, WA 98195.

John Clarkin, PhD, Department of Psychology, New York Hospital, Cornell Medical Center, 21 Bloomingdale Road, White Plains, NY 10605.

Donald B. Colson, PhD, Director of Psychology, C. F. Menninger Memorial Hospital, Box 829, Topeka, KS 66601.

Lolafaye Coyne, PhD, C. F. Menninger Memorial Hospital, Box 829, Topeka, KS 66601.

Marjorie Crago, PhD, Department of Psychiatry, Arizona Health Sciences Center, Tucson, AZ 85724.

Paul Crits-Christoph, PhD, University of Pennsylvania, Department of Psychiatry, Hospital of the University of Pennsylvania, 309 Piersol Building, 3400 Spruce Street, Philadelphia, PA 19104-4283.

John T. Curtis, PhD, Department of Psychiatry, Mount Zion Hospital, Box 7921, San Francisco, CA 94120.

Dietmar Czogalik, PhD, Forschungsstelle für Psychotherapie, Christian-Beiser-Strabe 79a, W-D-7000 Stuttgart 70, Federal Republic of Germany.

Christine V. Davidson, PhD, Department of Psychiatry and Behavioral Science, Northwestern University Medical School, Evanston, IL 60201.

Alice Dazord, MD, PhD, SCRIPT-INSERM, Hospital Saint Jean de Dieu, 290 Route de Vienne, 69 008 Lyon, France.

Judith C. Dean, PhD, Psychiatry Department, College of Medicine, University of Arizona, 1501 North Campbell, Tucson, AZ 85724.

Annette Demby, MSW, Harvard Community Health Plan, Management Offices, One Fenway Plaza, Boston, MA 02215.

Robert Elliott, PhD, Department of Psychology, University of Toledo, Toledo, OH 43606.

Paul M. G. Emmelkamp, PhD, Klinische Psychologie, Academisch Ziekenhuis, Oestersingel 59, 9713 EZ Groningen, the Netherlands.

David Engle, PhD, Department of Psychiatry/College of Medicine, Unviersity of Arizona, Tucson, AZ 85724.

Frank J. Floyd, PhD, University of Denver, 2460 S. Vine Street, Denver, CO 80202.

Siebolt H. Frieswyk, PhD, Karl Menninger School of Psychiatry, Box 829, Topeka, KS 66601.

Richard Fritsch, PhD, Chestnut Lodge Research Institute, 500 W. Montgomery Avenue, Rockville, MD 20850.

Glen O. Gabbard, MD, Director, C. F. Menninger Memorial Hospital, Box 829, Topeka, KS 66601.

Paul M. Gedo, PhD, Chestnut Lodge Research Institute, 500 W. Montogmery Avenue, Rockville, MD 20850.

Paul Gerin, MD, SCRIPT-INSERM, Hospital Saint Jean de Dieu, 290 Route de Vienne, 69 008 Lyon, France.

Michael Geyer, MD, Karl-Marx-Universität Leipzig, Abt für Psychotherapie, Karl-Tauchnitz-Strabe 25, O-DDR 7010 Leipzig, Federal Republic of Germany.

Wells Goodrich, MD, Chestnut Lodge Research Institute, 500 W. Montgomery Avenue, Rockville, MD 20850.

T. Grande, PhD, Ruprecht-Karls-Universität Heidelberg, Psychosomatische Klinik, W-6900 Heidelbert 1, den Thibautstrabe 2, Federal Republic of Germany.

Klaus Grawe, PhD, University of Berne, Institute of Psychology, Gezellschaftsstrasse 49, CH 3012 Berne, Switzerland.

Leslie S. Greenberg, PhD, York University, 4700 Keele Street, North York, Ontario, Canada M3J1P3.

Kurt Hahlweg, PhD, B. Berckhan, Universität Hamburg, Fachbereich Erziehungswissenschaften (06), Von-Melle-Park 8, W-2000 Hamburg 13, Federal Republic of Germany.

Sarah A. Hall, University of California, Department of Psychology, Berkeley, CA 94720.

Gillian E. Hardy, University of Sheffield, MRC/ESRC Social & Applied Psychology, Sheffield S102TN England.

Heather Harper, University of Sheffield, MRC/ESRC Social & Applied Psychology, Sheffield S102TN England.

William P. Henry, PhD, Center for Psychotherapy Research, Vanderbilt University, Nashville, TN 37240.

Clara C. Hill, PhD, Department of Psychology, University of Maryland, College Park, MD 20742.

Mardi J. Horowitz, MD, University of California, Department of Psychiatry & Langley Porter Psychiatric Institute, 401 Parnassus Avenue, San Francisco, CA 94143.

Leonard M. Horowitz, PhD, Psychology Department, Stanford University, Stanford, CA 94305.

Leonard Horwitz, PhD, C. F. Menninger Memorial Hospital, Department of Psychology, Box 829, Topeka, KS 66601.

Arthur C. Houts, PhD, Department of Psychology, Memphis State University, Memphis, TN 38152.

Kenneth I. Howard, PhD, Department of Psychology, Northwestern University, Evanston, IL 60201.

Neil S. Jacobson, PhD, 2456 4th Avenue West, Seattle, WA 98119.

Robin B. Jarrett, PhD, University of Texas, Southwestern Medical School, 5323 Harry Hines Blvd., Dallas, TX 75235-9070.

John Jochem, PsyD, Illinois School of Professional Psychology, One Quincy Court/220 South State Street, Chicago, IL 60604.

Enrico E. Jones, PhD, University of California, Berkeley, CA 94720.

Anthony S. Joyce, Department of Psychiatry, Faculty of Medicine, IE 1.01 MacKenzie Centre, University of Alberta, Edmonton, Alberta, Canada T6G 2B7.

Horst Kächele, MD, am Hochstresse 8. Universität Ulm, W-D-7900 Ulm/Donau, Federal Republic of Germany.

Mary Kadlec, Illinois School of Professional Psychology, One Quincy Court/220 South State Street, Chicago, IL 60604.

Nick Kanas, MD, Verterans Administration Medical Center, 4150 Clement Street, San Francisco, CA 94121.

Ellen Klass, PhD, Hunter College of the City University of New York, Department of Psychology, 695 Park Avenue, New York, NY 10021.

Gerald Klerman, Cornell University Medical College, 525 East 68th Street, New York, NY 10021.

C. Krause, Universität Hamburg, Fachbereich Erziehungswissenschaften (06), Von-Melle-Park 8, W-2000 Hamburg 13, Federal Republic of Germany.

William Kurtines, PhD, University of Miami, Department of Psychiatry, School of Medicine, 1425 N.W. 10th Avenue, Suite 302, Miami, FL 33136.

Michael J. Lambert, PhD, Brigham Young University, Provo, UT 84601.

Robert Langs, MD, Nathan S. Kline Institute for Psychiatric Research, Building 37, Orangeburg Road, Orangeburg, NY 10962.

Lester Luborsky, PhD, University of Pennsylvania, Department of Psychiatry, Hospital of the University of Pennsylvania, 3400 Spruce Street, Philadelphia, PA 19104-4283.

Paulo P. P. Machado, MA, Graduate School of Education, University of California, Santa Barbara, CA 93106.

Gayle Mann, Illinois School of Professional Psychology, One Quincy Court/220 South State Street, Chicago, IL 60604.

Howard S. Markman, PhD, Director of the Center for Marital and Family Studies, University of Denver, 2460 S. Vine Street, Denver, CO 80203.

Peter E. Maxim, MD, PhD, University of Washington, School of Medicine, Department of Psychiatry and Behavioral Sciences, RP-10, Seattle, WA 98195.

Mary McCallum, PhD, Department of Psychiatry, Faculty of Medicine, 1E 1.01 Mackenzie Centre, University of Alberta, Edmonton, Alberta, Canada T6G 2B7.

Leigh McCullough, PhD, Beth Israel Medical Center, Bernstein Pavilion, 2nd Floor, 10 Nathan D. Perlman Road, New York, NY 10003.

Thomas H. McGlashan, MD, Yale Psychiatric Institute, P.O. Box 12A, Yale Station, New Haven, CT 06520.

Erhard Mergenthaler, PhD, am Hochstrasse 8, Universität Ulm, W-D-7900 Ulm/Donau, Federal Republic of Germany.

Christopher M. Meshot, Department of Psychology, Miami University, Oxford, OH 45058.

Adolph-Ernst Meyer, MD, Freie Und Hansestadt Hamburg, Universitäts-Krankenhaus, Eppendorf, II. Medizinische Univ.-Klinik, Psychosomatische Abteilung, W-1 Hamburg 20 Martinistr. 52, Federal Republic of Germany.

Andrew W. Meyers, PhD, Department of Psychology, Memphis State University, Memphis, TN 38152.

David C. Mohr, Veteran's Administration Hospital, Psychology (116B), 3801 Miranda Avenue, Palo Alto, CA 94304.

Leslie A. Morrison, MA, University of Sheffield, MRC/ESRC Social & Applied Psychology, Sheffield S102TN England.

Robert Neimeyer, PhD, Department of Psychology, Memphis State University, Memphis, TN 38152.

Gavin E. Newsom, Director, Social Work, C. F. Menninger Memorial Hospital, Box 829, Topeka, KS 66601.

Michael T. O'Mahoney, PhD, Department of Psychiatry and Behavioral Science, Northwestern University Medical School, Northwestern University, Evanston, IL 60201.

David E. Orlinsky, PhD, Committee on Human Development, University of Chicago, Chicago, IL 60637.

Lesley A. Parke, Department of Psychology, University of California, Berkeley, CA 94720.

E. Lakin Phillips, PhD, George Washington University, 718 21st Street, NW, Bldg. N, Washington, DC 20052.

William E. Piper, PhD, Department of Psychiatry, Faculty of Medicine, 1E 1.01 Mackenzie Centre, University of Alberta, Edmonton, Alberta, Canada T6G 2B7.

Günter Plöttner, Director of Medicine, Karl-Marx-Universität Leipzig, Abt. für Psychotherapie, Karl-Tauchnitz-Strabe 25, O-DDr 7010 Leipzig, Federal Republic of Germany.

David L. Reinnie, PhD, York University, 4700 Keele Street, North York, Ontario, Canada M3J1P3.

Shirley Reynolds, University of Sheffield, MRC/ESRC Social & Applied Psychology, Sheffield, S102TN England.

Laura N. Rice, PhD, York University, 4700 Keele Street, North York, Ontario, Canada M3J1P3.

Arturo Rio, PhD, Department of Psychiatry/School of Medicine, 1425 N.W. 10th Avenue, Suite 302, Miami, FL 33136.

U. Röder, Universität Hamburg, Fachbereich Erziehungswissenschaften (06), Von-Melle-Park 8, W-2000 Hamburg 13, Federal Republic of Germany.

Saul E. Rosenberg, PhD, 838 Mandana Blvd., Oakland, CA 94610.

Bonnie Rudolph, PhD, Illinois School of Professional Psychology, One Quincy Court/220 South State Street, Chicago, IL 60604.

Gerd Rudolph, PhD, Ruprecht-Karis-Universität Heidelberg, Psychosomatische Klinik, W-6900 Heidelbert 1, den Thibautstrabe 1, Federal Republic of Germany.

Harold Sampson, PhD, Mt. Zion Hospital, Department of Psychiatry, Box 7921, San Francisco, CA 94115.

Stephen M. Saunders, PhD, Department of Psychology, Northwestern University, Evanston, IL 60208.

B. Schenk, Universität Hamburg, Fachbereich Erziehungswissenschaften (06), Von-Melle-Park 8, W-2000 Hamburg 13, Federal Republic of Germany.

U. Schütze, Universität Hamburg, Fachbereich Erziehungswissenschaften (06), Von-Melle-Park 8, W-2000 Hamburg 13, Federal Republic of Germany.

William R. Shadish, Jr., PhD, Department of Psychology, Memphis State University, Memphis, TN 38152.

David A. Shapiro, PhD, University of Sheffield, MRC/ESRC Social & Applied Psychology, Sheffield, S102TN England.

Varda Shoham-Salomon, PhD, Department of Psychology, University of Arizona, Tucson, AZ 85721.

George Silberschatz, PhD, Mount Zion Hospital, Box 7921, San Francisco, CA 94120.

William W. Sloan, Jr., PhD, Department of Psychology, Miami University, Oxford, OH 45056.

Ellen Somberg, Illinois School of Professional Psychology, One Quincy Court/220 South State Street, Chicago, IL 60604.

Scott M. Stanley, PhD, Center for Marital and Family Studies, University of Denver, 2460 S. Vine Street, Denver, CO 80202.

Mike Startup, PhD, University of Sheffield, MRC/ESRC Social & Applied Psychology, Sheffield S102TN England.

William B. Stiles, PhD, Department of Psychology, Miami University, Oxford, OH 45056.

Charles H. Stinson, MD, University of California, Department of Psychiatry & Langley Porter Psychiatric Institute, 401 Parnassus Avenue, San Francisco, CA 94143.

Mark Stone, PhD, Illinois School of Professional Psychology, One Quincy Court/220 South State Street, Chicago, IL 60604.

Hans H. Strupp, PhD, Vanderbilt University, A & S Department of Psychology, Nashville, TN 37203.

Ulrich Stuhr, PhD, Freie Und Hansestadt Hamburg, Universitäts-Krankenhaus, Eppendorf, II. Medizinische Univ. Klinik, Psychosomatische Abteilung, W-2 Hamburg 20 Martinistr. 52, Federal Republic of Germany.

José Szapocznik, PhD, University of Miami, Department of Psychiatry, School of Medicine, 1425 N.W. 10th Avenue, Suite 302, Miami, FL 33136.

Shaké G. Toukmanian, PhD, York University, 4700 Keel Street, North York, Ontario, Canada M3J1P3.

A. C. Wagner, Universität Hamburg, Fachbereich Erziehungswissenschaften (06), Von-Melle-Park 8, W-2000 Hamburg 13, Federal Republic of Germany.

Holly Weems, Illinois School of Professional Psychology, One Quincy Court/220 South State Street, Chicago, IL 60604.

Joseph Weiss, MD, Mount Zion Hospital, Department of Psychiatry, P.O. Box 7921, San Francisco, CA 94120.

James P. Whelan, PhD, Department of Psychology, Memphis State University, Memphis, TN 38152.

Peter Winiecki, OecD Karl-Marx-Universität Leipzig, Institut fur Medizinische, Statistik und Dokumentation, O-Liebigstrabe 27, DDR 7010 Leipzig, Federal Republic of Germany.

Arnold Winston, MD, New School for Social Research, 65 Fifth Avenue, New York, NY 10003.

1

Introduction to Psychotherapy Research

Michael J. Lambert
Brigham Young University

A fundamental commitment of psychology, psychiatry, and other mental health–related fields is the well-being of the client seeking services in applied settings. The ethics of treatment inspire the practitioner to make every effort to protect the welfare of those who seek services. The purpose of empirical research is to explore and verify the relationships that exist among variables that affect the well-being of clients. Specifically, psychotherapy research is largely aimed at evaluating the effects of treatment variables on patient functioning. Although most treatment approaches are based on naturalistic observations and intuition, the complexity of the natural situation and the limited perspective gained by examining the single case suggest the need for an experimental approach that provides an additional perspective from which to view clinical phenomena. Without such a perspective it is doubtful whether the client's welfare will be best served. Thus, psychotherapy research is a necessary component of the highest ethical practice and a fundamental aspect of psychotherapeutic services. Nevertheless, despite the importance of empirical research for the ethical practice of psychotherapy and the strong interest of professionals and the lay public in psychotherapy, conducting research on the effects of therapy is at best difficult and at worst impossible.

In recent reviews of contemporary psychotherapy research studies, two colleagues and I examined current instruments and procedures for measuring psychotherapy outcome (Froyd & Lambert, 1989; Ogles & Lambert, 1989). We were startled to discover the seemingly endless number of measures used to assess the effects of psychotherapy. In our first review, we examined 348 studies published in 20 selected journals between 1983 and 1989. We found a total of 1,430 outcome measures. Of this large number, 840 measures were used only once. This review considered a wide variety of patient diagnoses, treatment modalities, and therapy types (Froyd & Lambert, 1989). In our second review, we examined studies of agoraphobia outcome published during the 1980s. We located 106 studies that used no fewer than 98 unique outcome measures. In a well-defined, limited disorder, these instruments measured, with an equally narrow range of interventions, mainly behavioral and cognitive–behavioral therapies. The proliferation of outcome measures (a sizable portion of which are unstandardized scales) is overwhelming.

The number of therapies offered to patients is similarly expanding. The precise number is hard to estimate. Garfield (1982) found 60 different types in the 1960s. By the mid-1970s an estimate of more than 130 was given by the National Institute of Mental Health (1975), and Herink (1980) suggested the presence of more than 250 distinct techniques.

Finally, there is widespread concern about similar trends in the diagnostic nomenclature of the American Psychiatric Association. These changes can be noted over the last 40 years in revisions of the *Diagnostic and Statistical Manual of Mental Disorders (DSM)*. From approximately 100 disorders in 1952, the number of categories has mushroomed to more than 260 in the revised third edition of the *DSM* (American Psychiatric Association, 1987).

Despite the ethical imperative to investigate the effects of specific techniques with specific problems and to measure these effects adequately (if not consistently), psychotherapy researchers are faced with a seemingly impossible task. Basing therapeutic interventions on a firm empirical foundation appears to be farther than ever beyond the reach of our abilities. Nevertheless, psychotherapy research continues, albeit in an increasingly complex maze with shifting walls. The maze would be complicated enough if it could be solved from an ivory tower. However, the psychotherapy researcher is usually far from an ivory tower. First, psychotherapy research requires a good deal of clinical sensitivity, and researchers are often practitioners as well as scientists. They are on the front lines with their clients and experience the stress of entering the sometimes troubling and confusing world of the client. They feel the pressure to treat and care for the patient properly. Such a task is not just an academic exercise. Second, psychotherapy and psychotherapy research take place in a financial and political climate of accountability. Without demonstrable outcomes it seems unlikely that psychotherapy can continue to be covered by national or independent health care systems. The mounting pressure to find fast, effective, permanent cures is great.

The money to conduct research is scarce and requires considerable effort, not to mention patience, to acquire; this is a competitive and often thankless task. This book is in many ways a testimony to the efforts of those who are willing not only to participate in therapy but also to stand back and examine critically the nature of the process and to put cherished beliefs to the cold scientific test.

If we are ethically bound to conduct research on psychotherapeutic processes, then this research, no matter how difficult, must produce findings that contribute to patient welfare. What are some important findings that have come from the application of scientific methodologies to psychotherapy? What central findings have significant implications for the practice of therapy? What issues face psychotherapy research in the 21st century? It is to these questions that we now turn.

Findings of Significance for the Practice of Psychotherapy

Hundreds of studies have examined the effects of therapies on a wide variety of diverse patient populations and diagnoses. The results of these studies cannot be integrated and summarized easily in a brief review; thus, only the most important conclusions from studies of adult outpatients are discussed. The interested reader may want to consult the *Handbook of Psychotherapy and Behavior Change* (Garfield & Bergin, 1986) for more extensive reviews of a broader range of disorders, treatment modalities, and critical issues.

Psychotherapy Is Effective

A question that occupied the minds of those undertaking the earliest studies of psychotherapy was: Can psychotherapy be shown to have positive effects? The earliest studies (from the 1930s to the 1960s) aimed at answering this question were uncontrolled and quasi-experimental, and their interpretations have been ambiguous. The resulting controversies (Bergin & Lambert, 1978; Rachman & Wilson, 1980) were sustained by disagreements over the "spontaneous" change noted in untreated patients. As the methodology of studies increasingly included appropriate control groups that took into account spontaneous improvement, and as the body of studies became more substantial, it became increasingly clear that many psychotherapies (that underwent empirical study) have clinically significant effects on clients. It is also true that not everyone benefits to a satisfactory degree and that the outcomes are not always stable. This conclusion is supported by traditional reviews of the literature (Lambert, Shapiro, & Bergin, 1986; Meltzoff & Kornreich, 1970) and by the host of quantitative reviews undertaken in the last decade (e.g., Nicholson & Berman, 1983; Quality Assurance Project, 1983; Shapiro & Shapiro, 1982; Smith, Glass, & Miller, 1980). The studies contributing to this conclusion number in the hundreds and report data on thousands of therapists and patients across the United States and Europe.

So strong is the evidence favoring the general effectiveness of therapy that this question is no longer of interest in many psychotherapy studies, although it should be of concern to those persons who are developing and practicing techniques that do not rest on a firm empirical base. It is surprising to see that so many new therapies are developed and strongly advocated before any empirical investigations are conducted, and it is disheartening to see practitioners apply them gladly without even asking for research support. The latter is even more disturbing than the former and raises serious questions about clinical training and practice.

Psychotherapy Is More Effective Than Placebo Interventions

Another important question raised in psychotherapy research is the following: Do the effects of therapy exceed those that can be obtained when patients merely believe that they are undergoing a bona fide treatment? This question derives directly from empirical methodology that seeks to eliminate rival causal hypotheses for the treatment effects that are so frequently reported in outcome studies. The situation is analogous to that in clinical drug trials that use placebo control groups as an essential methodological feature to compare an active chemical agent with a pharmacologically inert substance. This contrast makes good sense in medicine, allowing as it does attributions of success to pharmacological rather than psychological agents. It makes less sense when extended to psychotherapy research, in which the effects of treatments and placebos depend on psychological mechanisms.

The results of psychotherapy compared with placebo control studies are based on a smaller set of studies and are more controversial than the results of general outcome studies. As expected, patients in so-called placebo control groups typically show greater improvement than patients assigned to waiting-list or no-treatment control groups. At the same time the gains in patients undergoing psychotherapy are greater than those attained by patients in placebo control conditions (e.g., Blanchard, Andrasik, Ahler, Teders, & O'Keefe, 1980; Miller & Berman, 1983; Quality Assurance Project, 1983).

The placebo control issue raises many interesting questions about what causes improvement in patients and is not without controversy (cf., Prioleau, Murdock, & Brody, 1983; Shepard, 1984; Bloch & Lambert, 1985; Lambert, Shapiro, & Bergin, 1986). Before addressing questions of causality two other important issues must be addressed: Are the changes stable, and are there any negative effects and contraindications for psychotherapy?

Many Patients Who Improve in Therapy Maintain That Improvement for Extended Periods

Psychotherapy research has focused primarily on the immediate posttreatment status of patients who have participated in therapy. What kinds of change persist? What intervention methods increase the durability of improvements? What factors influence the likelihood of relapse and maintenance? Long-term follow-up studies carry with them a host of difficult and expensive problems to solve. Despite this, it appears that follow-up studies on some disorders lead to the conclusion that the changes attained are surprisingly stable.

There is no reason to believe that a single course of psychotherapy should inoculate a person forever against psychological disturbance. Yet, even people who have a long history of recurrent problems gain a relatively stable improvement. At the same time, there is clear evidence that a portion of patients who improve do relapse and continue to seek help from various mental health professionals, their former therapists, and the public. In fact, problems such as addictions, alcohol abuse, smoking, obesity, and depression are so likely to recur that they are not considered properly studied without data collection 1 year after treatment.

One of the most interesting reviews on this subject was published by Nicholson and Berman (1983), who sought to answer the following question: Is follow-up necessary in evaluating psychotherapy? After reviewing the 67 studies that provide stable evidence on this question, they concluded that " . . . our findings indicate that for a broad range of disorders this improvement stands the test of time"(p. 275). Their review did not focus on some of the more difficult problems to treat, however, such as addictions. Although we have reason to be optimistic about the lasting effects of therapy for some people, additional research needs to be done on this topic. Particularly, research on systematic efforts to maintain treatment gains (cf., Imber, Pilkonis, Harway, Klein, & Rubinsky, 1982) represents an area that needs immediate attention, especially with regard to brief therapeutic interventions.

Some Psychotherapy Has a Negative Effect on Some Patients

Bergin (1966) proposed the term *deterioration effect* to describe the general finding that a certain portion of psychotherapy patients are worse after treatment. Although there is controversy over the use of this term and the causal link between patient worsening and therapeutic variables (Mays and Franks, 1980, 1985; Rachman and Wilson, 1980; Strupp, Hadley, and Gomes-Schwartz, 1977), there is ample research evidence that more than suggests that some patients get worse as a result of the very interventions that are intended to help them.

In early work (Bergin & Lambert, 1978; Lambert, Bergin, & Collins, 1977), evidence based on more than 50 studies about the incidence, prevalence, and magnitude of negative change was described. The evidence amounts to a piecing together of obscure bits of information because there are few, if any, definitive studies on the subject. There has been considerable hesitance to address this issue directly; many studies do not provide the opportunity for outcomes to be categorized as "worse." As research methodology has improved this situation has changed, and research itself has stimulated better quality control through the selection, supervision, and monitoring of therapy in outcome studies.

For now, it can be concluded that negative effects are extensive, occurring across modalities (individual, group, marital, and family therapies), diagnoses, and treatment techniques (Lambert et al., 1977). The likely causes of negative effects are a function of clinician, technique, and client factors. Some patients appear to be especially susceptible to worsening (e.g., borderline and schizophrenic diagnoses); particularly when treatment methods are aimed at breaking down, challenging, or undermining habitual coping strategies and defenses. More ambiguous therapies appear to be more risky with such patients than therapies and techniques that provide high task structure as well as clearly defined and limited goals, unless this structured therapy is highly confrontative.

Of considerable significance is the role of the therapist in certain critical issues in the therapeutic process. An issue of great significance in all therapy is the termination of treatment, whether through completion or referral. The possibilities of client-perceived rejection and self-blame are especially likely at this time.

Some of the strongest evidence for therapy-induced negative effects favors the causal link between therapist attitudes (toward the client) and deterioration. Dislike, disrespect, and low empathy have been found to correlate with lack of improvement and negative change. This research has been summarized in a number of reports (e.g., Lambert, et al., 1977; Truax & Mitchell, 1971) and has clear implications for training of therapists and supervision of therapeutic practice.

Information about negative consequences of therapist maladjustment, exploitiveness, and immaturity can be gathered with ease from client self-reports. Striano (1982), in a consumer report study, examined the personal experiences of 25 selected clients who had been to more than one therapist, one of whom was reported as being helpful and one of whom was said to be unhelpful or harmful. She documented through the reports of these clients various "horror stories" of the type that are often shared privately among clients and professionals but are rarely published. A number of such reports are also recounted by Bergin and Lambert (1978) and Lambert et al. (1977). Grunebaum (1985) added to this repertoire of reports through a survey of mental health professionals who described therapy that they had undergone. Of these professionals, 10% reported being harmed by therapy. Such accounts lack documentation independent of client report, so that they could be laden with subjective biases to an unknown degree; such complaints are of social and clinical importance, however, and they provide reasons to continue inquiries into therapist contributions to negative change.

Further research in this area is badly needed. Especially useful would be research into the various factors that could affect supervision of trainees because it is at this level that the most effective interventions could be undertaken. It is also a time at which it may prove most easy to direct a person away from the practice of psychotherapy.

Common Factors and Specific Therapy Interventions Have Been Found to Affect Client Posttherapy Status

A significant portion of contemporary research is aimed at clarifying the factors associated with therapeutic improvement. To a large extent this research employs designs that are aimed at discovering the effects of specific therapeutic factors by contrasting an established treatment with a new treatment, an effective treatment with one or more of its component factors, or an effective treatment with a completely different treatment on a group of patients with special characteristics that could suggest an interaction effect. Other studies correlate therapy process variables with patient outcomes. Contemporary research has moved toward the application of well-defined techniques to well-defined problems and the measurement of limited therapeutic goals. As with strictly medical diseases, specific treatments are sought for specific disorders. The treatment technique is hypothesized to cause the improvement.

Despite the interest and effort put into such research, the link between technique and improvement is elusive. This conclusion has been reached in numerous traditional reviews (e.g., Bergin & Lambert, 1978; Bergin and Suinn, 1975; Beutler, 1979; Luborsky, Singer, & Luborsky, 1975; Meltzoff & Kornreich, 1970) as well as in recent meta-analytic studies (e.g., Dush, Hirt, & Schroeder, 1983; Smith et al., 1980). The conclusion drawn by most of these reviews of comparative outcome studies is that none of the therapies are superior; as Luborsky et al. (1975) suggest, "Everyone has won and all must have prizes" (p. 995). Within this conclusion are small areas of superiority for some of the therapies that have been tested. Notably, in the largest meta-analytic reviews (Smith et al., 1980; Shapiro & Shapiro, 1982) behavior and cognitive therapies were found to have the largest effect when contrasted to verbal therapies, a finding that disappears when the data are adjusted for the reactivity (or "softness") of the outcome measures often used in studies of behavior therapy.

Another issue of interest to practitioners and researchers is the relative effectiveness of cognitive compared with behavioral methods. The Shapiro and Shapiro (1982) report showed a significantly larger effect for cognitive therapy compared with desensitization, yet Berman, Miller, and Massman (1985), who used a larger sample of studies, showed no difference between cognitive and desensitization therapies. The combination of cognitive therapy with desensitization did not yield increased effects beyond what either treatment obtained alone.

The foregoing meta-analyses reveal a mixed picture. There is a strong trend toward no difference among techniques in the amount of change they produce that is counterbalanced by evidence indicating that under certain circumstances cognitive and behavioral techniques are superior to traditional verbal therapies, even though they do not differ from each other in efficacy. Still, most comparative studies show no difference in the outcome experienced by clients.

When the differences among therapies are tested and no difference in client outcome is found, there is a host of possible reasons. Thus, interpretation of the meaning of results that do not reject the null hypothesis should be done with considerable caution. Certainly the practicing clinician makes hundreds of decisions about actions to be taken with the client for the client's benefit. Could most of these decisions be irrelevant to constructive personality change? Could one consistent set of decisions have no advantage over another different set of decisions? Could there really be no important consequences of different therapeutic techniques and activities? Some argue that the failure to find significant differences in outcome could be the result of methodological shortcomings rather than an accurate reflection of reality. Methodological factors loom large in explaining the relatively weak findings reported in comparative outcome studies.

Kazdin and Bass (1989), for example, examined the statistical power of comparative outcome studies to address the question of whether the number of treatment subjects in each group is sufficiently large to detect differences in outcome after psychotherapy. They examined psychotherapy outcome studies in nine relevant journals over a 3-year period (1984–1986). Effect sizes were calculated for posttreatment and follow-up periods, and these were compared with sample size to evaluate power in relation to Cohen's (1977) criteria. Given the effect sizes that resulted, they estimated that fewer than half the studies (and fewer than one third of the studies at follow-up) had an adequate sample size at termination to detect differences between two or more active treatments. They concluded that both individual studies and comparative therapy outcome reviews may have overlooked problems with sample size by interpreting the lack of difference without giving due weight to methodological factors.

The power of a study to detect differences involves many factors, such as sample size, care and consistency in patient selection (homogeneity), use of standardized assessment conditions, integrity of treatment, choice of outcome measure, and the like. The result is a host of possible explanations for the appearance of similarity. In addition to methodological explanations, there are explanations that are sensible and congenial with respect to various theories about behavior change and its causes.

The failure to find remarkable differences among seemingly disparate treatments has led many researchers and reviewers to conclude that factors that are common across therapies may cause behavior change and account for the relative equivalence of diverse therapies. Typical of this view is that expressed by Kornblith, Rehm, O'Hara, and Lamparski (1983), who conducted a series of studies in which they evaluated a cognitive–behavioral approach to the treatment of depression. After several applications of their self-control therapy, they compared results with a didactic condition (without the usual homework assignments), the usual treatment without the self-reinforcement element, and a problem-oriented therapy (psychodynamic group psychotherapy). All four treatments were equally effective, leading the authors to ponder anew the commonalities among these diverse treatments for depression:

> Looking across cognitive and behavioral therapy procedures for treating depression generally, it is apparent that these packages have at least three important characteristics in common. First, they each present a concrete rationale. This rationale includes a vocabulary for describing and defining the problems of depression in ways that may be very new to participants. Rationales also provide a vocabulary for describing the mechanisms of change. Second, all of these therapy programs are highly structured. They provide clear plans for producing change in a logical sequence of steps. Third, all of these programs provide feedback and support so that participants can clearly see changes in their own behavior and are reinforced for these changes . . . Research . . . needs to look more clearly at characteristics of packages such as these, rather than merely at details of procedure or abstract differences in underlying theories. (p. 525)

Despite the fact that clinicians emphasize the differences between their favorite therapeutic interventions and those of other therapists and that these techniques are subsequently emphasized in clinical training and supervision experiences, common factors are prominent ingredients in all forms of practice and appear to be more important than specific techniques. In addition to providing warm support, feedback, reassurance, suggestion, credibility, attention, and expectancy for improvement, many therapies can be interpreted as exposing people to their fears or as changing people's expectations for personal effectiveness, elements once regarded as unique to behavioral interventions. These and related factors common across therapies seem to make up a significant portion, if not the bulk, of what is therapeutic in the psychotherapies.

Among the common factors most frequently studied have been those identified by the client-centered school as necessary and sufficient conditions for patient personality change: accurate empathy, positive regard, nonpossessive warmth, and congruence or genuineness. Virtually all schools (Lambert, 1983) accept the notion that these or related therapist relationship variables are important for significant progress in psychotherapy and, in fact, are fundamental in the formation of a working alliance.

Studies showing both positive and equivocal support for the hypothesized relationships between therapist variables and outcome have been reviewed (cf., Beutler, Crago, & Arizmendi, 1986; Gurman, 1977; Orlinsky & Howard, 1986; Lambert, DeJulio, & Stein, 1978; Parloff, Waskow, & Wolfe, 1978; Patterson, 1984). Reviewers are nearly unanimous in their opinion that the therapist–patient relationship is crucial, but they point out that research support for this position is not as clear as it once was. Studies that use client-perceived ratings of the relationship rather than objective ratings obtain consistently more positive results, but the larger correlations with outcome are often between client process ratings and client self-reports of outcome, which possible inflate the correlations. In addition, it is becoming increasingly clear that the individual attributes of patients play an important role in determining the quality of therapist-offered conditions (e.g., Strupp, 1980a, 1980b, 1980c, 1980d).

A strong case can be made for the role of relationship factors in outcome (Lambert et al., 1986). Patients commonly attribute their success in treatment to personal qualities of the therapists. These qualities bear a surprising resemblance to each other across various studies and methodologies: Patients report positive outcomes with therapists who are understanding, supportive, encouraging, insight-producing, sensitive, honest, caring, interested, endowed with a sense of humor, and so forth. Patients seldom mention technical procedures as crucial to their improvement. Future research will need to take relationship factors into account despite the fact that research is primarily focused on theory-based technical procedures.

The discussion of common factors naturally raises interesting questions about the personal qualities of the therapist. The therapist, as a unique person, is often considered a confounding variable in psychotherapy studies; therefore, studies of the outcomes of particular therapists are not conducted. Instead several therapists are studied and their differential contribution to outcome treated as error variance, and in the most rigorously designed studies costly measures are taken (e.g., treatment manuals, supervision, monitoring, and feedback) to diminish the observed impact of the therapist as a unique person. Because the aim of a great deal of this research is to establish or discover which techniques and interventions are most powerful, therapist differences are a nuisance. Although this commonly accepted and necessary methodological procedure helps in the discovery of differences in technique, it may mask the most potent aspect of therapy: the therapist as person, that is to say the wisdom and humanity of the therapist.

Therapy outcome and process studies continue to examine the interaction of patient and treatment. Future research also must attend to the qualities of particular therapists that make them unusually effective.

The Patient Makes the Greatest Contribution to Psychotherapy Outcome

The search for active ingredients in psychotherapy outcome must include careful attempts to assess the client's contribution. Just as therapy techniques and common factors, including the therapist as a person, affect outcome, so do the myriad of factors brought into the interaction by the patient. Each kind of therapy, although effective, may be beneficial for different kinds of clients. Therapy research has focused considerable attention on the client and on client interactions with therapies and therapists (Beutler, 1979, 1983; Calvert, Beutler, & Crago, 1988; Garfield, 1986). Studies of demographics (gender, race, socioeconomic status, age, etc.), diagnosis, personality, style (defensiveness, values, ego strength, etc.) and in-therapy behavior have all been conducted with various degrees of success. This strategy is consistent with ethical ideals, scientific standards, and practical necessity.

Already mentioned is the interaction among patient diagnosis, clinical status, and therapy structure that increases the possibility of negative outcomes. This finding and related findings suggest the importance of continued investigation of patient characteristics that are associated with positive and negative outcomes. The result should be a better match between therapy and patient and a corresponding enhancement of client benefit. Despite efforts to match therapy with patient or therapist, few replicable substantive findings have been produced by outcome studies. Those clients who tend to do poorly in one therapy also do poorly in alternative treatments. Although treatment assignment decisions are constantly made, they are based most often on clinical judgment and "home remedies" rather than on a firm empirical base. An example of an empirically based assignment of patients to particular treatments and therapists suggests the possibilities in this area. Dougherty (1976) measured personality traits of both therapists and clients while observing and classifying clients on the basis of their response to counseling. After this correlational, naturalistic study was completed, an experimental manipulation of client–therapist matching was undertaken. As predicted, the optimally matched clients attained significantly greater gains than minimally matched clients.

Another example of research in this area is a study by Calvert et al. (1988), who tested the assumption that client style of psychological defense and reactance potential would interact with therapist procedures that were classified as directive and internal–external in focus. Specifically, they hypothesized that clients high in externalizing defensive styles would respond better to externally focused (behavioral) therapies and that patients with high reactance to directiveness would profit most from low-directive therapies. The results seemed to depend on the type of outcome measure used. As the investigators state, "Among internalizing patients, insight/awareness-focused therapies resulted in the patients' both feeling and behaving better. Among externally defended patients, however, compatible behaviorally oriented treatment matches resulted in the patients' feeling better but behaving worse" (p. 115). No support for the hypothesized positive effects of matching patient reactance and therapist directiveness were found. Enough support was found for the matching hypothesis to encourage further research, but overall the empirical base for making assignments was not substantial.

An area of considerable interest and great practical as well as theoretical import is the assignment of patients to brief therapy interventions. With the increased pressure for limits on treatment funded by insurance companies and government agencies, more and more therapists are forced to consider abbreviated treatments. This raises the important question: Which patients are well suited (and ill suited) to brief interventions? Numerous spokespersons for various brief therapies have outlined the selection criteria for their approach. The criteria have been reviewed by Lambert (1979) and the patient traits listed, but the lists usually correspond closely with those traits that characterize successful cases in all therapies: a recent, identifiable, focal problem that is readily verbalized; high motivation; circumscribed, nonsomatic symptoms; and an ability to relate effectively with the therapist. A history of positive, satisfying relationships suggesting an ability to be trusting in relationships is also among the criteria.

It appears that matching patients, therapists, and therapies remains more of an ideal than a reality. Nevertheless, therapists will be called on to make increasingly difficult decisions about the probable outcomes of their interventions, including the refusal to treat some patients and the referral of others. Psychotherapy research will be increasingly called on to provide useful data about such decisions and to play a central role in quality assurance. These practical tasks will not take the researcher too far from the examination of important long-range theoretical questions, but the practical demands for research in this area make ongoing and future research an urgent, timely quest.

Future Directions and Recommendations

Many therapies that have been empirically tested have been shown to have demonstrable effects on various clients. These effects have been shown to be not only statistically significant but clinically meaningful. Psychotherapy facilitates the remission of symptoms by speeding up the natural healing process and often provides additional coping strategies and methods for dealing with future problems. These effects tend to be lasting even in therapies that are not aimed at character or structural change in personality. The effects are clearly present when the contrasts are made with untreated patients, those who receive pseudotherapies, and placebo controls in whom support and expectancies are equivalent. The differences among the therapies that have been studied are

not as pronounced as has been expected. Behavioral and cognitive therapies and elective mixtures of these show superior outcomes in a number of instances with specific disorders, although this is by no means the general case. In contrast to their effect on general outpatient disorders, behavioral and cognitive therapies appear to add a significant increment to the outcome of several specific, difficult, anxiety-based problems. That a vast number of therapists have become eclectic in orientation appears to be a positive response to the growing body of empirical research that casts doubt on the superiority of particular schools of treatment.

Interpersonal, social, and affective factors common across therapies still loom large as stimulators of client improvement. It should come as no surprise that helping people deal with depression, inadequacy, anxiety, and inner conflicts that are often devastating to their interpersonal relationships and their quest for meaningful directions in their lives can be greatly affected by a therapeutic relationship that is characterized by understanding, acceptance, trust, warmth, and wisdom. These relationship factors are probably crucial even in technical directive therapies in which they are not emphasized.

Empirical research has been adequate to confirm the positive effect of many of the therapies that have been put to the test, but problems with methodology, especially the measurement of change, significantly diminish the comparison of therapies and the search for the active ingredients of therapeutic influence.

Although these broad, positive statements about psychotherapy can be made with more confidence than ever before, it is important to point out that there is wide variability among outcomes experienced by patients undergoing psychotherapy. Many therapies go untested, and large, well-attended conferences on psychotherapy can be held with hardly a mention of empirical support for even the most controversial techniques (cf., the Annual Psychotherapy Conference of the Ericson Foundation). It is as if the scientist-practitioner model were not a part of our training or professions.

Much more research needs to be conducted (and will always need to be conducted) before the exact relationship between the process of therapy and its outcome will be known. Mention can be made of a few of the topics that should be of immediate concern to psychotherapy researchers, and the consuming public:

• evaluation of those therapies that are not based on a body of empirical research as well as eclectic therapies that lack empirical support;

• further tests of the limits of brief therapy approaches, especially those that are not aimed at limited, circumscribed, skill-deficiency problems that respond well to structured treatments;

• identification and study of nonresponders, including guidelines for early referral or modification of approach;

• continued process–outcome research on those aspects of therapy that are central to the espoused efficacy of a theoretical approach (an example of this research would be the theoretical and empirical research on analysis of the core conflict relationship theme conducted by Luborsky and his colleagues [Luborsky, McClellan, Woody, O'Brien, & Auerbach, 1985]. This research program could easily serve as a prototype for future theory-based research.);

• attention to the individual therapist who has especially positive results rather than the currently common analysis of therapist effects as secondary variables pursued when the intervention of interest proves nonsignificant (process studies of the behavior of the unusually effective therapist are badly needed);

• continued research on the maintenance of therapeutic gains so that therapists are more able to expend systematic efforts at helping clients solidify gains and cope with future problems (this is especially crucial with those disorders most prone to relapse and with the personality-disordered client whose presenting symptoms often mask underlying propensities to relapse or develop another Axis I problem);

• clearer specification of those problems and disorders that are especially suitable for treatment by paraprofessional and lay therapists who are supervised by licensed practitioners;

• chaos reigns in the assessment of outcome (little agreement has been reached about the most viable measures for even the most commonly studied problems. To some degree, meta-analytic techniques have brought order to the great diversity among studies. Nevertheless, even meta-analysis cannot completely overcome the results of such diversity and adds additional interpretive problems by implying that equivalent effect sizes suggest equivalent magnitudes and meaningfulness of underlying change. Even small effect sizes on some measures may indicate clinically important changes, and large effect sizes on other measures may not indicate clinically important improvement. A new uniformity myth may be in the making. There is a clear need for coordination of assessment strategies not only so that adequate assessments of change will be conducted but to facilitate the integration of research projects conducted by different researchers across the United States and throughout the world. A professional body such as the National Institute of Mental Health or the Society for Psychotherapy Research is in a position to help bring order to the current chaos that characterizes outcome measurement. Despite some efforts, little progress has been made.).

It is time for psychotherapy researchers and academicians to direct their attention to programmatic research that emphasizes systematic experimentation rather than the single-shot study. Knowledge from single studies is highly limited and often difficult to integrate into past research. Programmatic research, on the other hand, builds a knowledge base gradually and systematically by addressing a series of logically related questions. Good examples of systematic and programmatic research are contained in the studies of simple phobias, compulsive disorders, agoraphobia, and depression that have been conducted by investigators such as Marks (1977), Emmelkamp (1986), Rehm et al. (1981), and Beck, Rush, Shaw, and Emery (1979). As this book testifies, there are many programmatic efforts underway that have already had an important impact on the field, and many of these programs promise to be influential centers for continuing progress in psychotherapy research.

The public deserves treatments that are based not only on our best clinical judgment but also on systematic research conducted under controlled situations. This research is an integral aspect of quality services and the highest ethical principles. Like other areas of scientific research, psychotherapy research is an ongoing, never-ending process of learning and discovery in which final answers are unlikely and unnecessary. The search for truth is meaningful as a process and contributes significantly to our understanding of therapy without providing final answers. This fact is probably what makes it possible for persons to face the difficulties and challenges of such a complex and fluid area of inquiry. One can only hope that the mental health professions will be equal to the challenging questions, addressed in this book, that are being asked as we enter the 21st century.

References

American Psychiatric Association. (1987). *Diagnostic and statistical manual of mental disorders* (rev. 3rd ed.). Washington, DC: Author.

Beck, A. T., Rush, A. J., Shaw, B. F., & Emery, G. (1979). *Cognitive therapy of depression.* New York: Guilford Press.

Bergin, A. E. (1966). Some implications of psychotherapy research for therapeutic practice. *Journal of Abnormal Psychology, 71,* 235–246.

Bergin, A. E., & Lambert, M. J. (1978). The evaluation of therapeutic outcomes. In S. L. Garfield & A. E. Bergin (Eds.), *Handbook of psychotherapy and behavior change: An empirical analysis* (2nd ed., pp. 139–189). New York: Wiley.

Bergin, A. E., & Suinn, R. M. (1975). Individual psychotherapy and behavior therapy. *Annual Review of Psychology, 26,* 509–556.

Berman, J. S., Miller, R. C., & Massman, P. J. (1985). Cognitive therapy versus systematic desensitization: Is one treatment superior? *Psychological Bulletin, 97,* 451–461.

Beutler, L. E. (1979). Toward specific psychological therapies for specific conditions. *Journal of Consulting and Clinical Psychology, 47,* 882–892.

Beutler, L. E. (1983). *Eclectic psychotherapy: A systematic approach.* New York: Pergamon Press.

Beutler, L. E., Crago, M., & Arizmendi, T. G. (1986). Therapist variables in psychotherapy process and outcome. In S. L. Garfied & A. E. Bergin (Eds.), *Handbook of psychotherapy and behavior change: An empirical analysis* (3rd ed., pp. 257–310). New York: Wiley.

Blanchard, E. B., Andrasik, F., Ahler, T. A., Teders, S. J., & O'Keefe, D. O. (1980). Migraine and tension headache: A meta-analytic review. *Behavior Therapy, 11,* 613–631.

Bloch, S., & Lambert, M. J. (1985). What price psychotherapy? A rejoinder. *British Journal of Psychiatry, 146,* 96–98.

Calvert, S. J., Beutler, L. E., & Crago, M. (1988). Psychotherapy outcome as a function of therapist-patient matching on selected variables. *Journal of Social and Clinical Psychology, 6,* 104–117.

Cohen, J. (1977). *Statistical power analysis in the behavioral sciences* (2nd ed.). New York: Academic Press.

Dougherty, F. (1976). Patient therapist matching for optimal and minimal therapeutic outcome. *Journal of Consulting and Clinical Psychology, 44,* 889–897.

Dush, D. M., Hirt, M. L., & Schroeder, H. (1983). Self-statement modification with adults: A meta-analysis. *Journal of Consulting and Clinical Psychology, 94,* 408–422.

Emmelkamp, P. M. G. (1986). Behavior therapy with adults. In S. L. Garfield & A. E. Bergin (Eds.), *Handbook of psychotherapy and behavior change* (3rd ed., pp. 385–442). New York: Wiley.

Froyd, J. E., & Lambert, M. J. (1989). *A review of measures used to assess psychotherapy outcome.* Un-

published manuscript, Brigham Young University, Provo, UT.

Garfield, S. L. (1982). Eclecticism and integration in psychotherapy. *Behavior Therapy, 13,* 610–623.

Garfield, S. L. (1986). Research on client variables in psychotherapy. In S. L. Garfield & A. E. Bergin (Eds.), *Handbook of psychotherapy and behavior change: An empirical analysis* (3rd ed., pp. 213–256). New York: Wiley.

Garfield, S. L., & Bergin, A. E. (Eds.). (1986). *Handbook of psychotherapy and behavior change: An empirical analysis* (3rd ed.). New York: Wiley.

Grunebaum, H. (1985). Helpful and harmful psychotherapy. *Harvard Medical School Mental Health Newsletter, 1,* 5–6.

Gurman, A. S. (1977). The patient's perception of the therapeutic relationship. In A. S. Gurman & A. M. Razin (Eds.), *Effective psychotherapy: A handbook of research* (pp. 503–543). New York: Pergamon Press.

Herink, R. (Ed.). (1980). *The psychotherapy handbook: The A to Z guide to more than 250 different therapies in use today.* New York: Meridien.

Imber, S. D., Pilkonis, P. A., Harway, N. I., Klein, R. H., & Rubinsky, P. A. (1982). Maintenance of change in the psychotherapies. *Journal of Psychiatric Treatment and Evaluation, 4,* 1–5.

Kazdin, A. E., & Bass, D. (1989). Power to detect differences between alternative treatments in comparative outcome research. *Journal of Consulting and Clinical Psychology, 57,* 138–147.

Kornblith, S. H., Rehm, L. P., O'Hara, M. W., & Lamparski, D. M. (1983). The contribution of self-reinforcement training and behavioral assignments to the efficacy of self-control therapy for depression. *Cognitive Therapy and Research, 7,* 499–528.

Lambert, M. J. (1979). Patient characteristics and their relation to psychotherapy outcome in brief psychotherapy. *Psychiatric Clinics of North America, 2,* 111–124.

Lambert, M. J. (1983). *Psychotherapy and patient relationships.* Homewood, IL: Dorsey Press.

Lambert, M. J., Bergin, A. E., & Collins, J. L. (1977). Therapist induced deterioration in psychotherapy. In A. S. Gurman & A. M. Razin (Eds.), *Handbook of psychotherapy and behavior change: An empirical analysis* (pp. 157–211). New York: Wiley.

Lambert, M. J., DeJulio, S. S., & Stein, D. M. (1978). Therapist interpersonal skills: Process, outcome, methodological considerations, and recommendations for future research. *Psychological Bulletin, 85,* 467–489.

Lambert, M. J., Shapiro, D. A., & Bergin, A. E. (1986). The effectiveness of psychotherapy. In S. L. Garfield & A. E. Bergin (Eds.), *Handbook of psychotherapy and behavior change* (3rd ed., pp. 157–211). New York: Wiley.

Luborsky, L., McClellan, A. T., Woody, G. E., O'Brien, C. P., & Auerbach, A. (1985). Therapist success and its determinants. *Archives of General Psychiatry, 42,* 602–611.

Luborsky, L., Singer, B., & Luborsky, L. (1975). Comparative studies of psychotherapy. *Archives of General Psychiatry, 32,* 995–1008.

Marks, I. (1977). Behavioral psychotherapy of adult neurosis. In S. L. Garfield & A. E. Bergin (Eds.), *Handbook of psychotherapy and behavior change: An empirical analysis* (2nd ed., pp. 493–548). New York: Wiley.

Mays, D. T., & Franks, C. M. (1980). Getting worse: Psychotherapy or no treatment. The jury should still be out. *Professional Psychology, 11*, 78–92.

Mays, D. T., & Franks, C. M. (1985). *Negative outcome in psychotherapy and what to do about it.* New York: Springer.

Meltzoff, J., & Kornreich, M. (1970). *Research in psychotherapy.* New York: Atherton Press.

Miller, R. C., & Berman, J. S. (1983). The efficacy of cognitive behavior therapies: A quantitative review of the research evidence. *Psychological Bulletin, 94*, 39–53.

National Institute of Mental Health. (1975). *Research in the service of mental health* (DHEW Publication No. ADM 74-120). Rockville, MD: Department of Health, Education and Welfare.

Nicholson, R. A., & Berman, J. S. (1983). Is follow-up necessary in evaluating psychotherapy? *Psychological Bulletin, 93*, 261–278.

Ogles, B. M., & Lambert, M. J. (1989). *Agoraphobia research in the 1980s: A review and meta analysis.* Unpublished manuscript; Brigham Young University, Provo, UT.

Orlinsky, D. & Howard, K. I., (1986). Process and outcome in psychotherapy. In S. L. Garfield & A. E. Bergin (Eds.), *Handbook of psychotherapy and behavior change: An empirical analysis* (3rd ed., pp. 311-381). New York: Wiley.

Parloff, M. B., Waskow, I. E., & Wolfe, B. E. (1978). Research on therapist variables in relation to process and outcome. In S. L. Garfield and A. E. Bergin (Eds.), *Handbook of psychotherapy and behavior change: An empirical analysis* (pp. 233–282). New York: Wiley.

Patterson, C. H. (1984). Empathy, warmth, and genuineness in psychotherapy: A review of reviews. *Psychotherapy, 21*, 431–438.

Prioleau, L., Murdock, M., & Brody, N. (1983). An analysis of psychotherapy versus placebo studies. *Behavioral and Brain Sciences, 6*, 275–310.

Quality Assurance Project. (1983). A treatment outline for depressive disorders. *Australian and New Zealand Journal of Psychiatry, 17*, 129–146.

Rachman, S. J., & Wilson, G. T. (1980). *The effects of psychological therapy* (2nd ed.). New York: Pergamon Press.

Rehm, L. P., Kornblith, S. J., O'Hara, M. W., Lamparsky, D. M., Roman, J. M., & Volkan, J. (1981). Evaluation of major components in a self-control behavior therapy program for depression. *Behavior Modification, 5*, 459–489.

Shapiro, D. A., & Shapiro, D. (1982). Meta-analysis of comparative therapy outcome studies: A replication and refinement. *Psychological Bulletin, 92*, 581–604.

Shepherd, M. (1984). What price psychotherapy? *British Medical Journal, 288*, 809–810.

Smith, M. L., Glass, G. V., & Miller, T. I. (1980). *The benefits of psychotherapy.* Baltimore, MD: Johns Hopkins University Press.

Striano, J. (1982). Client perception of "helpful" and "not helpful" psychotherapeutic experiences. *Dissertation Abstracts International, 43*, 4303B. (University Microfilms No. 80-17, 382)

Strupp, H. H. (1980a). Success and failure in time limited psychotherapy: A comparison of two cases—Comparison 1. *Archives of General Psychiatry, 37*, 595–603.

Strupp, H. H. (1980b). Success and failure in time limited psychotherapy: A comparison of two cases—Comparison 2. *Archives of General Psychiatry, 37*, 708-716.

Strupp, H. H. (1980c). Success and failure in time limited psychotherapy: With special reference to the performance of a lay counselor. *Archives of General Psychiatry, 37*, 831–841.

Strupp, H. H. (1980d). Success and failure in time limited psychotherapy: A systematic comparison of two cases—Comparison 4. *Archives of General Psychiatry, 37*, 947–954.

Strupp, H. H., Hadley, S. W., & Gomes-Schwartz, B. (1977). *Psychotherapy for better or worse.* Northvale, NJ: Jason Aronson.

Truax, C. B., & Mitchell, K. M. (1971). Research on certain therapist interpersonal skills in relation to process and outcome. In A. E. Bergin & S. L. Garfield (Eds.), *Handbook of psychotherapy and behavior change* (pp. 299–344). New York: Wiley.

Large-Scale Programs: North America

The Beth Israel Psychotherapy Research Program

Leigh McCullough and Arnold Winston
Mount Sinai School of Medicine

Background and Aims

History

The Beth Israel Psychotherapy Research Program was first envisioned by Arnold Winston in the late 1970s. The work of Peter Sifneos (1979) provided the impetus, representing a form of psychotherapy that lent itself to empirical study. In contrast to longer-term approaches, this active, focused, time-limited treatment offered clearly delineated techniques as well as outcome results that could be obtained in a reasonable amount of time. Sifneos (from 1979 to 1981) and then Habib Davanloo (from 1981 to 1983) came to Beth Israel to train the clinical staff in the techniques of brief individual psychotherapy, using both live interviews and videotaped presentation in their instruction. Ten therapists became involved in the program, and two treatment conditions emerged. Short-term dynamic psychotherapy (STDP) followed Davanloo's (1980) approach, which used gentle but relentless confrontation of defenses and focused on underlying affect (Been & Sklar, 1985; Goldin & Winston, 1985; Winston, 1981; Winston & Goldin, 1985; Winston & Trujillo, 1985). The other treatment condition developed at Beth Israel was brief adaptational psychotherapy (BAP), which was designed to confront defenses at a more moderate level and to identify clients'

maladaptive patterns (Pollack & Horner, 1985; Flegenheimer, 1985; Flegenheimer & Pollack, 1989). Recently two additional treatment conditions were added: supportive psychotherapy, based on a reappraisal of supportive psychotherapy (Winston, Pinsker, & McCullough, 1986), and cognitive–behavioral treatment, based on an integration of a problem-solving approach described by D'Zurilla and Goldfried (1971) and a cognitive restructuring approach described by Beck and his associates (Beck, 1962; Beck & Emery, 1985).

A formal research program was initiated in 1982 (cf., Trujillo & McCullough, 1985), and two studies have been completed that examined process and outcome in the original two treatment conditions (BAP & STDP): Beth Israel Study 1 (1983–1985) and Beth Israel Study 2 (1985–1988). Beth Israel Study 3 was initiated in September 1988 with the addition of the supportive and cognitive–behavioral groups to examine process and outcome across a wider variety of theoretical orientations.

Overall Aims

The overall aim of the Beth Israel program is to study the relation between psychotherapy process and outcome in active, focused, time-limited psychotherapy for the treatment of individual clients with long-standing character pathology. It is commonly held that nonspecific factors (e.g., therapeutic alliance, client characteristics) are responsible for change in psychotherapy. The Beth Israel program is attempting to demonstrate that nonspecific factors carry the weight of research results only because psychotherapy techniques have not been sufficiently developed or refined. We hypothesize that the techniques developed in the brief psychotherapies may contribute equally to psychotherapeutic effectiveness.

Subareas of Investigation

There are three main subareas of investigation: (a) examination of the relative contribution of specific compared with nonspecific factors to psychotherapeutic outcome; (b) identification of specific techniques or common factors that span theoretical orientation; and (c) dissemination of our results in a format that will be useful to practicing clinicians (e.g., frequencies of interventions per session or description of client responding immediately after an intervention).

Method

Subjects and Selection

The clients are men and women aged 21–65 years with Axis II personality disorder diagnoses as defined by the revised third edition of the *Diagnostic and Statistical Manual of Mental Disorders (DSM-III–R*; American Psychiatric Association, 1987). In Beth Israel Study 1 ($N = 32$) only five personality disorders were selected for treatment: avoidant, dependent, compulsive, passive–aggressive, histrionic, and a mixture of these. In Beth Israel Study 2 ($N = 30$) we broadened the client selection criteria to include as test cases any Axis II disorder (e.g., borderline, narcissistic, paranoid, etc.) that has shown positive response to the brief psychotherapy approach when proper supportive interventions are included in treatment. Contraindications include the following: (a) evidence of psychosis, organic brain syndrome, or mental retardation; (b) active Axis III medical diagnosis; (c) evidence of current substance abuse; (d) active suicidal behavior; (e) history of violent behavior or destructive impulse control problems; and (f) psychotropic medication use within the past year.

Instruments

In keeping with well-known prescriptions for the standards of psychotherapy research (e.g., Waskow & Parloff, 1975), client assessment uses standard, widely recognized instruments chosen to represent both individualized and standardized measurement. Assessment is obtained from multiple sources and includes the following:

- Client Self-Report
  1. target complaints (Battle, Imber, Moehn-Saric, Stone, Nash, & Frank, 1966)
  2. Social Adjustment Scale (Weissman & Bothwell, 1976)
  3. SCL-90–R (Derogatis, 1977),
  4. Adult Norwicki–Strickland Internal–External Control Scale (Norwicki & Duke, 1974)
  5. Inventory of Interpersonal Problems (Horwitz, Rosenberg, Baer, Ureño, & Villaseñor, 1988)

- Therapist Assessment of the Client
  1. target complaints (Battle et al., 1966)
  2. Global Assessment Scale (Endicott, Spitzer, Fleiss, & Cohen, 1976)
  3. Inventory of Interpersonal Problems (Horwitz et al., 1988)

- Research Assistant Assessment
  1. Global Assessment Scale (Endicott et al., 1976)
  2. Structured Clinical Inventory (SCID) for the *DSM-III–R*, Axis I: SCID I (Spitzer, Williams, Gibbon, & First, 1988)
  3. Structured Clinical Inventory for the *DSM-III–R*, Axis II: SCID II (Spitzer, Williams, & Gibbon, 1987)
  4. Beth Israel videocoding system (McCullough et al., 1986).

Procedures

Screening and initial evaluation. The program secretary initially receives the applicant's call requesting treatment; this is typically in response to an advertisement in a local news-paper, an outside referral, or a referral from our outpatient clinic. Applicants are given a brief telephone screening by the secretary to rule out major contraindications as noted earlier and, if found to be suitable, are then invited to come to the office to complete a battery of instruments and to meet with a research assistant, who conducts an interview and administers the Structured Clinical Interview for *DSM-III–R* (SCID I and II; Spitzer et al., 1988). Applicants sign an informed consent form for all procedures including videotaping of all therapy sessions. Applicants for whom this type of treatment is not deemed suitable are assisted with a referral to an appropriate form of treatment. Applicants who are accepted into the program are randomly assigned to a treatment condition, which lasts for a maximum of 40 sessions.[1]

Midphase evaluation. At approximately the midpoint in treatment (Session 20), the therapist notifies the research team that the midphase evaluation may take place. Paper-and-pencil tests are mailed to the client, and the research assistant conducts a telephone interview with the client to make the required ratings. No diagnostic assessment is performed at this point.

Termination evaluation. Termination data are obtained approximately 1 month after the end of treatment to avoid the "halo effect" of recent cessation of treatment. Paper-and-pencil measures are mailed to the client for completion, and a research assistant conducts a telephone interview. Diagnostic assessment is performed with the SCID I and II modules on any diagnostic category found to be present at entry into treatment. Therapists also provide a termination assessment.

Follow-up interview. At the follow-up interviews (at 1 and 3 years), the research interviewer again contacts the client by telephone after the client has completed the paper and pencil battery and returned it through the mail.

No-treatment control group. The control groups in the Beth Israel Psychotherapy Research Program are quasi-controls because clients are not randomly assigned to a waiting list because of the ethical issues involved in withholding treatment to those in need.

In Study 1 there were more than 1,000 requests for treatment after an article appeared in the *New York Times Magazine* about our program, and a waiting list was inevitable because of the limited number of therapists ($N = 10$) available to provide treatment. We contacted each of these applicants, and referrals were given when needed. A group of applicants, whose test scores did not differ significantly from those of research sample, agreed to retake the battery of assessment instruments after an interval of approximately 4–6 months; this constituted the control sample.

In Study 2, we have had available to us a growing sample of clients who applied for treatment, completed our assessment battery, and were accepted but did not enter treatment because of (a) inability of the client and the therapist to find a mutually acceptable time to meet, (b) the client's being transferred outside the geographic area, or (c) inability of the client to stay for the full duration of treatment. These clients have agreed to fill out the paper-and-pencil tests a second time, thus providing an additional quasi-control group.

Coding of videotaped session. All sessions are videotaped by the therapist and stored with the program secretary in a videotape archive to be coded later by the research assistants. As mentioned in the Instruments section, additional instruments are used to code aspects of client and therapist activity; these include the Overview of Psychotherapy Interaction (OPI) Coding System (McCullough, 1990), which has been in development for the past 10 years. Because this instrument is important in understanding our specific findings, a general description of it is given here.

Eight therapist variables were chosen to coordinate with the variables reported by Elliot et al. (1987): questions, information, clarifications, confrontations, directives, support and reassurance, self-disclosure, and interpretations. Four categories of client variables were chosen from other process research areas: (a) levels of patient affective experience (static or blandly stated feeling, expressively stated feeling, and nonverbal concomitants of feeling (e.g., clinched fists, tears); (b) two levels of patient defensive behavior; (intermediate [e.g., intellectualization, rationalization] and immature [e.g., projection]) used to avoid or resist the topic under discussion (McCullough, Vaillant, & Vaillant, 1986; Vaillant, 1985); (c) three "person" references (therapist, parents or family, and significant others); and (d) four types of patient cognitive responding (insight and elaboration [e.g., meaningful continuation on a topic], recounting [e.g., concrete informative talk by the patient], fantasy and dreams, and problem solving).

Raters score videotapes by coding occurrences

---

[1]Although brief psychotherapy has been defined in the literature in the range of 26 sessions or fewer, because of the nature of our population we decided that 40 sessions is more appropriate. Thus, the term *brief psychotherapy* is something of a misnomer, and we prefer to use the term *time-limited psychotherapy.*

of verbal response modes for each minute of the session. This permits the evaluation of segments of sessions, sequences of client–therapist interaction, and patterns of change. This system represents a compilation of operationally defined and commonly used variables applicable to therapies of different theoretical orientations and thus allows comparisons across different therapies. Good reliability and validity have been demonstrated (Trujillo & McCullough, 1985; Joseph, 1988; McCullough et al., in press), and an additional reliability study on a revised version of the system is underway. To ensure reliability further, all sessions are coded by three separate raters, and no data are accepted for analysis unless at least two of three raters identify the occurrence of the variable in the same minute.

Research Accomplishments

Findings

In regard to the specific aims set forth in the creation of this program, our major accomplishments have been twofold. First, as we hypothesized, we have been able to demonstrate the efficacy of both forms of brief psychotherapy compared with a waiting-list control group (Winston, Pollack, Trujillo, et al., 1987). Second, we have been able to isolate client–therapist episodes that significantly predict improvement at outcome (McCullough et al., 1987).

In the first study, Winston, Pollack, Trujillo, and their colleagues (1987) demonstrated the efficacy of brief psychotherapy, a finding that is consistent with the abundant evidence provided by meta-analyses of psychotherapy research (e.g., Smith, Glass, & Miller, 1980). Even though our client population demonstrated a more severe level of pathology than the subjects often included in the meta-analyses (e.g., college students), our study yielded comparable results: effect sizes ranged from 1.4 (on target complaints) to 0.86 (on the Social Adjustment Scale), with the average effect size for the composite outcome being 0.98. This lends support to the premise that active, focused interventions in a time-limited format can be effective in the treatment of clients with severe, long-standing character problems.

The second major accomplishment has been the identification of therapist–client episodes (i.e., one example of a specific treatment factor) that predict outcome (McCullough et al., in press). The

initial interventions chosen for study were based on a dissertation completed by Porter (1988), which examined the immediate client response to transference interpretations and clarifications. In contrast to examining isolated variables (e.g., therapist interpretations alone or client affective response alone summed across a session), this turn-by-turn analysis yielded strong relationships to outcome. For all therapist interventions immediately followed by intermediate or immature defensiveness (i.e., patient behaviors used to avoid a topic), there were negative correlations with a composite outcome score ($M = -.32$, range $= -.13– -.50$). The strongest significant correlation was for all interventions followed by defense ($r = -.50$, $p = .05$). For all therapist interventions followed by affective responding (i.e., the client verbally stating a feeling with concomitant expressive vocal quality) there were strong positive correlations with outcome ($M = .40$, range $= +.04– -.60$). Two categories had significant correlations with improvement: transference interpretation followed by affect ($r = .60$, $p = .05$) and all interventions followed by affect ($r = .51$; $p = .05$). In conclusion, client affective and defensive responding showed no relation to outcome when examined alone. When the client responding was examined in the context of the immediately preceding therapist intervention, however, there was a strong significant relationship to outcome. This represented the first step toward identification of specific in-session interactions that showed a relation to outcome.

Therapist Adherence Scale

The senior clinical faculty at Beth Israel has been in the process of developing and testing a set of fidelity scales (Winston, Pollack, Flegenheimer, et al., 1987) specifically designed for each treatment group to test therapist adherence to treatment as set forth in each group's treatment manual and to alert us to therapists who are not performing at an adequate level. Initial research demonstrates that it is possible to reliably rate therapist adherence to technique in brief psychotherapy. The scales that were developed also demonstrate some validity by means of an independent videocoded variable (number of therapist interpersonal interventions) that correlates with the fidelity ratings. This suggests that the fidelity scales are measuring meaningful therapist activity in the interpersonal area. Although there was not a significant correlation between adherence to technique and outcome, a trend in the expected direction was evident. Perhaps with a larger number of clients a significant relation between purity of technique and outcome may emerge.

Research Programs in Progress

Ten research studies are presently in progress. These were designed to examine in greater detail the major goals of this program, that is, the relative contribution of specific technical factors and nonspecific factors to psychotherapeutic process and outcome.

Specific Technical Factors

In a dissertation for Rutgers University, Joseph (1988) compared therapist interventions preceding transference interpretations that elicited affect from the client with those that elicited defensiveness from the client. Joseph hypothesized that there would be increased confrontation before interpretations that elicited affective responding, but she found instead that confrontation before interpretation increased defensive responding. Clarification was the only variable that significantly preceded the transference interpretations that elicited affect. Apparently, the therapist's listening carefully and reflecting back what the client said before making an interpretation prepared the client to respond in a less defensive and more affective manner. Research now in progress that uses the process variables in relation to outcome have yielded initial analyses demonstrating that transference interpretations eliciting affect are the most strongly correlated to outcome ($r = .64$) (Winston, Pollack, Trujillo, et al., 1987).

A second study examining therapist interventions is being conducted by Makynen from Columbia University Teachers College. Her research follows directly from the dissertation of Salerno (1988), also from Columbia Teacher's College, which hypothesized that clients would respond affectively to confrontation but demonstrated instead that confrontation significantly predicted client defensive behavior in the 1 minute immediately following the therapist intervention. Makynen is extending the time period to be studied by examining confrontations that are sustained over several minutes. On the basis of the results of Salerno's study, Makynen is hypothesiz-

ing that confrontations of longer duration have a greater probability of eliciting client affective responding.

Two studies are examining client affect in the Beth Israel data set in greater detail. The first is being conducted by Sharir from New York University in collaboration with Dahl from Downstate Medical Center. Sharir is applying Dahl's (1988) Coding System for the Emotions, which is designed to make distinctions in emotional responding (e.g., sadness, anger, anxiety, etc.), to examine client defensiveness in relation to these different types of affect. In the other study (Taurke, Flegenheimer, McCullough, Winston, & Pollack, in press), the ratio of affective responding to defensive responding per session was used to examine the change in this ratio across phases of treatment and the relation of the change in this ratio and outcome. When clients were grouped according to high- and low-outcome scores, significant differences between groups emerged. Results showed that during the early phase of treatment clients in both groups showed an average of one affective response for every five defensive responses and that in the late phase of treatment, the low-outcome clients remained at the same level and the high-outcome clients showed a change to one affective response for every two defensive responses.

Nonspecific Factors

Three studies have begun to evaluate the effects of therapeutic alliance. Our initial studies revealed a pattern that gentler techniques (e.g., clarifications) were more predictive of affective responding that the more intrusive techniques (e.g., confrontation or interpretation). When the intrusive techniques did elicit affect, however, there were stronger relationships with improvement than with gentler techniques. We have thus hypothesized that the more intrusive techniques are indeed more powerful but may require a good alliance to "hit the mark," whereas the gentler techniques are less reliant on alliance or, perhaps, less likely to jeopardize the alliance. A master's thesis that began to examine these relationships was prepared by Foote from New York University (Foote, McCullough, Winston, Pollack, & Laikin, 1988). Foote is continuing to delineate these relationships in his doctoral dissertation by using client coordinating style (Westerman, Tanaka, Frankl, & Kahn, 1986) as a measure of alliance or misalliance and is examining differential client response to clarification and confrontation under variations in client coordination with the therapist. He hypothesizes that the greater the coordination between client and therapist, the greater the ability of the therapist to confront the client and to elicit a positive affective or elaborative response.

Another dissertation on therapeutic alliance, prepared by Marcelo Rubin of Columbia University Teachers College in collaboration with Charles Marmar at Langley Porter, is using the California Psychotherapy Alliance Scales instrument to assess therapeutic alliance (Marmar, Gaston, Gallagher, & Thompson, 1987). Rubin will perform an in-depth analysis of client in-session response (e.g., variation in affect and defense and elaboration) across different levels of therapeutic alliance.

A third therapeutic alliance study, for a master's thesis at New York University, was prepared by Nicholas Samstag, who used the Vanderbilt Psychotherapy Process Scale to assess client responding across variations in alliance. Samstag added another dimension to this analysis by examining the variation in alliance related to effects of severity of client pathology (Samstag, McCullough, & Winston, 1989).

Three studies examined obsessive and histrionic personality traits among clients. We hypothesized that the obsessive personality would respond more favorably to the STDP group; that is, the STDP group would confront the defenses and elicit affective responding in the typically isolated, intellectualizing personality more successfully than the more cognitively focused BAP group, which was hypothesized to be more successful with the histrionic client. Four senior clinicians judged each client on an obsessive-histrionic scale with a Likert-type rating of 1 to 10. Of the initial 16-client data set, 4 clients were judged to be strongly histrionic, 4 clients to be strongly obsessive, and the remaining 8 clients to have an admixture of both qualities. Initial results show trends in the expected direction. The two best outcomes in the BAP group were of two clients judged to be clearly histrionic, and the two best outcomes in the STDP group were of two clients judged to be obsessive. Conversely, the two worst outcomes in the STDP group were histrionic, and of the two worst outcomes in the BAP group one was obsessive and one a mixed-trait personality. These results were taken from a small sample, and additional subjects will have to be obtained before any firm conclusions can be drawn.

Two research assistants have chosen to examine differential responding between the obsessive and histrionic personality styles. Hanig from Columbia University is presently designing his dissertation on differential client responding in obsessive compared with histrionic clients in terms of affect, defense, and elaborative responding. He is hypothesizing that the obsessive personality will demonstrate more incidents of intellectualized defensive behavior and less affective responding than the histrionic personality. Conversely, the histrionic client is hypothesized to demonstrate more incidents of immature or regressive defenses and more affective behavior. The second study on this topic was conducted by Bortner for a master's thesis for Yeshiva University in which differential responses of obsessive and histrionic clients to transference interpretations were examined (Bortner, McCullough, Winston, & Pollack, 1989).

Another study of client characteristics is being conducted by Broner for her dissertation at Union Graduate School on locus of control, that is, the client's sense of internal and external mastery over his or her environment. Broner is comparing clients with internal and external locus of control in terms of their in-session responses as well as their change in locus of control across the span of treatment.

Programs Planned for the Future

There are three main areas of investigation planned for the future: (a) examination of process variables from multiple perspectives (e.g., combining specific factors, nonspecific factors, client and therapist characteristics, etc.); (b) working toward a common language for therapy process; and (c) content analysis (e.g., accuracy of interpretation).

Nature of the Research Organization

This research program has been possible because of volunteer contributions from research committee members, therapists, and graduate students. This program could not have been developed and maintained without their help.

Team Members and Roles

Research steering committee. This group meets on a weekly basis to discuss client flow and any outstanding clinical problems, research in progress, and future research directions. This meeting time is also used to practice and revise conference presentations and to review data analyses and publications in process. Arnold Winston, MD, is program director, and Leigh McCullough, PhD, is research director. Jerome Pollack, MD, is clinical director and coordinator of the BAP group, and Michael Laikin, MD, coordinates the STDP group. Henry Pinsker, MD, coordinates the supportive group, and Arlinza Turner, PhD, coordinates the cognitive–behavioral group.

Therapists. The members of the multidisciplinary group of therapists, with an average of 10 years' experience, volunteer several hours a week in addition to their professional duties. They typically see one client a week, participate in a weekly 2-hour peer supervision group, and frequently attend clinical workshops for additional training during the year. Thus, the clinicians have extensive training in active, focused, time-limited therapy.

Research assistants. Graduate students from universities throughout the New York City area, many of whom have been mentioned earlier, have contributed thousands of hours of help, volunteering a minimum of 6–8 hours per week (and often much more) over several years.

Funding Sources

The Beth Israel Psychotherapy Research Program is supported by volunteer contributions of time from therapists and research assistants as well as sliding-scale fees from clients. The fees average $40 (range = $30–$100). The active client caseload was originally 10 and has grown to 15–20 per month. These fees cover the partial payment of office space, utilities, equipment, supplies, and small stipends for research interviewers or statistical consultation.

Relation to Other Research Programs

Integration With Findings of Other Research

In addition to conducting extensive consultation with other research programs and incorporation

of many of their assessment instruments (as mentioned earlier), we are pleased to be collaborating with the following researchers: Hartvig Dahl, MD (Downstate Medical Center), on Dahl's Coding System for the Emotions; Charles Marmar, MD (Langley Porter), on therapeutic alliance; and Leslie Greenberg, PhD (York University), on sadness episodes in psychotherapy. Barry Farber, PhD (Columbia University Teacher's College), supervised our first 2 dissertations (Porter, 1988; Salerno, 1988) and is in the process of supervising an additional four, and Stanley Messer, PhD (Rutgers University), supervised Joseph's dissertation (Joseph, 1988).

Two international collaborative projects have begun. One study, in collaboration with Marianne Grawe-Gerber, PhD, at the Bern Psychotherapy Research Program, Bern, Switzerland, will compare the Structured Analysis of Social Behavior (coding of object relations) with the OPI videocoding system developed at Beth Israel by using transcripts from the PEP project (cf., Kachele, 1989). The other project, in collaboration with Martin Svartberg, MD, and his colleagues at the Ostmarka Psychotherapy Research Program, Trondheim, Norway, will use the OPI system to code and compare psychotherapy process in several forms of brief psychotherapy from both sites.

Impact on the Field of Psychotherapy

Because the program is young, our impact on the field of psychotherapy research is just beginning. We are one of the few programs actively studying four different treatment modalities. Furthermore, we have developed the OPI coding system designed to capture the common specific elements in these four modalities, and as noted earlier we hope that by studying variables common to different treatments in may different settings we can aid the effort to develop a common language among therapists and ultimately assist in contributing to an integrated psychotherapeutic approach.

References

American Psychiatric Association. (1987). *Diagnostic and statistical manual of mental disorders* (rev. 3rd ed.). Washington, DC: Author.

Battle, C., Imber, S., Hoehn-Saric, R., Stone, A., Nash, E., & Frank, J. (1966). Target complaints: A criterion of improvement. *American Journal of Psychotherapy, 20,* 184–192.

Beck, A. T. (1962). Thinking and depression: 2. Theory and therapy. *Archives of General Psychiatry, 10*, 561–571.

Beck, A. T., & Emery, G. (1985). *Anxiety disorders and phobias.* New York: Basic Books.

Been, H., & Sklar, I. (1985). Transference in short-term dynamic psychotherapy. In A. Winston (Ed.), *Clinical and research issues in short-term dynamic psychotherapy* (pp. 1–18). Washington, DC: American Psychiatric Press.

Bortner, J., McCullough, L., Winston, A., & Pollack, J. (1989, June). *Variation in patient affective and defensive responding to transference interpretations in three personality trait groups.* Paper presented at the Society for Psychotherapy Research conference, Toronto, Ontario, Canada.

Dahl, H. (1988). *Coding system for the emotions.* Unpublished manuscript, State University of New York Health Science Center, Brooklyn.

Davanloo, H. (1980). *Short term psychotherapy.* Northvale, NJ: Jason Aronson.

Derogatis, L. R. (1977). *The SCL-90 manual—I: Scoring and administrative procedures for the SCL-90.* Baltimore, MD: Clinical Psychometric Research.

D'Zurilla, T. J., & Goldfried, M. R. (1971). Problem solving and behavior modification. *Journal of Abnormal Psychology, 78*, 107–126.

Elliott, R., Friedlander, M., Hill, C., Mahrer, A.R., Margison, F. R., & Stiles, W. B. (1987). Primary therapist response modes: Comparison of six rating systems. *Journal of Consulting and Clinical Psychology, 2*, 218–223.

Endicott, J., Spitzer, R., Fleiss, J., & Cohen, J. (1976). The Global Assessment Scale. *Archives of General Psychiatry, 33*, 766–771.

Flegenheimer, W. (1985). History of brief psychotherapy. In A. Horner (Ed.), *Treating the oedipal client in brief psychotherapy* (pp. 7–24). Northvale, NJ: Jason Aronson.

Flegenheimer, W. V., & Pollack, J. (1989). Some aspects of the time limit in brief psychotherapy. *Bulletin of the Menninger Clinic, 53*, 44–51.

Foote, J., McCullough, L., Winston, A., Pollack, J., & Laikin, M. (1988, June). *Emergence of client affective responding as a result of specific therapeutic interventions.* Paper presented at the Society for Psychotherapy Research conference, Santa Fe, NM.

Goldin, V., & Winston, A. (1985). The impact of short-term dynamic psychotherapy on psychoanalytic psychotherapy. In A. Winston (Ed.), *Clinical and research issues in short-term dynamic psychotherapy* (pp. 19–43). Washington, DC: American Psychiatric Press.

Horowitz, L. M. Rosenberg, S. E. Baer, B. A. Ureño, G., & Villaseñor, V. S. (1988). The Inventory of Interpersonal Problems: Psychometric properties and clinical applications. *Journal of Consulting and Clinical Psychology, 56*, 885–892.

Joseph, C. (1988). Antecedents to transference interpretation in short-term psychodynamic psychotherapy. (Doctoral dissertation, Rutgers University, 1987). *Dissertation Abstracts International, 50*, 1648B.

Kachele, H. (1989, September). *Single case research in psychotherapy: The PEP project.* Paper presented at the Third European Conference on Psychotherapy Research, Bern, Switzerland.

Marmar, C. R., Gaston, L., Gallagher, D., & Thompson, L. W. (1987, June). *Therapeutic alliance and outcome in behavioral, cognitive, and brief dynamic psychotherapy in late-life depression.* Paper presented at the annual meeting of the Society for Psychotherapy Research, Ulm, Federal Republic of Germany.

McCullough, L. (1990). *Psychotherapy interaction coding system.* Unpublished manuscript, Department of Psychiatry, University of Pennsylvania, PA.

McCullough, L. Vaillant, C., & Vaillant, G. (1986). Toward reliability and identifying ego defense through verbal behavior. In G. Vaillant (Ed.), *Empirical studies of ego mechanisms of defense* (pp. 61–70). Washington, DC: American Psychiatric Press.

McCullough, L., Winston, A., Porter, F., Pollack, J., Farber, B. A., Vingiano, W., Laikin, M., & Trujillo, M. (in press). The relationship of client–therapist interaction to psychotherapeutic outcome. *Psychotherapy.*

Norwicki, S., & Duke, M. (1974). A locus of control scale for non-college as well as college adults. *Journal of Personality Assessment, 38*, 136–137.

Pollack, J., & Horner, A. (1985). Brief adaptation-oriented psychotherapy. In A. Winston (Ed.), *Clinical research issues in short-term dynamic psychotherapy* (pp. 41–60). Washington, DC: American Psychiatric Press.

Porter, F. (1988). The immediate effects of interpretation on client response in short-term dynamic psychotherapy (Doctoral dissertation, Columbia University Teachers College, 1987). *Dissertation Abstracts International, 48*, 87–24076.

Salerno, M. (1988). The immediate effects of confrontation versus clarification on client affective and defensive responding in short-term dynamic psychotherapy (Doctoral dissertation, Columbia University Teachers College, 1987). *Dissertation Abstracts International, 49*, 4557B.

Samstag, N., McCullough, L., & Winston, A. (1989, June). *The correlation of therapeutic alliance on the Vanderbilt Psychotherapy Process Scale with outcome in two forms of brief psychotherapy.* Paper presented at the Society for Psychotherapy Research conference, Toronto, Ontario, Canada.

Sifneos, P. E. (1979). *Short-term dynamic psychotherapy: Evaluation and technique.* New York: Plenum Press.

Smith, M. L., Glass, G. V., & Miller, M. I. (1980). *The benefits of psychotherapy.* Baltimore, MD: John Hopkins University Press.

Spitzer, R., Williams, J., & Gibbon, M. (1987). *Structured Clinical Interview for DSM-III–R personality disorders (SCID-II, 3/1/87).* New York: Biometric Research Department, New York State Psychiatric Institute.

Spitzer, R., Williams, J., Gibbon, M., & First, M. (1988). *Instruction manual for the Structured Clinical Interview for DSM III–R—Client version (SCID-P 6/1/88).* New York: Biometric Research Department, New York State Psychiatric Institute.

Taurke, E., Flegenheimer, W., McCullough, L., Winston, A., & Pollack, J. (in press). Change in affect/defense ratio from early to late sessions in relationship to outcome. *Journal of Clinical Psychology.*

Trujillo, M., & McCullough, L. (1985). Research issues in short-term dynamic psychotherapy: An overview. In A. Winston (Ed.), *Clinical and research issues in short-term dynamic psychotherapy* (pp. 81–102). Washington, DC: American Psychiatric Press.

Vaillant, G. E. (1985). Maturity of ego defenses in relation to DSM-III Axis II personality disorders. *Archives of General Psychiatry, 42,* 597–601.

Waskow, I. E., & Parloff, M. B. (Eds.). (1975). *Psychotherapy change measures.* Rockville, MD: National Institute of Mental Health.

Weissman, M. M., & Bothwell, S. (1976). Assessment of social adjustment by client self-report. *Archives of General Psychiatry, 33,* 111–115.

Westerman, M. A., Tanaka, J. S., Frankl, A. S., & Kahn, J. (1986). The coordinating style construct: An approach to conceptualizing client interpersonal behavior. *Psychotherapy, 23,* 540–547.

Winston, A. (1981). Use of transference in short-term dynamic psychotherapy. *Issues in Ego Psychology, 4,* 26–34.

Winston, A., & Goldin, V. (1985). Pathological mourning in short-term dynamic psychotherapy. In A. Winston (Ed.), *Clinical and research issues in short-term dynamic psychotherapy* (pp. 41–60). Washington, DC: American Psychiatric Press.

Winston, A., Pinsker, H., & McCullough, L. (1986). A review of supportive psychotherapy. *Hospital and Community Psychiatry, 37,* 1105–1114.

Winston, A., Pollack, J., Flegenheimer, W., Laikin, M., McCullough, L., Kestenbaum, R., & Trujillo, M. (1987, June). *A brief psychotherapy fidelity scale—reliability, validity and relation to outcome.* Paper presented at the Society for Psychotherapy Research conference, Ulm, Federal Republic of Germany.

Winston, A., Pollack, J., Trujillo, M., McCullough, L., Laikin, M., Flegenheimer, W., & Kestenbaum, R. (1987, June). *Brief dynamic psychotherapy: Process and outcome.* Paper presented at the Society for Psychotherapy Research conference, Ulm, Federal Republic of Germany.

Winston, A., & Trujillo, M. (1985). Working through. In A. Horner (Ed.), *Treating the oedipal client in brief psychotherapy* (pp. 141–158). Northvale, NJ: Jason Aronson.

3

The Chestnut Lodge Research Institute: An Investigation of the Process and Outcome of Long-Term Hospital Treatment

**Paul M. Gedo, Thomas H. McGlashan,
Wells Goodrich, and Richard C. Fritsch**
Chestnut Lodge Research Institute

Background and Aims

The Chestnut Lodge psychiatric staff began case study investigations of long-term dynamic inpatient treatment in the 1930s. Frieda Fromm-Reichmann, whose work established an innovative framework for psychoanalytic psychotherapy with psychotic patients, consolidated this tradition. In her papers concerning technique and her book *Principles of Intensive Psychotherapy* (1950), she advocated frequent face-to-face sessions and the use of guided associations. She treated the patient's illness as an extreme problem in living and forged an alliance with the portion of the patient's psyche that was striving toward health. Along with Harry Stack Sullivan and Dexter M. Bullard, Sr., she fostered the therapist–administrator split, a team approach in which the ward chief was responsible for day-to-day administrative decisions, thus freeing the therapist to do exploratory and interpretive work.

Chestnut Lodge's directors incorporated a research institute in 1947, which they hoped would foster an integrated research program to investigate schizophrenia. A $250,000 Ford Foundation grant funded several studies as well as constructions of an on-grounds research building. Clini-

cians such as Otto Will, Harold Searles, Donald Burnham, and Ping-Nie Pao continued Fromm-Reichmann's theoretical and technical experiments and used their findings with Chestnut Lodge clients as primary data. These authors explored a series of interrelated problems: the parameters necessary for effective psychodynamic therapy with psychotic patients, the ways in which such adjustments reflected on prevailing psychoanalytic (ego psychological) theory, the psychotic patient's ability to tolerate and profit from investigative therapy, countertransference and its effects, and schizophrenic persons' verbal and paraverbal modes of communication. Stanton and Schwartz (1954) made the first systematic empirical observations concerning the milieu's effect on patients and staff and the ways in which treatment participants knowingly and inadvertently affect the milieu and one another.

Thomas McGlashan expanded on this empirical tradition after his appointment as director of research in 1982. The hospital continued to treat many chronically ill patients, most of whom were

We thank the following people for their support and editorial advice: Linda B. Berman MA, Dexter M. Bullard, Jr., MD, Robert K. Heinssen, PhD, and Patricia Hoffman-Judd, PhD.

diagnosed as schizophrenic and had not improved in other settings. The staff continued to use milieu treatment and intensive individual psychodynamic psychotherapy as the central treatment modalities. McGlashan noted that although some patients made progress over time, others did not seem to change significantly.

McGlashan's initial empirical project aimed at retrospectively illuminating what characteristics differentiated the successful and less successful therapist-patient dyads. Chestnut Lodge had rich resources for a naturalistic descriptive psychotherapy process study. Its therapists had been using Fromm-Reichmann's methods for some 40 years, and a vast archive of therapist notes and transcribed treatment conference records existed that documented these efforts. Staff had included some leading theorist-practitioners of dynamic inpatient psychotherapy; the documentation of this work presumably included prototypic examples of effective and ineffective dyadic processes.

This proposed process study obviously required reliable independent outcome assessments. In turn, this raised issues regarding how to measure the outcome of long-term psychodynamic treatment. It also drew our attention to a patient's index admission clinical picture and to the question of how closely the presenting psychopathology and the initial prognosis correlated with long-term outcome. Were successful therapists merely better matched with appropriate patients? How likely (or unlikely) were schizophrenic patients as opposed to those with other difficulties such as bipolar or unipolar affective disorders or severe character pathology, to make significant gains in treatment? What were the course vicissitudes in each nosological category? We addressed these and other issues by conducting a long-term (15-year average) follow-up study (McGlashan, 1984a, 1984b).

A second research division grew out of Chestnut Lodge's adolescent and child inpatient treatment program, which opened in 1975. Wells Goodrich became director of adolescent and child research. In 1978, Goodrich and his colleagues began ongoing assessment of adolescent inpatients, using a prospective longitudinal design to explore the interactions among psychopathology, treatment processes, and outcome of long-term psychodynamic hospital treatment. One outgrowth of this effort was the elaboration of an integrated model of a multidimensional adolescent treatment course. Our prospective design allows repeated longitudinal assessments by the research, clinical, and nursing staffs and includes data

from the patients themselves. We have recently begun follow-up interviews of the earliest cohorts of Adolescent and Child Division patients.

The overall aims of the adult and adolescent research programs are to study the phenomenologies of person, disorder, and treatment process and to relate these to long-term course and outcome. We hope to illuminate and predict interplay between treatment process and natural history in patients with severe disorders who are undergoing intensive psychosocial treatment.

Method

Research Setting and Samples

Chestnut Lodge is a 130-bed private, long-term psychiatric hospital located in suburban Maryland. Most patients have severe, often chronic, schizophrenia or character pathology or both. The treatment philosophy is based on intensive psychodynamically oriented individual psychotherapy, milieu work, and active rehabilitation. In the past two decades, family therapy and psychotropic medications have also become central treatment components.

The adult follow-up sample included 532 patients without organic brain syndrome who remained at Chestnut Lodge 90 days or more and were discharged between 1950 and 1975 plus a group of long-term patients still in the hospital. The adolescent studies included all patients (170) admitted since the division opened.

Instruments and Procedures

The adult studies used measures designed to capture multiple dimensions of baseline functioning, course, and outcome. Where possible, we used existing scales; we assessed interrater reliability for all instruments and dropped variables for which we were unable to establish sufficient agreement. For baseline assessment, trained research assistants created a 25-page abstract from each subject's medical record. We then used this abstract to rate multiple domains such as demographics, family history, growth and development, premorbid functioning, illness onset and course, and sign and symptom presentation. We also used the abstracts to rediagnose patients on the basis of contemporary criteria , most by those of the revised third edition of the *Diagnostic and Statistical Manual of Mental Disorders (DSM-III-R;* American Psychiatric Association, 1987).

To obtain follow-up data, we interviewed patients and significant others in person or by telephone. Judges blind to the baseline data rated the interviews. They assessed multiple outcome dimensions including further treatment, work and school functioning, nuclear and marital family relationships, social activity, psychopathology (e.g., amount of time symptomatic, symptom severity, suicidal ideation, substance use), and global functioning.

At follow-up, particularly responsive patients were asked to participate in an additional extended interview. These semistructured sessions focused on dimensions of psychodynamic and defensive functioning such as functional developmental level, aspects of self, object relatedness, reality acceptance, fullness of experience, integrative capacity, self-analytic functioning, and symptomatology (McGlashan, 1984a).

The Adolescent and Child Division project also used a multidimensional measurement battery. Judges rated medical records for *DSM III–R* research diagnosis, demographic variables, history of assaultive and self-destructive behavior, and a life-events scale (Fullerton & Friedman, 1981). This scale focused on family relationships; evidence of psychiatric difficulties; and level of distress in infancy, latency, and adolescence. Family members completed a scale measuring family flexibility and cohesion. Records of intellectual and projective psychological testing and of Chestnut Lodge school performance were also available. Additional assessments were administered at 3 and 15 months of hospitalization and at discharge. These included a locus of control questionnaire and clinical staff ratings of severity of illness (Global Assessment Scale [GAS] score). An adapted version of the Summers Scale, now referred to as the Attachment Scale (Fritsch, de Marneffe, & Goodrich, 1987; copies available on request) assessed patient separation, possessiveness, emotional and instrumental dependency, and differentiation. We also developed instruments that measure treatment alliance and adaptation to the milieu; these are described. We currently engaged in a 5-year follow-up study.

Research Accomplishments

Instruments Developed

The adult study developed both standard and extended follow-up interviews (copies available on request). The latter are based explicitly on psychodynamic treatment process and outcome theories. We also developed operational rating criteria for a wide range of variables. We elaborated on the Prognostic Scale for Chronic Schizophrenia (Fenton & McGlashan, 1987a) and are currently constructing a prognostic scale for borderline personality disorder.

The adolescent study featured two new measures. The first is an aggression checklist. By using the adolescent's developmental history and the administrator's admission note as data, it evaluates the qualities of externally aggressive (e.g., fighting or stealing) and internally aggressive (e.g. suicidal acts or self-mutilative) behavior before admission. The second measure, the Chestnut Lodge Adolescent Interaction Report (CLAIR), is an elaboration of Lorr's Inpatient Multidimensional Psychiatric Scale. The unit staff member who best knows the client completes this 73-item questionnaire 1 month after admission and at discharge. The change score provides a measure of hospital behavioral shifts. We have achieved adequate reliability with these measures. Overall, we hope to develop and refine theoretically driven measures that will permit empirical study of long-term, multimodal psychodynamic treatment.

Findings

In the adult follow-up study, McGlashan (1984b) compared *DSM-III*–defined schizophrenic, depressed, and bipolar cohorts. Most clients had had long-term (more than 2 years) disability and had been hospitalized many times before coming to Chestnut Lodge. After index admission, schizophrenic patients tended to transfer to other hospitals and to receive additional somatic treatment; affective disorder patients used additional outpatient psychotherapy. Overall, most depressed patients made impressive, lasting gains in treatment; bipolar patients also tended to improve, whereas most schizophrenic patients remained chronically incapacitated (with two-thirds being chronically ill or marginally functional at follow-up). Nevertheless, some schizophrenic patients who ultimately functioned better had looked worse at admission. A small group (14%) of schizophrenic patients sustained a long-term remission without medications (Fenton & McGlashan, 1987b).

Overall, Chestnut Lodge's (chronically ill) borderline personality disorder patients made impressive gains (McGlashan, 1986a). Although most continued in various intermittent psychiatric treatments during the follow-up period and continued to experience symptoms frequently, most functioned quite well, especially instrumentally. Most sustained moderately close interpersonal relationships, and some were able to live with a long-term sexual partner, although a subgroup avoided intimate relationships entirely. Four-fifths of the borderline patients achieved a moderate, or better, global outcome. Unlike the improvement seen in schizophrenic or depressed patients some of the borderline personality disorder patients' improvement seemed to be a function of natural history; post-hoc analysis of variance showed that patients tended to do better the older they were and the longer the time since their discharge (Bardenstein & McGlashan, 1988).

McGlashan and Heinssen (1989) compared subgroups of the borderline cohort that showed antisocial, narcissistic, or neither set of traits. At baseline, the antisocial trait group showed poorer work functioning, earlier symptomatology, and more assaultive and criminal behavior; at follow-up, however, they were functioning as well as or better than the other two subgroups. It is unclear whether a specific treatment component helped the antisocial patients improve or whether treatment acted as a holding environment, containing a spiraling decline and facilitating positive maturational changes.

Compared with borderline personality disorder patients or mixed borderline and schizotypal personality disorder patients, pure schizotypal patients did not fare as well at follow-up (McGlashan, 1986b). They tended to remain socially isolated and looked worse than the borderline patients, but better than the schizophrenic patients, in terms of employment, social relations, and global outcome.

Patients with schizoaffective psychosis who met *DSM-III* criteria for both schizophrenia and a bipolar or unipolar affective disorder tended to fall between the outcomes of these respective disorders (Williams & McGlashan, 1987). Schizoaffective patients needed considerable postdischarge treatment and did poorly in work and social situations. Even so, they fared better than schizophrenic patients across these domains.

The team also investigated predictors of long-term outcome (McGlashan, 1986c). Schizophrenic patients with better outcomes tended to have higher premorbid functioning, better preservation of affect (e.g., depression), lower genetic loading, and enough reality testing that they had never been assaultive. Fenton and McGlashan (1986) found that a subgroup of schizophrenic patients displaying marked obsessive-compulsive symptoms along with schizophrenia were significantly more impaired at outcome. McGlashan (1986d) demonstrated that outcome predictors varied depending on length of follow-up. A prediction study of borderline patients (McGlashan, 1985) revealed that higher intelligence quotient, less affective instability at baseline, and less hospitalization before index admission predicted better global outcome.

McGlashan (1987) compared cohorts with unipolar depression, borderline personality disorder, and both disorders (comorbid group). Compared with the pure depressed patients the comorbid group developed pathology earlier, displayed psychotic symptoms more often, and was more likely to develop substance abuse problems and to seek additional treatment. Compared with the pure borderlines, the comorbid group developed pathology later, used more treatment, and was more likely to attempt suicide.

The follow-up study's manic cohort was almost evenly divided between adult and adolescent onset patients. McGlashan (1988) found that the two cohorts were equivalent in many ways. When differences existed, the adolescent onset patients were more impaired at baseline yet functioned at an equivalent or higher level at follow-up. McGlashan concluded that the younger onset patients may have had a less virulent illness that was temporarily exacerbated by adolescent developmental challenges or that their pathology was less fixed because of their greater youth and character flexibility.

In a recent book, McGlashan and Keats (1988) analyzed the psychotherapeutic treatment processes of two schizophrenic cases with good outcomes and two such cases with poor outcomes. They hoped to discriminate patterns associated with long-term success and failure. They viewed therapy as a complex, interactive process that facilitates epigenetic change along various developmental lines. They identified a range of treatment process levels that correlated with developmental (baseline) and outcome (follow-up) vicissitudes. Achieving more complex, developmentally advanced process levels is itself a therapeutic outcome, especially for archaically organized clients.

These authors offered hypothesized process and outcome correlates to maturity and relational complexity levels. They differentiated between engagement, which involves any sort of relatedness; attachment, in which the therapist becomes unique to the patient; and alliance, in which therapist and patient accept distinct roles and work toward a shared treatment aim. Most psychotherapy studies have assumed the presence of an alliance. With a chronically and severely impaired population, however, an alliance is often the outcome of months or years of work. Most patients who cannot engage continue to experience severe incapacitation, and those who manage engagement or attachment but cannot form a solid working alliance usually are functioning at outcome but at a moderately compromised level.

The alliance can range from allowing the therapist to supply missing psychological skills (supportive alliance), to creating a shared language to examine experience and to solve problems (instrumental alliance), to an analytic working alliance fostering introspection and insight, including exploration of the transference. The last of these marks the transition from a more anaclitic to a more autonomous relational level and correlates with long-term functional remission. An established analytic alliance permits exploration and integration of previously warded-off experience. These relationship-modifying processes can then facilitate internalizing of various aspects of the therapist and the functions that he or she has served for the patient. The most complex process involves mourning lost or nonexistent life options and personal abilities and anticipatory mourning for the therapist before termination. Patients who achieve such differentiated process levels are more likely to reach and maintain a full recovery.

Several factors cut across process levels. These include commitment to the work; dyadic match and other relationship parameters such as hedonic tone; containment (in Winnicott's [1954/1958] sense); and empathy for the patient's manifest illness, existential struggle, and psychodynamics.

The authors illustrated each case's process and dyadic factors with detailed description from the archival and follow-up material. They acknowledged the limits of this small retrospective study. They offered their hypothesized process levels for further exploration and testing, however, and concluded that prospective or comparative treatment and outcome studies should assess process level context more thoroughly. This would allow researchers to match samples better, especially for post hoc analyses. McGlashan and Keats (1988) integrated their findings regarding treatment with what is known about the natural history of schizophrenia and the effect of adjunctive treatments and estimated the main and interactive effects of each on outcome. They discussed how practitioners might differentially combine these elements to treat patients at different points along the schizophrenic, and therapy process, continuum.

The adolescent research group, using the methods of both Rinsley (1980) and Masterson (1978), has elaborated a multimodal, triphasic model of long-term inpatient treatment (Goodrich, 1985, 1987). The first phase is devoted to creating a working alliance within which the adolescent can tolerate symbiotic dependency. Like McGlashan and Keats (1988), Goodrich concluded that establishing an attachment and an alliance is itself an outcome of effective treatment process. In the second phase, the staff fosters the patient's self-observant focus on transference repetitions in the here and now. Staff also support the adolescent's positive identifications with team members and their functions. The final phase deals with termination as it evokes autonomy and dependency issues.

The research group has begun testing this process model. We predicted that ability to form a consistent dependent attachment, in which hospital personnel were viewed as helpful and supportive, by the 3rd month of treatment would be a positive prognostic sign. Fifteen-month symptomatic improvement data supported this hypothesis (Fritsch & Goodrich, 1990). Additionally, there were interesting differences within various diagnostic cohorts. For instance, a large percentage of patients with schizotypal organization who did not make a firm attachment by 3 months achieved attachment and intermediate outcome by 15 months that were similar to those of patients with good 3-month attachments. Analysis of variance indicated an interaction between attachment level and severity of illness.

Because attachment issues are so central to adolescent treatment process, Free and Goodrich (1985) compared early transitional object attachment patterns in our patient population with those of a control sample of private day school students. They found that the two groups did not differ significantly in the frequency or duration of their early childhood transitional object attachment. Nevertheless, it was significantly more likely that the patients' mothers had intervened actively to end their child's attachment. More patients evinced a continuing transitional object attachment as adolescents. This may have been due to their ongoing need to work through attachment and separation issues.

Fritsch, Holmstrom, Goodrich, and Rieger (1990) have elaborated an object-relations model in which patients vary from those who cannot maintain self-other boundaries (withdrawing autistically rather than acting out), to those who need and accept symbiotic assistance, to those who can form a mature alliance with staff members. Initial cluster analysis of CLAIR data on our adolescent patients indicated several distinct clusters that correlated with various milieu adjustment patterns. Two patient clusters reacted with autistic withdrawal, two with symbiotic attachment, and two with prosocial behavior in the milieu. Some of the prosocial patients had mature internalized object representations yet engaged in the most acting-out behavior, probably as an initial defense against attachment. There were also gender differences, with boys being more likely to act out and girls tending to turn away from staff and to look to peers. The authors concluded that active initial resistance, or acting-out behavior, coupled with positive peer relationships, may be an indirect sign of healthy internal capacities rather than a simple index of pathology.

Friedman, Goodrich, and Fullerton (1985) explored the diagnostic utility of a standard locus of control measure with Chestnut Lodge's chronically disturbed adolescent population. With effects of maturation and treatment length being partialed out, locus of control displayed a significant but modest correlation with overall pathology (GAS score).

The adolescent group has also focused on prognostic issues. Fullerton, Goodrich, and Berman (1986) compared the treatment resistances of adopted and nonadopted patients. After 1 month of hospitalization, adopted patients were more likely than nonadopted patients to form close bonds with peers and to reject ties with staff. Adopted patients were significantly more likely to run away from the hospital many times. They were also more likely to run away in groups, whereas those who were not adopted more often ran alone. The authors related these findings to possible dynamic meanings and conflicts regarding adoptive status. Goodrich and Fullerton (1984) found that patients who terminated treatment by running away were more likely to be peer-dependent than adult-dependent. These patients seemed to translate rage about treatment difficulties or losses (e.g., favored staff leaving the hospital) into ego-syntonic action. The more adult-dependent patients seemed to react to similar frustrations by becoming dysphoric and withdrawn; they were less likely to flee the treatment.

Berman and Goodrich (1990) found that several intuitively appealing variables (ego, level of pathology, age at admission, and gender) did not have prognostic significance for hospital elopements. History of running away from home did predict such escapes, however. Goodrich (1990) has detailed severe borderline adolescents' usual responses to provision of a symbiotic attachment in a secure hospital holding environment. This symbiosis allows them to acquire missing psychological and developmental skills and to gain insight concerning previous conflictual attachments. Goodrich pointed to the need for further study of those patients who are treatment-resistant or who only reach partial recovery, however, with an eye to refining treatment or admissions parameters.

Delga, Heinssen, Fritsch, Goodrich, and Yates (1989) explored the interrelationships among psychosis, externally and internally directed aggression, and patient gender in the Chestnut Lodge adolescent sample. These psychotic adolescents were not more likely to have had histories of violent or suicidal behavior than nonpsychotic adolescents. Boys were no more violent than girls. When less extreme behaviors were considered, nonpsychotic patients showed significantly higher aggression levels. These findings were at variance with those of the Bellevue Hospital study (Inamdar, Lewis, Siomopoulos, Shanok, & Lamela, 1982), which had examined a lower socioeconomic cohort.

Fritsch, Delga, Heinssen, Goodrich, and Yates (1987) found that history of external aggression is significantly associated with unmanageable hospital behavior. Younger adolescents and boys tended to present more administrative problems, although boys and girls did not differ in history of external aggression. Patients with high internally directed aggression did not seem to be more depressed than other adolescent patients. Adolescents with a history of external and internal aggression had severe personality disorders. They tended to conform initially but to present more milieu management problems as treatment progressed. Overall, adolescents seemed to enact similar pathological behavior patterns in the community and in the hospital.

Fullerton, Yates, and Goodrich (1990) explored effects of therapist-patient gender match and therapist experience level on outcome. There was an interaction effect: Inexperienced therapists were more effective with same-sex patients and experienced therapists did better work with opposite-sex patients. The team is expanding this study of therapist-patient matching and its effect on outcome.

Research Programs in Progress

The adult group continues to explore hypotheses concerning psychopathology, treatment process, and outcome. McGlashan and Heinssen are developing a prognostic scale for patients with borderline illness. McGlashan and Fenton are examining the risk of developing schizophrenia among character-disordered patients. Heinssen and McGlashan are also exploring the validity of schizophreniform psychosis as a distinct nosological entity. Initial analysis indicates that the schizophreniform cohort falls somewhere between the affective disorder and the schizophrenic cohorts in terms of premorbid functioning and long-term course.

The adolescent team continues to sharpen and explore their process measures. We are undertaking a factor analytic study of locus of control responses. We hope to subtype personality disordered patients on the basis of their attachment and aggression scale scores. We are developing methods to measure insight across treatment in hopes of relating insight to changes in overall functioning. We are also exploring ways to integrate psychological test data, especially regarding the patient's ego and superego functions and drive fixations, into our diagnostic and prognostic studies.

Programs Planned for the Future

The adult project plans to re-score the follow-up sample for illness subtypes and for long-term course patterns. We hope to develop reliable operational criteria for what constitutes a prototypic schizophrenic, unipolar or bipolar affective-disordered case, or personality-disordered case on the basis of long-term clinical profiles. Another study will involve the intensive description and analysis of several good- and poor-outcome borderline personality-disordered patients in hopes of explicating a model of treatment process analogous to that elaborated by McGlashan and Keats (1988). Future plans also include establishing a prospective longitudinal assessment system.

The adolescent project researchers have begun collecting follow-up data on patients discharged at least 5 years ago. We hope eventually to test the effects of multidimensional process variables (e.g., alliance, dependent attachment, self-esteem, acquisition of insight, quality of hospital separation) on long-term outcome. We also hope to compare the treatment course and follow-up adaptation of diagnostic cohorts, especially of personality-disordered, dysthymic, and conduct-disordered patients. Such comparisons do not exist in the adolescent treatment literature.

Nature of the Research Organization

Most research participants have full-time appointments, which include significant clinical responsibilities, at the hospital. Several doctoral-level psychology students are also involved in research. We have received funding from the Ford Foundation (1947, $250,000) for research projects and the research building; the National Institute of Mental Health (1981 to 1983, $100,000), the Fund for Psychoanalytic Research, American Psychoanalytic Association (1979, $5,000 to McGlashan, primary investigator), and the National Alliance for Research on Schizophrenia and Depression (1989 to 1991, $30,000 to Fenton, primary investigator) for the adult follow-up study; a research endowment from the Chestnut Lodge Research Institute for miscellaneous expenses; and indirect hospital support for the research institute budget (e.g., salaries, secretarial support, and equipment).

Relation to Other Research Programs

The adult study's findings have generally been consonant with those of other research regarding nosology, prognosis, and natural history for schizophrenia, affective disorder, and schizotypal and borderline personality disorders. The study has attempted to foster cross-study comparisons by using a multi-diagnosis sample and multidimensional measures by paying careful attention to reliability issues. Chestnut Lodge research has exerted great influence on clinical practice, beginning with Fromm-Reichmann's applications and emendations to psychoanalytic technique, which had a profound impact on psychodynamic psychotherapy. The adult follow-up study demonstrates the importance, and the complexities, of making accurate assessments of the patient's current condition and of establishing realistic, attainable treatment goals. The range of interventions that our clinicians actually use seems far wider than most other clinicians have acknowledged; this breadth is probably integral to optimal improvement.

The adolescent group is studying intensive treatment that builds on the research done at Timberlawn and Menninger hospitals. The patient populations are similar, and the research findings lend further subtlety and empirical support to the treatment model (Goodrich, 1985, 1987). The Chestnut Lodge research has also added an increased focus on prospective longitudinal process measures. Additionally, the group is pooling data with a Swedish research team; this cross-national comparison should enrich our knowledge regarding the cultural context of adolescent psychopathology and its treatment.

References

American Psychiatric Association. (1987). *Diagnostic and statistical manual of mental disorders* (rev. 3rd ed.). Washington, DC: Author.

Bardenstein, K., & McGlashan, T. (1988). The natural history of a residentially treated borderline sample: Gender differences. *Journal of Personality Disorders, 2,* 69–83.

Berman, L., & Goodrich, W. (1990). Running away from treatment: Observations and admission predictors for hospitalized adolescents. *Adolescent Psychiatry, 17,* 279–304.

Delga, I., Heinssen, R., Fritsch, R., Goodrich, W., & Yates, B. (1989). Psychosis, aggression, and self-destructive behavior in hospitalized adolescents. *American Journal of Psychiatry, 146,* 521–525.

Fenton, W., & McGlashan, T. (1986). The prognostic significance of obsessive-compulsive symptoms in schizophrenia. *American Journal of Psychiatry, 143,* 437–441.

Fenton, W., & McGlashan, T. (1987a). Prognostic scale for schizophrenia. *Schizophrenia Bulletin, 13,* 277–286.

Fenton, W., & McGlashan, T. (1987b). Sustained remission in drug-free schizophrenics. *American Journal of Psychiatry, 144,* 1306–1309.

Free, K., & Goodrich, W. (1985). Transitional object attachment in normal and in chronically disturbed adolescents. *Child Psychiatry and Human Development, 16,* 30–44.

Friedman, R., Goodrich, W., & Fullerton, C. (1985). Locus of control and severity of psychiatric illness in the residential treatment of adolescents. *Residential Group Care and Treatment, 3,* 3–13.

Fritsch, R., Delga, I., Heinssen, R., Goodrich, W., & Yates, B. (1987, October). *Predicting aggression in hospitalized adolescents.* Poster presented at the American Academy of Child Psychiatry, Washington, DC.

Fritsch, R., de Marneffe, C., & Goodrich, W. (1987). *The Chestnut Lodge Attachment Scale.* Unpublished manuscript.

Fritsch, R., & Goodrich, W. (1990). Adolescent in-patient attachment as a treatment process. *Adolescent Psychiatry, 17,* 246–263.

Fritsch, R., Holmstrom, R., Goodrich, W., & Rieger, R. (1990). Personality and demographic differences among different types of adjustment to adolescent milieu. *Adolescent Psychiatry, 17,* 202–225.

Fromm-Reichmann, F. (1950). *Principles of intense psychotherapy.* Chicago: University of Chicago Press.

Fullerton, C., & Friedman, R. (1981). *Family life events chart.* Unpublished manuscript.

Fullerton, C., Goodrich, W., & Berman, L. (1986). Adoption predicts psychiatric treatment resistances in hospitalized adolescents. *Journal of American Academy of Child Psychiatry, 25,* 542–551.

Fullerton, C., Yates, B., & Goodrich, W. (1990). The sex and experience of the therapist and their effects on intensive psychotherapy of the adolescent patient. *Adolescent Psychiatry, 17,* 273–278.

Goodrich, W. (1985). Symbiosis and individuation: The integrative process for residential treatment of adolescents. *Current Issues in Psychoanalytic Practice, 1,* 23–45.

Goodrich, W. (1987). Long-term psychoanalytic hospital treatment of adolescents. *Psychiatric Clinics of North America, 10,* 273–287.

Goodrich, W. (1990). The severe borderline adolescent: Hospital treatment process and patterns of response. *Adolescent Psychiatry, 17,* 226–245.

Goodrich, W., & Fullerton, C. (1984). Which borderline patients in residential treatment will run away? *Residential Group Care and Treatment, 2,* 3–14.

Inamdar, S., Lewis, D., Siomopoulous, G., Shanok, S., & Lamela, M. (1982). Violent and suicidal behavior in psychotic adolescents. *American Journal of Psychiatry, 139,* 932–935.

Masterson, J. (1978). *Treatment of the borderline adolescent: A developmental approach.* New York: Wiley.

McGlashan, T. (1984a). The Chestnut Lodge follow-up study: I. Follow-up method and study sample. *Archives of General Psychiatry, 41,* 573–585.

McGlashan, T. (1984b). The Chestnut Lodge follow-up study: II. Long-term outcome of schizophrenic and affective disorders. *Archives of General Psychiatry, 41,* 586–601.

McGlashan, T. (1985). The prediction of outcome in borderline personality disorder: Part V of the Chestnut Lodge follow-up study. In T. McGlashan (Ed.), *The borderline: Current empirical research* (pp. 61–98). Washington, DC: American Psychiatric Press.

McGlashan, T. (1986a). The Chestnut Lodge follow-up study: III. Long-term outcome of borderline personalities. *Archives of General Psychiatry, 43,* 20–30.

McGlashan, T. (1986b). Schizotypal personality disorder. The Chestnut Lodge follow-up study: VI. Long-term follow-up perspectives. *Archives of General Psychiatry, 43,* 329–334.

McGlashan, T. (1986c). The prediction of outcome in chronic schizophrenia: IV. The Chestnut Lodge follow-up study. *Archives of General Psychiatry, 43,* 157–176.

McGlashan, T. (1986d). Predictors of shorter-, medium-, and longer-term outcome in schizophrenia. *American Journal of Psychiatry, 143,* 50–54.

McGlashan, T. (1987). Borderline personality disorder and unipolar affective disorder: Long-term effects of comorbidity. *Journal of Nervous and Mental Disease, 175,* 467–473.

McGlashan, T. (1988). Adolescent versus adult onset of mania. *American Journal of Psychiatry, 145,* 221–223.

McGlashan, T., & Heinssen, R. (1989). Narcissistic, antisocial, and non-comorbid subgroups of borderline disorder: Are they distinct entities by long-term clinical profile? *Psychiatric Clinics of North America, 12,* 653–670.

McGlashan, T., & Keats, C. (1988). *Schizophrenia: Treatment, process, and outcome.* Washington, DC: American Psychiatric Press.

Rinsley, D. (1980). *Treatment of the severely disturbed adolescent.* Northvale, NJ: Jason Aronson.

Stanton, A., & Schwartz, M. (1954). *The mental hospital.* New York: Basic Books.

Williams, P., & McGlashan, T. (1987). Schizoaffective psychosis: I. Comparative long-term outcome. *Archives of General Psychiatry, 43,* 329–334.

Winnicott, D. (1958). Metapsychological and clinical aspects of regression within the psycho-analytical set-up. In D. Winnicott (Ed.), *Through Paediatrics to Psychoanalysis: Collected papers* (pp. 278–294). New York: Basic Books. (Original work published 1954)

4

Interpersonal Psychotherapy: Research Program and Future Prospects

Gerald L. Klerman
Cornell University Medical College

Myrna M. Weissman
New York State Psychiatric Institute

Background and Aims

The overall aim of this research program is the development and evaluation of interpersonal psychotherapy (IPT) for the treatment of depression and related clinical conditions. A major activity is a series of clinical trials in which the efficacy of the treatment is evaluated. On the basis of the results of those trials, refinement of technique and evaluation of process are undertaken.

IPT is a brief (usually 12–16 weeks) weekly psychotherapeutic treatment developed for the ambulatory, nonbipolar, nonpsychotic, depressed patient that is focused on improving the quality of the depressed patient's current interpersonal functioning and the problems associated with the onset of depression. It is suitable for use, after appropriate training, by experienced psychiatrists, psychologists, and social workers. It can be used alone or in combination with pharmacologic treatments.

History

IPT was developed as part of a research program and was primarily intended to be a standardized treatment for use in controlled clinical trials. The research on IPT was developed by the Boston-New Haven Collaborative Depression Project, which was undertaken initially by Gerald L. Klerman, MD, in New Haven and continued after his relocation to Boston in 1970. Through the 1960s and early 1970s, the New Haven collaborators included Myrna M. Weissman, PhD, Bruce Rounsaville, MD, and Eve Chevron. The Boston collaborators included Klerman at Harvard University and the late Alberto DiMascio, PhD, and Carlos Neu, MD, at Boston State Hospital-Tufts University Medical College. The initial studies were of the role of psychotherapy in relationship to the use of drugs in maintenance treatment of depressives after recovery from an acute episode (Klerman, DiMascio, Weissman, Prusoff, & Paykel, 1974). Subsequently, a randomized trial of brief IPT was undertaken for acutely depressed clients in a 12-week trial (Weissman, Prusoff, DiMascio, Neu, Gohlaney, & Klerman, 1979).

IPT is based on extensive evidence depicting most clinical depressions—regardless of symptom patterns, severity, biological vulnerability, or personality traits—occurring in an interpersonal context. Understanding and renegotiation of the interpersonal context thus can facilitate recovery from depression and reduce social morbidity.

The techniques and methods of IPT have been operationally described in a manual that has undergone a number of revisions. This manual, now in published final form (Klerman, Weissman, Rounsaville, & Chevron, 1984), was developed to standardize the treatment so that clinical trials could be undertaken. A training program for experienced psychotherapists of different disciplines providing the treatment for these clinical trials has also been developed (Weissman, Rounsaville, & Chevron, 1982). Because there is no ongoing training program for practitioners, although preliminary workshops are from time to time available, the book can serve as a guide for the experienced clinician who wants to learn IPT.

Aims

IPT has evolved over 20 years of experience in the research and treatment of ambulatory depressed patients. It has been tested alone and in comparison and combination with tricyclics in six clinical trials with depressed patients: three of acute treatment (Weissman et al, 1979; Sloane, Staples, & Schneider, 1985; Elkin et al, 1986) and three of maintenance treatment (Klerman et al., 1974; Kupfer & Frank, 1988; Reynold & Imber, 1988). Six studies have included a drug comparison group (Klerman et al., 1974; Kupfer & Frank, 1988; Reynold & Imber, 1988; Weissman et al., 1979; Sloane et al., 1985: Elkin et al., 1986), and four have included a combination of IPT and drugs (Klerman et al., 1974; Weissman et al., 1979; Sloane et al., 1985; Elkin et al., 1986). Two derivatives of IPT, conjoint marital (IPT-CM; Foley, Rounsaville, Weissman, Sholomskas, & Chevron, in press) and interpersonal counseling (IPC; Klerman et al., 1987), have been developed and evaluated in small studies.

Method

IPT developed in the 1960s and 1970s as part of a series of new developments in the psychological treatment of depression. A number of brief psychotherapies were developed, notably cognitive–behavioral therapy by Beck, Shaw, and Emory (1979) and various forms of behavior therapy. This interest in brief psychotherapy for depression arose against a background of renewed clinical interest in the psychopathology, diagnosis, and treatment of depression. Structured interviews and diagnostic algorithms were developed,

and more focused diagnostic procedures were applied in therapeutic research on drugs and psychotherapy during this decade.

In this context psychotherapy is seen as a treatment modality for specified clinical indications, in this case depression. This represents a departure from what is perhaps the mainstream of psychotherapy, emphasizing the general applicability of psychotherapy to personality conflicts rather than to specific disorders.

A major effort in our work has been testing for efficacy of treatment by applying the techniques of randomized clinical trials in assessing drugs, psychotherapy, and the combination of both. Table 4.1 lists the efficacy of IPT and its derivatives (Weissman, Jarrett, & Rush, 1987).

Research Accomplishments

IPT as Treatment of Acute Depression

In 1973 we initiated a 16-week study of the acute treatment of 81 ambulatory depressed patients, both men and women, comparing IPT and amitriptyline (each alone and in combination) against a nonscheduled psychotherapy treatment (DiMascio, Weissman, Prusoff, Neu, Zwilling, & Klerman, 1979; see Study 1 in Table 1). IPT was administered weekly by experienced psychiatrists. A specified procedural manual was developed. By 1973 the Schedule of Affective Disorders and Schizophrenia as well as Research Diagnostic Criteria were available for making more precise diagnostic judgments, thereby ensuring the selection of a more homogeneous sample of depressed patients.

Patients were randomly assigned to the IPT or the control group at the beginning of treatment, which was limited to 16 weeks because this was an acute and not a maintenance treatment trial (Weissman, Klerman, Prusoff, Sholomskas, & Padian, 1981). Patients were assessed up to 1 year after treatment had ended to determine any long-term treatment effects. The assessment of outcome was made by an independent clinical evaluator who did not know the treatment conditions. In the latter part of the 1970s, we reported the results on acute depression of IPT compared with tricyclic antidepressants alone and in combination. We demonstrated that both active treatments (IPT and the tricyclic's) were more effective than the control treatment and that combined

Table 4.1
Efficacy Studies of Interpersonal Psychotherapy (IPT) in Depression

Treatment condition	Diagnosis	Number of patients	Time	Study
Acute treatment studies				
1. IPT + amitryptiline with and without nonscheduled treatment	MDD	96	16 weeks	Weissman et al. (1979)
2. IPT or nortriptyline or placebo	MDD or dysthymia, age 60+ years	?	6 weeks	Sloane, Staples, and Schneider (1985)
3. IPT or CB or imipramine management or placebo + management	MDD	25	16 weeks	Elkin, Shea, Watkins, and Collins (1986)
Maintenance treatment studies				
4. IPT or low contact + amitryptiline, placebo, or no medication	Recovered MDD	150	32 weeks	Klerman, DiMascio, Weissman, Prusoff, and Paykel (1974)
5. IPT or IPT + placebo or IPT + imipramine management or imipramine management or placebo	Recovered and recurrent MDD	125	3 years	Kupfer & Frank (1988)
6. IPT for elderly depressed clients	Recovered and recurrent MDD	120	3 years	Reynold & Imber (1988)

Note. MDD = major depressive disorder and CB = combination of both.

treatment was superior to either treatment alone (Weissman et al., 1979; DiMascio et al., 1979).

In addition, we conducted a 1-year follow-up study that indicated that therapeutic benefit of treatment was sustained for most patients. Those who had received IPT alone or in combination with drugs were functioning better than those who had received either drugs alone or the control treatment (Weissman et al., 1981). A fraction of patients in all treatments relapsed and required additional treatment.

IPT as Maintenance Treatment

The first study of IPT as maintenance treatment began in 1967 (Study 4 in Table 1). In June 1967, it was clear that the tricyclic antidepressants were efficacious in the treatment of acute depression. It was unclear how long treatment should continue and what the role of psychotherapy was in maintenance treatment. Our study was designed to answer those questions.

A sample of 150 acutely depressed outpatients who had responded to a tricyclic antidepressant (amitriptyline) with symptom reduction were studied. Each patient received 8 months of maintenance treatment with drugs alone, psychotherapy (IPT) alone, or a combination of both. We found that maintenance drug treatment alone prevented relapse and that psychotherapy alone improved social functioning and interpersonal relations but had no effect on symptomatic relapse. Because of the differential effects of the treatments, the combination of drugs and psychotherapy was the most efficacious (Klerman et al., 1974); no negative interaction between drugs and psychotherapy was found.

In the course of that project, we became aware of the need for greater specification of the psychotherapeutic techniques involved and for careful training of psychotherapists for research. The psychotherapy had been described in terms of conceptual framework, goals, frequency of contacts, and criteria for therapist suitability. The techniques, strategies, and actual procedures had not been set out in a procedure manual, however, and there were no training programs.

Other Studies of IPT for Depression

Investigators have extended IPT to other aspects of depression. A long-term period of maintenance IPT is still underway at the University of Pittsburgh, conducted by Kupfer and Frank, to assess the value of drugs and psychotherapy in maintenance treatment of chronic recurrent depressions

(Kupfer & Frank, 1988; see Study 5 in Table 1). A similar study in a depressed geriatric patient population is also underway at the University of Pittsburgh (Study 6 in Table 1). Sloane (Study 2 in Table 1) completed a pilot 6-week trial of IPT compared with nortriptyline and placebo for depressed elderly patients. He found partial evidence that the efficacy of IPT over nortriptyline was due to elderly individuals not tolerating the medication. In elderly people the problem of tolerating medication, particularly anticholinergic effects, has led to increased interest in psychotherapy for this age group.

Further development of IPT is underway in two areas: IPT as conjoint marital therapy and the derivation of a brief form of counseling for use in primary health care settings.

IPT in a Conjoint Marital Context

Although the causal direction is unknown, clinical and epidemiologic studies have shown that marital disputes, separation, and divorce are strongly associated with the onset of depression (Weissman, 1987). Moreover, depressed patients in ambulatory treatment frequently cite marital problems as their chief complaint (Rounsaville, Weissman, Prusoff, & Herceg-Baron, 1979; Rounsaville, Prusoff, & Weissman, 1980). When psychotherapy is prescribed, however, it is unclear whether the patient, the couple, or the entire family should be involved. Some evidence suggests that individual psychotherapy for depressed patients involved in marital disputes may promote premature separation or divorce (Gurman & Kniskern, 1978; Locke & Wallace, 1976). There have been no published clinical trials comparing the efficacy of individual and conjoint psychotherapy for depressed patients with marital problems.

We found that marital disputes often remained a complaint of the depressed patient despite the patient's symptomatic improvement with drugs or psychotherapy (Rounsaville et al, 1980). Because IPT presents strategies for managing the social and interpersonal problems associated with the onset of depressive symptoms, we speculated that a conjoint version of IPT, which focused intensively on problems in the marital relationship, would be useful in alleviating those problems (Study 1 in Table 2).

Individual IPT was adapted to the treatment of depression in the context of marital disputes by concentrating its focus on interpersonal marriage disputes, a subset of one of the four problem areas associated with depression for which IPT was developed. IPT-CM extends individual IPT techniques for use with the identified patient and his or her spouse. The treatment incorporates aspects of currently available marital therapies, particularly those that emphasize dysfunctional communication as the focus of interventions. In IPT-CM, functioning of the couple is assessed in five general areas: communication, intimacy, boundary management, leadership, and attainment of socially appropriate goals. Dysfunctional behavior in these areas is noted, and treatment is focused on bringing about improvement in a small number of target problem areas. A treatment manual and training program similar to those used in IPT were developed for IPT-CM in the initial phase of this study.

Only patients who identified marital disputes as the major problem associated with the onset or exacerbation of a major depression were admitted into the pilot study. Patients were randomly assigned to IPT or IPT-CM and received 16 weekly therapy sessions. In IPT-CM the spouse was required to participate in all psychotherapy sessions, whereas in IPT the spouse did not meet the therapist. Patients and spouses in both treatment conditions were asked to refrain from taking psychotropic medication during the study before first discussing it with their therapists; therapists were discouraged from prescribing or arranging for prescriptions of any psychotropic medication.

Table 4.2
Research Studies in Progress

Treatment condition	Diagnosis	Time (in weeks)	Study
1. IPT-CM compared with individual IPT for marital disputes	MDD + marital disputes ($N = 18$)	16	Foley, Rounsaville, Weissman, Sholomskas, and Chevron (in press)
2. IPC	High GHQ score	6	Klerman et al. (1987)

Note. IPT = interpersonal psychotherapy, CM = conjoint marital therapy, MDD = major depressive disorder, and GHQ = General Health Questionnaire.

Three therapists (a psychiatrist, a psychologist, and a social worker) administered individual IPT to depressed married subjects. Three therapists (social workers) administered IPT-CM. All therapists had extensive prior experience in the treatment of depressed patients. At the end of treatment patients in both groups expressed satisfaction with the treatment, felt that they had improved, and attributed improvement to their therapy (see Table 4.2). Patients in both groups exhibited a significant reduction in symptoms of depression and social impairment at termination of therapy. There was no significant difference between treatment groups in the degree of improvement in depressive symptoms and social functioning at termination (Foley et al., in press).

Locke-Wallace Marital Adjustment Test scores at Session 16 were significantly higher (indicative of better marital adjustment) for patients receiving IPT-CM than for those receiving IPT (Locke & Wallace, 1976). Scores of Spanier's (1976) Dyadic Adjustment Scale also indicated greater improvement in marital functioning for patients receiving IPT-CM than for those receiving IPT. At Session 16, patients receiving IPT-CM reported significantly higher levels of improvement in affectional expession (i.e., demonstrations of affection and sexual relations in the marriage) compared with those receiving IPT.

The results should be interpreted with caution because of the pilot nature of the study, that is to say the small size of the sample, the lack of a no-treatment control group, and the absence of a pharmacotherapy or combined pharmacotherapy–psychotherapy comparison group. If the study is repeated we recommend that medication be freely allowed or used as a comparison condition and that there be more effort to reduce the symptomatic depression before treating the marital issues.

IPC for Stress or Distress in Primary Care

Previous investigations have documented high frequencies of anxiety, depression, and functional bodily complaints in patients in primary care settings (Goldberg, 1972; Brodaty and Andrews, 1983; Hoeper, Nyez, Cleary, Rogier, & Goldberg, 1979). Although some of these patients have diagnosable psychiatric disorders, a large percentage have symptoms that do not meet established criteria for psychiatric disorders. A mental health research program formed in a large health maintenance organization in the greater Boston area found that problems of living and symptoms of anxiety and depression were among the main reasons for individual primary care visits. These clinical problems contribute heavily to the high use of ambulatory services.

We developed IPC to deal with patients' symptoms of distress. IPC is a brief, focused, psychosocial intervention for administration by nurse practitioners working in a primary care setting (Weissman & Klerman, 1988). It was modified from IPT over a 6-month period through an interactive and iterative process in which the research team met with the nurse practitioners on a weekly basis to review previous clinical experience, to discuss case examples, to observe videotapes, and to listen to tape recordings.

IPC proved to be feasible in the primary care setting (Klerman et al., 1987). It was learned easily by experienced nurse practitioners in a short training program of from 8–12 hours. The brevity of the sessions and the short duration of treatment rendered IPC compatible with usual professional practices in a primary care unit. No significant negative effects of treatment were observed, and nurses were able with weekly supervision to counsel several patients whose levels of psychiatric distress would normally have resulted in direct referral to specialty mental health care. In comparison with a group of untreated subjects with initial elevations, in General Health Questionnaire (GHQ) scores, those patients receiving the IPC intervention showed greater reduction in symptom scores over an average interval of 3 months. Many IPC-treated patients reported significant relief of symptoms after only one or two sessions. Many of the patients met the criteria for depression when they entered the study.

This study provides initial evidence that early detection of distressed adults and subsequent brief treatment with IPC can, in the short term, reduce symptoms of distress as measured by GHQ scores. The main effect seems to occur in symptoms related to mood, especially in those forms of mild and moderate depression that are commonly seen in medical patients. Such outreach to distressed individuals may also result in the reduced use of health care services and may avoid the need for medication.

Although definitive evaluation of IPC awaits further study, and although its effect on health care service use is not yet determined, this report of short-term symptom reduction suggests that this approach to outreach and early intervention is an effective alternative to current practices. If so, then IPC may be a useful addition to the repertoire of psychosocial intervention skills that can be incorporated into routine primary care.

Programs Planned for the Future

In 1985 Klerman moved to Cornell University Medical College in New York, and Weissman moved to the New York State Psychiatric Institute at Columbia University College of Physicians and Surgeons in New York. Collaborations continue between the two senior investigators and their colleagues. At Payne Whitney Clinic, Cornell University Medical College, Mason is exploring the possible value of IPT in the treatment of depressed alcoholic patients. There is high comorbidity between alcoholism and depression, and IPT is being explored for this group. In addition, Markowitz, supported by a National Institute for Mental Health (NIMH) faculty scholar award, is working with Klerman to develop a modification of IPT for the treatment of patients with dysthymia as defined by the revised third edition of the *Diagnostic and Statistical Manual of Mental Disorders (DSM-III–R;* American Psychiatric Association, 1987).

At the New York State Psychiatric Institute, Weissman and Moreau are exploring the possible value of IPT in the treatment of depressed adolescents on an outpatient basis. The patients are being seen in a special adolescent depression clinic at Columbia University Medical Center.

Relation to Other Research Programs

The NIMH Collaborative Study of the Treatment of Depression

Having accumulated efficacy data on two specified psychotherapies for ambulatory depressives, in the late 1970s the NIMH, under the leadership of Parloff and Elkin, designed and conducted a multicenter controlled clinical trial of drugs and psychotherapy in the treatment of depression (Study 3 in Table 1). A sample of 250 outpatients was randomly assigned to four treatment conditions: cognitive therapy, IPT, imipramine, and a combination of placebo and clinical management. Each patient was treated for 16 weeks. Extensive efforts were made in the selection and training of psychotherapies. Outcome was assessed by a battery of scales that assessed

symptoms, social functioning, and cognition. The criterion for entry was a score of at least 14 on the 17-item Hamilton Rating Scale for Depression. Of the 250 patients who entered treatment, 68% completed at least 15 weeks and 12 sessions of treatment. The initial findings from three centers (Oklahoma City; Washington, DC; and Pittsburgh) were reported at the American Psychiatric Association annual meeting, May 13, 1986, in Washington, DC (Elkin et al., 1986). The full data have been published (Elkin et al., 1989). Overall, the findings showed that all active treatments were superior to placebo in the reduction of symptoms over a 16-week period:

1. The overall degree of improvement was highly significant clinically. More than two thirds of the patients were symptom free at the end of treatment.

2. More patients in the placebo-clinical management condition dropped out or were withdrawn; this was twice as many as for IPT, which had the lowest attrition rate.

3. At the end of 12 weeks of treatment, the two psychotherapies and imipramine were equivalent in the reduction of depressive symptoms and in overall functioning.

4. Pharmacotherapy had more rapid onset of action, but by 12 weeks the two psychotherapies produced equivalent results.

5. Although many of the patients who were less severely depressed at intake improved with all treatment conditions, including those in the placebo-clinical management group, the more severely depressed patients in that group did poorly.

6. Forty-four percent of the sample was moderately to severely depressed at intake. The criterion of severity used was a score of 20 or more on the Hamilton Rating Scale for Depression at entrance into the study. Patients in IPT and in the imipramine groups consistently had significantly better scores than the placebo group on the Hamilton Rating Scale. Only one of the psychotherapies, IPT, was significantly superior to placebo for the severely depressed group. For this group, IPT did as well as imipramine.

The Current Status of IPT in the Psychotherapy of Depression

Although the positive findings of the clinical trials of IPT in the NIMH Collaborative Study and in the other studies described are encouraging and have received considerable attention in the popular press (Boffey, 1986), we wish to emphasize a number of limitations in the possible conclusion regarding the place of psychotherapy in the treatment of depression. All of the studies, including those by our group and by the NIMH, conducted on ambulatory depressed patients or those experiencing distress. There are no systematic studies evaluating the efficacy of psychotherapy for hospitalized depressed patients or bipolar patients who are usually more severely disabled and often suicidal.

It is also important to recognize that these results should not be interpreted as implying that all forms of psychotherapy are effective for depression. One significant feature of recent advances in psychotherapy research is in the development of psychotherapies specifically designed for depression (i.e., time limited and of brief duration). Just as there are specific forms of medication, there are specific forms of psychotherapy; in addition, just as it would be an error to conclude that all forms of medication are useful for all types of depression, it would be an error to conclude that all forms of psychotherapy are efficacious for all forms of depression.

IPT and Drug Therapy Combined

A number of studies in the program just described compared IPT with medication; they also evaluated the combination of IPT and medication. Unlike other forms of psychotherapy, IPT has no ideological hesitation about the use of medication. The decision to use medication in the treatment of depression should be based on the patient's severity of symptoms, quality of depression, duration of disability, and response to previous treatments. It should not be based on the loyalties or training of the professional, as is too often the case in common clinical practice.

In our studies, IPT and medication (usually tricyclic antidepressants) have had independent and additive main effects; some measures have suggested synergistic effects. We have not found any negative interactions, and, in fact, patients treated with the combination of medication and psychotherapy have a lower dropout rate, a greater acceptance of the treatment program, and more rapid and pervasive symptom improvement. Contrary to many theoretical discussions, the prescription of medication does not interfere with the patient's capacity to participate in psychotherapy.

In fact, the opposite occurs. A reduced discussion of symptoms facilitates the patient's capacity to make use of social learning.

Various treatments may be suitable for depression. The depressed patient's interests are best served by the availability and scientific testing of different psychological as well as pharmacological treatments, which can be used alone or in combination. The ultimate aim of these studies is to determine which treatments are best for specific subgroups of depressed patients.

These investigations indicate that for outpatient ambulatory depression there is a range of effective treatments, including a number of forms of brief psychotherapy, as well as various medications, notably monoamine oxidase inhibitors and tricyclic antidepressants. These therapeutic advances have contributed to our understanding of the complex interplay of psychosocial and biological factors in the etiology and pathogenesis of depression, specifically of ambulatory depression.

References

American Psychiatric Association. (1987). *Diagnostic and statistical manual of mental disorders* (rev. 3rd ed.). Washington, DC: Author.

Beck, A. T., Shaw, B. F., & Emory, G. (1979). *Cognitive therapy of depression.* New York: Guilford Press.

Boffey, P. M. (1986, May 14). "Psychotherapy is as good as drug therapy in curing depression," study finds. *New York Times,* pp. A1, A7.

Brodaty, H., & Andrews, G. (1983). Brief psychotherapy in family practice: A controlled prospective intervention trial. *British Journal of Psychiatry, 143,* 11–19.

DiMascio, A., Weissman, M. M., Prusoff, B. A., Neu, C., Zwilling, M., & Klerman, G. L. (1979). Differential symptom reduction by drugs and psychotherapy in acute depression. *Archives of General Psychiatry, 36,* 1450–1456.

Elkin, I., Shea, T., Watkins, R., & Collins, J. (1986, May). *NIMH Treatment of Depression Collaborative Research Program: Comparative treatment outcome findings.* Paper presented at the meeting of the American Psychiatric Association, Washington, DC.

Elkin, I., Shea, M. T., Watkins, T., Imber, S. D., Sotsky, S. M., Collins, J. F., Glass, D. R., Pilkonis, P. A., Leber, W. R., Docherty, J. P., Fiester, J., & Parloff, M. B. (1989). National Institute of Mental Health Treatment of Depression Collaborative Research Program: General effectiveness of treatments. *Archives of General Psychiatry, 46,* 971–983.

Foley, S. H., Rounsaville, B. J., Weissman, M. M., Sholomskas, D., & Chevron, E. S. (in press). Individual versus conjoint interpersonal psychotherapy for depressed patients with marital disputes. *International Journal of Family Psychiatry.*

Goldberg, D. P. (1972). The detection of psychiatric illness by questionnaire. *Institute of Psychiatry Maudsley Monographs* (Whole No. 21).

Gurman, A. S., & Kniskern, D. P. (1978). Research on marital and family therapy: Progress, perspective and prospect. In S. Garfield & A. Bergin (Eds.), *Handbook of psychotherapy and behavior change* (2nd ed., pp. 817–902). New York: Wiley.

Hoeper, E. W., Nycz, G. R., Cleary, P. D., Rogier, D. A., & Goldberg, I. D. (1979). Estimated prevalence of RDC mental disorder in primary medical care. *International Journal of Mental Health, 8,* 6–15.

Klerman, G. L., Budman, S., Berwick, D., Weissman, M. M., Damico-White, J., Demby, A., & Feldstein, M. (1987). Efficacy of a brief psychosocial intervention of symptoms of stress and distress among patients in primary care. *Medical Care, 25,* 1078–1088.

Klerman, G. L., DiMascio. A., Weissman, M. M., Prusoff, B., & Paykel, E. S. (1974). Treatment of depression by drugs and psychotherapy. *American Journal of Psychiatry, 131,* 186–191.

Klerman, G. L., Weissman, M. M., Rounsaville, B. J., & Chevron, E. S. (1984). *Interpersonal psychotherapy of depression.* New York: Basic Books.

Kupfer, D., & Frank, E. (1988). Unpublished and untitled manuscript, University of Pittsburgh.

Locke, H. J., & Wallace, K. M. (1976). Short-term marital adjustment and prediction tests: Their reliability and validity. *Marriage and Family Living, 38,* 15–25.

Reynold, C., & Imber, S. (1988). Unpublished and untitled manuscript, University of Pittsburgh.

Rounsaville, B. J., Prusoff, B. A., & Weissman, M. M. (1980). The course of marital disputes in depressed women: A 48 month follow-up study. *Comprehensive Psychiatry, 21,* 111–118.

Rounsaville, B. J., Weissman, M. M., Prusoff, B. A., & Herceg-Baron, R. (1979). Marital disputes and treatment outcome in depressed women. *Comprehensive Psychiatry, 20,* 483–490.

Sloane, R. B., Staples, F. R., & Schneider, L. S. (1985). Interpersonal therapy versus nortriptyline for depression in the elderly. In G. D. Burrows, T. R. Norman, & L. Dennerstein (Eds.), *Clinical and pharmacological studies in psychiatric disorders* (pp. 344–346). London: Libbey.

Spanier, G. B. (1976). Measuring dyadic adjustment: New scales for assessing the quality of marriage and similar dyads. *Journal of Marriage and Family Living, 38,* 15–25.

Weissman, M. M. (1987). Advances in psychiatric epidemiology: Rates and risks for major depression. *American Journal of Public Health, 77,* 445–451.

Weissman, M. M., & Klerman, G. L. (1988) *Manual for interpersonal counseling for stress and distress.* Unpublished manuscript.

Weissman, M. M., Jarrett, R., & Rush, J. A. (1987) Psychotherapy and its relevance to the pharmacotherapy of major depression: A decade later (1976–1985). In H. Y. Meltzer (Ed.), *Psychopharmacology: A generation of progress* (pp. 1059–1069). New York: Raven Press.

Weissman, M. M., Klerman, G. L., Prusoff, B. A., Scholomskas, D., & Padian, N. (1981). Depressed outpatients: Results one year after treatment with drugs and/or interpersonal psychotherapy. *Archives of General Psychiatry, 38,* 52–55.

Weissman, M. M., Prusoff, B. A., DiMascio, A., Neu, C., Gohlaney, M., & Klerman, G. L. (1979). The efficacy of drugs and psychotherapy in the treatment of acute depressive episodes. *American Journal of Psychiatry, 136,* 555–558.

Weissman, M. M., Rounsaville, B. J., & Chevron, E. S. (1982). Training psychotherapists to participate in psychotherapy outcome studies: Identifying and dealing with the research requirement. *American Journal of Psychiatric, 139,* 1442–1446.

5

Harvard Community Health Plan Mental Health Research Program

Annette Demby and Simon H. Budman
Harvard University

Background and Aims

The Harvard Community Health Plan (HCHP) Mental Health Research Program (MHRP) began in 1975 at the initiation of Simon Budman, PhD, who was hired with the understanding that he would establish a program of psychotherapy research at HCHP. A number of convergent factors allowed the MHRP to take root quickly. The HCHP, a fledgling health maintenance organization (HMO) with strong ties to the Harvard Medical School, was struggling with ways of establishing its identity as more than "just a form of health insurance." In its 1975 mission statement, HCHP committed itself to the goals of offering high-quality innovative medical care as well as becoming a laboratory for research and teaching in regard to such approaches.

Furthermore, legislative changes in Massachusetts presented the HCHP MHRP with the challenge of providing cost-effective psychotherapeutic coverage for a broader population of patients than had been the case in the first 5 years of the plan's existence. A strong need was created for acquiring data on the efficacy and utility of various brief therapy approaches then under development in the organization.

Finally, before joining HCHP, Budman had submitted an HCHP-based grant application to the National Institute of Mental Health (NIMH) as a result of his interest in the examination of mental health treatment within HMOs. This grant was approved in 1976 and became the first of a series of mental health studies to be conducted at HCHP under Budman's leadership. Financial support for the MHRP has come from the HCHP Foundation and from the following external funding sources: NIMH, the John A. Hartford Foundation, the Robert Wood Johnson Foundation, and the W. T. Grant Foundation.

Over the years, the major focus of the MHRP has been studying time-effective psychosocial interventions in a comprehensive health care setting. Each project has reflected the needs and strengths of the setting, a large, 384,000-member, multisite HMO with great numbers of psychologically minded outpatients and a mental health program that emphasizes an array of brief psychotherapy approaches. The major themes that have been explored are examination of the effectiveness of brief or time-limited psychotherapy approaches; exploration of the associations among psychological distress, psychotherapeutic interventions, and medical care utilization patterns; clarification of the process dimensions of time-limited psychotherapies; and development and empirical examination of teaching programs to train therapists in the practice of time-limited group psychotherapy.

The MHRP has emphasized investigation of the effectiveness of various time-limited psychotherapy approaches, including a brief psychoeducational group intervention for recently separated individuals, 15-session and 18-month time-limited group psychotherapy, 15-session individual psychotherapy, a primary care-based psychosocial intervention (interpersonal counseling [IPC]) designed for patients who have elevated distress levels, and two models of a psychosocial educative treatment program for subacute low back pain.

We have also extensively examined the associations among psychological disturbance, mental health treatment approaches, and medical care utilization patterns in the HCHP closed system. Several MHRP studies have included this health-mental health link component in their design. An early study analyzed the impact on health care use of the stress of marital separation, comparing utilization patterns of recently separated individuals with those of married individuals. One study examined the health care use of three cohorts of group psychotherapy patients: those with extremely positive outcomes in therapy, those with extremely negative outcomes, and those who had dropped out of group treatment. Several studies examined health care utilization changes for psychotherapy patients before and after therapy. The Hartford Study examined epidemiological and health care utilization aspects of stress in the HCHP primary care population.

Beginning in 1980, we have been attempting to clarify the key process dimensions in group psychotherapy. An instrument measuring cohesiveness in group therapy was developed in the Cohesion Instrument Development in Group Therapy Study, and the relation between cohesion and outcome was explored. In building on this work, three instruments are currently under development in a continuation study of group therapy process elements and their relationship to outcome variables.

Another path that we have taken is teaching and training. A manual and training videotape of time-limited group psychotherapy have been produced, and a training program to teach clinicians about group psychotherapy is underway. The training program features the use of live actors improvising simulated group therapy sessions.

Other areas of investigation that have been undertaken include a study of relationships among stress, coping, health, and illness in school-aged children, an examination of methodological issues in the early detection of mental illness, a doctoral dissertation of the measurement of target problems in short-term therapy, a dissertation on process variables in individual psychotherapy, a study of loneliness in an outpatient population, and an examination of gender differences in the associations between friendship patterns and mental health indicators in an outpatient population.

The Marital Separation Project examined the life stress of marital separation in a controlled, prospective design. A sample of 237 subjects, half recently separated and half married, participated. A stratified random half of the separated cohort participated in a brief psychoeducational group intervention. Measures of psychosocial adjustment and medical utilization were compared to describe correlates of experiencing marital separation and to evaluate the intervention. This project paved the way for further therapy effectiveness studies and for continued exploration of the medical offset phenomenon (Wertlieb, Budman, Demby, & Randall, 1984).

The Short-Term Group Psychotherapy Project examined the effectiveness of 15-session, dynamic, short-term group therapy in a naturalistic pre-post study. The therapy groups studied focused on young adult developmental issues. An assessment battery was completed before, immediately after, and 4–6 months after treatment by 192 subjects. Three distinct outcome groups (dropouts, low changers, and high changers) were identified and their characteristics observed. Group participants made statistically and clinically significant improvements on most change measures. Interpersonal variables (interpersonal sensitivity, closeness to others, and primary involvement with family) were identified as potentially important dimensions to pursue in screening and preparing patients for a group. These findings challenged clinicians to generate subtler criteria for referrals to short-term groups and stimulated further work on experiential pre-group preparation of patients (Budman, Bennett, & Wisneski, 1981; Budman, Clifford, Bader, & Bader, 1981; Budman, Demby, and Randall, 1982).

The Controlled Outcome Study was an examination of the effects of time-limited group therapy on medical utilization. A sample of 36 nonpsychotic patients was randomly assigned to begin 15-session group therapy or, for that same 4-month period, to remain on a waiting list, receiving treatment on demand (TOD). Patients treated immediately and TOD clients reduced their medical utilization. TOD patients reduced their medical utilization more than immediate care patients and were more likely to have changed their patterns of utilization. Dropouts had the best medical offset outcomes. This and subsequent projects raised important issues about the so-called offset phenomena (Budman, Demby, & Feldstein, 1984; Budman, Demby, Feldstein, & Gold, 1984; Budman & Springer, 1987).

The Hartford Study, which was on depression in ambulatory care, investigated the epidemiological and health care utilization aspects of stress. The impact of IPC, a primary care-based psychosocial intervention on a population of clients who had elevated scores on the General Health Questionnaire (GHQ; Goldberg & Hillier, 1979) was analyzed. The GHQ scores of 1,649 new adult HCHP enrollees were analyzed. Elevated GHQ scores were strongly associated with the probability of both mental health and nonmental health care use within 12 months of enrollment. A significantly greater reduction in GHQ levels was found for untreated subjects (Berwick, Budman, Damico-White, Feldstein, & Klerman, 1987).

The Low Back Pain Study (Berwick, Budman, & Feldstein, 1989) compared three approaches to subacute low back pain: usual care in the HCHP delivery system, and usual care plus one of two models of a psychoeducative treatment program. A total of 222 subjects participated. No measurable effect was found for either of the treatment conditions compared with usual care. Health care utilization tended to be slightly higher for the usual care plus intervention groups.

The Comparative Outcome Study (COS; Budman et al., 1988) was a large randomized clinical trial of time-limited group psychotherapy compared with time-limited individual psychotherapy. Participants were 98 nonpsychotic outpatients. Pre-post assessment batteries were administered and analyzed for differential treatment effects. Both treatments had favorable outcomes, but subjective measures reflected a clear preference by patients for individual treatment. Members of specific therapy groups, however, were more satisfied than the average individual treatment subject. These results stimulated the MHRP staff to direct increased attention to process as well as outcome and to develop a systematic training program for group therapists.

The Cohesion Instrument Development in Group Therapy Project (Budman, Demby, et al., 1987; Budman, Soldz, Demby, Feldstein, Springer, & Davis, 1989) is a current study of the psychometric properties (reliability and validity) of three group therapy process scales. Videotapes of 18 psychotherapy groups will be rated with each scale. This study also continues to assess the

effectiveness of time-limited group treatment with a pre-post design as well as the relationships between process and outcome variables. Initial results with an early version of the HCHP Group Cohesiveness Scale (GCS) indicate that cohesion, as rated by clinician observers, is strongly related to outcome, as self-reported by patients. Cohesion is especially strongly associated with improvement on self-esteem and on global symptomatology as measured by the SCL-90-R.

Method

Subjects and Selection

Subjects in MHRP studies have all been HCHP members who have, in general, been employed, White, well educated, and well motivated for treatment. The subjects in most of the psychotherapy outcome projects have been young adults (aged 21–35 years); other studies have involved a wider range of adult ages, and one study involved school-aged children. Until recently, subjects have been symptomatic (e.g., anxious or depressed) but have not been psychotic or severely or chronically impaired in their level of functioning. Recently initiated studies have included more impaired patients.

Instruments

A wide range of instruments have been used to assess change and effectiveness from a number of perspectives. Our assessment batteries have included both standardized measures of symptomatology such as the SCL-90-R (Derogatis, 1977); the GHQ (Goldberg & Hillier, 1979); the Global Assessment Scale (Endicott, Spitzer, Fleiss, & Cohen, 1976); structured psychiatric interviews such as the Diagnostic Interview Survey (Robins, 1986); the Structured Clinical Interview for the revised third edition of the *Diagnostic and Statistical Manual of Mental Disorders* (American Psychiatric Association, 1987; Spitzer, Williams, Gibbon, & First, 1988); the Personality Disorder Examination (Loranger, 1988), measures of social and interpersonal adjustment such as the Social Adjustment Scale (Weissman & Paykel, 1974); the People in Your Life Scale (Marziali, 1987); the Inventory of Interpersonal Problems (Horowitz, 1987); the Millon Clinical Multiaxial Inventory (Millon, 1987); and measures of client ratings of change such as the Target Complaints

Measure (Battle, Imber, Hoehn-Saric, Stone, & Frank, 1966).

Several psychotherapy process scales have been used: the Vanderbilt Psychotherapy Process Scale (O'Malley, Suh, & Strupp, 1983), the Vanderbilt Negative Indicators Scale (Strupp et al., 1981), and the Helping Alliance measure (Luborsky, Crits-Christoph, Alexander, Margolis, & Cohen, 1983). We have developed three instruments: the HCHP GCS (Budman, Demby, et al., 1987), the Group Therapist Intervention Scale (Budman, Springer, and Bernstein, 1987), and the Individual Group Member Interpersonal Process Scale (IGIPS; Budman, Davis, & Rothberg, 1987). These scales were created after unsuccessful efforts to adapt process measures designed for individual psychotherapy to group therapy material.

Procedures

The types of designs and methodologies used in MHRP investigations include naturalistic studies (pre-post assessments of psychotherapeutic interventions or studies examining the sequelae of specific stressors), controlled studies (pre-post assessment of a treatment condition compared with a no-treatment or TOD condition), randomized clinical trials, epidemiological surveys, longitudinal studies, and examinations of therapy process dimensions, instrument development, and relations between therapy outcome and process dimensions, medical utilization patterns, or both.

Since 1981, the MHRP has used videotape equipment to record psychotherapy sessions to examine psychotherapy outcome and process variables and to clarify questions regarding instrument development. Presently, a large library of videotaped therapy sessions is archived (approximately 20 time-limited therapy groups in their entirety and a sampling of sessions from the therapy of approximately 40 individual patients).

Research Accomplishments

In the area of therapeutic effectiveness, results have indicated that subjects have made significant objective gains and have expressed subjective satisfaction with the treatment studied. Marital Separation Project subjects' feedback was overwhelmingly positive, resulting in HCHP instituting this program on an ongoing basis. The Hartford Study showed a significantly greater reduction in self-reported stress on the GHQ for the treated subjects and spurred HCHP to develop a mode of primary care supportive counseling. The COS results clearly indicated that subjects made substantial gains on almost all outcome measures as well as indicating subjective satisfaction with the treatment. This was an encouraging finding because there had been much discussion in the clinical literature up until that time disparaging the value of brief group therapy approaches.

The COS results indicated that both individual and group time-limited therapies showed similarly favorable outcomes. This similarity of outcome included every major measure in the large multidimensional outcome battery. When subjective outcomes were scrutinized, however, it became clear that subjects clearly preferred individual therapy. Group therapy subjects also "voted with their feet" by increasing their HCHP mental health visits in the 6 months after therapy (compared with the 6 months before therapy) by 27%, whereas individual patients decreased their use by 92% That is, group subjects apparently experienced a need for more therapy in contrast to individual subjects, who appeared to be more satisfied.

It is evident that although time-limited groups in this study were highly successful from various perspectives, there were some major problems regarding acceptability and satisfaction. Also, although on the average group subjects were not satisfied with their treatment as individual subjects, members of specific groups being far more satisfied than the average individual treatment subject. These results supported the overall efficacy of the HCHP group therapy model but indicated that some subjects were less positively disposed toward group therapy, and further, that some groups appeared to generate far greater satisfaction for members than did others. This finding, coupled with encouraging initial positive associations between the process dimension of group cohesiveness and individual group member outcome, stimulated us to investigate further the relations between process and outcome variables in group psychotherapy.

With regard to the impact of psychotherapeutic interventions on medical utilization, our findings have supported the generally held view that a mental health population tends to use medical services at a higher rate than a nonmental health population. Subjects who had recently experienced marital separation, for example, showed statistically significantly higher levels of health care utilization in the 12 months surrounding separation than the nonseparated sample in the

Marital Separation Project. The bulk of these visits were to mental health services, not general health care visits.

In examining health care use changes for subjects in short-term groups, it was found that both subjects with extremely positive outcomes and those with extremely negative outcomes maintained high levels of nonmental health medical use after group therapy. Dropouts, however, showed a different pattern: These subjects, who had the fewest number of mental health visits, significantly reduced their general health care utilization after therapy. This finding presaged our later work regarding the issue of medical utilization offset after psychotherapy. In fact, the initial hypothesized offset after therapy, which argued for mental health services, paying for themselves, slowly gave way to the notion that although certain types of interventions with specific populations may reduce inappropriate medical utilization, there are clear indications that some psychotherapeutic interventions may actually increase costs (Budman et al., 1982).

In the area of process-outcome work, we found strong relations among group cohesion as measured by the GCS (Version 1), improved self-esteem, and reduced symptomatology for group therapy subjects in the COS. Higher cohesion appears to be related to better outcome, even after controlling for pretherapy functioning. Group cohesiveness thus appears to be an important process variable related to patient improvement in group therapy.

Research Programs in Progress

Our current projects include the Cohesion Instrument Development in Group Therapy Study (described earlier) and the three following pilot projects:

1. The establishment of a training program for group therapists is underway. Our training manual and videotape, in future iterations, will be the focus of various clinical trials and experiments to test more fully the efficacy of the MHRP time-limited group therapy models. Subjects in this study are advanced psychotherapy trainees and staff from HCHP centers. We are testing the hypothesis that effectiveness in group therapy may be increased with improved, standardized training of group therapy therapists.

2. The development of a long-term manualized group psychotherapy approach for patients with severe personality disorders has also begun. In this study, it is hypothesized that Budman and Gurman's (1988) time-limited model of group therapy is transferrable to a longer-term, more severely disturbed population and that those in-group member behaviors that are associated with personality disorder diagnoses are modifiable through interpersonally oriented group psychotherapy.

3. Pilot work has begun on an investigation of repeat psychiatric hospitalizations in the HCHP system. It is hypothesized that repeat hospitalization rates are higher for patients with major depressive diagnoses with an associated personality disorder than for those without a personality disorder and that specific treatment strategies may be indicated for identifiable groups of psychiatric hospitalization repeaters.

Briefly, initial findings of these projects support our hypotheses that psychiatric hospitalizations are more frequent and occur earlier in a patient's life if there is comorbidity (specifically, a personality disorder or substance abuse disorder diagnosis) for patients with major depressive disorders. Also, with regard to the modification of behaviors associated with personality disorder diagnoses in group therapy, a recently developed version of the IGIPS (IGIPS-PD) appears to be able to discriminate between patients with personality disorders and those without. IGIPS-PD ratings have also demonstrated positive change over the course of long-term therapy in the behaviors displayed by avoidant patients in therapy groups.

Programs Planned for the Future

The MHRP plans to pursue several key areas of interest over the next 5 years: (a) continued immersion in probing the central processes of time-effective group psychotherapy; (b) expansion of Budman and Gurman's (1988) time-limited group psychotherapy model to different populations (e.g., patients with substance abuse problems); and (c) development of collaborative psychotherapy research efforts. Toward these ends, cooperative efforts have begun with William Beardslee, MD, at Children's Hospital, who has recently received a grant to develop and manualize a preventive intervention for children of HCHP parents with affective disorder. In addition, an expanded role for the MHRP at an affiliated inpatient psychiatric unit is presently being considered.

The MHRP has maintained an ongoing focus and a coherent program of research over the past 12 years, and its future plans are to elaborate further this focus. The HCHP comprehensive care setting has afforded us the unique opportunity of comparing not only the psychosocial outcomes of the therapies studied but health care utilization outcomes as well. We have contributed to the empirical knowledge base that supports models of short-term group therapy, an area that has been lacking in rigorous empirical support compared with the individual area. In addition, the research on cohesion and other dimensions of process in group psychotherapy has added clinical depth, relevance, and scientific rigor to this field of inquiry. The development of usable and clinically relevant process measures for group psychotherapy has the potential for building a more precise science of group treatment.

Relation to Other Research Programs

The MHRP has benefited from the contributions of several other psychotherapy research programs, including the Vanderbilt, the Langley-Porter, and the University of Pennsylvania groups, to name a few. This has been especially true in the area of instrument development because the MHRP has attempted to adapt individual treatment psychotherapy process scales for group treatment and, in so doing, has further clarified the specific salient characteristics of group treatment process dimensions.

Cross-fertilization of concepts and methodologies has occurred through the Society for Psychotherapy Research (SPR), which has been a source of considerable benefit over the years. Opportunities through SPR have resulted in numerous helpful exchanges, including a recent panel discussion regarding issues in choosing psychotherapy raters and a workshop presentation of the HCHP GCS scale applied to therapy sessions from other settings.

Clinical Practice

Because the MHRP has been so closely tied to clinical practice, its relevance to clinicians has been considerable. Virtually every MHRP staff researcher is also a clinician. Many of the research questions addressed by the MHRP have originated with HCHP clinicians who have been challenged to provide quality time-limited therapeutic services to a large HMO population. *The Theory and Practice of Brief Therapy*, by Budman and Gurman (1988), makes extensive use of findings emerging from the MHRP and other psychotherapy research programs. That book is used extensively throughout the United States as a standard reference for therapists conducting brief treatment.

Clinical Training

There is a considerable need for systematic, empirically based clinical training in the field of time-limited therapies. We are frequently requested to offer training programs and to provide information about brief therapies. This is especially true because our work is so closely linked with the practicalities of clinical practice. Current work on a systematic training program for therapists conducting time-limited group therapy is a major step toward further dissemination of this knowledge base.

References

American Psychiatric Association. (1987). *Diagnostic and statistical manual of mental disorders* (rev. 3rd ed.). Washington, DC: Author.

Battle, C. C., Imber, S. D., Hoehn-Saric, R., Stone, A. R., & Frank, J. D. (1966). Target complaints as criteria of improvement. *American Journal of Psychiatry, 120,* 184–192.

Berwick, D. M., Budman, S., Damico-White, J., Feldstein, M., & Klerman, G. (1987). Assessment of psychological morbidity in primary care: Explorations with the General Health Questionnaire. *Journal of Chronic Disease, 40,* 71s–79s.

Berwick, D. M., Budman, S., & Feldstein, M. (1989). No clinical effect of back schools in an HMO: A randomized prospective trial. *Spine, 14,* 338–344.

Budman, S. H., Bennett, M. J., & Wisneski, M. (1981). An adult developmental model of short-term group psychotherapy. In S. H. Budman (Ed.), *Forms of brief therapy* (pp. 305–342). New York: Guilford Press.

Budman, S. H., Clifford, M., Bader, L., & Bader, B. (1981). Experiential pre-group preparation and screening. *Group, 5,* 19–26.

Budman, S. H., Davis, M., & Rothberg, P. C. (1987). *The Individual Group Member Interpersonal Process Scale (IGIPS)*. Boston: Harvard Community Health Plan.

Budman, S. H., Demby, A. B., & Feldstein, M. L. (1984). A controlled study of impact of mental health treatment on medical care utilization. *Medical Care, 22,* 216–222.

Budman, S. H., Demby, A., Feldstein, M., & Gold, M. (1984). The effects of time-limited group psychotherapy: A controlled study. *International Journal of Group Psychotherapy, 34,* 587–603.

Budman, S. H., Demby, A., Feldstein, M., Redondo, J., Scherz, B., Bennett, M. J., Koppenaal, G., Daley, B. S., Hunter, M., & Ellis, J. (1987). Preliminary findings on a new instrument to measure cohesion in group psychotherapy. *International Journal of Group Psychotherapy, 37,* 75–94.

Budman, S. H., Demby, A., & Randall, M. (1982). Psychotherapeutic outcome and reduction in medical utilization: A cautionary tale. *Professional Psychology, 13,* 200–207.

Budman, S. H., Demby, A., Redondo, J. P., Hannan, M., Feldstein, M., Ring, J., & Springer, T. (1988). Comparative outcome in time limited individual and group psychotherapy. *International Journal of Group Psychotherapy, 38,* 63–87.

Budman, S. H., & Gurman, A. S. (1988). *The theory and practice of brief therapy.* New York: Guilford Press.

Budman, S. H., Soldz, S., Demby, A., Feldstein, M., Springer, T., & Davis, M. S. (1989). Cohesion, alliance and outcome in group psychotherapy: An empirical examination. *Psychiatry, 52,* 339–350.

Budman, S. H., & Springer, T. (1987). Treatment delay, outcome and satisfaction in time-limited group and individual psychotherapy. *Professional Psychology: Research and Practice, 18,* 647–649.

Budman, S. H., Springer, T., & Bernstein, E. (1987). *The Group Therapist Intervention Scale (GTIS).* Unpublished manuscript.

Derogatis, L. R. (1977). *SCL-90 administration, scoring and procedures manual I for the revised version.* Baltimore, MD: John Hopkins University of Medicine, Clinical Psychometrics Research Unit.

Endicott, J., Spitzer, R. L., Fleiss, J. L., & Cohen, J. (1976). The Global Assessment Scale—A Procedure for measuring overall severity of psychiatric disturbance. *Archives of General Psychiatry, 33,* 776–771.

Goldberg, D. P., & Hillier, V. F. (1979). A scaled version of the General Health Questionnaire. *Psychological Medicine, 9,* 139–145.

Horowitz, L. (1987). *Inventory of Interpersonal Problems.* Stanford, CA: Stanford University Department of Psychology.

Loranger, A. (1988). *Personality Disorder Examination (PDE) manual.* Department of Psychiatry, Cornell University Medical College, Westchester, NY.

Luborsky, L., Crits-Christoph, P., Alexander, L., Margolis, M., & Cohen, M. (1983). Two helping alliance methods for predicting outcomes of psychotherapy. *Journal of Nervous and Mental Disease, 171,* 480–491.

Marziali, E. A. (1987). People in your life: Development of a social support measure for predicting psychotherapy outcome. *Journal of Nervous and Mental Disease, 175,* 327–338.

Millon, T. (1987). *Manual for the Millon Clinical Multiaxial Inventory II.* Minneapolis, MN: National Computer Systems.

O'Malley, S. S., Suh, C. S., & Strupp, H. H. (1983). The Vanderbilt Process Scale: A report on the scale development and a process–outcome study. *Journal of Consulting and Clinical Psychology, 51,* 581–586.

Robins, L. N. (1986). The development and characteristics of the NIMH Diagnostic Interview Schedule. In M. M. Weissman, J. Myers, and C. Ross (Eds.), *Community surveys of psychiatric disorders* (pp. 403–427). New Brunswick, NJ: Rutgers University Press.

Spitzer, R. L., Williams, J. B., Gibbon, M., & First M. B. (1988). *Structured Clinical Interview for DSM-III–R—Patient Version (SCID-P).* Biometrics Research Department, New York State Psychiatric Institute, New York.

Strupp, H. H., Moras, K., Sandell, J., Waterhouse, G., O'Malley, S., Keithly, L., & Gomes-Schwartz, B. (1981). *Vanderbilt Negative Indicator Scale.* Unpublished manuscript, Vanderbilt University, Nashville, TN.

Weissman, M. M., & Paykel, E. S. (1974). *The depressed woman: A study of social relationships.* Chicago: University of Chicago Press.

Wertlieb, D., Budman, S., Demby, A., & Randall, M. (1984). Marital separation and health: Stress and intervention. *Journal of Human Stress, 10,* 18–26.

6

Psychotherapy of Borderline Patients at the Menninger Foundation: Expressive Compared With Supportive Interventions and the Therapeutic Alliance

Leonard Horwitz, Jon G. Allen, Donald B. Colson,
Siebolt H. Frieswyk, Glen O. Gabbard, Lolafaye Coyne,
and Gavin E. Newsom
The Menninger Foundation

Background and Aims

History

The Treatment Interventions Project was begun at the Menninger Clinic in 1980 with the aim of differentiating patients who profit most from an expressive exploratory approach from those who require a more supportive approach. This issue divides the psychotherapy field as represented by Kernberg (1976), Gill and Muslin (1976), and Gunderson (1984) on the more expressive side and of Stone (1987), Masterson (1976), and Adler (1985) on the more supportive side. Either strategy may be appropriate depending on the specific type of patient, and a refinement of indications and contraindications for each approach is a significant issue for research.

The selection of this research area was a direct spinoff of the Menninger Psychotherapy Research Project. Perhaps the most widely touted finding of the study (Kernberg, Burstein, Coyne, Appelbaum, Horwitz, & Voth, 1972), as judged from the quantified variables, was that supportive psychotherapy is ineffective with borderline patients. This finding, however, was not corroborated by Horwitz (1974), who examined all of the clinical data. He found that a supportive, nontransference approach with patients who showed various degrees of ego weakness yielded more extensive and more stable change than had been predicted. The final report on the project by Wallerstein (1986) was in substantial agreement with Horwitz's finding. The discrepancy among these reports probably resulted from a failure to scrutinize individual cases in the quantitative study. Hence, in the present research, we opted for an intensive study of single cases.

The therapeutic alliance is our major dependent variable for three reasons. First, Horowitz (1974) hypothesized that the alliance played a major role in the favorable outcomes of some supportive cases. Second, reports from several research centers have demonstrated that the therapeutic alliance, often assessed in the first few sessions of treatment, was a key variable in predicting the eventual treatment outcome (Frieswyk et al., 1986). Finally, given the conspicuous difficulty that borderline patients have in forming stable and trusting collaborative relationships, the clinical literature emphasizes the key role of the alliance in their treatment (Kernberg, 1976; Masterson, 1976).

In the course of two pilot studies that used transcripts of recorded sessions of 2 patients, we developed a set of measures to enable a study of the relationship between the therapist's interventions and the patient's alliance in the therapy process. In 1986 we initiated a formal reliability study of these measures by using typescripts of 39 recorded psychotherapy sessions with borderline patients. As of this writing we are beginning to embark on the main study, which initially will consist of an intensive examination of the audiotaped psychotherapy process of 3 borderline patients.

Overall Aims

Our principal objectives are to assess what type of borderline patient, at which phase of treatment, responds best to a supportive treatment and, conversely, what type of patient benefits from an exploratory, uncovering treatment. We will use two time perspectives, longitudinal and cross-sectional, to generate a running profile of the therapist's interventions along an expressive-supportive continuum during the entire course of treatment. In so doing, we will examine how the therapist's strategies interact with the patient's characteristics and how both relate to the therapeutic outcome. We will also endeavor to link within-session shifts in the alliance to prior therapeutic interventions within that session, keeping in mind that patients' reactions in a given session are often related to long-range effects and to the quality of the therapeutic relationship itself. On the basis of our pilot studies, however, we believe that some of the shifts in the alliance may be related to immediately preceding therapeutic work.

Method

Subjects and Selection

Patients must be at least 18 years of age, in psychotherapy at least twice a week for most of their treatment, of at least average intelligence, and have no indication of organic brain pathology. Patients should carry a primary diagnosis of borderline personality disorder, as defined by the revised third edition of the *Diagnostic and Statistical Manual of Mental Disorders (DSM–III–R;* American Psychiatric Association, 1987) determined by the usual intake diagnostic procedure of the Menninger Clinic, which includes a psychiatric case study, a social history, and psychological testing. In addition, the research team will conduct an initial research assessment, including Gunderson's Diagnostic Interview for Borderlines, and will reach a consensus diagnosis of borderline personality. Finally, therapists will have at least 5 years of psychotherapy experience beyond their residency or specialty training.

Instruments

Therapeutic alliance measures. A review of prior research and theory led us to focus on the degree of the patient's collaboration in the process, that is, the extent to which the patient is making optimal use of the therapy as a resource for constructive change (Frieswyk, Colson, & Allen, 1984). By focusing on the patient's contribution to the alliance we were able conceptually to separate a key facet of the alliance from various aspects of the patient-therapist relationship (e.g., transference) and the therapist's technique, thus paving the way for an investigation of how the relationship and technique influence the evolution of the alliance. Out of this thinking, we developed a global collaboration scale (a 7-point, example-anchored rating scale) that could be rated reliably with the use of transcripts of psychotherapy sessions (Allen, Newsom, Gabbard, & Coyne, 1984).

Our major research aim is to study, in a highly molecular fashion, the relation between the interventions of therapists and the collaboration of patients; that is, to link changes in patients' collaboration in sessions to specific interventions. Accordingly, we developed measures (Allen, Gabbard, Newsom, & Coyne, in press) that could be applied to relatively small segments of sessions (i.e., 50 lines of transcript, which yields an average of 10 segments per session). To rate segments we subdivided collaboration into two key components, which involve the extent to which the patient (a) raises significant issues and (b) makes optimal use of the therapists's interventions. For each component, we developed a 5-point, example-anchored rating scale. In addition, we detect momentary shifts in collaboration (i.e., for each segment, indicating an upward or downward shift or no shift). We developed a manual that defines shifts and illustrates them with numerous vignettes from a pilot study.

Interventions measures. Beginning with Gill and Hoffman's (1982) process coding categories, we engaged in several successive efforts to develop categories of therapist interventions suitable for this research. The resulting Interventions Categories Inventory (Colson, Horwitz, Frieswyk, & Coyne, 1989) is a manual designed to help assign each intervention to one of seven categories: (a) interpretation, (b) confrontation, (c) clarification, (d) encouragement to elaborate, (e) empathy, (f) advice and praise, and (g) simple affirmations. In addition, each intervention (except affirmation) is assigned a score indicating whether it includes reference to the patient-therapist relationship.

The category system assesses the supportiveness or expressiveness of each intervention in three ways. First, the six categories (i.e., excluding affirmation) are arranged on a continuum, with interpretation being the most expressive intervention and advice and praise the most supportive. A second measure of this dimension is inherent in the distinction between relationship- or transference-focused (more expressive) and non-transference-focused (more supportive) interventions. For a third measure of supportive compared with expressive emphasis, we developed two 7-point scales, one for overall expressiveness and the other for overall supportiveness.

Finally, because of the crucial role played by the skillfulness with which interventions are formulated, our judges rate the suitability of each intervention. This involves a competence of interventions scale, which is a 6-point scale ranging from seriously deficient to excellent. A similar scale is used to rate the therapist's overall competence during the entire session.

Procedures

The audiotaped sessions are randomly selected and transcribed. We rate approximately 15–20 sessions over the course of the entire treatment, in each instance selecting 2–3 successive sessions. The selection of successive sessions results in a more representative picture of the patient's state and provides an opportunity to examine more than the patient's immediate reaction to the therapist's interventions.

Two teams of three experienced clinical researchers rate the sessions: One team rates the alliance measures, and the other team rates the interventions categories. One team reaches a consensus (after members make independent judgments) about the junctures at which shifts in collaboration occurred, and the other team reaches a consensus about the classification of each intervention. Then the two teams meet as a combined group to make judgments, first independently and then by consensus, about the preceding intervention or interventions that contributed to the positive or negative shift in collaboration.

We plan to evaluate the treatment outcome on the basis of the following procedures: (a) an examination of the typescripts of sessions from the termination phase compared with a sample from the initial phase; (b) assessment interviews at a follow-up point with both patient and therapist; (c) a follow-up videotaped Gunderson Diagnostic Interview for Borderlines for comparison with the initial interview; and (d) repeat psychological testing at a follow-up point for comparison with the initial testing. We also plan to incorporate some standardized outcome measures with the use of raters who were not involved in rating the various process measures.

Research Accomplishments

Pilot Studies

We completed two pilot studies with the transcripts of the psychotherapy process with two patients. The first study (Horwitz & Frieswyk, 1980) examined a recorded 18-month supportive–expressive psychotherapy with a college student diagnosed with borderline personality disorder. The research team concluded that the patient could have made greater gains if the therapist had pursued a more consistent strategy of interpreting the latent negative transference that inhibited the development of a strong alliance. The second pilot study (Gabbard et al., 1988) examined the therapy of a professional man in his mid-30s with borderline personality disorder who was hospitalized for a moderate depression with suicidal ideation. At that time, he had been in a mainly expressive psychotherapy for more than 2 years at a frequency of three times per week. During this work, we experimented with attempting to link within-session shifts in the alliance to preceding therapeutic interventions. This method clearly indicated that transference interpretations were useful to the patient by enhancing the therapeutic alliance.

Reliability of Therapeutic Alliance Measures

We have completed a reliability study of our measures to assess changes in collaboration within psychotherapy sessions (Allen et al., in press). We studied transcripts of single sessions from the psychotherapy of 39 patients with borderline disorders. We divided this sample into two groups, discussing the results from the first set of 20 cases (and refining our measures slightly) before rating the second set of 19 cases.

We assessed changes within sessions in two ways. First, to assess the drift in collaboration (upward or downward) from each one third of the session to the next, we averaged the collaboration component ratings (significant issued and making use of interventions) across segments for each third of each session. Our reliability for most of these ratings was adequate for the first group of 20 cases, but some of the reliabilities were marginal for the second group of 19 cases. The ratings for the second group of cases might have been poorer because they were completed over a long period, during which the raters had not worked together closely.

The second method of assessing changes involved assessing shifts in collaboration. Assessing collaboration with adequate reliability was difficult for two reasons. First, the preponderance of ratings was of no shift, yielding a high base rate of no-shift ratings. Second, for a substantial proportion of segments only one rater detected a shift, presumably for idiosyncratic reasons. Nevertheless, the raw data indicated numerous clusters of shift ratings where, idiosyncratic ratings aside (and in the context of predominantly no-shift ratings), two or three raters independently detected a shift at the same point. Moreover, in the great majority of instances when more than one rater detected a shift, there was complete agreement about its direction (upward or downward).

Notwithstanding the difficulties in attaining independent agreement, we discovered that changes in patients' collaboration occur with sufficient frequency to constitute a feasible focus for research (i.e., clear-cut changes occurred in most sessions). Because of the relatively high frequency of idiosyncratic ratings, however, we concluded that we must use consensus judgments by two or three judges and that our subsequent studies of single cases should use individualized criteria for shifts in collaboration. That is, we will study a subsample of sessions for a given patient to select patient-specific criteria (from our manual containing many criteria) that we will then use in the sessions to be researched.

Reliability of Intervention Categories

We completed a reliability study of our intervention categories (Colson et al., 1989) with the same sample of patients and sessions used to study the alliance measures. We also divided the sample into two groups, discussing results from the first 20 cases, slightly refining our manual for categorizing interventions, and then rating the second set of 19 cases.

When reliabilities were assessed category by category for all seven categories, the estimates were disappointingly low. On the other hand, when we assessed the reliability of the total number of each category in each session, the figures were, for the most part, at or above acceptable levels for both the first and second series of sessions. Similarly, reliabilities for the six primary intervention categories, arranged on a continuum from expressive to supportive, were at acceptable levels or better. The reliability of overall ratings of supportiveness and expressiveness was also quite satisfactory.

The reliability calculations of the transference-focused compared with the non-transference-focused interventions are more complicated because they cover thirds of sessions. We encountered difficulty with reliability for the first third of the sessions because transference interventions occur infrequently in the beginning of any therapy session. Most reliabilities of this transference compared with nontransference distinction were at acceptable levels or better for the second and last thirds of the sessions, however.

Overall, with regard to interrater reliability of the intervention categories, we stand on fairly solid ground for the use of category totals in the sessions, for the transference compared with non-transference distinction, and for the use of the categories as an expressive–supportive continuum. The part of our research plan that rests on a category-by-category, examination of therapy sessions will require additional methodological refinement, however.

Research Programs in Progress

We are beginning our main study to assess the kinds of interventions most suitable for various types of borderline patients. Our method will be both molecular and molar. We will use the linkage between interventions and within-session shifts in patients' collaboration in a fine-grained microscopic approach. In addition, we will relate treatment outcome to thrapeutic strategy, as assessed by a profile of interventions over the entire course of treatment.

Hypotheses

Because our method consists of an intensive study of single cases, we will not be engaged in hypothesis testing but rather in hypothesis finding. We believe that a wide variety of personality characteristics in the borderline population may contribute to or detract from the effectiveness of an interpretive approach. We assume that there is a borderline spectrum (Grinker & Werble, 1977; Meissner, 1984) ranging from high-level borderline patients close to the neurotic border to low-level patients nearer the psychotic end of the continuum. This kind of gross differentiation is probably the major general factor determining the appropriateness of supportive compared with expressive methods. It may also reflect a greater linkage of the high-level patient to the conflict model, whereas the low-level patient is more closely related to the deficit model. Like the closely related quality of ego strength, this continuum provides a useful approximation of the level of ego functioning that is basic to planning treatment and predicting outcome. In the present study, however, we are attempting to discover finer differentiations that determine the optimal treatment approach.

By using the dimension of closeness compared with distance, Horwitz (1985) has spelled out in some detail hypotheses regarding the indications for different intervention strategies. Most generally, we hypothesize that patients who manifest either behavioral extreme are not candidates for interpretation; those who alternate between the two poles are more ready for uncovering work. Patients who consistently maintain a close, symbiotic tie with their therapist indicate a weak self–object differentiation and a need to use the treatment relationship to supply functions that they are unable to fulfill themselves. Such patients are seeking a symbiotic union with a maternal part–object, a merger with the "good breast." They view the therapist as the soothing, magical protector from whom all good things derive. Their conscious or unconscious treatment contract is that they will be compliant, "good children" as long as the therapist will reciprocate with unending nurturance. Interpretations of their needs and unrealistic expectations, which may highlight the separateness of patient and therapist may be viewed as a poor substitute for the gratifications they seek and as a repetition of maternal failure and rejection.

Distant patients are rigidly fixed in a defensive posture against seeking symbiotic gratification. Modell (1976) has characterized them as being encapsulated in a plastic bubble or glass jar; they feel constrained to remain affectively uncommunicative. Their hunger for a relationship is often indicated by their seeking treatment, but their anxiety about the dangers of trusting themselves or others in a close relationship makes them maintain a barrier. Interpretations to such patients unduly intrude into their private domains, as if destroying their carefully protected islands of safety. Therapists who trespass on this forbidden territory risk angry retaliation or a ruptured treatment.

These two extremes heuristically illustrate the dimensions that must be considered in assessing a patient's readiness to use interpretations. Obviously, degrees of both closeness and distance must also be considered.

The primary indicators of the borderline patient's amenability to interpretation are not only attenuated degrees of closeness–distance behavior but are also manifestations of flexibility in the patient's response pattern. A patient who alternates between the two behaviors, for example, is likely to be ready to accept both the intimacy and the separateness involved in a transference interpretation.

Therapists must also attempt to differentiate between pathological and healthy alternation. At the pathological extreme is the involuntary, automatic, poorly controlled alternation of ego states that characterizes many borderline patients (Kernberg, 1976). These patients oscillate between split self-object representations because of poorly integrated good and bad polarities. When the split between these ego states is profound, the reactions are more pathognomonic and relatively impervious to interpretation. On the other hand, oscillations that have the earmarks of greater integration between good and bad internal representations are a positive sign. In these instances, the patient is likely to be communicating a readiness for the intimacy of transference exploration while retaining a necessary sense of separateness and autonomy. This manner of functioning constitutes a more adaptive alternation between closeness and distance.

The closeness–distance dimension is a multifaceted variable manifested by various behavioral as well as intrapsychic representations. Our ultimate aim is to strengthen or weaken the closeness–distance hypothesis while at the same time explicating its manifestations.

Tentative Findings

Certain tentative findings relevant to these hypotheses have emerged from our pilot studies to date (Horwitz, 1988).

Both patients who have been studied so far gave evidence of alternating between closeness and distance in dealing with their therapist. Both showed clear-cut signs of latent negative transference in the form of anger at being in a submissive position and of competitive strivings to attain the upper hand. On the other hand, both patients were excessively compliant and agreeable, rarely expressing overt disagreements or challenging the therapist's vaunted position. One received systematic interpretation of the transference accompanied by considerable resolution of his sadomasochistic conflicts. The other patient, despite evident readiness to deal with negative feelings, was not offered systematic work with the transference; this patient's moderate improvement at termination proved relatively unstable.

With regard to the patient treated profitably with an expressive modality, the following characteristics emerged as special indications for transference work (Horwitz, 1988): (a) minimal propensity for lapsing into transient psychotic thinking consistent with a high-level borderline disorder; (b) life-long strong yearning for a close bond with a male parental figure that was gratified by transference work, even when hostile content was uncovered; (c) tendency to internalize rather than externalize, which aids the transference work (albeit enhancing any masochistic

submissiveness) insofar as it tends to reduce paranoid distortions of the therapist, and (d) fluctuating desire for closeness or distance without being restricted to either polarity.

Programs Planned for the Future

New Directions and Hypotheses

As mentioned in the previous section, the closeness–distance dimension is a complex, multifaceted interpersonal and intrapsychic dimension worthy of study in its own right, and we hope to explore it in other contexts in the future. A similar distinction was made by Balint (1968), who designated the ocnophilic and philobatic types as manifestations of an underlying basic fault. More recently, Blatt and Shichman (1983) introduced a similar typology of anaclitic and introjective, which are likewise characterized by excessive clinging or excessive distancing.

Our findings in this project emphasize the necessity in process studies to evaluate the suitability of the therapist's interventions. Although accuracy is, of course, a sine qua non that has recently been related to outcome (Crits-Christoph, Cooper, & Luborsky, 1988), other facets of an interpretation must be taken into account. Such subtle factors as timing, tact, and empathy should be considered. Some members of our team have already begun to develop methods for assessing the suitability of interventions, particularly transference interpretations.

Significance

Because of the diversity of views on the indications and contraindications for transference work in psychoanalytic psychotherapy, it is important to refine our knowledge in this area, particularly with patients who show significant ego defects. Thus, we are attempting to develop a method of studying the treatment process and outcome in a way that combines clinical meaningfulness with objective research methods. As a result, we hope to contribute to a more accurate understanding and measurement of the supportive–expressive distinction.

Finally, our objective is to contribute to the more effective understanding and treatment of this highly challenging and difficult population. Patients with borderline disorders represent about one half the patient population in the C. F.

Menninger Memorial Hospital; they were the major diagnostic group to show negative effects in response to treatment in the Menninger Psychotherapy Research Project (Colson, Lewis, & Horwitz, 1985). The instability of their functioning in the workplace and in family settings often places burdens on others and produces pain for themselves. Any addition to the technical and scientific knowledge for helping such people will constitute an important contribution.

Relation to Other Research Programs

Integration of Findings With Other Research

Most measures of therapeutic alliance in the research literature pertain to the contributions of both the patient and the therapist, sometimes lumping the two factors into one composite score. On the other hand, the clinical and research literature on the alliance tend to emphasize that the strength of the alliance is mainly determined by the patient's pathology. The more disturbed the patient, the more difficult it is to establish a reliable alliance. By focusing on the patient's collaboration with the therapist as the final common pathway for their mutual contributions to the alliance (Colson et al., 1988), our measure reflects our clinical sense of the principal determinants of the alliance.

Our reliability study included Luborsky's (1976) helping alliance measure alongside our own alliance measures. Without any special training, our raters achieved an average reliability of .80 for the Luborsky scale. At this point, however, we have not fully analyzed the similarities and differences between the two sets of measures.

Our original intention was to adapt Gill's process coding categories (Gill & Hoffman, 1982) to our particular interest. Ultimately, however, we decided to eliminate Gill's patient content categories entirely and instead to base our system on his therapist categories. We already rate patient content in terms of the patient's collaboration, and we experienced difficulty reaching consensus judgments on one particularly important score: the patient's indirect allusion to the transference. We ultimately concluded that, to some degree or other, practically every comment that patients make about their external life could be construed as allusion to the relationship with the therapist.

Impact on the Field of Psychotherapy

Because we have not yet embarked on our main study, we do not have any clear-cut research findings that are likely to influence the current practice of psychotherapy. Nevertheless, the research instruments we developed have been used in a few other studies. The McLean group (Frank, 1988) has adopted affect expression, one of our mediating variables, into their Therapeutic Alliance Scale. Locally, Allen, Deering, Buskirk, & Coyne (1988) adapted the Therapeutic Alliance Scale to study the process of hospital treatment. In addition, Colson, Eyman, and Coyne (1988), in a study of the psychotherapy of difficult-to-treat hospital patients, used an adaptation of our therapeutic alliance measure to assess the patient's response to psychotherapy.

References

Adler, G. (1985). *Borderline psychopathology and its treatment.* Northvale, NJ: Jason Aronson.

Allen, J. G., Deering, C. D., Buskirk, J. R., & Coyne, L. (1988). Assessment of therapeutic alliances in the psychiatric hospital milieu. *Psychiatry, 51,* 291–299.

Allen, J. G., Gabbard, G. O., Newsom, G. E., & Coyne, L. (in press). Detecting patterns of change in patients' collaboration within psychotherapy sessions. *Psychotherapy.*

Allen, J. G., Newsom, G. E., Gabbard, G. O., & Coyne, L. (1984). Scales to assess the therapeutic alliance from a psychoanalytic perspective. *Bulletin of the Menninger Clinic, 48,* 383–400.

American Psychiatric Association. (1987). *Diagnostic and statistical manual of mental disorders* (rev. 3rd ed.). Washington, DC: Author.

Balint, M. (1968). *The basic fault: Therapeutic aspects of aggression.* London: Tavistock.

Blatt, S. J., & Shichman, S. (1983). Two primary configurations of psychopathology. *Psychoanalysis and Contemporary Thought, 6,* 187–254.

Colson, D. B., Eyman, J., & Coyne L. (1988, October). *Rorschach correlates of the therapeutic alliance and treatment difficulty in psychotherapy with long-term psychiatric hospital patients.* Paper presented at the Austen–Riggs Center Conference on Psychological Testing and the Psychotherapeutic Process, Stockbridge, MA.

Colson, D. B., Horwitz, L., Allen, J. G., Frieswyk, S. H., Gabbard, G. O., Newsom, G. E., & Coyne, L. (1988). Patient collaboration as criterion for the therapeutic alliance. *Psychoanalytic Psychology, 5,* 259–268.

Colson, D. B., Horwitz, L., Frieswyk, S. H., & Coyne, L. (1989). *A system for categorizing therapist interventions: Interrater reliability.* Manuscript submitted for publication.

Colson, D. B., Lewis, L., & Horwitz, L. (1985). Negative outcome in psychotherapy and psychoanalysis. In D. T. Mays & C. M. Franks (Eds.), *Negative outcome in* psychotherapy and what to do about it (pp. 59–75). New York: Springer.

Crits-Christoph, P., Cooper, A., & Luborsky, L. (1988). The accuracy of therapists' interpretations and the outcome of dynamic psychotherapy. Journal of Consulting and Clinical Psychology, 56, 490–495.

Frank, A. (1988, June). Problems in studying treatment of borderlines. Paper presented at the annual meeting of the society for Psychotherapy Research, Santa Fe, NM.

Frieswyk, S. H., Allen, J. G., Colson, D. B., Coyne. L., Gabbard, G. O., Horwitz, L., & Newsom, G. (1986). Therapeutic alliance: Its place as a process and outcome variable in dynamic psychotherapy research. Journal of Consulting and Clinical Psychology, 54, 32–38.

Frieswyk, S. H., Colson, D. B., & Allen, J. G. (1984). Conceptualizing the therapeutic alliance from a psychoanalytic perspective. Psychotherapy, 21, 460–464.

Gabbard, G. O, Horwitz, L., Frieswyk, S., Allen, J. G., Colson, D. B., Newsom, G., & Coyne, L. (1988). The effect of therapist interventions on the therapeutic alliance with borderline patients. Journal of the American Psychoanalytic Association, 36, 697–727.

Gill, M. M., & Hoffman, I. Z. (1982). A method for studying the analysis of aspects of the patient's experience of the relationship in psychoanalysis and psychotherapy. Journal of the American Psychoanalytic Association, 30, 137–167.

Gill, M. M., & Muslin, H. (1976). Early interpretation of transference. Journal of the American Psychoanalytic Association, 24, 779–794.

Grinker, R., & Werble, B. (1977). The borderline patient. Northvale, NJ: Jason Aronson.

Gunderson, J. G. (1984). Borderline personality disorder. Washington, DC: American Psychiatric Press.

Horwitz, L. (1974). Clinical prediction in psychotherapy. Northvale, NJ: Jason Aronson.

Horwitz, L. (1985). Divergent views on the treatment of borderline patients. Bulletin of the Menninger Clinic, 49, 525–545.

Horwitz, L. (1988). Indications for transference interpretation with a borderline patient. Unpublished manuscript.

Horwitz, L., & Frieswyk, S. H. (1980, December). The impact of interpretation on therapeutic alliance in borderline patients. Paper presented at the meeting of the American Psychoanalytic Association, New York.

Kernberg, O. F. (1976). Object-relations theory and clinical psychoanalysis. Northvale, NJ: Jason Aronson.

Kernberg, O. F., Burstein, E. D., Coyne, L., Appelbaum, A., Horwitz, L., & Voth, H. (1972). Psychotherapy and psychoanalysis: Final report of the Menninger Foundation's psychotherapy research project. Bulletin of the Menninger Clinic, 36, 3–275.

Luborsky, L. (1976). Helping alliances in psychotherapy. In J. L. Claghorn (Ed.), Successful psychotherapy (pp. 92–116). New York: Brunner/Mazel.

Masterson, J. F. (1976). Psychotherapy of the borderline adult: A developmental approach. New York: Brunner/Mazel.

Meissner, W. W. (1984). The borderline spectrum: Differential diagnosis and developmental issues. Northvale, NJ: Jason Aronson.

Modell, A. H. (1976). "The holding environment" and the therapeutic action of psychoanalysis. Journal of the American Psychoanalytic Association, 24, 285–307.

Stone, M. H. (1987). Psychotherapy of borderline patients in light of long-term follow-up. Bulletin of the Menninger Clinic, 51, 231–247.

Wallerstein, R. S. (1986). Forty-two lives in treatment: A study of psychoanalysis and psychotherapy. New York: Guilford Press.

Mount Zion Hospital and Medical Center: Research on the Process of Change in Psychotherapy

George Silberschatz, John T. Curtis, Harold Sampson,
and Joseph Weiss
Mount Zion Hospital and Medical Center

Background and Aims

The broad objective of the Mount Zion Psychotherapy Research Group (MZPRG) is to increase the effectiveness of psychotherapy by discovering fundamental principles about how the psychotherapist helps the patient to make progress. Under the direction of Sampson and Weiss, the research program began 17 years ago with clinical and empirical studies of psychoanalyses. These early studies addressed how patients develop control over their unconscious impulses, affect, and defenses (Sampson, Weiss, Mlodnosky, & Hause, 1972); insight into previously warded-off mental contents (Gassner, Sampson, Weiss, & Brumer, 1982; Horowitz, Sampson, Siegelman, Wolfson, & Weiss, 1975); and control over symptomatic behaviors (Horowitz, Sampson, Siegelman, Weiss, & Goodfriend, 1978). In the last 10 years, we have extended our research to the study of brief (16-session) psychodynamic psychotherapy. The studies of the MZPRG have tested and led to further refinement of a theory of psychopathology and psychotherapy developed by Weiss (1967, 1971, 1986).

The concept of unconscious pathogenic beliefs is central to Weiss's (1967, 1971, 1986) theory. According to the theory, psychopathology stems from unconscious pathogenic beliefs that usually develop from traumatic childhood experiences. Patients come to therapy with a plan (which is often unconscious) to master their conflicts. The patient's plan may be viewed as a strategy for disconfirming pathogenic beliefs by developing greater understanding of them in therapy and by testing them in the relationship with the therapist. The therapist may help the patient to disconfirm pathogenic beliefs through interpretations or by responding appropriately to the patient's tests (Curtis & Silberschatz, 1986; Silberschatz & Curtis, 1986; Weiss, 1986). The theory does not suggest a particular technique; rather, it explains how therapy works.

In planning studies on how the therapist influences the process and outcome of psychotherapy, the MZPRG was confronted with a fundamental problem in the field: how to determine whether a particular intervention appropriately addresses an individual patient's problems and therapy goals. The MZPRG responded to this problem by developing a method for creating reliable, individualized case formulations that could then be applied to determine whether any given intervention suitably addresses a patient's problems. The formulation method, *plan diagnosis,* was initially used on psychoanalyses (Caston, 1980, 1986) and was subsequently refined and applied to the study of brief dynamic psychotherapy (Curtis & Silberschatz, 1989; Curtis, Silberschatz, Sampson, Weiss, & Rosenberg, 1988; Rosenberg, Silberschatz, Curtis, Sampson, & Weiss, 1986).

The plan diagnosis method paved the way for developing a measure that could be used to rate the goodness of fit between therapist behaviors and the problems and goals of a patient. Two suitability measures have been developed. The first, the degree to which the therapist passes the patient's tests, assesses the appropriateness of a therapist's response during a moment in the therapy (i.e., when the patient is testing a pathogenic belief). A second measure developed by Caston (1980, 1986), the Plan Compatibility of Interventions Scale (PCIS), has been used to rate the suitability of therapist interpretations (Bush & Gassner, 1986; Fretter, 1984; Silberschatz, Fretter, & Curtis, 1986). Both of these measures have been applied with high interjudge reliabilities to therapy transcript data, and both have proven to be sensitive predictors of shifts in therapy process. Throughout our research we have compared our methods and concepts with those of other investigators, and we have also tested competing hypotheses about the process of psychotherapy (Silberschatz, 1978; Silberschatz, Sampson, & Weiss, 1986).

Our research effort is divided into four subareas of investigation: (a) reliable and replicable methods of formulating patients' plans, (b) studies of the patient's efforts to disconfirm pathogenic beliefs through testing of the therapist, (c) the effects of the therapist's interventions on the patient's progress, and (d) the development of new process and outcome measures that are sensitive indicators of therapeutic progress. Each of these areas of investigation, along with a summary of our findings, is described.

Method

The MZPRG has been studying the effective ingredients of psychotherapy, particularly how therapist behaviors influence the therapeutic process. Our concepts and measures cut across different types of patients and different types of therapy. Consequently, we have not focused on a particular therapy modality for targeted patient populations, nor have we used treatment manuals. Typically, treatment manuals define how a particular type of therapy (e.g., cognitive therapy,

interpersonal therapy) should be conducted. We have developed a different kind of manual (the patient plan diagnosis) that is case specific and defines each patient's problems and goals and how the therapist can best respond to that patient. Consequently, in our efforts to identify effective ingredients in psychotherapy we use the patient plan formulation as a case-specific "treatment manual." The PCIS represents an individually tailored adherence measure that can quantify how much of an effective ingredient was delivered by the therapist. On the basis of the plan formulation of each patient, we have devised new instruments (described later) that measure the degree to which the patient has used or incorporated the effective agent.

Subjects

The patients studied in our research reflect a range of diagnostic categories, ages, educational backgrounds, and socioeconomic status levels. Therapies were drawn from our own archives as well as from those of other investigators. The patients whose psychoanalyses we studied were young, well-educated individuals with neurotic disorders. Our brief therapy sample includes young, middle-aged, and older patients (ranging in age from 18 to 88 years) who met the following acceptance criteria: a history of positive interpersonal relationships, no evidence of psychosis, organic brain syndrome, or mental deficiency, no evidence of serious substance abuse, and no evidence of suicidal or homicidal potential. Although they differed in presenting complaints, all patients in our brief therapy sample were diagnosed as having neurotic or character disorders or both. The brief therapy sample consisted predominantly of White, lower middle-class, and middle-class patients.

In all of the therapies we have studied, the therapists were experienced clinicians. The psychoanalysts had completed psychoanalytic training at accredited psychoanalytic institutes, and the therapists in the brief therapy studies all had at least 5 years of postdoctoral experience as well as training in brief dynamic psychotherapy. Most cases were treated by therapists who did not adhere to our particular theory of psychotherapy. Indeed, for the brief therapy studies we deliberately chose therapists with various psychodynamic orientations (e.g., Sifneos, Davanloo, Malan). When the therapies were recorded, the therapists were unaware of our hypotheses.

A total of 38 patients were treated as part of our brief therapy study. Patients received 16 weekly sessions of psychodynamically oriented psychotherapy; all sessions lasted 45 minutes, and all were audiotaped. Each patient received intake, termination, and 6-month and 1-year follow-up interviews by an independent clinical evaluator. Pretherapy and posttherapy test batteries were completed by patients, therapists, and the clinical evaluator. Verbatim transcripts of all therapy sessions, pretreatment interviews, test scores, and process data collected on each case were entered into the computerized Mount Zion Psychotherapy Data Archive.

Instruments

The instruments used in our research are aimed at answering the following questions:

• What does the patient hope to accomplish in treatment? What obstacles have stood in the patient's way? How is the patient likely to work in therapy to overcome these obstacles (plan formulation)?

• Did the patient make progress during a particular session or group of sessions (process or within-session change)?

• How did the therapist's interventions influence the patient's progress (process studies)?

• How much did the patient change from pretherapy to posttherapy status (outcome)?

Plan diagnosis. The MZPRG has developed a protocol for preparing the formulation of a patient's plan for therapy (Curtis & Silberschatz, 1989; Curtis et al., 1988). Plan formulations contain the following four components: the patient's conscious as well as unconscious *goals;* the *obstructions* or pathogenic beliefs preventing the attainment of goals; the means by which the patient is likely to *test* the therapist to disconfirm pathogenic beliefs; and the *insights* that would be particularly useful in helping the patient to disconfirm pathogenic beliefs. Studies of psychoanalysis (Caston, 1980, 1986) and of brief dynamic psychotherapy (Curtis & Silberschatz, 1989; Curtis et al., 1988; Rosenberg et al., 1986) have focused on methods for assessing the interjudge reliability of plan formulations. These studies show that excellent interjudge reliability can be achieved with this method.

Process measures. The patient plan formulation is used in our process research to evaluate the suitability of therapist behaviors and the amount of progress that the patient is making within the session. Two kinds of therapist process measures have been used the Test Passing Scale, a 7-point Likert-type scale that measures the degree to which the therapist passes or fails the patient's tests (Silberschatz, 1978, 1986); and the PCIS, a 7-point Likert-type scale that assesses the extent to which the therapist's interpretations are compatible with the patient's plan (Bush & Gassner, 1986; Caston, 1980; Fretter, 1984; Silberschatz, Fretter, et al., 1986). Interjudge reliabilities for both measures have been good (ICCs > .75).

The patient's responses to therapist interventions (i.e., immediate changes from preintervention to postintervention status) have been measured with instruments developed by the MZPRG as well as by other researchers. One measure that we have used in most of our studies is the patient Experiencing Scales (Klein, Mathieu-Coughlan, & Kiesler, 1986), a widely used and well-validated instrument that taps the patient's level of involvement in therapy. Other process instruments used in our research include the Penn Helping Alliance Rating Method, the Vanderbilt Psychotherapy Process Scale, the Gottschalk–Gleser Anxiety Scale, and the Morgan Patient Insight Scale. The instruments developed by the MZPRG are described in the Research Accomplishments section.

Outcome measures. The outcome battery for the brief therapy sample includes Target Complaints, Goal Attainment Scaling, SCL-90–R, the Global Assessment Scale, the Brief Psychiatric Rating Scale, the Overall Change Rating Scale, the Adjective Checklist, and the Loevinger Sentence Completion Test. We have also developed a psychodynamic measure of outcome—the Plan Attainment Scale (Nathans, 1988; Silberschatz, Curtis, & Nathans, 1989)—that is derived from the patient plan formulation (see the Research Accomplishments section).

Procedures

Most of our studies involve testing hypotheses about how therapy works. We have typically used a repeated measures, single-case design with patients serving as their own controls. The research design entails (a) identifying the crucial incidents in therapy (e.g., therapist interpretations, the emergence of previously warded-off mental contents, the patient's testing of the therapist); (b) measuring the patient's behavior before, during, and after the crucial event; and (c) replicating findings in other cases. For example, to study the effects of the therapist's passing or failing the patient's tests (Silberschatz, 1986) the following steps were taken: key patient tests (crucial incident) were identified; the therapist's responses to these tests were rated for the degree to which they disconfirmed the belief that the patient was testing (passing or failing the test); and the patient's behavior and affect immediately before and after the test were measured to determine whether the patient changed in the predicted direction. A similar procedure was used in studies of the immediate impact of therapist interpretations on the patient's in-session progress (Bush & Gassner, 1986; Silberschatz, Fretter, et al., 1986).

Research Accomplishments

Findings

All theories of psychotherapy assume that the therapist plays a significant role in the change process. Nevertheless, there has been little empirical evidence that the therapist has any systematic impact on therapeutic progress or outcome. It has been difficult to demonstrate therapist effects because investigators have not had a way of measuring whether therapist activities are appropriately suited to the particular patient's problems and goals. Consequently, most research has tended to count the frequency of types of interventions (e.g., interpretations, questions, and reflections) without taking into account the suitability of the intervention. The plan concept provides a framework for evaluating the patient's problems and goals, the obstacles to their realization, the means by which the patient will work in therapy to overcome these obstacles, and, most important, how the therapist can best help the patient.

The main findings of the MZPRG research program are as follows:

• It is possible to identify reliably a patient's plan.

• The plan formulation has predictive validity; that is, it correctly specifies how a patient will work and how he or she will respond to the therapist's interventions.

• The patient's tests can be reliably identified.

• Reliable judgments can be made about whether a therapist has passed or failed a test or whether an interpretation is well suited to the particular patient (i.e., whether it is plan compatible).

• Therapist behaviors have a significant impact on the patient's therapeutic progress: When a therapist passes the patient's tests or makes plan-compatible interpretations, the patient shows signs of progress. When the therapist fails tests or makes plan-incompatible interpretations, the patient shows signs of retreat.

The plan diagnosis method has proved to be a reliable procedure for developing individually tailored psychodynamic case formulations. The method has been applied to 3 psychoanalyses and 11 brief therapies drawn from the Mount Zion Psychotherapy Data Archive as well as from other investigators' studies. Interjudge reliabilities (intraclass correlations of pooled judges' ratings) in the .80–.90 range are typical (Curtis & Silberschatz, 1989; Curtis et al., 1988; Rosenberg et al., 1986). Recent studies indicate that the plan concept can be taught to relatively inexperienced judges who can then apply it reliably (Curtis & Silberschatz, 1989). The plan diagnosis method has also been used by investigators who used a theoretical framework different from that of the MZPRG with comparably high levels of reliability (Collins & Messer, 1988).

Our studies show that plan formulations can be used to identify significant events in psychotherapy. Judges have been able reliably to identify key tests by the patient (i.e., instances in which the patient is testing a central pathogenic belief) and to rate the degree to which a therapist's interpretation helps the patient carry out his or her plan (intraclass correlations for these ratings range from .78 to .89; see Silberschatz, 1986; Silberschatz, Fretter, et al., 1986). In addition, plan formulations have been used as case-specific measures to assess how much progress a patient makes in the session (plan progressiveness) and in the therapy overall (Plan Attainment Scale; both measures are described later). In short, plan formulations can be reliably used to assess the meaning of patient and therapist behaviors and to provide a clinically meaningful template for evaluating therapeutic progress (Silberschatz, Curtis, & Nathans, 1989).

Our studies show that there are consistent significant correlations between ratings of therapist behaviors and immediate patient progress. Horowitz et al. (1975) found that the patient's level of discomfort (as measured by a speech disruption measure) dropped when the therapist passed a test and that new (previously warded-off) content tended to follow passed tests. Silberschatz (1978, 1986) found that the patient became significantly more involved, productive, and relaxed when the therapist passed key tests. In addition to finding empirical support for the concept of testing and for the importance of the therapist's passing the patient's tests, Silberschatz compared the predictive validity of an alternative psychoanalytic model (based on traditional psychoanalytic theory) with that of Weiss's model (Silberschatz, Sampson, & Weiss, 1986). Interestingly, the two models made opposite predictions. The results provided strong support for the testing model: All of the correlations were in the direction predicted by the testing model and opposite to the direction predicted by the alternative model. This research is distinctive in the psychoanalytic literature in that it is the first study to show that competing hypotheses can be empirically evaluated.

In studies of brief dynamic therapies we have replicated and expanded on our findings concerning testing in psychoanalysis. We have found significant correlations between the degree to which a therapist passes a patient's tests and immediate changes in the patient's levels of experiencing (Silberschatz, Curtis, & Kelly, 1989), adaptive regression (Bugas, 1986), and voice stress levels (Kelly, 1986, 1988; see the Instruments Developed section for a description of measures). The fact that results from studies of psychoanalyses have been replicated in research on brief therapies with different patients and various measures of patient progress lends strong empirical support to the hypothesis that passing a patient's tests is an important factor in determining therapeutic progress.

Comparable results have also been obtained in research relating the plan compatibility of therapist interpretations (PCIS scores) with immediate patient improvement. In a study of more than 200 therapist interpretations drawn from 3 brief therapy cases, we found that PCIS ratings correlated significantly with changes in patient experiencing levels across all 3 cases (Silberschatz, Fretter, et al., 1986). We also sought to determine whether another measure of therapist interpretations—Malan's transference and nontransference classification method—would predict changes in the patient (see Silberschatz, Fretter, et al., 1986). PCIS scores (averaged for each session) explained 30%–60% of the variance in patient experiencing levels, whereas the transference classification was not predictive. The data suggest that patients who received a high proportion of plan-compatible interpretations had better treatment outcomes than those who received a low proportion of such interpretations.

Instruments Developed

In addition to the plan diagnosis method and the plan-based rating scales already discussed, the following measures have been developed by the MZPRG.

Plan Progressiveness Scale. This scale measures the degree to which, at any given time in the therapy, the patient's productions reflect progress or retreat with respect to his or her plan. The Plan Progressiveness Scale differs from other measures of therapeutic involvement (e.g., the Experiencing Scales) in that it is a case-specific scale that focuses on the content of the patient's productions rather than on the manner of their delivery. Thus, segments of patient speech that might be rated high on a measure such as the Experiencing Scales could be rated low on plan progressiveness. The scale was initially developed by Silberschatz and Curtis (1986) on 32 segments of patient speech (varying in length from 3 to 6 minutes); the intraclass correlation for the mean of 4 judges' ratings was .89. We found significant correlations between therapist test passing ratings and patient plan progressiveness.

The Plan Attainment Scale. The Plan Attainment Scale is a psychodynamic outcome measure that is based on the patient's plan formulation. It measures the patient's progress in three areas: the degree to which the patient achieved the goals for therapy, overcame the obstructions to attaining these goals (disconfirmation of pathogenic beliefs), and developed pertinent insights. Each of these three sections contains individualized items (taken from the plan formulation) that are rated on a 7-point Likert-type scale. In addition to rating individual items, judges make global ratings of goals, obstructions, and insights as well as a global rating for overall plan attainment. Trained judges first read the intake interview and plan formulation for the case to be rated; they then read the posttherapy evaluation interview and rate the patient's progress from pretherapy to posttherapy status on the Plan Attainment Scale. After the patient's progress is rated, a 6-month follow-up interview is also rated. In a study of seven cases, the measure was shown to be reliable and to correlate with other outcome measures such as the SCL-90–R and Target Complaints (Nathans, 1988; Silberschatz, Curtis, & Nathans, 1989).

Voice Stress Measure (VSM). The VSM is a psychophysiological measure that has been shown to be a sensitive indicator of emotional arousal and stress as reflected in voice characteristics (Scherer, 1982). Kelly (1986, 1988) adapted the VSM to study brief segments of psychotherapy data (2–5 minutes of speech). Kelly validated the VSM on 111 segments of patient speech drawn from three different brief therapies by correlating patient VSM scores with ratings of the degree to which therapists passed patients' tests. Passed tests tended to be followed by a decrease in voice stress, whereas failed tests tended to be followed by an increase in stress.

Adaptive Regression Scale. Based on Holt's system of scoring primary process thought on the Rorschach, the Adaptive Regression Scale (Bugas, 1986) is designed to measure both the expression of and the degree of control over primary process thinking manifested in psychotherapy sessions. The scale taps how comfortably and freely a patient can gain access to and use unconscious material in a therapeutic way; in this respect, the scale may be viewed as a measure of Kris's concept of regression in the service of the ego. The scale has been applied with good interjudge reliability ($ICCs > .85$). Bugas (1986) found significant correlations between changes (from pretest to posttest segments) in patients' levels of adaptive regression and ratings on the therapist Test Passing Scale.

The Boldness Rating Scale. The Boldness Rating Scale, developed by Caston (1986), is a 5-point rating scale that assesses the degree to which the patient is able to confront or elaborate on nontrivial material; that is, the extent to which he or she boldly tackles issues or retreats from them. At the low end of the scale, the patient is anxious and generally inhibited, and may express dissatisfaction about his or her handling of the material. At the high end of the scale, the patient seems able to plunge ahead and confront various issues even if they are painful or distressing. The scale has been used in studies of psychoanalyses and brief psychotherapies with high interrater reliability. Silberschatz (1986) found that boldness ratings correlated positively with ratings of test passing.

The Relaxation Rating Scale. This 5-point Likert-type scale measures the patient's degree of freedom and relaxation in the psychotherapy session. Originally developed to rate entire sessions (Curtis, Ransohoff, Sampson, Brumer, & Bronstein, 1986), the scale was adapted for rating 2- to 8-minute segments of patient transcript material Silberschatz, 1978, 1986). The sale ranges from the patient's seeming uncomfortable, constricted, beleaguered, and tense at the low end to feeling spontaneous, relaxed, and free at the high end. High interrater reliability has been achieved with psychoanalytic data as well as data from brief therapy. Relaxation has been shown to correlate with test passing (Silberschatz, 1978, 1986).

The Therapy Shame and Guilt Scale. This 33-item psychotherapy process measure was designed to assess manifestations of patients' shame and guilt in psychotherapy sessions. The scale was developed by Nergaard (1985). Alpha reliabilities for the individual items ranged from .45 to .98 (the average reliability was .80). A principal-components factor analysis yielded two distinct factors of shame and guilt items. In a study of 38 brief therapy cases from the Mount Zion Psychotherapy Data Archive, Nergaard and Silberschatz (1989) found that guilt ratings correlated significantly with posttherapy outcome.

Research Projects in Progress

Three main areas of work are currently in progress: (a) continuing research on the relation between the plan compatibility of therapist interpretations and patients' in-session progress, (b) relating the plan compatibility of interventions to therapy outcome, and (c) encouraging replications of our methods and procedures by other research groups.

In our studies of the psychotherapeutic process, we found consistent significant correlations between the suitability (plan compatibility) of therapist behaviors and immediate patient progress. We assumed, on the basis of these findings, that if the therapist made a preponderance of good or suitable (i.e., plan-compatible) interventions then the outcome of the treatment would be favorable. That is, if a clinician repeatedly confirms the patient's pathogenic beliefs (i.e., by failing the patient's tests or behaving in a plan-incompatible manner), the outcome is likely to be poor. If the therapist helps the patient disconfirm pathogenic beliefs (by passing tests or intervening in plan-compatible ways), the patient is likely to make significant progress toward achieving therapy goals, and the outcome is likely to be favorable.

Pilot data from our testing and interpretation studies are consistent with this hypothesis. For instance, in one case with a poor therapy outcome, the average rating of the therapist's responses to the patient's tests throughout the therapy was 1.5 on a 7-point scale ranging from *therapist fails the test* (1) to *a clear instance of passing the patient's test* (7). By contrast, in a second case with a successful outcome, the average of the therapist's responses to tests was 5.5. Similarly, in our interpretation study (Silberschatz, Fretter, et al., 1986), we found that the case with the highest percentage of plan-compatible interpretations had the best outcome, whereas the case with the highest percentage of plan-incompatible interpretations had the worst outcome.

A study to assess the relation between plan compatibility of therapist interventions and treatment outcome is currently underway at Mount Zion Hospital. In this research, the verbatim transcripts of 38 completed brief dynamic psychotherapies are being studied. All therapist interventions from a sample of five therapy sessions are being rated for their degree of plan compatibility. Mean ratings will be computed for each of the five sessions, and these averaged plan-compatibility ratings will then be correlated with outcome assessment.

The plan diagnosis method has now been sufficiently streamlined so as to be usable by researchers outside of the MZPRG. To familiarize interested colleagues with our concepts and methods, the MZPRG has been hosting week-long intensive annual workshops. Stanley Messer and colleagues from Rutgers University attended one of our workshops to learn our plan diagnosis procedures. They then applied the plan diagnosis method to cases of their own as well as to cases from the Mount Zion Psychotherapy Data Archive. Although their conceptual framework differs sharply from our own, they have been able to apply our method with good interjudge reliabilities (Collins & Messer, 1988). A study comparing the formulations developed by the Rutgers and Mount Zion groups is currently underway. Each group is rating the plan diagnosis items identified for a given case by the other group in order to identify areas of overlap and disagreement in the formulations. By using the research design developed by Silberschatz (1978;

Silberschatz, Sampson, et al., 1986) to study competing psychoanalytic hypotheses of the analytic process, the predictive power of these different formulations will be tested.

Programs Planned for the Future

The research of the MZPRG has focused exclusively on psychodynamic therapy. An important new research direction is to apply our concepts and to test our hypotheses on other schools of therapy. We are currently planning research on cognitive therapy to determine how well ratings of plan compatibility of therapist behaviors predict progress in cognitive therapy. Initial reviews of cognitive therapy hours indicate that the plan diagnosis method can be applied to this form of treatment and that the PCIS can be adapted to cognitive therapies.

Nature of the Research Organization

The MZPRG was organized in 1972 by Sampson and Weiss to study the process of psychoanalytic therapy. At its inception the group had 10 members, and it has grown over the years to include more than 50 active members. The group includes clinically experienced psychoanalysts, psychiatrists, psychologists, social workers, research psychologists, and doctoral-level students (to date, 15 doctoral dissertations have been carried out in collaboration with the MZPRG). In 1979, Rosenberg and Silberschatz established the Brief Therapy Project as part of the larger MZPRG. Rosenberg subsequently left Mount Zion, and in 1982 Silberschatz and Curtis became codirectors of the Brief Therapy Project and organized the Mount Zion Psychotherapy Data Archive.

The National Institute of Mental Health (NIMH) has been a major source of funding for the MZPRG (NIMH grants MH-13915, 1967–1976; MH-34052, 1979–1981; and MH-35230, 1981 to the present). We have also received funding from Mount Zion Hospital, the American Psychoanalytic Association's Fund for Psychoanalytic Research, and the Chapman Research Fund.

Relation to Other Research Programs

Our main research focus has been to develop our concepts and methods, to demonstrate that our measures are reliable, and to test the predictive validity of our measures. Having established the reliability of our instruments, we have recently started to compare our measures with those of other investigators. We have compared our plan diagnosis method with Luborsky's core conflictual relationship theme and Perry's dynamic formulation method (Perry, Luborsky, Silberschatz, & Popp, 1989). We have used the Vanderbilt Psychotherapy Process Scale (Windholz & Silberschatz, 1988) and the Vanderbilt Negative Indicators Scale (Nergaard & Silberschatz, 1989) on the sample of 38 brief therapies in the Mount Zion Psychotherapy Data Archive. Finally, we have compared the predictive validity of our Test Passing Scale and the PCIS with several process measures: the Penn helping alliance rating method (Hamer, 1987), the Vanderbilt Psychotherapy Process Scale (Kale, 1986), and Malan's classification of interpretations (Fretter, 1984; Silberschatz, Fretter, et al., 1986).

The research of the MZPRG supports the value of developing and testing theories of change processes in psychotherapy. The theory that we have been testing and the case-specific research approach that we use have the potential to bridge the wide gap between the practice of psychotherapy and research on psychotherapy. Although many investigators have suggested that psychotherapy research methods must be geared to the specific dynamics of particular patient–therapist interactions, empirical studies that use such case-specific methods are extremely rare. Many of the studies carried out by the MZPRG illustrate how such methods can be applied to study psychoanalysis and brief therapies. Our findings provide strong empirical support for the plan concept and for the therapeutic value of interventions that are compatible with the patient's plan.

The MZPRG was designed to improve the effectiveness of psychotherapy. Our studies have led to the refinement and further development of Weiss's (1967, 1971, 1986) theory of psychotherapy. The theory and its clinical applications have been widely taught in the San Francisco Bay Area and "exported" to other areas of the country through presentations, publications, and the yearly workshops held at Mount Zion Hospital and the San Francisco Psychoanalytic Institute. We have found that even relatively novice therapists can be trained in developing plan formulations and in applying them (in both clinical practice and research) to the understanding of clinical phenomena. Consequently, our research findings are both informed by and have had a strong impact on the theory and practice of psychotherapy.

Although the MZPRG research studies grew out of Weiss's (1986) cognitive-psychodynamic theory, our concepts and methods cut across various types of therapy and explain how the therapist's behavior, regardless of the type of therapy practiced, affects the patient's progress. Our techniques for developing reliable case formulations, for measuring the therapist's adherence to these formulations, and for measuring the impact of therapist behaviors on the process and outcome of therapy can be used by investigators with differing theories.

References

Bugas, J. S. (1986). *Adaptive regression and the therapeutic change process.* Unpublished doctoral dissertation, Pacific Graduate School of Psychology, Menlo Park, CA.

Bush, M., & Gassner, S. (1986). The immediate effect of the analyst's termination interventions on the patient's resistance to termination. In J. Weiss, H. Sampson, & the Mount Zion Psychotherapy Research Group (Eds.), *The psychoanalytic process: Theory, clinical observation, and empirical research* (pp. 299–322). New York: Guilford Press.

Caston, J. (1980). Manual on how to diagnose the plan. In J. Weiss, H. Sampson, J. Caston, & S. Gassner (Eds.), *Further research on the psychoanalytic process* (pp. 31–35). San Francisco: Department of Psychiatry, Mount Zion Hospital.

Caston, J. (1986). The reliability of the diagnosis of the patient's unconscious plan. In J. Weiss, H. Sampson, & the Mount Zion Psychotherapy Research Group (Eds.), *The psychoanalytic process: Theory, clinical observation, and empirical research* (pp. 241–255). New York: Guilford Press.

Collins, W., & Messer, S. (1988, June). *Development of case formulations employing the Mount Zion plan formulation method.* Paper presented at the 19th annual Society for Psychotherapy Research meeting, Santa Fe, NM.

Curtis, J. T., Ransohoff, P., Sampson, F., Brumer, S., & Bronstein, A. (1986). Expressing warded-off contents in behavior. In J. Weiss, H. Sampson, & the Mount Zion Psychotherapy Research Group (Eds.), *The psychoanalytic process: Theory, clinical observation, and empirical research* (pp. 187–205). New York: Guilford Press.

Curtis, J. T., & Silberschatz, G. (1986). Clinical implications of research on brief dynamic psychotherapy: I. Formulating the patient's problems and goals. *Psychoanalytic Psychology, 3,* 13–25.

Curtis, J. T., & Silberschatz, G. (1989). *The plan formulation method: A reliable procedure for case formulation.* Manuscript submitted for publication.

Curtis, J. T., Silberschatz, G., Sampson, H., Weiss, J., & Rosenberg, S. E. (1988). Developing reliable psychodynamic case formulations: An illustration of the plan diagnosis method. *Psychotherapy, 25,* 256–265.

Fretter, P. B. (1984). The immediate effects of transference interpretations on patients' progress in brief, psychodynamic psychotherapy. *Dissertation Abstracts International, 46,* 1415A. (University Microfilms No. 85-12, 112)

Gassner, S., Sampson, H., Weiss, J., & Brumer, S. (1982). The emergence of warded-off contents. *Psychoanalysis and Contemporary Thought, 5,* 55–75.

Hamer, F. M. (1987). *The therapeutic alliance and the process of psychotherapy.* Unpublished doctoral dissertation, University of California, Berkeley.

Horowitz, L. M., Sampson, H., Siegelman, E. Y., Weiss, J., & Goodfriend, S. (1978). Cohesive and dispersal behaviors: Two classes of concomitant change in psychotherapy. *Journal of Consulting and Clinical Psychology, 46,* 556–564.

Horowitz, L. M., Sampson, H., Siegelman, E. Y., Wolfson, A. W., & Weiss, J. (1975). On the identification of warded-off mental contents. *Journal of Abnormal Psychology, 84,* 545–558.

Kale, C. (1986). The therapist's effect on patient progress in brief psychodynamic psychotherapy. *Dissertation Abstracts International, 47,* 3959. (University Microfilms No. 86-23, 649)

Kelly, T. J. (1986, June). *The immediate effect of therapist interventions on patient stress as measured by long-term voice spectrum.* Paper presented at the 17th Annual Meeting of the Society for Psychotherapy Research, Wellesley, MA.

Kelly, T. J. (1988). *Do therapists' interventions matter?* Unpublished doctoral dissertation, New York University.

Klein, M. H., Mathieu-Coughlan, P., & Kiesler, D. J. (1986). The experiencing scales. In L. S. Greenberg & W. M. Pinsof (Eds.), *The psychotherapeutic process: A research handbook* (pp. 21–72). New York: Guilford Press.

Nathans, S. (1988). *Plan attainment: An individualized measure for assessing outcome in psychodynamic psychotherapy.* Unpublished doctoral dissertation, California School of Professional Psychology, Berkeley.

Nergaard, M. (1985). The effects of shame, guilt, and the negative reaction in brief dynamic psychotherapy. *Dissertation Abstracts International, 46,* 2464. (University Microfilms No. 85-18, 799)

Nergaard, M., & Silberschatz, G. (1989). The effects of shame, guilt, and the negative reaction in brief dynamic psychotherapy. *Psychotherapy, 26,* 330–337.

Perry, J. C., Luborsky, L., Silberschatz, G., & Popp, C. (1989). An examination of three methods of psychodynamic formulation based on the same videotaped interview. *Psychiatry, 52,* 302–322.

Rosenberg, S. E., Silberschatz, G., Curtis, J. T., Sampson, H., & Weiss, J. (1986). A method for establishing reliability of statements from psychodynamic case formulations. *American Journal of Psychiatry, 143,* 1454–1456.

Sampson, H., Weiss, J., Mlodnosky, L., & Hause, E. (1972). Defense analysis and the emergence of warded-off mental contents: An empirical study. *Archives of General Psychiatry, 26,* 524–532.

Scherer, K. R. (1982). Methods of research on vocal communication: Paradigms and parameters. In K. R. Scherer & P. Ekman (Eds.), *Handbook of methods in nonverbal behavior research* (pp. 136–198). Cambridge, England: Cambridge University Press.

Silberschatz, G. (1978). Effects of the analyst's neutrality on the patient's feelings and behavior in the psychoanalytic situation. *Dissertation Abstracts International, 39,* 3007-B. (University Microfilms No. 78-24, 277)

Silberschatz, G. (1986). Testing pathogenic beliefs. In J. Weiss, H. Sampson, & the Mount Zion Psychotherapy Research Group (Eds.), *The psychoanalytic process: Theory, clinical observation, and empirical research* (pp. 256–266). New York: Guilford Press.

Silberschatz, G., & Curtis, J. T. (1986). Clinical implications of research on brief dynamic psychotherapy: II. How the therapist helps or hinders therapeutic progress. *Psychoanalytic Psychology, 3,* 27–37.

Silberschatz, G., Curtis, J. T., & Kelly, T. J. (1989). *Therapist test passing as a predictor of patient progress in psychotherapy.* Manuscript submitted for publication.

Silberschatz, G., Curtis, J. T., & Nathans, S. (1989). Using the patient's plan to assess progress in psychotherapy. *Psychotherapy, 26,* 40–46.

Silberschatz, G., Fretter, P. B., & Curtis, J. T. (1986). How do interpretations influence the process of psychotherapy? *Journal of Consulting and Clinical Psychology, 54,* 646–652.

Silberschatz, G., Sampson, H., & Weiss, J. (1986). Testing pathogenic beliefs versus seeking transference gratifications. In J. Weiss, H. Sampson, & the Mount Zion Psychotherapy Research Group (Eds.), *The psychoanalytic process: Theory, clinical observation, and empirical research* (pp. 267–276). New York: Guilford Press.

Weiss, J. (1967). The integration of defenses. *International Journal of Psychoanalysis, 48,* 520–524.

Weiss, J. (1971). The emergence of new themes: A contribution to the psychoanalytic theory of therapy. *International Journal of Psychoanalysis, 52,* 459–467.

Weiss, J. (1986). Introduction. In J. Weiss, H. Sampson, & the Mount Zion Psychotherapy Research Group (Eds.), *The psychoanalytic process: Theory, clinical observation, and empirical research* (pp. 3–21). New York: Guilford Press.

Windholz, M. J., & Silberschatz, G. (1988). Vanderbilt Psychotherapy Process Scale: A replication with adult outpatients. *Journal of Consulting and Clinical Psychology, 56,* 56–60.

8

Northwestern University–University of Chicago Psychotherapy Research Program

Kenneth I. Howard
Northwestern University

David E. Orlinsky
University of Chicago

Stephen M. Saunders, Elizabeth Bankoff,
Christine Davidson, and Michael O'Mahoney
Northwestern University

Background and Aims

Our research program has had two major goals. The first is an intensive investigation of the process of psychotherapy—what happens in therapy or in the therapeutic environment (both inter- and intrapersonally, both in and between sessions—and how such processes are related to therapeutic effectiveness. The second is to gather information about the psychotherapy service delivery system—who uses psychotherapy, under what circumstances, in what manner, and the like.

A grant-supported study of long-term psychotherapy is the umbrella project under which all other studies are being conducted. Although the substudies in our program are as varied and diverse as the individuals involved, investigations can be grouped into general subcategories on the basis of whether they address therapeutic process or service delivery. One area of process research is generated by a generic model of psychotherapy (Orlinsky & Howard, 1987b). The experiences of

the participants in therapy has been another major area of research; both intrasession (e.g., experiences in the affective environment) and intersession (e.g., awareness of therapy between sessions) experiences have been investigated. Pretherapy determinants of the process of treatment (e.g., symptoms, social support, psychologic assets for intensive therapy) is another general category of research. All of this process research has been conducted with the goal of elucidating the determinants of effective therapy, a goal demanding integration of process and outcome measures.

Our research program has also focused intensively on the psychotherapy service delivery system, and these studies can also be grouped into general subcategories. Of course, these categories overlap somewhat with the process research. One area of interest has been in predicting treatment duration (service utilization) and treatment effec-

This program is partially supported by Research Grant R-01-MH42901 from the National Institute of Mental Health (1988–1993).

tiveness by means of early therapy indicators, such as the quality of the early therapeutic bond or the initial level of symptomatic distress. Interest in the relationships among length of treatment, phases of therapy, and treatment effectiveness culminated in a prospective, long-term study aimed at uncovering the relationships among determinants, phases, and effectiveness of short- compared with long-term treatment. Other projects, completed and current, are described later, including a project to compile data from the best existing surveys of the service delivery system.

The goals of the program are investigated, for the most part, from the perspective of the participant observer. Which observational perspective one uses is a crucial methodologic issue that has been discussed in more detail elsewhere (Orlinsky & Howard, 1986), and it is generally agreed that multiperspective work is necessary. Our work complements the work conducted in programs emphasizing nonparticipant observers, such as the Berkeley, Penn, and Vanderbilt psychotherapy research programs.

Method

Northwestern Memorial Hospital's Institute of Psychiatry in downtown Chicago is home to the research program. The institute houses one of the busiest community mental health centers in the country. Among the various programs in the institute are an eating disorders program, an older adult program, an aftercare program, a chemical dependence program, and several inpatient units. The psychotherapy research program is coordinated by Kenneth Howard, PhD, and is located in the outpatient psychotherapy program. In a typical year this program accepts more than 500 new clients into individual psychotherapy.

The patients who enter the institute's psychotherapy program are highly selected. To become a patient in this program, one must first call the clinic. A brief telephone interview is conducted by an intake worker who inquires into the nature of the problem, determines whether or not the person seems suitable for intensive individual psychotherapy, and then arranges a screening interview. The screening interview is conducted by a clinician (usually a psychology or psychiatry trainee) and takes 1–2 hours. If the screening interviewer concludes that the client is suitable for intensive psychotherapy (rather than some other treatment or some other program, a summary of the interview is sent to the director of the psycho-

therapy program (Michael O'Mahoney, PhD), who assigns a therapist. The therapist contacts the patient to arrange the first session.

Two thirds of the patients in the psychotherapy program are women, and 85% are 20–39 years old. Eight-three percent are not currently married, and 57% are employed full-time (another 14% are students). The patients tend to be fairly well educated: 83% have at least some college education, and 26% have attended graduate school.

At any one time there are about 80 therapists in the psychotherapy program. Most of these are in some stage of training (e.g., psychology practicum students, psychology interns, psychiatry residents), although most already have had considerable experience. Sixty percent of the therapists are psychologists, 29% psychiatrists, and 11% social workers. Ninety-four percent are 20–39 years of age; 54% are men, and 54% are married. Eighty-three percent of the therapists at the institute have had personal therapy.

The orientation of the institute is psychodynamic. Supervisors espouse this therapeutic approach, case presentations follow this model, and attempts are made to conceptualize each case from this perspective.

Data collection at the institute has been fairly intensive since the mid-1980s, and the amount of data available is extensive. The research program is now in its fourth wave of data collection, a wave defined as a specific, coherent set of questionnaires. The first wave consisted of Therapy Session Report (TSR) data collected for a dissertation by Rone Marshel in 1983. The second wave began in 1983 and ended in 1985 and consisted of questionnaires completed by patients after the initial screening interview and after each of the first 6 therapy sessions. The third wave, begun in 1985 and completed in 1988, saw numerous questionnaires revised or replaced; it resembled the second wave in that extensive data were collected after each of the early sessions. The fourth and current wave of data collection is described in detail later.

Research Accomplishments

Much of the work we presented has been based on two models of psychotherapy: the dosage model (Howard, Kopta, Krause, & Orlinsky, 1986) and the generic model (Orlinsky & Howard, 1987b). In a meta-analysis (Howard et al., 1986), a lawful positive linear relation between dose (log of number of sessions) of psychotherapy and percentage improvement (normalized) was demonstrated. The study showed that 8 sessions is the median effective dose of individual psychotherapy and that by 26 sessions, an effective dose of 75% is obtained. The dosage model has been important in helping to define short-term as opposed to long-term treatment, a conceptualization that has been important to numerous studies.

The generic model of psychotherapy (Orlinksy & Howard, 1987b) has also generated considerable research attention. This model postulates that certain input variables, process events, and outcome realizations are common to all therapies. The generic model distinguishes five major process components: (a) the therapeutic contract, which specifies the terms under which therapy is to be carried out; (b) therapeutic interventions; (c) the therapeutic bond; (d) personal self-relatedness, which is how the individuals manage self-directed aspects of the encounter; and (e) therapeutic realizations, which represent the yield of the therapeutic process (e.g., insight, catharsis, etc.). The generic model offers a conceptualization of the interrelationships among input, process, and outcome variables, providing a theory of psychotherapy that can guide empiric investigation.

One general group of studies concerns the process of psychotherapy. As noted earlier, the generic model of psychotherapy identifies five process variables. One of the initial studies of this model investigated the therapeutic bond. Saunders, Howard, and Orlinsky (1989) developed the Therapeutic Bond Scales to measure the three components of the bond: working alliance, empathic resonance, and mutual affirmation. The scales were found to be internally consistent and were predictive of patients ratings of session quality. Saunders (1988a) confirmed the prediction that the rated quality of the bond in an early session (Session 3) would be predictive of therapeutic effectiveness. There was also some evidence that patients who have high working alliance scores (i.e., who seem to be putting considerable effort into their role as patient) but low mutual affirmation and empathic resonance scores do more poorly.

The generic model suggests specific interrelations among the components of psychotherapeutic process. Kolden (1988b) constructed self-relatedness, therapeutic realizations, and immediate postsession outcome measures from the TSR. With these and the therapeutic bond scales, he found that the propositions of the generic model held up well under empirical scrutiny. Winfrey (1988) found that successful short-term patients

had the highest scores on the therapeutic bond measure. Moreover, if the therapeutic bond declined from the third to the eighth session, treatment tended to fail.

With the Therapeutic Procedures Inventory (Orlinsky, Lundy, Howard, Davidson, & O'Mahoney, 1987), McNeilly and Howard (1988) devised a method of monitoring the integrity of the treatment. They obtained descriptions from supervisors of ideal sessions of therapy of a psychodynamic orientation. Item profiles indicated that ideal early sessions differ from ideal late sessions and that it is possible to identify a guiding ideology for the clinic. It is possible to describe this ideology further by what is not done in a psychotherapy session. Trainee and supervisor descriptions of actual sessions of individual psychotherapy can now be compared with these ideal profiles (see also Newman, Kopta, McGovern, Howard, & McNeilly, 1988).

Carone (1986) investigated patient and therapist perceptions of the patient's presenting symptoms and functioning in an effort to evaluate the degree of consensus in the dyad in the early phase of therapy. She found that healthier, treatment-wise, educated, young patients and their therapists tended to agree in their perceptions. After six sessions, however, agreement tended to occur when therapists lowered their estimation of patients' problems to match the patients' perceptions, suggesting that agreement during the early phase of therapy may reflect a mutual minimization of problems rather than a collaborative understanding. In a similar study, Frommelt (1988a, 1988b) examined the widely held belief that treatment is generally more successful if the participants accept and work toward similar goals. After conducting a survey of the session-by-session psychotherapy goals of outpatients and therapists, she found that dyads tended to have different views of what goals were important at different times in treatment but did agree that gaining insight, talking about concerns, and establishing a therapeutic relationship were important. Results suggested that goal congruence was correlated with the participants' ratings of progress but only moderately correlated with treatment outcome.

In another study, Saunders and Howard (1987) investigated the patient's perception of the affective environment of an early session and its relationship to treatment effectiveness. The two feeling sections of the TSR ("How did you feel during this session?" and "How did your therapist seem to be feeling?") were combined and factor analyzed. The six resulting factors were all significantly related to the patient's rating of in-session progress but were not substantially predictive of treatment duration or outcome. When the sample was categorized according to treatment duration, however, there was a relatively strong correlation between affect and outcome when therapy was brief (fewer than 8 sessions) and a weak correlation when treatment was relatively lengthy (more than 26 sessions).

Robinson (1988) compared the demographic characteristics and early therapeutic process of patients who underwent successful, naturally occurring short-term psychotherapy (9–25 sessions) with those of patients who underwent successful treatment that lasted 26 sessions or more. She found that successful short-term patients were more likely to be married and employed men and were less likely to have had previous therapy. Successful long-term patients were more likely to be concerned (in Session 3) about being lonely, isolated, worthless, and unlovable and about angry feelings and fearful experiences. Successful short-term clients were more likely to report seeing the therapist as cheerful, pleased, and optimistic and receiving more encouragement from the session.

Tarragona and Orlinsky (1988) investigated the impact of the therapy session on the patient. Specifically, they looked at the relationship between patients' experiences in the therapeutic session (operationalized with the patient TSR) and their therapy-related experiences during the week after the session (operationalized with the Intersession Experience Questionnaire [Orlinsky & Tarragona, 1986]). More than 80% of the patients had thoughts, feelings, memories, or images of therapy between sessions, and such intersession experiences were most frequent when people were facing a difficult situation and were feeling bad. Patients' imagery about the therapist frequently evoked feelings of acceptance and confidence. Patient ratings of the therapeutic bond correlated positively with feeling remoralized between sessions, suggesting that intersession experiences are related to the quality of the alliance.

Pretherapy determinants of process and outcome have also been investigated. Daskovsky (1988) investigated the relation between patients' psychological assets (level of object relations, capacity to delay gratification, willingness to engage in treatment, degree of distress, and psychological mindedness) for psychotherapy and their capacity to enter into a therapeutic relationship, to remain in therapy, and to benefit from treatment. He developed scales to measure these pre-

therapy assets. One finding indicated that the level of the therapeutic bond in the third session and ratings of object relations at intake were inversely related. This finding was interpreted as indicating that some patients (those with poor object relations) may need the therapeutic relationship too much and may idealize the therapist during this early phase of treatment. Results also indicated that capacity to delay gratification, willingness to engage in treatment, and psychological mindedness were all predictive of dosage. Capacity to delay gratification, willingness to engage in treatment, and level of object relations were significant predictors of outcome.

There have been a number of studies investigating correlates of initial (pretherapy) symptomatic distress as measured with symptom checklists similar to the SCL-90–R (Derogatis, 1977). Kolden and Howard (1988) examined the relation between presenting symptoms and ultimate length of treatment. Results indicated that symptoms of hostility were most predictive of discontinuation of treatment. A different study was prompted by epidemiological research that indicates that a sizable minority of individuals who visit mental health professionals do not exhibit significant psychic distress or qualify for a psychiatric diagnosis. Noel (1988) tried to determine the extent to which such individuals are seeking self-fulfillment (in contrast to problem resolution) by examining differences between presenting problem statements for the most and least distressed outpatients. Results indicated that types of presenting problems and initial level of distress were relatively independent.

Another pretherapy patient characteristic that has been researched is dysfunctional attitudes and dysfunctional interpersonal attitudes. Kolden (1988a) used the Dysfunctional Attitudes Scale (Weissman, 1979) and other available measures to examine the relations among stress, dysfunctional attitudes, and depression in a group of outpatients. The Beck et al. (1979) model of depression predicts that dysfunctional attitudes are potentiated by stress and lead to clinical depression. In this study it was found that stress and dysfunctional attitudes were related, but dysfunctional attitudes did not seem to be uniquely characteristic of depressives.

The psychotherapy service delivery system has also been investigated in our program. For instance, it is known that most psychotherapy patients are early terminators or dropouts in that they do not remain in therapy for the prescribed amount of time. There are two prevailing beliefs about such patients: they leave treatment dissatisfied and remain in psychological distress or, conversely, they got what they wanted from this brief contact. In a study by Schwartz and Howard (1988), telephone interviews were conducted with persons who were scheduled for an intake appointment in the psychotherapy program but declined treatment before the third therapy session (44% of the patients). These persons either (a) had not shown for the intake, (b) came to the intake but did not have a session of psychotherapy, or (c) had one or two sessions of psychotherapy. Of the first group (the no-shows) about 50% had entered treatment elsewhere, and only 11% had done nothing about their problems. Of the latter two groups, those patients who had only completed a screening interview or had attended one or two sessions of therapy and then terminated (dropouts), 32% had entered therapy elsewhere within 3 months of their initial contact with the institute. Overall, of no-shows and dropouts fully 40% had entered treatment elsewhere; only 9% were functioning at a low level and had not entered psychotherapy. One patient indicated that she had benefited from her limited contact with the institute. The major lesson is that early terminators are not necessarily rejecting psychotherapy but may be selecting treatment in an alternative setting.

In another study investigating determinants of early termination of treatment, Noel and Howard (1989) investigated the impact of being assigned to a clinician for treatment different from the one who conducted the initial interview. They found that a higher proportion of patients who were assigned a different therapist did not return for a first session of psychotherapy. Those who were screened by one clinician and treated by another, however, were more likely to remain in treatment beyond eight sessions. One implication of these findings is that the existence of some barriers to entry into psychotherapy serve to deflect less needy or less motivated patients. This is analogous to findings that insurance coverage serves to lower entry barriers to treatment but is not related to level of use (e.g., Knesper, Belcher, & Cross, 1988).

A study conducted by Brown (1988) sheds more light on utilization of outpatient mental health services. By using survival analysis to achieve a better description of individual patterns of use, he examined individual treatment episodes at the institute. About 82% of patients who proceeded beyond the initial screening interview remained in treatment after 4 sessions, 64% after 8 sessions,

and 48% after 16 sessions. Results indicated that members of health maintenance organizations were no less likely than nonmembers to become long-term patients and, in fact, were less likely to terminate between Sessions 10 and 24.

Research Programs in Progress

Noel (1988) used the system of classifying patients' responses to an open-ended question (completed by patients before the initial screening interview) about their reasons for seeking therapy developed by Yoken (1988). This system includes six main categories of problems: emotionalness, self-concept, interpersonal relationships, achievement, physical complaints, and trauma. It appears to be reliable and is being assessed for validity. Such information about problems will be useful in planning treatment, assessing outcome, and defending the inclusion of psychotherapy services in third-party payment programs.

There is considerable evidence that the patient's earliest feelings toward the therapist are important precursors of the therapeutic bond. Bankoff (1988) is investigating the ways in which social support (operationalized with the Social Support Questionnaire [Bankoff, 1985]) affects the earliest phase of the bonding process. Initial findings based on a sample of 24 patients suggests that social support does influence the development of the therapeutic bond but in a fairly complex way. That is, whether the influence is positive, negative, or neutral seems to be dependent on the source and quality of the support.

Extending her earlier work, Carone (1986) is investigating the hypothesis that agreement in the dyad may be less important than awareness of the two perspectives, that is to say explicit awareness of both discrete and overlapping elements of patient and therapist viewpoints. The various indices of consensus will be related to the quality of the therapeutic relationship and therapeutic progress.

The most comprehensive work currently being conducted through the research program is a longitudinal study of long-term psychotherapy in terms of patients, processes, and outcomes, which was awarded a 5-year grant from the National Institute of Mental Health. One rationale for this study is that epidemiological research consistently indicates that although the median length of treatment is 5–8 sessions (Garfield, 1986), a small minority of the persons who make a mental health visit in a year use the great majority of the outpatient mental health visits provided in that year (Taube, Kessler, & Feuerberg, 1984). Although treatment of this small group of long-term patients constitutes the bulk of psychotherapeutic practice, because their treatment covers a considerable span of time and because they are a small fraction of those who enter treatment, these cases are difficult to study in clinical settings that do not have both a large patient population and a commitment to providing long-term treatment. Accordingly, long-term psychotherapy has received little attention in the research literature. Northwestern Memorial Hospital's Institute of Psychiatry has both a large patient population and a commitment to long-term treatment. The focus of our study is an investigation of (a) the distinctive clinical and demographic characteristics of successful and unsuccessful short- and long-term patients; (b) the early therapeutic experiences of successful and unsuccessful short- and long-term patients; and (c) changes in therapeutic process (i.e., phases of therapy) over the course of successful and unsuccessful long-term treatment.

All psychotherapy program patients are asked to participate in the study. After an individual is given an appointment for a screening interview, the telephone intake worker informs the research project administrator, who mails the person the first set of questionnaires. On the day of the screening interview, after registration, prospective psychotherapy patients are brought to the research office, where they are informed of the research project, asked to sign an informed consent for participation, and given the second set of questionnaires (post-screening interview questionnaires).

Consenting research patients are asked to complete a self-report set of questionnaires after each of their first seven therapy sessions. These questionnaire sets are distributed by the cashier, the one person at the institute with whom all patients will have contact before each therapy session. The cashier is informed of the need to give a particular patient the appropriate questionnaire set by means of an automated warning system that has been established on the institute's financial information computer.

All consenting research patients who remain in therapy are mailed a questionnaire set after sessions 15, 16, 17, 25, 26, 27, and so on. This "three-session on, seven-session off" distribution schedule continues throughout the course of the treatment episode. Enclosed with each of the mailed questionnaires is a postage-paid addressed envelope for return mailing. The research patients are instructed to complete each questionnaire set as soon after the specified session as possible.

The research instruments have been designed to assess the extent and type of psychopathology, pathology proneness, environmental stress, and readiness for treatment. The process of therapy is also being assessed from the patient's perspective. The TSR, developed by Orlinsky and Howard (1966; see also Orlinsky & Howard, 1987a), as a general survey of the experiences of patients in individual psychotherapy, is completed by patients after Sessions 1, 3, 5, and 6 and every 10th session thereafter. Outcome is assessed with numerous self-report inventories included in questionnaire packets distributed before the first therapy session, after each of several early sessions, every 10 sessions thereafter, and at termination. Table 8.1 shows a summary of the input, process, and outcome measures currently being used in the study.

Table 8.1

Instruments in the Northwestern University–University of Chicago Psychotherapy Research Program

Type of measure
Input (patient and therapist characteristics) instruments
General measures
DSM-III–R Axes I, II, III, IV, and V ratings from the SCID (Spitzer, Williams, & Gibbon, 1988)
Presenting problems (patient self-report; see Yoken, 1988)
Extent and type of psychopathology measures
Symptom checklist (patient self-report; adapted from Derogatis, 1977)
Interpersonal symptoms (patient self-report; adapted from Horowitz, Rosenberg, Baer, Ureño, & Villaseñor, 1988)
Current life functioning (patient self-report; Howard, 1988)
Level of functioning (Carter & Newman, 1980)
Global Assessment Scale (Endicott, Spitzer, Fleiss, & Cohen, 1976)
Pathology proneness measures
Dysfunctional Attitudes Scale (patient self-report; adapted from Weissman, 1979)
Self-esteem (patient self-report; Rosenberg, 1979)
Coping style (patient self-report; adapted from Tobin, Holroyd, Reynolds, & Wigal, 1989)
Environmental stress measures
Life Stress Inventory (patient self-report; adapted from Holmes & Rahe, 1967)

Table 8.1 continued on next page

Table 8.1 continued

Social Support Scales (patient self-report;
Bankoff, 1985)

Readiness-for-treatment measures
Therapeutic experience (patient self-report)
Readiness for Treatment Questionnaire (patient
self-report)
Process of Seeking Therapy Questionnaire
(patient self-report; Saunders, 1988b)

Process instruments
Therapeutic Contract Questionnaire—Session and
Segment Forms (report; Orlinsky, Howard,
Davidson, & O'Mahoney, 1986)
Therapeutic Procedures Inventory (therapist report;
Orlinsky, Lundy, Howard, Davidson, & O'Mahoney,
1987)
Therapy Session Report (patient self-report;
Orlinsky & Howard, 1966)
Closeness to Therapist Questionnaire (patient
self-report)
Inter-session Experience Questionnaire (patient
self-report; Orlinsky & Tarragona, 1986)

Outcome instruments (change on input instruments
also used as an outcome measurement)
Patient Rating of Improvement Scale
Therapist Rating of Improvement Scale
Independent Rating of Improvement Scale

Note. *DSM-III–R* = revised third edition of the *Diagnostic
and Statistical Manual of Mental Disorders*; SCID = Structured Clinical Interview for *DSM-III–R*.

The study is unusual in the amount of information required of the therapists. After the screening interview, the interviewer (and the therapist)
provides diagnoses based on the revised third edition of the *Diagnostic and Statistical Manual of
Mental Disorders* (*DSM-III–R*; American Psychiatric Association, 1987 [Axes I, II, IV, and V]),
plus Level of Functioning Scale and Global Assessment Scale ratings (see Table 1 for references). Therapists complete the Therapeutic Procedures Inventory and the Therapeutic Contract
Questionnaire—Session Form regularly at 10-
week intervals. Because it is necessary to have
reliable and valid diagnoses of patients, interviewers have been trained in the use of the Structured Clinical Interview for DSM-III-R (SCID-
III–R; Spitzer, Williams, & Gibbon, 1988).

Treatment integrity lately has become a frequently heard term in psychotherapy research,
underscoring the need to ensure that planned
treatments are implemented. As a means of assessing the conformity of each treatment with the

guiding orientation of the clinic, the Therapeutic
Procedures Inventory (Orlinsky et al., 1987) is
completed by clinicians at various points in treatment. In addition, supervisors rate supervisees'
sessions on the basis of the skillfulness of their
case handling. At termination, the therapist provides DSM-III–R diagnoses and rates the success
of therapy, the amount of patient change, level of
functioning, and Global Assessment Scale scores.

Programs Planned for the Future

Research on the psychotherapy service delivery
system is multifaceted and complex, and the research program has begun to embrace the issue in
earnest. An attempt is currently underway to
synthesize epidemiologic surveys that are relevant to the utilization of psychotherapeutic services. Of particular interest are surveys concerned with the potential patient population, the
real patient population, the service providers, and
utilization patterns. Data tapes from the Epidemiologic Catchment Area survey and other surveys
are being compiled at Northwestern University's
Computer Center under the direction of our programmer and data analyst. To construct an adequate archive of data on patients who receive at
least six sessions of individual psychotherapy, ag-
gregation across surveys is necessary.

Yoken is working on the analysis of questionnaire data regarding patients' and normal controls' experiences of feelings such as anxiety, sadness, and anger. One focus is the change in
emotional differentiation over the course of therapy. Yoken is also collecting data from both patients and therapists to investigate their respective levels of emotionality, activity, and
sociability. Additionally, she is analyzing data
(patient and therapist TSRs) investigating the
role of emotional attunement between patient
and therapist as it relates to outcome.

Conron will extend the work of Daskovsky
(1988) by investigating the patient's experience of
the therapist in relationship to the patient's level
of psychological functioning (e.g., level of object
relations, delay of gratification, etc.). The hypothesis is that low-functioning patients have more
intense interpersonal needs that they attempt to
defend against or to gratify in treatment, whereas
high-functioning patients have a more balanced
experience that includes a realistic desire to
achieve psychological health.

McNeilly will be investigating the hypothesis
that *DSM-III–R* diagnoses are not optimally rele-

vant for categorizing patients treated in outpatient settings. Diagnoses will be compared with presenting problems, symptoms, life functioning, duration of treatment, and treatment outcome. She is particularly interested in differences between patients who qualify or do not qualify for Axis I diagnoses.

Saunders will use the Process of Seeking Therapy Questionnaire (Saunders, 1988b) to investigate the routes that people use to enter therapy (including previous treatment) and how they make this decision. The questionnaire is based on the work of Kadushin (1969) and Veroff and colleagues (e.g., Veroff, Kulka, & Douvan, 1981), and findings will be compared with those of the large samples.

Nature of the Research Organization

The following is a list of current team members and their roles: Elizabeth Bankoff, PhD, Northwestern University (NV), project coordinator; Mac Brachman, MA University of Chicago (UC), investigator; Bruce Briscoe, data analyst and programmer; Kevin Brown, PhD, NU, investigator; Beth Carone, PhD, NU, investigator; Jane Conron, MA, NU, investigator; David Daskovsky, PhD, NU, investigator; Christine Davidson, PhD, NU, co-principal investigator; Norma Davilla, MA, UC, investigator; Alix Derefinko, NU, graduate research assistant; Marge Epstein, MA, UC, investigator; Michael Horowitz, PhD, NU, investigator; Judith Gillard-Kaufman, MA, De Paul University, investigator; Eve Gordon, NU, graduate research assistant; Ann Horn, NU, graduate research assistant; Mary Hortatsos, NU, project administrator; Kenneth Howard, PhD, NU, principal investigator; Sheryl Jones, NU, graduate research assistant; Rebecca Koehler, investigator; Marta Lundy, PhD, University of Illinois at Chicago, investigator; Mark McGovern, PhD, NU, investigator; Cheryl McNeilly, MA, NU, investigator; Susan Noel, MA, University of Wisconsin–Milwaukee, investigator; Michael O'Mahoney, PhD, NU, co-principal investigator; Fred Newman, PhD, University of Illinois at Chicago, investigator; David Orlinsky, PhD, UC, co-principal investigator; Kevin Perry, NU, investigator; Janet Robinson, PhD, NU, investigator; Stephen Saunders, MA, NU, investigator; David Schwartz, MA, NU, investigator; Margarita Tarragona, PhD, UC, investigator; LaPearl Winfrey, PhD, NU, investigator; and Carol Yoken, PhD, Loyola University of Chicago, investigator. Our team also includes six to seven undergraduate research assistants.

References

American Psychiatric Association. (1987). *Diagnostic and statistical manual of mental disorders* (rev. 3rd ed.). Washington, DC: Author.

Bankoff, E. (1985). *Social Support Scales.* Evanston, IL: Department of Psychology, Northwestern University.

Bankoff, E. (1988, June). *The relationship between psychotherapy patients' support systems and therapeutic bonding.* Paper presented at the 19th Annual Meeting of the Society for Psychotherapy Research, Santa Fe, NM.

Beck, A. T., Rush, A. J., Shaw, B. F., & Emery, G. (1979). *Cognitive therapy of depression.* New York: Guilford Press.

Brown, K. P. (1988, June). *Patterns of psychotherapy utilization: A survival analysis of length of treatment.* Paper presented at the 19th Annual Meeting of the Society for Psychotherapy Research, Santa Fe, NM.

Carone, B. (1986). *Consensus in the therapeutic relationship.* Unpublished doctoral dissertation, Northwestern University, Evanston, IL.

Carter, D. E., & Newman, F. L. (1980). *A client-oriented system of mental health service delivery and program management: A workbook and guide* (National Institute of Mental Health Series FN No. 4, DHHS Publication No. ADM 80-307). Washington, DC: U.S. Government Printing Office.

Daskovsky, D. (1988). *The patient's assets for psychotherapy.* Unpublished doctoral dissertation, Northwestern University, Evanston, IL.

Derogatis, L. R. (1977). *SCL-90: Administration and procedures manual-I for the revised version.* Baltimore, MD: Clinical Psychometrics Research.

Endicott, J., Spitzer, R. L., Fleiss, J. L., & Cohen, J. (1976). The Global Assessment Scale: A procedure for measuring overall severity of psychiatric disturbance. *Archives of General Psychiatry, 33,* 766–771.

Frommelt, G. M. (1988a, June). *The relationship between patient-therapist goal congruence and therapy outcome.* Paper presented at the 19th Annual Meeting of the Society for Psychotherapy Research, Santa Fe, NM.

Frommelt, G. M. (1988b, June). *Patient and therapist goals: A descriptive study of psychotherapy.* Paper presented at the 19th Annual Meeting of the Society for Psychotherapy Research, Santa Fe, NM.

Garfield, S. L. (1986). Research on client variables in psychotherapy. In S. L. Garfield & A. E. Bergin (Eds.), *Handbook of psychotherapy and behavior change* (3rd ed., pp. 213–256). New York: Wiley.

Holmes, T. H., & Rahe, R. H. (1967). The social readjustment rating scale. *Journal of Psychosomatic Research, 11,* 213–218.

Horowitz, L. M., Rosenberg, S. E., Baer, B. A., Ureño, G., & Villaseñor, V. S. (1988). Inventory of Interpersonal Problems: Psychometric properties and clinical applications. *Journal of Consulting and Clinical Psychology, 56,* 885–892.

Howard, K. I. (1988). *Current Life Functioning*. Department of Psychology, Northwestern University, Evanston, IL.

Howard, K. I., Kopta, S. M., Krause, M. S., & Orlinsky, D. E. (1986). The dose–effect relationship in psychotherapy. *American Psychologist, 41, 159–164.*

Kadushin, C. (1969). *Why people go to psychiatrists.* New York: Atherton Press.

Knesper, D. J., Belcher, B. E., & Cross, J. C. (1988). Variations in the intensity of psychiatric treatment across markets for mental health services in the United States. *Health Services Research, 22,* 797–819.

Kolden, G. G. (1988a). *Dysfunctional attitudes and depression in an outpatient psychiatric sample.* Manuscript submitted for publication.

Kolden, G. G. (1988b). *Orlinsky and Howard's "Generic Model of Psychotherapy": An empirical examination in the early sessions of therapy.* Unpublished doctoral dissertation, Northwestern University, Evanston, IL.

Kolden, G. G., & Howard, K. I. (1988). *Presenting symptoms and length of treatment.* Manuscript submitted for publication.

McNeilly, C., & Howard, K. I. (1988, June). *The therapeutic procedures inventory as a measure of therapeutic ideology in an outpatient clinic.* Paper presented at the 19th Annual Meeting of the Society for Psychotherapy Research, Santa Fe, NM.

Newman, F., Kopta, S. M., McGovern, M., Howard, K. I., & McNeilly, C. (1988). Evaluating the conceptualizations and treatment plans of interns and supervisors during a psychological internship. *Journal of Consulting and Clinical Psychology, 56,* 659–665.

Noel, S. B. (1988, June). *A comparison of presenting problems for the most and the least distressed individuals seeking psychotherapy.* Paper presented at the 19th Annual Meeting of the Society for Psychotherapy Research, Santa Fe, NM.

Noel, S. B., & Howard, K. I. (1989). Initial contact and engagement in therapy. *Journal of Clinical Psychology, 45,* 798–805.

Orlinsky, D. E., & Howard, K. I. (1966). *Therapy Session Report, Form P(atient) and Form T(herapist).* Chicago: Institute of Juvenile Research.

Orlinsky, D. E., & Howard, K. I. (1986). Process and outcome in psychotherapy. In S. L. Garfield & A. E. Bergin (Eds.), *Handbook of psychotherapy and behavior change* (3rd ed., pp. 311–381). New York: Wiley.

Orlinsky, D. E., & Howard, K. I. (1987a). The psychological interior of psychotherapy: Explorations with the therapy session report questionnaires. In L. S. Greenberg & W. M. Pinsoff (Eds.), *The psychotherapeutic process: A research handbook* (pp. 477–501). New York: Guilford Press.

Orlinsky, D. E., & Howard, K. I. (1987b). A generic model of psychotherapy. *Journal of Integrative and Eclectic Psychotherapy, 6,* 6–27.

Orlinsky, D. E., Howard, K. I., Davidson, C. V., & O'Mahoney, M. T. (1986). *Therapeutic Contract Questionnaire.* Chicago: Northwestern Memorial Hospital.

Orlinsky, D. E., Lundy, M., Howard, K. I., Davidson, C. V., & O'Mahoney, M. T. (1987). *Therapeutic Procedures Inventory.* Chicago: Northwestern Memorial Hospital.

Orlinsky, D. E., & Tarragona, M. (1986). *Intersession Experience Questionnaire.* Chicago: University of Chicago.

Robinson, J. (1988). *Naturally occurring short-term psychotherapy.* Unpublished doctoral dissertation, Northwestern University, Evanston, IL.

Rosenberg, M. (1979). *Conceiving the self.* New York: Basic Books.

Saunders, S. M. (1988a). Correlation between therapeutic bond and treatment effectiveness as a function of amount of time between their assessments and level of role investment. *Psychotherapy Bulletin, 23,* 23–25.

Saunders, S. M. (1988b). *The Process of Seeking Therapy Questionnaire.* Evanston, IL: Department of Psychology, Northwestern University.

Saunders, S. M., & Howard, K. I. (1987). *Correlates of patients' affective experience of the psychotherapy session.* Paper presented at the 17th Annual Meeting of the Society for Psychotherapy Research. Ulm, Federal Republic of Germany.

Saunders, S. M., Howard, K. I., & Orlinsky, D. E. (1989). Therapeutic Bond Scales: Psychometric characteristics and relationship to treatment effectiveness. *Psychological Assessment: A Journal of Consulting and Clinical Psychology, 1,* 323–330.

Schwartz, D., & Howard, K. I. (1988, June). *Follow up study of very early terminators from an outpatient clinic.* Poster presented at the 19th Annual Meeting of the Society for Psychotherapy Research, Santa Fe, NM.

Spitzer, R. L., Williams, J. B. W., & Gibbon, M. (1988). *The Structured Clinical Interview for DSM-III-R—Patient version.* New York: Biometrics Research Department, New York State Psychiatric Institute.

Tarragona, M., & Orlinsky, D. E. (1988, June). *During and beyond the therapeutic hour: An exploration of the relationship between patients' experiences of therapy within and between sessions.* Paper presented at the 19th Annual Meeting of the Society for Psychotherapy Research, Santa Fe, NM.

Taube, C. A., Kessler, L., & Feuerberg, M. (1984). *Utilization and expenditure for ambulatory mental health care during 1980. National Medical Care Utilization and Expenditure Survey, data report 5.* Washington, DC: Department of Health and Human Services.

Tobin, D. L., Holroyd, K. A., Reynolds, R. V., & Wigal, J. K. (1989). The hierarchical factor structure of the Coping Strategies Inventory. *Cognitive Therapy and Research, 13,* 343–361.

Veroff, J., Kulka, R. A., & Douvan, E. (1981). *Mental health in America: Patterns of help-seeking from 1957–1976.* New York: Basic Books.

Weissman, A. N. (1979). *The Dysfunctional Attitudes Scale: A validation study.* Unpublished doctoral dissertation, University of Pennsylvania, Philadelphia.

Winfrey, L. L. (1988). *The relationship of client perception of early therapeutic experience to duration and outcome in psychotherapy.* Unpublished doctoral dissertation, State University of New York, Stonybrook.

Yoken, C. (1988, June). *Classifying patients' self reported presenting problems.* Paper presented at the 19th Annual Meeting of the Society for Psychotherapy Research, Santa Fe, NM.

The University at Albany, State University of New York Center for Stress and Anxiety Disorders: Psychotherapy Research at the Phobia and Anxiety Disorders Clinic

Ellen Tobey Klass
Hunter College, City University of New York

David H. Barlow
Center for Stress and Anxiety Disorders,
University at Albany, State University of New York

Background and Aims

History

The Phobia and Anxiety Disorders Clinic (PADC) of the University at Albany, State University of New York, was established by David H. Barlow in 1979. Its first purpose was to conduct a controlled trial that tested the utility of including spouses directly in behavioral treatment of agoraphobia. As the PADC became a popular referral source for patients with a wide range of anxiety disorders, research projects developed on generalized anxiety disorder and panic disorder with limited and no avoidance (1981), social phobia (1982), and childhood anxiety disorders (1983). Research on all these disorders is ongoing, along with single-case studies of other anxiety disorders. A classification project, begun in 1981, has yielded nu-

merous studies of assessment and descriptive psychopathology.

In 1982, the Center for Stress and Anxiety Disorders was organized within the university as an umbrella organization for the PADC and the Stress Disorders Clinic, which is directed by Edward B. Blanchard and studies psychophysiological disorders. The center has departmental status, with Barlow and Blanchard acting as codirectors. It is a vehicle for sharing resources and fostering collaborative research.

Overall Aims

Anxiety confronts health and mental health practitioners in quantities that dwarf other psychological and psychiatric problems. Sophisticated epidemiological research has indicated that anxiety disorders are the largest mental health problem in the United States, as determined from 6-month population prevalence rates (Myers et al., 1984). Yet anxiety has been poorly understood and most often treated with largely unproven therapies, and it has been markedly understudied compared to other major psychological disorders. The central aims of PADC treatment research are to develop and evaluate effective psychological (nondrug) therapies for anxiety disorders and to delineate crucial factors in effective treatment. Another major goal is to characterize the nature of anxiety and panic within and across anxiety disorders. PADC research uses a behavioral conceptual model that specifies factors believed to be involved in each disorder.

Subareas of Investigation

Our agoraphobia treatment research is divided into studies of couples treatment and treatment for patients without cooperative partners. The couples project is now studying a comprehensive treatment targeting avoidance behavior, panic attacks, and the social system in which the symptoms occur. Research on agoraphobics treated alone examines the impact of attentional focus on panic symptoms on maintenance of treatment gains from standard behavior therapy. The agoraphobia research also studies predictors of treatment response, especially physiological responsivity in phobic situations. The current panic disorder project examines the separate and combined effects of information–cognitive therapy, breathing retraining, and systematic exposure to interoceptive cues, all of which to date have always been combined in psychosocial treatment of panic disorder.

The generalized anxiety disorder project compares the effects of applied relaxation training, cognitive therapy, and a combined relaxation–cognitive condition to a waiting-list control group. The social phobia project, directed by Richard G. Heimberg of the university's psychology department, examines cognitive–behavioral group therapy (CBGT) that includes both exposure to phobic situations and cognitive restructuring. The current research compares the effects of CBGT and phenelzine (Nardil). The childhood anxiety project, directed by Wendy K. Silverman of the university's psychology department, studies phobic disorders (comparing contingency management and self-control therapies) and school refusal. The classification project has developed measures and

examined the phenomenology, reliability, and validity of the anxiety disorder categories of the third edition of the *Diagnostic and Statistical Manual of Mental Disorders* (*DSM-III*; American Psychiatric Association, 1980) and its revised version (*DSM-III–R*; American Psychiatric Association, 1987). Findings are summarized by Barlow (1988). All of these projects have been funded by the National Institute of Mental Health (NIMH).

Method

Subjects and Selection

Subjects in all PADC studies are outpatients who are referred by community practitioners or self-referred for treatment. Each year, many hundreds of patients who contact the PADC are screened by detailed telephone procedures. Exclusions include current substance use disorders, symptoms of psychosis, organicity, or suicidal ideation; subjects must also be 18–65 years old. Patients using psychotropic medication cannot have begun drug treatment in the recent past and must agree to maintain a stable medication regimen throughout treatment (so as not to confound treatment effects). Approximately 300 patients a year meet initial inclusionary criteria and receive an intake evaluation; the rest are referred to appropriate community resources.

At intake, patients are administered the Anxiety Disorders Interview Schedule–Revised (ADIS–R; DiNardo & Barlow, 1988), which is a structured interview for diagnosis and confirmation of inclusionary criteria developed at the PADC. Approximately 80% of the 300 patients interviewed each year receive a primary anxiety disorder diagnosis, making the PADC one of the largest anxiety research clinics in the United States. After undergoing psychophysiological and self-report assessment, patients are triaged into treatment research projects. Patients not qualifying for ongoing projects are referred out to appropriate community resources with their workups.) The childhood project follows a similar procedure, with telephone screening being followed by assessment with the child and parents.

Instruments

The PADC uses a multimodal assessment strategy, tapping subjective, behavioral, and physiological aspects of anxiety through interview, behavioral observation, self-report scales, self-monitoring, and psychophysiological monitoring. The ADIS–R is the central instrument for diagnosis and clinical ratings. It permits differential diagnosis among *DSM-III–R* anxiety, affective, and somatoform disorders and screens for substance abuse and psychosis. The Hamilton Anxiety Scale and the Hamilton Rating Scale for Depression are embedded in the ADIS, which also collects additional data and thus permits a full *DSM-III–R* five-axis diagnosis (American Psychiatric Association, 1987). Patients who are physically able receive a psychophysiological examination that includes anxiety-relevant challenges: voluntary hyperventilation, response and habituation to unexpected tones, and a carbon dioxide provocation procedure. Self-report measures of anxiety-relevant features are also collected at intake.

Patients assigned to research projects receive additional pretreatment assessment. Parallel data are collected after treatment and at follow-up intervals of up to 2 years. Assessment includes (a) self-monitoring of anxiety, depression, pleasant feelings, and medication use on a daily diary form for 2 weeks. Patients with panic disorders (with and without agoraphobia) also record fear of panic and complete a simple separate form for each panic attack (see Barlow, 1988, p. 389–390). (b) After treatment and in follow-up, an independent clinician administers an abbreviated ADIS and rates the severity of the treated disorder. A staff member reviews the interview material and makes a second rating. (c) The patient rates interference of symptoms with life spheres such as work and leisure activities. (d) The patient rates treatment credibility after the treatment rationale has been presented.

For agoraphobia and social phobia, avoidance of phobic-related activities is tracked by (a) self-monitoring of phobic-related activities in the natural environment on a daily diary form for 2 weeks; and (b) an individualized behavioral avoidance test, which taps personally relevant phobic stimuli in a standard fashion. The patient is asked to perform several personally relevant phobic activities while self-rated distress is recorded. In the agoraphobia studies, heart rate during the behavioral avoidance test is monitored with a portable psychophysiological recording system; the same data were collected in the social phobia research until the current study.

The Anxiety Disorders Interview Schedule for Children (ADIS–C; Silverman & Nelles, 1988) is used in the childhood project for screening and diagnosis. Measures include clinician and parent ratings of severity of disorder, the child's self-monitoring data, self-report scales, and a behavioral avoidance task. For school refusal, school attendance is also assessed.

Procedures

In our controlled trials, patients are always randomly assigned to treatment condition. All treatment procedures are manualized in detailed session-by-session protocols. All sessions are tape-recorded, and therapist adherence is monitored by procedural adherence ratings of randomly selected tapes. Because specific parameters have been varied in studies described later, we describe the core elements of treatments here.

Agoraphobia: Couples treatment. Therapy is conducted in groups of four to six agoraphobics with their spouses (or cohabiting partners, if they have been living together for more than 1 year) with two co-therapists for 12 sessions. Agoraphobia is explained in terms of avoidance of panic and attribution theory, and the treatment rationale and coping self-statements for use during exposure tasks are presented. The spouse's role in possibly maintaining agoraphobic behavior and as coach during exposure practices are discussed. Therapy then focuses on gradual patient-controlled exposure tasks. Patients choose items from their individualized fear and avoidance hierarchies to practice at least three times weekly, including at least once, but not more than twice, with the spouse (to build independent exposure). Therapy sessions focus on discussing the previous week's practices, reinforcing coping methods, and planning subsequent practices. Barlow and Waddell (1985) provide a detailed description with clinical illustrations.

Agoraphobics alone. Therapy is conducted in groups of four to six patients with two therapists for 10 sessions. A conceptualization and rationale like those in the couples treatment (without reference to the spouse) are presented. Patients are trained either to focus on or to distract themselves from panic sensations. In the third and fourth sessions, therapists accompany patients to an outside site and coach them in exposure tasks. Therapy then emphasizes gradual patient-controlled exposure tasks, which patients are asked to practice at least three times weekly. Therapy sessions focus on discussing the previous week's practices, reinforcing coping methods, and planning subsequent practices.

Panic disorder. Treatment is conducted individually for 11 sessions (current) or 15 sessions (Barlow, Craske, Cerny, & Klosko, 1989). In the project conducted by Barlow and colleagues (1989), the following three conditions were compared with each other and with a waiting-list control: (a) applied relaxation, targeting somatic aspects of anxiety; (b) exposure–cognitive therapy, which arranged for interoceptive exposure and addressed catastrophic misinterpretations of sensations; and (c) combined relaxation and exposure–cognitive treatment. As in Ost's (1988) work, applied relaxation involved training in progressive muscle relaxation and its use as a coping skill. The exposure–cognitive therapy condition modified the work of Beck and Emery (1985). It included information about the physiology of panic and specific techniques to identify and modify cognitive errors. Exposure to the physical sensations associated with panic, breathing retraining, and planned practices framed as behavioral experiments were also used. Barlow and Cerny (1988) describe the treatment in detail. Our most recent protocol, in workbook format suitable for distribution to patients working under clinical supervision, is available by writing to Barlow in care of the PADC.

Generalized anxiety disorder. Treatment is conducted individually for 15 sessions with applied relaxation, cognitive therapy, and a combined condition; a waiting-list group serves as a control. As in the Barlow and Cerny (1988) panic disorder protocol, applied relaxation is used as a coping skill. In the cognitive treatment, didactic procedures are used, followed by cognitive and behavioral strategies for coping with anxiety, including imaginal rehearsal and thought stopping.

Social phobia. Therapy is conducted in groups of 6 patients with two co-therapists for 12 sessions. Social phobia is explained as involving a cycle of physiological arousal, negative cognitions, and behavioral avoidance. Patients are taught to identify and modify negative automatic thoughts. Individualized exposures to phobia-relevant situations are conducted in the group, with therapists and group members playing relevant roles. Cognitive restructuring has two components. Before exposure, the patient is helped to identify negative automatic thoughts and to develop alternative self-statements to use during exposure. After exposure, the patient evaluates the accuracy of the negative automatic thoughts. Weekly behavioral practices, including cognitive restructuring, are assigned. Heimberg and Becker (1984) provided a detailed treatment manual.

Research Accomplishments

Findings

Agoraphobia. Our posttreatment findings indicate the superiority of treatment that includes the spouse compared with the identical treatment administered without the spouse's presence (Barlow, O'Brien, & Last, 1984). At 24-month follow-up, the advantage was maintained, and on some measures an additional increment emerged (Cerny, Barlow, Craske, & Himadi, 1987). Our findings also suggest that marital satisfaction may predict outcome (Barlow et al., 1984): Agoraphobic wives in previously satisfactory marriages did equally well regardless of whether the husbands were included, but wives with unhappy marriages did significantly better after therapy if the husbands were included. (The small number of agoraphobic men precluded similar analyses.) These findings underline the importance of considering the interpersonal system that is the context for behavior change. Our research also suggests that physiological responsiveness may predict outcome (Craske, Sanderson, & Barlow, 1987). Compared with nonresponders, treatment responders had higher heart rates in behavioral avoidance tests before treatment, after treatment, and at 6-month follow-up, although their heart rates decreased over time. Thus, physiological arousal can co-exist with a nonfearful subjective state, and a willingness to tolerate feared situations may contribute to treatment success.

For agoraphobics treated alone, initial results indicate the same positive posttreatment effects for behavior therapy regardless of whether it included focus on or distraction from panic symptoms. Follow-up data bearing on the major hypothesis of better maintenance of gains with focused exposure are currently being analyzed.

Panic disorder. In the comparison study conducted by Barlow et al. (1989) of applied relaxation, exposure–cognitive therapy, a combined condition, and a waiting-list control, all three active treatments had the same general positive effect relative to the waiting list. Some differential effects on specific symptoms were found: The exposure–cognitive and combined treatments, which targeted panic, had more impact on panic frequency than applied relaxation, which, conversely, had more impact on generalized anxiety.

Another controlled trial (Klosko, Barlow, Tassinari, & Cerny, 1990) compared combined treatment, alprazolam (Xanax), and a pill placebo administered in double-blind fashion with a waiting-list control. Of study completers, alprazolam and therapy patients improved more than waiting-list controls. Therapy, but not alprazolam, completers had a higher degree of freedom from panic than placebo and waiting-list groups.

For social phobia a controlled trial compared CBGT with an educative–supportive group therapy, which has been conceptualized as a credible psychological alternative (Heimberg, Dodge, Hope, Kennedy, Zollo, & Becker, 1990). After treatment and at follow-up, CBGT had more impact on clinician-rated severity and anxiety experienced in the behavioral avoidance test.

Instruments Developed

The ADIS (DiNardo, O'Brien, Barlow, Waddell, & Blanchard, 1983; DiNardo & Barlow, 1988) has been a central result of PADC research. Reliability studies that used the stringent criterion of diagnostic agreement between two independent interviews showed satisfactory kappa coefficients for agoraphobia, obsessive–compulsive disorder, and social phobia; a satisfactory kappa for panic disorder; and weaker results for generalized anxiety disorder and simple phobia (DiNardo & Barlow, 1988). Subsequent changes in the generalized anxiety disorder criteria have substantially improved diagnostic reliability. A recently completed revision (DiNardo & Barlow, 1988) has made the ADIS fully compatible with the *DSM-III–R* (American Psychiatric Association, 1987) diagnostic criteria. Other instruments have refined earlier measures (e.g., self-monitoring forms for mood and medication use and the panic attack record; cf., Barlow, 1988, pp. 389–390). The childhood project has developed a parallel ADIS for children that yields reliable diagnoses (Silverman & Nelles, 1988).

Research Programs in Progress

Our current research on couples treatment of agoraphobia and individual treatment of panic

disorder and generalized anxiety disorder are projected for completion in 1992, and the completion date for the current social phobia project is 1993. The couples project is evaluating a comprehensive therapy of avoidance behavior and panic attacks and the social system in which the symptoms occur. Despite the demonstrated advantages of couples treatment, like other researchers, we have found that relatively few agoraphobic patients attain high end-state (basically normal) functioning. Recent conceptualizations of agoraphobia have emphasized the role of panic attacks as well as avoidance, and advantages of couples treatment may be conferred by improved communication and problem-solving skills. Our current project incorporates these considerations by evaluating the individual and combined advantage of adding two therapeutic modules to the standard couples treatment: (a) cognitive–behavioral treatment that targets the panic attack directly, as in our panic-control protocol; and (b) couples communication training focused on phobic-related issues. A combined condition adds both panic control and communication training to the standard treatment.

Our current panic disorder project replicates and extends our research by comparing three procedures currently thought by some to be crucial in the nondrug treatment of panic. To date all psychosocial approaches have included all three of the following treatment components to some degree, so that the relative contribution of each has been unclear: (a) A basic information–cognitive therapy is directed at misperceptions and cognitive distortions regarding panic without any specific techniques to alter physiological responsiveness. Two procedures are added to it: (b) breathing retraining, predicated on the hypothesis that proneness to hyperventilation is the basis for panic attacks; or (c) systematic exposure to interoceptive cues, which is thought by many to be essential in psychosocial treatment of panic. Repeated controlled exposure to feared physical sensations is used to weaken conditioned emotional responses and anticipatory fear, and cognitive techniques are applied to control anxiety on exposure. A combined treatment condition involves all three protocols.

The outcome study of generalized anxiety disorder, described earlier, is ongoing. Initial findings are promising (Rapee, Adler, Craske, & Barlow, 1988). Although conclusions are tentative, it appears that the active treatments (applied relaxation, cognitive therapy, and combined condition) are superior to waiting-list controls on measures of anxiety, including clinician ratings, self-report, and self-monitoring.

Results of a recently completed study of social phobia comparing CBGT with exposure without cognitive restructuring a waiting-list control group suggest that the cognitive component is important for successful outcome (Heimberg & Hope, 1988). A controlled trial of CBGT compared with phenelzine (Nardil) has just begun in a two-site collaboration between Heimberg and Liebowitz of the New York State Psychiatric Institute. Patients are treated with group therapy, phenelzine, or one of two control conditions: educational–supportive therapy or pill placebo. After 12 weeks responders to active treatments receive 6 months of maintenance therapy with lessened contact, as in typical drug studies. After six treatment-free months, follow-up evaluation examines long-term maintenance. Another central question is cross-site replicability given the commitment of one site (PADC) to psychological treatment and the other (Psychiatric Institute) to drug treatment.

In the childhood project, current research involves a controlled trial of contingency management compared with self-control therapy for phobias with two age levels: younger (8–10-year-olds) and older (11–13-year-olds). Treatment that relies on external controls (contingency management) may be more effective with younger patients, and the more cognitive, internal focus of self-control therapy may have more impact on older children. The school refusal study compares prescriptive treatment (on the basis of structured idiographic assessment) and standardized treatment in a clinical series that uses single-case methods.

Programs Planned for the Future

Although completion dates for most projects are several years away, some additional research directions are planned. A multisite study of the treatment of panic disorder is being developed. It will compare the Albany panic-control treatment with standard drug treatment with imipramine as well as the two treatments combined. Appropriate control groups will also be included. Research questions include cross-site replicability and comparative outcome and maintenance.

There are also some logical next studies if additional personnel are available. For instance, an important question in treating agoraphobia is whether direct psychological treatment of panic can affect avoidance behavior. By using single-case methods, we hope to treat the panic symptoms directly with the panic-control protocol while probing for effects on avoidance. If avoidance is reduced, it would suggest more efficient treatments. If exposure to feared situations must be arranged, it would confirm that avoidance must be systematically targeted. We also hope to explore the usefulness of including in treatment persons older than the spouse for those agoraphobics, single and married, without a cooperative partner. Conceptually, the only requirement is that the partner be an integral part of the patient's interpersonal system.

Nature of the Research Organization

Team Members and Their Roles

Professional team members at the clinic all conduct initial assessments, administer protocol therapy, and analyze and write up research. David H. Barlow, Professor of Psychology, is Co-director of the Center for Stress and Anxiety Disorders and director of the PADC. Barlow also trains, supervises, and monitors therapists, directs the research efforts, and acts as a liaison to other anxiety research clinics.

During the 1989–1990 year, six clinical psychologists and one psychiatrist were engaged in full-time research at the PADC. Included in this group are Michelle G. Craske, who as associate director, was responsible for day-to-day operations, along with Karla Moras, Tim Brown, Rick Zinbarg, and Jennifer Jones. Rob Hertz, a psychiatrist who trained at the PADC, handles medical and pharmacological aspects of our clinical research. Richard G. Heimberg, Associate Professor of Psychology, directs the Social Phobia Project, and Craig Holt oversees its day-to-day operation. Wendy K. Silverman, Associate Professor of Psychology, directs the child and adolescent fear and anxiety treatment project, with similar responsibilities. Peter A. DiNardo is a consultant, monitoring diagnostic procedures and the classification project and providing additional clinical supervision. Robert Athanasiou is the clinic physician, participating in research projects and providing medical consultation.

The PADC is also staffed by 10–12 doctoral-level students in clinical psychology. They collect and manage data, and advanced students perform intake assessments and conduct protocol therapy under supervision. Undergraduates also participate in data management. Full-time staff includes a clinic coordinator and a laboratory technician for psychophysiological assessments. Several professionals have visited the PADC, typically on sabbaticals, long enough to participate in the work of the clinic. Jerome A. Cerny of Indiana State University helped develop the panic disorder protocol, worked on agoraphobia research, and was Associate Director for a year. Paul A. Martin of the University of Western Australia investigated the overlap of psychophysiologic and anxiety disorders, and Tian Oei of the University of Queensland investigated patterns of panic symptoms. Ellen Tobey Klass of Hunter College studied anxiety patients with co-occurring personality disorders and predictors of outcome in panic disorder treatment.

Funding and Support

The NIMH and the University at Albany, State University of New York have supported the PADC. The NIMH has made a series of grants that have supported the research on couples treatment of agoraphobia, individual treatment of panic and generalized anxiety disorder, and group treatment of social phobia as well as work on the classification of anxiety disorders. These grants have been used for full-time staff and graduate student support, equipment, consultation, and facility leasing costs. The NIMH has also awarded a 10-year MERIT (method to extend research in time) grant to Barlow that ensures continuity of research efforts. The University at Albany provides maintenance and support services and funds a doctoral clinical psychology student. The Upjohn Corporation partially funded the comparison of behavioral and drug therapy for panic disorder (Klosko et al., 1990), and Bristol–Myers Corporation is funding a comparison of behavioral and drug treatment for patients presenting with both anxiety and depression. Through efficient use of resources, it has been possible to carry on many unfunded research projects as well.

Relation to Other Research Programs

Integration With Findings of Other Research

Our findings can be integrated with those of both interpersonally and biologically oriented researchers. Our couples results confirm those of uncontrolled studies of this method and converge with the increasing emphasis of clinical investigators on the interpersonal system of the patient (cf., Barlow, 1988, pp. 460–472). Our panic disorder treatment is linked to work by biologically oriented psychiatrists on the distinctiveness and ethological features of the panic attack (cf., Barlow, 1988, pp. 209–234). Experience with the ADIS structured interview at the PADC led to two changes that have been adopted in the *DSM-III–R:* specifying the fear of experiencing panic as a central feature in panic disorder and changing the criteria for generalized anxiety disorder to require two spheres of worry other than areas related to other anxiety diagnoses. This makes generalized anxiety disorder something other than a residual diagnosis. The ADIS has evidently made a contribution to the scientific community. It is in use in more than 150 clinical and clinical research settings around the world and has been translated into four languages. In addition, our treatment protocols are in use in several other clinical research settings.

Impact on the Field of Psychotherapy

PADC research has influenced training and practice by providing empirical support for problem-oriented, nondrug treatments of anxiety disorders. Numerous clinical psychology programs, and some psychiatry and social work programs, provide such training. The desirability of including the agoraphobic's spouse in treatment is a specific result of our findings. PADC staff have disseminated treatment models developed at the clinic through publishing detailed treatment manuals for couples treatment of agoraphobia (Barlow & Waddell, 1985) and individual treatment of panic disorder (Barlow & Cerny, 1988) and through professional workshops.

As we hope this chapter has demonstrated, team research at the PADC has fostered productivity and creativity through the exchange of ideas and sharing of resources. Especially as we move to cross-site collaboration, questions arise as to whether researchers with strongly differing viewpoints can collaborate successfully and obtain similar results with each others' treatments. Such collaborative research certainly will be successful and will lead to new developments in efficient and effective treatments for anxiety disorders.

References

American Psychiatric Association. (1980). *Diagnostic and statistical manual of mental disorders* (3rd ed.). Washington, DC: Author.

American Psychiatric Association. (1987). *Diagnostic and statistical manual of mental disorders* (rev. 3rd ed.). Washington, DC: Author.

Barlow, D. H. (1988). *Anxiety and its disorders.* New York: Guilford Press.

Barlow, D. H., & Cerny, J. A. (1988). *The psychological treatment of panic.* New York: Guilford Press.

Barlow, D. H., Craske, M. G., Cerny, J. A., & Klosko, J. S. (1989). Behavioral treatment of panic disorder. *Behavior Therapy, 20,* 261–282.

Barlow, D. H., O'Brien, G. T., & Last, C. G. (1984). Couples treatment of agoraphobia. *Behavior Therapy, 15,* 41–58.

Barlow, D. H., & Waddell, M. T. (1985). Agoraphobia. In D. H. Barlow (Ed.), *Clinical handbook of psychological disorders: A step-by-step treatment manual* (pp. 1–68). New York: Guilford Press.

Beck, A. T., & Emery, G. (1985). *Anxiety disorders and phobias.* New York: Basic Books.

Cerny, J. A., Barlow, D. H., Craske, M. G., & Himadi, W. G. (1987). Couples treatment of agoraphobia: A two-year followup. *Behavior Therapy, 18,* 401–415.

Craske, M. G., Sanderson, W. C., & Barlow, D. H. (1987). How do desynchronous response systems relate to the treatment of agoraphobia: A follow-up evaluation. *Behavior Research and Therapy, 25,* 117–122.

DiNardo, P. A., & Barlow, D. H. (1988). *Anxiety Disorders Interview Schedule–Revised (ADIS–R).* Albany, NY: Phobia and Anxiety Disorders Clinic, University at Albany, State University of New York.

DiNardo, P. A., O'Brien, G. T., Barlow, D. H., Waddell, M. T., & Blanchard, E. B. (1983). Reliability of DSM-III anxiety disorder categories using a new structured interview. *Archives of General Psychiatry, 40,* 1070–1074.

Heimberg, R. G., & Becker, R. E. (1984). *Cognitive–behavioral treatment of social phobia in a group setting.* Albany, NY: Phobia and Anxiety Disorders Clinic, University at Albany, State University of New York.

Heimberg, R. G., Dodge, C. S., Hope, D. A., Kennedy, C. R., Zollo, L., & Becker, R. E. (1990). Cognitive–behavioral group treatment for social phobia: Comparison to a credible placebo control. *Cognitive Therapy and Research, 14,* 1–23.

Heimberg, R. G., & Hope, D. A. (1988, October). *Group treatment for social phobia: A cognitive–behavioral approach.* Paper presented at the meeting of the Phobia Society of America, Boston.

Klosko, J., Barlow, D. H., Tassinari, R. A., & Cerny, J. A. (1990). Comparison of alprazolam and cognitive behavior therapy in the treatment of panic disorder. *Journal of Consulting and Clinical Psychology, 58,* 77–84.

Myers, J. K., Weissman, M. M., Tischler, C. E., Holzer, C. E. III, Orvaschel, H., Anthony, J. C., Boyd, J. H., Burke, J. D. Jr., Kramer, M., & Stoltzman, R. (1984). Six-month prevalence of psychiatric disorders in three communities. *Archives of General Psychiatry, 41,* 959–967.

Ost, L. G. (1988). Applied relaxation in the treatment of panic disorder. *Behaviour Research and Therapy, 26,* 13–22.

Rapee, R. M., Adler, C., Craske, M. G., & Barlow, D. H. (1988, November). *Cognitive restructuring and relaxation in the treatment of generalized anxiety disorder: A controlled study.* Paper presented at the meeting of the Association for Advancement of Behavior Therapy, New York.

Silverman, W. K., & Nelles, W. B. (1988). The Anxiety Disorders Interview Schedule for Children. *Journal of the American Academy of Child and Adolescent Psychiatry, 27,* 772–778.

10

The University of Alberta Psychotherapy Research Center

William E. Piper, Hassan F. A. Azim,
Mary McCallum, and Anthony S. Joyce
University of Alberta

Background and Aims

History

The Psychotherapy Research Center, Department of Psychiatry, University of Alberta (Edmonton) is the product of clinical and research traditions that developed in separate geographical regions of Canada. The clinical tradition is represented by the evolution of the Division of External Psychiatric Services, University of Alberta Hospitals. The division is a large, multifaceted outpatient service for psychiatric patients that is located in an 800-bed university hospital. Last year the walk-in clinic component of the division assessed 2,400 new patient referrals. The day and evening hospital programs had an average daily census of 40 and 25 patients, respectively.

The division has grown steadily under the leadership of its director, Hassan F. A. Azim, since its inception in 1973. The service began as a pilot day hospital program and soon added an evening hospital program. Continuation of financial support from the provincial government was contingent on submission of evaluative reports concerning the effects of the programs. To accomplish program evaluation a Master's level evaluator was funded. In 1975 a proposal for a multipurpose walk-in clinic to provide a full range of complementary services in relation to the day and evening hospital programs was approved. It too was

funded conditionally on submission of evaluative reports.

Included among the funded staff were full-time positions for a research psychologist and a research technician. Soon a secretarial position was converted to an additional research technician position. Thus at an early stage the tripartite clinical division (walk-in clinic, day hospital, and evening hospital) included a substantial (four-member) evaluation unit that monitored clinical activities and provided documentation that justified the continued functioning of the clinical services.

An ongoing, integrated evaluation unit is one of the unique features of the division. It helped create a tradition of collaboration between clinicians and researchers that facilitated an eventual shift of emphasis from program evaluation projects to randomized clinical-trial research projects. That shift was also facilitated by the arrival of a new research director in 1985, William E. Piper, who brought with him a tradition of conducting psychotherapy research.

The tradition was cultivated in the Individual and Group Psychotherapy unit of the Allan Memorial Institute (Montreal, Quebec, Canada). Since 1973 the unit has carried out a series of clinical trial investigations that focused on the efficacy of different forms of psychotherapy with psychiatric outpatients. The four major clinical investigations that were carried out between

1973 and 1985 concerned outcome comparisons among (a) long-term group therapy and no treatment (waiting-list control group); (b) types of pretherapy training and no pretherapy training for patients entering long-term group therapy; (c) high, low, and mixed on-task behavior patient compositions in long-term group therapy; and (d) short-term individual, short-term group, long-term individual, and long-term group forms of psychotherapy. Associated with several of these projects were process analyses, primarily from the perspective of external raters. They included a focus on such variables as type of therapist intervention, objects addressed in therapist interventions, and psychodynamic work. The investigations spawned an interest in the relation between initial patient characteristics and both process and outcome variables.

The present Psychotherapy Research Center in Edmonton thus represents the confluence of distinct clinical and research traditions. The clinical tradition (Edmonton) led to the creation of a large multifaceted outpatient service staffed by well-trained clinicians that includes a substantial evaluation unit. The research tradition (Montreal) led to the completion of a number of clinical trial investigations of psychotherapy that focused on patient characteristics and therapy process as well as therapy outcome. The combination of the two traditions in 1985 led to the initiation of three large-scale clinical trial investigations and a fourth extensive process analysis investigation based on the clinical material provided by one of the three clinical trials.

Overall Aims

The general aim of the research program at the University of Alberta is to conduct a series of controlled clinical-trial investigations involving individual and group forms of psychodynamically oriented psychotherapy for ambulatory psychiatric patients, including a partial hospitalization population. The investigations will permit the study of various predictor–process–outcome relations. Of particular interest is the investigation of interactions between patient characteristics and treatment variables. Although each of the therapies chosen for study are short term in duration (ranging from 3 to 5 months), the projects are relatively long term in nature (ranging from 3 to 5 years). Most of the projects involve detailed process analysis, and all involve an interdisciplinary team of therapists, assessors, and research coordinators.

Major Areas of Investigation

Each of the four investigations had a distinct area of focus. The first investigation was a controlled study of patient suitability and outcome in short-term individual psychotherapy. The primary purpose of the project was to study the effects of short-term, dynamically oriented individual therapy in a randomized control group design with two samples of psychiatric outpatients that differed on a selection criterion (quality of object relations). Interest in carrying out the project stemmed directly from the findings of the Montreal comparative study of psychotherapy. The study indicated that short-term individual therapy was the most cost-effective treatment when both therapist and patient time were considered. In addition, quality of object relations was found to be significantly related to both process and outcome scores of the patients. The recent Edmonton investigation involved 144 patients and 8 therapists. Data collection spanned more than 3 years (October 1985 to February 1989).

The second investigation was a controlled study of effectiveness and client suitability for short-term group psychotherapy. One purpose was to conduct a controlled clinical-trial investigation of short-term, dynamically oriented group psychotherapy with psychiatric outpatients who are experiencing difficulties after the loss of a person. Another was to investigate the personality characteristic of psychological mindedness in terms of its potential value as a selection criterion and a prognostic variable. A pilot study in Montreal indicated promising psychometric properties for this new interview measure of psychological mindedness. The project involved approximately 160 patients, 3 therapists, and 16 therapy groups. Data collection spanned more than 4 years (November 1986 to December 1990).

Both the first and second investigations reflect recent interest among mental professionals in short-term, dynamically oriented psychotherapies. Despite considerable interest, there has been relatively little in the way of scientific evidence based on controlled studies to support, qualify, or refute the rather optimistic clinical reports about the usefulness of such therapies.

The third investigation is a controlled evaluation of a day treatment program. One of its objectives is to conduct a controlled, clinical trial investigation of a day treatment program for patients with serious, chronic mental disorders. A second is to identify patient characteristics that are related to favorable outcome. A third is to identify patient characteristics that are associated with working in and completing the day treatment program. This project is expected to involve approximately 300 patients and to span a data collection period of more than 3 years (September 1988 to October 1991).

The fourth investigation concerns preconditions and responses to psychodynamic interpretations in short-term individual psychotherapy. The purpose of the project is to identify precondition (patient verbalization), interpretation (therapist verbalization), and response (patient verbalization) features that are associated with successful and unsuccessful interpretation episodes in short-term individual psychotherapy. Methodological objectives of the study include (a) the measurement of a set of process variables (state of anxiety, self-involvement, interpersonal intent, and verbal content) that are more comprehensive than those that have been used in most previous process analysis studies; and (b) the control of important covariates (patient dynamic capacity, degree of pathology, and therapy alliance), which often has been neglected in previous studies. The data set is being selected from the audiotaped therapy sessions of 60 patients from the first investigation. This project will span approximately 3 years (April 1987 to March 1989).

Method

Subjects and Selection

In the short-term individual therapy project patients were matched according to quality of object relations, sex, and age. The mean age of the patients was 31 years; 65% were women. Examination of their target objectives revealed a familiar set of psychiatric outpatient difficulties concerning depression, anxiety, self-esteem, and interpersonal functioning. Most patients received an Axis I diagnosis of affective or adjustment disorder as defined by the revised third edition of the *Diagnostic and Statistical Manual of Mental Disorders (DSM-III-R;* American Psychiatric Association, 1987). One third of the patients also received an Axis II diagnosis (usually dependent or avoidant personality disorder).

In the short-term group therapy project patients were matched according to psychological mindedness, sex, and age. The patients were adults who had lost a significant other in the re-

cent past through death, separation, or divorce. They were not adapting well to the change and were interested in examining the reasons with others who had had a similar experience. Depressive symptomatology, social isolation, and loneliness were typical features of the patients. Data from the first 8 therapy groups revealed that 53% of the patients received a *DSM-III-R* Axis I diagnosis of affective disorder, 23% adjustment disorder, and 6% anxiety disorder. In addition, 24% of the patients received an Axis II diagnosis of personality disorder (usually dependent personality disorder). The mean patient age was 36 years; and 67% were women.

In the day hospital project patients were matched according to diagnosis (assessed by the Diagnostic Interview Schedule), sex, and age. The program was designed for persons who need comprehensive care but do not require 24-hour inpatient hospitalization. The patients evidenced long-term patterns of social and educational–vocational maladaptation. Nearly half had reported previous psychiatric hospitalizations. Of the patients who completed the program in 1986 56.3% received a *DSM-III-R* Axis I diagnosis of affective disorder, and 62.4% received on Axis II diagnosis of personality disorder. Many (38.9%) received both. The mean patient age was 30 years; 58% were women.

Procedure

The three clinical-trial investigations follow the same general procedure. Client referrals for the first and second investigations have come from the large pool of patients who receive intake assessments in the walk-in clinic of the division. The therapies of each investigation represent treatment alternatives in a larger set that are available at the clinic. If the patient and intake assessor agree that the patient should pursue one of the treatments, the patient signs a consent form and receives an information form that describes the procedures. The patient is then scheduled for interview and questionnaire assessments. Each investigation uses a pretest–posttest control group design as defined by Campbell and Stanley (1963). Thus, patients are randomly assigned to an immediate-treatment or delayed-treatment condition. Before condition assignment patients are matched in pairs on a few variables, as discussed later. They receive a follow-up assessment after the completion of therapy.

Dependent Measures

Each investigation includes a comprehensive battery of outcome measures that is assessed at repeated intervals. Outcome is assessed in several areas: interpersonal and personality functioning, self-esteem, psychiatric symptomatology, personalized target objectives, and satisfaction with treatment. The sources of evaluation include the patient, the therapist, and an independent outcome assessor. The batteries include standard measures that have been used in other psychotherapy outcome studies and specific measures that are believed to be sensitive to changes associated with the particular patients and treatments.

Research Accomplishments

Instruments Developed

The development of special instruments for use in the current investigations in Edmonton has been a major priority. In most cases they represent a continuation of work begun in Montreal.

Quality of object relations. This variable is defined as a patient's internal enduring tendency to establish certain kinds of relations with others. The patient's relationships with important figures throughout life are explored with reference to criteria that characterize five levels of object relations: genital, oedipal, obsessive, depressive, and narcissistic-borderline. The criteria refer to behavioral manifestations, regulation of affect, regulation of self-esteem, and historical antecedents. The assessment, which is a semistructured interview, usually requires 2 hours. When it is completed, the interviewer assigns 100 points along the 5 anchor points of the scale and an overall rating that ranges from 1 to 9.

Psychological mindedness. This variable is defined as the ability to identify dynamic, conflictual components and to relate them to a person's difficulties. The interview measure is administered individually and requires approximately 30 minutes. The test stimulus is a videotape of a simulated patient–therapist interaction. After the tape is viewed it is stopped, and the person being assessed is asked "What seems to be troubling this women?" The person's responses are scored according to his or her ability to identify dynamic, conflictual components (e.g., wishes, anxiety, defenses, and affects) and to relate them to the man's difficulties. A rating on a scale ranging from 0 to 9 is assigned to the person.

Therapist Intervention Rating Scale (TIRS). The TIRS is a content analysis system that assigns each therapist intervention to 1 of 10 categories. The 10 categories range from simple facilitative remarks such as "mm-hm" to complex constructions about the patient's internal conflicts. Categories 7–10 are defined as interpretations because they contain one or more types of dynamic components. A dynamic component is defined as one part of a patient's conflict that exerts an internal force on some other part of the patient, (e.g., a wish, anxiety, or defense). In addition to categorizing the type of intervention, the TIRS assesses the type of object (person) included in the intervention.

Response to interpretation. We have also developed a four-category response to interpretation scale. Three of the categories are defined as work. In those cases the patient preserves a focus on himself or herself, preserves a focus on the meaning of the interpretation, and adds something important to the interpretation. Descriptive work provides additional detail (or documentation) to the interpretation. Relational work provides additional objects or situations that have a similar dynamic relationship to the patient. This is what some investigators define as linking. Dynamic work provides one or more additional dynamic components to those that are included in the interpretation. The fourth category is defined as nonwork. In this case the patient does not add something important to the interpretation.

Psychodynamic Work and Object Rating System (PWORS). The PWORS is a system for assessing psychodynamic work and reference to objects in group psychotherapy. Psychodynamic work is an effort to understand a problem in terms of conflict among dynamic components that belong to one or more units of the group. Units of the group refer to a patient, the therapist, a dyad, a subgroup, or the group as a whole. Objects refer to people inside or outside the group. Dynamic components are wishes, anxiety, defenses, or dynamic expressions (affect, behaviors, and cognitions) that belong to a unit of the group. Statements are part of a sentence, a sentence, or several sentences spoken by a group member that are separated by a statement by another group member or by a silence longer than 10 seconds. Each statement is placed into one of two nonwork categories or one of two work categories.

Major Hypotheses

The hypotheses associated with the first two investigations are similar in nature. This is largely a result of the investigations' similar designs. Each involves the evaluation of a treatment modality, the examination of the effects of a patient personality characteristic, and the interaction between the treatment modality and the patient characteristic. Hypotheses concerning outcome criteria are as follows (the specific variables for the first and second investigations are indicated in parentheses):

1. The best results will be obtained by highly suitable patients (quality of object relations or psychological mindedness) who were treated (short-term individual or group therapy).

2. The next best results will be obtained by marginally suitable patients (quality of object relations or psychological mindedness) who were treated (short-term individual or group therapy) and by highly suitable patients (quality of object relations or psychological mindedness) who were not treated immediately (short-term individual or group therapy).

3. The poorest results will be obtained by marginally suitable patients (quality of object relations or psychological mindedness) who were not treated (short-term individual or group therapy).

4. Highly suitable patients (quality of object relations or psychological mindedness) will have a more positive therapy process than marginally suitable patients (quality of object relations or psychological mindedness).

5. There will be a direct relation between therapy process and therapy outcome.

Hypotheses for the third investigation are as follows:

1. For most outcome variables, particularly those that focus on social functioning and self-esteem, significantly greater improvement will be reported by patients in the day hospital program compared with those in the nontherapy treatment condition.

2. For several of the patient characteristic measures (e.g., quality of object relations and psychological mindedness), there will be a significant relation with ratings of patient work in the small dynamic therapy group of the day hospital.

3. There will be a significant relation between the work ratings and outcome variables.

Some of the hypotheses for the fourth investigation are as follows:

1. The greater the correspondence between the content of an interpretation and the therapist's initial formulation of the patient's focal conflict, the greater the work in response to the interpretation.

2. Higher ratings of quality of object relations, dynamic capacity, and therapeutic alliance and lower ratings of patient pathology will be associated with more productive responses to interpretation.

3. Readiness for interpretation in patient material before an interpretation will be reflected by a flexible involvement in internal subjective material as represented by high-level experiencing scores, focused voice quality, and use of the disclosure verbal response mode.

Tentative Findings

The four research investigations just described will preoccupy the attention and major resources of the Psychotherapy Research Center during the next several years. In the case of the first investigation, which was recently completed, several findings have emerged. Considerable support for the efficacy of short-term individual therapy was found. Compared with control patients, treated patients evidenced significantly greater improvement in areas of interpersonal functioning, psychiatric symptomatology, self-esteem, and life satisfaction. The effect sizes for the statistically significant scores ranged from moderate to large. Approximately 60% of the treated patients achieved criteria of clinical significance on several measures for which normative data were available. The benefits were maintained for 6 months after therapy. Some evidence was also found for an independent effect of quality of object relations on scores of interpersonal functioning and symptomatology. As hypothesized, the best results were found for treated patients who had high quality of object relations and the poorest results for untreated patients with low quality of object relations. The results suggest that an optimal match between type of patient and type of therapy may have been found and that quality of object relations should be considered a patient selection criterion.

The interview measure of quality of object relations was also compared with measures of recent interpersonal functioning with respect to the prediction of therapeutic alliance and therapy outcome. Of the patients who had completed short-term individual therapy, 64 were chosen to form a sample that was evenly balanced according to quality of object relations, treatment condition, and therapist. Quality of object relations was found to be the best predictor. It was significantly related to client-rated and therapist-rated therapeutic alliance and to improvement of both general symptomatology and specific target problems. Currently, a series of analyses is being conducted that focuses on the relations among quality of object relations, transference interpretations, patient work in response to interpretations, and outcome.

Tentative findings for the short-term group therapy investigation are based on data from the first 8 groups. One finding concerns the phenomenon of remaining or dropping out. A dropout is defined as someone who started therapy (i.e., attended at least one session) and then dropped out prematurely. The overall dropout rate for the eight groups was 28%. Dropping out was not significantly related to being assigned to the immediate-therapy condition as opposed to the delayed-therapy condition. Dropping out was related to the patient characteristic that we defined as psychological mindedness, however. Of the first 8 groups, only 2 of 33 highly psychologically minded patients (6%) were dropouts, whereas 13 of 21 minimally psychologically minded patients (62%) were dropouts. A chi-square analysis was significant, and the proportion of variance accounted for was 32%.

Thus, we may have identified an important predictor of premature termination in short-term, dynamically oriented group therapy. The selection implication of the findings is that patients with little psychological mindedness should not be referred to this type of therapy. We do not have sufficient data, however, to know whether such patients who remain in therapy evidence desirable therapy process and favorable outcome. If so, the implication would be that special methods of retaining such patients should be developed. This may involve pretherapy training or technical procedures in therapy itself.

A second finding concerns the outcome results. Substantial benefits for the treatment method (i.e., dynamically oriented, short-term group therapy for patients who experienced a person loss) were found. The benefits, which held up over a 6-month follow-up period, include areas of interpersonal functioning, psychiatric symptomatology, self-esteem, and general life satisfaction. In contrast, a significant main effect for psychological mindedness was not found, nor was there substantial evidence for an interaction effect between treatment and psychological mindedness. The study is continuing, and we look forward to determining whether these findings hold as well as discovering others.

Clinical Significance

In regard to the clinical significance (relevance) of the first two investigations, mental health clinics frequently experience demands for therapy that exceed their resources. Offering a few supportive sessions or placing patients on lengthy waiting lists is often felt to be unsatisfactory. Short-term forms of therapy have been regarded as a promising solution.

In addition to providing data that address basic effectiveness issues, the first 2 investigations provide information relevant to patient selection. Data concerning relations between patient characteristics and therapy process as well as therapy outcome will be available. The third investigation focuses on a partial hospitalization therapy program that was designed to treat patients who evidence serious, chronic mental disorders. Such patients usually have a history of long-term maladaptation and have made frequent demands on social and medical facilities. Despite the prevalence of such patients (affective and personality disorders), their high morbidity, their significant cost to society, and the apparent appropriateness of treating them in intensive day treatment programs, controlled studies of such programs and patients are virtually absent in the research literature.

The fourth investigation will meet the need of practicing psychotherapists for an empirically based understanding of when and how to provide dynamic interpretations and how to evaluate their impact on patients. In addition, suggestions for intervening with patients who differ on initial levels of suitability may be forthcoming; these would contribute to criteria for tailoring treatment to specific patients.

The four investigations also have the potential to provide a number of useful tools as well as information relevant to clinical training. The interview measures of quality of object relations and psychological mindedness could be used to teach trainees how to assess patients for psychotherapy. Familiarity with and use of the process analysis systems could be most valuable in teaching trainees when to make an intervention, how to make an intervention, and how to assess its impact. Anecdotal reports from clinicians who have used these instruments suggest that they do have a useful impact conceptually and technically.

Nature of the Research Organization

Membership of the Psychotherapy Research Center

The clinical staff of the division comprises 8 psychiatrists, 4 of whom are full-time practitioners in the center's immediate vicinity, and the equivalent of more than 30 full-time therapists from the disciplines of psychology, social work, occupational therapy, and nursing. In addition, there are 7 full-time secretarial support staff positions and 4 full-time research positions. Various treatments, including both short- and long-term forms of individual and group therapy as well as child, marital, and family therapy, are provided. Substantial clinical teaching also takes place. In 1988 7 psychiatric residents, 22 family medicine residents, 8 medical interns, 4 medical students, 1 psychology intern, and 5 occupational therapy students rotated through the division. One feature that is essential to conducting large-scale clinical trial investigations is the availability of a steady source of patient referrals and a sizable staff of collaborative clinicians (assessors and therapists). The clinic clearly achieves those capacities.

The center's codirectors are William E. Piper, PhD, and Hassan F. A. Azim, MB, BCh. Research associates are Anthony S. Joyce, MA; George W. H. Nixon, MB, BCh; John S. Rosie, MB, BCh; Mary McCallum, PhD; Perry M. Segal, MD; and Robert S. Lakoff, MD. Research technicians are Hillary L. Morin, RN; Nancy C. Hurst, BA; Doris Ryan, BA; Bonnie L. Stephanson, BA; Karen A. Evans, BA; Vuokko van der Veen, BA; and Sherryl L. Basarab, BA. Daniel S. K. Szeto, MSc, is the staff statistician, and Jane C. Carr, BSc, is an honors student who provides technical support.

Funding Sources

Funding for the Psychotherapy Research Center is provided by an ongoing internal (hospital) budget and a number of time-limited external (public and private) operating grants. As indicated earlier, the internal budget has supported four full-time positions (two psychologists and two research technicians) for more than 10 years. This "hard" money ($141,834 in 1987) has made it possible to do basic program evaluation work while laying the groundwork that is required to conduct large-scale clinical-trial investigations of psychotherapy. It has sustained the core personnel of the research team.

Funding from external grants ($388,457 acquired between July 1985 and June 1988) has made it possible to expand considerably the number of members of the research team. This has enabled the team to perform time-intensive tasks (e.g., process analyses and individual patient interviews) for large numbers of patients. The external granting agencies include Health and Welfare Canada (public, federal government), which is analagous to the National Institute of Mental Health in the United States; the Alberta Provincial Mental Health Advisory Council (public, provincial government); and the Canadian Psychiatric Research Foundation (private, national). Current external monies will provide funding for approximately five full-time research technicians during the next 3 years. Thus, the center has a secure financial base to carry out the four research investigations just described.

Relation to Other Research Programs

Currently, we are not involved in multisite investigations with other psychotherapy research centers. Collaboration on a small scale with the Individual and Group Psychotherapy Unit of the Allan Memorial Institute in Montreal continues. The questions we are addressing in our four major investigations are closely related to those being addressed by a number of other psychotherapy research teams. Focus on short-term psychotherapy has become a priority in many settings. Consideration of context and sequence in the investigation of therapy process is also a current emphasis. As our center becomes more established, the possibilities for more direct and elaborate collaboration are expected to increase.

References and Bibliography

American Psychiatric Association. (1987). *Diagnostic and statistical manual of mental* disorders (rev. 3rd ed.). Washington, DC: Author.

Azim, H. F. A., & Joyce, A. S. (1986). The impact of data-based program modifications on the satisfaction of outpatients in group psychotherapy. *Canadian Journal of Psychiatry, 31,* 119–122.

Azim, H. F. A., Piper, W. E., Segal, P. M., Nixon, G. W. H., & Duncan, S. (1990). *The quality of object relations scale: An object relations assessment (theoretical considerations and clinical and research implications).* Unpublished manuscript.

Campbell, D. T., & Stanley, J. C. (1963). *Experimental and quasi-experimental designs for research.* Chicago: Rand McNally.

Joyce, A. S., Azim, H. F. A., & Morin, H. (1987). Brief crisis group psychotherapy versus the initial sessions of long-term group psychotherapy: An exploratory comparison. *Group, 12,* 3–19.

Joyce, A. S., & Piper, W. E. (1990). An examination of Mann's model of time-limited individual psychotherapy. *Canadian Journal of Psychiatry, 35,* 41–49.

McCallum, M., & Piper, W. E. (1988). Psychoanalytically-oriented short-term groups for outpatients: Unsettled issues. *Group, 12,* 21–32.

McCallum, M., & Piper, W. E. (in press-a). A controlled study of effectiveness and patient suitability for short-term group psychotherapy. *International Journal of Group Psychotherapy.*

McCallum, M., & Piper, W. E. (in press-b). *The psychological mindedness assessment procedure. Psychological Assessment: A Journal of Consulting and Clinical Psychology.* Unpublished manuscript.

Piper, W. E., Azim, H. F. A., Joyce, A. S., & McCallum, M. (in press). Transference and interpretation, therapeutic alliance and outcome in short-term individual psychotherapy. *Archives of General Psychiatry.*

Piper, W. E., Azim, H. F. A., Joyce, A. S., McCallum, M., Nixon, G. W. H., & Segal, P. S. (in press). *Quality of object relations vs. interpersonal functioning as predictors of therapeutic alliance. Journal of Nervous and Mental Disease.*

Piper, W. E., Azim, H. F. A., McCallum, M., & Joyce, A. S. (1990). *Patient suitability and outcome in short-term individual psychotherapy. Journal of Consulting and Clinical Psychology, 58,* 475–481.

Piper, W. E., Debbane, E. G., Bienvenu, J. P., & Garant, J. (1984). A comparative study of four forms of psychotherapy. *Journal of Consulting and Clinical Psychology, 52,* 268–279.

Piper, W. E., Debbane, E. G., Bienvenu, J. P., & Garant, J. (1986). Relationships between the object focus of therapist interpretations and outcome in short-term, individual psychotherapy. *British Journal of Medical Psychology, 59,* 1–11.

Piper, W. E., de Carufel, F. L., & Szkrumelak, N. (1985). Patient predictors of process and outcome in short-term individual psychotherapy. *Journal of Nervous and Mental Disease, 173,* 726–733.

11

University of Arizona: Searching for Differential Treatments

Larry E. Beutler, David Engle, Varda Shoham-Salomon,
David C. Mohr, Judith C. Dean, and Edward M. Bernat
University of Arizona Health Sciences Center

Background and Aims

The psychotherapy research project at the University of Arizona Health Sciences Center began in 1979 under two development grants from the university with the establishment of parallel programs emphasizing naturalistic and controlled studies. Subsequent progression of the program has led to blending of the two arms through an interactive data base.

Under the first grant, a naturalistic data base was developed to track and assess treatment in the psychiatry department's outpatient training clinic. Historical and test data from both trainees and patients were included in the data base. Trainees completed questionnaires regarding their theoretical beliefs, personality patterns, and perceptual styles at the beginning and end of each training year. Patients completed intake inventories to assess symptom severity, coping patterns, perceptual style, belief systems, personality style, and treatment preferences. At the end of treatment, both patients and therapists were asked to rate the treatment relationship, process, and outcome, and patients again completed inventories regarding their symptoms, perceptual style, beliefs, and values. Six to twelve months after termination of treatment, patients were asked to complete a similar battery of rating forms. In 1984 a shift of emphasis toward controlled investigations resulted in discontinuation of the routine baseline data collection for three years.

A controlled studies research arm was established under the second development grant. Initially, three group psychotherapy models (cognitive-behavior, interactional-supportive, and experiential-gestalt) and a milieu only control condition (no group therapy) were compared. Acute psychiatric inpatients were randomly assigned to one of the conditions. Symptom and behavior change measures were made both before and after therapy (Beutler, Frank, Schieber, Calvert, & Gaines, 1984). Closure of the inpatient psychiatry clinic at University Hospital in June 1985 required terminating the inpatient project. At that time, the controlled study and naturalistic data were incorporated into a common data base.

Two subsequent events have integrated the controlled and naturalistic arms of the psycho-

Work on this chapter was supported by National Institute of Mental Health grant MH39359 and by the faculty and staff of the Department of Psychiatry, to whom we express our thanks.

Larry E. Beutler is now the director of training, Counseling Psychology Program, Graduate School of Education, University of California, Santa Barbara, California 93106.

A substantial portion of this program has been moved to or is run jointly with the University of California, Santa Barbara.

therapy research project in the outpatient clinic. First, an award from the National Institute of Mental Health in 1985 commissioned us to develop and compare psychotherapies for the treatment of depression. Under this grant a manual developed for group cognitive therapy (CT; Yost, Beutler, Corbishley, & Allender, 1986) was used as a model for the development of a manual for a form of group experiential psychotherapy (Daldrup, Beutler, Engle, & Greenberg, 1988), which was then used to assess treatment efficacy in patients with chronic pain and depression. Second, in 1988 the psychiatry outpatient clinic was reorganized in an effort to integrate clinical training and research. This reorganization has emphasized the development of specialty clinics whose nature and role are dictated by the requirements of existent research programs. With the reorganization came a mandate to establish a data base to serve as a foundation for naturalistic research studies and to supplement the controlled studies conducted in the several specialty clinics.

Since July 1988 intake data have been gathered on all patients to monitor patients, therapists, and therapies. This allows tracking of treatment-induced changes and has resulted in an applied study of psychotherapy in the outpatient setting. Baseline patient data from the naturalistic arm can then be provided to specialty clinics for research use. Each clinic is designed to accommodate controlled research protocols, thereby facilitating much of the pilot data needed in the development of funded research programs. There are active research protocols in the behavioral gerontology, depression, eating disorders, and medical psychiatry clinics.

Aims of the naturalistic arm of the research program include use of the accumulating data base to provide an archive of patient and treatment data for research and training programs, to provide data management and statistical services for research studies, to provide data for development of measurement devices and algorithms to identify optimally compatible patients and therapists, to assess pretreatment and process predictors of effectiveness in naturally occurring psychotherapy, and to identify therapist qualities that contribute to effectiveness.

Method

The University of Arizona Psychiatry Department training clinic receives no public funds to support patient care. All patients receiving services from this clinic are enrolled in the naturalistic research protocol as a condition of their treatment. Participation in the controlled studies in any specialty clinic is voluntary. External funding for controlled studies partially underwrites service cost in these programs, providing an incentive for participation. Fees in the general clinics are adjusted on the basis of patient need; a portion of fees provides support for research activities.

Clinical evaluation teams manage the specialty clinics. Each team has a psychiatrist and a clinical psychologist as core members, one of whom also serves as the team director. A triage committee composed of the administrative director, medical director, clinical evaluation team directors, training program directors, the data base coordinator, patient services coordinator, and social service and pharmacy specialists administers the psychiatry clinic. This committee assigns research and training priorities, maintains quality assurance, and ensures that each patient is assigned to an appropriate program.

After a brief telephone screening by a nurse practitioner, patients are given appointments for a two-part intake evaluation. First, an intake interview is scheduled with the specialty clinic team whose research criteria most closely fit the presenting problems of the patient. The second appointment is with the data base coordinator, who administers the psychological assessment battery; this currently comprises the Diagnostic Interview Schedule, Brief Symptom Inventory, Minnesota Multiphasic Personality Inventory (MMPI), Social Support Questionnaire (Sarason, Levine, Basham, & Sarason, 1983), Outpatient Attitudes Questionnaire (a pilot measure of expectancies and resistance), and additional instruments required for the controlled research protocols.

For patients who meet the entrance requirements and agree to participate in one of the controlled research studies, the length, type, and intensity of treatment are determined by the protocol. All other patients are assigned to a trainee in psychiatry, clinical psychology, or social work for treatment on a rotating schedule.

Research Accomplishments

Eight doctoral dissertations and nearly a dozen empirical psychotherapy studies have been supported by the naturalistic data base. Included are investigations of patient-therapist matching

(Beutler, Arizmendi, Crago, Shanfield, & Hagaman, 1983; Calvert, Beutler, & Crago, 1988), contributors to treatment maintenance (Schramski, Beutler, Lauver, Arizmendi, & Shanfield, 1984), dropout predictors (Kolb, Beutler, Davis, Crago, & Shanfield, 1985), how trainee orientations and beliefs change with training (Guest & Beutler, 1988), and characteristics of more and less effective clinicians (Lafferty, Beutler, & Crago, 1989).

The psychotherapy for depression project demonstrates the productivity of controlled studies in the outpatient clinic. This project has resulted in six doctoral dissertations, more than 15 empirical studies; four books, numerous chapters in books, and several theoretical articles. Publications have included treatment manuals for CT (Yost et al., 1986), focused expressive psychotherapy (Daldrup et al., 1988), and eclectic or combination psychotherapies (Beutler, 1983; Beutler & Clarkin, 1990) as well as empirical studies assessing treatment efficacy of these various approaches (Beutler et al., 1984; Beutler, Daldrup, Engle, Guest, Corbishley, & Meredith, 1988; Beutler, Daldrup, Engle, Oro-Beutler, Meredith, & Boyer, 1987; Beutler, Scogin, et al., 1987; Scogin, Hamblin, & Beutler, 1987), the utility of various outcome measures (Scogin, Hamblin, & Beutler, 1986), and the nature of effective psychotherapy processes (Hill, Beutler, & Daldrup, 1989).

We have developed instruments for assessing therapist compliance with experiential psychotherapy, degree of goal-directed arousal, and patient coping style (Daldrup et al., 1988). Application of algorithms for patient-therapist and patient-therapy matching has also been demonstrated (Beutler, 1983; Beutler et al., 1984; Calvert et al., 1988).

Research Programs in Progress

Controlled Research Arm

The psychotherapy for depression project is the organizing project in the depression clinic and is the most developed controlled study in the outpatient clinic. For this reason it is used for illustration in the ensuing discussion.

Psychotherapy for depression project. Objectives of the psychotherapy for depression project are to (a) develop and test the relative efficacy of several models of group and individual therapy, including a form of nondirective self-help therapy (supportive/self-directed [S/SD] therapy; (b) assess how the level of emotion aroused in psychotherapy contributes both to treatment mainte-

nance and to alterations in depression; and (c) determine whether there are differential effects when different therapies and therapists are matched to patients who vary in coping style (externalization) and resistance propensity (reactance).

Three psychotherapies for depression are currently being compared in the project: (a) focused expressive psychotherapy (FEP), a gestalt-based group therapy that encourages affective arousal by intensifying awareness and facilitating expression of unwanted emotions (Daldrup et al., 1988); (b) CT a treatment that enhances emotional control through identifying, challenging, and then reframing distorted thought patterns that are presumed to be the root of the emotional conflict (Yost et al., 1986); and (c) S/SD therapy which involves brief telephone sessions along with structured readings. This last treatment contrasts with the others in that it attempts neither to increase nor to decrease the intensity or form of emotional expression.

FEP and CT are conducted in groups of 4–8 patients that meet weekly over 20 weeks. Each 1½ hour session is videotaped. The groups are led by experienced psychologists who are trained in one of the two therapies. Compliance with the therapeutic model is facilitated by weekly supervision of therapists, completion of weekly compliance checklists, and compliance rating of videotapes by external reviewers.

Method. Eligibility criteria for the psychotherapy for depression protocol are as follows: The subject meets diagnostic criteria for major depression as outlined in the revised third edition of the *Diagnostic and Statistical Manual of Mental Disorders (DSM-III-R*; American Psychiatric Association, 1987); scores 16 or higher on the 17-item form of the Hamilton Rating Scale for Depression (HRSD); and demonstrates no psychotic features, suicidal ideation, or evidence of substance abuse. Subjects are recruited through the outpatient psychiatry clinic, media announcements, and referrals. Eligible patients are then randomly assigned to one of the three treatment groups.

Screening instruments and interviews are given within 2 weeks before treatment is assigned. Treatment process variables and depression are measured weekly with the Beck Depression Inventory (BDI) and session report forms. More intensive assessments including self-report instruments and structured interviews are administered every 5 weeks, at termination, and at 3-, 6-, and 12-month follow-up periods.

Initial findings. Because most psychotherapy research has not found differences in effectiveness even among psychotherapies in which there are clearly observed differences in internal processes, we have neither expected nor found that the treatments used in this project differ remarkably in overall effectiveness. Nevertheless, we are finding support for our hypothesis that differential effectiveness rates emerge when treatment is cross-matched to compatible patients. Depressed patients who cope with unwanted emotions by acting out and projecting (externalizing) tend to do best in CT because their behavioral objectives contrast with the introspective and awareness methods of the other treatments. On the other hand, both S/SD and FEP tend to favor nonexternalizing depressed patients (internalizers), although we expect and are finding that this pattern is more inconsistent for FEP than for S/SD.

Initial data on the role of resistance propoposensity (reactance) also tends to confirm our hypothesis that directive treatments (CT and FEP) are of greatest benefit to patients who have little propensity for resistance. S/SD is remarkable in the extent to which it appears to be effective among patients who are highly disposed to resist therapeutic influence attempts.

In addition, we have found that FEP and CT are distinguishable in terms of both the methods used and the degree of arousal induced as rated by patients and external observers. Ratings by patients is done in postsession evaluations of process and satisfaction. Arousal level is measured by an instrument developed for this project to catalog and rate nonverbal expressions (Burgoon, Kelley, Newton, & Keely-Dyreson, 1987), including vocal or kinesic behavior (body posture, gestures, level of bodily activity, etc.) from videotaped sessions.

Our initial findings indicate that FEP induces greater increases in composite indicators of patient vocal arousal, although some specific contributors to this measure of vocal arousal such as loudness, pitch, or latencies do not discriminate FEP from CT. Indicators of bodily arousal have also been found to be greater in FEP than CT. We continue to test the hypothesized positive relation between arousal level and end of treatment depression among patients who are characterized as overcontrolled, constrained, and internalizing. Similarly, we are testing the hypothesized negative relation between arousal and improvement among patients who are undercontrolled and externalizing. Assessing rates of differential outcomes among the treatments is in progress.

Related projects. *Assessment of externalized hostility.* Self-report instruments that are currently available to measure overcontrolled hostility, such as the Multidimensional Anger Inventory (Siegel, 1986) or the Overcontrolled Hostility scale on the MMPI, are not specific enough for predicting response to the specific demands of psychotherapy. Overcontrolled emotions are outside the individual's immediate awareness, making them difficult to tap through self-report measures alone. We are now attempting to assess overcontrolled emotions through measures of nonverbal vocal and behavioral expressions.

Four methods of rating anger and hurt in patient's speech have been examined (Mohr, Shoham-Salomon, Engle, & Beutler, 1988). Content and vocal quality were found to be separate but related entities that operate independently. By using content-filtered speech, we have found that raters can reliably assess emotions expressed in speech quality independently of language content. By using transcripts, raters also can assess the emotion expressed in speech content independently of speech quality. Raters have great difficulty focusing on either content or voice quality alone when using unmodified audiotaped speech, especially when the two modalities are discrepant. Other research has noted that voice quality is less under conscious control than the speech content (Zuckerman, DePaulo, & Rosenthal, 1986). Therefore, we anticipate that ratings of emotions that use content-filtered speech will more accurately assess underlying and overcontrolled emotions than ratings on the basis of speech content.

Measurement of depression. We are also focusing on the measurement of various aspects of depression as tapped by different instruments, including the BDI and the HRSD. The BDI and HRSD correlate at low levels at pretreatment, but the relationship increases by treatment's end. It is hypothesized that this difference in pretreatment and posttreatment correlations is due to increasing variability of depression in an initially homogeneous sample because some patients improve and others do not. BDI scores seemed to reflect dysthymia more than major depression in our sample, whereas the reverse was true for the HRSD scores. The BDI appears to be more sensitive to lower levels of depression than the HRSD, suggesting that the two instruments are measuring different aspects of depression. By examining the measurement qualities and changes throughout the course of therapy, we hope to clarify these differences.

FEP: Process–outcome links. We have begun to study factors contributing to the efficacy of FEP. Hill et al. (1989) found that patient participation, self-exploration, distress level, dependency, and experiencing are related to positive outcome in this form of treatment. Also related to outcome is the degree to which the therapist encourages exploration and demonstrates empathy and regard. Ratings of depth and smoothness in the session are related to positive postsession feelings. As the FEP model would predict, the degree to which a patient's initial expressions of hurt are transformed to expressions of anger during treatment is related to in-session improvement (Mohr et al., 1988).

Another study in our program has analyzed the spontaneous speech content of depressed psychogenic pain patients being treated in psychotherapy (Corbishley, Hendrickson, Beutler, Engle, and Daldrup, 1988). Content indicators suggest that these patients see themselves as responsible, conscientious, compliant, passive, and rulebound. They view life and emotional expression as dangerous, avoid conflict or risk, and deny their own emotional needs while feeling responsible for meeting the needs of others. Despite initial inhibitions against the expression of negative emotions, these patients respond well to FEP.

Negative outcome. Much of psychotherapy research has examined patients who improve. One of the current projects in our program focuses on those who did not improve. Treatment failure occurs in three ways: Patients may drop out before symptomatic improvement, have no symptomatic improvement at the end of therapy, or experience negative or deterioration effects. We anticipate that patients who overcontrol emotions and internalize conflict will be more likely to remain in FEP than those who are undercontrolled and externalized. A reversal of this pattern is expected among patients in CT and S/SD. Initial results indicate that FEP may produce negative effects in more severely disturbed patients at a higher rate than CT, suggesting that there may be an interaction between the benefits of arousal-inducing (i.e., abreactive) therapies and the severity or pervasiveness of the patient's pathology.

Naturalistic Research Arm

A major objective of our naturalistic investigations is to identify dimensions of patient-therapist compatibility. One aspect of this objective has led to the development of a multifactorial instrument, the Outpatient Attitudes Questionnaire (Dean, Meredith, & Beutler, 1989), which is being pilot tested in the psychiatric outpatient clinic. This questionnaire is designed to examine elements that influence resistance-receptivity to either therapist directiveness or treatment modality. Currently, the factor structure of this instrument is being established through item selection and modification. Once the factor structure is defined, the instrument will be field tested to determine reliability as well as the predictive, divergent, convergent, and descriminant aspects of validity.

Other research has focused on patient and supervisor variables that contribute to the therapist developing a guiding model of treatment (Guest & Beutler, 1988). Still other research has focused on similar characteristics of the patient and therapist as predictors of treatment benefit (Lafferty et al., 1989).

Among the more revealing naturalistic studies has been one that assessed patient coping style compatibility in terms of therapist directiveness and treatment orientation (Calvert et al., 1988). Findings of this study generally support an interaction between patient coping (internal or external) and therapist style of intervention (insight or action). The nature of this relation is consistent with that being investigated in the clinical study of treatments for depression.

Programs Planned for the Future

We plan to continue blending naturalistic and controlled studies in two main areas: differential psychotherapy outcome and psychotherapy process.

Differential Outcome Studies

We have become interested in the early responses of patients. Some patients respond well to treatment, and others do not respond significantly to the treatment assigned. We believe that treatment efficacy can be improved by combining treatments in ways that provide optimal compatibility among the treatment methods, patient coping styles, and reactance levels. Because of our expected demonstration that FEP and CT (selected because of their widely contrasting methods and models of change) are differentially effective for externalizing and internalizing patients, we would like to extend our investigations to the efficacy of combined treatments.

The general hypothesis we are seeking to test is as follows: Treatment efficacy can be increased among patients who ordinarily have responded most poorly to the cognitive and the experiential treatments studied in our program by matching three aspects of the patient's functioning that are associated with this poor rate of response to characteristic interventions of each treatment package. We hypothesize that two corresponding patient and treatment dimensions will constitute an optimal fit for maximizing patient response to treatment. The first of these matching dimensions is between patient coping style and therapy type, and the second dimension is between patient reactance levels and therapist directive style.

In our proposed study, patients will be stratified to represent relatively good and poor prognoses on the basis of their levels of initial motivation distress, a dimension that we have found is predictive of improvement. Patients in both groups will be provided with one of three manualized treatments: standard GCT, S/SD therapy, or a prescriptive psychotherapy that is tailored to fit each patient's coping style and reactance levels by adding or emphasizing arousal-induction, paradoxical, and self-help procedures from FEP and S/SD therapies in CT. The following specific hypotheses will be tested:

1. Prescriptive therapy will show enhanced effects compared with either cognitive therapy or S/SD alone, especially among poor-prognosis patients.

2. The strength of treatment effect will be directly proportional to the degree to which treatments fit therapy procedures to patient motivational arousal levels, coping styles, and reactance levels. A good match will be one in which

  • the early application of experiential strategies for inducing arousal inversely corresponds to the patient's initial level of motivation arousal
  • the use of paradoxical interventions proportionately corresponds to the patient's reactance level
  • use of directive, nonparadoxical therapeutic interventions corresponds with the patient's reliance on an externalizing coping style
  • therapists use of reflective and self- exploratory interventions corresponds inversely with the patient's reliance on an externalizing coping style.

3. Among patients who become or remain symptomatic within a month of ending brief CT or prescriptive treatment, S/SD therapy will be an effective buffer against further relapse, especially among high-reactant patients.

Patients meeting criteria for major depression will make up the sample and will be assigned to one of three treatments. The CT and S/SD treatments will represent the high and low standards against which prescriptive treatments will be assessed. The prescriptive treatment will combine aspects of FEP to enhance motivational distress levels early in treatment, with cognitive reframing and paradoxical interventions being used to overcome high reactance levels. In selecting these combined procedures, we will follow the guidelines developed by Beutler and Clarkin (1990). This model is presented as a manualized method for selecting procedural menus rather than global treatment types and is designed to tailor the treatment to particular coping styles, variations in problem complexity, and reactance levels.

A randomly selected sample of those who begin to show declines in mental status after termination of either CT or prescriptive therapy will be given additional S/SD intervention by telephone, supplemented by guided readings. This procedure will provide an initial test of a cost-effective relapse prevention procedure.

Psychotherapy Process

Our psychotherapy process studies will attempt to expand current understanding of different types of psychotherapies. It will focus on verbal and nonverbal aspects of therapeutic relationships and on how they develop in different types of therapy. We will study the nature of therapeutic relationships at different phases of therapy, including the acute, prechange phase and the posttherapy relapse prevention phase.

Relation to Other Research Programs

Within the last several years, several intra-institutional and interinstitutional collaborative research projects have been initiated. Within the University of Arizona, active collaboration exists on several small projects between the Department of Psychiatry at the Arizona Health Sciences Center and the Department of Psychology on the main campus. These liaisons facilitate data analysis and coordination of recruitment efforts.

A project designed by Hal Arkowitz of the Department of Psychology is developing an integrated psychotherapy for depression by combining methods of the psychodynamic and cognitive-behavioral models. Exploration of family patterns that contribute to and maintain depression has been a special aspect of this project (Arkowitz, Holliday, & Hutter, 1982).

The Department of Psychiatry has established collaborative relationships with both Varda Shoham-Salomon and Elizabeth Yost of the Department of Psychology. Yost has been associated with the Arizona psychotherapy research program for several years; she helped to develop the CT treatment manual and continues as both a psychotherapist and a CT trainer. In 1987 Shoham-Salomon became coinvestigator on the psychotherapy for depression project while she was a visiting assistant professor in the Department of Psychiatry. She is currently a faculty member in the Department of Psychology and continues in her role as coinvestigator.

Three interinstitutional collaborative programs have been established, and another is planned. The first of these was initiated with Clarkin at the Westchester Division of Cornell University. We are planning to use similar methods for gathering intake and exit data on patients for a cross-institutional comparison. To date, the collaboration has resulted in a coauthored volume on integrative psychotherapy (Beutler & Clarkin, 1990).

To assess the utility and efficacy of the FEP model across cultures, a multiphased effort among several western European countries began in 1987. The first phase of this program provides training through intensive workshops that use a didactic approach accompanied by experiential learning, and the second phase monitors treatment integrity. Treatment sessions are audiotaped and sent to the University of Arizona re-search team for analysis, and written evaluations are returned to the therapists in Europe. Initial data suggest that therapists can learn the model and apply it effectively in various cultures. Training programs have been initiated in Great Britain (David Shapiro and Michael Barkin at the University of Sheffield and Jenny Firth-Cozens and Roxane Agnew in Liscester), Belgium (Winfrid Huber and Anne Tracey), and Greece (Danay Papadatou and Eugenia Nida-Vazakas). Plans are underway to conduct training in Düsseldorf and Hamburg, Federal Republic of Germany, and in Zurich, Switzerland.

Finally, we are attempting to compare our own findings on differential treatment predictors to cross-cultural samples. We have begun extracting data from the University of Bern (Klaus Grawe) and Heidelberg University (Gerd Rudolph) to allow comparison with variables that we have found to be predictive of differential efficacy rates among diverse psychotherapies. Initial findings suggest that coping style and resistance propensity variables interact in a similar way with cognitive-behavior and insight-oriented approaches across cultures.

Moderate and large psychotherapy research projects such as ours often necessitate the use of a team research approach. This format can provide an intellectual exchange that has a synergistic effect, providing opportunities for individual expertise to be exploited more fully by the group. Working as a team can keep enthusiasm and productivity higher for many participants than working in isolation. Team research can also provide training for inexperienced researchers and clinicians through modeling and direct exposure.

References

American Psychiatric Association. (1987). *Diagnostic and statistical manual of mental disorders* (rev. 3rd ed.). Washington, DC: Author.

Arkowitz, H., Holliday, S., & Hutter, M. (1982, November). *Depressed women and their husbands: A study of marital interaction and adjustment.* Paper presented at the meeting of the Association for the Advancement of Behavior Therapy, Los Angeles.

Beutler, L. E. (1983). *Eclectic psychotherapy: A systematic approach.* New York: Pergamon Press.

Beutler, L. E., Arizmendi, T. G., Crago, M., Shanfield, S., & Hagaman, R. (1983). The effects of value similarity and client persuasibility on value convergence and psychotherapy improvement. *Journal of Social and Clinical Psychology, 1,* 231–245.

Beutler, L. E., & Clarkin, E. (1990) *Systematic treat-*

ment and selection: Toward targeted therapeutic interventions. New York: Brunner/Mazel.

Beutler, L. E., Daldrup, R., Engle, R., Guest, P., Corbishley, A., & Meredith, K. (1988). Family dynamics and emotional expression among patients with chronic pain and depression. *Pain, 32,* 65–72.

Beutler, L. E., Daldrup, R. J., Engle, D., Oro-Beutler, M. E., Meredith, K., & Boyer, J. T. (1987). Effects of therapeutically induced affect arousal on depressive symptoms, pain and beta-endorphins among rheumatoid arthritis patients. *Pain, 29,* 325–334.

Beutler, L. E., Frank, M., Schieber, S. C., Calvert, S., & Gaines, J. (1984). Comparative effects of group psychotherapies in a short-term inpatient setting: An experience with deterioration effects. *Psychiatry, 47,* 66–76.

Beutler, L. E., Scogin, F., Kirkish, P., Schretlen, D., Corbishley, M. A., Hamblin, D., Meredith, K., Potter, R., Bamford, C. R., & Levenson, A. I. (1987). Group cognitive therapy and alprazolam in the treatment of depression in older adults. *Journal of Consulting and Clinical Psychology, 55,* 550–556.

Burgoon, J. K., Kelley, D. L., Newton, D. A., & Keeley-Dyreson, M. P. (1987, November) *The nature of arousal and nonverbal indices.* Paper presented at the annual meeting of the Speech Communication Association, Boston.

Calvert, S. J., Beutler, L. E., & Crago, M. (1988). Psychotherapy outcome as a function of therapist-patient matching on selected variables. *Journal of Social and Clinical Psychology, 6,* 104–117.

Corbishley, A., Hendrickson, R., Beutler, L. E., Engle, D., & Daldrup, R. J. (1988). *Behavior, affect and cognition among psychogenic pain patients in group expressive therapy.* Manuscript submitted for publication.

Daldrup, R. J., Beutler, L. E., Engle, D., & Greenberg, L. S. (1988). *Focused expressive psychotherapy: Freeing the overcontrolled patient.* New York: Guilford Press.

Dean, J. C., Meredith, D. E., & Beutler, L. E. (1989, June). *Development of a measure of receptivity-resistance to therapy.* Paper presented at the annual meeting of the Society for Psychotherapy Research, Toronto, Ontario, Canada.

Guest, P. D., & Beutler, L. E. (1988). Impact of psychotherapy supervision on therapist orientation and values. *Journal of Consulting and Clinical Psychology. 56,* 653–658.

Hill, D. C., Beutler, L. E., & Daldrup, R. (1989). The relationship of process to outcome in brief experiential psychotherapy for chronic pain. *Journal of Clinical Psychology, 45,* 951–956.

Kolb, D. L., Beutler, L. E., Davis, C. S., Crago, M., & Shanfield, S. B. (1985). Patient and therapy process variables relating to dropout and change in psychotherapy. *Psychotherapy, 22,* 702–710.

Lafferty, P., Beutler, L. E., & Crago, M. (1989). Differences between more and less effective psychotherapists: A study of select therapist variables. *Journal of Consulting and Clinical Psychology, 57,* 1–5.

Mohr, D. C., Shoham-Salomon, V., Engle, D., & Beutler, L. E. (1988, June). *Anger in focused expressive psychotherapy: Its measurement and role.* Paper presented at the meeting of the Society for Psychotherapy Research, Santa Fe, NM.

Sarason, I. G., Levine, H. M., Basha, R. B., & Sarason, B. R. (1983). Assessing social support: The Social Support Questionnaire. *Journal of Personality and Social Psychology, 44,* 127–138.

Schramski, T. G., Beutler, L. E., Lauver, P. J., Arizmendi, T. A., & Shanfield, S. B. (1984). Factors that contribute to posttherapy persistence of therapeutic change. *Journal of Clinical Psychology, 40,* 78–85.

Scogin, F., Hamblin, D., & Beutler, L. E.(1987). Bibliotherapy for depressed older adults: A self-help alternative *Gerontologist, 27,* 383–387.

Scogin, F., Hamblin, D., & Beutler, L. E. (1986). Validity of the cognitive error questionnaire with depressed and nondepressed older adults. *Psychological Reports, 59,* 267–272.

Siegel, J. M. (1986). The Multidimensional Anger Inventory. *Journal of Personality and Social Psychology, 51,* 119–200.

Yost, E., Beutler, L. E., Corbishley, A., & Allender, J. (1986). *Group cognitive therapy: A treatment approach for depressed older adults.* New York: Pergamon Press.

Zuckerman, M., DePaulo, B. M., & Rosenthal, R. (1986). Humans as deceivers and lie detectors. In P. D. Blanck, R. Buck, & R. Rosenthal (Eds.), *Nonverbal communication in the clinical context* (pp. 13–35). University Park: Pennsylvania State University Press.

12

The Process of Change: The Berkeley Psychotherapy Research Group

Enrico E. Jones, Sarah A. Hall, and Lesley A. Parke
University of California, Berkeley

Background and Aims

History

During the past decade, the focus of inquiry of the Berkeley Psychotherapy Research Group has evolved from an examination of the impact of demographic and social factors on psychotherapy outcome to the description and explication of the process and mechanisms of change in psychotherapy. This shift in our research from a more external focus (i.e., on such social markers as socioeconomic status, gender, age, ethnicity, and culture) to one that is more internal (i.e., centered on the psychology of the individual) has grown out of a series of empirical investigations demonstrating that the patient's psychological distress, characterological problems, and emotional conflicts are most predictive of treatment outcome.

A number of our early conceptual studies (Jones, 1974, 1982a, 1985b; Jones & Matsumoto, 1982) challenged the notion that psychological treatments, and in particular expressive psychotherapies, are ineffective with people who are economically disadvantaged or members of minority groups. Being based on a careful reconsideration of previous research as well as on our empirical investigations (Jones, 1978, 1982b), these studies underscore the fact that socioeconomic status and culture are highly unreliable predictors of therapy outcome. Demographic categories are not psychological variables; they include individuals

with a wide range of problems and do not inform us about personality structure, psychological conflict, or aspirations and goals in therapy. An important theoretical study (Jones & Thorne, 1987) critically examined proposed solutions to problems in intercultural assessment, such as the construction of new norms for conventional measures or the development of new, culture-specific instruments. We argue that in intercultural assessment a comprehension of the direct experience of the subject is essential for understanding what psychological assessments yield, and we have explored strategies for gaining access to the subjective experience of the patient by obtaining introspective, narrative accounts during various phases of the assessment procedure.

In addition to investigating the association between ethnic status and therapeutic outcome, we directed research efforts at another demographic variable: gender. In two large-sample studies on the effects of gender in psychotherapy (Jones & Zoppel, 1982) we found that female therapists rated their treatments as having been more successful, particularly with female patients. Further corroborating this finding, posttherapy interviews demonstrated that patients, regardless of gender, agreed that female therapists formed more effective therapeutic alliances. Nevertheless, both male and female patients of male therapists reported significant improvement as a result of therapy. Our results suggested that although therapist gender does show some effect on psychotherapy, the term *sex bias* does not do justice to the complexity of the impact of gender in psychotherapies.

Overall Aims

The limited discoveries yielded by studies that focused simply on demographic variables began to direct our attention to the nature of the therapist-patient interaction itself. The problem of how to go about investigating the actual process of psychotherapy led to the construction of the psychotherapy process Q set (Jones, 1985a), which is designed to provide a basic language for the description and classification of the therapy process in a form suitable for quantitative analysis. This instrument, which is described more fully later has become the fulcrum on which our subsequent research has been based.

A crucial question for psychotherapy research is the association between process and outcome. Since its inception the field has been preoccupied with demonstrating the efficacy of psychotherapies, and comparatively little has been done in the way of systematically describing the processes of psychotherapy and how they lead to particular outcomes. Recently the study of process has begun in earnest. The question is no longer whether psychotherapy is effective but how and why change occurs. Many methodological and conceptual problems beset formal investigations of this sort, however. The psychotherapy process Q set provides a promising response to some of the dilemmas currently facing the field of process research.

Method

During the last several years, the psychotherapy process Q set has enabled us to investigate a number of issues of central importance to the field of psychotherapy research: the description of the therapeutic process, the relation of process to outcome, and the analysis of change or evolution in the therapy process over time. The Q set comprises three types of items: items describing patient attitudes, behavior, or experience; items reflecting the therapist's actions and attitudes; and items attempting to capture the nature of the interaction in the dyad, or the climate or atmosphere of the encounter. A manual (Jones, 1985a) details instructions for Q sorting and provides the items and their definitions along with examples

to minimize potentially varying interpretations. The Q method requires judges to sort the 100 items into nine piles ranging from least characteristic (Category 1) to most characteristic (Category 9). Q items sorted into the middle pile (Category 5) are characterized as either neutral or irrelevant for the particular therapy hour being rated. The number of cards to be sorted into each pile conforms to a normal distribution, which requires judges to make multiple evaluations among items, thus avoiding either positive or negative halo effects.

The Q sort is an *ipsative* method; that is, the items are ordered in a unique case from those most characteristic of the person or situation being described to those least characteristic. The distinctiveness of this procedure is perhaps best understood by contrasting it to the more conventional *normative* mode of scaling, in which comparisons are made between individuals on some dimension of variation. On an ipsative scale the following question is posed "Is Mr. A more anxious or resistant than he is insightful?" On a normative scale, the question would be as follows: "Is Mr. A more psychologically minded than Mr. B?" The special values of the Q method are that it provides a way of quantifying the qualitative data of a therapy interaction and that it can capture the uniqueness of each case while also permitting the assessment of the similarities or dissimilarities between cases (see J. Block, 1961; J. H. Block & Block, 1980).

Psychometric Properties of the Process Q Set

A number of studies have examined the reliability and validity of the psychotherapy process Q set. In each case, the Q set has consistently demonstrated high levels of interrater reliability, item reliability, and test-retest reliability (Jones, Cumming, & Pulos, in press). The 100 items in the Q set are more or less independent measures of specific process variables. The relatively large number of items increases the possibility of a Type I error (finding a relation in a sample that is not true in the population). Although techniques exist for minimizing Type I errors, such procedures increase the probability of a Type II error (dismissing a relation observed in the sample as a result of chance when a real relation does exist in the population). We are not inclined to impose stringent controls for Type I errors because we prefer to avoid the premature rejection of potentially important associations that might otherwise be lost to subsequent investigation. A relatively liberal set of selection criteria can be balanced by certain safeguards, such as replication, aggregations over time, statistical significance levels, magnitude of variance accounted for, and thematic replications in which emphasis is given to items that fit theoretically meaningful patterns. Most univariate and multivariate techniques may be used in analyses of the psychotherapy Q set if such safeguards are adopted. The instrument permits unusual flexibility in terms of research designs and data analytic strategies, including the usual group comparisons or nomothetic designs (in which Q ratings of groups of hours are compared) as well as idiographic or $N = 1$ designs. The possibility of moving between these two kinds of research strategies with the process Q set allows the testing of hypotheses of various degrees of specificity.

The Q Set in Relation to Issues in Process Research

As a method for the systematic inquiry into the therapy process, the psychotherapy process Q set attempts to address a number of problems confronted by all process researchers: decisions regarding the size of the unit of analysis, temporal range and content domain, level of inference, and the problematic role of theory. In the section that follows, the process Q set is discussed in terms of how it addresses these crucial issues or decision points.

Unit of measurement. A longstanding question for process research has been the level or size of the unit for analysis. Level or unit of analysis refers to the degree of generality or specificity of the material to be examined. The unit chosen—whether it is a vocal quality, utterance, problem area, or phase of treatment—depends on the construct or the particular research question being investigated. Some studies have selected units at the micro level, such as patient vocal quality, whereas others have investigated macro level units, such as the therapeutic alliance (which refers to a wide range of therapist and patient behaviors). This has made it difficult to compare findings from different studies and to draw general conclusions from process research. By contrast, the psychotherapy process Q items represent a language that, like all idioms, contains multiple size descriptors. The purposes of such a

system are to avoid merely signifying the presence or absence of a particular event and thereby to achieve a comprehensive and clinically meaningful description of the therapy process. The Q set provides, then, a language that readily allows us to compare our results with those of other studies, regardless of whether these studies use more specific or more general units.

Temporal range. Most process rating scales use 4–10 minute segments of therapy hours, and judges are asked to rate a dimension of presumed relevance on the basis of relatively brief impressions. These data typically are aggregated without consideration of meaningful factors of timing and context. It has become increasingly clear that aggregate data analyses that use rates, frequencies, or ratios of units across time segments cannot capture change processes. Aggregations obliterate the context; it is the patterning of variables more than their simple occurrence that indicates the therapeutic significance of what is occurring. With the Q technique an entire treatment hour, not just a small segment, is rated. The therapy hour might be termed a *natural time frame*; it is a segment of time that has practical utility for researchers as well as inherent meaning for clinicians and patients. Moreover, the process Q set can be used to study either single hours or samples or blocks of treatment hours, making possible the empirical investigation of treatment phases that have thus far only been described clinically. Psychotherapy has typically been researched as if it were static rather than "in motion" despite the fact that the natural framework for the observation of process would appear to be longitudinal (i.e., one that takes into account time and the effect of previous hours on succeeding hours).

Content domain. Because there are a number of theories of therapy and the process of change, there is no one system that includes the complete array of therapist and patient behaviors that might be considered important in psychotherapy. Some filter is needed to select units from the nearby infinite number of attributes that can be used to describe the therapy process. The items included in the Q set represent an empirical selection from a pool of several hundred items garnered from already existing process measures as well as new items constructed by research-oriented clinicians. Pilot ratings were conducted on videotapes and audiotapes of psychotherapies representing a wide range of theoretical orientations, including client-centered, gestalt, rational-emotive, psychodynamic, and cognitive-behavioral. New items were constructed where necessary. Items were eliminated if they showed little variation over a wide range of subjects and therapy hours, were redundant, or had low interrater reliability. The final version of the Q set describes a broad range of therapeutic phenomena capturing relevant and salient events in the domain of psychotherapy process.

Level of inference. Closely related to choices of unit of analysis, temporal range, and content domain is the problem of level of inference in process research. As research moves from micro to macro levels of analysis; there is typically a greater need to rely on inferential judgment; problems arise when such judgments are informal, implicit, or intuitive. The process Q set manual addresses this problem with explicit rules governing raters' use of inference. The Q items themselves, as defined in the manual, are anchored to behavioral and linguistic cues that can be identified in recordings of hour. The use of abstract terms or jargon is avoided whenever possible. For example, clinical judges are not asked to identify the presence or absence of a "dysfunctional cognition" in the patient's mind; instead, they are asked to notice whether the therapist corrects a distortion that patient holds about reality.

The role of theory. A persistent dilemma in the field of psychotherapy process research concerns the extent to which investigations should be theory driven, or at least tied to theoretical constructs. Investigators who accept different paradigms vary a great deal in the concepts that they use and in their descriptive language; indeed, they may not even consider the same dimensions. Pantheoretical instruments are needed that can be applied to therapies representing different theoretical orientations. The psychotherapy process Q items were written, as far as possible, in theoretically neutral form. Although a broad interpersonal orientation underlies the Q set, the items themselves are not committed to a special theoretical stance, so that formulations can be derived from the Q items that are compatible with different theoretical viewpoints.

Q items can be used validly and reliably to distinguish among different treatment modalities. In a test of discriminant validity, a videotape of three therapy sessions conducted with the same patient by well-known proponents of their respective treatment forms (Albert Ellis, Fritz Perls, and Carl Rogers) were rated by 10 therapists with various theoretical orientations and a range of experience. Fifty-two Q items were found to differentiate rational-emotive from gestalt therapy, 47 items distinguished rational-emotive from client-centered therapy, and 38 items differentiated client-centered from gestalt therapy. The 10 items designated most and least characteristic for each form of therapy were then presented to another group of five therapists familiar with these treatment modalities, who successfully matched ($p <$ .001) the sets of Q items with the type of therapy from which they had been derived (Pulos & Jones, 1987). This "back translation" of the Q set indicates that the instrument distinguished among treatment modalities not only in terms of statistical significance but also in a manner that accurately captured the nature of the theoretical orientations represented.

Psychotherapy process is obviously complex and multidimensional. Measures of sufficient complexity to reflect adequately the phenomena that they are attempting to assess—instruments that can tap configurations, patterns, or interrelationships in process—must be developed. It is imperative that clinicians move beyond the unidimensional and static approaches to the measurement of process that have been used thus far to methodologies that instead allow for the discovery of associations or relationships among various aspects of therapy.

Findings

Recently we have focused on the systematic examination of factors contributing to successful outcome in diverse treatment modalities. Treatments of various types and lengths have been studied, including crisis intervention (Jones, Wynne, & Watson, 1986; Shonkoff & Jones, 1982), brief dynamic psychotherapies (Jones, Cumming, & Horowitz, 1988; Jones, Krupnick, & Kerig, 1987; Jones, Parke, & Pulos, in press; Soo-Hoo, Jones, & Pulos, 1988), and an intensive investigation of a single psychoanalytic case (Jones & Windholz, 1990). Emprical and conceptual studies addressing method and measurement problems reflect our abiding interest in these issues (Jones, 1980; Jones & Pulos, 1987).

In this section we highlight some of the findings from studies that have involved the application of the psychotherapy process Q sort to records of actual therapy hours. The first study, which applied the process Q set to explore gender effects in psychotherapy (Jones et al., 1987), both extended and concluded our series of investigations on patient demographic characteristics and psychotherapy. Pretherapy and posttherapy assessments showed that patients treated by female therapists experienced a significantly greater degree of symptomatic improvement and reported more satisfaction with treatment than those treated by male therapists. The magnitude and pervasiveness of therapist gender effects on outcome was, however, modest. Patient age accounted for twice, and patient pretreatment level of disturbance more than three times, the outcome variance explained by gender. This finding is consistent with several major psychotherapy outcome studies (e.g., Luborsky et al., 1980), which conclude that the single best predictor of posttherapy adjustment is the patient's initial level of personality functioning. Despite the modest outcome effects, the Q data revealed that female therapists were judged to arouse less negative affect in female patients and seemed to encounter fewer interpersonal difficulties. Even so, our findings did not support the notion that what occurs in therapy is simply a recapitulation of stereotypic sex-role dynamics between men and women.

Another study (Jones et al., 1988) examined the effects of therapist actions and techniques and patient behaviors and attitudes on psychotherapy outcome. Forty patients diagnosed as having stress-response syndromes after a traumatic event or a bereavement were treated in a brief (12–session) psychodynamic psychotherapy. Transcripts of therapy hours from each of the cases were rated with the Q set. Results demonstrated that an expressive approach was associated with better outcomes among less disturbed patients and that a more supportive stance on the part of the therapist correlated with more successful outcomes with more disturbed patients. The study suggests that patient change is more complex than the nonspecific hypothesis of therapeutic effectiveness implies. Previous failures to identify consistent correlations between specific aspects of process and treatment outcomes seem to be a product of the attempt to find simple, direct associations to the neglect of more complex research conceptualizations of process that adequately reflect the interaction of multiple influences in clinical treatments.

A second study derived from the same data set (Soo-Hoo et al., 1988) examined the therapeutic alliance construct by investigating the relationship between Q ratings and ratings made with the Vanderbilt Therapeutic Alliance Scale (VTAS). Consistent with findings of other studies (e.g., Hartley, Strupp, 1983), therapeutic alliance scores did not predict outcome. What, we asked, is this scale measuring? We found that 28 Q items correlated significantly with the VTAS; furthermore, a stepwise multiple regression yielded 3 Q items that explained 69% of the variance on the VTAS. The single biggest predictor, the Q item "Patient feels understood by the therapist," accounted for 51% of the variance. The remaining two items, "The patient is committed to the work of therapy" and "The therapist is responsive and affectively involved," accounted for 18% of the variance. Additional analyses showed that the patient's feeling understood was predicted by Q items such as "Therapist's own emotional responses do not intrude into the relationship" and "Therapist conveys a sense of nonjudgmental acceptance." This kind of "unpacking" of the therapeutic alliance by means of the Q set suggests that therapeutic alliance can be considered an interactive product of what has transpired between patient and therapist.

In another investigation of brief psychotherapy, we studied the treatments of 30 patients diagnosed as having a range of neurotic disorders who were treated in 16–session psychodynamic therapies (Jones, Parke, & Pulos, in press). Transcripts of the 1st, 5th, and 14th therapy hours were rated with the psychotherapy process Q set. Results confirmed the special role of some technical features commonly considered essential for successful brief treatments, particularly transference interpretations and a focus on the therapy relationship, attention to defensive maneuvers and the reformulation of patients' in-therapy behavior, and an emphasis on the patient's affective experience. In general, these treatments were characterized by what might be described as a gradual shift from an outer focus (an external, reality-oriented construction of personal difficulties and problems in relationships) to an inner focus (on intrapsychic issues and on the relationship with the therapist).

An intensive investigation of a single psychoanalytic case (Jones & Windholz, 1990) has served as our prototype for the study of single-case and long-term treatments. Blocks of 10 sessions of 6-year analysis were selected at regular intervals over the course of the treatment, and transcripts of these hours were rated in randomized order with the process Q set. Consistent with theoretical and clinical expectations, the patient's discourse over time became less intellectualized and dominated by rational thought, became more reflective, and showed a greater access to emotional life and a developing capacity for free association. With time, too, the analyst became increasingly active in challenging the patient's understanding of an experience or event, in identifying recurrent patterns in her life experience or behavior, in interpreting defenses, and in emphasizing feelings that the patient considered wrong, dangerous, or unacceptable. The results of the study demonstrate that the intensive investigation of the single case serves as an important complement to group comparison designs and in the study of process.

Research Programs in Progress

The efforts of the Berkeley Psychotherapy Research Group are currently focused on a study of process in brief (16-session) cognitive-behavioral therapy. The research is based on archival records for 32 depressed outpatients, 16 of whom were treated with cognitive-behavioral therapy and 16 with cognitive-behavioral therapy plus antidepressants (Hollon, DeRubeis, Evans, Tuason, Weimer, & Garvey, 1983). Patients receiving therapy and antidepressant medication showed slightly greater (although nonsignificant) improvement than those receiving therapy alone. Of the entire patient sample, 44% demonstrated clinically significant improvement on two of three symptom change measures (a conservative estimate of patient change). Q ratings of treatment hour transcripts showed few differences in the nature of the therapy process between treatment groups, suggesting that antidepressant medication had little effect on the nature of patients' involvement in the therapy process. Q correlates of outcome suggest that treatment-specific techniques as well as more general relationship factors contributed to successful outcome (Jones, Pulos, & Tunis, 1989).

We are also conducting a comparison of our brief psychodynamic therapy and brief cognitive-behavioral therapy data sets with the process Q set. The former treatment sample consists of 30 patients, the latter 32; treatments in both modalities were 16 sessions in length. Q ratings were conducted for the 1st, 5th, and 14th sessions for all patients in both modalities. Of 100 Q items 61 significantly distinguished psychodynamic and cognitive-behavioral treatments, with almost all of these differences being in the direction that would have been predicted on the basis of familiarity with the treatment types (e.g. "Discussion centers on cognitive themes, i.e., about ideas and

belief systems" and "Therapist is neutral" were more descriptive of cognitive-behavioral and dynamic treatments, respectively). The Q items that did not distinguish the two treatment modalities were also noteworthy (e.g., "Therapist is sensitive to the patient's feelings, attuned to patient; empathic" and "Therapist conveys a sense of nonjudgmental acceptance"). These results begin to address an important question for the field today: What features are specific to a treatment type, and what factors are common across modalities? These data also demonstrate the Q set's capacity to function as a discriminator between types of therapy process and to contribute toward providing a language for operationalizing what is currently being referred to as *psychotherapy integration*.

Programs Planned for the Future

A new project is being launched that extends the investigation of therapy process and outcome to an as yet insufficiently studied treatment modality: long-term, intensive, dynamic psychotherapy. This new direction represents an effort to develop measures and procedures for the study of long-term therapies. It aims (a) develop a manual for the conduct of long-term dynamic treatments with a specified patient population; (b) develop treatment outcome measures that move beyond assessing symptom improvement and toward assessing what might be termed *change in psychologic structure*; and (c) begin to accumulate an archive of recorded long-term dynamic treatments. The manual will be empirically grounded; that is, it will be derived from empirical descriptions of the therapy process in actual treatments obtained through the application of the psychotherapy process Q set. Patients meeting Research Diagnostic Criteria for a major depressive disorder are being seen in an intensive dynamic psychotherapy consisting of two sessions per week over a 24-month period. Treatments will be conducted at the Psychology Clinic at the University of California, Berkeley. Extensive initial as well as ongoing evaluations will be conducted with an emphasis on obtaining individualized repeated outcome measures. Each treatment will be videotaped in its entirety.

Q ratings of therapy hours over the treatment course will provide the empirical and descriptive base for a treatment manual that will begin to define psychodynamic treatments with such patients. In addition, these data will allow the intensive analysis of each case in a manner that can address the question of individual differences in response to treatment. These same treatments will also generate initial data concerning the construct and convergent validity of new methods for assessing nonsymptom change in patients that we have already begun to evaluate in pilot studies: the Inventory of Psychological Functioning, which is an observer rating measure (Hall, 1989); and text analysis (Mergenthaler, 1985) of the patient-therapist discourse, which is aimed at discovering change in patients' language or use of speech reflecting shifts in modes of experiencing, patterns of affective response, and reflexive forms of cognition.

Nature of the Research Organization

Team Members

The Berkeley Psychotherapy Research Group is directed by Enrico E. Jones, Professor of Psychology. The research team comprises members of the Department of Psychology at the University of California, Berkeley, graduate students in Berkeley's clinical psychology program, and research-oriented psychotherapists in private practice. Current members include Janice Cumming, PhD, research psychologist; Sara A. Hall, MA, research assistant; Lisa Marchitelli, research assistant; Georgine Marrott, PhD, adjunct lecturer in psychology; Lesley A. Parke, MA, research assistant; Steven M. Pulos, PhD, research psychologist; and Sandra Tunis, PhD, postdoctoral scholar.

Funding Sources

Our research program has received support from various sources throughout the years, most importantly from the National Institute of Mental Health (NIMH). The early work on the role of patient social and demographic characteristics in psychotherapy was in part supported by NIMH Grant 2-RO1-MH26104 (psychological studies of minority mental health, 1974–1977), NIMH Grant 2-RO1-MH3311 (1979–1980), and Grant 1-RO1-MH38348 (gender and psychotherapy: studies of process and outcome, 1983–1985). More recent investigations of the psychotherapy process have been supported by NIMH Grant 1-RO1-MH3848 (comparative studies of psychotherapy process, 1985–1990). Biomedical research

support grants administered intramurally by the University of California, Berkeley, permitted the undertaking of pilot research and provided continuity during the periods when NIMH support was not available (1979–1980, 1982–1983, and 1988–1989).

Relation to Other Research Programs

Collaborative Arrangements With Other Investigators

The research on psychotherapy process that we have undertaken in the last years has relied on collaborative arrangements with other research groups who have provided us with records of psychotherapies. Mardi Horowitz, MD, and his colleagues at the Center for the Study of Neuroses, Langley Porter Psychiatric Institute, University of California, San Francisco, granted access to a large archive of treatments of stress-response disorders. George Silberschatz, PhD, and John Curtis, PhD, of the Mount Zion Psychotherapy Research Project in San Francisco provided their archive of brief psychodynamic treatments. Steve Hollon, PhD, shared the treatment records of a sample of cognitive-behavioral therapies. Much of the work of the Berkeley group would not have been possible without the collaborative support of these other research programs.

Impact on the Field of Psychotherapy

Investigations of the relation between treatment process and outcome have encountered formidable difficulties, such that compelling associations between dimensions of process and treatment efficacy have yet to be adduced. The significance of the ongoing work of the Berkeley Psychotherapy Research Group lies in its programmatic effort to further understanding about the relation between process and outcome in diverse treatment modalities. Insufficient attention has been given to developing a valid descriptive methodology for psychotherapy research or to the explication of how and why change occurs (Greenberg, 1986). What is needed are efforts that will systematically identify, describe, and explain change processes through investigations in which associations between variables (technique or relationship) and outcome are examined. The psychotherapy process Q set reflects an advance in process research methodology. Our investigative efforts have begun to link dimensions of process to outcome in both cognitive-behavioral and brief dynamic psychotherapies in a multidimensional and context-sensitive fashion by exploiting the Q set's ability to tap simultaneously aspects of treatment alliance, technique, and interactional dimensions of process. Future plans lay the groundwork for extending this descriptive effort to include long-term dynamic psychotherapies, which have barely begun to be studied. This new effort will allow us to investigate similarities and differences between long-term treatments and brief treatments and to address the question of whether similar therapist actions lead to corresponding effects in different modalities. The development of new methods for assessing non-symptomatic patient change and of a treatment manual for the long-term dynamic therapy of depression represent important innovative approaches to the study of psychotherapy.

References

Block, J. (1961). *The Q-sort method in personality assessment and research.* Springfield, IL: Charles C Thomas.

Block, J. H., & Block, J. (1980). The role of ego-control and ego-resiliency in the organization of behavior. In W. A. Collings (Ed.), *Minnesota Symposia on Child Psychology* (Vol. 13, pp. 39–101). Hillsdale, NJ: Erlbaum.

Greenberg, L. S. (1986). Research strategies. In L. S. Greenberg & W. M. Pinsof (Eds.), *The psychotherapeutic process: A research handbook* (pp. 707–734). New York: Guilford Press.

Hall, S. A. (1989). *The Inventory of Psychological Functioning: An observer rating scale for patient change.* Unpublished manuscript, University of California, Berkeley.

Hartley, D. E., & Strupp, H. H. (1983). The therapeutic alliance: Its relationship to outcome in brief psychotherapy. In M. Masling (Ed.), *Empirical studies of psychoanalytic theories* (pp. 1–27). Hillsdale, NJ: Analytic Press.

Hollon, S. D., DeRubeis, R. J., Evans, M. D., Tuason, V. B., Weimer, M. J., & Garvey, M. J. (1983, December). *Cognitive therapy, pharmacotherapy, and combined cognitive pharmacotherapy in the treatment of depression: Differential outcome.* Paper presented at the 16th Annual Meeting of the Association for the Advancement of Behavior Therapy, Washington, DC.

Jones, E. E. (1974). Social class and psychotherapy: A critical review of research. *Psychiatry, 37,* 307–320.

Jones, E. E. (1978). The effects of race on psychotherapy process and outcome: An exploratory investigation. *Psychotherapy: Theory, Research and Practice, 15,* 226–236.

Jones, E. E. (1980). Multidimensional change in psychotherapy. *Journal of Clinical Psychology, 36,* 544–547.

Jones, E. E. (1982a). Minority mental health: Perspectives. In E. E. Jones & S. J. Korchin (Eds.), *Minority mental health* (pp. 3–36). New York: Praeger.

Jones, E. E. (1982b). Psychotherapists' impressions of treatment outcome as a function of race. *Journal of Clinical Psychology, 38,* 722–731.

Jones, E. E. (1985a). *Manual for the psychotherapy process Q-set.* Unpublished manuscript, University of California, Berkeley.

Jones, E. E. (1985b). Psychotherapy and counseling with black clients. In P. Pederson (Ed.), *Handbook for cross-cultural counseling and therapy* (pp. 173–179). Westport, CT: Greenwood.

Jones, E. E., Cumming, J. D., & Horowitz, M. J. (1988). Another look at the nonspecific hypothesis of therapeutic effectiveness. *Journal of Consulting and Clinical Psychology, 56,* 48–55.

Jones, E. E., Cumming, J. D., & Pulos, S. (in press). The psychotherapy process Q-set: Applications in single case research. In N. Miller, L. Luborsky, J. Barber, & J. Docherty (Eds.), *Handbook of psychodynamic research and treatment.* New York: Basic Books.

Jones, E. E., Krupnick, J. L., & Kerig, P. K. (1987). Some gender effects in a brief psychotherapy. *Psychotherapy, 24,* 336–352.

Jones, E. E., & Matsumoto, D. R. (1982). Psychotherapy with the underserved: Recent developments. In L. R. Snowden (Ed.), *Reaching the underserved: Mental health needs of neglected populations* (pp. 207–228). Beverly Hills, CA: Sage.

Jones, E. E., Parke, L. A., & Pulos, S. M. (in press). How therapy is conducted in the private consulting room: A multivariate description of brief dynamic treatments. *Psychotherapy Research.*

Jones, E. E., Pulos, S. M. (1987). *On process research in psychotherapy.* Unpublished manuscript, University of California, Berkeley.

Jones, E. E., Pulos, S. M., & Tunis, S. (1989). *Cognitive-behavioral therapy for depression: An empirical description of the therapy process.* Unpublished manuscript, University of California, Berkeley.

Jones, E. E., & Thorne, A. (1987). Rediscovery of the subject: Intercultural approaches to clinical assessments. *Journal of Consulting and Clinical Psychology, 55,* 488–495.

Jones, E. E., & Windholz, M. J. (1990). The psychoanalytic case study: Toward a method of systematic inquiry. *Journal of the American Psychoanalytic Association, 38,* 985–1009.

Jones, E. E., Wynne, M. F., & Watson, D. D. (1986). Client perception of treatment in crisis intervention and longer-term psychotherapies. *Psychotherapy, 23,* 120–132.

Jones, E. E., & Zoppel, C. L. (1982). Impact of client-therapist gender on psychotherapy process and outcome. *Journal of Consulting and Clinical Psychology, 50,* 250–272.

Luborsky, L., Mintz, J., Auerbach, A., Christoph, P., Bachrach, H., Todd, T., Johnson, M., Cohen, M., & O'Brien, C. P. (1980). Predicting the outcome of psychotherapy: Findings of the Penn Psychotherapy Project. *Archives of General Psychiatry, 37,* 480–491.

Mergenthaler, E. (1985). *Textbank systems: Computer science applied in the field of psychoanalysis.* New York: Springer-Verlag.

Shonkoff, A. D., & Jones, E. E. (1982). Hot-line volunteer response to moments of distress. *Crisis Intervention, 11,* 85–96.

Pulos, S. M., & Jones, E. E. (1987, May). *A study of the differential validity of the psychotherapy process Q-set.* Paper presented at the 67th Annual Convention of the Western Psychological Association, San Diego.

Soo-Hoo, T., Jones, E. E., & Pulos, S. M. (1988, June). *An empirical investigation of the therapeutic alliance construct.* Paper presented at the Society for Psychotherapy conference, Santa Fe, NM.

13

University of California, San Francisco Center for the Study of Neuroses: Program on Conscious and Unconscious Mental Processes

Mardi J. Horowitz and Charles Stinson
Langley Porter Psychiatric Institute

Background and Aims

Scientists collaborating in the University of California, San Francisco (UCSF), psychotherapy research program have as their shared goal the development of new theory, methods, and techniques having to do with intrapsychic, nonconscious variables of person schemas and control processes. It is anticipated that in the future psychotherapy will take a more integrative form that will include new methods of formulation and combined techniques. These new methods and techniques will seek to facilitate change in person schemas including role-relationship models, self-schemas and schemas of others, and control processes such as those that affect the conscious selection of alternatives among conflicting aims or purposes. This program takes both a psychodynamic and a cognitive perspective and aims toward the development of new theory that may direct methods of assessment and therapeutics in such directions.

The precursor of the present program was the Psychotherapy Evaluation and Study Center, established at UCSF in 1973, in the Langley Porter Psychiatric Institute. The Center for the Study of Neuroses was funded as a clinical research center by the National Institute of Mental Health (NIMH) from 1977 to 1984. It has been funded as the Program on Conscious and Unconscious Mental Processes by the John D. and Catherine T. MacArthur Foundation from 1983 onward. Mardi Horowitz, MD, directed these programs from their inception; before Charles Stinson, MD, was codirector, Nancy Kaltreider, MD, and Charles Marmar, MD, successively occupied that position.

The Psychotherapy Evaluation and Study Center focused on how people processed and adapted to recent traumatic events that had precipitated symptom formation. This focus led to research on the diagnosis and explanation of stress-response syndromes, which in turn contributed to development of the official diagnosis of posttraumatic stress disorder in the third edition of the *Diagnostic and Statistical Manual of Mental Disorders (DSM-III*; American Psychiatric Association,

The Center for the Study of Neuroses of the Langley Porter Psychiatric Institute is the open-door research center of the program on conscious and unconscious mental processes of the John D. and Catherine T. MacArthur Foundation.

1980) later in the 1970s (such a diagnosis was not included in the *DSM-II*). As a part of that effort, instruments were developed for the empirical assessment of the trajectory of change with persons who had the signs and symptoms of such disorders.

State theory (Horowitz, 1979, 1987), schema theory (Horowitz, 1988a), and control process theory (Horowitz, 1976, 1986, 1988a) led to new ideas about how to understand the assimilation of traumatic experiences. We developed some new techniques for brief psychotherapy specifically for stress-response syndromes that incorporated both cognitive and dynamic viewpoints (Horowitz, 1986; Horowitz, Marmar, Krupnick, et al., 1984).

Center research and subsequent international studies found this treatment to be effective. Research findings suggested an interaction of the level of self-organization and therapeutic process in leading to outcomes of better or worse symptom reduction (Horowitz, Marmar, Weiss, DeWitt, & Rosenbaum, 1984). The center became progressively more directed toward research to clarify mental processes, such as those having to do with self-organization, and research on control over which multiple self-schemas could organize how sequences of ideas and emotions might be represented consciously or communicated to others.

Currently, we focus on basic issues of conscious and unconscious mental processes involved in the formation and resolution of symptoms in persons with pathological grief and social phobia. In terms of phenomena, we have maintained a focal interest in intrusive representations of ideas and feelings, both in consciousness and in social communication, as well as the apparent opposite, that is, phenomena of omission of expectable ideas and feelings in conscious representation or communication.

Intrusions and omissions are special foci of interest because, in the psychotherapeutic context, these phenomena point to the topics of importance. By influencing the patient's regulatory functions, the therapist can help the patient reduce both intrusive breakthroughs of warded-off topics and excessive defensive avoidances of themes that are important to confront and make choices about to solve problems and to resolve conflicts.

Method

As mentioned, two psychopathological syndromes were selected for our current main study. One of

these two conditions is pathological grief, a type of event-related stress-response syndrome. According to person schemas theory, mourning progresses slowly because it involves change in durable and unconscious schemas of self and other. The death of a loved one permits a clear focus on a recent external situation as a partial cause of psychological events and suggests what topics of thought to follow in the exploration of mental reactions and changes in memories and fantasies over time (Horowitz et al., 1981; Windholz, Marmar, & Horowitz, 1985; Windholz, Weiss, & Horowitz, 1985).

The second condition is social phobia, one of the important anxiety disorders. In such conditions, anxiety in anticipating social interactions is often experienced as an unwanted, irrational reaction. In contrast to the situation with pathological grief, the inciting stressful event lies in the anticipated future. The theory, methods, and strategies developed in the study of pathological grief and social phobias potentially lead to new approaches to understanding and treating other conditions.

The choices for research in the center are recorded in the form of two agendas, one on person schemas, and the other on the control of ideas and feelings. Both agendas begin with efforts at theory formulation, move to the development of new methods, and end with potential changes in how psychological treatments of selected mental disorders may be conducted. The focus of both agendas is intrusions into or omissions from conscious representation of specific emotional topics and the conscious or unconscious control of this representation (Horowitz, 1988b).

Work on the initial stages of the center's agendas has led to evolving theory that each person has some means of regulating thought about the nearly limitless topics available for contemplation, that these thoughts are not equally accessible, and that this differential access is sometimes a consequence of certain schematized thoughts being more warded off in consciously or unconsciously purposive manners and not solely of unfamiliarity or nonspecific effects of information or arousal overload. More specifically, theory arising from the agenda on person schemas states that each person has repertoire of multiple self-schemas, differently accessible to consciousness, that function unconsciously in parallel-distributed processing to organize the implications of events.

Persons with either pathological grief or social phobia often describe anxious states of mind with consciously elaborated views of the self as weak, vulnerable, defective, and abandoned. These states of mind, organized by schemas of the self as weak, are often in striking contrast to stronger views of the self in other situations. Psychoanalytic contribution to this theory implies that persons in each condition sometimes have warded-off constellations of ideas and emotions organized by schemas of the self as too strong in which the activities or wishes of the self include envious, hostile, or competitive strivings that might harm another person.

Existing dynamic theory predicts that topics related to such schemas of the self as too strong might be the principal targets of inhibition at an unconscious level of induced control to prevent guilt. Warded-off schemas and topics might sometimes break through control processes, leading to symptomatic intrusive experiences. At other times, the control processes would prevent such dreaded states. Control processes might be used excessively, leading to maladaptive omission of contemplation or communication of important topics.

Patients with either condition, pathological grief or social phobia, often change during a brief psychotherapy. In the safety of a therapeutic relationship the person may reduce purposive unconscious controls or consciously override them, bringing forth to deliberate communication a topic that is usually intrusive or omitted. Such manifestations during the course of research therapy permit analysis of change in the interactions of schemas, ideas, emotions, and controls over time.

In considering such interactions, we have found that neither classical psychoanalytic theory nor cognitive theory provides explanatory foundations that are completely satisfactory for our purposes. Cognitive science has focused mainly on theory and empirical study of normal function of basic cognitive processes and less on pathology. Conversely, psychoanalytic theory has examined pathology in highly complex generalizations about the development of drives and defenses and has not taken advantage of important concepts of cognitive and neurobehavioral science.

Current cognitive theory offers powerful explanatory models about the elements of mental processing but at disparate levels, focusing on low-level processing and mostly without making a distinction between purposive conscious and unconscious processes. Consequently, intrusions and omissions would be considered meaningless noise and disorganized errors of a system overloaded by information or emotional state. On the other

hand, psychoanalytic theory provides powerful ideas to explain the clinically common observations that intrusions and omissions are rarely meaningless and often reveal important information: that the intrusive and omissive phenomena of psychopathology are not merely random. It does not, however, present a solid, mechanistic explanatory base about how functional cognitive operations do occur.

Our theoretical position incorporates concepts from cognitive science (e.g., parallel-distributed processing, neural net dynamics, schema theory, and especially person schemas theory) with psychoanalytic theory. The cognitive elements provide an infrastructure that can lead to important model building and empirical testing. The psychodynamic elements contribute nontrivial, clinically face-valid descriptions of intrapersonal and interpersonal dynamics. In a sense, whereas cognitive science has focused on representation of ideas *about* objects, psychodynamics has focused on the idea *as* object. Taking both together, it is possible to address the consequences not only of objects that are feared but also of ideas that are themselves feared. Processing that leads to unconscious anticipation of dreaded consequences of ideas or intentions may naturally give rise to purposive unconscious controls responsible for the formation of intrusions and omissions.

With this more powerful theory, we can reframe the concept of purposive unconscious control of conscious representation and make important contrasts with theories that do not posit the existence of such controls. Omissions may be due to active inhibitions rather than mere deficits in functioning resulting from system overload. Intrusions may be breakthroughs of purposive, motivated representations in spite of inhibitions rather than mere products of disinhibition resulting from fatigue. In other words, there can be more organization in the apparent disorganization of conscious experience than is accounted for by cognitive theory alone.

We expect one of the most potent factors influencing conscious and unconscious processing to be the instantiation of a dreaded schema of self or of self in relation to other. The psychodynamic contribution to our theory postulates that warded-off anger and guilt may result in intrusive symptoms in pathological grief and that warded-off envy and competitiveness may result in symptomatic omission of rational behavior in social phobia. If so, these too-strong person schema themes might be identified and related to the formulation and emergence of psychiatric signs and symptoms; the approach of these themes to consciousness would be accompanied by behavior, cognitive, and biologic sequelae of warding-off operations.

Our center is geared to search for and identify such cryptic organization to support or refute the construct of purposive unconscious processing in a joint psychodynamic and cognitive model. We use a battery of rating scales that cover not only the issue of specific and general symptoms but also areas of interpersonal functioning, self-appraisal, the development level of self-concept, and aspects of current concerns. General symptoms are recorded on a symptom checklist; specific symptoms are recorded on instruments such as the Impact of Event Scale (Horowitz, Wilner, & Alvarez, 1979; Zillberg, Weiss, & Horowitz, 1982) and the Stress Response Rating Scale (Weiss, Horowitz, & Wilner, 1984).

Process variables include measures of the therapeutic alliance (Foreman & Marmar, 1985; Marmar, Marziali, Horowitz, & Weiss, 1986) and the therapist's actions as well as the patient's actions during the therapy (Hoyt, Marmar, Horowitz, & Alvarez, 1981; Hoyt, Xenakis, Marmar, & Horowitz, 1983; Weiss, Marmar, & Horowitz, 1988; Xenakis, Hoyt, Marmar, & Horowitz, 1983). At present, new variables are being explored that have to do with shifts in state of mind, changes in control processes as assessed both verbally and nonverbally, and shifts in autonomic physiology (heart rate, skin temperature, and skin resistance, as now being measured on both therapist and patient; exceptional emotional expressions; and various measures having to do with the narrative topic at a given point in time).

We emphasize videotape and graphic display of variables as close to the time of taping as possible. This graphic display uses a PSYCLOPS system now under development (primarily by Stinson) that allows inspection of a large number of primary and secondary data sets relevant to issues of schemas, emotions, and controls. The system will include techniques for examining the temporal interaction of various variables, zooming in and out to see larger and smaller temporal segments of the data, and adjustable time lags to see possible order effects among variables over time.

Research Accomplishments

Findings

In the center there has been a successful demonstration of the validity of certain stress syndromes (Horowitz, 1976; Horowitz, Wilner, Kaltreider, & Alvarez, 1980), the efficacy of a brief dynamic treatment directed at these syndromes (Horowitz, Marmar, Krupnick, et al., 1984; Marmar, Horowitz, Weiss, Kaltreider, & Wilner, 1988), and evidence for cognitive processes that lead to symptom formation of these syndromes. The best summaries of these investigations are in the following books: *Stress Response Syndromes* (Horowitz, 1986), *States of Mind: Configurational Analysis of Individual Psychology* (Horowitz, 1987), and *Introduction to Psychodynamics: A New Synthesis,* (Horowitz, 1988a).

Instruments Developed

Important empirical instruments developed in our center include the Impact of Event Scale (Horowitz Wilner, & Alvarez, 1979; Zilberg, Weiss, & Horowitz, 1982), a life events questionnaire that is weighted for remoteness or recentness of events (Horowitz, Schaefer, & Cooney, 1974; Horowitz, Schaefer, Hiroto, Wilner, & Levin, 1977), a coping scale (Horowitz, & Wilner, 1980), the Stress Response Rating Scale (Horowitz, 1986; Weiss et al., 1984), a patient's state of mind segmentation (Horowitz, Marmar, & Wilner, 1979), a therapist action scale (Horowitz, Marmar, Krupnick, et al., 1984; Hoyt, Marmar, Horowitz, & Alvarez, 1981; Hoyt, Xenakis, Marmar, & Horowitz, 1983), the Therapeutic Alliance Scales (Marmar, Marziali, Horowitz, & Weiss, 1986; Marziali, Marmar, & Krupnick, 1981), patterns of individualized change scales (Horowitz, Marmar, Weiss, Kaltreider, & Wilner, 1986; Kaltreider, DeWitt, Lieberman, & Horowitz, 1981; Kaltreider, DeWitt, Weiss, & Horowitz, 1981; Weiss, DeWitt, Kaltreider, & Horowitz, 1985), a motivation scale (Rosenbaum & Horowitz, 1983), a difficulty scale (Rosenbaum, Horowitz, & Wilner, 1986), a dilemmas dictionary and scale (Horowitz, Rosenbaum, & Wilner, 1988), a positive states of mind scale (Horowitz, Adler, & Kegeles, 1988), clinical formulation consensus test (DeWitt, Kaltreider, Weiss, & Horowitz, 1982) and a role-relationships model configuration format (Horowitz, 1989).

Research Programs in Progress

Our program's principal hypothesis now involves the assumption of purposive unconscious control of conscious representation in interpersonal communications, including those that are pathological. In our convergent theoretical position we assume that as a conflictual strong schema becomes activated, schematic processing outside of the person's consciousness may anticipate entry into a dreaded state of mind or anticipate negative feedback from another person; controls of various sorts are activated to avoid entry into an undermodulated state of mind and its associated intense surges of negative emotions. These controls may range from conscious to unconscious alterations of schemas, associational networks, memories, emotions, modes of representation, and aspects of the social context.

Examples of possible dreaded, undermodulated states of mind may include disrupted processing capacity, as in cognitive theory; embarassment, as in social learning theory; and states of out-of-control impulses, as in psychodynamic theory. Our research oriented around this hypothesis and the convergence of its psychodynamic and cognitive science variance are organized by the two agendas already mentioned. The steps of these agendas are as follows.

Agenda on Person Schemas

Step 1: We explore cognitive and psychodynamic models of meaning structures and their effects on the organization and maintenance of views of self and other that may give rise to situationally discrepant behavior patterns.

Step 2: We identify, describe, and classify, with the use of existing models, selected clinically relevant phenomena including omissions and intrusions of conscious ideas and feelings about self and other.

Step 3: We systematically investigate person schemas and their relation to clinically relevant interpersonal behavior patterns that may be adaptive or maladaptive.

Step 4: We study intensively individuals with maladaptive interpersonal behavior patterns to investigate the stability and variability of the inferred person schemas.

Step 5: We explore the implications of person schema constructs for the classification and explanation of psychopathology.

Step 6: We develop long-range plans for using the person schema construct for the development of new intervention strategies.

Agenda on Control of Ideas and Feelings

Step 1: We examine and revise theories of defense and their relationship to conscious and unconscious control processes (Horowitz, 1988a; Singer, 1990).

Step 2: We monitor themes so that alterations in the thematic progression of communication can be studied. We link theories of control of themes and ideas to methods of measuring flow of topics and points in verbal and nonverbal communication.

Step 3: We study the sequential flow of emotional expressions in various verbal and nonverbal channels and develop theory about control over emotion communication and conscious experience.

Step 4: We examine the relation between emotional expression and thematic progression and seek to explain observed patterns in terms of control theory.

Step 5: We construct ways of altering control processes and studying the effects of those interventions on thematic progression and emotional expression.

Step 6: We explore the implications of revised control theory for the classification and explanation of psychopathology.

Step 7: We develop long-range plans for using the theory of control processes for development of new intervention strategies.

Nature of the Research Organization

Between 1977 and 1984, the program was funded as a clinical research center of NIMH. For 1984 to 1994 the center is funded as the Program on Conscious and Unconscious Mental Processes of the John D. and Catherine T. MacArthur Foundation. In addition, NIMH funds training of two postdoctoral fellows.

Extramural scientists are involved with the program through tasks forces on defenses, topics, and person schemas. The Defenses Task Force works to examine and revise theories of defense and their relationship to conscious and unconscious control processes. Plans call for these theoretical revisions to move toward a unified control theory focusing on regulation of mental set and person schemas. Integrations of traditional psychodynamic theory and newer cognitive methods are sought in the many conferences that characterize this program. The Defenses Task Force has also accepted the charge to develop the official position statement on defenses for the American Psychiatric Association for the *DSM-IV*. This task force now includes Michael Bond, MD; Steven Cooper, PhD; Bram Fridhandler, PhD (Chair); Mardi Horowitz, MD; J. Christopher Perry, PhD; and George Vaillant, MD.

The Topic Task Force aims at developing convergent methods for identifying and defining different topics in a two-person dialog and for defining which topics are more or less emotional, conflictual, or stressed. The purpose is to develop means to identify topics, measures of topic onset, measures of shifts in narrative mode, and ratings of the production or avoidance of information about a particular topic. This task force now includes Wilma Bucci, PhD; Roy D'Andrade, PhD; Mardi Horowitz, MD; Steven Reidbord, MD; Catherine Snow, PhD; Charles Stinson, PhD (chair); Dennie Wolf, PhD; Constance Millbrath, PhD; and Erhard Mergenthaler, PhD.

The aim of the Person Schemas Task Force is the assessment of person schemas and how they affect information processing, conscious representation, and social interaction, especially in dyad and triad groups. The task force aims to develop measures that can be used in designating where situationally discrepant behaviors occur on a videotape or in a narrative, the pattern involved, and how one might infer various self-concepts and interpersonal schemas that are wished, feared, warded off, or used to ward off some other more dreaded schema. The nucleus of this new force now includes Paul Crits-Christoph, PhD; Tracy Eells, PhD; Leonard Horowitz, PhD; Mardi Horowitz, MD; Lester Luborsky, PhD; Connie Milbrath, PhD (co-chair); Peter Salovey, PhD; Jerome Singer, PhD (co-chair); Susan Andersen, PhD; Daniel Hart), EdD; John Kihlstrom, PhD; and Zindel Seagel, PhD.

We maintain an open door research center where scientists from the task forces can come and go, focusing inspection on the same sets of recorded information provided and maintained by the center's staff. These scientists share membership on task forces, attend workshops, and correspond through electronic mail. The recordings of subjects expressing conflictual emotional themes in dynamic psychotherapy and probing research sessions are thus opened to scrutiny by persons who ordinarily do not have the ability to share such observations. Essential features of the center include having subjects give written informed consent to use such materials, using procedures to evoke frank expressions of usually private topics, maintaining archives that record such information as completely as possible, and developing support systems that foster centralized and collaborative efforts.

We record and collect time-coded video, audio, and other data for each evaluation, therapy, and research session of subjects. These data are merged for inspection and analysis. Our laboratories are continually renovated as we strive to develop the best methods to gather and maintain records. We have chosen to have a centralized, specialized support staff rather than, for example, research assistants assigned to particular scientists. Thus we have word processors, an audio-video specialist, archival-textual research associates, computer programmers, a statistical associate, a program manager, administrative assistants, and central clerical staff.

Resident scientists plan and conduct research in accordance with the agendas, with a particular focus on on-line approaches to the intensive study of single subjects. In addition, some resident scientists have administrative assignments that include liaison with visiting and consulting scientists and coordination of task forces and organization of workshops.

The task forces meet regularly. Scheduled annual joint meetings should prove interesting because the three task forces deal with different methods for the assessment of variables related to the hypothesis of unconscious warding-off operations and because all apply their approaches to the same cases from the open-door research center. These joint meetings of task forces will show where exciting progress has been made with our interesting archive of records and new variables.

The program will stage yearly didactic conferences with outreach to academic and clinical scientists. The expense of the conference itself is covered by our program budget. Invited audiences pay only their own travel and lodging. The conferences have two purposes: to use the intensively studied cases to teach emotional, cognitive, or neural science academic faculty about psychodynamically relevant phenomena and their possible explanation; and to use the same material to challenge psychodynamic clinicians with the evidence for and possibilities of new theories. Although the invitees will not be expected to present material in any formal way, ample time for discussion after careful presentation of the materials will be part of the design of such programs.

Training and collaborative work in the center have also led to important work by colleagues now in other programs. Marmar and Weiss are now developing a separate program for the study of Vietnam veterans and posttraumatic stress disorder, as well as those in psychotherapeutic treatment, at the San Francisco Veterans Administration Hospital. Weiss directs a NIMH training program for fellowships in psychotherapy research, which involves training in the present program at UCSF as well. Rosenbaum and Hoyt conduct research in the context of the Kaiser Foundation hospital system in Northern California.

Our program currently makes available long postdoctoral fellowships (up to 3 years) for persons already trained as clinicians to learn the complexities of psychotherapy and process research at the level of new basic variables such as those concerned with person schemas and control processes. There also is a funded position in the program for a senior cognitive scientist who has not previously had the experience of reviewing clinical records and who can bring advanced cognitive science perspectives into the arena of highly charged and conflictual emotional themes.

Participation in the task forces also involves this program with other universities. Transcription standards have been developed jointly by program researchers at UCSF and by Erhard Mergenthaler and colleagues at the University of Ulm. Joint studies on person schemas have involved scientists such as Lester Luborsky and Paul Crits-Christoph at the University of Pennsylvania and Jerome Singer and Peter Salovey at Yale University; work on the Defenses Task Force has involved scientists at UCSF with Harvard University's Christopher Perry and Steven Cooper, Michael Bond at the University of Montreal, and George Vaillant at Dartmouth University. Roy D'Andrade of UC San Diego, Gordon Bower, Kraemer and Spiegel of Stanford University, Steven Palmer of UC Berkeley, Robert Emde of the University of Colorado, Peter Knapp of Boston University, Matt Erdelye of Brooklyn College, Wilma Bucci of Adelphi University; Helena Kraemer of Stanford University, Ben Libet of UCSF, David Spiegel of Stanford University, and Charles Yingling of UCSF are among a larger list of scientists who have been involved with the program. These scientists are familiar enough with

the program that acquainted colleagues could discuss its possibilities with them.

References

DeWitt, K., Kaltreider, N., Weiss, D. S., & Horowitz, M. J. (1982). Judging change in psychotherapy: The reliability of clinical formulation. *Archives of General Psychiatry, 40,* 1121–1128.

Foreman, S. A., & Marmar, C. R. (1985). Therapist actions that address initially poor therapeutic alliances in psychotherapy. *American Journal of Psychiatry, 142,* 8.

Horowitz, M. J. (1976). *Stress response syndrome.* Northvale, NJ: Jason Aronson.

Horowitz, M. J. (1986). *Stress response syndromes* (2nd ed.). Jason Aronson. Northvale, NJ: Jason Aronson.

Horowitz, M. J. (1987). *States of mind: Configurational analysis of individual psychology* (2nd ed.). New York: Plenum Press.

Horowitz, M. J. (1988a). *Introduction to psychodynamics: A new synthesis.* New York: Basic Books.

Horowitz, M. J. (Ed.). (1988b). *Psychodynamics and cognition.* Chicago: University of Chicago Press.

Horowitz, M. J. (1989). *Nuances of techniques in dynamic psychotherapy.* Hillsdale, NJ: Jason Aronson.

Horowitz, M. J., Adler, N., & Kegeles, S. (1988). A scale for measuring the occurrence of positive states of mind. *Psychosomatic Medicine, 50,* 477–483.

Horowitz, M. J., Krupnick, J., Kaltreider, N., Wilner, N., Leong, A., & Marmar, C. (1981). Initial psychological responses to parental death. *Archives of General Psychiatry, 38,* 310–323.

Horowitz, M. J., Marmar, C., Krupnick, J., Wilner, N., Kaltreider, N., & Wallerstein, R. (1984). *Personality styles and brief psychotherapy.* New York: Basic books.

Horowitz, M. J., Marmar, C., Weiss, D., Dewitt, D., & Rosenbaum, R. (1984). Brief psychotherapy of bereavement reactions: The relationship of process to outcome. *Archives of General Psychiatry, 41,* 438–448.

Horowitz, M. J., Marmar, C., Weiss, D., Kaltreider, N., & Wilner, N. (1986). Comprehensive analysis of change after brief dynamic psychotherapy. *American Journal of Psychiatry, 143,* 582–589

Horowitz, M. J., Marmar, C., & Wilner, N. (1979). Analysis of patient states and state transitions. *Journal of Nervous and Mental Disease, 167,* 91–99.

Horowitz, M. J., Rosenbaum, R., & Wilner, N. (1988). Dilemmas of relationship: A new psychotherapy research process measure. *Psychotherapy, 25,* 241–248.

Horowitz, M. J., Schaefer, C., & Cooney, P. (1974). Life event scaling for recency of experience. In E. K. Gunderson & R. H. Rahe (Eds.) *Life stress and illness.* Springfield, IL: Charles C Thomas.

Horowitz, M. J., Schaefer, C., Hiroto, D., Wilner, N. & Levin, B. (1977). Life event questionnaire for measuring presumptive stress *Psychosomatic Medicine, 39,* 413–431.

Horowitz, M. J., & Wilner, N. (1980). Life events, stress, and coping. In L. Poon (Ed.), *Aging in the 80s* (pp.

363–374). Washington, DC: American Psychological Association.

Horowitz, M. J., Wilner, N., & Alvarez, W. (1979). The impact of event scale: A measure of subjective stress. *Psychosomatic Medicine, 41,* 209–218.

Horowitz, M. J., Wilner, N., Kaltreider, N., & Alvarez, W. (1980). Signs and symptoms of post-traumatic stress disorder. *Archives of General Psychiatry, 37,* 85–92.

Hoyt, M., Marmar, C., Horowitz, M. J., & Alvarez, W. (1981). The Therapist Action Scale and the Patient Action Scale: Instruments for the assessment of activities during dynamic psychotherapy. *Psychotherapy, Theory, Research and Practice, 18,* 109–116.

Hoyt, M., Xenakis, S., Marmar, C., & Horowitz, M. J. (1983). Therapists' actions that influence their perceptions of "good" psychotherapy sessions. *Journal of Nervous and Mental Disease, 171,* 400–404.

Kaltreider, N., DeWitt, K., Lieberman, R., & Horowitz, M. J. (1981). Individualized approaches to outcome assessment: A strategy for psychotherapy research. *Journal of Psychiatric Treatment Evaluation, 3,* 105–111.

Kaltreider, N., DeWitt, K., Weiss, D., & Horowitz, M. J. (1981). Patterns of individual change scales. *Archives of General Psychiatry, 38,* 1263–1269.

Marmar, C., Horowitz, M. J., Weiss, D., Kaltreider, N., & Wilner, N. (1988). A controlled trial of brief psychotherapy and mutual help group treatment of conjugal bereavement. *American Journal of Psychiatry, 145,* 203–209.

Marmar, C., Marziali, E., Horowitz, M. J., & Weiss, D. S. (1986). The development of the therapeutic alliance rating system. In L. Greenberg & W. Pinsof (eds.) *The psychotherapeutic process: A research handbook* (pp. 36–390). New York: Guilford Press.

Marziali, E., Marmar, C., & Krupnick, J. (1981). Therapeutic Alliance Scales: Development and relationship to psychotherapy outcome. *American Journal of Psychiatry, 138,* 3.

Rosenbaum, R., & Horowitz, M. J. (1983). Motivation for psychotherapy: A factoral and conceptual analysis. *Psychotherapy: Theory, Research, and Practice, 20,* 346–354.

Rosenbaum, R., Horowitz, M. J., & Wilner, N. (1986). Clinician assessment of patient difficulty. *Psychotherapy: Theory, Research, and Practice, 23,* 417–425.

Singer, J. (Ed.). (1990). *Repression and dissociation: Implications for personality theory, psychopathology, and health.* Chicago: University of Chicago Press.

Weiss, D., DeWitt, K., Kaltreider, N., & Horowitz, M. J. (1985). A proposed method for measuring change beyond symptoms. *Archives of General Psychiatry, 42,* 703–708.

Weiss, D., Horowitz, M. J., & Wilner, N. (1984). Stress Response Rating Scale: A clinician's measure. *British Journal of Clinical Psychology, 23,* 202–215.

Weiss, D., Marmar, C., & Horowitz, M. J. (1988). Do the ways in which psychotherapy process ratings are made make a difference: The effects of mode of presentation, segment and rating format on interrater reliability. *Psychotherapy, 25,* 44–50.

Windholz, M., Marmar, C., & Horowitz, M. J. (1985). Review of research on conjugal bereavement: Impact on health and efficacy of intervention. *Comprehensive Psychiatry, 26,* 433–447.

Windholz, M., Weiss, D., & Horowitz, M. J. (1985). An empirical study of the natural history of time limited psychotherapy for stress response syndromes. *Psychotherapy: Theory, Research, and Practice, 26,* 433–447.

Xenakis, S., Hoyt, M., Marmar, C., & Horowitz, M. J. (1983). Reliability of self reports by therapists using the Therapist Action Scale. *Psychotherapy: Theory, Research, and Practice, 20,* 314–320.

Zilberg, N. Weiss, D., & Horowitz, M. J. (1982). Impact of event scale: A cross validation study and some empirical evidence. *Journal of Consulting and Clinical Psychology, 50,* 407–414.

14

Prevention of Divorce and Marital Distress

Howard J. Markman and Scott M. Stanley
University of Denver

Frank J. Floyd
Michigan State University

Kurt Hahlweg
Max Planck Institute
Munich, Federal Republic of Germany

Susan Blumberg
University of Denver

Background and Aims

History

This program began 15 years ago when Markman, working along with John Gottman and Clifford Notarius at Indiana University, began investigating the causes of marital distress. The initial studies indicated that the quality of couples' communication clearly discriminated between distressed and nondistressed couples. In particular, distressed couples showed a tendency to escalate negatively during discussions of marital issues, whereas nondistressed couples were able to exit the beginning stages of negative interaction cycles (e.g., Gottman, Markman, & Notarius, 1977). On the basis of these early studies the group developed a treatment program for couples, summarized in *A Couple's Guide to Communication* (Gottman, Notarius, Gonzo, & Markman, 1976).

At the same time, Markman began a series of longitudinal studies to test the hypothesis that the communication variables that discriminated between distressed and nondistressed couples would predict the development of marital distress and divorce. Longitudinal studies were essential because of the possibility that the differences in communication between distressed and nondistressed couples were a result of distress caused by other factors, rather than communication itself being a significant etiological factor in the development of distress. The results of the longitudinal studies indicated that the quality of communication before marriage and before distress developed was one of the best predictors of future marital distress, with correlations ranging up to .60 between premarital communication quality and subsequent marital adjustment (Markman, 1981). On the basis of these earlier studies, Markman, Stanley, and Floyd developed an intervention program designed to prevent marital distress and divorce by teaching premarital couples the skills associated with marital success. From its inception the intervention program, called the

The research reported in this chapter is supported by National Institute of Mental Health Grant R02-MH35525.

Prevention and Relationship Enhancement Program (PREP), departed from earlier efforts in this area, which were based on armchair speculation and untested assumptions and had not documented any actual long-term preventive effects. Instead, we emphasized the necessity of an empirical foundation to describe the nature of the problem, to evaluate etiological factors, and to demonstrate the short- and long-term effectiveness of intervention strategies. To accomplish these objectives we began a program of longitudinal research to evaluate the possibilities for preventing marital discord and divorce as well as to identify the predictors of divorce and marital distress.

Overall Aims

Clearly, marital distress and family disruption are among the most far-reaching problems in this country, affecting all segments of society. At present rates, divorce and the resulting stress on spouses and children can be expected to occur for 50% of newlyweds in the United States (National Center for Health Statistics, 1987). Additionally, many other couples remain in stable but distressed relationships, living in varying degrees of stress and misery over long periods of time. Although there is empirical evidence that early signs of future marital distress are potentially identifiable in premarital interaction, the primary method of intervention with marital distress is to treat relationship problems after they have become severe enough for the couple to seek therapy, usually after there have already been negative effects on spouses and children. Even for those who seek help, research suggests that most couples in therapy usually become less distressed but not necessarily happy (Storaasli & Markman, in press).

The rationale for divorce prevention is similar to that of other forms of prevention in that efforts are directed toward teaching the competencies associated with successful adjustment before problems develop. We intervene during the planning-marriage period or the first year of marriage because during such transitions motivation to learn new skills is relatively high, and destructive interaction patterns have not yet solidified. Like the architects who prepared the San Francisco skyscrapers to survive the recent earthquake, we attempt to provide couples with foundations on which to build a successful marriage that is able to withstand and prepare for the ground swells of married life.

Intervention Program

PREP is designed to teach couples communication skills and ground rules for handling conflict and promoting intimacy. The program is described briefly here; a detailed description is given by Markman, Floyd, Stanley, and Lewis, 1986. PREP can be distinguished from marital therapy in that the goal is not the alleviation of current dysfunction, and it can be distinguished from marital relationship enhancement programs in that the central goal is not the enhancement of present functioning. Rather, the primary goal of PREP is to modify dimensions of couple functioning to help happy couples remain happy. Hence, couples are taught skills that they may not need so much now as later, such as how to exit constructively from interactions in which negative communication is escalating.

PREP is typically conducted in five sessions, each lasting approximately 2½ hours. Couples spend some time with other couples listening to lectures presented by the group leader, with the bulk of the session time being spent away from the group, practicing skills or discussing various issues with the aid of a consultant. Couples are given homework, including assignments to read from *A Couple's Guide to Communication* (Gottman et al., 1976).

In Sessions 1 and 2, couples are taught various communication skills, with the greatest focus being placed on the importance of proper listening and feedback for both accuracy in communication and validation of one another's viewpoints. In Session 3, couples are taught how to solve problems and disagreements. They learn how to monitor behaviors, to make specific requests for behavioral change, and to use skills such as brainstorming as problem-solving techniques. We seek to help couples develop a sense of relationship efficacy (Notarius & Vanzetti, 1984), that is to say confidence in their ability to handle problems that will inevitably arise in the future. The focus in Session 4 is on identifying and discussing major expectations for their partner, their relationship, and the institution of marriage (Sager, 1976). Couples also explore and discuss levels of relationship commitment and commitment to other areas of life (e.g., careers). The final session focuses on sensual and sexual education and enhancement as well as the general role and importance of fun in relationships. The program ends with couples agreeing on a set of ground rules that they will use to handle issues in their marriage.

Method

Subjects

The subjects for the longitudinal study are 135 couples planning their first marriage and 20 couples planning remarriage. Subjects were recruited through communitywide publicity offering couples who were planning marriage participation in three sessions over a 3–4 month period with the possibility of future involvement. Couples were not informed at this time about the option of participating in an intervention program. Couples were matched on variables predictive of divorce (Markman, 1981), and one or two couples from each matched set were randomly selected to be invited to participate in a premarital intervention program.

The PREP results we discuss summarized below are mainly for 21 couples who accepted and completed the program (the intervention group) and their matched counterparts (the control group; Storaasli & Markman, in press). Some of the results are from a larger sample of 33 PREP couples and 50 control couples (Markman, 1981). The demographic characteristics of the subsample of 42 subjects at Time 1 were as follows: months known, 30 (range = 4–84); age of women, 23 years (range = 18–31 years); age of men, 24 years (range = 18–32 years); years of education, 15.5 (range = 12–18); and personal income level, $10,500 (range = $5,000–$20,000+). Furthermore, the relationship satisfaction score was 123 (SD = 14.4), which places the group in the non-distressed range (Locke & Wallace, 1959). There were no significant differences between groups on these variables and no differences between the subsample and the larger sample.

Instruments

The following inventories were completed independently by both partners at each assessment point: the Marital Adjustment Test (Locke & Wallace, 1959), the Relationship Program Inventory (Knox, 1971), and the Sexual Satisfaction Inventory (Snyder, 1979). Two measures were designed to assess communication skills and deficits, representing "insiders" (couples) and "outsiders" (observers), and microanalytic and global perspectives on the couples' interactions: The Communication Box (Markman & Floyd, 1980) was used to obtain couples' self-ratings of the emotional impact of their partner's statements;

and the Interaction Dimensions Coding System (Julien, Markman, & Lindahl, 1989), a global coding system, was used to assess four positive (e.g., support and validation) and five negative (e.g., withdrawal) dimensions of communication identified by previous research as central components of constructive and destructive communication.

Procedures

To date there have been seven points of contact with the couples: preassessment (Time 1), intervention, postassessment (Time 2), 1.5-year follow-up (Time 3), 3-year follow-up (Time 4), 4-year follow-up (Time 5), and 5-year follow-up (Time 6). The procedures for each stage differ according to the specific aims of the assessment at that point, but all sessions require the couples to complete a set of questionnaires (including those just described) and to participate in videotaped problem-solving interaction tasks. The tasks involve discussions of typical marital and family problem situations as well as discussions of their own relationship problem areas. To ensure that couples in the control group were unaware of their status and to reduce possible treatment selection effects, couples assigned to the intervention group were invited to complete PREP at the close of the preassessment, and couples assigned to the control group were not informed about the intervention program.

Research Accomplishments

The Short- and Long-Term Effects of PREP

Relationship stability. A global yet fundamental index of the effectiveness of the premarital intervention is the stability of the couples' relationships. A comparison of the two groups of couples revealed that at each follow-up point more of the couples in the PREP group were intact than those in the control group. By Time 6 (5 years after the program), 12% of the couples in the PREP group had dissolved their relationship, whereas 41% of the couples from the control group had done so. The above figures include break-ups before marriage, so relationship stability was also calculated in terms of divorce and separation rates. Once again, PREP couples were more stable than control couples, with divorce or separation rates being 8% and 19%, respectively.

Short-term effects. The short-term effects of the program were assessed by comparing the intervention and control groups at the postassessment on a set of measures of relationship functioning. Intervention couples compared with control couples improved their levels of communication skills from pretest to posttest status. Thus, the couples appeared to learn the skills taught in the program. Nevertheless, all other measures of relationship quality failed to show similar immediate effects.

Long-term effects (Times 3–4). The results at Time 3 generally indicated that control couples evidenced declines in levels of relationship quality, including decreased satisfaction, greater problem intensity, and less positive communication impact, whereas the intervention couples maintained or improved their already high level of functioning. By Time 4 (3 years after the intervention), the results for the entire collection of variables were even stronger. Although both groups evidenced a decline in satisfaction over time, the control group declined more than the intervention group. Consistent with the goals of prevention, the relationship satisfaction differences apparent at Time 3 not only were maintained 1.5 years later but expanded to other domains of relationship functioning (problem intensity and sexual problems).

Changes in communication. Next we addressed the question of whether the changes in communication skills apparent after the test were maintained over time. Results indicated that intervention couples demonstrated significantly lower levels of negative communication (i.e., conflict, denial, and negative affect) than control couples 4 years after the program. There were no significant differences in terms of positive communication.

Long-term effects on marital satisfaction. Time 4 and Time 5 (5 years after the program) results indicate that although the intervention men had higher levels of relationship satisfaction than control men, the control women and the intervention women had about the same level of satisfaction. Thus, the long-term effects of intervention appear to be attenuating for the women. Longer term follow-up is necessary to determine whether this pattern continues over time or whether it is a function of the point in the family's life cycle and to understand why decay in effects occurs.

Selection effects. Although the results support the effectiveness of the intervention program, an alternative explanation—that unmeasured self-selection factors may have produced or contributed to the findings—must be acknowledged. Approximately 60% of the couples assigned to the intervention group declined or did not complete the intervention, producing nonequivalent groups. Were couples who decided to complete the intervention more likely to function better in the first place? We compared decliners with acceptors on premarital variables and found no differences. Nevertheless, we suspected that acceptors might be different from decliners in terms of commitment to the relationship (especially the men).

Commitment. Building on the work of Johnson (1982), we conceptualized commitment as a metaconstruct with subconstructs called *personal dedication* and *constraint commitment*. Personal dedication refers to commitment in the sense of an intrinsic desire to work on, improve, and stick with the relationship. Constraint commitment refers to more extrinsic forces that serve to make relationships more likely to continue, such as the financial and emotional costs of ending a relationship. To assess these dimensions, we developed the Commitment Inventory (Stanley, 1986).

Prediction of Marital Distress

The present research program combines a longitudinal study of communication patterns in couples with a long-term evaluation of a program designed to prevent marital discord. Our results to date on the prediction of divorce indicate that negative premarital communication (negative escalation and withdrawal) predicts future marital distress and divorce and that men's withdrawal from conflict is especially predictive. Thus, we suggest that couples at risk for divorce have problems handling their own and their partners' negative emotions. These findings dovetail with the prevention results, which show that when partners learn constructive ways of dealing with conflict they enjoy higher levels of relationship stability and satisfaction (especially men).

We periodically revise PREP as we continue to learn more about the causes of marital distress in our ongoing longitudinal study. We also modify the intervention program on the basis of the results of the outcome study.

Discussion

The results of the research program thus far show promise for the possibility of preventing declines in relationship functioning that normally occur over time. Although some evidence for decay of effects is starting to emerge, intervention couples are significantly happier with their marriages and communicate better during the early years of marriage when the foundations are laid for successful child and family development. Although the results to date are promising, longer term follow-up is needed as the couples enter the primary risk period for divorce. Most important, additional studies are needed to assess the extent to which the findings replicate and generalize to other populations, especially high-risk populations. Nevertheless, the results strongly suggest that increased attention must be paid to preventing marital problems and divorce.

Programs in Progress and Planned for the Future

Booster Sessions

One important implication of these findings is that PREP booster sessions should be included in future versions of the program. Family transition periods (e.g., birth of the first child) are a natural time to schedule booster sessions. If the initial program inoculates couples against certain declines in functioning, it follows directly that an occasional "booster shot" should reinforce the preventive effects.

Religious Beliefs and PREP

Most premarital relationship counseling takes place in religious settings, usually being conducted by a pastor, priest, or rabbi. Although PREP is not a substitute for this experience, traditional premarital religious counseling typically does little or nothing in the way of actual skill building in a manner that research would suggest is likely to prevent future relationship problems. There is a possibility of enhancing the value of PREP for couples who are inclined to work more directly on religious issues as part of preparation for marriage. Although not replacing what religious leaders can provide, PREP can be tailored to include experiences that encourage couples to evaluate, discuss, and deal more directly with the

religious framework for their relationship and marriage. To accomplish this objective, we are developing an optional sixth session that helps couples better understand their marriage in the context of their faith by applying the communication skills taught in PREP.

Extension and Replication, Federal Republic of Germany (FRG)

In 1981, Markman was invited to an international conference sponsored by the Max Planck Institute in Munich, FRG; and at this conference, an international collaboration between Markman and Kurt Hahlweg developed. This collaboration has resulted in a German version of PREP called Ehevorbereitung Ein Partnerschaftliches Lernprogramm (EPL). The FRG and the Catholic Church in Germany are currently funding a study (Hahlweg is the primary investigator for this study) evaluating the effects of the German version of PREP in 10 dioceses in the FRG.

We are also forging links with colleagues in community, university, and religious settings throughout the United States who are or will be implementing and, in many cases, evaluating the program in their own settings. For example, plans are underway to evaluate the effects of the program with U.S. Navy couples planning marriage and couples who are mildly abusive. We have developed a detailed set of training materials for leaders, consultants, and researchers (available from the authors).

Extension and Replication, United States: Evaluation of Placebo Effects

In addition to selection effects, an alternative explanation of our findings is the effect of unmeasured nonspecific factors that are as likely to affect prevention as they are treatment programs. A study is underway that compares a revised version of PREP with "engaged encounter" to evaluate the impact of nonspecific (placebo) factors. Engaged encounter is similar in many respects to PREP (length, contact with religious leaders, and focus on marital issues relevant to couples planning marriage or remarriage) but differs in that no communication training is involved. Because communication training is hypothesized to be the key effective ingredient in PREP, this design is the strongest test to date of the effects of PREP and similar programs.

Delivering PREP to High-Risk Couples

Given the present divorce rate of 50% in the United States, all couples are at risk for divorce and marital distress. Yet, there are groups of couples at higher risk than average. Three major research efforts are planned that target high-risk couples. In the first, Daniel O'Leary (Stonybrook) and Markman are collaborating on a study of the effects of PREP on abusive couples who are planning marriage. Our previous work has found that the rate of partner abuse premaritally is more than 40% and that these couples are at increased risk for marital distress even though they generally report that they are currently happy with their relationship and do not define abuse as a problem. In the second, Hahlweg and Markman are consulting on a project in Holland, headed by Cas Schaap, that will offer EPL and PREP to couples who are children of divorce and have high levels of depression. Both factors are associated with current and future marital distress. Third, the transition to parenthood has been found to have a negative effect on the marital satisfaction of first-time parents. Fortunately, first-time parents appear to be unusually motivated to participate in intervention programs, and low-cost childbirth preparation programs are readily available. Thus, a "marriage" between PREP and childbirth preparation programs appears to be a promising approach for further efforts toward the prevention of marital distress (see Markman & Kaduschin, 1986, for details). A study in the FRG headed by Hahlweg is planned to evaluate the effects of a combined Lamaze and PREP (EPL) intervention for couples having their first child.

Nature of the Research Organization

Team Members and Their Roles

The research program is housed in the Center for Marital and Family Studies, which is part of the psychology department at the University of Denver. The center is supported by the department and the university, and the research program is supported by the National Institute of Mental Health (NIMH).

The following individuals are members of the program: Howard J. Markman, PhD, University of Denver (principal investigator); Scott Stanley, PhD, University of Denver (coprincipal investigator; involved in the ongoing design and evalua-

tion of the longitudinal study, refinement of PREP, and research on commitment); Mari Jo Renick, PhD, University of Denver (staff member responsible for data analyses and the child and family phase of our recruitment); Frank Floyd, PhD (former coprincipal investigator who helped design the longitudinal study and was involved in evaluating results and writing reports on the results); Kurt Hahlweg, PhD, University of Braunschweig, Max Planck Institute of Psychiatry (principal investigator, FRG project); Susan Blumberg, MA, University of Denver (project director, placebo study); Danielle Julien, PhD, University of Quebec at Montreal (postdoctoral research fellow on the project who developed the Interaction Dimensions Coding System and continues to have ongoing input into the coding system); Wayne Duncan, PhD, University of Washington (program project director for 3 years who is involved in the design of follow-up stages of the project and writing reports on the results); Ragnar Storaasli, MA (research associate and data analyst); Kristin Lindahl, MA (research associate, interviewer and data analyst); Wendy Wainright, BA (research assistant and interview team leader who administrates follow-up stages of the project); Lisa LaViolette-Hoyer (research assistant and coding team leader); Karen Dykes, BA (research assistant and coding team leader); Mari Clements, BA (research assistant, coding team leader, interviewer, and data analyst); and Audi Novak (office manager and administrative assistant who is responsible for the day-to-day operation of the research center).

Funding

NIMH has provided funding for the study of long-term effects of premarital intervention (grant R02-MH35525-03, principal investigator, January 1985 to July 1990) and $750,000 for direct costs).

Relation to Other Research Programs

Integration With Findings of Other Research

The short-term results are consistent with other evaluations of prevention programs for couples (e.g., Guerney 1977; Miller, Nunnally, & Wackman, 1975). A meta-analysis shows, however, that our effect sizes are somewhat smaller than those of programs designed to enhance relationships (see Hahlweg & Markman, 1988, for details). Because the goal of PREP is not to enhance current relationship functioning but to prevent future distress, such differences in short-term effect sizes are not surprising.

The long-term results cannot be compared directly with those of other marital and family therapy outcome studies (either prevention or treatment) because this is the longest outcome evaluation to date in the marital and family areas. The longest evaluation of a marital therapy intervention is 2 years with the use of self-report measures and 1 year with the use of interactional measures (Jacobson, personal communication, November 1989). At this point, our research program evaluates marital satisfaction and divorce 5 years after the program and evaluates the effects on communication 3 years after the program. Given the similarity between PREP and typical cognitive–behavioral marital therapy programs (e.g., Epstein & Baucom, 1988; Jacobson & Margolin, 1979; Stuart, 1980) and other prevention programs (the Minnesota Couples Communication Program and Relationship Enhancement), our findings provide evidence for the long-term effectiveness of such programs beyond that already established. Moreover, as noted in a recent NIMH report (NIMH, 1989), "preventive interventions require a protracted period of evaluation to ensure the dysfunction is prevented . . . the long-term evaluation of impact is especially critical, because the magnitude and scope of intervention efforts can vary greatly over time" (p. 202). This study will provide the longest-term evaluation of the outcome of a cognitive–behavioral intervention in the marital and family area and is the only study to address the question of whether we prevent divorce and increase the chances of marital success through a cost-effective, empirically based skills training program.

The relatively robust effects of a five-session intervention aimed at teaching skills at a key time in development lends support to theory and research on the importance of communication in determining marital success, intervening at times of transition in family development, and directing large-scale federal resources to programs designed to prevent divorce and marital distress.

Impact on the Field of Psychotherapy

Clinical practice. There are at least two ways in which this program of research can have an impact on clinical practice. First, although more research is needed, our results demonstrate that there is merit in trying to prevent severe marital distress before it develops. If evidence accumulates that this is indeed possible, such work could stimulate the professional community to greater interest in the possibilities for prevention in many areas. With increased interest and more research and programs focused on prevention, we look forward to the time when public and professional opinions favor spending money on cost-effective programs that save both financial and psychologist costs in the future. (As the Fram Oil Filter person said in a recent commercial, "Pay me now, or pay me later.") Second, as noted earlier, the dissemination of PREP in an organized, understandable manner will enable others to make use of well-researched and developed programs with couples in their local community.

Given the severe negative effects of marital conflict and divorce, if mental health professionals could devote a portion of their time to helping keep happy couples happy through preventive efforts (such as PREP), we can achieve a positive and significant impact on the emotional well-being and mental health of spouses and children alike.

Clinical training. The most specific impact on clinical training that can be claimed so far is the effect on the many individuals who have in some way worked with PREP in this laboratory. Over the years, perhaps 40 or more consultants have been trained in the principles of the program. Although it is impossible to gauge the actual impact of this training on these people or on the field as a whole, there is frequently feedback from these people as to the value of their experiences with PREP in their subsequent clinical work. Certainly, these people learn the rationale and the skills for preventing marital problems before they develop. As PREP is further disseminated, it is expected that there could be an effect on the clinical training of others around the country. Ultimately, the effect of any program such as PREP on the clinical practice and training of others will rest partly on the results of ongoing research in determining the value of such a program in the prevention of divorce and marital distress.

References

Epstein, N. & Baucom, D. H. (1988). Outcome research on cognitive behavioral marital therapy: Conceptual and methodological issues. *Journal of Family Psychology, 1,* 378–384.

Gottman, J. G., Markman, H. J., & Notarius, C. I. (1977). The topography of marital conflict: A sequential analysis of verbal and nonverbal behavior. *Journal of Marriage and the Family, 39,* 461–478.

Gottman, J., Notarius, C., Gonzo, J., & Markman, H. (1976). *A couple's guide to communication.* Champaign, IL: Research Press.

Guerney, B. G. (1977). *Relationship enhancement.* San Francisco: Jossey-Bass.

Hahlweg, K., & Markman, H. J. (1988). Effectiveness of behavioral marital therapy: Empirical status of behavioral techniques in preventing and alleviating marital distress. *Journal of Consulting and Clinical Psychology, 56,* 440–447.

Jacobson, N. S., & Margolin, G. (1979). *Marital therapy: Strategies based on social learning and behavior exchange principles.* New York: Brunner/Mazel.

Johnson, M. P. (1982). The social and cognitive features of the dissolution of commitment to relationships. In S. Duct (Ed.), *Personal relationships: Dissolving personal relationships.* (pp. 51–74). New York: Academic Press.

Julien, D., Markman, H. J., & Lindahl, K. (1989). A comparison of global and microanalytic coding system: Implications for future trends in studying interactions. *Behavioral Assessment, 11,* 81–100.

Knox, D. (1971). *Marriage happiness.* Champaign, IL: Research Press.

Locke, H., & Wallace, K. (1959). Short marital adjustment and prediction tests: Their reliability and validity. *Marriage and Family Living, 21,* 251–255.

Markman, H. J. (1981). The prediction of marital distress: A five year follow-up. *Journal of Consulting and Clinical Psychology, 49,* 760–762.

Markman, H. J., & Floyd, F. (1980). Possibilities for the prevention of marital discord: A behavioral perspective. *American Journal of Family Therapy, 8,* 29–48.

Markman, H. J., & Kaduschin, F. S. (1986). Preventive effects of Lamaze training for first-time parents: A short-term longitudinal study. *Journal of Consulting and Clinical Psychology, 54,* 872-874.

Markman, H. J., Floyd, F., Stanley, S., & Lewis, H. (1986). Prevention. In N. Jacobson & A. Gurman (Eds.), *Clinical handbook of marital therapy.* (pp. 173–195). New York: Guilford.

Miller, S., Nunnally, E. W., & Wackman, D. B. (1975). *Alive and aware: Improving communication in relationships.* Minneapolis, MN: Interpersonal Communication Programs.

National Center for Health Statistics. (1987). Births, marriages, divorces, and deaths for February, 1986. *Monthly Vital Statistics Report, 35.*

National Institute of Mental Health. (1989). *Research on children and adolescents with mental, behavioral, and developmental disorders: Mobilizing a national initiative.* (Report of a study by a Committee of the Institute of Medicine, Division of Mental Health and Behavioral Medicine). Washington, DC: National Academy Press.

Notarius, C. I., & Vanzetti, N. (1984). The marital agenda protocol. In E. Filsinger (Ed.), *Marital and family assessment* (pp. 209–227). Beverly Hills, CA: Sage.

Sager, C. J. (1976). *Marriage contracts and couple therapy: Hidden forces in intimate relationships.* New York: Brunner/Mazel.

Snyder, D. K. (1979). *Marital Satisfaction Inventory.* Los Angeles: Los Angeles Western Psychological Services.

Stanley, S. M. (1986). Commitment and the maintenance and enhancement of relationships (Doctoral dissertation, University of Denver). *Dissertation Abstracts International.*

Storaasli, R. D., & Markman, H. J. (in press). Relationship problems in the premarital and early stages of marriage: A test of family development theory. *Journal of Family Psychology.*

Stuart, R. B. (1980). *Helping couples change: A social learning approach to marital therapy.* New York: Guilford Press.

15

University of Miami School of Medicine: Brief Strategic Family Therapy for Hispanic Problem Youth

José Szapocznik and Arturo Rio
University of Miami School of Medicine

William Kurtines
Florida International University

Background and Aims

The Spanish Family Guidance Center was begun at the University of Miami in 1972 with funds from the Office of Economic Opportunity, Department of Health, Education and Welfare to provide services to the local Hispanic community. A structural family systems approach was adopted in 1973. In 1974 a programmatic research effort was launched to investigate the application of structural family therapy to mental health and multiple drug abuse problems among Hispanic youths. The program that emerged from these activities is a laboratory to develop, refine, and test both theory and application in the structural family therapy tradition. The center's long-term strategy is to affect the field of child and adolescent treatment by furthering a strategic structural family systems approach and its applications.

Method

Theory and treatment development takes place at the Spanish Family Guidance Center with primarily Hispanic subjects from the Greater Miami area. The emphasis of the program has been on

the structural family treatment of behavior problem children with an emphasis on drug-abusing youth (Szapocznik & Kurtines, 1989). The approach we have been developing represents a refinement of previously existing structural family systems therapy such as that of Minuchin (Minuchin, 1974; Minuchin & Fishman, 1981) and the strategic approaches of Haley (1976) and Madanes (1981). To address some of the difficulties encountered with conventional family therapy, we have done extensive work on developing treatment methods that are both strategic (i.e., planned, problem-focused, and pragmatic) and time limited. Family therapy can be difficult to implement when it requires engaging and retaining entire families in therapy over an extended period of time. In contrast, brief strategic family therapy (BSFT), which has become our central modality for implementing the strategic structural systems approach, is designed to be implemented in 12–15 sessions.

The theoretical basis for BSFT is three central concepts: systems, structure, and strategy. As in structural family therapy (Minuchin, 1974; Minuchin & Fishman, 1981), BSFT's major therapeutic techniques fall into three major structural family therapy interventions categories: joining, diagnosing, and restructuring. To enhance the replicability of the BSFT approach as well as that of a number of refinements that are described in subsequent sections, a published user-oriented manual is available (see Szapocznik & Kurtines, 1989).

Clients seen in the research projects of the center are Hispanic, about 80% are Cuban-American, and all are typically lower or middle-class as assessed by Hollingshead's (1957) index of social position. Recently, there has been a marked increase in the number of Latin-American clients other than Cubans. Most of the behavior problem, drug-using youths are male (up to 33% are female in some studies conducted at the center). The drug-abusing youths range in age from 12 to 21 years, with the majority falling in the 14–17-year-old age range, and all are still attending school.

Research Accomplishments

The work of the center has comprised a number of studies investigating the impact of various treatment intervention modalities developed within a common theoretical and conceptual framework and that have been adapted to meet a number of specific population needs and characteristics (Szapocznik, Kurtines, Santisteban, & Rio, in press). In addition, diagnostic aids and outcome evaluation instruments have been developed as needed.

The main research and development activities of the center occurred in two phases: the initial exploratory and treatment identification phase, and the theory development and testing phase. The first phase, from 1972 to 1978, was aimed at the identification of the special characteristics and problems of the Cuban population as well as the identification of a theoretical and clinical framework to match these characteristics and to address the special problems. A major study on value orientation (Szapocznik, Scopetta, Aranalde, & Kurtines, 1978) determined that an approach in which therapists take an active, directive, present-oriented leadership role matched the expectations of the population. In work with families with children and adolescents, intergenerational conflicts were frequently intermingled with culturally determined behavioral and value conflicts (Szapocznik, Scopetta, Kurtines, & Aranalde, 1978; Szapocznik, Kurtines, & Fernandez, 1980; Szapocznik, Santisteban, Kurtines, Perez-Vidal, & Hervis, 1984). On the basis of this research, structural family therapy was

identified as a particularly well-suited approach for this population (Szapocznik, Scopetta, Kurtines, et al., 1978). Through extensive clinical experience and a series of pilot research studies, structural family therapy was adapted to enhance its acceptability and effectiveness by adding a number of elements, some of the most important of which include strategic and time-limited aspects. To distinguish the particular family therapy approach that emerged from this phase of our work, we termed it *BSFT*.

The second phase of our work, since 1978, has aimed at extending structural family theory and application by developing, refining, and testing new concepts and strategies. By challenging some of the basic concepts of conventional structural systems family therapy, we have developed and refined theoretical insights that have led to new breakthroughs in application. To carry out this work, we conducted a number of major research studies, four of which we describe.

BSFT: Conjoint Compared With One Person

A major study was funded by the National Institute on Drug Abuse (NIDA; grant DA03224) from 1977 to 1981 to develop and investigate a strategy for conducting family therapy when it is not possible to bring the entire family into treatment. A national survey sponsored by NIDA revealed that family therapy was in fact widely viewed as a treatment of choice for behavior problem, drug-abusing adolescents. Even so, the vast majority of counselors who work with this population reported that they were not able to bring whole families into treatment. In response to this problem, we developed an intervention modality for achieving the goals of family therapy without having the whole family present. In responding to this problem, however, it was necessary to challenge some of the basic assumptions of family therapy.

A basic assumption of structural family systems therapy is that drug abuse in youths is a symptom of maladaptive interactional patterns in the family. That is, the family may be unwittingly supporting or encouraging the symptomatic behavior or, alternatively, the family may be incapable of behaving in ways that would eliminate the undesirable behavior. Additionally, structural family therapy assumes that to eliminate problem behaviors a change to more adaptive family interactions is required. Finally, a basic assumption of conventional family systems theory has been that to bring about changes in family interactions it is necessary to work directly with the conjoint family. Moreover, the available family intervention strategies are designed for work with the conjoint family.

One-person family therapy (OPFT), as tested in this study, challenges the assumption of conventional family therapy that it is necessary to work directly with the conjoint family to bring about changes in family interactions. OPFT differs from conjoint family therapies (CFTs) in that it attempts to achieve the goals of family therapy while working primarily with only one family member.

What made OPFT possible was the novel application of the *principle of complementarity*. This basic system's principle establishes the nature of the interdependency of the behaviors of the members of a system by postulating that a change in the behavior of one family member will require corresponding changes in the behavior of other family members. What is novel about OPFT is the deliberate and strategic use of this principle in directing the identified patient in therapy to change her or his behavior in ways that will require an adjustment in the behavior of other family members toward the identified patient.

OPFT is thus unique as an approach to family therapy in that it attempts to bring about therapeutic changes in both the behavior problem, drug-abusing adolescent and the adolescent's family while working primarily with the adolescent. To conduct family therapy through one person, it was necessary to adapt the BSFT conjoint techniques for use in working through one person. A significant advantage of OPFT is that it makes available powerful family intervention techniques in those cases in which the entire family cannot be induced into therapy.

Method. To challenge the assumption that it is necessary to have the entire family present to bring about changes in family interaction, we conducted an experimental study comparing the conjoint and one-person modalities of BSFT (Szapocznik, Kurtines, Foote, & Perez-Vidal, 1983, 1986). Considerable work was done in describing the one-person modality (OPFT) to ensure its standardization and replicability (Szapocznik, Hervis, Kurtines, & Spencer, 1984; Szapocznik, Foote, Perez-Vidal, Hervis, & Kurtines, 1989).

An experimental design was achieved by randomly assigning 72 Hispanic-American families with drug-abusing adolescents to a CFT or OPFT modality. Both modalities were time limited (12–15 sessions). In CFT therapists were restricted to no more than 2 individual sessions; in OPFT therapists were restricted to no more than 2 conjoint sessions. Client families were extensively tested at the time of intake (pretesting), termination (posttesting), and 6-month follow-up. Instruments were selected such that outcome could be examined from several different perspectives, including an independent rating of the identified patient's functioning, parents' reports of problem behaviors observed in the identified patient, family members' report of family climate, and independent ratings of structural family functioning (see Szapocznik, Kurtines, et al., 1983, 1986, for a detailed discussion of the psychometric properties of the measures).

Findings. Data were analyzed by means of a mixed-design analysis of variance. The results (Szapocznik, Kurtines, et al., 1983, 1986) indicated not only that OPFT was as effective as CFT in bringing about significant improvement in behavior problems and drug abuse in the youths but also that it was as effective as CFT in bringing about and maintaining significant improvements in family functioning. These results demonstrated that it is possible to change family interactions even when the whole family is not present.

Structural Systems Engagement

OPFT was developed to address the problem of bringing the entire family into therapy by working with one person to orchestrate family change without working with the entire family. This problem can also be approached from an alternative and equally useful perspective, however, namely developing techniques and methods for more effectively bringing entire families into therapy. The latter alternative is particularly useful in those cases in which the drug-abusing, problem youth is the family member that refuses to come into therapy. The result of the previous study provided direct data on how extensive is the problem of getting families to come into treatment. In the previous study only 250 client families of approximately 650 initial contacts came in for a screening interview. Of this number only 145 completed the intake procedure, and only 72 completed treatment. Clearly, a large proportion of client families who seek treatment are never engaged into therapy.

A second major study was funded by NIDA (grant DA02059) from 1982–1986 to develop and investigate the efficacy of a procedure for engaging hard-to-reach cases and bringing them to therapy completion. Strategic structural systems engagement (SSSE) was designed to engage resistant families in treatment more effectively. SSSE is based on the premise that resistance to change in the family results from two systems properties: First, family systems will attempt to maintain structural equilibrium or the status quo, which in the case of drug-abusing youth can be accomplished by staying out of therapy. Second, although the presenting symptom may be drug abuse, the initial obstacle to change is resistance to treatment. From a structural systems perspective, when resistance to coming into treatment is defined as the symptom to be targeted by the intervention, the resistance is redefined as a symptom that is maintained by the family's current pattern of interaction. Therefore, the same systemic and structural principles that are used in understanding and treating the family once it is in therapy can also be used in understanding and treating the family's resistance to engagement (Szapocznik, Perez-Vidal, et al., 1989).

From a structural systems perspective, the solution to overcoming the undesirable symptom of resistance is to restructure the family's patterns of interaction that permit the symptom of resistance to continue to exist. OPFT techniques become useful because the person making the call for help becomes our "one person" through whom we can potentially work to restructure the family's pattern of interaction that is maintaining the symptom of resistance. Hence, in so called hard-to-reach families, in order to have the opportunity to intervene, the therapist must begin therapy with the first telephone call. That is, in SSSE therapy does not begin with the first office session; rather, it is extended forward to the initial contact. Once the symptom of resistance is overcome and a family has agreed to come to therapy, the focus of the intervention shifts to overcoming the presenting symptoms of problem behavior and drug abuse.

Method. To test the effectiveness of SSSE in engaging and bringing to therapy completion families with drug-abusing youths, Szapocznik et al. (1988) conducted an experimental study by randomly assigning 108 Hispanic families of adolescents who were suspected of or were observed using drugs to one of two conditions: SSSE and engagement as usual (EAU). EAU was the control condition. In this control condition, the clients were approached in a way that closely resembled the kind of engagement that usually takes place in outpatient centers. In SSSE, on the other hand, client families were engaged by means of techniques developed specifically for use with families that resist therapy. Considerable work was done in describing the nature of SSSE to ensure its standardization and replicability (Szapocznik & Kurtines, 1989; Szapocznik, Perez-Vidal, et al., 1989). The basic outcome measures for this study were engagement and maintenance through treatment completion. In addition, preoutcome to postoutcome measures of individual and structural family functioning were obtained (see Szapocznik et al., 1988, for a detailed discussion of the psychometric properties of the measures).

Treatment integrity guidelines and checklists were developed for both conditions, and six levels of engagement effort were defined a priori. To monitor for treatment integrity, all contacts were logged and all sessions reviewed and rated by an independent clinical research supervisor who was blind to condition. Treatment integrity analyses revealed that interventions in both conditions adhered to guidelines and that the two modalities were clearly distinguishable by the level of engagement effort applied.

Findings. There were two basic sets of findings from the study (Szapocznik et al., 1988). The first had to do with the effectiveness of the SSSE intervention. The effects of the experimental condition were dramatic. More than 57% of the families in EAU failed to be engaged into treatment. In contrast, only 7.15% (four families) in SSSE were lost to treatment. The differences in the retention rates were also dramatic. In EAU, dropouts represented 41% of the cases that were engaged, whereas dropouts in SSSE represented 17% of the engaged cases. Thus, of all of the cases that were initially assigned, 25% in EAU and 77% in SSSE were successfully terminated. For families that completed both conditions, there were highly significant improvements both in the problematic adolescent's functioning and in family functioning as assessed by the structural family systems measure, and these improvements were not significantly different across conditions. Thus, the crucial distinction between the conditions was in their differential rate of retention.

A second major finding of the project (Szapocznik et al., 1988) was the identification of a number of types of resistant families and the development of intervention strategies for engaging these families. There were four general types of resistant families that were identified in the population under study: (a) Families who were characterized by a powerful identified client. In these families, the powerful identified patient was joined, usually on his or her own "turf," in order to bring the family into treatment, (b) Families who were characterized by an ambivalent mother. Although she had called for help, she was also likely to protect the identified patient and to be ambivalent about having her husband involved in the therapy process. In these cases, the therapist circumvented the mother and went directly to the father (with the mother's permission) and placed the father in a more central role in bringing the family into treatment. (c) Families in whom the mother and son tended to be strongly allied and the father was disengaged or distant. In this type of family, the therapist worked with the mother to encourage and coach her to behave in ways that would bring the father closer to her and thus make him willing to attend treatment. (d) Families in whom one or more members were concerned that some family secret would be revealed in therapy. In these cases, the therapist would work to establish a treatment contract, accepted by all parties involved, that would restrict the problems to be addressed in therapy.

Bicultural Effectiveness Training

In addition to breakthroughs in treating hard-to-reach families, our program of research has also resulted in breakthroughs in novel applications of other structural concepts. Structural family therapies, including BSFT, are characterized by a strict adherence to process and the content dictated by the uniqueness of each family is used only as a circumstantial vehicle for achieving the process goals. In the case of immigrant Hispanic families in the Miami area, it became apparent that a large number of families with adolescents were presenting intergenerational conflicts in which parental authority became invalidated and in which the content seemed to be remarkably consistent from family to family. More specifically, the nature of the content took on a cultural flavor in which parents and youths developed different cultural alliances (Hispanic and American, respectively). The etiology of this kind of cultural gap is reflected in the differential rate of acculturation between parents and youngsters, with the youngsters acculturating more rapidly than their parents (Szapocznik, Scopetta, Kurtines, &

Aranalde, 1978). The most important implication is that in families in which members are characterized by culturally related differences, the typical intergenerational differences found families of adolescents are exacerbated by cultural differences (Szapocznik, Scopetta, Kurtines, & Aranalde, 1978; Szapocznik, Kurtines, & Fernandez, 1980). A recent comprehensive review of the literature by Rogler, Malgady, and Rodriguez (1989) has strongly endorsed our pioneer paradigm of bicultural adjustment.

A major study was funded by the National Institute of Mental Health (NIMH; grant MH31226) from 1979 to 1982 to develop and investigate the efficacy of a structural intervention for addressing this problem. For this purpose we took advantage of the structural systems emphasis on changing family process while using content as a vehicle to achieve the desired changes in family interactions. Because for these families content seemed to remain remarkably consistent in terms that could be defined with regard to differences along cultural lines or alliances, a set of psychoeducational interventions was designed that aimed at restructuring the family to reduce intergenerational conflict while using culture as a standard content.

The bicultural effectiveness training (BET) approach was developed to be conducted in 12 conjoint sessions. The process that BET uses to bring about structural family change involves two change strategies developed specifically for the BET modality and derived from structural family therapy concepts (Szapocznik, Santisteban, et al., 1984). The initial change strategy is temporarily to detour family conflict by placing the focus of both the intergenerational differences and the intercultural differences on the cultural conflict. Detouring is done by placing the cultural conflict in the identified patient role. Placing the cultural conflict in an identified patient role is brought about by reframing the family's perception of the conflict. Reframing in turn is accomplished by providing the family with a transcultural perspective that emphasizes the commonalities between parents and their children, and by deemphasizing the intergenerational differences (e.g., by teaching that each member has a value position or point of view that is culturally determined). The purposes of this technique are to establish boundaries around the family and to foster a new interactional pattern between parents and adolescents by detouring the intergenerational conflict through the cultural conflict. Thus, when the intergenerational conflict is deemphasized and the cultural conflict is emphasized, the family's perspective of the problem has been reframed.

From a process perspective, the initial change strategy (i.e., detouring) is a useful means of loosening the existing rigid generational–cultural alliances (parent-Hispanic and adolescent–acculturated Americanized). This strategy, however, only loosens existing alliances. The purpose of BET is to bring about more permanent structural changes in family interaction patterns, which is accomplished through the second strategy.

The second BET change strategy, establishing crossed alliances, provides a means of creating new cross-alliances between family members and cultures. This is done through exercises designed to make both parents and youth more comfortable with both cultures. Through these exercises, parents are encouraged to accept and understand the value of certain aspects of the American culture represented by their child, and the adolescents are encouraged to accept and understand the value of certain aspects of the Hispanic culture represented by their parents. From a structural perspective, then, at a process level enhancing biculturalism in family members is accomplished by creating cross-alliances between generations and cultures. The expected outcome after the second change strategy is a reduction in intergenerational conflict and firmer boundaries around the family. Corresponding to the intrafamily change is a new set of family generational–cultural relationships with flexible alliances between parents and both cultures as well as youth and both cultures.

Method. The effectiveness of BET was tested in a treatment outcome study (Szapocznik, Santisteban, Rio, Perez-Vidal, Kurtines, & Hervis, 1986) by means of an experimental design in which families were randomly assigned to one of two treatment conditions: BET and CFT. The subjects were 31 Cuban-American families who presented with a complaint about a behavior or conduct disorder. The BET intervention was developed as a standardized, time-limited (12-session) psychoeducational modality. To standardize the intervention, lesson plans were developed for each of the 12 sessions as well as an overall description of the program (Szapocznik, Santisteban, et al., 1984). CFT served as a control condition for this project. In both CFT and BET, the aim was to promote more adaptive patterns of family interaction. CFT, however, focused on the

family's presenting problem as the context around which to produce change and thus did not specifically address the issue of culture conflict in the family. BET aimed specifically at the promotion of family functioning by regarding culture conflict as a focal problem. All client families in the study were extensively tested at intake and termination by means of an independent measure of the identified patient's functioning, parent's reports of behavior problems observed in the identified patient, and independent ratings of structural family functioning (see Szapocznik, Santisteban, et al., 1986, for a detailed discussion of the psychometric properties of the measures). In addition, to ascertain changes in cultural orientation measures of acculturation (Szapocznik, Scopetta, Kurtines, et al., 1978) and bicultural involvement (Szapocznik et al., 1980) were also obtained.

Treatment integrity guidelines and checklists were developed for both conditions. To monitor for treatment integrity all sessions were videotaped, and randomly selected sessions were rated on the checklist. Treatment integrity analyses revealed that therapists adhered to guidelines and conducted interventions in a fashion consistent with their respective modes of interventions and that the two modalities were applied in a clearly distinguishable fashion.

Findings. Data were analyzed by means of a mixed-design analysis of variance. The results of the analyses indicated that families in both conditions improved significantly on all three clinical measures. These findings indicate that it was possible to bring about those changes sought through structural family therapy even in the case of BET, in which the content (i.e., culture and culture conflict) used as a vehicle for interactional change was standardized in a psychoeducational modality. A further check on the mechanism for change revealed that, as would have been expected, families in BET evidenced greater cultural change.

Structural Family Compared With Individual Psychodynamic Therapy

Our previous research concentrated on the development, refinement, and testing of structural family theory and strategies. The question of the relative effectiveness of a structural systems family approach compared with other widely used modalities, however, also needs to be addressed. Because outpatient care of children and adolescents in our community has been strongly psychodynamic in orientation, the best available expertise for a comparative study in this community was with psychodynamic treatment. In discussion with experts in the field, it appeared that it would be a fairer test of the psychodynamic approach if it were applied to a latency-age population rather than adolescents.

For these reasons, a major study was conducted under funding from NIMH (grant MH34821) from 1981 to 1986 to investigate the relative effectiveness of structural family therapy, individual psychodynamic child therapy, and a recreational activity control group in latency-age Hispanic boys. In addition to comparing treatment effectiveness, a particular focus of this study was to investigate the impact of structural family therapy on psychodynamic ratings of child functioning and vice versa (i.e., the impact of child psychodynamic therapy on structural ratings of family functioning). Both theoretical approaches, structural family and child psychodynamic, assume underlying etiologies to symptoms. They postulate different processes as being primarily responsible for the symptom resolution, however. Both treatment modalities aim at symptom reduction. The child psychodynamic approach postulates that child psychodynamic functioning is the intervening variable that needs to be modified to eliminate the symptom. Structural family therapy, on the other hand, postulates that family interactions represent the intervening variable that needs to be modified to eliminate the symptom. Because of these important differential theoretical predictions, one aim of this study was to explore the impact of each theoretical modality on theoretically sensitive measures of functioning and change. The study thus sought to address two complementary research aims: an investigation of efficacy, and an exploratory articulation of mechanisms that may account for effectiveness.

Method. The basic design was a mixed-experimental design (within and between). The between factor was intervention condition with three levels (family therapy, child therapy, and control). The within dependent variable was three repeated measures at pretherapy, posttherapy, and 1-year follow-up. An experimental design was achieved by randomly assigning all subjects to one of these intervention conditions (Szapocznik, Rio, et al., 1989).

Five types of measures were used in the study; the first three were presumed to be theoretically neutral: attrition rates, behavioral observation measures, self-report of symptom measures, a theoretically based psychodynamic measure, and a theoretically based structural family measure (see Szapocznik, Rio, et al., 1989, for a detailed discussion of the psychometric properties of the measures).

Treatment integrity guidelines and checklists were developed for both treatment conditions. To monitor for treatment integrity all sessions were videotaped, and randomly selected sessions were rated on the checklist. Treatment integrity analyses revealed that therapists adhered to guidelines and conducted interventions in a fashion consistent with their respective modes of interventions and that the two treatment modalities were applied in a clearly distinguishable fashion.

Findings. Attrition data were analyzed by means of chi-square, and outcome data were analyzed by means of a mixed-design analysis of variance. The results of the analyses revealed several important findings, the first 3 of which involved treatment outcome and relative effectiveness of the conditions. The fourth finding concerns the articulation of a mechanism that may account for the specific effects of differential treatments.

First, with respect to efficacy, the control condition was significantly less effective in retaining cases than the two treatment conditions. Second, the two treatment conditions, structural family therapy and psychodynamic child therapy, were both apparently equivalent in reducing behavior and emotional problems based on parent reports and self-reports. Third, greater effectiveness of family therapy was found compared with child therapy in protecting family integrity in the long term. This finding provides support for the structural family therapy assumption that treating the whole family is important because it improves the symptoms and protects the family, whereas treating only the child may result in deteriorated family functioning.

The fourth important finding revealed that there is a complex relationship between specific mechanisms and related outcome variables. For both treatment conditions there was a significant pretest to posttest improvement in psychodynamic functioning and symptom reduction, and these improvements were maintained at follow-up. In contrast, there were no pretest to posttest changes in family functioning for either condition. By the time of follow-up, however, families in the family condition improved significantly in the measure of family functioning, whereas families in the psychodynamic condition deteriorated significantly on this measure. This finding, on the one hand, is consistent with some of the underlying assumptions of psychodynamic theory and, on the other, does not support some of the underlying assumptions of family therapy because changes in family functioning were not necessary for symptom reduction.

Research Programs in Progress

The center is currently conducting a major 5-year (1987–1992) study funded by NIDA (grant DA5334) to test experimentally the effectiveness of the strategic structural systems approach to engagement and therapy in the treatment of behavior problem, drug-abusing Hispanic youths. Building on our previous work, we have developed an integrated concept of BSFT that incorporates interventions beginning with the initial contact of a family member requesting help from the center and carrying through therapy and the completion of treatment. The study is designed to test separately, together, and in relation to each other each of the two components of the BSFT approach (i.e., the engagement component aimed at overcoming the problem of resistance to treatment and the therapy component aimed at overcoming the problem of drug abuse and related behavior problems in adolescents). This study is organized to test two hypotheses: (a) the BSFT approach to engagement is effective in overcoming resistance to treatment and (b) BSFT is effective in reducing or eliminating drug abuse and related behavior problems.

Method

To test these hypotheses, 180 Hispanic families with a drug-abusing adolescent member are being randomly assigned to one of three conditions: SSSE plus BSFT, EAU plus BSFT, and EAU plus group therapy control.

The first hypothesis will be tested by comparing the first two conditions, and the second hypothesis will be tested by comparing the last two conditions. The engagement outcome measures will consist of rates of engagement and maintenance to treatment completion. The treatment outcome measures, obtained at pretest, posttest, 9-month follow-up, and 18-month follow-up, will consist of independent measures of identified patient functioning, parent ratings of identified patient functioning, measures of family structural functioning, family member reports of family climate and communication, self-reported drug use, and objective assessments of drug use (urine analysis at random therapy sessions as well as at pretest, posttest, and follow-ups and hair analysis at pretest, posttest, and follow-ups).

Programs Planned for the Future

Three kinds of programs are currently under development. One program is in the training area, a second program is in process research, and the third consists of applications of our prior work to new populations. With regard to training and dissemination activities, we are currently developing a structural family therapy training track for the child and adolescent psychiatry fellowship program in our Department of Psychiatry. With regard to dissemination activities, we are collaborating with the National Coalition on Hispanic Health and Human Services (COSSMHO) in conducting a national training program for Bachelor's- and Master's-level counselors using our BSFT approach. The program is currently planned for eight heavily Hispanic cities in the United States and Puerto Rico.

In the planning stages are a set of secondary analyses of our data using multiple regression methods to investigate the relative contribution of structural family changes and psychodynamic child functioning on symptom reduction. In addition, we are beginning an analysis of archived family therapy sessions applying Benjamin's structural analysis (Benjamin, 1977; Benjamin, Foster, Giat-Roberto, & Estroff, 1986).

The center has began to explore the generalizability and adaptability of our findings to other populations and problem areas. For example, we have become increasingly involved in serving non-Cuban Hispanics. This population, comprised of recent immigrants mostly from Central America, presents a different idiosyncracy than our more traditional target population of Cuban immigrants. For work with recent immigrant, non-Cuban Hispanics, we are developing an adaptation of our BSFT approach that includes ecological features. In this approach, the therapist directly intervenes both in the family as well as in interactions at the interface between the family and societal systems that have an impact on the family. We have also been exploring the adaptability of our work to other inner-city populations.

Nature of the Research Organization

The center is organizationally part of the Department of Psychiatry of the University of Miami School of Medicine. The center generates its financial support through competitive research grant awards primarily from the NIMH and NIDA. We are increasingly strengthening our ties to the Office of Substance Abuse Prevention.

The research team is headed by José Szapocznik, PhD, Professor of Psychiatry of Psychology and Director of the Spanish Family Guidance Center. Other members of the team include William Kurtines, PhD; Daniel Santisteban, PhD; Angel Perez-Vidal, PsyD; Mercedes Scopetta, PhD; Raquel Cohen, MD; Olga Hervis, MSW; and Edward Murray, PhD. Therapists are brought into the Center and become part of the research team as needed by the research projects.

Relation to Other Research Programs

Investigators from our center collaborate with investigators at other universities who are conducting investigations modeled after our own. In recent years, for example, we have collaborated with investigators at diverse sites around the country (e.g., Louisiana State University, Purdue University, University of New Mexico, etc.) attempting to replicate our findings or utilizing modalities developed at our center. In particular, there has been great interest in replicating our study on structural systems engagement and in using our "one person family therapy modality" as an experimental condition in studies with substance abusers. There has also been much interest in the usefulness of our Structural Family Systems Ratings as a diagnostic, outcome, or process measure.

Impact of Our Work on Psychology

Undoubtedly the strongest impact of our work has occurred in services to Hispanic populations throughout the United States. Our family therapy work was selected by an independent committee of the COSSMHO as the most thoroughly researched and documented model for use with Hispanic youths with behavior problems. We receive invitations to train hundreds of mental health professionals every year on family therapy with drug-abusing and behavior-problem youths. Our leadership in the Hispanic field has resulted in the 1978 Outstanding Community Agency Award and the 1982 National Leadership Award for Academic Excellence of the COSSMHO; and the 1989 Rafael Tavares Award for Academic Excellence from the Association of Hispanic Mental Health Professionals. Our work on acculturation, biculturalism, and adjustment, which was not reviewed here, has been the inspiration for hundreds of Master's theses and doctoral dissertations around the country, both with Hispanic as well as with other immigrant populations. Most recently, our interest in mechanisms mediating the effectiveness of family therapy was cited as an important reason for selecting our article *Structural Family and Psychodynamic Child Therapy for Problematic Hispanic Boys* (Szapocznik, Rio, et al., 1989) to receive the 1990 Outstanding Research Publication Award of the American Association of Marriage and Family Therapy. The Structural Family Systems Ratings is receiving increasing attention as a theoretically based procedure for systematic diagnosis (Szapocznik & Kurtines, 1989) and assessment of treatment outcome.

References

Benjamin, L. S. (1977). Structural analysis of a family in therapy. *Journal of Consulting and Clinical Psychology, 45,* 391–406.

Bengamin, L. S., Foster, S. W., Roberto, L. G., & Estroff, S. E. (1986). Breaking the family code: Analysis of videotape of family interactions by structural analysis of social behavior (SASB). In L. S. Greenberg & W. M. Pinsof (Eds.), *The psychotherapeutic process: A research handbook.* New York: Guilford Press.

Haley, J. (1976). *Problem-solving therapy.* San Francisco: Jossey-Bass.

Hollingshead, A. B. (1957). *Two factor index of social position.* New Haven, CT.

Madanes, C. (Ed.). (1981). *Strategic family therapy.* San Francisco: Jossey-Bass.

Minuchin, S. (1974). *Families and family therapy.* Cambridge, MA: Harvard University Press.

Minuchin, S., & Fishman, H. C. (1981). *Family therapy techniques.* Cambridge, MA: Harvard University Press.

Rogler, L. H., Malgady, R. G., & Rodriguez, O. (1989). *Hispanics and mental health: A framework for research.* Malabar, FL: Kreger.

Szapocznik, J., Foote, F., Perez-Vidal, A., Hervis, O., & Kurtines, W. M. (1989). One person family therapy. In R. A. Wells and V. A. Gianetti (Eds.), *Handbook of brief psychotherapy* (pp. 493–510). New York: Plenum Press.

Szapocznik, J., Hervis, O., Kurtines, W. M., & Spencer, F. (1984). One person family therapy. In B. Lubin and W. A. O'Connor (Eds.), *Ecological approaches to clinical and community psychology* (pp. 335–355). New York: Wiley.

Szapocznik, J., & Kurtines, W. M. (1989). *Breakthroughs in family treatment*. New York: Springer.

Szapocznik, J., Kurtines, W. M., & Fernandez, T. (1980). Bicultural involvement and adjustment in Hispanic-American youth. *International Journal of Intercultural Relations, 4*, 353–366.

Szapocznik, J., Kurtines, W. M., Foote, F., & Perez-Vidal, A. (1983). Conjoint versus one person family therapy: Some evidence for the effectiveness of conducting family therapy through one person. *Journal of Consulting and Clinical Psychology, 51*, 889–899.

Szapocznik, J., Kurtines, W. M., Foote, F., & Perez-Vidal, A. (1986). Conjoint versus one person family therapy: Further evidence for the effectiveness of conducting family therapy through one person. *Journal of Consulting and Clinical Psychology, 54*, 395–397.

Szapocznik, J., Kurtines, W. M., Santisteban, D. A., & Rio, A. T. (in press). The interplay of advances among theory, research, and application in treatment interventions aimed at behavior problem children and adolescents. *Journal of Consulting and Clinical Psychology*.

Szapocznik, J., Perez-Vidal, A., Brickman, A. L., Foote, F. H., Santisteban, D., Hervis, O., & Kurtines, W. M. (1988). Engaging adolescent drug abusers and their families into treatment: A strategic structural systems approach. *Journal of Consulting and Clinical Psychology, 56*, 552–557.

Szapocznik, J., Perez-Vidal, A., Hervis, O., Brickman, A. L., & Kurtines, W. M. (1989). Innovations in family therapy: Overcoming resistance to treatment. In R. A. Wells & V. A. Gianetti (Eds.), *Handbook of brief psychotherapy* (pp. 93–115). New York: Plenum Press.

Szapocznik, J., Rio, A., Murray, E., Cohen, R., Scopetta, M., Rivas-Vazquez, A., Hervis, O., Posada, V., & Kurtines, W. (1989). Structural family versus psychodynamic child therapy for problematic Hispanic boys. *Journal of Consulting and Clinical Psychology, 57*, 571–578.

Szapocznik, J., Santisteban, D., Kurtines, W. M., Perez-Vidal, A., & Hervis, O. (1984). Bicultural effectiveness training: A treatment intervention for enhancing intercultural adjustment. *Hispanic Journal of Behavioral Sciences, 6*, 317–344.

Szapocznik, J., Santisteban, D., Rio, A., Perez-Vidal, A., Kurtines, W. M., & Hervis, O. (1986). Bicultural effectiveness training (BET): An intervention modality for families experiencing intergenerational/intercultural conflict. *Hispanic Journal of Behavioral Sciences, 8*, 303–330.

Szapocznik, J., Scopetta, M. A., Aranalde, M. A., & Kurtines, W. M. (1978). Cuban value structure: Clinical implications. *Journal of Consulting and Clinical Psychology, 46*, 961–970.

Szapocznik, J., Scopetta, M. A., Kurtines, W. M., & Aranalde, M. A. (1978). Theory and measurement of acculturation. *Interamerican Journal of Psychology, 12*, 113–130.

16

University of Pennsylvania: The Penn Psychotherapy Research Projects

Lester Luborsky, Paul Crits-Christoph, and Jacques Barber
University of Pennsylvania

Background and Aims

History

The research programs we describe in this chapter represent the collaborative and separate research projects constructed by the three authors, who are all full-time faculty in the Department of Psychiatry, University of Pennsylvania. Luborsky's program began in 1967 with a 5-year National Institute of Mental Health (NIMH) project on the factors influencing outcomes of dynamic psychotherapy. The findings are summarized in Luborsky, Crits-Christoph, Mintz, and Auerbach (1988). The data and findings have become known as the Penn Psychotherapy Project, and the data have recurrently served as a basis for much of our research ever since, whenever we have new ideas to examine. The data consist of the pretests, posttests, and tape recordings of dynamic psychotherapy for 73 patients, most of whom are from the outpatient psychiatric clinic of the Department of Psychiatry and a smaller number being referred from private practitioners affiliated with the department. Data sets from other projects have been added to the collection: drug dependence (VA [Veterans Administration]–Penn Project), major depression (Penn Depression Project), and patients' preference for therapists (Patient's Preference Project).

Crits-Christoph joined the faculty of the Department of Psychiatry in 1984. He participated collaboratively with Luborsky in the Penn Psy-

chotherapy Project and the study on major depression in addition to pursuing his own interests in methodological issues in psychotherapy research and comparative models of change in different psychotherapies. In 1988 Barber joined the faculty and collaborated with Luborsky and Crits-Christoph on studies of dynamic psychotherapy. He has also continued his own line of research on the change process in cognitive therapy.

Aims

Our interests cover various topics. The most persistent general aims are as follows: (a) to find the factors influencing the outcomes of psychotherapy; (b) to develop operational measures of the propositions about curative factors in dynamic psychotherapy; (c) to investigate the effectiveness of different treatments for different disorders (mainly drug dependence and depression); (d) to compare models of change in different forms of psychotherapy; (e) to examine relationships among changes in moods, measures of the competence of the immune system, and illness; and (f) to develop specific manuals for the treatment of various psychological disorders.

Method

Subjects and Selection

The Penn Psychotherapy Project. This project ($N = 73$) investigated the factors influencing outcomes of psychotherapy. Most patients had a diagnosis of major depression or anxiety disorders as defined by the revised third edition of the *Diagnostic and Statistical Manual of Mental Disorders* (*DSM-III–R*; American Psychiatric Association, 1987).

The VA–Penn Psychotherapy Project. This project ($N = 110$) is part of the collaboration with George Woody, Thomas McLellan, and Charles O'Brien on factors that influence outcomes of psychotherapy and comparison of the effectiveness of drug counseling with two forms of psychotherapy: dynamic psychotherapy (supportive–expressive) and cognitive–behavioral psychotherapy. The patients were all drug dependent, but many had various other diagnoses including depression and antisocial personality. This sample has also been used for studies of therapists' success in treating clients (Luborsky, McLellan, Woody, O'Brien, & Auerbach, 1985; Luborsky, Crits-Christoph, et al., 1986).

The Dynamic Psychotherapy for Major Depression Project. Three studies are being performed on this sample of patients ($N = 40$) with a *DSM-III–R* diagnosis of major depression: the factors that influence outcomes of dynamic psychotherapy for depression; the associations among mood, immunocompetence, and illness; and changes in psychodynamic variables as a result of psychotherapy.

The Preference for Therapists Project. This study ($N = 47$) includes investigation of the factors that influence outcomes of psychotherapy and the factors that influence the patient's preference for a particular therapist (Alexander, Luborsky, & Auerbach, 1990). The design of the treatment consists of two sessions with a first therapist and two sessions with a second therapist. At the end of the fourth session the patient must express a preference to continue with one of the two therapists. The patients were all drawn from the outpatient clinic of the hospital of the University of Pennsylvania.

Statistical Implications of Therapist Effects Project. For research on the statistical implications of therapist's effects, Crits-Christoph has obtained new data from 10 comparative outcome studies.

Assessing psychodynamic constructs in cognitive therapy. The data from the depression study conducted by Hollon et al. (1989) have been lent to Crits-Christoph for a study of the

relevance of psychodynamic measures of change to cognitive therapy.

Mechanisms of change in cognitive therapy. Barber (1989) studied the mechanisms of change in cognitive therapy. To examine the specific mechanisms of change in cognitive therapy, he compared depressed patients who received cognitive therapy, supportive–expressive psychotherapy, medication, and pill placebo on various cognitive and coping measures.

Instruments

The instruments (described later) include measures of psychological health or sickness (the Health–Sickness Rating Scale [Luborsky, 1975] and its slightly revised and renamed version, the Global Assessment Scale [Endicott, Spitzer, Fleiss, & Cohen, 1976]), therapeutic alliance, central relationship pattern (core conflictual relationship theme [CCRT] method), accuracy of interpretation, self-understanding, and pervasiveness of conflicts in the central relationship pattern. The Ways of Responding Questionnaire, a new measure of compensatory skills, has also been developed (Barber & DeRubeis, 1989).

Research Accomplishments

The Penn Psychotherapy Project

Therapeutic alliance measures. These operational measures come in three forms: a rating method (Morgan, Luborsky, Crits-Christoph, Curtis, & Solomon, 1982) a counting of signs method (Luborsky, Crits-Christoph, Alexander, Margolis, & Cohen, 1983), and a questionnaire that is to be filled out by a patient and therapist independently (Luborsky, 1984; Luborsky et al., 1985). The counting of signs and the questionnaire methods are based on a set of signs of an alliance, including the experience of the patient that therapy is helping, the patient's feeling understood, and the patient's feeling hopeful about benefits. Since the first operational measure of the alliance was applied to psychotherapy sessions (Luborsky, 1976), other studies have shown that the alliance can predict the outcomes of psychotherapy. In total, eight predictive studies have reported findings with alliance measures, and all eight have shown significant predictions of outcome (mean correlation = .5; Luborsky et al.,

1988; Luborsky & Auerbach, 1985). This is an impressive performance for an area of research in which all findings are rarely in the same direction and are rarely all significant. It should also be noted that it is not just the therapeutic alliance measures that are significantly predictive but many related measures of the broader category of positive relationship qualities (Luborsky, Crits-Christoph, Mintz, & Auerbach, 1988). The relation between alliance and outcome has been examined mainly in short-term or moderate-length dynamic psychotherapy and not yet in psychoanalysis.

Central relationship pattern measures. These measures are the product of a new assessment venture in the field of psychotherapy research in the past dozen years (Luborsky, Crits-Christoph, & Mellon, 1986) that has resulted in the development of 15 central relationship pattern measures. The data base for these measures is a sample of the person's relationship interactions in narratives from psychotherapy sessions, from other interviews, or from actual behavioral samples of such interactions. From these narratives the most pervasive pattern is abstracted through clinical judgment. The first of these central relationship pattern measures that fits these criteria was the CCRT method (Luborsky, 1977; Luborsky & Crits-Christoph, 1990). The method can be applied reliably by independent CCRT judges (Crits-Christoph, Cooper, & Luborsky, 1988), or the method can be used clinically by the clinician during the sessions to formulate the central relationship pattern, which in turn helps focus the interpretations. Because the method represents a formalization of what dynamic therapists generally do in formulating transference patterns, therapists report that they can comfortably use the basic structure of the method in the course of therapy (Fried, 1989).

An example is presented to illustrate the method of deriving the CCRT version of the central relationship pattern. The example is from Session 5 of Ms. Cunningham, a young married woman with sexual inhibition and problems in being close. The narratives that she gave in that session (in highly condensed form) about her interactions with other people are as follows:

1. *About her assistant*: I am annoyed by her. I don't want to share her because she might prefer the other worker to me.

2. *About her husband*: I got home in a funny mood about what I'd done with the boys (a group

under her supervision). I wanted his approval or direction. He didn't give it, so I got furious.

3. *About a boy's group*: I was upset. Two boys in the group stick together rather than mix. I'm trying to separate them. I'm annoyed. I spoke to one parent—I hadn't intended to—but then I couldn't stop. I tried to control myself.

4. *About her therapist*: (Therapist: You didn't express wanting reassurance *here* yesterday.) Patient: I won't get reassurance here. I want to be reassured you're listening.

5. *About her professor*: I noticed his tie was coarse woven. I reached out and held it and said "This is a wonderful texture."

Each of the self–other narratives was scored to locate the types of these three components: wishes, the responses from the other person, and the responses of the self. The most frequent of each of the three types of components across all narratives constitutes the CCRT. Ms. Cunningham's CCRT was as follows:

- Wish 1: to be assertive by exerting control over the other person; to be dominant
- Wish 2: to control herself
- Wish 3: to be reassured; to get approval
- Responses from other: dominates; controls; disapproves; does not reassure
- Responses of self: fear of poor self-control; self-blame; feelings of anger, upset, and inhibition.

We are now engaged in validity studies of what is measured by the CCRT and, more broadly, of its convergence with Freud's (1912/1958) basic clinical observations about the transference pattern. One of Freud's (1895/1955, 1905/1953) observations was that the pattern is expressed across multiple modes both in the patient's dreams and in his or her narratives about events. We have begun to examine this observation by comparing the CCRT for dreams with the CCRT for waking narratives (Popp, Luborsky, & Crits-Christoph, 1990). Another of Freud's (1905/1953) basic observations about the transference is that the general relationship pattern comes to involve the therapist. We examined this hypothesis (Fried, Crits-Christoph, & Luborsky, 1990) by comparing the narratives about the therapist with the CCRT for other people. A significant parallel emerged. Our aim is eventually to examine the degree of parallel between each of the 22 observations Freud made about his concept of the "transference template" and relevant evidence from the CCRT (Luborsky, 1990). So far we have shown evidence for the parallel in nine of these and probable evidence for the parallel in seven others for which we have done only an initial study. For the observation about insight we have mixed results. For the remaining five we have not yet fashioned an operational definition of Freud's observation.

Accuracy of interpretation measures. Dynamic psychotherapists have a long tradition of striving to achieve accurate interpretations. It has been difficult to do quantitative research on this topic, however, although initiative has been taken (Auerbach & Luborsky, 1968). The problem has been to find an operational measure of accuracy that makes sense clinically and is reliably measurable. Crits-Christoph, Cooper, et al. (1988) developed a measure on the basis of a two-step process. In the first step, one set of judges identifies the essence of the patient's message in terms of the CCRT; in the second step, another set of judges establishes the degree of accuracy of each of the therapist's main interpretations in terms of their congruence with the patient's CCRT. These judgments were made with good levels of reliability, and the measure showed a moderately good level of correlation with the outcomes of psychotherapy for 43 patients ($r = .44$, $p < .01$). The implication of this correlation is consistent with clinical theory: The greater the accuracy of the interpretation, the greater the benefit provided to the patient.

Self-understanding and insight measures. It is one of the basic propositions of psychoanalytic psychotherapy and psychoanalysis that the greater the insight, the greater the patient's improvement. Of the four findings reported in research studies, however, only one showed significant results in relation to outcome. Crits-Christoph and Luborsky (1990b) reported that the early level of self-understanding was related to outcome ($r = .31$, $p < .05$) in the patients from the Penn project. Nevertheless, they did not assess the more theoretically relevant hypothesis that gain in self-understanding over the course of therapy is associated with good outcome.

Change in central relationship patterns. A theoretical proposition about a curative factor in psychotherapy is that the greater the change in the transference pattern, the greater the patient's benefits from psychotherapy. In the Penn project we studied the change for 33 patients in the per-

vasiveness of the CCRT across narratives about relationship interactions, both early and late in therapy, and its relation to more usual measures of change, such as change in symptoms and in the psychological health–sickness dimension (Crits-Christoph & Luborsky, 1990a). The main results were as follows:

1. The CCRT pervasiveness scores showed a high degree of agreement among judges.

2. The CCRTs of each case about 1 year later remained recognizably similar in pervasiveness to the early CCRTs. As an example of long-term consistency, the CCRT for Ms. Cunningham presented earlier remains similar to the CCRT in Session 1028 about 4 years later.

3. Nevertheless, there were also meaningful changes in CCRT pervasiveness from early to late. These differed for the different components of the CCRT; the wishes did not change significantly, but the responses did. The largest changes were a decrease in negative responses of self, a decrease in negative responses from other, and an increase in positive responses from other.

4. The change in CCRT pervasiveness correlated significantly with the change in symptoms for three of the five CCRT measures. As an example, change in the psychological health–sickness measure, a measure of psychological health, correlated significantly and in the expected direction with change in the CCRT's negative responses of self.

These data have implications for psychoanalytic theories of change. They do not support the view that the transference pattern is dissolved through therapy. They do lend support to clinical theories that much of the transference pattern will remain and will still be apparent even after successful treatment but that some aspects will change.

The VA–Penn Psychotherapy Project. This project (Woody et al., 1983) investigated many of the same factors that influence outcomes that were included in the Penn Psychotherapy Project (Luborsky et al., 1988), including psychological health and sickness (McLellan, Woody, & Luborsky, 1986) and the therapeutic alliance (Luborsky et al., 1985). The major aim of this project has been to compare three forms of treatment: supportive–expressive, cognitive–behavioral, and treatment as usual (drug counseling). Both of the psychotherapies produced results superior to those of drug counseling (Woody et al., 1983) and were generally but not significantly different from each other in their benefits. A significant and usual correlation appeared between psychological health and the benefits of the three treatments: Better initial psychological health was associated with greater benefits from the therapy.

A special factor that was investigated in this project was the success of each therapist in helping patients. The method was to compare the outcomes of each therapist in terms of the benefits attained by the patients in his or her caseload. Three reports have been completed:

1. Nine therapists, each treating about 6 patients, showed large differences in the outcomes of their caseloads. These differences tended to be associated with the quality of the helping alliance that their patients established with them (Luborsky et al., 1985).

2. Two counselors who each started with new equivalent caseloads later showed important differences in their patients' outcomes (McLellan, Luborsky, & Woody, 1988).

3. The data from four studies (at Penn, Johns Hopkins, the University of Pittsburgh, and the University of Montreal) were assembled, with each containing a set of therapists and the treatment outcomes of their caseloads. Therapist differences were found in the outcomes in each study (Luborsky, Crits-Christoph, McLellan, et al., 1986).

The Dynamic Psychotherapy for Major Depression Project. Although this project is still incomplete, two findings have emerged with sufficient clarity to be worth reporting. First, with a partial sample of 18 patients, moderate benefits were found from the 16-session time-limited dynamic psychotherapy. Second, patients with a single diagnosis of major depression were found to benefit from psychotherapy more than those with an additional diagnosis such as personality disorder. Having an additional diagnosis probably implies greater psychiatric severity, which would limit the benefits from psychotherapy.

The Preference for Therapists Project. In this study we examined patients' preferences for therapists after the patients had had two sessions with each of two therapists. At the outset we considered two contradictory expectations: (a) Patients would choose the first therapist because their main attachment had been established with the first therapist and (b) patients would remain with the second therapist primarily because they were already seeing the second therapist and there would be an incumbent affect. Initial results from 47 patients (Alexander et al., 1990) showed that more than two thirds of the patients who were given the choice of the two different therapists whom they had seen preferred to stay with the incumbent, that is, the second of the two therapists.

Statistical Implications of Therapist Effects Project. Findings from the project on statistical implications of therapist effects for conducting comparative treatment studies have been reported at the Society for Psychotherapy Research meetings (Crits-Christoph, 1987), and a final report is near completion (Crits-Christoph & Mintz, 1989). This project first reviewed the psychotherapy outcome research literature to determine how researchers have treated the therapist as a factor in the design and analysis of their studies. It is argued that the therapist should be considered a random term, rather than a fixed factor, or ignored completely (as is commonly done). The importance of this issue depends on the typical size of therapist effects and the amount of bias introduced in significance testing for treatment differences by not specifying the therapist as a random term. To examine the size of therapist effects, the data from 10 psychotherapy outcome studies were analyzed for the percentage outcome variance due to therapists. The results indicated that therapist effects vary considerably but at times can be large. Computer simulation studies revealed that considerable bias can be introduced by not specifying the therapist as a random term. On the basis of these findings, we give recommendations for the design and analysis of psychotherapy outcome studies.

Assessing psychodynamic constructs in cognitive therapy. The study that used the data from the sample of Hollon et al. (1989) is in progress, and findings are not yet available.

Assessing cognitive changes in cognitive therapy. Barber and DeRubeis (1989) developed an open-ended thought-listing assessment (Ways of Responding Questionnaire) to measure the acquisition of compensatory skills supposedly taught during cognitive therapy. In the initial comparison of patients who received medication or cognitive therapy or supportive–expressive therapy, Barber (1989) found that patients' skills improved with treatment regardless of the type of treatment. Patients who began treatment with a high level of compensatory skills did not benefit as much from treatment. Similar results were obtained with other cognitive measures, such as the Attributional Style Questionnaire (Peterson, Semmel, von Baeyer, Abramson, Metalsky, & Seligman, 1982; Seligman et al., 1988) and the Dysfunctional Attitudes Scale (Weissman, 1979). These results, together with existing findings, seem to suggest the intricate interrelation of the cognitive, affective, and biochemical components of depression.

Research Programs in Progress and Planned for the Future

Tests of Propositions of Dynamic Therapy

We plan to continue the study of the factors influencing outcomes of psychotherapy with the data of the Penn project and other ongoing projects because it is essential for dynamic therapy to increase the body of tested information about the validity of its propositions about curative factors. We have outlined the progress so far in a recent review (Luborsky, Barber, & Crits-Christoph, 1990). Our further research agenda includes the study of combinations of scores on measures of curative factors (e.g., the helping alliance, accuracy of interpretations, self-understanding) so that we can learn how they interact in predicting the outcomes of dynamic psychotherapy.

The Development of Operational Measures

We are continuing with the psychometric development of operational measures of the curative factors. These include the following: (a) Conduct further validity studies for the CCRT method along the lines suggested in Luborsky and Crits-Christoph (1990). Within these projected studies, a high priority is the further development of standard categories for scoring the CCRT (Barber, Crits-Christoph, & Luborsky, 1990) and the further construction of measures of insight with the CCRT method. (b) Systematically develop a measure of adherence to the manual for supportive–expressive psychotherapy (Luborsky, 1984; Barber, Crits-Christoph, & Luborsky, 1989). (c) Construct a questionnaire-based measure to assess the pervasive central relationships (Barber, Crits-Christoph, & Luborsky, 1990).

Development of Time-Limited Dynamic Therapy for Major Depression

The sample will be enlarged to follow through with reevaluation of the main hypotheses that have received support so far: a moderate benefit from short-term dynamic psychotherapy and a significant contribution to the benefit of the initial psychiatric severity of the patients.

Mood, Immunocompetence, and Illness of Depressed Patients in Psychotherapy

The hypothesis will be examined that the level of depression is associated with the level of immunocompetence and the frequency of certain physical illnesses (Luborsky, Barber, et al., 1990).

Testing of Theories of Change in Two Therapies

A study is underway comparing the theories of change in dynamic and cognitive–behavioral psychotherapy. The results of this study should provide guidance in the further testing of theories of change in different forms of psychotherapy.

Comparative Studies of Cognitive and Dynamic Therapies

Crits-Christoph is leading an effort to bring together investigators in both cognitive and psychodynamic therapies at Penn (including Luborsky, Aaron Beck, and Barber from the Psychiatry Department and Martin Seligman and Robert DeRubeis from the Psychology Department). This research program would evaluate the efficacy of the two therapies with various disorders in an attempt to discover the best match of patient types with modes of treatment. Initial disorders to be studied include chronic depression, generalized anxiety disorders, obsessive–compulsive personality disorder, avoidant personality disorder, and dependent personality disorder. The significance of these studies is heightened by the fact that we will be controlling more carefully than is usual for the factors influencing treatment outcomes.

Nature of the Research Organization

NIMH provided funding for developing the CCRT method (Luborsky, principal investigator) and for studying the benefits of accuracy of interpretation (Crits-Christoph, principal investigator). The Office of Naval Research funded the study of mood–immune system relationships (Luborsky, principal investigator), and the National Institute on Drug Abuse funded the comparative study of curative factors in two different psychotherapies (Crits-Christoph, principal investigator). The Fund for Psychoanalytic Research supported the examination of the immediate impact of accurate interpretations on patients' levels of resistance (Crits-Christoph, principal investigator) and the study of the relation between dream and waking narratives (Carol Popp, principal investigator). Studies of the CCRT and of unconscious and conscious processes are being carried out in collaboration with the MacArthur Program at the University of California, San Francisco (Horowitz, principal investigator). Finally, Luborsky has received an NIMH Research Scientist Award, and Crits-Christoph has received an NIMH Research Career Development Award. NIMH support is being pursued for the comparative treatment studies as well.

Relation to Other Research Programs

The findings from the Penn psychotherapy projects are now sufficient in quantity to have an impact on clinical practice and training (Luborsky, 1987). Each of the operationalized measures of patient and treatment has an implication for clinical practice. For example, the degree of psychiatric severity, such as an Axis II diagnosis, should have an implication for clinicians about the outcomes of treatment, and psychiatric severity should also be used as a basis for equating patients to be compared in different treatments. Therapists should be encouraged to monitor or at times to develop a good therapeutic alliance. Therapists should recurrently formulate the central relationship pattern and the conflicts in it and then guide their interpretations by this formulation to achieve more accurate interpretations. The knowledge of these factors should become part of clinical training (Fried, 1989)

because of their known relationship with the outcomes of psychotherapy.

References

Alexander, L., Luborsky, L., Crits-Christoph, P., & Auerbach, A. (1990, June). *What happens when patients choose therapists?* Paper presented at the annual meeting of the Society for Psychotherapy Research, Wintergreen, VA.

American Psychiatric Association. (1987). *Diagnostic and statistical manual of mental disorders* (rev. 3rd ed.). Washington, DC: Author.

Auerbach, A. H., & Luborsky, L. (1968). Accuracy of judgements of psychotherapy and the nature of the "good hour." In J. Shlien, H. F. Hunt, J. P. Matarazzo, & C. Savage (Eds.), *Research in psychotherapy* (Vol. 3, pp. 155–168). Washington, DC: American Psychological Association.

Barber, J. P. (1989). *What is learned in cognitive therapy? An initial validation of the Ways of Responding Questionnaire and a test of the compensatory model of change.* Unpublished doctoral dissertation, University of Pennsylvania, Philadelphia.

Barber, J. P., & DeRubeis, R. J. (1989). On second thought: Where the action is in cognitive therapy for depression. *Cognitive Therapy and Research, 13,* 441–457.

Barber, J. P., & DeRubeis, R. J. (1990). *The Ways of Responding: Development and initial validation of a scale to assess compensatory skills.* Manuscript submitted for publication.

Barber, J. P., Crits-Christoph, P., & Luborsky, L. (1990). A guide to CCRT standard categories and their classification. In L. Luborsky & P. Crits-Christoph, (Eds.), *Understanding transference: The core conflictual relationship theme method* (pp. 37–50). New York: Basic Books.

Barber, J. P., Crits-Christoph, P., & Luborsky, L. (1989). *The Penn Adherence Scales for Supportive–Expressive Psychotherapy (PAS-SE).* Unpublished manuscript, University of Pennsylvania, Department of Psychiatry, Philadelphia.

Barber, J. P., Crits-Christoph, P., & Luborsky, L. (1990). *The Central Relationship Questionnaire.* Unpublished manuscript, University of Pennsylvania, Department of Psychiatry, Philadelphia.

Crits-Christoph, P. (1987, June). *The size of therapist effects and the problem of non-independence in psychotherapy outcome research.* Paper presented at the annual meeting of the Society for Psychotherapy Research, Ulm, Federal Republic of Germany.

Crits-Christoph, P., Cooper, A., & Luborsky, L. (1988). The accuracy of therapists' interpretations and the outcome of dynamic psychotherapy. *Journal of Consulting and Clinical Psychology, 56,* 490–495.

Crits-Christoph, P., & Luborsky, L. (1990a). The changes in CCRT pervasiveness during psychotherapy. In L. Luborsky & P. Crits-Christoph (Eds.), *Understanding transference: The core conflictual relationship theme method* (pp. 133–146). New York: Basic Books.

Crits-Christoph, P., & Luborsky, L. (1990b). The measurement of self-understanding. In L. Luborsky & P. Crits-Christoph (Eds.), *Understanding transference: The core conflictual relationship theme method,* (pp. 189–196). New York: Basic Books.

Crits-Christoph, P., & Mintz, J. (1989). *Statistical implications of therapist effects for conducting comparative studies of psychotherapies.* Unpublished manuscript, University of Pennsylvania, Philadelphia.

Endicott, J., Spitzer, R., Fleiss, J., & Cohen, J. (1976). The Global Assessment Scale: A procedure for measuring overall severity of psychiatric disturbances. *Archives of General Psychiatry, 33,* 766–771.

Freud, S. (1953). Fragment of an analysis of a case of hysteria. In J. Strachey (Ed. and Trans.), *The standard edition of the complete psychological works of Sigmund Freud* (Vol. 7, pp. 15–122). London: Hogarth Press. (Original work published 1905)

Freud, S. (1955). Psychotherapy of hysteria. In J. Strachey (Ed. and Trans.), *The standard edition of the complete psychological works of Sigmund Freud,* (Vol. 2, pp. 255–305). London: Hogarth Press. (Original work published 1895)

Freud, S. (1958). The dynamics of the transference. In J. Strachey (Ed. and Trans.), *The standard edition of the complete psychological works of Sigmund Freud* (Vol. 12, pp. 99-108). London: Hogarth Press. (Original work published 1912)

Fried, D. (1989). *Therapists' evaluation of their utilization of the CCRT in practice.* Unpublished manuscript, Yale University, New Haven, CT.

Fried, D., Crits-Christoph, P. & Luborsky, L. (1990). The parallel of the narratives about the therapist vs. the CCRT about others. In L. Luborsky & P. Crits-Christoph (Eds.), *Understanding transference: The core conflictual relationship theme method,* (pp. 147–157).

Hollon, S. D., DeRubeis, R. J., Evans, M. D., Wiemer, M. J., Garvey, M. J., Grove, W. M., & Tuason, V. B. (1989). *Cognitive therapy, pharmacotherapy, and combined cognitive–pharmacotherapy in the treatment of depression: I. Differential outcome in the CPT Project.* Manuscript submitted for publication.

Luborsky, L. (1975). Clinicians' judgments of mental health: Specimen case descriptions and forms for the Health–Sickness Rating Scale. *Bulletin of the Menninger Clinic, 35,* 448–480.

Luborsky, L. (1976). Helping alliances in psychotherapy: The groundwork for a study of their relationship to its outcome. In J. L. Claghorn (Ed.), *Successful psychotherapy* (pp. 92–116). New York: Brunner/Mazel.

Luborsky, L. (1977). Measuring a pervasive psychic structure in psychotherapy: The core conflictual relationship theme. In N. Freedman & S. Grand (Eds.), *Communicative structures and psychic structures* (pp. 367–395). New York: Plenum Press.

Luborsky, L. (1984). *Principles of psychoanalytic psychotherapy: A manual for supportive-expressive (SE) treatment.* New York: Basic Books.

Luborsky, L. (1987). Research can now affect clinical practice—A happy turnaround. *Clinical Psychologist, 40,* 56–60.

Luborsky, L. (1990). The convergence of Freud's observations about transference with CCRT evidence. In L. Luborsky & P. Crits-Christoph (Eds.), *Understand-*

ing transference: The core conflictual relationship theme method. (pp. 251–266).

Luborsky, L., & Auerbach, A. (1985). The therapeutic relationship in psychodynamic psychotherapy: The research evidence and its meaning for practice. In R. Hales & A. Frances (Eds.), *Psychiatry update: The American Psychiatric Association annual review* (Vol. 4, pp. 550–561). Washington, DC: American Psychiatric Press.

Luborsky, L., Barber, J. P., & Crits-Christoph, P. (1990). Theory-based research for understanding the process of dynamic psychotherapy. *Journal of Consulting and Clinical Psychology, 58,* 281–287.

Luborsky, L., Barber, J., Levinson, A., Prystowsky, M., Cacciola, J., Gleser, R., & Bastian, J. (1990). *Antibody levels in relation to changes in depression after psychotherapy.* Unpublished manuscript.

Luborsky, L., & Crits-Christoph, P. (1990). *Understanding transference: The core conflictual relationship theme method.* New York: Basic Books.

Luborsky, L., Crits-Christoph, P., Alexander, L., Margolis, M., & Cohen, M. (1983). Two helping alliance methods for predicting outcomes of psychotherapy: A counting signs versus a global rating method. *Journal of Nervous and Mental Disease, 171,* 480–492

Luborsky, L., Crits-Christoph, P., & Mellon, J. (1986). The advent of objective measures of the transference concept. *Journal of Consulting and Clinical Psychology, 54,* 39–47.

Luborsky, L., Crits-Christoph, P., McLellan, T., Woody, G., Piper, W., Imber, S., & Liberman, B. (1986). Do therapists vary much in their success? Findings from four outcome studies. *American Journal of Orthopsychiatry, 66,* 501–512.

Luborsky, L., Crits-Christoph, P., Mintz, J., & Auerbach, A. (1988). *Who will benefit from psychotherapy? Predicting therapeutic outcomes.* New York: Basic Books.

Luborsky, L., McLellan, A. T., Woody, G. E., O'Brien, C. P., & Auerbach, A. (1985). Therapist success and its determinants. *Archives of General Psychiatry, 42,* 602–611.

McLellan, A. T., Luborsky, L., & Woody, G. (1988). Is the counselor an "active ingredient" in methadone treatment? An examination of treatment success among four counselors. *Journal of Nervous and Mental Disease, 176,* 423–430.

McLellan, A. T., Woody, G., & Luborsky, L. (1986). "Psychiatric severity" as a predictor of outcome from substance treatments. In R. Meyer (Ed.), *Psychiatric aspects of opiate dependence.* New York: Guilford Press.

Morgan, R., Luborsky, L., Crits-Christoph, P., Curtis, H., & Solomon, J. (1982). Predicting the outcomes of psychotherapy by the Penn helping alliance rating method. *Archives of General Psychiatry, 39,* 397–402.

Peterson, C., Semmel, A., von Baeyer, C., Abramson, L., Metalsky, G., & Seligman, M. (1982). The Attributional Style Questionnaire. *Cognitive Therapy and Research, 6,* 287–299.

Popp, C., Luborsky, L., & Crits-Christoph, P. (1990). The parallels of dream narratives and waking narratives. In L. Luborsky & P. Crits-Christoph (Eds.), *Understanding transference: The core conflictual relationship theme method* (pp. 158–172). New York: Basic Books.

Seligman, M., Castellon, C., Cacciola, J., Schulman, P., Luborsky, L., Ollove, M., & Downing, R. (1988). Explanatory style change during cognitive therapy for unipolar depressed patients. *Journal of Abnormal Psychology, 97,* 13–18.

Weissman, A. N. (1979). *The Dysfunctional Attitudes Scale: A validation study.* Unpublished manuscript, University of Pennsylvania, Philadelphia.

Woody, G., Luborsky, L., McLellan, A. T., O'Brien, C., Beck, A. T., Blaine, J., Herman, I., & Hole, A. V. (1983). Psychotherapy for opiate addicts: Does it help? *Archives of General Psychiatry, 40,* 639–645.

CHAPTER

17

University of Texas Southwestern Medical Center at Dallas: Psychosocial Research Program in Mood Disorders

Robin B. Jarrett
Mental Health Clinical Research Center
University of Texas Southwestern Medical Center at Dallas

Background and Aims

History

In 1978, A. John Rush, MD, established a descriptive research program involving mood disorders in the Department of Psychiatry at the University of Texas (UT) Southwestern Medical Center at Dallas. Polysomnographic studies of depressed clients before treatment were being conducted under the direction of Howard P. Roffwarg, MD, and dexamethasone challenges were assayed under the direction of Paul J. Orsulak, PhD. Descriptive studies of biological dysregulation in depression were ongoing. Questionnaires regarding psychological functioning were routinely administered, and a pilot study of cognitive therapy was underway.

In 1984, Robin B. Jarrett, PhD, joined this established collaborative research group, which had been having an impact primarily in the area of biological psychiatry. Her arrival brought the energy needed to ensure that the research agenda included a systematic examination of the role of psychosocial factors in mood disorders. Study of the role of psychosocial variables includes issues

relevant not only to treating depression but also to the psychopathology of depression. Thus, the broad agenda became, and continues to be, the intensive study of all variables—both biological and psychological—important in the pathogenesis, course, and treatment of mood disorders.

In 1987, the research group successfully obtained funding through the National Institute of Mental Health (NIMH). It was christened and continues as the Mental Health Clinical Research Center (MHCRC). Presently, the focus of MHCRC research is to identify and understand variables important in producing and preventing relapses and recurrences of mood disorders. To accomplish this broad aim, additional recruiting occurred. Monica A. Basco, PhD, was recruited to collaborate in psychosocial research, particularly on the role of interpersonal factors in mood disorders.

I wish to express my appreciation to David Savage for secretarial assistance and to Kenneth Z. Altshuler, MD, Stanton Sharp Professor and Chairman, for his administrative support.

Preparation of this chapter was supported in part by a National Institute of Mental Health grant (MH-41115) to the Department of Psychiatry, University of Texas Southwestern Medical Center at Dallas.

Christina M. Gullion, PhD, was recruited to collaborate and provide statistical support. Collaboration continues with other established researchers, junior investigators, and students interested in psychosocial variables and mood disorders. The psychosocial research program in mood disorders enjoys the support of the MHCRC, including collaboration with Cores (psychiatric assessment, sleep studies, data management and statistics, psychiatric clinical diagnostic laboratory, brain imaging, and administration).

To date, psychotherapy research in Dallas has centered primarily on the treatment of depression with cognitive therapy. Even so, we think of our program not only as one of psychotherapy research but also as one with a broad interest in the psychosocial factors involved in mood disorders. In so doing, we have been particularly interested in studying the potential relations between and the roles of biological and psychological variables in mood disorders. Studying distinct sets of psychosocial variables as well as their association with biological variables may prove relevant to understanding the pathogenesis and course of mood disorders; these variables may or may not be relevant to treatment, or vice versa.

Training in cognitive therapy has centered primarily around educating cognitive therapists who participate in research protocols. In the past 5 years, we have developed a systematic program for training protocol therapists and have an extensive library of videotapes that are useful in this training process. G. Greg Eaves, PhD, has been actively involved with the program since 1982, and Brian F. Shaw, PhD (of Toronto, Canada), provides off-site consultation in our training effort. In recent years, as our study of the role of psychological factors in mood disorders continues to expand, our cadre of research cognitive therapists has grown to include psychologists, psychiatrists, psychiatric fellows, psychiatric residents, psychology graduate students, and social workers.

Overall Aims

Specific aims of the Psychosocial Research Program in Mood Disorders presently include (a) studying the interaction between psychological and biological dysregulation in mood disorders; (b) predicting which depressions respond to cognitive therapy; (c) developing cognitive therapy methods aimed at new patient populations (e.g., depressed outpatients with marital or relationship discord, depressed children and adolescents, and pharmacologically stabilized bipolar patients); (d) identifying psychosocial factors that relate to relapse and recurrence and their prevention; (e) developing psychological measures of cognitive and interpersonal variables that may affect the course of mood disorders or response to treatment; and (f) developing new and improving on currently established methods to train cognitive therapists to participate in research on depression.

Rationale

Why study the interaction between psychological and biological dysregulation? One of the unique aspects of our research program is that we have the opportunity to collaborate with investigators interested in biological psychiatry (e.g., those interested in sleep or brain imaging research). Through such collaboration, which by definition involves different levels of analysis, we hope to better understand the course of mood disorders.

What is cognitive therapy and why study it? We have focused on cognitive therapy, a short-term psychological treatment that is based on the phenomenological model of human behavior (Beck, Rush, Shaw, & Emery, 1979). We have elected to study cognitive therapy because it reduces depressive symptoms in an unidentified subtype of unipolar nonpsychotic depressed outpatients more than it does in a waiting-list or a nonspecific treatment control condition (Jarrett & Rush, 1986) and because it shows promise as a maintenance or prophylactic treatment under some unidentified conditions (Blackburn, Eunson, & Bishop, 1986).

Why innovate in or extend cognitive therapy? These early but promising findings regarding the efficacy of cognitive therapy were important in the treatment of depression because cognitive therapy offered an effective alternative or adjunct to medication treatment and may prove to be prophylactic. As a result of such promise, we have queried whether cognitive therapy might be adaptable to new patient populations and other important variants of or clinical problems associated with depressive illness. We will adapt and apply cognitive therapy to new patient populations (e.g., depressed children and adolescents, pharmacologically stable bipolar depressed patients, patients with marital or relationship discord) as well as to currently unsolved clinical problems (e.g., relapse and recurrence).

Why develop booster sessions after cognitive therapy? Booster sessions after an acute trial of cognitive therapy for the treatment of depression are an important adaptation because it is unclear under what conditions cognitive therapy is, in fact, prophylactic. Our own data have shown that the positive effects of short-term cognitive therapy may be short lived (Jarrett, Gullion, Basco, & Rush, 1989). These findings have motivated us to evaluate whether the high rate of relapse and recurrence obtained in our pilot study is replicable and to design maintenance or booster sessions in an ongoing cognitive therapy trial.

Why develop new measures to assess cognitive and interpersonal factors relevant to the course of mood disorders? Psychological researchers of mood disorders have searched for psychological markers of depressive illness in a manner similar to that of biological researchers, who are interested in locating variables associated with vulnerability for mood disorders and the onset of illness. Theoretically, one of the most important questions is whether psychological factors correlated with depressive illness are antecedents and thus have causal roles or whether they are consequences of the illness (i.e., simple concomitants). Finding answers to these questions has been hampered by poor measurement, which has confused theoretical issues and methodology, and has resulted in controversy. In the field of psychological research, investigators have relied heavily on self-report questionnaires. Bias in and difficulties with obtaining information from patients with self-reports (e.g., reliance on retrospective reporting, unreliability, and poor internal validity) makes them a precarious basis for forming scientific conclusions. At the same time, the field has been slow to develop new measures (e.g., behavioral samples of factors important in the course of illness) because of the labor-intensive nature of such endeavors.

We have elected to develop behavioral samples of cognitive and interpersonal variables, which were chosen as the area of study because they are important in the psychopathology and course of illness and may be related to relapse and recurrence. We have selected behavioral sampling as the method for assessment because it may have higher external validity than other measures (i.e., the behavior in question is sampled rather than recorded retrospectively). The measurement of cognitive distortion or biased attributions that

is currently under development is called the Worst Event Test (WET; Casenave, Gullion, & Jarrett, 1990; D'Arcangelis, Casenave, Kolodner, Peterson, & Jarrett, 1990). The measure of interpersonal communication skill also under development is called the Clinician Rating of Adult Communication (CRAC; Basco, Birchler, Kalal, Talbott, & Slater, in press).

Why is it necessary to improve methods for training cognitive clinicians to participate in research? To conduct psychotherapy research, it is first necessary to have available a cadre of psychotherapists who can competently and validly provide the studied treatment. Our efforts in Dallas, as well as those in Philadelphia, Pittsburgh, and Toronto, reveal that training, supervision, and quality control of cognitive therapists are continuous, labor-intensive processes. Improved training methods may decrease the associated time and costs involved.

To the extent that psychotherapy is an independent variable in a study, training, supervision, and longitudinal quality control provide checks on the manipulation and thus increase the likelihood that optimal conditions for testing the therapy exist. Only when a psychotherapy has "integrity" (i.e., when the manual has been followed and is representative of the studied intervention rather than an alternate brand of psychotherapy) and the clinician is competent (i.e., demonstrates an acceptable level of skill) has the clinical trial been conducted under optimal conditions.

Experts in cognitive therapy agree that not all competent psychotherapists can become good cognitive therapists. Thus, selection and training of therapists are necessary. After a cognitive therapist has been trained to meet a criterion, it is common for therapist competence and treatment integrity to be influenced by the difficulty of the patient (Shaw & Dobson, 1988), exposure to alternative therapies through continued education, and personal life events. Such drift necessitates longitudinal quality control, which consists of monitoring treatment integrity and therapist competence over time. Such monitoring allows empirical demonstration that the treatment is valid and pure (has integrity), that the therapist is competent, and that the intervention occurs when a therapist is performing below the criterion.

Once a cadre of competent therapists is developed, training them to treat depression is a continuous process for the following reasons: The skills of therapists who have met the criterion can deteriorate without stimulation or with difficult patients, some attrition of therapists is to be expected as their professional goals change over time, and more therapists are needed as the number of protocols involving cognitive therapy increases. We are in the process of systematizing the training and longitudinal quality control of protocol cognitive therapists.

Method

Subjects

Because our research program operates in a medical center in a large metropolitan area, the types of patients who could be studied span most psychologic disorders and medical and psychiatric illnesses. Most subjects who have been studied to date include adult outpatients presenting with depression to the Mood Disorders Outpatient Program. Potential subjects undergo a psychiatric evaluation using structured interviews: the Schedule for Affective Disorders and Schizophrenia (Endicott & Spitzer, 1978) and the Structured Clinical Interview for DSM-III–R (*Diagnostic and Statistical Manual of Mental Disorders*, revised third edition, American Psychiatric Association, 1987; Spitzer, Williams, & Gibbons, 1986). Detailed histories of the subjects' course of illness are obtained. Medical tests are routinely performed, and medical consultation is sought when indicated.

Instruments

Both biological and psychosocial assessments are performed. Biological assessment includes sleep polysomnographic studies conducted under the direction of Howard P. Roffwarg, MD, dexamethasone suppression testing with assay quality control conducted under the direction of Paul J. Orsulak, PhD, and selected brain imaging conducted under the supervision of Michael D. Devous, Sr, PhD. A wide range of psychosocial questionnaires are administered to subjects. These include the Dysfunctional Attitudes Scale (Weissman, 1979), the Attributional Style Questionnaire (Seligman, Abramson, Semmel, & von Baeyer, 1979), the Automatic Thoughts Questionnaire (Hollon & Kendall, 1980), the Self-Control Scale (Rosenbaum, 1980), the Dyadic Adjustment Scale (Spainer, 1976), and the Social Adjustment Scale (Weissman & Bothwell, 1976).

Severity of client symptoms is assessed with the 17-item Hamilton Rating Scale for Depression (Hamilton, 1960, 1967), the Beck Depression Inventory (Beck, Ward, Mendelson, Mock, & Erbaugh, 1961) and the Inventory for Depressive Symptomatology (Rush, Giles, Schlesser, Fulton, Weissenburger, & Burns, 1986).

As already mentioned, our research group is currently involved in attempting to develop new methods of assessing cognitive distortions with the WET and verbal and nonverbal communication in dyads with the CRAC.

Selected patients receive the Personality Disorders Examination (Loranger, Susman, Oldham, & Russakoff, 1987) and participate in a study investigating the potential relationship between personality disorders and mood disorder.

Procedures

Cognitive therapy is conducted according to the treatment manual of Beck et al. (1979). Competence and adherence are evaluated both locally and off site with the Cognitive Therapy Scale (Young & Beck, 1980; Vallis, Shaw, & Dobson, 1986) after videotaped sessions are observed. Supervision of therapists occurs weekly in a group format. Individual therapist supervision and consultation occur as needed. Supervision includes lectures, role plays, case conferences, and discussion of issues relevant to psychotherapy in general and to cognitive therapy in particular. In addition, we have developed an extensive archive of videotaped cognitive therapy sessions that is available for process studies.

Research Accomplishments

To date, our major research finding is that reduced rapid eye movement (REM) latency has not been associated with a positive or negative response to cognitive therapy (Jarrett, Rush, Khatami, & Roffwarg, in press). Furthermore, these results suggest that some patients with biological dysregulation (as indicated by reduced REM latency) show a favorable response to an acute trial of cognitive therapy. Limitations of this initial finding include a small sample of patients who exhibit REM latencies less than 51 minutes and few endogenous depressions. Data collection continues with an effort to enter more endogenous depressions, as defined by Research Diagnostic Criteria (Spitzer, Endicott, & Robins, 1978).

A second research finding is that the rate of relapse or recurrence after an acute trial of cognitive therapy is much higher than expected (Jarrett et al., in press). We are in the process of attempting to identify variables associated with this high rate of relapse or recurrence and are adapting cognitive therapy to decrease the probability of relapse and recurrence.

In the area of the role of psychosocial factors in the psychopathology of mood disorders, we have examined the extent to which depressed outpatients experience dysfunctional guilt. We have found that depressed outpatients report significantly more guilt than normal controls in most types of situations. A positive family history of depression was related to a higher overall level of guilt in depressed patients than in those without such a history. Course of illness, severity of depression, and the endogenous subtype were not related to the amount of guilt reported by depressed patients (Jarrett & Weissenburger, 1990).

Research Programs in Progress

We continue our attempts to predict response to cognitive therapy by examining the broad question "Who responds to cognitive therapy?" We are investigating this question by examining subgroups of depressed outpatients. In May 1989, we received funding from NIMH to conduct a 5-year, controlled, randomized comparison of cognitive therapy, phenelzine, and pill placebo in the treatment of atypical depression. In this study, atypical depression is operationalized as a major depressive disorder (as defined by the *DSM-III–R*) with atypical features, which include a reactive mood or consummatory pleasure and two or more of the following: increased appetite or weight gain, hypersomnia, leaden paralysis, or lifetime rejection sensitivity (Liebowitz et al., 1984, 1988).

Programs Planned for the Future

New directions in our research will include evaluating applications of cognitive therapy to new populations and targets and a systematic evaluation of the potential prophylactic effects of cognitive therapy with this recurrent illness. Special attention will continue to be given to the potential association between biological and psychological dysregulation in mood disorders with the rationale that such data will generate hypotheses regarding the pathogenesis of major depressive disorder.

Implications of our current research include identifying which patients with mood and related disorders are best treated with psychosocial interventions, specifically cognitive therapy. If we are successful in identifying a priori the responsive subtype(s), the human suffering and economic cost of depression could be reduced. We are in the process of extending this effort to include systematic monthly longitudinal follow-up for the purpose of evaluating the extent and predictors of relapse and recurrence after an acute trial of cognitive therapy. We also hope to evaluate the cost-effectiveness of cognitive therapy and to develop methods or adaptations that make cognitive therapy truly prophylactic for this serious recurrent illness.

Nature of the Research Organization

Funding

Our research program is funded directly through R01 grants from NIMH and by an MHCRC grant. Application and review of grants in departmental, federal, and private foundations is an ongoing process.

Team Members and Their Roles

The following is a list of the primary team members and their roles: Kenneth Z. Altshuler, MD (psychiatrist), Stanton Sharp Professor, chair of the Department of Psychiatry, UT Southwestern Medical Center; A. John Rush, MD, Betty Jo Hay Chair in Mental Health, director of the MHCRC; Robin B. Jarrett, PhD (clinical psychologist), director of the MHCRC Psychosocial Core and Mood Disorders Outpatient Program (studies the role of psychosocial variables in mood disorders and directs research and training on cognitive therapy); Monica Basco, PhD (clinical psychologist and cognitive and marital clinician), co-director of the Psychiatric Assessment Core (studies the role of interpersonal variables in mood disorders); Howard P. Roffwarg, MD (psychiatrist), director of the Sleep Studies Unit at UT Southwestern; Paul J. Orsulak, PhD (biochemist), director of the Psychiatric Clinical Diagnostic Laboratory at Dallas Veterans Affairs Medical Center; Christina M. Gullion, PhD (quantitative psychologist), director of the MHCRC Data Management and Statistics Core; Rodger Kobes, MD, PhD (psychiatrist and biochemist), staff psychiatrist at Timberlawn Psychiatric Hospital and cognitive therapist who collaborates and provides therapy; G. Greg Eaves, PhD (clinical psychologist), private practice psychologist who collaborates and provides therapy; Fred Petty, MD, PhD (psychiatrist), co-director of the Psychiatric Assessment Core (collaborates and conducts studies of mood disorders at the Veterans Affairs Medical Center Mood Disorders Program); Carroll Hughes, PhD (psychologist, conducts longitudinal studies on adolescents with mood disorders); Paul Silver, PhD (clinical psychologist interested in anxiety and personality disorders who collaborates with the MHCRC Psychosocial Core); Robert Gatchel, PhD (clinical psychologist, studies behavioral medicine, particularly the treatment of chronic pain, and provides a liaison with the Division of Psychology); and Brian F. Shaw, PhD (clinical psychologist), off-site consultant. Students (e.g., undergraduates, medical students, graduate students, residents, and fellows) who are studying at UT Southwestern and other Dallas area institutions ask questions that challenge our assumptions and stimulate new ideas.

Relation to Other Research Programs

We communicate and exchange ideas with other researchers in our area by attending professional meetings and publishing our research results in both psychiatric and psychological journals. We communicate with other researchers in our university by participating in research seminars, grand rounds, and working scientific task forces both locally and nationally.

Our research findings should affect clinical practice if we are able to identify which depressed patients should be treated with what psychosocial interventions. We hope to examine methods for increasing the prophylactic effects of cognitive therapy, which would decrease the probability and consequences of relapse and recurrence. At present, we could influence clinical training through a methodology developed for training protocol-appropriate cognitive therapists.

References

American Psychiatric Association. (1987). *Diagnostic and statistical manual of mental disorders* (rev. 3rd ed.). Washington, DC: Author.

Basco, M. R., Birchler, G. R., Kalal, B., Talbott, R., & Slater, M. A. (in press). *The Clinician Rating of Adult Communication (CRAC): A clinician's guide to the assessment of interpersonal communication skill. Journal of Clinical Psychology.*

Beck, A. T., Rush, A. J., Shaw, B. F., & Emery, G. (1979). *Cognitive therapy of depression.* New York: Guilford Press.

Beck, A. T., Ward, C. H., Mendelson, M., Mock, J. E., & Erbaugh, J. K. (1961). An inventory for measuring depression. *Archives of General Psychiatry, 4,* 561–571.

Blackburn, I. M., Eunson, K. M., & Bishop, S. (1986). A two-year naturalistic follow-up of depressed patients treated with cognitive therapy, pharmacotherapy and combination of both. *Journal of Affective Disorders, 10,* 67–75.

Casenave, D., Gullion, C. M., & Jarrett, R. B. (1990, June). *Important design factors in the investigation of the role of attributions in depression: A critical piece to the puzzle.* Paper presented at the meeting of the Society for Psychotherapy Research, Wintergreen, VA.

D'Arcangelis, R. M., Casenave, G., Kolodner, R. M., Peterson, L. L., & Jarrett, R. B. (1990, June). *A computer-assisted content analytic approach to rating biased attribution.* Paper presented at the meeting of the Society for Psychotherapy Research, Wintergreen, VA.

Endicott, J., & Spitzer, R. L. (1978). A diagnostic interview: The Schedule for Affective Disorders and Schizophrenia. *Archives of General Psychiatry, 35,* 837–844.

Hamilton, M. (1960). A rating scale for depression. *Journal of Neurology, Neurosurgery, and Psychiatry, 12,* 56–62.

Hamilton, M. (1967). Development of a rating scale for primary depressive illness. *British Journal of Social and Clinical Psychology, 6,* 278–296.

Hollon, S. D., & Kendall, P. C. (1980). Cognitive self-statements in depression: Development of an automatic thoughts questionnaire. *Cognitive Therapy and Research, 4,* 383–397.

Jarrett, R. B., Gullion, C. M., Basco, M. R., & Rush, A. J. (1989, November). *Are the effects of short-term cognitive therapy short-lived?* Paper presented at the meeting of the Association for Advancement of Behavior Therapy, Washington, DC.

Jarrett, R. B., & Rush, A. J. (1986). Psychotherapeutic approaches to depression. In J. O. Cavenar (Ed.), *Psychiatry* (pp. 1–35). Philadelphia: Lippincott.

Jarrett, R. B., Rush, A. J., Khatami, M., & Roffwarg, H. P. (in press). *Prognostic value of the polysomnogram in cognitive therapy of depression: A preliminary report. Psychiatry Research.*

Jarrett, R. B., & Weissenburger, J. E. (1990). Guilt in depressed outpatients. *Journal of Consulting and Clinical Psychology, 58,* 495–498.

Liebowitz, M. R., Quitkin, F. M., Stewart, J. W., McGrath, P. J., Harrison, W., Rabkin, J., Tricamo, E., Markowitz, J. S., & Klein, D. F. (1984). Phenelzine v imipramine in atypical depression: A preliminary report. *Archives of General Psychiatry, 41,* 669–677.

Liebowitz, M. R., Quitkin, F. M., Stewart, J. W., McGrath, P. J., Harrison, W. M., Markowitz, J. S., Rabkin, J. G., Tricamo, E., Goetz, D. M., & Klein, D.

F. (1988). Antidepressant specificity in atypical depression. *Archives of General Psychiatry, 45,* 129–137.

Loranger, A. W., Susman, V. L., Oldham, J. M., & Russakof, L. M. (1987). The Personality Disorders Examination: A preliminary report. *Journal of Personality Disorders, 1,* 1–13.

Rosenbaum, M. (1980). Individual differences in self-control behaviors and tolerance of painful stimulation. *Journal of Abnormal Psychology, 89,* 581–590.

Rush, A. J., Giles, D. E., Schlesser, M. A., Fulton, C. L., Weissenburger, J. E., & Burns, C. T. (1986). The Inventory for Depressive Symptomatology (IDS): Preliminary findings. *Psychiatry Research, 18,* 65–87.

Seligman, M. E. P., Abramson, L. Y., Semmel, A., & von Baeyer, C. (1979). Depressive attributional style. *Journal of Abnormal Psychology, 88,* 242–247.

Shaw, B. F., & Dobson, K. S. (1988). Competency judgments in the training and evaluation of psychotherapists. *Journal of Consulting and Clinical Psychology, 56,* 666–672.

Spainer, G. B. (1976). Measuring dyadic adjustment: New scales for assessing the quality of marriage and similar dyads. *Journal of Marriage and the Family, 38,* 15–28.

Spitzer, R. L., Endicott, J., & Robins, E. (1978). Research Diagnostic Criteria: Rationale and reliability. *Archives of General Psychiatry, 36,* 773–782.

Spitzer, R. L., Williams, J. B. W., & Gibbons, M. (1986). *Structured Clinical Interview for DSM-III–R (SCID).* New York: New York State Psychiatric Institute, Biometrics Research Department.

Vallis, T., Shaw, B. F., & Dobson, K. D. (1986). The Cognitive Therapy Scale: Psychometric properties. *Journal of Consulting and Clinical Psychology, 54,* 381–385.

Weissman, A. W. (1979). The Dysfunctional Attitudes Scale: A validation study. *Dissertation Abstracts International, 40,* 1389B-1390B.

Weissman, M. M., & Bothwell, S. (1976). Assessment of social adjustment by patient self-report. *Archives of General Psychiatry, 33,* 1111–1115.

Young, J., & Beck, A. T. (1980). *Cognitive Therapy Scale: Rating manual.* Unpublished manuscript, Center for Cognitive Therapy, Philadelphia.

18

University of Washington Health Science Center: Studies on the Representation and Structure of Knowledge in Psychotherapy

Peter E. Maxim and John E. Carr
University of Washington

Background and Aims

History

Since 1963, a number of faculty at the University of Washington Department of Psychiatry and Behavioral Sciences have functioned as a loosely organized research group interested in the representation and organization of psychologic constructs important to client change during psychotherapy. On joining the faculty of the University of Washington in 1963, Carr established a research program aimed at operationally defining the component factors in the patient–therapist interaction and empirically demonstrating their relationship to treatment outcome. Working within the framework of Kelly's "personal construct system" and especially the "sociality corollary," Carr and his colleagues concluded that the literature with regard to patient–therapist similarity in attitudes, beliefs, and personality was inconclusive, largely as the result of confounding content and structure in "cognitive process" and of a methodological mixing of "own" and "provided" constructs in measures of "conceptual structure."

On joining the faculty in 1973, Maxim began research into the methods of representing observed behavior and the basic structures that correlate with them. This work initially focused on primate models of social behavior and the limbic system reinforcement sites that modified ongoing behavior. By 1984, Maxim's interest in quantification and categorization of behavioral categories and brain representation of these knowledge structures shifted from nonhumans to humans and to the patient–therapist interaction dyad.

The goal of this current work is to develop an information modeling system with levels of hierarchical structure, decision making, and dynamic adaption over time. The specific medical area to be modeled is patient–therapist interaction because enough is understood about this interaction that we can make a successful simulation of these interactional ideas. Furthermore, it is a rich enough environment to produce a complex and interesting information model. In developing the model, qualitative simulation of patient–doctor interaction, we are addressing the issues of knowledge representation, of modeling time-oriented processes and dynamic interactions, and of system validation. We hypothesize that a qualitative simulation can successfully describe and predict patient–therapist interaction dialog as it changes over time.

Both principal investigators in this group have focused initially on patient outcome research. A series of empirical investigations was begun, focusing on the role of patient–therapist similarity in the differentiation of cognitive structure as a predictor of treatment efficacy (Carr, 1970). Subsequent investigations focused on other issues relevant to increased understanding of the therapeutic relationship, such as differences in cognitive structures of successful and less successful therapists, cognitive differences associated with diagnosis, and the impact of positive compared with negative constructs on self-perception and the perception of others. Other investigations were conducted on student–teacher interaction, group interactions, mechanisms of change in cognitive structure, and cognitive compared with ethnic or sex role matching as predictors of outcome (Carr, 1980).

Maxim's work initially used a variant of repertory grid analysis and the semantic differential in combination with measures of change in patient coping. An information-processing model was developed that centered on the patient's maladaptive belief as the focal point around which patient and therapist organized their knowledge of the patient's world. Maxim and Hunt (1990) demonstrated that patients' appraisal of and coping with people and issues important to their initial maladaptive beliefs developed a stable, predictable relationship to one another as patients improved. Appraisal and coping appear to be the main feedback structures that can be changed in how patients process information during therapy. Changing them leads to changes in the patient's beliefs and knowledge structures supporting these beliefs. On initiating therapy patients have a large number of maladaptive belief conflicts, as measured by the Inventory of Interpersonal Problems (IIP). At the same time, plotted appraisal and coping measures for issues and people relevant to these beliefs generally do not correlate. Over sessions, as patients improve, IIP scores of their belief conflicts decrease. This decrease correlates directly with an increase in correlation between the measured appraisal and coping relationship for each person and issue (Maxim, 1990).

Overall Aims

Carr and associates developed the Interpersonal Discrimination Task (IDT), the principal measure of cognitive structure used in their research (Carr, 1965b, 1980). IDT scores have proven to be reflec-

tive of an overall level of differentiation for the individual, measuring change in situational demands, developmental process, and cognitive shifts by the individual. By the early 1970s, these investigators were demonstrating the role of cognitive structure in various forms of psychopathology and treatment. Maladaptive cognitive structures and avoidance of anticipatory anxiety appeared to be consistently reinforced through a drive-reduction mechanism. Attention in the 1980s turned to the possible role of endogenous opioids as the mechanism underlying this drive-reduction mechanism. Most recently, attention has been focused on the interaction of neurohormonal systems, cognitive process, and behavior in affecting the outcome of behavioral therapies (Egan, Carr, Hunt, & Adamson, 1988).

Maxim and associates have developed a comprehensive structural model of the implicit and explicit communications occurring during patient–therapist interactions (Maxim & Sprague, 1988). Two coding schemas have been developed to catalog the psychologic information carried in this model: the Seattle psychotherapy language analysis schema (SPLASH) and the metacommunication in interactive sequences in therapy (MIST). These schemas are being used to address two hypotheses: (a) The salient psychologic features of patient–therapist verbal interaction that cause change in patients' appraisal and coping with people and issues about which they have conflicts can be identified with our coding schemas and (b) strings of patient–therapist interactions can be assembled into treatment protocols that describe the necessary interactions that must occur at different therapy stages to produce change. These protocols will take into account the patient's diagnosis and type of maladaptive beliefs and will indicate the temporal order in which patient–therapist interactions must be made.

Studies to investigate these hypotheses are of two types: (a) process–outcome correlations with multiple measures of change in a small number of intensively studied patients and (b) expert system modeling of the knowledge structures being used by patients and therapists in verbal interactions that lead to these changes.

Method

Subjects have varied among medical students, residents, experienced clinicians, lay professionals, and various diagnostic groups. The Minnesota Multiphasic Personality Inventory

(MMPI) and SCL-90 have been the main personality assessment measures used with the IDT studies. Outcome measures consisted of change scores on the Cornell Medical Index; the Hamilton Rating Scale for Depression; the Beck Depression Inventory; the SCL-90; the Fear Survey Schedule; patient, therapist, and observer perceptions of outcome; and behavioral measures such as missed appointments and premature termination.

Similarly, the patient–therapist interaction coding schemas have been developed from published verbatim texts of prominent therapists conducting therapy and videotapes of numerous patients treated in our clinic. Validation studies of the appraisal–coping relationship measure include nonpatient, paid subjects, patients receiving psychotherapy only, and matched patients receiving only pharmacotherapy (Maxim, 1990). In Maxim's studies of patient–therapist interaction, initial assessment measures included the SCL-90, the Beck Depression Inventory, the IIP, sexual and physical abuse questionnaires, and the MMPI. Change measures included the Personal Orientation Inventory, the Beck Depression Inventory, the Therapy Session Report, the IIP, a semantic differential for appraisal scores, and the Ways of Coping Checklist.

In studies of patient–therapist matching, patients were either randomly assigned to therapists or assigned on a standard clinical rotating basis. During the first session, both patient and therapist were administered the IDT. Patients completed pretests of all outcome measures. At periodic intervals these tests were repeated, that is, at the end of therapy (a fixed number of weeks) and at follow-up (1 and 3 months). Patient data were then grouped according to client–clinician match or degree of mismatch (one to three groups), and group means on outcome measures were statistically compared with t tests, analysis of variance, or nonparametrics depending on the distribution characteristics of the data. Variations on this design included prospective assignment to groups. In most studies, however, outcome data were collected blind to the patient or therapist IDT scores.

In studies on patient–therapist verbal interaction, patients have been matched by diagnosis, initial scores on the IIP, or the initial skew in their appraisal–coping relationships. Most of the process design focuses on within-subjects repeated measures, however. Data from patient–therapist interaction are indexed to a particular structure in our model, such as the belief conflict,

that is under study. Expert system modeling of these interactions uses programs that make inferences on the basis of predicted logic. Patient–therapist categorical data are used with their accompanying certainty factors in a rule-and-frame-based logic system (M.1 or IXL) to construct protocols for treatment.

Research Accomplishments

The Work of Carr's Group

Past work in developing the IDT focused on different aspects of dyadic interaction and cognitive structure. Initial studies were concerned with the development of the IDT, resolving methodological problems inherent in outcome research, and delineating further the components of cognitive structure involved in interpersonal perception (Carr, 1965a, 1965b, 1969, 1974; Carr & Whittenbaugh, 1968, 1969; Carr & Post, 1974; Carr & Townes, 1975).

Patient–therapist compatibility. In the first major program investigation, Carr (1970) found that matched patient–therapist pairs (in terms of differentiation of cognitive structure) have significantly better treatment outcomes than unmatched pairs. The finding has been replicated with medical student therapists (Montgomery & Carr, 1971), psychiatric residents, and psychology interns and faculty (Hunt, Carr, Dagadakis, & Walker, 1985) and was independently confirmed by Craig (1973) and McLachlan (1972, 1974). The matching effect on outcome appears to be maximal within the first 12–15 sessions. Thereafter, differences between matched and mismatched group means decrease as a result of premature termination of poor outcome cases and shifts in structure by patients and therapists toward one another (Carr, 1980).

This replicated finding supported Kelly's sociality corollary and suggested an operationally definable cognitive mechanism to account for the empathic phenomenon of the doctor–patient relationship. It also suggested a crucial role of the phenomenon in the assignment of patients to therapists, especially for short-term therapy relationships.

Group compatibility. Were groups matched in terms of differentiation of cognitive structure more likely to have a successful outcome than mismatched groups? The hypothesis was first put to the test in a major community action project under the auspices of the Seattle school board (Posthuma & Carr, 1974). Community discussion groups were organized throughout the city to discuss the range of emotional and practical issues associated with a school busing plan. On the basis of IDT scores, randomly selected participants were assigned to high-, medium-, and low-matched groups or to mixed groups balanced for race and sex and were assigned both abstract (e.g., ethnicity) and concrete (e.g., school lunch program) topics for discussion. At the completion of the workshop participants rated the outcome in terms of its impact on racial cooperation and understanding of school-related problems. The number of participants (compared with nonparticipants) who volunteered to enroll their children in the busing plan was noted.

Of participants discussing abstract topics, 61% indicated satisfaction with the outcome compared with only 38% of concrete topic discussants. When it came to actual busing, however, matched group parents were more likely to bus their children than mismatched group parents, as anticipated. Surprisingly, in the matched groups, the most highly differentiated parents seemed *less* likely to bus. Interviews of these parents revealed that recently acquired community control of local school programs had resulted in a marked improvement in quality of education and a surge in local pride. The tendency to oppose busing among this group of parents, which was highly differentiated and predominately Black, seemed to reflect an appreciation of a complex sociopolitical process. Participants with lower differentiation scores on the IDT seemed to focus more on the global objectives of racial harmony and quality education throughout the larger metropolitan community. Both positions were legitimate and defensible and were increasingly articulated as the project unfolded.

The findings had implications for community leaders as well as mental health professionals. If treatment outcome is to be measured only in terms of verbal endorsement for public consumption, then organizers should have participants discuss abstract concepts such as "brotherhood," "peace," or "the American way." If one desires behavioral change with concrete solutions to concrete problems, however, then attention to group composition and topic specificity is required.

Modifying cognitive structure. Our next series of investigations confirmed that accuracy of interpersonal perception is modifiable in response to incoming validating or invalidating information if the information is domain relevant (Post-

huma & Carr, 1975). On the basis of this premise, the use of videotape playback had been widely advocated as a therapeutic and training aid. Feedback with regard to personal performance and "seeing ourselves as others see us" was presumed to be especially beneficial for self-development and behavioral change.

A second study in this series attempted to determine whether playback effected changes in cognitive structure and, if so, under what conditions. Subjects were assigned to four groups: viewing themselves in a relevant task (personal interview), viewing themselves in an irrelevant task (counting backward from 100), viewing someone else in a relevant task, and viewing someone else in an irrelevant task. Only subjects who viewed themselves in the relevant task showed significant changes in cognitive structure (IDT) and accuracy of self-perception as measured by the Interpersonal Check List before and after the test, the change being in the direction of greater congruency between self as seen by self and self as seen by others. Heart rate measures taken throughout the experiment showed significantly greater cardiac deceleration for the self-relevant group than all other groups. Because autonomic reactivity is generally regarded as a reliable indicator of cognitive attention to internal and external stimuli, the physiological findings are consistent with the hypothesis of changes in cognitive structure in response to personally relevant feedback.

Cognitive factors in phobic avoidance. As in patients with depression, patients with phobic anxiety demonstrated distinctive perceptions of abnormal behavior and self relative to others. In such patients all incoming information is generally interpreted as validating the view of personal incompetence in controlling one's life, emotions, and behavior. These patients also were highly avoidant, which appeared to be consistently reinforced through a drive-reduction mechanism.

A treatment protocol incorporating interfacing cognitive and behavioral change procedures was developed and clinically tested. It was observed that patients able to report and manifest fear responses to imagined stimuli inevitably proved to be successful in exposure therapies within predictably short periods of time (i.e., 12–15 weeks). It was further observed that if asked to concentrate on the feared image, patients reported within 1–2 minutes a diminution of the anxiety, often to their own surprise.

It was suspected that the observed reduction in

fear had little to do with relaxation instructions and that the only correlated events were exposure to a fear-inducing stimulus and the fear response itself. If the fear reduction were automatic, then any event immediately preceding it should be reinforced by drive reduction. If that behavior were avoidant, it would explain the self-maintaining and generalizing avoidant behavior of the phobic patient. What then could account for the automatic reduction in anxiety?

Attention was turned to developments in endocrinology that were then in the scientific limelight. Especially intriguing was the discovery of the endogenous opioid neurotransmitters such as the endorphins. Certain literature of the time indicated that the body's responses to stress include the release of beta-endorphin, which has analgesic properties. Furthermore, beta-endorphin is released in response not only to physical pain or injury but also to perceived threat, psychological stress, and conditioned fear. Was this the mechanism of drive reduction?

A carefully controlled, double-blind study was designed by Kelly Egan and Carr and carried out by Daniel Hunt and Richard Adamson. It was reasoned that if beta-endorphin were involved in the efficacy of exposure therapies, then blockade of the endorphin release by an antagonist should have an observable effect on treatment outcome. Twelve patients meeting criteria for simple phobia as outlined in the revised third edition of the *Diagnostic and Statistical Manual of Mental Disorders* (*DSM-III-R*; American Psychiatric Association, 1987) were admitted for behavioral treatment of their phobic condition. All patients completed pretherapy the SCL-90 and the Beck Depression Inventory and then underwent eight successive, twice-weekly sessions of systematic desensitization. Patients then completed posttherapy measures and 1- and 3-month follow-up measures. Before each session, each patient received a 1-mL intravenous injection. Unknown to the patient, the therapist, or the physician administering the injections, patients received a dose of either naloxone (an endorphin antagonist) or saline. The dose of naloxone (1 mg/mL) was low enough that no significant physiological effect was anticipated. Physiological recordings were taken throughout to provide any indication of autonomic reactivity, however. There were no significant differences in autonomic reactivity, and subjective reports indicated no difference in patient's perceptions of injection reactivity. The two groups were balanced for sex and age.

As expected, the patients injected with saline demonstrated a marked reduction in symptomatology on both the SCL-90 and the Beck Depression Inventory. In contrast, the group injected with naloxone showed no change. The results of the study clearly indicated that the endorphins play a role in exposure therapies and suggested support for the hypothesis that stress-induced analgesia (endorphin release) may be the mechanism of drive reduction (Egan et al., 1988; Hunt, Adamson, Egan, & Carr, 1988).

The research program in this area continues to clarify the nature of the mechanisms involved. A review of the relevant literature strongly suggests a complex linkage among behavioral, cognitive, and neurochemical systems and raises the possibility that the demonstrated coeffectiveness of pharmacological and behavioral treatments of anxiety disorders may be due to their effects on a final common neurochemical pathway.

Instruments developed. The IDT was first developed by Carr (1965b) in response to a need for a measure of cognitive structure that, like the Role Construct Repertory Test, was derived from the subject's own constructs but was simpler and less time consuming. The instrument had the added advantage of demonstrating the ease with which the subject could operate within his or her own conceptual framework by making discriminations among known persons along his or her own conceptual dimensions. The instrument is easily scored, yielding four quantitative measures, an overall differentiation score (O-A), and three specific scores: other–other (O–O), self–other (S–O), and self-distinctiveness (S–D). Scoring details are given in Carr (1965b, 1970, 1980).

Of the various scores, O-A is most frequently used as a general index of cognitive differentiation. The other measures permit the researcher to examine in greater detail the interpersonal differentiation process in terms of who is being differentiated from whom, to what degree, and along what dimensions (e.g., positive or negative). The IDT is easily administered and is generally completed in 15–30 minutes. The statistical properties of the IDT plus its use of subjects' conceptual dimensions and significant social figures has made it a valuable research instrument in clinical settings. It is readily adaptable to group, family, and couples settings.

Test–retest reliability after 1 day is .82–.84 and after 2 months is .58–.65. With regard to validity, the IDT has been shown to relate significantly to the Conceptual Level Test, the Halstead Category Test, the Remote Associates Test, the Embedded

Figures Test, the Repression–Sensitization Scale, and the Level of Aspiration–Expectancy Measure. The IDT is not related significantly to intelligence quotient, School and College Abilities Tests, the Edwards Personal Preference Schedule, or the Marlowe–Crowne Social Desirability Scale.

The Work of Maxim's Group

Previous work on patient–therapist interaction. We have developed and tested the two coding schemas SPLASH and MIST, which form the basis for the modeling development that we are proposing. These capture the levels of psychologic knowledge that inform each speaker's utterances. Development of a hierarchical knowledge representation of the patient–doctor interaction at any point in therapy treatment is accomplished by the systematic encoding of utterances from typed transcripts. This representation derives from a concrete level (i.e., the utterances) and generates a composite frame that identifies the patient's state-space at an abstract level. The state-space is refined over time as more information is provided through the interaction between patient and doctor.

The SPLASH schema. The model of how one processes this information is given in the equation in Figure 1. As one moves toward a particular goal, one has an expectation of receiving information that one's current role and tactic behavior is appropriate on the basis of past memories of successful and unsuccessful outcomes. In the current thought and behavioral chain, this expected information is compared with an incoming stream of current information. Mismatch between the two sets of information, coupled with the strength of the motive force, determine the degree of stress experienced by the person in the current effort. This stress is experienced as an affect of different shadings and causes one to generate beliefs about how to modify future role and tactic efforts to reduce stress. It also leads one to utilize internal compensatory mechanisms of reappraisal and coping strategies, which act in a feedback manner to modify any part or all three parts of the information-processing model. Patients come to therapy complaining about the output from these equations: maladaptive beliefs, negative affect, and ineffective behavior in dealing with the world. When patients are successful in their reappraisal and use different coping methods, their symptoms of maladaptive beliefs, affect, and behavior disappear (Maxim & Hunt, 1990; Maxim, 1990).

This model of information processing is contained in a model of interpersonal conflict. That is, conflict arises between competing goals or competing coping strategies that will satisfy one goal but inhibit achieving another, or conflict arises between competing types of expected or perceived information about one's role or tactics that may fit one but contradict another view of oneself or of others that one wishes to retain. One will then develop a set of constraining beliefs about what one can accomplish and will be using maladaptive coping and appraisal mechanisms in attempting to deal with these people. One will bring these maladaptive beliefs, appraisals, and coping mechanisms to new relationships as well.

Both of these models, as well as SPLASH (Maxim, Strauss, Hodun, & Rosenfarb, 1986), can be seen as contained within a larger model of metacommunication that forms the basis for MIST (Maxim & Sprague, 1988). These two catalogs, SPLASH and MIST, contain the items that make up the full range of semantic categories used by the patient and therapist to organize their world and to interact with others and with each other. By using them, the researcher can describe what is going on in the spoken utterances

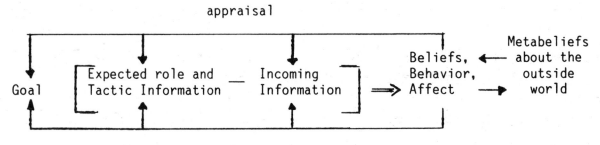

Figure 18.1. Belief conflict equation.

between patient and therapist as therapy progresses.

The SPLASH category items were derived in part from work by Gottschalk and Gleser, Haan, Chance, Russell and Styles, and Malan. The schema consists of five major categories with attendant category items: affects (48 items), impulses (15 items), coping strategies (58 items), the speaker's view-object-frame of reference (two sets of 20 and 27 items used in combination), and interpersonal messages (38 items).

The MIST schema. The goals and beliefs categories of these models that are generally implicitly but not explicitly in the speaker's utterances are contained in the MIST catalog because it reflects the larger model of communication. The MIST catalog begins at the level of anecdotal memory organization of goals, roles, and tactics. Persistent failure in meeting goal expectations through failed tactics leads to belief constructs about how one structures future goal pursuits. A belief conflict is a patient-generated three-part linkage among an antecedent goal, the role one is in when pursuing it, and the consequential tactic one can or cannot carry out to meet the goal.

What one decides to communicate about a belief in the intentional interactive process and concrete utterance levels connect to three categories at the MIST abstract level of communication, which makes up the rest of the speaker's state-space: strategies, plans, and models. Plans represent the ideational components and strategies the enactment components of the level above the interactional process. Their functions are to complete the procedural search for appropriate contextual planning and then to enact those plans strategically to pursue the belief conflict equation elements of an explicit goal, a given role, and a particular tactic. The top level category is the patient's personal model of the world, which consists of an ideational component, or personal myths, and enactment components called *rituals*. This personal model level is derived from experience while growing up as well as from family and cultural models. It gives one a sense of one's rights, privileges, and values and functions to provide one with declarative programming (i.e., knowledge about where to look for procedures to handle a specific interaction). The top level patient-specific model of conflict and the accompanying therapist model of correction is the material often consciously used by the therapist in directing a therapy session.

We have drawn on the work of many others, including Shapiro, Frank, Becker, Blatt, and Ar-

ieti, in condensing patient psychopathology into the MIST categories. The therapist has a structurally corresponding set of plans and strategies through which to modify the patient's belief conflict. The therapist is also oriented across many discussion topics by a metaplan. The MIST categories for therapist metaplans, plans, and strategies for change are derived from Freud, Jung, Adler, Rogers, Beck, Perls, Ellis, and many others. The MIST catalog consists of seven major categories and their attendant category items: belief codes consisting of belief goals (19 items), belief roles (18 items), and belief tactics (29 items); maladaptive plans (8 items); maladaptive strategies (24 items); metaplans (3 items); plans for change (17 items); strategies for change (25 items); and the interactional process code consisting of process goals (7 items), category elements (10 items), reframing operators (5 items), and relation elements (10 items).

To summarize, then, the patient and therapist interactions in a therapy session center around a series of discussion topics, each of which is focused on a patient belief conflict. Each belief is an example of a metabelief that is constrained by the patient's maladaptive plans and strategies of how to get along in the world. These in turn are partly formed from the patient's personal, familial, and cultural models. Appreciation of these models as therapy progresses allows the therapist to construct a patient-specific *model-of-conflict* and a corresponding *model-of-correction*. This latter model shapes the therapist's choice of plans and strategies for change. Examination of the patient's maladaptive plans, strategies, and beliefs is carried out through an interactional process that the patient initiates, and the therapist responds to the patient's belief with a corrective interactional process.

Toward a unified model. Unlike a simple model of the understanding of a story in which there is just one theme, therapy sessions contain different theme content sections called *discussion topics*. Each discussion topic contains a belief conflict for which the patient has sought treatment. Each utterance in a discussion topic section of a session is SPLASH coded for the utterance variables and MIST coded for the belief model, plan, strategy, and interactional process that are implicit to it.

Different discussion topics, however, have an interrelationship in a session that must be followed by the therapist to produce change and must be modeled by us to give accurate simulation. Broadly speaking, the major points in therapy for the therapist are to identify the patient's specific belief conflicts, to see how they connect throughout the session, and then to seek to modify the appraisal and coping strategies that the patient is using that perpetuate those beliefs.

In trying to induce change, therapists cannot get patients to change through first-order change attempts, that is to say by using a hierarchical category that is on the same level as the one to be changed. Instead, the therapist must structurally use a higher category to produce second-order change (Watzlawick, Weakland, & Fish, 1974). These second-order changes are induced by reframing the conflict issue. Within a discussion topic and bridging from one topic to another, the patient presents arguments in support of specific beliefs about people or issues, and the therapist tries to make countering arguments. We want to simulate what goes on in each discussion topic in a session, how the interactions bridge from one discussion topic to another across the session, and then how the interactions bridge from session to session.

We have used these catalogs to score single transcripts from Malan, Davanloo, Beck, Perls, Rogers, and our own therapists to ensure their wide applicability (Maxim et al., 1986; Maxim & Sprague, 1988; Maxim, 1990). Face validity of the categories has been checked by comparing the frequency of particular plan, strategy, and interactional process items against these therapists' descriptions of their theoretical orientation and rules for conducting therapy (Maxim, 1990).

Research Programs in Progress

Our verbal interaction categorical data present two major modeling challenges: structural relationship representation and dynamic decision change over time. Our previous work has focused on structural relationship representation. We have found that with combinations of five SPLASH categories we need more than 250 rules to code just 1 hour of therapy and that we need increasing numbers of memos to explain rule usage. We then tried frame-based and certainty factor models to cut down on the number of rules needed. Modeling with frames has helped us develop ideas about how to cluster our coded categories, and certainty factor calculations have given us clues about which categories are most closely related. Frames alone have proved too inflexible to model changing constellations of SPLASH utterance variables, however. Certainty factors, aside from issues of the statistical uncertainty of

bidirectionality and assumed modularity, cause us to lose knowledge about sequential ordering of arguments when we agglomerate data for computation.

Programs Planned for the Future

We currently propose modeling these categorical relationships with a combination of networked frames linked by production rules and containing production rules and attached predicates. The modeling of dynamic interactions between the patient and doctor needs to simulate a goal-directed interaction that is time based and adaptive. This modeling will lead to the development of a "response sequence advisor system" that will simulate the interaction and provide reports about the protocols currently being used and those that might be used next. It will be able to adapt its protocol decisions to changes in the patient's state-space and history of previous interaction.

We are designing a response sequence advisor by adapting ideas from the Oncocin temporal network. The advisor will operate from starting knowledge about the patient's diagnosis; initial IIP, MMPI, and Beck Depression Inventory scores; and appraisal–coping values. It will then identify the appropriate patient model of conflict and accompanying sequence of beliefs. This model and its beliefs will be related to the therapist model of correction and to the appropriate response protocol sequences. These response frames contain slots for appropriate plans and strategies and determine which SPLASH variables will be instantiated to make up appropriate arguments. We will use a number of modeling features to develop these declarative programming procedures in the advisor, including the following:

• backward chaining in each participant space after receiving concrete variables uttered by the other speaker to identify inductively the abstract state-space variables that locate that speaker

• responding with forward chaining from one's own abstract state-space variables and knowledge rules about the history of the relationship to decide what concrete variables to utter next

• problem decomposition of the patient's complaints in a session into a series of discussion topics centered on a particular person and a maladaptive belief about that person

• heuristic search strategies used initially by

the therapist space to find a possible solution domain each time a new subprogram is defined

• inductive inference to tie subprograms to higher abstract variables

• dependency-directed backtracking from concrete to abstract variables to contradict assumptions in the abstract variables.

The advisor will keep track of what beliefs are addressed and what protocols are used in each block of four sessions. At the end of every fourth session, IIP metabelief change scores and change scores in appraisal–coping values will be used by the advisor to adjust the array and sequence of beliefs still to be addressed and the protocol sequences to be used.

Nature of the Research Organization

Organization Members

As noted at the beginning of this chapter, our organization is informal and collaborative because we are interested in each other's research problem areas. Currently, the faculty involved are John E. Carr, PhD, principal investigator; Peter E. Maxim, MD, PhD, principal investigator; Kelly Egan, PhD; D. Daniel Hunt, MD, collaborating psychiatrist to both programs outlined; Gary Cox, PhD, research psychologist and statistical consultant; Eugene Lee, MA, computer specialist and consultant in artificial intelligence; and Joseph Becker, PhD, expert psychotherapist.

Funding

Funding sources for our programs have varied over their history, with most funding coming from the National Institute of Mental Health as research grants in response to RFAs or initiated de novo. Other sources have included the University of Washington Biomedical Research Support Grant Program, Veteran's Administration Career Development Award, the Boeing Medical Research Program, and a number of private research donations. Current grant proposals include funding support requests for postdoctoral fellowships and support in medical informatics research with the National Library of Medicine.

References

American Psychiatric Association. (1987). *Diagnostic and statistical manual of mental disorders* (rev. 3rd ed.). Washington, DC: Author.

Carr, J. E. (1965a). Cognitive complexity: Construct descriptive terms versus cognitive process. *Psychological Reports, 16,* 133–134.

Carr, J. E. (1965b). The role of conceptual organization in interpersonal discrimination. *Journal of Psychology, 59,* 159–176.

Carr, J. E. (1969). Differentiation as a function of source characteristics and judges conceptual structure. *Journal of Personality, 37,* 378–386.

Carr, J. E. (1970). Differentiation similarity of patient and therapist and the outcome of psychotherapy. *Journal of Abnormal Psychology, 76,* 361–369.

Carr, J. E. (1974). Perceived therapy outcome as a function of differentiation between and within dimensions. *Journal of Clinical Psychology, 30,* 282–285.

Carr, J. E. (1980). Personal construct theory and psychotherapy research. In A. W. Landfield & L. W. Leitner (Eds.), *Personal construct psychology: Psychotherapy and personality* (pp. 223–270). New York: Wiley.

Carr, J. E., & Post, R. (1974). Repression sensitization and self–other discrimination in psychotic patients. *Journal of Personality Assessment, 38,* 48–51.

Carr, J. E., & Townes, B. D. (1975). Interpersonal discrimination as a function of age and psychopathology. *Child Psychiatry and Human Development, 5,* 209–215.

Carr, J. E., & Whittenbaugh, J. (1968). Volunteer and nonvolunteer characteristics in an outpatient population. *Journal of Abnormal Psychology, 73,* 16–17.

Carr, J. E., & Whittenbaugh, J. (1969). Sources of disagreement in the perception of psychotherapy outcome. *Journal of Clinical Psychology, 25,* 16–21.

Craig, W. R. (1973). The effects of cognitive similarity between client and therapist upon quality and outcome of the psychotherapy relationship (Doctoral dissertation, University of Missouri Columbia, 1972). *Dissertations Abstracts International, 34,* 1272B.

Egan, K. J., Carr, J. E., Hunt, D. D., & Adamson, R. (1988). Endogenous opiate system and systematic desensitization. *Journal of Consulting and Clinical Psychology, 56,* 287–291.

Hunt, D. D., Adamson, R., Egan, K., & Carr, J. E. (1988). Opioids: Mediators of fear or mania. *Biological Psychiatry, 23,* 426–428.

Hunt, D. D., Carr, J. E., Dagadakis, C., & Walker, E. (1985). Cognitive match as a predictor of psychotherapy outcome. *Psychotherapy, 22,* 718–721.

Kelly, J. A. (1955). *The psychology of personal constructs.* New York: Norton.

Maxim, P. E. (1990). *The relationship between appraisal, coping and the Inventory of Interpersonal Problems.* Manuscript submitted for publication.

Maxim, P. E., & Hunt, D. D. (1990). appraisal and coping during patient change. *Journal of Nervous and Mental Disease, 178,* 235–241.

Maxim, P. E., & Sprague, M. (1988). *Metacommunication through interactive sequences in therapy (MIST).* Seattle: University of Washington Press.

Maxim, P. E., Strauss, M., Hodun, A., & Rosenfarb, I.

(1986). *Seattle psychotherapy language analysis schema (SPLASH)*. Seattle: University of Washington Press.

McLachlan, J. F. (1972). Benefit from group therapy as a function of patient-therapist match on conceptual level. *Psychotherapy: Theory, Research and Practice, 9,* 317–323.

McLachlan, J. F. (1974). Therapy strategies, personality orientation and recovery from alcoholism. *Canadian Psychiatric Association Journal, 19,* 30–35.

Montgomery, F., & Carr, J. E. (1971). *Differentiation,* similarity and outcome of treatment: A replication. Unpublished manuscript. University of Washington, Seattle.

Posthuma, A., & Carr, J. E. (1974). Differentiation matching and desegregation workshops. *Journal of Applied Social Psychology, 4,* 36–46.

Posthuma, A., & Carr, J. E. (1975). Differentiation matching in psychotherapy. *Psychologie Canadienne, 16,* 34–43.

Watzlawick, T., Weakland, J., & Fish, R. (1974). *Change.* New York: Norton.

19

The University of Washington: A Research Program on Marital Therapy and Depression in the Center for the Study of Relationships

Neil S. Jacobson
University of Washington

Background and Aims

The Center for the Study of Relationships (CSR) at the University of Washington was created in the fall of 1979 to continue work that I began as a graduate student in Chapel Hill, North Carolina, and continued at Brown University and at the University of Iowa. The main focus of the research at that time was on attempting to understand the determinants of and developing effective treatment programs for marital problems. These goals continue to serve as the impetus for much of our work. Most of this work has been designed to test the limits of a social learning theoretical perspective as a framework for understanding and treating marital distress (Jacobson & Margolin, 1979).

In the course of carrying out this research program the scope has expanded, and thus so have our aims. For the past 5 years, we have become interested in major depression as a target problem. This focus began as an outgrowth of clinical, theoretical, and empirical observations that marital problems were frequently associated with depression, especially in women (e.g., Jacobson, Holtzworth-Munroe, & Schmaling, 1989). This led

to the aim of attempting to elucidate the nature of the relation between marital problems and depression. We also began to investigate the value of marital therapy as a treatment for depression in married women.

As an outgrowth of this relatively new focus on depression, investigating the value of marital therapy has become a second spoke in our center's wheel. That is, it can now be said that we have a second program of research underway in the area of depression because much of the current work focuses on depression above and beyond its connection to interpersonal or relationship variables. We have become intrigued by questions related to both the etiology and the successful treatment of depression. The aim here is to study the change mechanisms of Beck's cognitive–behavioral treatment, a widely used, highly effective treatment for depression (Beck, Rush, Shaw, & Emery, 1979); our hope is that through the intensive study of cognitive–behavioral therapy much will be learned about how depressed people change and that suggestive information will be gathered regarding the etiology of depression.

Another body of research that has been spawned by the initial focus on marital therapy is an interest in wife abuse or battering. We are about to embark on a major longitudinal study in collaboration with John Gottman, Amy Holtzworth-Munroe, and Peter Fehrenbach. The study examines cognitive, interactional, and psychophysiological variables as antecedents and consequences of battering. The aim is to build a theory that helps explain the onset, offset, increase, and decrease of battering in marital relationships.

Finally, the focus on various types of psychotherapy research (evaluating treatments for marital problems and depression) has led to a keen interest in psychotherapy research methodology independently of how it is applied to the particular problems we are currently studying. The aim is to maximize the relevance of psychotherapy research for practitioners by contributing to innovative methodologies that bridge the gap between research and practice.

Method

Our basic tactic for studying the change process in psychotherapy has been the randomized clinical trial. The marital therapy research began with comparisons between the original social learning-based treatment package (Jacobson & Margolin, 1979) and a waiting-list control group (Jacobson, 1977). This first study also included a single-subject experimental design for each treated subject embedded in the randomized trial. Subsequent studies included randomized trials involving a nonspecific control group (Jacobson, 1978), a study that dismantled the communication training portion of our treatment package (Jacobson & Anderson, 1980), a study that dismantled the entire treatment package (Jacobson, 1984; Jacobson & Follette, 1985; Jacobson, Schmaling, & Holtzworth-Munroe, 1987), and a study that compared research structured with clinically flexible versions of our marital therapy package (Jacobson, Schmaling, Holtzworth-Munroe, Katt, Wood, & Follette, 1989). Finally, a series of replicated single-subject designs was conducted to evaluate the importance of communication and problem-solving training above and beyond behavior exchange procedures (Jacobson, 1979).

As these clinical trials were being conducted, various questions were posed regarding the determinants of marital satisfaction and distress. These questions have been investigated by using treatment subjects as our samples of maritally distressed couples and by recruiting happily married couples from the community. Most of the experimental questions were tested by comparing distressed and nondistressed couples on variables of interest. For example, our model predicts that distressed couples will be more reactive to immediate events than happily married couples above and beyond differences between distressed and nondistressed couples in the base rates of those events. To test this hypothesis, distressed and nondistressed couples were compared in their tendency to be reactive to recently occurring positive and negative behaviors delivered by the partner (Jacobson, Follette, & McDonald, 1982; Jacobson, Waldron, & Moore, 1980). As another example, in a series of studies we predicted that distressed couples would be more likely to attribute their partner's behavior to causes that were likely to maintain marital distress (Camper, Jacobson, Holtzworth-Munroe, & Schmaling, 1988; Holtzworth-Munroe & Jacobson, 1985, 1988; Jacobson, McDonald, Follette, & Berley, 1985). Thus, distressed and nondistressed couples were compared on various measures that probe for causal attributions.

Similar methodologies have been used in our depression research: randomized clinical trials to compare the relative efficacy of various treatments; comparisons between depressed subjects and various control groups to uncover variables that are associated with, and may bear some causal relationship to, depression; and dismantling studies to answer questions regarding the active ingredients of the treatment programs.

Research Accomplishments

Major Findings

Marital therapy. An approach that I initially developed on the basis of pioneering work by Richard Stuart, Gerald Patterson, and Robert Weiss (Stuart, 1969; Weiss, Hops, & Patterson, 1973) combined contingency management procedures (now referred to as *behavior exchange*) with communication and problem-solving training in a treatment package for married couples on the basis of a social learning theoretical perspective. An initial pilot study found that this treatment package was effective relative to a waiting-list control treatment (Jacobson, 1977). This was the first randomized clinical trial establishing the efficacy of any marital therapy procedure with a clinical population of distressed couples. This study was followed by a second clinical trial in which it was discovered that the efficacy of this treatment program could not be attributed to the nonspecific aspects of marital therapy per se but had something to do with the specific treatment package provided in this approach (Jacobson, 1978). Thus, on the basis of these first 2 studies, evidence was provided that the package that had come to be known as *behavioral marital therapy* worked and that its effects could not be attributed to nonspecific factors.

A series of studies expanded on these findings in a number of ways. First, a series of single-subject experimental designs with a population of severely distressed couples replicated the earlier findings with a much more difficult population and provided evidence that the communication and problem-solving training component of the procedure contributed above and beyond the behavior exchange directives most commonly associated with a behavioral approach (Jacobson, 1979). Second, an analog study with a young group of happily married couples seeking an enrichment experience demonstrated that communication and problem-solving training requires behavior rehearsal combined with instructions and feedback in order to be effective (Jacobson & Anderson, 1980). Approximations of this elaborate package had no impact on the communication skills of the couples receiving the training. Despite the analog nature of this study, it provided evidence that couples need the opportunity to practice directly and to receive feedback from the therapist about the skills taught. Minimalist communication training procedures based on suggestions alone without the opportunity for supervised practice are virtually no better than no treatment at all. Thus, one would not expect self-help manuals to be effective in the absence of therapy, nor should one expect couples to acquire better communication simply from a therapist's suggestions alone.

Third, a component analysis of the marital therapy treatment package found that the communication and problem-solving training component promotes relatively enduring changes in marital satisfaction relative to behavior exchange procedures alone (Jacobson, 1984; Jacobson & Follette, 1985). This finding was in accord with our theory about how change occurs in behavioral marital therapy. We expected behavior exchange procedures to have strong immediate effects (which they did), but we also expected the effects to be relatively short term (which they were). Because the communication

training component of behavioral marital therapy is prevention oriented and designed to help couples learn to be their own therapists, it was supposed to lead to sustained changes. It seemed to accomplish this, at least through a 6-month follow-up. However, as we continued to follow-up couples for 1 year (Schmaling & Jacobson, 1990) and then 2 years (Jacobson, Schmaling, & Holtzworth-Munroe, 1987), relapses became more prevalent among couples receiving either communication training or communication training in combination with behavior exchange. By the 2-year follow-up, there were no longer differences in efficacy between groups, although the couples receiving both major treatment components were still doing relatively well. Few of them had separated or divorced, and at least half of them remained significantly better off than they had been when they entered therapy. Nevertheless, 30% of the couples who had recovered initially had, by the 2-year follow-up, deteriorated to the point where they were no better or even worse off than they had been when therapy began.

The one variable that strongly predicted relapse in the component analysis study was stressful life events subsequent to therapy termination. The best predictor of short-term treatment response was the extent to which the two spouses in a given relationship wanted comparable levels of intimacy. Couples who were traditional in the sense that husbands wanted less intimacy and wives wanted more tended not to do well in therapy.

Finally, we have some evidence that a clinically flexible version of behavioral marital therapy does a better job of maintaining treatment gains than the typically invariant modular approach used in clinical trials (Jacobson, Schmaling, et al., 1989). Thus, past outcome studies may be providing a conservative estimate of the efficacy of behavioral marital therapy.

To conclude, we have learned that our treatment approach works and that it appears to be something about this approach per se that accounts for its effects. It clearly does not help all couples, however, and when stringent criteria for clinically significant change are applied our success rate appears to be somewhere between one half and two thirds; in other clinical research laboratories the success rate may be lower (Jacobson, Follette, Revenstorf, Baucom, Hahlweg, & Margolin, 1984). Sustained treatment gains seem to be fostered by individually tailored treatment plans, including communication and problem-solving training as a major (although not the sole) treatment component, and selecting couples with relatively egalitarian relationships. The avoidance of stressful life events seems to be crucial to maintaining treatment gains over a 2-year period, given the limits of our current treatment technology.

Determinants of marital satisfaction and distress. Most of the researchers, who have contributed to a social learning theoretical perspective on marital satisfaction or distress have attempted to differentiate between distressed and nondistressed married couples on various theoretically relevant variables. In the bulk of this research, the communication styles of these two groups of couples were compared and it was found that relative to nondistressed couples, distressed couples engage in higher frequencies of negative behavior and lower frequencies of positive behavior, have a greater tendency to reciprocate negative behavior, and show impaired abilities in conflict resolution.

Our primary contribution has been to supplement these basic findings by adding to the features that differentiate between distressed and nondistressed couples. Three sets of findings should be mentioned. First, we discovered a process that we have labeled *reactivity*, and have found it to be associated with marital distress. Reactivity refers to the tendency for spouses to react at the affective level to some immediate stimulus from the partner. We have found that distressed couples are characterized by heightened reactivity to immediate positive and negative events in the relationship, even after partialing out base rate differences between distressed and nondistressed couples in the frequency of these events (Jacobson et al., 1982; Jacobson et al., 1980). Nondistressed couples' marital satisfaction appears to be relatively independent of immediate rewarding and punishing events in the relationship, whereas by comparison people in generally unhappy relationships seem to fluctuate day to day according to what has just happened.

Second, we consistently found differences between distressed and nondistressed couples in the causal explanations that they invoke to explain their partner's as well as their own behavior (Camper, et al., 1988; Holtzworth-Munroe & Jacobson, 1985; Jacobson, McDonald, et al., 1985). Basically, distressed couples tend to make the kinds of causal attributions that would be expected to maintain marital distress: Positive events are written off, and partners are blamed

for their negative behavior, which is attributed to intentional, global, stable, and internal factors. In contrast, nondistressed couples tend to make relationship-enhancing causal attributions that give their partners credit for their positive behavior and exonerate them for negative behavior.

More recently, the investigation of these attributional processes has been extended to violent couples, and the attempt has been to understand how female victims of battering explain their husbands' violent behavior and how male batterers explain it. Thus far, it appears that there are some interesting differences between the kinds of attributions made for violent behavior and those made for nonviolent but negative behavior. For example, whereas distressed couples typically attribute their partner's negative behavior to internal, stable, and global factors, violent behavior is attributed to unstable and specific factors despite the fact that the partner is held responsible and blamed for the violence (Holtzworth-Munroe, Jacobson, Fehrenbach, & Fruzzetti, 1988).

Third, we completed a series of studies examining spouses as observers of their own and their partner's behavior (Elwood & Jacobson, 1982, 1988; Jacobson & Moore, 1981). These studies have shown that spouses are not reliable reporters of relationship events, that distressed couples are less reliable than nondistressed couples, and that it makes more sense to think of spouses as reacting to perceptions or recollections of partner behaviors than to the behaviors themselves.

Treatment of and factors related to depression. As part of a major study still in progress, we have recently found that our marital therapy package is effective at alleviating depression in married depressives as long as the marriages are also maritally distressed (Jacobson, Dobson, Fruzzetti, Schmaling, & Salusky, 1989). In fact, marital therapy works as well or better than Beck's highly effective cognitive–behavioral treatment (Beck et al., 1979). Despite the equivalence in efficacy, we have initial evidence that the change mechanisms might be different in the expected ways. In the marital therapy treatment, change in depression correlates strongly with change in marital satisfaction, whereas such correlations are nonexistent in the cognitive–behavioral treatment.

Another major finding from the study is that, contrary to predictions, marital therapy did no better than cognitive–behavioral therapy in improving the quality of the marital relationships. In general, the depressed couples were more difficult to treat than garden variety maritally distressed couples. The primary hypothesis of the study, that marital therapy would be associated with less relapse than individual therapy, cannot be evaluated at this time because the follow-up is still in progress.

Factors associated with depression. Basically, three major findings have emerged from our research thus far on the relationships among cognitive variables, interpersonal variables, and depression.

First, a study with college students found depressed subjects to be both self-preoccupied and self-effacing in interpersonal encounters with strangers; these effects were specific to depression and not attributable to nonspecific emotional discomfort (Jacobson & Anderson, 1982). Second, in a study examining the relationship between depression and marital interaction we found, in contrast to previous research, that most of the dysfunctional interaction patterns typically observed in depressed couples were due to marital distress rather than to the impact of depression per se (Schmaling & Jacobson, 1990). Third, two studies have found data inconsistent with theories positing dysfunctional cognitive processes as variables that predispose people to depression (Follette & Jacobson, 1987; Fruzzetti & Jacobson, 1988). One of these studies found interpersonal factors to be highly predictive of depression after relationship dissolution despite the failure of predisposing cognitions to emerge as significant predictors (Fruzzetti & Jacobson, 1988).

Methodology and Clinical Significance

We have developed statistics for determining the proportion of subjects in a given sample who have changed to a clinically significant degree as a result of psychotherapy (Jacobson, Follette, & Revenstorf, 1984, 1986; Jacobson & Revenstorf, 1988). These statistics are based on an operational definition of clinical significance that roughly approximates what most people think of as recovery. The statistics have been adopted by other psychotherapy researchers (Jacobson & Revenstorf, 1988), and the concept—which has been discussed for years, long before the development of our statistics—has become a popular one (see Jacobson, 1988). These points are important because the statistical management of outcome data has become a research topic in its own right.

We have used our statistical procedures to perform our own type of meta-analysis and have applied this analysis to three bodies of literature: the behavioral marital therapy literature (Jacobson, Follette, Revenstorf, et al., 1984), the agoraphobia treatment outcome literature (Jacobson, Wilson, & Tupper, 1988), and the research on parent training (Schmaling & Jacobson, 1990). The basic finding in all three of these areas is that therapy impact is much less impressive when examined under the clinical significance microscope than it appears when viewed through what we believe to be the misleading prism of traditional inferential statistics.

Research Programs in Progress and Planned for the Future

Marital Therapy

Mark Whisman and I are in the middle of a clinical trial investigating the additive impact of a maintenance treatment after the acute treatment phase on long-term outcomes. This research follows from the findings that life stress subsequent to termination is highly predictive of relapse; the maintenance treatment attempts to extend the influence of therapy by having resources available for clients during times of need after formal therapy. There is a plan to follow-up this pilot study with a more extensive examination of maintenance treatments beginning about 2 years from now. This seems to be the most promising place to look for enhanced efficacy. All variations of our basic treatment package yield approximately the same short-term effects. On the other hand, differential effects at follow-up do appear to be sensitive to experimental manipulations of treatment variables.

We are also analyzing some process data examining therapist and client variables as predictors of outcome by testing a model that expects five types of therapist behavior and two types of client behavior to account for significant variance in outcomes (Holtzworth-Munroe, Jacobson, DeKlyen, & Whisman, 1988). Thus far, client factors, especially in-session involvement and between-session compliance with assigned tasks, seem to predict outcome better than therapist behaviors.

Domestic Violence

As mentioned earlier, in early 1989 we started a 4-year longitudinal study examining cognitive, interactional, and psychophysiological variables as antecedents to and consequences of wife abuse. Various hypotheses are being tested regarding factors expected to be associated with increases, decreases, initiations, and cessations of battering. Wife-abusing couples will be compared with distressed but nonabusive and nondistressed control groups. The eventual aim is to build a multivariate model to explain the onset and offset of battering. From this model, we hope that treatment implications, and ultimately more effective treatments, for battering will be developed.

Depression Research

Marital therapy and depression. The examination of marital therapy as a treatment for depression continues with the collection of follow-up data designed to test the hypothesis that involvement of the nondepressed spouse in treatment will significantly reduce the likelihood of relapse or recurrence of depression after recovery from an acute episode. On the basis of data collected so far, combined with results from other laboratories, it is beginning to look as if there is a subpopulation of depressed couples for whom marital therapy is the current treatment of choice. Our best guess, judging from current findings, is that marital therapy is the preferred psychosocial treatment only for couples who identify themselves as having marital problems *and* who view the marital problems as being causally related to the depression. Testing these hypotheses will require a follow-up clinical trial study in which couples are stratified according to level of distress as well as their perspective on the causal connection between the marital distress and depression.

A component analysis of cognitive–behavioral treatments for depression. As a way of understanding better how depressed people change during the course of cognitive–behavioral therapy, a dismantling study will began in the spring of 1989. Cognitive–behavioral therapy is being dismantled in such a way as to test competing hypotheses regarding its efficacy. This study focuses on change processes, potential change mechanisms, and analyses of therapist, client, and relationship process variables and their relationship to outcome.

References

Beck, A. T., Rush, A. J., Shaw, B. F., & Emery, G. (1979). *Cognitive therapy of depression.* New York: Guilford Press.

Camper, P. M., Jacobson, N. S., Holtzworth-Munroe, A., & Schmaling, K. B. (1988). Causal attributions for interactional behaviors in married couples. *Cognitive Therapy and Research, 12,* 195–205.

Elwood, R. W., & Jacobson, N. S. (1988). The effects of observational training on spouse agreement about events in their relationship. *Behavior Research and Therapy, 26,* 159–167.

Elwood, R. W., & Jacobson, N. S. (1982). Spouse agreement in reporting their behavioral interactions: A clinical replication. *Journal of Consulting and Clinical Psychology, 50,* 783–784.

Follette, V. M., & Jacobson, N. J. (1987). Importance of attributions as a predictor of how people cope with failure. *Journal of Personality and Social Psychology, 52,* 1205–1211.

Fruzzetti, A. E., & Jacobson, N. S. (1988). *Predicting depressed mood following relationship dissolution: A multivariate test of the hopelessness theory of depression.* Unpublished manuscript.

Holtzworth-Munroe, A., & Jacobson, N. S. (1985). Causal attributions of married couples: When do they search for causes? What do they conclude when they do? *Journal of Personality and Social Psychology, 48,* 1398–1412.

Holtzworth-Munroe, A., & Jacobson, N. D. (1988). Toward a methodology for coding spontaneous causal attributions: Preliminary results with married couples. *Journal of social and Clinical Psychology, 7,* 101–112.

Holtzworth-Munroe, A., Jacobson, N. S., DeKlyen, M., & Whisman, M. (1988). *Effective ingredients in social learning-based marital therapy: The prediction of therapy outcome from process variables.* Manuscript submitted for publication.

Holtzworth-Munroe, A., Jacobson, N. S., Fehrenbach, P., & Fruzzetti, A. E. (1988). *Causal attributions offered by violent and nonviolent married couples for relationship behaviors.* Manuscript submitted for publication.

Jacobson, N. S. (1977). Problem solving and contingency contracting in the treatment of marital discord. *Journal of Consulting and Clinical Psychology, 45,* 92–100.

Jacobson, N. S. (1978). Specific and nonspecific factors in the effectiveness of a behavioral approach to the treatment of marital discord. *Journal of Consulting and Clinical Psychology, 46,* 442–452.

Jacobson, N. S. (1979). Increasing positive behavior in severely distressed adult relationships. *Behavior Therapy, 10,* 311–326.

Jacobson, N. S. (1984). A component analysis of behavioral marital therapy: The relative effectiveness of behavior exchange and problem-solving training. *Journal of Consulting and Clinical Psychology, 52,* 295–305.

Jacobson, N. S. (1988). *The efficacy of psychotherapy: Fact or fiction.* Manuscript submitted for publication.

Jacobson, N. S., & Anderson, E. A. (1980). The effects of behavior rehearsal and feedback on the acquisition of problem solving skills in distressed and nondistressed couples. *Behavior Research and Therapy, 18,* 25–36.

Jacobson, N. S., & Anderson, E. A. (1982). Interpersonal skill and depression in college students: An analysis of the timing of self-disclosures. *Behavior Therapy, 13,* 271–282.

Jacobson, N. S., Dobson, K., Fruzzetti, A., Schmaling,

K. B., & Salusky, S. (1989). *Marital therapy as a treatment for depression.* Unpublished manuscript.

Jacobson, N. S., & Follette, W. C. (1985). Clinical significance of improvement resulting from two behavioral marital therapy components. *Behavior Therapy, 16,* 249–262.

Jacobson, N. S., Follette, W. C., & McDonald, D. W. (1982). Reactivity to positive and negative behavior in distressed and nondistressed married couples. *Journal of Consulting and Clinical Psychology, 50,* 706–714.

Jacobson, N. S., Follette, W. C., & Revenstorf, D. (1984). Psychotherapy outcome research: Methods for reporting variability and evaluating clinical significance. *Behavior Therapy, 15,* 336–352.

Jacobson, N. S., Follette, W. C., & Revenstorf, D. (1986). Toward a standard definition of clinically significant change. *Behavior Therapy, 17,* 308–311.

Jacobson, N. S., Follette, W. C., Revenstorf, D., Baucom, D. H., Hahlweg, K., & Margolin, G. (1984). Variability in outcome and clinical significance of behavioral marital therapy: A reanalysis of outcome data. *Journal of Consulting and Clinical Psychology, 52,* 497–504.

Jacobson, N. S., Holtzworth-Munroe, A., & Schmaling, K. B. (1989). Spouse involvement in the treatment of depression, agoraphobia, and alcoholism. *Journal of Consulting and Clinical Psychology, 57,* 5–10.

Jacobson, N. S., & Margolin, G. (1979). *Marital therapy: Strategies based on social learning and behavior exchange principles.* New York: Brunner/Mazel.

Jacobson, N. S., McDonald, D. W., Follette, W. C., & Berley, R. A. (1985). Attributional processes in distressed and nondistressed married couples. *Cognitive Therapy and Research, 9,* 35–50.

Jacobson, N. S., & Moore, D. (1981). Spouses as observers of the events in their relationship. *Journal of Consulting and Clinical Psychology, 49,* 269–277.

Jacobson, N. S., & Revenstorf, D. (1988). Statistics for assessing the clinical significance of psychotherapy techniques: Issues, problems, and new developments. *Behavioral Assessment, 10,* 133–145.

Jacobson, N. S., Schmaling, K. B., & Holtzworth-Munroe, A. (1987). Component analysis of behavioral marital therapy: Two-year follow-up and prediction of relapse. *Journal of Marital and Family Therapy, 13,* 187–195.

Jacobson, N. S., Schmaling, K. B., Holtzworth-Munroe, A., Katt, J. L., Wood, L. F., & Follette, V. M. (1989). Research-structured versus clinically flexible versions of social learning-based marital therapy. *Behavior Research and Therapy, 27,* 173–180.

Jacobson, N. S., Waldron, H., & Moore, D. (1980). Toward a behavioral profile of marital distress. *Journal of Consulting and Clinical Psychology, 48,* 696–703.

Jacobson, N. S., Wilson, L., & Tupper, C. (1988). Clinical significance of treatment effects resulting from exposure-based treatments for agoraphobia: A reanalysis of outcome data. *Behavior Therapy, 19,* 539–552.

Schmaling, K. B., & Jacobson, N. S. (1990). Marital interaction and depression. *Journal of Abnormal Psychology, 99,* 229–236.

Stuart, R. B. (1969). Operant-interpersonal treatment for marital discord. *Journal of Consulting and Clinical Psychology, 33,* 675–682.

Weiss, R. L., Hops, H., & Patterson, G. R. (1973). A framework for conceptualizing marital conflict, technology for altering it, some data for evaluating it. In L. A. Hamerlynck, L. C. Handy, & E. J. Mash (Eds.), *Behavior change: Methodology, concepts, and practice* (pp. 309–342). Champaign, IL: Research Press.

20

Vanderbilt University: The Vanderbilt Center for Psychotherapy Research

William P. Henry and Hans H. Strupp
Vanderbilt University

Background and Aims

The Vanderbilt Center for Psychotherapy Research, founded by Strupp, has been in operation since the early 1970s and has been the site of a series of major process and outcome studies. The project has attracted a number of graduate students, postdoctoral fellows, and other researchers who have functioned for almost two decades as a stable, integrated research group. The studies conducted at the center trace their philosophical lineage to Strupp's early work, which was marked by a special interest in the therapist's contribution to the treatment process. He believed that the person of the therapist played an important role in determining the quality and outcome of therapy (Strupp, 1960a, 1960b). Hence, describing psychotherapy solely in terms of its theoretical orientations and techniques provides too truncated and simplistic a view of what is basically a complex human relationship occurring in a specific context. The overall aim of the center's research program has been to investigate intensively the therapeutic process in dynamic interpersonal psychotherapy as it relates to differential therapeutic outcome. In this regard, particular emphasis has been placed on studying the nature, effects, and measurement of the therapeutic relationship.

A number of interrelated subareas of investigation have followed from this basic emphasis on therapeutic process:

1. *Process–outcome links.* Our chief thrust has been to focus on the quality and determinants of the therapeutic relationship and how this relationship relates to other aspects of process, technique, and outcome. In attempting to measure the nature of the alliance, we have moved progressively from scales designed to tap the general affective and attitudinal climate of the participants to a more highly structured examination of moment-by-moment interpersonal dyadic process by using Benjamin's structural analysis of social behavior (SASB; Benjamin, 1974).

2. *Therapist variables.* On the basis of our central belief in the importance of the person of the therapist, we have been carrying out studies (many in progress) attempting to relate the therapist personal characteristics to therapeutic process and outcome. In particular, we have focused on the interpersonal patterns in the therapists' own families of origin as reflected in the structure of the therapists' introject and in instances of problematic interpersonal process engaged in by these therapists.

3. *Outcome measurement.* In order to render process research more intelligible, we have come to believe that the principle of problem–treatment–outcome (PTO) congruence should be followed where possible (Strupp, Schacht, & Henry, 1988). That is, the conceptualization and measurement of a patient's presenting problem, the therapeutic interventions, and resultant change

should all be placed in a common metric. Thus, we have begun to develop intrapsychic and interpersonal outcome measures based on the same measurement system (SASB) used to chart the patient's initial interpersonal patterns and the interpersonal process occurring in therapy.

4. *Effects of training.* A recurrent observation made in our research has been that even well-trained, experienced therapists often have difficulty managing the therapeutic relationship with difficult patients. We thus initiated a major study designed to explore the extent to which this problem might be ameliorated by specialized training. We are currently involved in the analysis of the complex effects (both positive and negative) of this training. This has led to a focus on the development of measures designed to operationalize therapist competence in a manner that transcends simple technical adherence to a manualized treatment protocol. We are also exploring the effects of training procedures on the manner in which novices to a given approach acquire and initially implement complex skills.

5. *Research ecology.* An area of particular concern in psychotherapy research is the potential extent to which the phenomena studied are altered by, and interact with, the research procedures designed to study them. In our most recent project, we conducted extensive posttherapy interviews with patients in an attempt better to understand such variables as the extent to which patients felt obligated to stay in therapy or to report favorable outcomes because they were involved in a research project, the effect of videotaped sessions on therapeutic process, the potential positive or negative effects of extensive assessment batteries, and the like.

6. *Training technology.* The development of improved training methods based on empirical process research and on our previous experience in training therapists in time-limited dynamic psychotherapy (TLDP) is the logical next step in bridging the gap between clinical research and clinical practice. Toward this end, we are engaged in the study of alternative training methods that for some purposes might be superior to the didactic coursework and supervision traditionally employed. In this regard, we are attempting to extract relevant principles from cognitive and educational research that address the acquisition of complex skills.

Method

Subjects and Selection

The Vanderbilt Center for Psychotherapy Research is based in the university's Department of Psychology, which does not operate its own clinic. Hence, we have had to recruit and screen patients specifically for each of our major projects. We have encountered no major problems with this procedure, which has allowed us to tailor the subject population precisely to meet the needs of the research. In the Vanderbilt I Project, some patients were applicants to the university's Psychological and Counseling Center, and the larger number came in response to letters sent to random samples of the undergraduate student body. In an attempt to construct a somewhat homogeneous patient sample, all patients were 17–24-year-old men with a 2-7-0 (depression-psychasthenia-social introversion) profile on the Minnesota Multiphasic Personality Inventory (MMPI).

In the Vanderbilt II Project, patients were recruited through newspaper announcements offering low-cost therapy by experienced clinicians; 80 patients were selected from the 449 respondents. The patients selected had to meet specific inclusion and exclusion criteria such as a minimum score of 40 on the SCL-90-R's Global Severity Index (GSI), difficulties that were interpersonally based, no evidence of psychosis or drug abuse, no concurrent participation in therapy, and no use of psychotropic medication. In this sample, the mean GSI score was equivalent to the normative symptomatic mean score of outpatients nationwide. The patients ranged in age from 24 to 64 years ($M = 41$ years), 77.5% were women, and 48.8% were married. Finally, 87% of the sample received at least one Axis I diagnosis and 67% received an Axis II diagnosis according to criteria set forth in the revised third edition of the *Diagnostic and Statistical Manual of Mental Disorders* (*DSM-III-R*; American Psychiatric Association, 1987).

Psychotherapists participating in the study were either licensed psychiatrists (criteria: MD, residency, and at least 2 years of full-time postresidency experience) or psychologists (criteria: PhD, clinical internship, and at least 2 years of full-time postdoctoral clinical experience). All therapists were graduates of fully accredited programs in psychology or psychiatry and had received reasonable training in psychodynamic principles and techniques but no specialized training in short-term dynamic psychotherapy. They were highly reputable, both personally and professionally.

Instruments and Procedures

A guiding principle of research conducted at the center has been to construct large data sets based on comprehensive assessment batteries, extensive clinical interviews, and audio and video recordings of individual sessions. The objective was to document each case fully from as many viewpoints as possible. In this manner we assured ourselves of a flexible, rich data base that will support continued investigations beyond the scope of the original hypotheses. The Vanderbilt II Project alone has generated over 2,000 audiotaped sessions, over 600 videotaped interviews and therapy sessions, and over 80,000 pages of raw data on the project therapists and patients. We have attempted to use well-recognized instruments (e.g., the MMPI, Global Assessment Scale, and the SCL-90–R) that permit our results to be compared with those of other studies while simultaneously developing and testing new assessment measures (e.g., a measure of intrapsychic change based on SASB).

Given the number and range of studies published under center auspices in the last two decades, it is feasible to discuss methodology only in the broadest sense. The Vanderbilt I and II Projects (and probably our future work as well) have followed the same general research algorithm.

A broad question of interest is first identified, and a large-scale project is planned that uses appropriate grouping variables. Vanderbilt I (1972–1980) investigated the effects of therapist training and experience on process and outcome with the then-dominant paradigm of specific compared with nonspecific factors by studying trained therapists as opposed to lay counselors (college professors). Vanderbilt II (1983–1989) studied the effects of advanced training on process and outcome with experienced therapists being used as their own controls in a pretest–posttest training design.

Differential outcome, and especially process-outcome links, are then explored at the group level. For this purpose, two main process rating instruments designed for use by independent raters have been developed. The Vanderbilt Psychotherapy Process Scale (VPPS; Suh, O'Malley, & Strupp, 1986) was developed as a general pur-pose instrument for assessing patient and therapist attitudes and behaviors that capture the salient features of their interaction. The VPPS comprises 80 items, each of which is rated on a 5-point Likert-type scale and is designed to be used on selected therapy segments (15–20 minutes average) so that a balance is achieved between global impressions of a full hour and atomistic analyses of single communications. Eight replicated factors have been identified: Patient Participation, Patient Hostility, Patient Exploration, Patient Psychic Distress, Patient Dependency, Therapist Warmth and Friendliness, Therapist Exploration, and Negative Therapist Attitude.

In addition, the Vanderbilt Negative Therapist Indicator Scale (VNIS; Suh, O'Malley, & Strupp, 1986), a scale structurally and procedurally similar to the VPPS, was developed from the assumption that the presence of an appreciable number of negative indicators in early therapy sessions will be predictive of poor therapeutic outcome. One VNIS subscale, Errors in Technique (failure to focus the session, failure to address resistance, failure to examine the patient–therapist interaction, etc.) has proven particularly useful. More recently, we have developed instruments to measure therapist adherence to specific TLDB technical dictates (the Vanderbilt Therapeutic Strategies Scale).

We have also extensively used Benjamin's (1974) SASB system to measure moment-by-moment interpersonal transactions in the therapeutic dyad. The SASB system is capable of differentiating extremely fine-grained interpersonal processes, such as multiple and complex communications, on the basis of as little as several words of dialog. SASB has provided a useful complement to the other more global process measures described and has permitted theoretically coherent PTO links to emerge.

We have increasingly come to rely on multiple process rating instruments and sources measured concurrently in the same therapeutic session. Our early work often used correlations between single scales or factors measured on a selected early session (typically the third) and eventual outcome. We are now using cluster-analytic techniques to select groups of dyads sharing similar features based on a number of process ratings taken across time. In this manner, each process rating helps to provide context for the others, enhancing the explanatory value of process research.

After promising process–outcome links are identified at the group level, single-case exemplars of these group trends are then selected for intensive study. Proceeding from group data that are based on independent ratings to single-case study data has provided a procedure for empirically based, instrument-guided observation of clinical phenomena that can be replicated across cases. The isolation of replicated phenomena may then be used to construct rating scales designed to be applied back at the group level to test hypotheses generated by this process. Although large data sets are useful for the initial exploration of patterned regularities in phenomena, it is the phenomena themselves at the single-case level that are crucial to the fundamental steps in the development of any science (observation, discovery, and description). We agree with the position that encourages discovery-oriented research paradigms and emphasizes the importance of the identification of shared phenomena as the subject matter of psychotherapy research.

Research Accomplishments

Beginning in 1953, Strupp initiated a series of empirical studies to shed light on the therapist's contribution to the treatment process, a topic on which little systematic work had been done at that time. In an analog situation, therapists were asked to respond to printed statements made by patients early in therapy. Responses were content analyzed, and categories were related to such variables as the therapist's professional affiliation, level of experience, and theoretical orientation (Strupp, 1957a, 1957b, 1957c). The investigative technique was subsequently refined by using a film of an initial interview that had been adapted for research purposes by insertion of the title "WHAT WOULD YOU DO?" at a number of choice points. In addition to giving hypothetical communications to the film patient, therapists were asked to give their diagnostic impressions and to formulate treatment plans.

Results showed systematic relationships between therapists' personal reactions to the patient (an angry, depressed, and provocative middle-aged man) on the one hand and the quality of their communications, diagnostic impressions, and treatment plans on the other. Specifically, the studies adduced evidence that negative attitudes toward the patient tended to be associated with unempathic communications and unfavorable clinical judgments, whereas the opposite was true of respondents who felt more positively toward

the patient. Extensive analyses of the data led to the belief that psychotherapy is least effective when the therapist cannot relate to the patient in a warm, empathic manner, regardless of the therapist's level of technical expertise (Strupp, 1960a). This research focused attention on the phenomenon that, at a later stage, we came to term *negative complementarity*. Broadly speaking, it referred to therapists' difficulties in dealing with hostile, negativistic, and provocative aspects of a patient's behavior that might lead to deterioration of the therapeutic relationship, premature termination, or unfavorable outcomes.

Another series of studies dealt with the development of a system for analyzing the therapist's communications, which was subsequently applied to various therapy protocols (Strupp, 1957a, 1957b, 1957c). The emphasis on analyzing salient aspects of the therapist's behavior and its consequences to the development of the therapeutic relationship as well as its outcome led to a project dealing with patients' retrospective accounts of their therapy experience (Strupp, Fox, & Lessler, 1969). Results showed that patients' positive attitudes toward the therapist were closely associated with success in therapy, irrespective of how success was measured. Successful patients described their therapists as warm, attentive, interested, understanding, and respectful. They also perceived the therapist as experienced and active in the therapeutic situation. In short, the composite picture of the "good" therapist drawn by our respondents was more "human" compared with the stereotype of the impersonal, detached analyst.

With respect to the nature of therapeutic change, patients placed relatively minor emphasis on alleviation of common neurotic symptoms such as anxiety, depression, and physical disturbances, and they focused on improvements in the areas of interpersonal relations and self-esteem. One of therapy's most striking accomplishments according to the patients was the transformation of mysterious and mystifying symptoms into phenomena with explainable antecedents. Patients came to view their difficulties in the context of their interpersonal relations, and this new understanding was accompanied by the development of techniques for more adaptive, less conflictual, and more satisfying ways of relating to others. An integral part of this learning experience was a sense of mastery over what had hitherto been seen as events to be endured passively.

Our study also provided evidence on the durability of therapeutic change. Two years or more after their last therapeutic contact, a large proportion of respondents had found it unnecessary to seek further therapy. On the whole, they reported that they had developed a greater tolerance for frustration and a greater willingness to accept limitations in themselves, in others, and in their life situation.

Linked to these empirical studies was a series of theoretical articles that sought to explore and conceptualize the therapist's contribution to the treatment process (Strupp, 1959, 1960a, 1960b, 1962, 1968, 1969, 1970, 1972a, 1972b, 1973a, 1973b, 1977). The problem of therapeutic outcome and its measurement was addressed in several publications (Strupp, 1963, 1978; Strupp & Bloxom, 1975; Strupp & Hadley, 1977).

Collaboration with Allen E. Bergin over a period of several years was aimed at exploring the feasibility of large-scale collaborative studies in psychotherapy (Bergin & Strupp, 1972). This work eventually led to the design of the Vanderbilt I Project. In addition, another series of studies dealt with the topic of role induction in psychotherapy, particularly with lower class patients (Strupp & Bloxom, 1973, 1974, 1975).

Among the topics addressed by members of the Vanderbilt research team in the 1970s was the problem of negative effects in psychotherapy (Hadley & Strupp, 1976; Strupp, Hadley, & Gomes-Schwartz, 1977; Hartley & Strupp, 1978; Strupp, 1978). Our investigation indicated that practicing psychotherapists, along with researchers and theoreticians, had become increasingly conscious of the ramifications and implications of the outcome problem in psychotherapy, including the issue of potential negative effects. Our response to the question "Are there negative effects of psychotherapy, and, if so, how can we identify them?" was that it depends on what we measure, what facets of the patient's functioning we emphasize, and how members of society (and mental health professionals) choose to define a negative effect. To aid our understanding of the issue, we developed a tripartite model of mental health and therapeutic outcomes (Strupp & Hadley, 1977) from a survey of prominent therapists, theoreticians, and other experts (Hadley & Strupp, 1976).

In formulating a set of recommendations, we placed significant emphasis on the quality of training itself and on the need for students to gain an appreciation that the quality of the patient–therapist relationship is at least as important for a good therapy outcome as any technique. This focus on the quality of training and the need for developing more effective training programs

has come full circle in our conclusions from the Vanderbilt II Project, which was carried out a decade later.

Vanderbilt I Project

As noted earlier, the Vanderbilt I Project investigated the incremental effectiveness of professional training on process and outcome by attempting to separate specific and nonspecific factors. We contrasted a group of neurotic patients (MMPI profile 2-7-0) treated by college professors selected for their understanding and warmth (thought to represent the nonspecific factors common to all psychotherapies) with a comparable group of patients treated by experienced professional therapists (who were thought to contribute additional or specific technical factors). Both treated groups had outcomes superior to untreated controls, but our original group analyses did not demonstrate statistical superiority in outcomes for the professional therapists.

The absence of the predicted group difference was a highly provocative finding that required further explanation. Intensive process studies were conducted with the VPPS, VNIS, and intensive analyses of individual cases to shed light on the factors differentiating successful from unsuccessful outcomes (Gomez-Schwartz, 1978; Hartley & Strupp, 1983; Sachs, 1983; Strupp, 1980a, 1980b, 1980c, 1980d). Selected highlights of research findings include the following:

1. The group data had obscured the finding that professional therapists were often more effective than lay therapists with patients showing such characteristics as high motivation for psychotherapy, ability quickly to form a good working alliance, and relative absence of long-standing maladaptive patterns of relating to others.

2. Neither group was notably effective in treating patients with more characterological problems such as pronounced hostility, pervasive mistrust, negativism, inflexibility, and so forth.

3. The nature of the patient–therapist working alliance seems to be formed rather quickly (by the end of the 3rd session) and is an important predictor of outcome in a time-limited context (approximately 25 sessions). In addition, we obtained evidence that reasonably good predictions of process can be made from the first session, particularly judgments relating to the patient's motivation for therapy (Keithly, Samples, & Strupp, 1980). Most

important, we found little evidence that an initially negative or ambivalent therapeutic alliance was significantly altered in the course of the therapies under study.

4. Professional therapists gave little evidence of adapting their therapeutic approach or techniques to the specific characteristics and problems of individual patients and did not formulate specific therapeutic goals that were systematically pursued. Therefore, there was compelling evidence that the quality of the therapeutic relationship was determined to a significant degree by patient characteristics (i.e., the patient's ability to relate comfortably to and to work productively within the therapist-offered conditions).

5. Professional therapists who were well versed in the concepts of countertransference nonetheless often reacted negatively and countertherapeutically to patient hostility.

Strupp (1980a, 1980b, 1980c, 1980d) isolated eight cases in which four therapists each saw a good and a poor outcome case. The third session of these eight cases was later subjected to an extremely fine-grained (utterance by utterance) interpersonal process analysis with the SASB (Henry, Schacht, & Strupp, 1986). Results indicated that the therapists, although using similar techniques in their good and poor outcome cases, differed markedly in the quality of the interpersonal processes established. Furthermore, although technique varied substantially across the four therapists studied, the actual interpersonal processes differentiating high-change and low-change outcomes were markedly similar across dyads. In the poor-outcome cases the therapist engaged in a surprising amount of subtle controlling blame of the patient (which was usually responded to by the patient in complementary fashion, namely with hostile submission). Finally, therapist and patient complex communications (mixed messages containing simultaneous affiliative and disaffiliative components) were relatively common in the poor-outcome cases but virtually absent with the same therapist in the good-outcome case.

The experience gained in the Vanderbilt I Project crystallized four principles that guided the Vanderbilt II Project:

1. The global paradigm of specific compared with nonspecific factors could not be relied on as an instructive guide to understanding process–outcome relationships.

2. The interpersonal dimension was central to understanding the nature of psychotherapy. Interpersonal processes occurring between patient and therapist were central factors that could either therapeutically ameliorate or pathologically confirm a patient's dysfunctional self-system.

3. Time-limited therapies, which were at the time of the study highly controversial forms of intervention, appeared to be potentially viable forms of treatment.

4. The vulnerability of well-trained therapists to countertherapeutic process with difficult patients made it clear that therapists would benefit from additional training in the technical management of the therapeutic relationship.

Vanderbilt II Project

After the Vanderbilt I Project was completed, a 3-year period of pilot work was undertaken that included development and testing of a manual and adherence scale for TLDP (Strupp & Binder, 1984). The TLDP manual, which was based on psychodynamic and interpersonal principles, was explicitly intended to assist therapists in working with interpersonally difficult patients. The Vanderbilt II Project was designed to focus on the manner in which specialized training might improve the quality of the patient–therapist relationship and the therapeutic process. The research plan required 16 experienced therapists (clinical psychologists and psychiatrists) to treat 2 patients before and 2 patients after training in TLDP (during which time they saw an additional training case). Because planned analyses of the data are just now being completed, the following summary of major conclusions should be considered preliminary.

One overarching conclusion seems clear: The effects of manualized training are complex, involve potentially positive and negative effects, and do not lead to a straight-line function between technical adherence and outcome. First, the training program was successful in teaching a manualized form of therapy (TLDP) to independently judged technical adherence criteria. Second, there was evidence that some elements of general interviewing style not directly related to specifically taught techniques were also improved after training. For example, therapists showed greater encouragement of the experience and expression of in-session affect and increased their use of open-ended questions. Thus, training altered both specific and general technical operations associated with improving the quality of dynamic interpersonal psychotherapy.

The relationship between TLDP training and enhanced outcome was not as straightforward as predicted. The 16 participating therapists were divided into two subgroups, each headed by a different teaching team. Although the teaching materials had been developed jointly by the team leaders, one subgroup showed significantly higher technical adherence after training. When the posttraining outcomes of the two subgroups were compared, the group with the higher technical adherence produced superior outcomes across most measures. The relation between adherence to a manualized protocol and improved outcome was not as direct as we had hoped, but it clearly indicated that training in and adherence to TLDP techniques can enhance treatment efficacy. The pronounced differences between training subgroups were unexpected and served to point up the centrality of the training process as well as the training content. An initial informal analysis of the training process has suggested that the low-adherence group engaged in discussions of patient characteristics at a much higher level of abstraction (similar to much of traditional supervision), whereas the group with higher adherence focused more consistently on concrete patient–therapist transactional behaviors.

Another finding of potentially great importance to understanding the effects of training was obtained: Therapists who described themselves (on the SASB intrex introject questionnaire) as self-controlling and self-blaming had by far the greatest technical adherence. Previous research (Henry, 1986) has shown that this pattern of therapist introject is associated with a greater likelihood of poor interpersonal process in the therapeutic dyad. Further analysis has suggested that therapists with self-indicting introjects displayed the least warmth and friendliness and that their patients showed the highest level of hostility as measured by the VPPS. These relationships hold up even when the variance accounted for by level of technical adherence is partialed out. This puzzling interaction will require further study, but it appears possible that therapists most likely to adhere to the dictates of a training protocol are also more likely to engage in certain forms of problematic process, a situation that potentially works against the demonstration that training improves outcome.

The various relationships among training, technical adherence, and therapeutic process (as measured by SASB, VPPS, VNIS, and participant self-reports such as the Barrett–Lenard questionnaire) are too numerous to detail in this format. It is clear from initial analyses, however, that the process changes included both positive and negative aspects that probably interacted in complex ways. The training clearly increased the activity level of the therapists. As therapist verbal activity increased, so did the opportunity for countertherapeutic interpersonal process. Thus, the number of disaffiliative and complex statements by the therapists (as judged by independent raters with the SASB) increased after training, although the absolute percentage of such statements did not (i.e., technical adherence neither fostered nor prevented such clinician interpersonal behaviors per se). Even so, the patient's level of disaffiliative process and resistant behaviors (measured by the VPPS) appeared to increase as a result of technical adherence. This raises the provocative hypothesis that when therapists apply learned techniques in an unskillful manner training may actually have some negative effects.

The changes in the perceptions of the same therapists by their patients' before and after training are most intriguing. On the one hand, patients seen after training described their therapists as more genuine and at ease in the relationship. The largest difference was the increase in the degree to which patients felt that they could be openly critical of their therapist without causing the therapist to feel differently toward them. On the other hand, with higher technical adherence the patients also felt that their therapists were more impatient with them, and they felt that they (the patients) often had greater difficulty making themselves understood. These and other seemingly contradictory process changes suggest that defining and imparting therapeutic skill (as opposed to technical adherence) and altering a therapist's underlying interpersonal behaviors are demanding and complex problems, that may necessitate a complete reconceptualization of training procedures. It is clear that training therapists in manualized therapies to technical adherence criteria does not specify "the therapist variable" to the extent hoped for with the advent of this approach. Although a number of positive benefits seem to have accrued as the result of specific training, we continue to confront an observation of major importance that may be described as the central theme of the Vanderbilt group: the pronounced inability of therapists to avoid countertherapeutic processes with difficult patients.

Research Programs in Progress and Planned for the Future

We plan to continue extensive process analyses of the Vanderbilt II data set to identify subsets or clusters of dyads sharing common process and outcome characteristics across a range of measures. Instances of recurrent problematic processes will be studied with an events paradigm. These events are hypothesized to pose therapeutic risks or dilemmas. For example, we have observed that therapists have difficulty working with, and often eventually establish poor interpersonal processes with, patients who are chronically self-indicting. We plan to develop a taxonomy of these potential therapeutic risk situations, which are thought to be commonly recurring across different therapies and have been empirically linked to poor process.

These analyses and identified clinical vignettes along with the experience gained in Vanderbilt II will help to form the foundation for the development of a new approach to training. We have become convinced that current methods of training psychotherapists are not sufficiently robust to produce the desired skill in trainees. Our recent experience in training therapists has driven home the discrepancy between their conceptual knowledge of therapeutic principles and procedures on the one hand and their ability to translate that knowledge into consistently skillful performance (which transcends technical adherence per se) on the other. We consider it essential to develop training programs that are aimed at imparting fundamental interpersonal skills as a base for other forms of training. At the heart of this training will be efforts to increase trainees' abilities to perceive and act on the nuances of interpersonal in-session transactions as they occur.

Traditional didactic instruction and supervised casework do seem to impart general knowledge principles and to produce a certain level of skill. Nevertheless, new instructional methods may be required to teach optimal knowledge utilization in action. We are currently exploring recent developments in cognitive and educational psychology relevant to the domain of expert skill acquisition. For instance, one principle, "contrast-set teaching" (Bransford, Sherwood, Vye, Rieser, 1986), provides examples in contrasting sets or alternative responses to problem situations that illustrate a continuum from novice to expert and allow the student to learn what is relevant in judging the quality of a performance. In our de-velopmental work on new training procedures, we plan to use computerized videodisc technology to present such contrasting sets culled from our basic process research into "risk events". In addition, we are currently planning studies aimed at providing more precise definitions of therapeutic skill by making controlled comparisons between experts and novices. Our overarching aim as we conduct further process analyses and develop new instructional approaches is to continue to narrow the gap between basic psychotherapy research and its application to clinical practice and training.

If we and other research groups are to realize our aims, a number of challenges must be faced and overcome. Over the years, primary support for our center has come from research and training grants awarded by the National Institute of Mental Health. For various reasons, this support has not kept pace with inflation and has become increasing difficult to obtain, discouraging some young investigators from entering the field. In an era in which psychotherapy research has increasingly required substantial teamwork, problems surrounding the continuity of financial support have had serious effects on the maintainance of sustained team research. Centralized, collaborative data archives may be one way of reducing costs and furthering the goal of identifying shared phenomena for study by multiple research teams. Perhaps the greatest challenge for the future will be methodological, as we attempt to incorporate the best aspects of nomethetic and idiographic approaches to provide sustained, coherent, and clinically relevant empirical research.

References

American Psychiatric Association. (1987). *Diagnostic and statistical manual of mental disorders* (rev. 3rd ed.). Washington, DC: Author.

Benjamin, L. S. (1974). Structural analysis of social behavior. *Psychological Review, 81,* 392–425.

Bergin, A. E., & Strupp, H. H. (1972). *Changing frontiers in the science of psychotherapy.* Chicago: Aldine-Atherton.

Bransford, J. D., Sherwood, R., Vye, N., & Rieser, J. (1986). Teaching thinking and problem solving: Research foundations. *American Psychologist, 41,* 1078–1089.

Gomez-Schwartz, B. (1978). Effective ingredients in psychotherapies: Prediction of outcome from process variables. *Journal of Consulting and Clinical Psychology, 46,* 1023–1035.

Hadley, S. W., & Strupp, H. H. (1976). Contemporary views of negative effects in psychotherapy: An integrated account. *Archives of General Psychiatry, 33,* 1291–1302.

Hartley, D. E., & Strupp, H. H. (1978). The new psychotherapies: Caveat emptor. *New York University Educational Quarterly, 9,* 17–22.

Hartley, D. E., & Strupp, H. H. (1983). The therapeutic alliance: Its relationship to outcome in brief psychotherapy. In J. Masling (Ed.), *Empirical studies of psychoanalytical theories (Vol. 1,* pp. 1–38). Hillsdale, NJ: Analytic Press.

Henry, W. P. (1986). *Interpersonal process in psychotherapy.* Unpublished doctoral dissertation, Vanderbilt University.

Henry, W. P., Schacht, T. E., & Strupp, H. H. (1986). Structural analysis of social behavior: Application to a study of interpersonal process in differential psychotherapeutic outcome. *Journal of Consulting and Clinical Psychology, 54,* 27–31.

Keithly, L. J., Samples, S. J., & Strupp, H. H. (1980). Patient motivation as a predictor of process and outcome in psychotherapy. *Psychotherapy and Psychosomatics, 33,* 87–97.

Sachs, J. S. (1983). Negative factors in brief psychotherapy: An empirical assessment. *Journal of Consulting and Clinical Psychology, 51,* 557–564.

Strupp, H. H. (1957a). A multidimensional system for analyzing psychotherapeutic techniques. *Psychiatry, 20,* 293–306.

Strupp, H. H. (1957b). A multidimensional analysis of techniques in brief psychotherapy. *Psychiatry, 20,* 387–397.

Strupp, H. H. (1957c). A multidimensional comparison of therapist in analytic and client-centered therapy. *Journal of Consulting Psychology, 21,* 301–308.

Strupp, H. H. (1959). Toward an analysis of the therapist's contribution to the treatment process. *Psychiatry, 22,* 349–362.

Strupp, H. H. (1960a). Nature of psychotherapist's contribution to treatment process: Some research results and speculations. *Archives of General Psychiatry, 3,* 219–231.

Strupp, H. H. (1960b). *Psychotherapists in action: Explorations of the therapist's contribution to the treatment process.* New York: Grune & Stratton.

Strupp, H. H. (1962). Patient–doctor relationships: Psychotherapist in the therapeutic process. In A. J. Bachrach (Ed.), *Experimental foundations of clinical psychology* (pp. 576–615). New York: Basic Books.

Strupp, H. H. (1963). Psychotherapy revisited: The problem of outcome. *Psychotherapy, 1,* 1–13.

Strupp, H. H. (1968). Psychoanalytic therapy of the individual. In J. Marmor (Ed.), *Modern psychoanalysis: New directions and perspectives* (pp. 293–342). New York: Basic Books.

Strupp, H. H. (1969). Toward a specification of teaching and learning in psychotherapy. *Archives of General Psychiatry, 21,* 203–212.

Strupp, H. H. (1970). Specific vs. nonspecific factors in psychotherapy and the problem of control. *Archives of General Psychiatry, 23,* 393–401.

Strupp, H. H. (1972a). Needed: A reformulation of the psychotherapeutic influence. *International Journal of Psychiatry, 10,* 114–120.

Strupp, H. H. (1972b). On the technology of psychotherapy. *Archives of General Psychiatry, 26,* 270–278.

Strupp, H. H. (1973a). On the basic ingredients of psychotherapy. *Journal of Consulting and Clinical Psychology, 41,* 1–8.

Strupp, H. H. (1973b). Toward a reformulation of the psychotherapeutic influence. *International Journal of Psychiatry, 11,* 263–354.

Strupp, H. H. (1977). A reformulation of the dynamics of the therapist's contribution. In A. S. Gurman & A. M. Razin (Eds.), *Effective psychotherapy: A handbook of research* (pp. 1–22). New York: Pergamon Press.

Strupp, H. H. (1978). Psychotherapy research and practice: An overview. In S. L. Garfield & A. E. Bergin (Eds.), *Handbook of psychotherapy and behavior change: An empirical analysis* (2nd ed., pp. 3–22). New York: Wiley.

Strupp, H. H. (1980a). Success and failure in time-limited psychotherapy: A systematic comparison of two cases. *Archives of General Psychiatry, 37,* 395–603.

Strupp, H. H. (1980b). Success and failure in time-limited psychotherapy: A systematic comparison of two cases. *Archives of General Psychiatry, 37,* 708–716.

Strupp, H. H. (1980c). Success and failure in time-limited psychotherapy: With special reference to the performance of a lay counselor. *Archives of General Psychiatry, 37,* 831-841.

Strupp, H. H. (1980d). Success and failure in time-limited psychotherapy: Further evidence. *Archives of General Psychiatry, 37,* 947–954.

Strupp, H. H., & Binder, J. L. (1984). *Psychotherapy in a new key: A guide to time-limited dynamic psychotherapy.* New York: Basic Books.

Strupp, H. H., & Bloxom, A. L. (1973). Preparing lower-class patients for group psychotherapy: Development and evaluation of a role induction film. *Journal of Consulting and Clinical Psychology, 41,* 373–384.

Strupp, H. H., & Bloxom, A. L. (1974). Role induction for psychotherapy: A promising technique for the rehabilitation client. In A. B. Cobb (Ed.), *Special problems in rehabilitation* (pp. 98–140). Springfield, IL: Charles C Thomas.

Strupp, H. H., & Bloxom, A. L. (1975). Therapists' assessments of outcome. In I. E. Waskow & M. B. Parloff (Eds.), *Psychotherapy change measures* (pp. 170–180). Rockville, MD: National Institute of Mental Health.

Strupp, H. H., Fox, R. E., & Lessler, K. (1969). *Patients view their psychotherapy.* Baltimore, MD: Johns Hopkins University Press.

Strupp, H. H., & Hadley, S. W. (1977). A tripartite model of mental health and therapeutic outcomes: With special reference to negative effects in psychotherapy. *American Psychologist, 32,* 187–196.

Strupp, H. H., Hadley, S. W., & Gomes-Schwartz, B. (1977). *Psychotherapy for better or worse: An analysis of the problem of negative effects.* Montvale, NJ: Jason Aronson.

Strupp, H. H., Schacht, T. E., & Henry, W. P. (1988). Problem-treatment-outcome congruence: A principle whose time has come. In H. Dahl, H. Kachele, & H. Thoma (Eds.), *Psychoanalytic process research strategies* (pp. 1–14). New York: Springer-Verlag.

Suh, C. S., O'Malley, S. S., & Strupp, H. H. (1986). The Vanderbilt process measures: The Vanderbilt Psychotherapy Process Scale (VPPS) and the Vanderbilt Negative Indicators Scale (VNIS). In L. S. Greenberg & W. M. Pinsof (Eds.), *The psychotherapeutic process: A research handbook* (pp. 285–324). New York: Guilford Press.

CHAPTER

21

York University Psychotherapy Research Program

Leslie S. Greenberg, Laura N. Rice,
David L. Rennie, and Shaké G. Toukmanian
York University

Background and Aims

The research efforts at York University have been characterized by the investigation of how change takes place in psychotherapy. This research entails many commonalities in perspectives and approaches among the members of the center as well as some differences. In common is an interest in the process of change in humanistic and experientially oriented psychotherapies, in viewing change theoretically from a constructive information-processing perspective, in measurement construction, in the development of systematic research methods, and in the manualization of training in therapy.

Our interest in constructive information-processing theory has led us to recast experientially oriented psychotherapies as the systematic facilitation, in a supportive relationship, of different types of cognitive and affective information processing at particular times and for particular kinds of difficulties (Greenberg, 1984a; Greenberg, Elliott, & Foerster, 1990; Rennie, 1986, 1990; Rice, 1974, 1984; Rice & Greenberg, 1990; Toukmanian, 1986, 1990). In this view the therapist is seen as engaging in process diagnoses and identifying in-session processing problems that are currently amenable to intervention. The therapist is also viewed as being directive of the client's process, with each intervention having the

potential to alter the client's mode of processing. In addition to the therapist's directing the client's processing on a moment-by-moment basis to deepen experience and to gain access to new information, new processing tasks are suggested at particular times to facilitate particular types of affective problem resolution. The process directive approach is seen as being best facilitated in a relationship characterized by the therapeutic attitudes of empathy, respect, and genuineness and by a present-centered orientation in which the therapist focuses on the client's current processing of experience.

This view grew out of Rice and Wagstaff's (1967) work at the University of Chicago Counseling and Psychotherapy Research Center, in which they studied the process of change in client-centered therapy. In listening to tapes of client-centered therapy, they found that therapist interventions that were more stimulating and evocative led to more productive client explorations. This led to the development of process measures that could assess different levels of client and therapist process.

This study of process required an exquisite sensitivity to the moment-by-moment nature of client states and processes and the manner in which particular therapist statements affected these states and processes. This resulted in a perspective on the need to study the moment-by-moment interactive process and to capture possible causal links between particular types or styles of interventions and subsequent client manner of information processing.

Rice moved to York University in the late 1960s and developed a counseling and therapy program infused with this research spirit. In the early 1970s Toukmanian and Rennie joined the faculty and helped in developing this program. Greenberg worked as a doctoral student with Rice and in 1975 moved to the University of British Columbia but kept up a close collaboration with York. Out of this association grew the current Psychotherapy Research Center, which was established in 1986 when Greenberg returned to York.

Method

Most of the members at the center subscribe to a research approach informed by a rational–empirical methodology that promotes the integration of clinical theory and experience with rigorous observation. The approach is discovery oriented, requiring that the investigator remain close to the clinical data and retain freshness of observation but that rigorous cumulative observation and measurement be made of the therapeutic process under study. The rational phase of this approach allows tapping of the rich source of ideas drawn from theory and clinical experience in experiential therapy to develop rational models of possible change processes. The empirical phase allows engagement in a process of increasingly rigorous observation and measurement against which to compare rational conjectures. This approach, which involves moving back and forth between explicit and implicit theory and empirical observation of concrete phenomena in order to reflect more accurately the phenomena under study, is described in *Patterns of Change* (Rice & Greenberg, 1984).

The approach has been used to identify and understand specific classes of change events that seem to recur within and across clients in client-centered and gestalt therapy. Events have been construed as consisting of client markers indicating opportunities for particular types of interventions plus the interventions and the subsequent client responses to the interventions. A study of these events has allowed us to map client paths to resolution of the problem indicated by the marker and then to identify the ways in which these resolution performances could best be facilitated by the therapist. The research initiatives following from this approach are described below.

Research Accomplishments

Conflict Split and Two-Chair Dialog

A change event from gestalt therapy involving the resolution of conflict by means of two-chair dialog was studied by Greenberg (1984a, 1984b) using the rational–empirical method of task analysis. This event addresses a class of processing difficulties in which two aspects of the self are in opposition and is most clearly manifested when clients present verbal statements of splits indicating an experienced conflict between the two aspects of self (Greenberg, 1979). Although differing greatly in content, such statements possess structural similarity. The marker of a split has four features. The first 2 are statements of the two conflicting aspects of self. The third is a juxtaposition indicator, which places the two aspects in opposition, and the fourth is an indicator that the client is currently experiencing struggle. These markers have been shown to be identifiable with high reliability (100% agreement between raters; Greenberg, 1984a).

The basic theoretical assumption concerning the schematic processing difficulty at this marker is that two conflicting schematic structures involving incompatible behaviors, thoughts, feelings, and desires are being simultaneously evoked. Of special significance in disturbed functioning are two sets of conflicting schemata, one involving an automatic emotional response to one's own needs and desires and the other involving negative evaluations of this kind of experience, including expectations and injunctions about how one should behave. These "shoulds" have been introjected over the course of development but are not truly assimilated into the self-structure. Failure to attend to the biologically adaptive signals or to respond in ways dictated by the person's own needs and desires leaves the person confused and unclear; failure to meet the standards incorporated in the "shoulds" produces negative self-evaluation and loss of self-worth. When such conflicting self-schemas are relevant to important areas of life, they can cause immobilization and lead to confusion and anxiety or depression.

Splits lend themselves to a form of intervention in which the two aspects of self, a "critic" and an experiencing self, are clearly separated, often spatially, in two chairs. A dialog between them is instigated, with the therapist promoting active expression of each side of the conflict and encouraging a confrontation between the two conflicting aspects of self. The dialog promotes the creation of a new schematic structure that integrates the two previously disparate experiences. The client's self-evaluations and negative expectations are positively resolved through self-confrontation and by some form of integrative self-acceptance (Greenberg, 1983, 1984a).

A number of studies of two-chair dialog have been completed with the rational and empirical task analytic strategy devised for this purpose (Greenberg, 1984b). This research program yielded the following results: (a) verification of the efficacy of the two-chair intervention in resolving splits; (b) the development of an empirically grounded performance model of the processes in which a client needs to engage to achieve successful task resolution; (c) the verification that components of the performance model were related to treatment outcome; and (d) a therapist manual describing in detail the way in which the therapist facilitates the process of change.

Two-chair dialog at a conflict split offered within a good working alliance by a therapist perceived by the client as empathic has been shown in three separate studies to lead to deeper experiencing and superior session outcomes than those achieved with empathic responding to a split (Greenberg & Clarke, 1979; Greenberg & Dompierre, 1981) and to deeper experiencing than that achieved with focusing (Greenberg & Higgins, 1980). Two-chair dialog has also been shown to be more effective than cognitive problem solving in resolving decisional conflict (Clarke & Greenberg, 1986).

Intensive analysis of a number of successful conflict resolution performances led to the construction of a model of resolution in which the two chairs were shown to engage in different performances over time in the dialog (Greenberg, 1980, 1984a), performances that could be reliably demonstrated to be associated with resolution (Greenberg, 1983). Finally, the occurrence of three process components (measured by structural analysis of social behavior [Benjamin, Foster, Roberto, & Estroff, 1986], the experiencing scale [Klein, Mathieu-Coughlan, & Kiesler, 1986], and client vocal quality [Rice & Kerr, 1986])—*harsh criticism* and the eventual *softening* of the criticism in one chair, and the expression of *felt wants* from the experiencing chair—was shown to predict treatment outcome, goal attainment, and decision implementation at follow-up for 29 clients with anxiety over decisional conflict (Greenberg & Webster, 1982).

Evocative Unfolding of Problematic Reactions

Another event was identified in the context of client-centered therapy (Rice, 1974, 1984). This change event addresses a class of schematic processing difficulties that control a person's interactions with other people and situations in the environment. Although various contents may be involved, the reliably identifiable "marker" for such events has a particular structure involving three features: a particular incident; a reaction (internal, external, or both) on the part of the client; an indication that the client viewed his or her reaction as puzzling, unexpected, maladaptive, or otherwise problematic. That the client is aware of a discrepancy between his or her expected reaction and actual reaction indicates a current readiness to examine such interactions. At this marker the therapist encourages the client to describe the incident as vividly as possible, thus revoking the sights, sounds, and feelings experienced at the time. The therapist then assists the client in getting in touch with the edges of his or her affectively toned experience and thus in discovering and synthesizing crucial elements of the experience that had not been fully processed in awareness.

The assumption underlying this process of systematic experiential search is that if the incident can be vividly reevoked under conditions of safety, empathic understanding, and systematic experiential exploration, the incident can be reprocessed by the client more slowly and completely. It is this new, self-discovered information that will force reorganization of the inadequate or distorted self-in-world schemata that are involved. Successful resolution is defined as new awareness of important aspects of the client's own mode of functioning in a way that restructures the issue. Although still experientially involved, the client now has a sense of what he or she wants to change and a sense of having the power to instigate change.

A rational–empirical task analysis of the resolution of problematic reaction points (PRPs) was performed (Rice & Saperia, 1984; Wiseman, 1986). In an analog study, evocative unfolding at the PRP marker was rated significantly higher by the clients than were the interviews in which the PRP marker was followed by usual client-centered interventions, verifying that some important change processes worthy of further intensive analysis were occurring in this event. Task analyses of resolution performance have yielded a performance model of the processes in which the client needed to engage to reach successful resolution and a therapist manual describing the ways in which the therapist can best facilitate the client's engagement in the different steps leading to resolution.

Another clinical study demonstrated that the number of steps in the model actually completed (as assessed by predesignated clusters of process measures) was significantly related to client and therapist postsession ratings of the degree to which resolution had been achieved (Lowenstein, 1985). Task sessions were rated by clients as being deeper and more valuable than nontask sessions on the Session Evaluation Questionnaire (Lowenstein, 1985; Wiseman, 1986). In a brief therapy administered to 12 clients (Lowenstein, 1985), those who successfully resolved the PRP task session had significantly better outcomes on two outcome measures (state anxiety and target complaints) than those who did not. There was, however, no significant difference in scores on the Tennessee Self-Concept Scale. Confirmation for the effectiveness of the prescribed therapist operations in facilitating the essential client processes was obtained in sequential analyses involving three single-case studies (Wiseman, 1986; Wiseman & Rice, 1989).

The Perceptual Processing Perspective

Another line of research has focused on the investigation of the nature of clients' inferential processes that mediate change in a perceptually based schematic processing model of experiential psychotherapy (Toukmanian, 1986, 1990). In this framework, the targets of therapeutic interventions are model-specified client process markers. Essentially, these represent several dysfunctional patterns of client perceptual operations that are discernible from the differential quality of clients' verbal participation in therapy. The assumption underlying this treatment is that engaging clients in the controlled (i.e., slow, more reflective, and deliberate) processing of information associated with significant life events results in the development of structurally more complex and functionally more flexible self-schemata leading to meaningful changes in clients' perceptions of self in interpersonal situations and therapeutic improvement.

Evidence from several projects indicates that therapeutic improvement is associated with iden-

tifiable changes in clients' manner of schematic processing. For example, Toukmanian (1986) compared the processing characteristics of most- and least-improved clients using segments from early, middle, and late therapy sessions. She found that successful cases tended to move gradually away from using undifferentiated, categorical, and stereotypical construals in favor of more differentiated and indiosyncratic schematic representations that were formulated on the basis of information generated ostensibly from an internal frame of reference.

Changes before and after treatment in the content and structure of clients' self-schemata have also been investigated using a recognition memory paradigm for a list of positive and negative self-referent adjectives. In one study (Toukmanian, 1990), it was found that after receiving a brief, perceptually based experiential therapy, clients tended to incorporate more positive content in their self-schemata and to respond to schema-consistent adjectives faster or more efficiently than they did before starting treatment. Results from a second study (Toukmanian, 1990) indicated that, compared with the performance of clients in a treatment control group, those who had received this short-term experiential therapy had significantly less negative content in their self-schemata and significantly better outcome scores on various standard clinical instruments (e.g., the Beck Depression Inventory, State-Trait Anxiety, Inventory, and Tennessee Self-Concept Scale).

The Descriptive–Qualitative Approach

As the fourth member of the team, Rennie is using a descriptive research approach to access the client's and therapist's subjective experiences of psychotherapy. In this approach, interpersonal process recall is used to stimulate participants' recollections of the subjective experience of moments in therapy identified by them as being meaningful. The researcher interviews the participant about each such moment. The accounts thus given by the respondent are transcribed and subjected to a qualitative analysis. The analysis is replicated across events and individuals, and an overall structure of the respondents' experience of therapy is derived. Rennie's focus has been on the client's subjective experience of an entire therapy session (Rennie, 1990). His students have addressed clients' identifications of the sources of change over an entire course of therapy (Phillips, 1984; Rennie, Phillips, & Quartaro, 1988) and of both the client's and therapist's subjective experience of metaphor in therapy (Angus & Rennie, 1988, 1989).

There are two especially compelling aspects of the returns from this line of research. First, the approach has provided access to the therapy participants' self-awareness in the therapeutic encounter. Here it is apparent that clients and therapists actively monitor their thoughts and feelings and take executive action in response to that monitoring. Second, it is evident that much of the client's processing of experience is kept private during the interaction with the therapist. Both findings are seen as having implications for both the practice of and research into psychotherapy.

Measurement Construction

To study the change process, measures of the client's performance and experience need to be constructed to capture particular features of the therapeutic process that are regarded as important in change. A number of measures have been developed by our group. Rice devised measures of both client and therapist vocal quality, and a number of studies that used vocal quality as an index of productive therapy have been completed (Rice & Kerr, 1986). Toukmanian (1986) devised a measure of client perceptual processes for evaluating the client's manner of processing information. Studies have shown that the instrument is sensitive to expected changes in the manner in which clients process information across therapy sessions and that these changes are predictive of therapy outcome (Toukmanian, 1986, 1990).

A measure of the client's and therapist's perspectives on the working alliance have also been devised (Horvath & Greenberg, 1986). This inventory—the Working Alliance Inventory—measures Bordin's (1979) conceptualization of the three components of the working alliance: goals, tasks, and bonds. This measure has been shown to have good psychometric properties and has been tested in four studies relating process to outcome (Horvath & Greenberg, 1986, 1989). Finally, the qualitative research studies conducted by Rennie and his students have resulted in a taxonomy pertaining to the aspect of the subjective experience addressed by the particular study (Rennie et al., 1988), and work on the reliability of this taxonomy is currently underway.

Research Programs in Progress

A manual of a process-diagnostic, process-directive, experiential therapy has been devised in which the therapeutic interventions from five different change events have been specified (Greenberg & Rice, 1988). These focused interventions are embedded in a relationship that is characterized by the client-centered conditions of empathy, positive regard, and congruence. A number of additional general and specific relationship skills have been specified as well as the skills utilized in each change event.

Toukmanian (1984) has developed a manual for training therapists in a perceptually oriented experiential treatment that focuses on changing the manner in which clients construe themselves and the world. The manual specifies and describes the steps involved in the identification of client process markers that suggest the presence of an automated or overly constricted pattern of schematic processing. Rennie (1986) has developed a manualized psychotherapy training program integral to his research findings on self-reflectivity in which the therapist's tasks are to facilitate the client's awareness of the intentions and actions entailed in the cognitive and affective processing of experience and to judiciously direct that processing. Three key skills are process identification, process directives, and metacommunication.

Programs Planned for the Future

A major initiative in the center is being mounted by Greenberg and Rice to compare the effects of process-diagnostic, process-directive, experiential treatment with a purely client-centered treatment that provides the therapeutic attitudes but not the intentional actions to influence modes of processing. The aim here is to study different types of processing difficulties and the types of processing that lead to particular types of change specifically relevant to each type of processing difficulty. Five different types of change occurring in experiential therapy have been identified: recognition of one's own mode of functioning, self-acceptance, self-empowerment, understanding and acceptance of the other, and the creation of new meaning. Each of these types of change is most relevant to one type of in-session problem state: problematic reactions, self-evaluative splits, interruption of expression, unfinished business, and being on the surface of something meaningful, respectively. It is being hypothesized that each of the types of change represents the resolution of one of the change events, which begins with a particular problem state that is best facilitated by a specific intervention. These interventions are evocative unfolding for problematic reactions (Rice, 1984), two-chair dialog for self-evaluative splits (Greenberg, 1984a), two-chair enactment for self-interruption (Greenberg & Minden, 1988), empty-chair dialog for unfinished business (Greenberg & Minden, 1988; Greenberg & Safran, 1987), and focusing for being on the surface (Gendlin, 1981). These hypotheses will be tested by comparing the process and in-session outcomes of these marker intervention events in the experiential treatment, with the same marker being followed by the relationship conditions alone.

There are also a number of research projects that are currently being pursued with reference to the perceptual processing approach to experiential therapy. One major goal of this work, which is being carried out by Toukmanian and her team of student associates, is the refinement of this treatment method. Finally, Rennie's research will focus on the subjective experience of particular incidents of change and of the therapist's operations designed to instigate such incidents. The question of interest here is the relationship between cognitive or affective change processes and the client's metacognitive engagement in those processes.

References

Angus, L. E., & Rennie, D. L. (1989). Envisioning the representational world: Metaphoric expressiveness in psychotherapy. *Psychotherapy, 26,* 372–379.

Angus, L. E., & Rennie, D. L. (1988). Therapist participation in metaphor generation: Collaborative and non-collaborative relationships. *Psychotherapy, 25,* 552–560.

Benjamin, C., Foster, S., Roberto, L., & Estroff, S. (1986). Breaking the family code: Analysis of videotapes of family interactions by structural analysis of social behavior (SASB). In L. Greenberg & W. Pinsof (Eds.), *The psychotherapeutic process: A research handbook* (pp. 391–438). New York: Guilford Press.

Bordin, E. (1979). The generalizability of the psychoanalytic concept of working alliance. *Psychotherapy: Theory, Research and Practice, 16,* 252–260.

Clarke, K., & Greenberg, L. (1986). The differential effects of Gestalt two chair and cognitive problem solving in resolving decisional conflict. *Journal of Counseling Psychology, 33,* 11–15.

Gendlin, E. T. (1981). *Focusing.* New York: Bantam Books.

Greenberg, L. (1979). Resolving splits: Use of the two chair technique. *Psychotherapy: Theory, Research and Practice, 16,* 310–318.

Greenberg, L. (1980). The intensive analysis of recur-

ring events from the practice of Gestalt therapy. *Psychotherapy: Theory, Research and Practice, 17,* 143–152.

Greenberg, L. (1983). Toward a task analysis of intrapsychic conflict resolution. *Psychotherapy: Theory, Research and Practice, 20,* 190–201.

Greenberg, L. S. (1984a). Task analysis of intrapersonal conflict. In L. N. Rice & L. S. Greenberg (Eds.), *Patterns of change: Intensive analysis of psychotherapy process* (pp. 67–123). New York: Guilford Press.

Greenberg, L. S. (1984b). Task analysis: The general approach. In L. N. Rice & L. S. Greenberg (Eds.), *Patterns of change: Intensive analysis of psychotherapy process* (pp. 124–148). New York: Guilford Press.

Greenberg, L. S., & Clarke, K. (1979). The differential effects of gestalt two chair dialogue and empathic reflections at a conflict marker. *Journal of Counseling Psychology, 26,* 1–8.

Greenberg, L. S., & Dompierre, L. (1981). The specific effects of Gestalt two-chair dialogue on intrapsychic conflict in counselling. *Journal of Counseling Psychology, 29,* 468–477.

Greenberg, L. S., Elliot, R., & Foerster, K. (1990). Experiential processes in the psychotherapy of depression. In D. McCann & N. Endler (Eds.), *Depression: New directions in research, theory and practice* (pp. 157–185). Toronto, Ontario, Canada: Wall & Thompson.

Greenberg, L., & Higgins, H. (1980). The differential effects of two chair dialogue and focusing on conflict resolution. *Journal of Counseling Psychology, 27,* 221-225.

Greenberg, L., & Minden, R. (1988). *Manual for three specific interventions from Gestalt therapy.* Unpublished manuscript, York University, Toronto, Ontario, Canada.

Greenberg, L., & Rice, L. N. (1988). *Change processes in experiential psychotherapy.* Unpublished manuscript, York University, Toronto, Ontario, Canada.

Greenberg, L., & Safran, J. (1987). *Emotion in psychotherapy.* New York: Guilford Press.

Greenberg, L. S., & Webster, M. (1982). Resolving decisional conflict: Relating process to outcome. *Journal of Counseling Psychology, 29,* 468–477.

Horvath, A., & Greenberg, C. (1986). The development of the Working Alliance Inventory. In L. Greenberg & B. Pinsof (Eds.), *The psychotherapeutic process: A research handbook* (pp. 529–556). New York: Guilford Press.

Horvath A., & Greenberg, L. (1989). Development and validation of the Working Alliance Inventory. *Journal of Counseling Psychology, 36,* 223–233.

Klein, M. H., Mathieu-Coughlan, P., & Kiesler, D. J. (1986). The Experiencing Scales. In L. S. Greenberg & W. Pinsof (Eds.), *The psychotherapeutic process: A research handbook* (pp. 21–71). New York: Guilford Press.

Lowenstein, J. (1985). *A test of performance model of problematic reaction points and an examination of differential client performance in therapy.* Unpublished Master's thesis, York University, Toronto, Ontario, Canada.

Phillips, J. R. (1984). Influences on personal growth as viewed by former psychotherapy patients. *Dissertation Abstracts International, 46,* 2820B.

Rennie, D. L. (1986). *A training guide for second-gener-*

ation, person-centred psychotherapy. Unpublished manuscript, York University, Toronto, Ontario, Canada.

Rennie, D. L. (1990). Toward a representation of the client's experience of the psychotherapy hour. In G. Lietaer (Ed.), *Client centered and experiential psychotherapy: Toward the nineties* (pp. 155–172). Leuven, Belgium: Leuven University Press.

Rennie, D. L., Phillips, J. R., & Quartaro, J. K. (1988). Grounded theory: A promising approach to conceptualization in psychology? *Canadian Psychology, 29,* 139–150.

Rice, L. N. (1974). The evocative function of the therapist. In D. A. Wexler & L. N. Rice (Eds.), *Innovations in client-centered therapy* (pp. 289–311). New York: Wiley.

Rice, L. N. (1983). The relationship in client-centered therapy. In M. J. Lambert (Ed.), *Psychotherapy and patient relationships* (pp. 36–60). Homewood, IL: Irwin.

Rice, L. N. (1984). Client tasks in client-centered therapy. In R. Levant & J. Shlien (Eds.), *Client centered therapy and the person-centered approach* (pp. 261–277). New York: Praeger.

Rice, L. N., & Greenberg, L. S. (1984). The new research paradigm. In L. N. Rice and L. S. Greenberg, (Eds.), *Patterns of change: Intensive analysis of psychotherapy process* (pp. 7-26). New York: Guilford Press.

Rice, L. N., & Greenberg, L. S. (1990). Fundamental dimensions in experiential therapy: New directions in research. In G. Lietaer (Ed.), *Client centered and experiential psychotherapy: Toward the nineties* (pp. 397–414). Leuven, Belgium: Leuven University Press.

Rice, L. N., & Kerr, G. (1986). Measures of client and therapist vocal quality. In L. S. Greenberg & W.

Pinsof (Eds.), *The psychotherapeutic process: A research handbook* (pp. 73–105). New York: Guilford Press.

Rice, L. N., & Saperia, E. P. (1984). Task analysis of the resolution of problematic reactions. In L. N. Rice & L. S. Greenberg (Eds.), *Patterns of change: Intensive analysis of psychotherapy process* (pp. 29–66). New York: Guilford Press.

Rice, L. N., & Wagstaff, A. K. (1967). Client voice quality and expressive style as indexes of productive psychotherapy. *Journal of Consulting Psychology, 31,* 557–563.

Toukmanian, S. G. (1984). *Therapist manual: Perceptual processing method of therapy.* Unpublished manuscript, York University, Toronto, Ontario, Canada.

Toukmanian, S. G. (1986). A measure of client perceptual processing. In L. S. Greenberg and W. Pinsof (Eds.), *The psychotherapeutic process: A research handbook* (pp. 107–130). New York: Guilford Press.

Toukmanian, S. G. (1990). A schema-based information processing perspective on client change in experiential psychotherapy. In G. Lietaer (Ed.), *Client-centered and experiential psychotherapy: Toward the nineties* (pp. 309–326).

Wiseman, H. (1986). *Single-case studies of the resolution of problematic reactions in short-term client-centered therapy: A task-focused approach.* Unpublished doctoral dissertation, York University, Toronto, Ontario, Canada.

Wiseman, H., & Rice, L. N. (1989). Sequential analyses of therapist–client interaction during change events: A task-focused approach. *Journal of Consulting and Clinical Psychology, 57,* 281–286.

Large-Scale Programs: Europe

22

Free University of Berlin: Berlin Psychotherapy Study

Gerd Rudolf
Psychosomatisch Klinik der Universität Heidelberg

Background and Aims

History

From 1978 to 1981, the German federal government advertised a support program on therapy and rehabilitation studies dealing with psychic illnesses. The Berlin Psychotherapy Study was designed as a response to this call. The main point of interest of our university department, then newly established, consisted of developing standardized descriptive instruments for the diagnosis and therapy of neurotic and psychosomatic patients on the basis of psychoanalytic experience. Our intention was to investigate the process leading to a decision on indication and the commencement of therapy with the aid of instruments previously developed in our working group. Furthermore, we were interested in studying the therapeutic relationship between patient and therapist and its inference on therapy outcome. After an appraisal was made by an international panel of experts, the preliminary phase (1983) and the main phase (1984–1986) of the project were implemented with the initial government financial support. In 1987 a follow-up project was approved; the objective of this project was a comparative study of the development of patients who underwent therapy and those who received no treatment.

In the preliminary phase the instruments of the study, developed by Rudolf, Grande, and Porsch, were revised in collaboration with the participating therapists; the use of these instruments was

then practiced with video support. Forty-seven participating therapists contributed to developing the research design, and the project received methodological support through the advice and collaboration of scholars such as U. Baumann (Kiel), U. Hentschel (Mainz), H. Ihm (Marburg), and H. H. Studt (Berlin).

Two psychologists and a secretary were hired early in 1984, when we began collecting data at all the participating institutions. In 1986, initial results were reported. In 1987, a comprehensive research report (about 500 pages) was published. A number of publications have appeared in the interim, and a monograph summarizing the project's results is currently being prepared.

Overall Aims

The Berlin Psychotherapy Study is an observation study in the field of analytic psychotherapy. Its purpose is twofold: to make a comprehensive inventory of existing conditions and to investigate the inner contexts of psychotherapy. The focal point of interest is the means by which psychotherapy comes about: the establishment of therapeutic contact from the initial diagnostic interview, to planning of the therapy, to actual treatment and outcome. As part of this study, patients who are not treated are tracked in their further development.

Particular attention is paid to the interplay between the patient's request for therapy and the therapist's offer to provide therapy. The criterion for materialization of the promise of psychotherapy is the quality of the working therapeutic relationship. Careful recording and evaluation of this relationship is therefore a particular concern of the study.

Therapy studies based on experimental designs frequently include in their randomized samples small groups of highly selected patients, who amount to only a few percent of the original overall sample. In contrast, the Berlin Psychotherapy Study included all patients, who established contact with typical representatives of psychotherapeutic institutions in the region of West Berlin within a 1-year period. The day-to-day diagnostic–therapeutic routine of analytic psychotherapists and the behavior of the patients were investigated under naturalistic conditions. The follow-up observation, over a 3-year period, has made it possible to look into the prognostic assessments made by therapists and patients and to investigate the conditions under which the development of the therapeutic context can be predicted. Because the study also included patients who were not referred to psychotherapy or who withdrew from treatment, the limits of the psychotherapeutic offer of treatment can also be demonstrated.

The following topics and questions are the most significant of the study:

1. The system of psychotherapeutic care
   • How can patients who turn to the various psychotherapeutic institutions (psychoanalytic practice; municipal, university, or private clinics) be characterized clinically, psychologically, and sociologically?
   • How can we characterize the therapy offer and the therapy practice of the various institutions, and which patients profit from them?

2. Conditions for planning and selecting psychotherapy
   • What findings of the initial examination represent conditions for making a decision about psychotherapy (inpatient, outpatient, frequent outpatient, brief, or no therapy)?
   • What conditions contribute to the materialization of planned therapies?

3. The working therapeutic relationship
   • What patterns of the working therapeutic relationship can be recognized in the interrelationship of patient and therapist perspectives?
   • What findings of the initial examination represent conditions for the quality of the working therapeutic relationship?
   • What connection exists between the working therapeutic relationship and the outcome of therapy?

4. The outcome of therapy
   • What patterns of therapy-related changes can be observed from the perspectives of the therapist and the patient, and how convergent or divergent are these two perspectives?

5. The personality of the psychotherapist
   • What personality characteristics are typical of psychotherapists, and how do these characteristics influence their working style?
   • What sort of relationship exists between the patient's readiness to develop a transference reaction and the therapist's countertransference reaction?

6. The course of the therapy
   • What patterns of recovery efforts and illness behavior are shown by treated and untreated patients after 3 years have elapsed?

The Field of the Study: Patients, Therapists, and Therapy

Unlike those in many other therapy studies, the therapists participating in the Berlin project have, for the most part, a great deal of professional experience. Most of them completed their postgraduate psychoanalytic training long ago, several are active in senior positions, many are in practices, and only a small group is still in postgraduate psychotherapeutic training.

The therapists participating in the Berlin Psychotherapy Study represent the sectors of psychotherapeutic care typically represented in a major city: psychoanalytic practices, outpatient university clinics and hospitals, inpatient psychotherapy in private and university clinics, and psychosomatic consulting services in general hospitals. The spectrum of therapy types offered varies in the outpatient sector from classical individual psychoanalysis to group psychotherapy and focal therapy, and the inpatient therapy types include individual therapy, group therapy, and nonverbal therapy methods. Common to all of the therapy types examined in the study was the patient's decision to participate in a therapeutic process aimed at uncovering problems and the therapist's decision to support the patient in this endeavor. We were interested in the various developments and conditions that lead up to these positions of patient and therapist.

Method

Subjects and Selection

Randomizing the assignment of patients to therapies or other interventions would have rendered the collaboration of most therapists impossible. Our wish was therefore simply to observe the participating therapists in the course of their routine work without unduly modifying the situation.

For one year, the 47 psychotherapists participating documented their findings for all newly examined clients. Their tasks also included motivating the clients to fill out self-evaluation questionnaires. The study included all adult patients older than 18 years of age whose *International Classification of Diseases*, ninth edition (*ICD-9*; Revisionist Press, 1984), diagnosis numbers ranged from 300 to 319 (neurosis, personality disorders, and psychosomatic disorders). Patients with acute psychosis were excluded from the study. Table 22.1 outlines the characteristics of the patients examined and treated in the individual institutions.

Observation Levels, Time Sequence, and Study Instruments

The research tradition of our department favors the use of instruments such as evaluation and self-evaluation sheets developed from clinical-therapeutic experience that can be enhanced with the use of video. The present study focused on the joint relationship of patient and therapist as reflected in outside evaluations and self-evaluations. Therefore, findings were documented on various levels of observation (see Figure 22.1).

Participants were assessed with equivalent or comparable instruments. The instruments for evaluation and self-evaluation were also designed symmetrically. Thus, for instance, the central neurosis finding made by the therapist, as measured by the Psychic and Social Communicative Inventory (PSCI), was, in terms of its content, identical to the patient's self-evaluation (PSCI-Se). The same was true for the evaluation of the working therapeutic relationship seen from the view of the patient and therapist.

In the initial examination, the basis for the evaluation was the semistructured diagnostic interview. This interview gives the patient an opportunity to describe himself or herself and offers the therapist the opportunity to jointly compile all of the significant anamnestic facts involved in the illness, the patient's current social reality, and a biography in the context of the transference–countertransference relation. As a rule, the diagnostic interview took two to five sessions. The aim of the interview was not only to understand the dynamics of the patient's illness, but also (and above all) to fathom the possibilities of therapeutic cooperation, to attempt a prognosis, and to begin planning for an adequate therapy.

The various inventory questionnaires and rating scales were completed after the initial examination interviews. The patient's self-evaluation was also made after the initial interview. The therapist's self-evaluation was performed once at the onset of the study.

The most significant areas investigated are presented in Figure 22.2. The most important inventory and self-evaluation scales for the topics referred to in Figure 22.2 can be summarized briefly as follows.

Table 22.1
Characteristics of Psychotherapy Practice

Institution	Therapy	No. of clinicians	No. of clients Examined	No. of clients Treated
Psychoanalytic practices	Inpatient	17	147	78
University psychotherapeutic polyclinic	Outpatient	6	115	38
University psychosomatic clinic	Inpatient	7	29	29
General hospital, psychosomatic consultant	Outpatient	5	207	44
Psychosomatic clinic I	Inpatient	5	32	32
Psychosomatic clinic II	Inpatient	5	90	90
University psychiatric polyclinic	Inpatient	2	119	32
Total		47	739	343

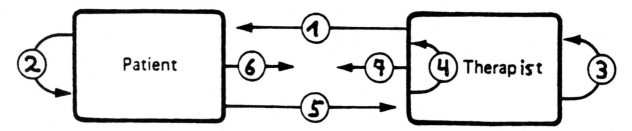

Figure 22.1. Schematic representation of levels of patient and therapist observation. (1 = level of expert evaluation [therapist views patient]; 2 = level of self-evaluation [patient views self]; 3 = level of self-evaluation [therapist views self]; 4 = level of counter-transference [therapist reacts to patient]; 5 = level of transference [patient views therapist]; 6 = level of therapeutic relationship [patient's view]; and 7 = level of therapeutic relationship [therapist's view].)

• *Illness:* list of physical symptoms, psychic and social symptoms, illness behavior, therapy expectation, scheme of diagnosis per *ICD-9*

• *Social reality:* training and vocation, economic situation, partnership situation, institutional situation of the therapist

• *Biography:* birth status, sibling situation, loss of loved ones, illnesses of parents, family's social and economic situation, emotional attitude to the most significant genesis persons

• *Personality structure:* interaction patterns, representation of self and objects, relationship to reality, characteristics

• *Working therapeutic relationship:* therapeutic cooperation, relationship dynamics, adaptability and defensive attitudes, therapy expectations

• *Therapy:* institution, therapy setting, goals of therapy.

A smaller portion of the scales was adapted from other authors' instruments and some were revised from our earlier studies, but most of them were developed specifically for the present study.

Data Storage and Management

The data were stored and managed with a data base of the SIR II type. The system, built with the support of the Center for the Methodological Support of Therapy Studies (ZMBT) based in Heidelberg, Federal Republic of Germany (FRG), contains interfaces with various evaluation systems such as the Statistical Package for the Social Sciences. Moreover, a network structure permits therapist–patient contexts to be represented. Because of the large and complex quantity of data, computer-controlled completeness checks were performed in the ZMBT at certain intervals to maintain data quality during data collection

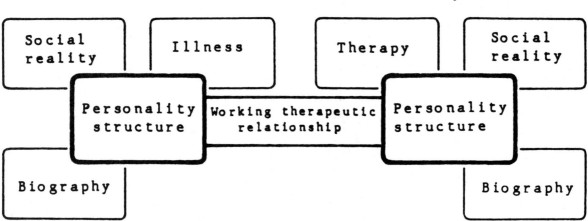

Figure 22.2. Areas investigated for the therapist and patient variables.

and input. To ensure privacy, no data were stored that permit a personal identification of the patients or therapists; instead, the persons involved were multiply coded. The patients were also asked to provide consent. The system was examined and accepted by Berlin's data commissioner.

The following criteria were selected to identify relevant inventory data: the identification decision, the materialization of therapy, the performance of therapy, the quality of the working therapeutic relationship, the quality of therapy results, and the quality of follow-up findings. Alpha adjustments were made in accordance with the number of checks to be performed. In most cases, multivariate methods were used in examining the interplay of several variables: regression analyses to determine the common connection of different variables with a target criterion and discrimination analyses to differentiate groups of criteria. Cluster analyses were calculated to develop types in the overall patient group (and therapist groups). Cluster analyses make it possible to include simultaneously many variables to establish a concise grouping of cases. In a second step, these groups could be selected as a point of departure for additional multivariate evaluation runs (for example, discrimination analyses and variance analyses). Aside from the probability of error (with appropriate adjustment of the alpha level), the practical weight of an effect (for example, share of declared variance) was also considered during the substantive evaluation of the results because, aside from theoretical questions, our attention was above all directed toward developing recommendations for action for psychotherapists active in practical fields.

Research Accomplishments

Findings

Patients in the system of psychotherapeutic care. The patients in psychoanalytic practices are not the type of upper-class patients whom we had assumed we would find. Although they are young and well educated, only 12% live in economically secure situations and work at a high vocational level. Approximately half of them live alone without a steady partner and without a secure vocational orientation. Presumably, the fact that psychotherapy in the FRG is financed by health insurance companies is the reason why many young persons are treated during the period of their search for personal and vocational identity.

Patient selection is most advanced in psychoanalytic practices: 87% of the patients are offered therapy, and 77% actually begin therapy (compared with an outpatient clinic, where therapy was offered to 62% of the patients and begun by 35%). The patients of the inpatient psychosomatic clinics are older on average and less well trained. They have had more frequent previous psychiatric (33%) and psychotherapeutic (52%) experience than patients in other services. The patients examined in the psychosomatic consulting services of general hospitals show the highest number of social problems. Their notion of their illness is frequently oriented in terms of organic medicine, and their motivation to participate in psychotherapy is not highly developed. Here the offer of therapy is the lowest (44%), with only 22% of the patients beginning treatment. All in all, patients appear less inclined to seek psychotherapeutic aid the more their problems are attributed to external social conflicts or to somatic diseases. Our results on the topic of psychotherapeutic institutions give a detailed description of the psychological and sociological characteristics of patients, their path through the health service, therapy offer, therapy realization and dropout, and the different types of outpatient and inpatient services.

Conditions for Initiating Psychotherapy

Of the data from the initial examination, 127 variables were investigated in terms of their predictive significance for deciding on an indication or for commencing psychotherapy. Significant relations resulted for 25 variables; together these accounted for 34% of the total variance. This information primarily came from information that therapists provided about patients.

Of central interest were evaluations of therapists emphasizing the suitability and willingness of patients to cooperate in psychotherapy. In this context, we also noted expressions made by therapists regarding their esteem for the patient and the patient's commitment to participating in therapy. This motivational factor seems to be of a much greater predictive value than diagnosis, symptoms, and other clinical data. On the other hand, traits of social disintegration, dependence, and somatization may be seen as negative predicting factors for indication and therapy commitment.

The working therapeutic relationship. The quality of the working therapeutic relationship in the course of therapy was rated by patient and therapist on the basis of a 40-point scale. Patterns of therapeutic cooperation of patient and therapist were formed with the aid of cluster analysis. Above all, it is the interactional readiness of the patient, registered by both patient and therapist, that determines the nature of the working relationship. Traits of contact anxiety and emotional avoidance, as well as attitudes of disappointment, render the establishment of a working alliance more difficult. As the social burden increases, the tendency toward denying conflicts and fixation on medical treatment also grows, which interferes with the working relationship.

Seen from the viewpoint of the therapist, the working relationship has the aspect of a personal relationship; seen from the viewpoint of the patient, it has the aspect of work borne by hope and confidence. The highest correlation between working relationship and the outcome of therapy is found in the therapist's perspective of both evaluations.

The outcome of therapy. The absolute rate of positive therapy results was calculated on the basis of plausible clinical considerations. It can be demonstrated within the framework of these calculations, however, that a slight modification of the criteria definition can vary the positive outcome rate between 50% and 80%.

We placed the emphasis on a multidimensional, differentiated description of the quality of personality changes in the course of therapy. The formation of change patterns with the aid of cluster analysis again shows the prognostic significance of the initial interaction readiness of patients.

Differences in patient and therapist perspective are also considerable in the outcome rating. Only 63% of the patients and therapists were able to reach agreement about the rough classification of the outcome of therapy. As we could show, this was due to the difference in the way the interactional patterns of the patients were seen by themselves and by the therapists.

Generally, we tried to interpret findings from an interactional point of view. This means that throughout the therapy the interactional pattern of the patient tends to be more a separation pattern or a cooperation pattern and that the expertise of the therapist tends to be a cognitive and emotional response to this offer.

The personality of the psychotherapist. A psychotherapist typology was established with the aid of a psychoanalytic character rating sheet and cluster analysis. We demonstrated that therapists in different clusters developed a different style of cooperation with their patients. Therapists and patients with different structures cooperate better initially but later develop more critical attitudes. In contrast, patients and therapists with discrepant characteristics begin more skeptically but go on to achieve a higher degree of therapeutic commitment.

The sex of both patient and therapist proved significant for the evaluation of the working relationship and the outcome of therapy: As a rule, friendlier evaluations were given by female therapists.

The initial emotional attitude of the therapist proved prognostically significant to the interplay of patient transference readiness and therapist countertransference reaction. On the side of the patients, critically distant transference attitudes also achieved positive therapy results.

Follow-up observation. The follow-up studies of the long-term patients (in individual and group psychoanalysis) demonstrated the good results of the therapy. The follow-up of the inpatient treatment showed that in 64% of the patients former complaints had been reduced but that in 78% other complaints were reported.

The group of patients who had no psychotherapy at all after the diagnostic interviews 3.5 years earlier seemed to be in an astonishingly good condition. The analysis of the data showed that these patients were not less ill or less in need of treatment but tended to express relatively few symptom complaints.

Out of a list of life events and activity reported from the 3.5-year follow-up period, we found five factors that correlate in a different way with the assessments of the follow-up. The factor reorientation (intrapsychic and social) intensified concern with one's own interests, establishing new contact, and vocational qualification had the strongest correlation with actual well-being and prognostic assessment.

Newly Developed Instruments

The inventory scale that we developed (the PSCI) and the equivalent self-evaluation scale (PSCI-Se) proved their clinical distinctiveness and prognostic predictiveness. The scales contain dimensions of interpersonal feelings and behavior that change in the course of therapeutic treatment. The substantive equivalence of both scales made it possible to examine the differences between patient and therapist perspectives.

The scale on the working therapeutic relationship that we developed (the TAB) for patients and therapists is suited to rate the quality of the working relationship relatively simply. The fact that the core of the working relationship can be detected as early as in the initial diagnostic interview is of particular significance. The TAB scale facilitates good predictions about the development of a working relationship and the outcome of therapy.

Our motivation and adaptability scale and defensive attitudes scale not only describe objective aptitudes or therapy problems of patients but also detect what the therapist believes the patient to be capable of. The therapy expectation scale affords insights into the patient's therapy concept with regard to his or her active commitment or passive expectations.

The semantic differential of object representations, derived with the help of Uwe Hentschel from the Kelly grid, permits a characterization of self-image and a weighting of transference and countertransference readiness in the interaction of patient and therapist evaluation.

The structural modification scale describes changes in the personality of the patient as rated by the therapist at the end of treatment. The data of the initial examination and the working relationship of therapist and patient correlate best with this outcome criterion. The illness behavior index that we developed reflects the orientation of the patient in terms of medical measures and has proved to be a prognostic indicator for a predominately somatic understanding of illness on the part of the patient.

Research Programs in Progress and Planned for the Future

Our investigations initially had focused on the analysis of the diagnostic situation and the initial therapeutic development in psychotherapeutic institutions under natural conditions. We then proceeded to analyze patterns of change in different types of psychotherapy. The team of the Berlin Psychotherapy Study has meanwhile changed its place of work and moved to Heidelberg. This clinic has a long tradition of investigating its special setting (psychoanalytically oriented inpa-

tient therapy with two subsequent years of outpatient psychotherapy). Compiling the experiences of the Berlin and the Heidelberg study, we plan to investigate therapeutic process elements in the treatment of severely disturbed persons.

Nature of the Research Organization

Members of the Research Group and Their Tasks

The organization of the research project was directed by the Department of Psychotherapy and Psychosomatic Medicine of the Berlin Charlottenburg University Clinic. The project director was Rudolf who, along with staff members Tillman Grande, Udo Porsch, Christina Ri, and Elke Großklaus, was assisted by other members of the department (Cornelia von Essen and Stefanie Wilke). These individuals formed the inner circle that organized the study, ensured data communication with the other clinics, took care of data storage and management, and interpreted and evaluated the data. Methodological support was provided by staff members of the ZMBT. Here, above all, the completeness controls of the data were performed and the data entered into the SIR II data base system.

Colloquia were held on a regular basis with the cooperating clinic members and practitioners. Cooperation with the Psychosomatic University Clinic in Berlin Steglitz (Hans Henning Studt and Astrid Riehl) was particularly close. Methodological support in evaluating the individual instruments has been provided by colleagues from outside, such as Uwe Hentschel. A large number of younger colleagues participated in detailed evaluations of the study in the framework of their dissertations.

Funding

The FRG's Federal Ministry for Research and Technology provided funding for the three full-time project staff members and the additional documentation work of the 47 therapists. The Free University of Berlin supported the methodological work. Furthermore, the research project was integrated into the routine work of the Department of Psychotherapy and Psychosomatic Medicine of the Berlin University Clinic.

Relation to Other Research Projects

In its search for predictors of promising or successful courses of therapy the project touches on the work of therapy investigators who use other methods and other samples, such as the work of the members of the Society for Psychotherapy Research. Examples are the studies of Howard et al. (chap. 8); Luborsky, Crits-Christoph, and Barber (chap. 16); and Henry and Strupp (chap. 20). Our project shares with these studies the conviction of the central significance of the working therapeutic relationship. What distinguishes our approach is the equal inclusion of the patient and therapist perspectives. Luborsky's emphasis on the central relationship conflict corresponds with the great weight that we assign to the patient's interaction readiness and its effects on therapeutic cooperation.

Another distinguishing aspect of our project involves the social and economic conditions of patients and their value postures, illness concepts, and therapy expectations in connection with these conditions. Although our project cannot actually be termed *epidemiological*, it does, in its emphasis on the social realm, touch on social-epidemiological studies such as those performed in Germany by Schepank and Dilling and their colleagues and in Austria by Strotzka.

Our findings also have a number of implications for psychotherapeutic practice. First, they highlight the extraordinary prognostic significance of the initial contact between patient and therapist. Because in our experience the therapeutic relationship does not simply grow over the course of many hours of therapy but rather is established quickly and at an early point in time, it is particularly important for the therapist to recognize and react early to the interactional signals, particularly in cases of disorders.

Second, it is important in prognostic terms for the therapist to attempt to grasp the illness concepts and therapy expectations of their patients at an early point in time and to realize that these concepts are heavily dependent on the patient's socioeconomic situation and on the value convictions of his or her social stratum. Thus, it appears to be important to view internalized object relations and the interaction readiness resulting from them not as an outcome of individual learning processes but instead within the context of the social situation of the individuals involved. These interactional and social perspectives are important aids for the therapist wishing to awaken in the patient that hopeful readiness to cooperate that is essential to a positive course of therapy. The practical example of our therapeutic institutions has convinced us that young therapists can improve their therapeutic competence by taking into account these aspects.

References

International classification of diseases (9th ed.). (1984). Brooklyn, NY: Revisionist Press.

Bibliography

Essen, C. von (1987, June). *About the validity of a diagnostic category system.* Paper presented at the meeting of the Society for Psychotherapy Research, Ulm, Federal Republic of Germany.

Grande, T., & Rudolf, G. (1989, September). *Follow-up investigations in patients treated by psychotherapy and those having received no psychotherapeutic treatment in different kinds of psychotherapeutic institutions.* Paper presented at the Third European Conference on Psychotherapy Research, Bern, Switzerland.

Grande, T. (1987, June). *The therapeutic relationship as a predictor of psychotherapy outcome.* Paper presented at the meeting of the Society for Psychotherapy Research, Ulm, Federal Republic of Germany.

Grande, T., Porsch, U., & Rudolf, G. (1986). Die biographische Anamnese als Ergebnis der Therapeut-Patient-Interaktion und der Einfluß auf Prognose und Indikationsentscheidungen. In F. Lamprecht (Ed.), *Spezialisierungen und integration in psychosomatik und psychotherapie.* Berlin, Federal Republic of Germany: Springer-Verlag.

Grande, T., Porsch, U., & Rudolf, G. (1988). Muster therapeutischer Zusammenarbeit und ihre Beziehung zum Therapieergebnis. *Zeitschrift Psychosomatiche Medicine, 34,* 76–106.

Grande, T., & Rudolf, G. (1989, September). *Patterns of cooperation and separation in the therapeutic relationship.* Paper presented at the Third European Conference on Psychotherapy Research, Bern, Switzerland.

Porsch, U. (1987, June). *Reciprocal effects to therapist's and patient's personality and characteristics of the psychotherapeutic relationship.* Paper presented at the annual meeting of the Society for Psychotherapy Research, Ulm, Federal Republic of Germany.

Porsch, U., Grande, T., & Rudolf, G. (1987). Die Person des Therapeuten als Einflußgrße bei der Befunddokumentation psychotherapiesuchender Patienten. In F. Lamprecht (Ed.), *Spezialisierung und integration in psychosomatik und psychotherapie.* Berlin, Federal Republic of Germany: Springer-Verlag.

Porsch, U., Rudolf, G., & Grande, T. (1988). Formen der therapeutischen Arbeitsbeziehung. *Zeitschrift Psychosomatische Medicine, 25,* 1–16.

Rudolf, G. (1987, June). *The development of the therapeutic relation: Approaches and results.* Paper presented at the annual meeting of the Society for Psychotherapy Research, Ulm, Federal Republic of Germany.

Rudolf, G. (1988, June). *Neurotic patterns of interaction and their clinical relevance: An overview based on the psychic and social communicative inventory (PSKB).* Paper presented at the annual meeting of the Society for Psychotherapy Research, Santa Fe, NM.

Rudolf, G. (in press). Die therapeutische Arbeitsbeziehung. *Ergebnisse der Berliner Psychotherapiestudie.*

Rudolf, G., von Essen, C., Porsch, U., & Grande, T. (1988). Psychotherapeutische Institutionen und ihre Patienten. *Zeitschrift Psychosomatische Medicine, 34,* 19–31.

Rudolf, G., & Grande, T. (1989, September). *Central issues of the Berlin Psychotherapy Study.* Paper presented at the Third European Conference on Psychotherapy Research, Bern, Switzerland.

Rudolf, G., Grande, T., & Porsch, U. (1988). Die Berliner Psychotherapiestudie. *Zeitschrift Psychosomatische Medicine, 34,* 2–18.

Rudolf, G., Grande, T., & Porsch, U. (1987). Indikationsstellung und therapeutische Interaktion bei dynamischer Psychotherapie und analytischer Standortbehandlung. *Zeitschrift Psychosomatische Medicine, 33,* 221–237.

Rudolf, G., Grande, T., & Porsch, U. (1988). Die initiale Patient-Therapeut-Beziehung als Prediktor des Behandlungsverlaufs. *Zeitschrift Psychosomatische Medicine, 34,* 32–49.

Rudolf, G., & Porsch, U. (1986). Neurotische Interaktionsmuster: Die Bildung von Befundskalen aus dem PSKB. *Zeitschrift Psychosomatische Medicine, 32,* 117–139.

Rudolf, G., Porsch, U., & Wilke, S. (1987). Prognose und Indikation—Von der Objektivierung der Patienteneigenschaften zur Analyse der Arzt-Patienten-Interaktion. In F. Lamprecht (Ed.), *Spezialisierung und integration in psychosomatik und psychotherapie.* Berlin, Federal Republic of Germany: Springer-Verlag.

Wilke, S., Grande, T., Rudolf, G., & Porsch, U. (1988). Katamnese nach stationrer Psychotherapie. *Zeitschrift Psychosomatische Medicine und Psychoanalysis, 34,* 107–124.

CHAPTER

23

Karl Marx University: The Leipzig Psychotherapy Process Research Program

Michael Geyer, Günter Plöttner, and Peter Winiecki
Karl Marx University

Background and Aims

History

Since 1968, Geyer has been interested in studying patterns of interaction in psychotherapy. In 1972, a team of researchers consisting of two physicians and two psychologists was formed to evaluate different systems of self-assessment and assessment by others in treatment-oriented groups. Since 1978, this approach has been applied to individual psychotherapy as well. The studies cover three types of groups: both open and closed groups of inpatients receiving treatment in psychotherapy wards (Geyer & Plöttner, 1985; Geyer, Plöttner, & Winiecki, 1987; Plöttner & Winiecki, 1989), and encounter groups treated in the framework of training group psychotherapists (Ott, Geyer, & Böttcher, 1980).

In 1974 the program became part of the government-financed national research programs of the German Democratic Republic. From 1974 to 1985 it was called the Cardiovascular Research Program; since 1986 has been called the Psychoneural Disorders Research Program. The program has had its current focus since 1976. A total of 8 physicians, 12 psychologists, and more than 30 medical students participated in individual projects at the Medical Academy of Erfurt from 1974 to 1983, and they have been involved in the research at Karl Marx University since 1983.

Overall Aims

The research program at Karl Marx University is based on the concept of dynamic interactional psychotherapy (Geyer, 1989), which considers the nature of the therapist–patient relationship to be the crucial factor in the therapy process. The therapy process may be described in terms of a succession of different patterns in the therapy relationship. Therefore, the main objectives of our research are to identify, describe, and control the sociodynamic constellations that are of therapeutic relevance.

Theoretically, the approach described here is based on the psychodynamic concept of psychotherapy (e.g., Luborsky, 1984; Kächele, 1985; Thomä & Kächele, 1985). The complementary therapy relationship construct that we use has been conceptualized in various forms by several psychotherapy schools (see the aforementioned authors as well as Tscheulin, 1983). As far as the underlying group therapy scheme is concerned, our position is akin to both group dynamic and group analytical conceptions (Foulkes, 1975).

The subareas of our investigation can be described by three questions: (a) How can an individual's sociodynamic position be defined? (b) Are there characteristic changes in the individual's sociodynamic position as a result of therapy? (c) Which therapy effects correlate with the various sequences of interaction in individual and group therapy?

In assessing the first of these questions, the quality of the therapeutic relationship is viewed as a complementary function of several parameters. These parameters include the distribution of control functions in the relationship, the attitude of both the patient and the therapist toward the therapy situation (e.g., motivation for therapy), and differences in the form of activities. From an analysis of these parameters emerges a picture of psychotherapy that captures the interrelationships among variables and the hierarchical structure of these variables. Such an analysis allows a number of individual variables such as resistance, defense strategies, and the impact of the therapy technique to be evaluated.

In addressing the question of whether there are characteristic changes in the psychotherapy patient's sociodynamic position with respect to others, we have attempted to identify typical sequences of interactional patterns that characterize treatment phases. This procedure has allowed us to begin assessing the relationship between a given interaction and other treatment processes. If particular regularities can be detected, the process can be modeled mathematically when its fundamentally stochastic nature is considered.

Method

Subjects and Selection

This project involved an initial core sample of patients undergoing group psychotherapy. Diagnostically, these patients represented *International Classification of Diseases* (9th edition, 1984) diagnoses 300 (neuroses), 301 (personality disturbance), and 306 (psychosomatic functional disorders). Fifty-eight percent of the sample were female. The average age of the subjects was 34.5 years. Therapy lasted 10 weeks, and the follow-up period was at least 15 months and averaged 18 months.

The main study included all of the patients receiving treatment in the psychotherapy ward of Karl Marx University's Psychiatric Clinic from 1985 to 1987 and who were specifically referred there for group psychotherapy ($N = 40$). The treatment group consisted of 158 patients. There were 21 dropouts before the beginning of treatment and 11 dropouts during the course of treatment.

The treatment group. All 158 patients received dynamic interactional group therapy from one of four therapists. Maximum group size was 12 patients. Therapy groups met daily from Monday through Friday for an average of 10 weeks.

Control groups. Two different control groups were studied. In the waiting-list group ($N = 40$), the criteria of efficacy specified below were used to analyze change over a 2-month period with no therapy. In the other control group, changes in patterns of interaction were examined in a group of 19 patients undergoing autogenic training for 12 weeks.

Instruments

The Feldes Polarity Profile. The set of rating scales standardized by Feldes and Hochauf (1978) serves to identify interpersonal relations in the social domain by means of the social potency (assertion of self) and social valence (e.g., social attraction and popularity) dimensions that may be described either as general mental qualities or universal dimensions of psychosocial processes. We used this instrument in every fifth therapy session to record qualitative changes in therapy relations. The instrument is based on the self-ratings of group members using semantic differentials, each comprising six ratings of potency and valence. The scores were plotted as points on a potency–valence diagram. The self-ratings cover the following aspects: (a) the individual's self-concepts (how potent and attractive he or she perceives himself or herself to be); (b) the individual's ideal (what he or she wishes to be like); (c) the individual's perception of the way in which the group perceives him or her; (d) the individual's perception of the therapist; and (e) the individual's perception of the group.

These ratings yielded five constellations of interaction. The clinical validity of these constellations was determined in an initial study of 31 patients who were receiving group therapy (Fischer, Scherler, & Zocher, 1987).

Motivation Questionnaire. Motivation for psychotherapy is measured in terms of the individual's perceived stress, the discrepancy between self-concept and ideal, and the degree of deviation from the norm, readiness to cooperate, and anxiety. The Motivation Questionnaire (Geyer & Plöttner, 1985) is a rating device measuring an individual's current motivation for therapy in the following ways: (a) the patient's general attitude toward therapy ("I need help"), (b) the patient's expectation that he or she will benefit from psychotherapy ("I need special psychotherapeutic help"), (c) the patient's ability to perceive pathogenetic relationships ("I am prepared to see relationships between my symptoms and my life situation"), (d) the ability to influence pathogenetic aspects of self ("I see possibilities of actively influencing things myself"), and (e) the patient's readiness to apply that ability outside therapy ("I believe that I am competent to change my situation for the better and would like to see that positive change maintained in the face of adversity").

Emotionality Inventory. In a standardized rating scale, the Emotionality Inventory (Ullrich & Ullrich-de Muynick, 1975) contains items from which six classes of clinically relevant emotional relations can be extracted: fatigue, aggressiveness, perceived somatic fear, inhibition, mental anxiety, and depression. With this instrument, the extent of a patient's tenseness or inhibition in situations is assessed in each therapy session on the basis of the Inhibition factor of the Emotionality Inventory. This assessment is achieved by using a 10-item semantic differential.

Closeness versus distance evaluation. By *socioemotional distance* we mean the perceived internal distance between two persons as indicated by a feeling of intimacy, emotional closeness, and the ability for identification with or sense of aloofness from another person (Ott et al., 1980). Socioemotional distance is measured by a semantic differential rating having a closeness–distance polarity. In every fifth therapy session each patient's internal distance, as he or she currently perceives it, and his or her desired distance from all those involved in the therapy situation is assessed on the basis of a 10-item scale.

Outcome measures. The 470-F Test (Stephen, Hess, & Höck, 1971; Zeller & Höck, 1973) was used to extract a general outcome variable. This measure comprises the 3 validity scales and 10 clinical scales of the Minnesota Multiphasic Personality Inventory, standardized and adapted for use in the German Democratic Republic (Spreen, 1963).

The Disorder Inventory. The Disorder Inventory (Beschwerdenfragebogen [BFB]; Höck & Hess, 1972; Hess, 1976, 1984) contains 88 symptom items, of which 63, subdivided into bodily and mental disturbances, make up the Neurosis subscale. The number of symptoms presented and the relation between mental and bodily symptoms are regarded as global criteria relevant to neu-

rosis. The BFB lends itself to documenting and objectifying the presence of neurotic and functional disorders but is of limited utility in the case of simultaneously present organic diseases. Its variants, the BFB-B, which permits the severity of the disorder to be evaluated, and the BFB-C, which charts the course of the individual's disorder, are suitable tools for efficacy assessment.

The Conflict Management Matrix. This rating scale is based on Malan's (1969) psychodynamic minimal hypothesis and allows a five-step inventory of the extent of conflict management. It requires pretherapy assessment of the individual's conflict constellation, which is controlled for the purpose of evaluating treatment outcome at the end of therapy.

The Inventory of Change in Experience and Behavior. This inventory (Zielke & Kopf-Mehnert, 1978) provides a quantitative estimate of perceived subjective change in experience and behavior and may be used to examine relevant treatment processes in individuals or in groups. Besides being a record of individual statements about change, it permits the computation of a total score from the items. The total score reveals something about the direction of change as a result of therapy and about the strength of that change.

Procedures

Methods for classifying patients. The patients were classified into groups for comparison by means of cluster analyses. These analyses were applied according to the following principles.

1. *Standardization of the data:* To attach equal weight to all of the variables involved, we standardized scores across the different tests (as in the detection of clusters of effectiveness; Winiecki, 1984).

2. *Selecting the clustering criterion:* We used the generalized degree of homogeneity (criterion of variance) because it takes into account the interdependency of the variables (Rao, 1973).

3. *Discovering initial groupings:* To optimize the clustering criterion, we selected various initial groupings (e.g., Ward's hierarchical clustering, the average linkage procedure, principal-components analysis) and initial clusters formed by change (Metzler, 1977) to prevent a clustering so-

lution from leading only to a local extremum of the clustering criterion.

4. *Defining cluster assignment procedures*: We defined cluster assignment procedures such as discriminant analysis that could classify cases in terms of maximum likelihood but also could identify cases defying classification (Plöttner & Winiecki, 1989).

Methods of process analysis. This aspect of our methods chiefly covered procedures for typifying processes (process cluster analysis), methods for analyzing processes over time (trend analysis and univariate and multivariate analyses of variance [ANOVAs] for repeated measurements), and methods of comparing different processes (multivariate ANOVA). Because most of the variables were of rank nature, we developed a multivariate rank ANOVA procedure permitting comparison of processes in terms of both intensity and form (Lehmacher, 1987; Plöttner & Winiecki, 1989).

Measures of efficacy of the therapy process. In addition to using methods for comparing pretherapy and posttherapy measurements, posttherapy and catamnesis findings (methods of ANOVA) and modern procedures for defining categories of success (methods of cluster analysis), we also used methods for analyzing relations among variables to identify variables that had a direct or indirect impact on the efficacy of the process.

Research Accomplishments

Our study has demonstrated that it is possible to describe the therapy process from three perspectives:

1. As a formal description of an interactional constellation, this approach asks such questions as, Is the pattern of relationship complementary or based on equality? Is it symmetrical or asymmetrical? Do typical constellations exist in psychotherapy?

2. From a longitudinal perspective, we can determine whether it is possible to detect typical sequences of interactional constellations.

3. A perspective that assesses the effectiveness of a type of sequence allows us to determine whether the types of treatment sequences differ with regard to the degree of therapy success.

A Formal Description of the Constellation of Interactions From the Patient's Perspective

On the basis of self-ratings of potency and valence with the Feldes Polarity Profile, 133 patients (1,264 measurements) described the relations among their self-concept, ideal, views about how others perceived them, perception of the group, and perception of the therapist. By means of cluster analysis, six well-defined homogeneous clusters were obtained. They represent all the essential constellations or patterns that are of therapeutic relevance from the patient's point of view. Cluster 1 includes all the parameters that are positively interrelated in a complex with regard to potency and valence. It expresses a symmetrical type of interaction.

These symmetrical or equality-based patterns of interaction may be attributed to a therapy relationship that has progressed. Frequently, however, they reflect an initially inadequate amount of structure existing in the interaction and represent the patient's lack of susceptibility to therapeutic influence.

Four other clusters represent different levels of asymmetrical or complementary constellations. Clinically, they correspond to those therapy constellations in which the patient clearly accepts the therapist's and the group's competence in helping him or her, experiences his or her own incompetence, develops a motive for change in the sense of a therapy goal, and responds to the therapy process. These constellations can also be related to the extent of therapeutic regression.

The sixth cluster describes a type of interaction in which the parameters are largely isolated. Clinically, this pattern depicts a situation in which the relationship becomes restructured toward more equality after a period in which the patient has been in a dependent position. The types of constellations described relate to stages in the therapy process of short or long duration. The mere frequency and direction of the structuring processes reflect the quality of the process.

Different Process Types

The succession of the clusters just described, defines for each patient the pattern of interactional relations that occur during therapy from the patient's perspective. In our main study, we used a multivariate rank ANOVA procedure to identify seven types of processes that can be combined into four basic types, which are in turn distinguished by potency scores computed for the patient's self-concept and characteristics of the patient's perception of the group and of the therapist. Thus, Process Type I is characterized by a frequent alteration between moderate- and high-potency scores with regard to the patient's self-concept and perceptions of how others see him or her. This pattern indicates that distinct changes are present in the patient's position during the therapy interaction, which in turn leads to a symmetrical relationship constellation.

In Process Type II, the potency scores stay in the negative range throughout the process. This pattern suggests that the patient is incapable of outgrowing the clinically marked state of dependence and of establishing a relationship based on equality.

Process Type III is characterized by a continuous shift from low to high levels of potency associated with the patient's self-perception and perception of the way in which others perceive him or her. This pattern indicates a trend toward more autonomy in the patient's relationship with the therapist.

Process Type IV is represented as a consistent, asymmetrical pattern of relationship that, in spite of frequent signs of movement toward more asymmetry, changes only slightly over time and treatment.

Relationship Between Type of Process and Therapy Success

More research into the therapy effects is needed to elucidate the significance of differences among the types of processes described. The therapy effects measured in terms of pretreatment and posttreatment comparisons on the 470-F-Test, the Disorder Inventory (BFB-C), the Conflict Management Matrix, and a change inventory can be related to more than the interaction clusters and types of processes discussed thus far. The variables socioemotional distance, motivation for therapy, and assessment of the therapist's behavior by the patient also prove to correlate strongly with therapy outcome.

Process Types I and II show the most impressive relationship with success or failure of therapy. Process Type I reflects a small degree of complementarity in the relationship between the patient and the group or therapist. At the same time, there is a strong correlation between Process Type I and a small amount of social distance, high satisfaction scores, and clear alteration in social inhibition scores.

Process Type II obtains consistent weak and negative correlations; respectively, between asymmetry or complementarity between the patient and the group or the therapist and the lack of success in therapy. This pattern is an indication of the unfavorableness of factors such as patient dependence and regressive tendencies in affecting outcome. Low levels of therapy success are also associated with social distance and low patient ratings of satisfaction. High self-concept scores, favorable perceptions of how others perceive the patient, and a positive perception of the therapist, form a relatively good prediction that a good helping alliance will emerge. Similarly, a close relationship exists among the potency scores of the patient's self-concept, perceived potency of the group, and the patient's adjustment as a group member.

From the beginning of therapy, successful patients show less socioemotional distance than unsuccessful ones. Apparently, a relationship marked by socioemotional closeness enables them to benefit from therapy at an early stage. Similarly, high satisfaction scores indicate the patient's feeling that they will get help. The motivation scale that we employ is an excellent measure of the effectiveness of the process.

Our research suggests that the therapist's attitude toward the patient is of particular relevance when it is assessed by the patient. The successful patient perceives himself or herself as much more accepted by the therapist than a less successful one (see also the findings of Cierpka, 1988; Eichhorn, 1984; Rudolf, Grande, & Porsch, 1988; Senf, 1986).

Research Programs in Progress

Hypotheses

Our research is currently testing the following hypotheses. First, the sociodynamic course of the therapy process correlates more strongly with baseline scores than with end-of-process scores. In other words, initial parameters are more closely related to therapy outcome than the course that the therapy process takes. Second, different baseline constellations call for different types of intervention to achieve similar results.

Tentative Findings

It may not be possible to maintain the first hypothesis in its present form. The strongest predictive factor is the dynamic nature of the process, which, although largely determined by initial parameters, is also affected by intervention strategies. It seems crucial, therefore, that clinicians have work to do to achieve an effective process dynamic. Before such an adaptive type of psychotherapy can be used, we need further research and more refined methods of representing crucial moments in therapy, especially when therapeutic relationships are restructured.

Programs Planned for the Future

New Directions and Hypotheses

Optimizing therapeutic interventions. Our future research efforts will focus on the problems of controlling the therapy process and optimizing the planning of therapeutic interventions. For example, mathematical modeling of the therapy process must evolve to where it can be computer generated. This would yield a new dimension of supervision that could be controlled in advance: It would stop short of computerized supervision but provide therapy control under the direction of experienced observers who may fall back on the resources of computers for assistance and direction.

The model will be extended in two directions. First, it will be extended with consideration of the stochastic aspect of treatment selection so that probabilities may be assigned to types of curves and constellations. This would better account for the true variety of processes. On the other hand, continual updating of the probabilities will help us determine the limitations of the model. Second, it will be extended with development of a set of instruments for computer-assisted clinical training. By using the aforementioned stochastic model and by adding more units, we hope to model a therapy group throughout the course of treatment. The beginning therapist will be informed of the results of the concurrent daily and weekly diagnosis, which will enable him or her to make certain interventions. The internal model will "process" that information for the subsequent process.

Pursuing these directions could lead to a training phase involving preparing the trainee to watch and control therapy groups in such a way that in a given therapy situation various possibilities for the intervention plan could be simulated by computer. Thus, computer-assisted training with an information phantom (resembling existing training situations in which students are taught medical dexterities) is likely to evolve, albeit sometime in the future.

Incorporating new process instruments. A second aim of our future research will be to use objective methods for representing major process characteristics. These include procedures that identify crucial variables independent of the individuals involved, such as analyses for classifying formal and content aspects of verbal communication during the psychotherapeutic interaction, analyses of nonverbal communication, and collection of psychophysiological data such as fluctuations in speaking frequency, muscle tone, and heart rate patterns. It must be stressed, however, that we do not as yet have reliable information as to whether these data can replace adequately those used to date.

Significance

The chief purpose of computer-assisted process modeling and the use of objective assessment devices is to help the therapist tailor his or her therapeutic techniques and strategies to the given conditions. Overall, the balance of self-control and external control should conform to that which is customary in other fields of medicine. In our experience, the fear that subtle process control might deprive the therapist–patient relationship of its unique character is unwarranted. On the contrary, such control facilitates constructive exchanges.

Relation to Other Research Programs

Impact on the Field of Psychotherapy: Clinical Practice

We have shown that the instruments we have described and used provide methods for detecting individual changes during the course of therapy, but in their present form they are incapable of capturing subtle content peculiarities and changes in attitudes and behavior. Although the present approach so far has uncovered only part of a subtle and complex process, its advantages for research and practice are obvious. Although all scientifically minded therapists work with a model of the therapy process in their heads, only a few establish order in the process before comparing it with the postulates of their models. Without an explicit mathematical model, no one is in a position to use the observation data effectively because bias cannot be controlled when the observation data are incorporated into the structure of the process model. This qualifies clinical training, under systematic supervision, as one suitable area of application of our approach.

Impact on the Field of Psychotherapy: Clinical Training

On the basis of the instruments described and the research findings obtained, we can attempt to answer the following questions: (a) How does the therapist promote or interfere with the emergence of the sociodynamic setting that is therapeutically necessary? (b) How should the dialectic relationship between the individual aspect and the group aspect specific to group therapy be handled? Supervision and clinical training require regular data analyses and an uncluttered system of records. Despite the fascination with the group dynamic, the individual's progress must remain the primary criterion of success.

Our general notion of an optimal process (a notion that can be controlled by the available methods) should be broad enough to facilitate a basic discussion of any given case. A specific supervision situation is characterized by questions that concern the cause of an individual's static position in the group; the persistence of various relation patterns; distorted perceptions of the emotional distance among group members, individuals, and therapists; and the distance that therapists perceive between individual patients and themselves. Thus, the content of therapeutic intervention is elucidated with concrete process data. By bringing the trainees face to face with the actual therapy process, we bring home to them the objectives of clinical training: achieving empathy, process analysis, and self-reflection.

In summary, the practical advantages of our approach include the following: interpretation of a therapy study on the basis of relatively objective data with assisted, speculative interpretation and the potential for mathematical modeling of the process; the potential for integrating findings from given situations into the entire process (lon-

gitudinal section), which can be related to the individual-group relationship (cross-section); and prediction and control of supervision effects in a concrete way.

References

Cierpka, M. (1988). Uberblick uber familiendiagnostische Fragebogeninventare. In M. Cierpka (Ed.), *Familiendiagnostick.* Heidelberg, Federal Republic of Germany: Springer-Verlag.

Eichorn, H. (1984). Uber die Effektivitat stationarer Gruppenpsychotherapie unter besonderer Berucksichtigung des Vergleiches offener and geschlossener Gruppen. *Med. Prom. B. Jena.*

Feldes, D., & Hochauf, R. (1978). Empirische Untersuchungen zur Stellung des Therapeuten in psychotherapeutischen Gesprachsgruppen. *Psychiat. Neurol. Med. Psychol., 30,* 648–656.

Fischer, A., Scherler, B., & Zocher, D. (1987). *Zusammenhange zwischen fremdbeurteilung und selbsteinschatzung im verlauf der stationaren gruppenpsychotherapie.* Leipzig: Dipl.-Arb.

Foulkes, S. (1975). *Group-analytic psychotherapy.* London: Gordon & Breach.

Geyer, M. (1989). *Methodik des psychotherapeutischen Einzelgesprachs.* Leipzig: Johann Ambrosius Barth.

Geyer, M., & Plöttner, G. (1985). Veranderungen der Therapiemotivation im Verlauf des psychotherapeutischen Prozesses. Mat. XI. PsychotherapiekongreB der DDR mit internat. Beteiligung Neubrandenburg. *Druckhaus Weimar, S.,* 158–162.

Geyer, M., Plöttner, G., & Winiecki, P. (1987). Zur Abbildung inter- aktioneller Konfigurationen mit Hilfe Prozebbegleitender semantischer Differentiale. *Mat. Internati. Psychotherapie-Symposium Erfur, S. Psychother. med. Psychol. (Stuttgart) 38,* 211–217.

Hess, H. (1976). *Entwicklung von Siebtestverfahren zur Erfassung neurotischer und funktioneller Storungen.* Berlin, Federal Republic of Germany: Math. Nat. Prom.

Hess, H. (1984). *Subskalaentwicklung fur differentielle Aussagen in der Neurosendiagnostik.* Ber. Psychoth. Neurosenf. HdG Berlin 25.

Höck, K., & Hess, H. (1972). Zur Eignung des Beschwerdenfragebogens (BFB) als Teilaspekt des standardisierten Interviews. In H. Rennert, K. Liebner, & H. D. Rosler (Eds.), *Zu aktuellen problemen der medizinischen psychologie.* Leipzig.

International classification of diseases (9th ed.). (1984). Brooklyn, NY: Revisionist Press.

Kächele, H. (1985). Was ist psychodynamische Kurztherapie? *Prax. Psychother. Psychosom., 30,* 119–127.

Lehmacher, W. (1987) Verlaufskurven und Crossover. In K. Uberla, P. L. Reichertz, & N. Viktor (Eds.), *Medizinische informatik und statistik. Bd. 67.* Berlin, Federal Republic of Germany: Springer-Verlag.

Luborsky, L. (1984). *Principles of psychoanalytic psychotherapy—A manual for supportive–expressive treatment.* New York: Basic Books.

Malan, D. (1969). *Psychoanalytische Kurztherapie: Eine Kritische Untersuchung.* Hamburg, Federal Republic of Germany: Rowoldt, Reinbeck.

Metzler, P. (1977). Clusteranalyse—Einfuhrung, Methoden, Anwendungsbeispiele. *Probl. u. Ergebn. d. Psychologie, 63*, 19–36.

Ott, J., Geyer, M., & Böttcher, H. P. (1980). Die Personlichkeit des Therapeuten—Zielstellung und Realisierungsmoglichkeiten auf den vershiedenen Ebenen der psychotherapeutischen Ausbildung. In H. Hess, W. Konig, & J. Ott (Eds.), *Zur integration der psychotherapie in die medizin* (pp. 46–57). Leipzig: Johann Ambrosius Barth.

Plöttner, G., & Winiecki, P. (1989). *Untersuchungen zur begleitenden diagnostik des psychotherapeutischen prozesses.* Leipzig.

Rao, C. R. (1973). *Lineare statistische methoden und ihre anwendungen.* Berlin, Federal Republic of Germany: Akademie-Verlag.

Rudolf, G., Grande, T., & Porsch, U. (1988). Die Berliner Psychotherapiestudie. *Psychosomatic Medicine, 34*, 2–18.

Senf, W. (1986). Behandlungsergebnisse bei 111 Patienten mit stationar-ambulanter psychoanalytisch-orientierter Psychotherapie. In H. Heinemann & H. J. Gartner (Eds.), *Das Verhaltnis der Psychiatrie zu ihren Nachbardisziplinen.* Berlin, Federal Republic of Germany: Springer-Verlag.

Spreen, O. (1963). *MMPI-Saarbrucken. Handbuch der dt. ausgabe des MMPI.* Bern: Huber.

Stephen, A., Hess, H., & Höck, K. (1971). Adaption und Reduzierung des MMPI-Saarbrucken. *Psychiatry, 23*, 695–702.

Thomä, H., & Kächele, H. (1985). *Lehrbuch der psychoanalytischen Therapie. Bd. 1 (Grundlagen).* Berlin, Federal Republic of Germany: Springer-Verlag.

Tscheulin, D. (1983) Differentielle Gesprachstherapie—Kontradiktion oder Innovation? In G. Bittner (Ed.), *Personale Psychologie* (pp. 241-257). Göttingen, Federal Republic of Germany: Hogrefe.

Ullrich, R., & Ullrich-de Muynick, R. (1975). Das Emotionalitatenin- ventar (EMI). *Diagnostica, 21*, 84.

Winiecki, P. (1984). *Statistische Merkmalsreduktion und Personen-Klassifikation bei der Ermittlung der Psychotherapiebedurftig-keit.* Leipzig.

Zeller, G., & Höck, K. (1973). Der 470-F-Test. Normierung eines adaptierten und reduzierten MMPI (Saarbrucken). *Mat. 7. KongreB d. Ges. f. Arztl. Psychotherapie d. DDR Erfurt.*

Zielke, M., & Kopf-Mehnert, C. (1978). Der Veranderungsfragebogen des Erlebens und Verhaltens (VEV). *Diagnostica, 24.*

24

University of Bern: Differential Psychotherapy Research

Klaus Grawe
University of Bern

Background and Aims

The history of the Differential Psychotherapy Research Program goes back to the 1970s. From 1969 to 1979, Grawe, the founder of the current program, worked as a clinical psychologist at the psychiatric clinic of the University of Hamburg in the Federal Republic of Germany. There, he was primarily involved with the development of inpatient psychotherapy programs. During this time Grawe conducted three comparative treatment studies in close collaboration with a number of other clinical psychologists and psychiatrists of different theoretical orientations. From the very beginning of our collaborative research we were not interested in determining whether one form of therapy was better than another. Our daily clinical experience had convinced us that all of the therapy forms conducted in our programs were effective in some way. At the same time, however, it seemed obvious that the therapies differed in terms of the quality of effects they produced, their mechanisms of change, and effects with different types of patients. Thus, the design of the comparative treatment studies that were conducted at the time was focused on finding out more about the qualitative effects, mechanisms of change, and differential indications of the therapy forms being compared. These studies have appeared in German in the form of books, contributions to edited volumes, and articles. They have

not been translated into English and thus are virtually unknown in the English-speaking world.

One of the above-mentioned studies compared client-centered therapy and behavior therapy (Grawe, 1976). The other two investigated different forms of behavioral group therapy for inhibited and socially anxious psychiatric patients (Grawe, Dziewas, Brutscher, Schaper, & Steffani, 1978; Dziewas, Grawe, & Wedel, 1980). As a result of these latter studies a form of therapy was developed that we designated *interactional behavior therapy* (Grawe & Dziewas, 1978). This conceptualization differed from the usual behavioral understanding by placing a much greater emphasis on what was happening in interpersonal relationships inside and outside the therapy.

A new method of therapeutic problem analysis also was developed that derived, on the basis of the patient's interactional behavior, a hierarchical structure of his or her most important interactional plans. The functional relations between these interactional plans and the patient's symptoms were then analyzed. Interactional behavior therapy focused on changing the most important problematic interactional plans. This conceptualization was at first used primarily in group therapy. These interactional problem-solving groups (Grawe, Dziewas, & Wedel, 1980) proved in several studies to be an effective therapeutic environment for patients with disturbances in interactional behavior.

In 1979 Grawe became the head of the Department of Clinical Psychology at the University of Bern. Since then, he has been working in Bern continuously and simultaneously has developed four research programs that are described later. The projects are related, but each project is being conducted by a different research group with a separate institutional and financial infrastructure. The first research program consists of comparative treatment studies in which the therapy form that we have developed is compared with other forms of therapy. The second research program deals with the further development of our therapeutic conceptualization. This conceptualization is designated *schema theory and heuristic psychotherapy*. The third program comprises an evaluation from a differential perspective of all controlled therapy outcome studies with clinical populations. This program is referred to as differential meta-analysis. The fourth program aims at the development of a methodology for psychotherapeutic single-case research.

Methods, Research Accomplishments, and Research Programs in Progress

Comparative Treatment Studies

In 1980, a comparative treatment study was begun. Sixty-three patients with interpersonal problems but otherwise varied symptoms were randomly assigned to the following four treatment conditions: (a) interactional behavior therapy in groups (the form of group therapy developed earlier at the psychiatric clinic of the University of Hamburg); (b) interactional individual therapy (based on the same conceptualization as group therapy but in the form of individual therapy); (c) broad-spectrum behavior therapy (behavior therapy as it is usually applied in clinical practice based on a functional behavior analysis and using different methods determined by the behavior analysis); and (d) client-centered therapy.

Ten therapists conducted each of the individual treatments, and four therapists conducted the group treatments. All therapies were audiotaped and partially videotaped. Extensive effect and course measurements were assessed from different perspectives with a large number of different instruments. Since 1985 we have been working on the analysis and evaluation of these therapies. The evaluation is centered on the following two questions: (a) Do therapies conducted along the lines of interactional behavior therapy in individual and group form differ in comparison to establish forms of broad-spectrum behavior therapy and client-centered therapy in terms of their effects, mechanisms of change, and indications? (b) Which measurement procedures and methods of analysis are most suitable for disclosing differential effects, mechanisms of change, and indications?

In the analyses of variance comparing the four therapy conditions for a total of more than 60 effect measures, only minimal differences were found among the four therapy forms. Comparative treatment studies have repeatedly produced the same general finding (Stiles, Shapiro, & Elliott, 1986).

Not convinced that these results gave an adequate picture of the actual comparative effects of the therapies being studied, however, we subsequently focused on developing methods with which the whole pattern of the interrelated effects of the therapies could be uncovered and compared, not limiting our perspective to changes in single variables. The calculation of effect sizes for all measures permitted a quantitative comparison of the changes in the different change areas. On this basis we found that the four therapies produce their main effects in different areas. An analogous standardized measure was developed for the distribution of the changes in the treatment groups. This resulted in differential therapy effects being found at different points in time in the four therapy conditions.

A detailed course analysis of measurement points over time showed that although the four different therapy forms reached approximately the same extent of global change over the whole therapy period (30–40 sessions), the course of these changes was different. These different courses continued during the follow-up period of 1 year. The patterns of change—the intercorrelation of the changes in the different areas—proved to be totally different. This suggests that changes produced by the therapy forms examined occur in different functional relationships.

Equally clear differences were found in the comparison of the correlations between pretherapy patient characteristics and therapeutic outcome. For broad-spectrum behavior therapy and client-centered therapy, clear statements could be made about which patients would profit from therapy and which would not. The indications and contraindications for the four therapy forms varied greatly, at times being exactly opposite. Both client-centered therapy and broad-spectrum behavior therapy were unsuccessful with socially more disturbed patients. Broad-spectrum behavior therapy was also unsuccessful with psychopathologically more disturbed patients. This was not the case with interactional individual and group therapy. The client-centered therapists were more successful with patients who had especially good interpersonal skills and the clear wish and ability to decide autonomously for themselves. Behavior therapists, on the other hand, were more successful with patients who tended toward dependency in interpersonal relationships. Thus, a clear differential indication for broad-spectrum behavior therapy and client-centered therapy was found.

On the whole, indications for client-centered therapy and broad-spectrum behavior therapy were more extensive than for the two forms of interactional therapy. In the two interactional therapy conditions the outcome was not related to pretherapy patient characteristics. This raised the question as to which factors actually accounted for the variance in therapy outcome in these latter treatment groups. One guess was that the therapy effects in these conditions were more closely related to the therapeutic process itself than to patient characteristics. This suspicion has been confirmed in process analyses.

Up until now, the four therapeutic conditions have been compared with each other by means of four forms of process analysis: the structural analysis of social behavior (Benjamin, 1974), postsession questionnaires for therapists and patients, rating scales that we developed for the interactional behavior of therapist and patient, and rating scales that assessed the extent to which the therapist applied certain therapeutic heuristics. The heuristics assessed with these scales were derived from our therapeutic conceptualization, schema theory and heuristic psychotherapy.

These process analyses showed on the one hand that the therapy conditions, as one would expect, did actually differ. On the other hand, they showed that the process factors in the different therapy forms were differentially related to outcome. Thus we see that in the four different therapy forms different factors of the therapeutic process are important for the outcome. On the whole, the therapeutic outcome in both interactional therapy conditions was much more closely related to what happened in the therapy sessions than was the case in broad-spectrum behavior therapy and client-centered therapy. In these the outcome was more closely related to pretherapy patient characteristics.

With the use of all of the results of our effect and process analyses, a differentiated image of each therapy form could be developed that specified the areas in which they had their main effects, in what way, and with whom. The fact that we found many differences among the different therapy forms in their effects, mechanisms of change, and indications contrasts greatly with the usual conclusions deriving from comparative treatment studies (Stiles et al., 1986). Thus, we do not agree with the position currently popular in psychotherapy research that holds that the time for large comparative treatment studies is past and that instead we should turn to a detailed analysis of the therapy process (Rice & Greenberg, 1984). A detailed analysis of the therapy process is certainly desirable. We emphasize it in our own current research programs. Nevertheless, such an analysis is especially fruitful if different procedures that have been carried out in an experimental design can be compared.

At present this research program is being continued in the following two ways: (a) We are analyzing the 63 therapies in this comparative treatment study with further methods of process analysis with the goal of being able to make even more detailed statements about the mechanisms of change in the four therapy forms, and (b) we have begun a new research project in which a fifth quasi-experimental condition is being added to the four other conditions. The therapies in this fifth condition are being conducted along the lines of our current therapeutic conceptualization, schema theory and heuristic psychotherapy, under the same experimental conditions as the 63 cases in the other completed therapies to permit a comparison between our present conceptualization and the other four well-studied therapy conditions.

Schema Theory and Heuristic Psychotherapy

While in Hamburg, Grawe developed a new method of therapeutic problem analysis. In contrast to learning-theory-based behavior analysis, this method does not examine the relation between the problem behavior and the antecedent and subsequent conditions but rather relates the observable behavior to the client's superordinate goals derived from his or her behavior. This method was designated *vertical behavior analysis* in contrast to *horizontal behavior analysis*, which focuses on relationships on the time axis.

Later in Bern, in collaboration with Caspar, Grawe developed the method further and designated it *plan analysis*. The method of plan analysis was systematically applied in the therapy conditions designated as interactional behavior therapy in developing the case formulation and served as the basis for the planning of the therapeutic procedure. The systematic application of the method in the context of a research program resulted in the continued development and systematization of the method. The different stages of this conceptual and methodological development can be found in diverse German publications (e.g., Grawe & Dziewas, 1978; Caspar & Grawe, 1982; Caspar, in press). The systematic application of the method to a large number of cases in a controlled clinical context resulted in a greatly revised and elaborated conceptualization. This conceptualization was first put in writing in 1986 (Grawe, 1986) and is now also available in English (Grawe, 1989). Since 1986 our therapeutic and research activity has been based on this conceptualization.

Psychotherapy is construed as a heuristic process that is focused on therapeutic goals instead of specific methods. The goals are derived on the basis of an understanding of the patient's current psychological functioning. We view the process of change as a process of the development of schemata. The therapist's tasks are to activate the schemata that are relevant to the problem and to stimulate their further development.

Three ways of stimulating the development of schemata are differentiated. These correspond to three therapeutic heuristics whose goal is to further the development of a particular schema.

1. *Reflective abstraction.* This process is set in motion by disturbances in the patient's regulatory activity. In that the patient's awareness is focused on the connection between the disturbance and his or her own regulatory activity, new contents of consciousness develop that permit new processes of control. Thus, in the process of reflective abstraction both new awareness and new regulatory possibilities develop.

2. *Processing emotions.* A negative emotional schema, directed to avoid a particular aversive emotion, is activated by stimulating the previously avoided emotions, making them become consciously experienced and furthering their processing. To the extent that the individual's behavior is no longer focused on avoiding certain negative emotions, the individual's positive goals can be pursued in the previously avoided areas.

The way is thus cleared for new experiences and developmental processes.

3. *Competence enhancement.* The individual's abilities to fulfill his or her goals is increased by improving his or her skills. This involves primarily the differentiation of already existing schemata rather than the development of new schemata.

These three processes or heuristics only become effective when the patient is open to the corresponding influences and developmental processes. This openness, in turn, presupposes a good therapeutic alliance. Thus, a fourth heuristic is specified, the heuristic of the *therapeutic alliance*. This heuristic is focused on furthering, at the relationship level, the best conditions for the development of schemata along the lines of the three processes or heuristics mentioned earlier.

In early 1988 we began a new research project in which this therapeutic conceptualization was applied in a highly systematic manner to 16 cases. The treatment is being conducted under the same conditions as those for the comparative treatment study mentioned above, and the same measures are being assessed. These new cases thus represent a quasi-experimental therapy condition in our original experimental design. By keeping the conditions the same, a statistical comparison of the newly conducted therapies with the original four therapy conditions will be possible.

The emphasis of the new research project, however, is on the theoretical and methodological development of this therapeutic conceptualization. Extensive schema analyses of each therapy are being carried out for research purposes. Schema analysis is a development of our original method of plan analysis. A case formulation based on schema analysis is developed by a three-member research team, and the results of this analysis are used by the therapist for conceiving his or her goals and procedures in the following therapy sessions. Furthermore, repeated schema-theoretical change analyses (analyses of the therapy process from a schema-theory perspective) take place as the therapy progresses. A rating system has been developed for this purpose. Still in development is an even more detailed coding system. Besides these two quantifying analyses, a systematized hermeneutic analysis from a schema-theory perspective of change also takes place.

The findings from these process analyses are also fed back into the therapy in that they are used systematically by the therapist for determining his or her subsequent goals and procedures. In this way two research colleagues besides the therapist are intensely involved in the analysis and planning of the respective therapy. Someone who is involved in the research analysis in one therapy serves as the therapist in another therapy, and vice versa. Altogether eight people are involved in conducting the therapies in this project.

We plan to conduct therapy with 16 new subjects over a period of 3 years with an average duration of 30–40 sessions. Each patient's therapy will be accompanied by the intensive research analyses described earlier. Considerably more time is invested in the research analyses than in conducting the therapies. We make this additional investment of time and energy for the research analyses to test our therapeutic conceptualization as systematically as possible against clinical practice and to develop it further in a continued interchange with therapeutic reality. At the same time, we want to find out whether the effectiveness of therapies can be increased through such an intensive accompanying analysis. Our original four experimental conditions will serve as a basis for comparison.

Another goal of the project is to develop research methods based on schema theory. Toward this aim we have initiated a systematic conceptualization and practical guide for carrying out and presenting schema analyses. We have also completed a rating system for assessing the therapeutic process from a schema-analysis perspective. Ten-minute segments are assessed from video recordings, and coding occurs on-line. We also plan to use this new instrument to assess the therapies conducted earlier in our comparative treatment study to permit process comparisons. A larger number of publications as well as diploma and doctoral theses dealing with our conceptualization and the schema-theory analyses of change are already available (e.g., Ambhl & Grawe, 1989; Grawe, 1988a; Heiniger & Jost, 1987; Thierstein, 1988; Thommen, 1988; Wthrich, 1987; Zingg, 1988). There is also a number of presentations in English (Ambhl, 1989a; Balmer & Heiniger, 1989; Caspar, 1988; Doblies, 1989; Grawe, 1988b, 1989).

Differential Meta-Analysis

In all four comparative treatment studies that we have conducted, significant differences have been found in the effects, mechanisms of change, and differential indication of the therapy forms examined. This appears to stand in contradiction to the general findings of comparative psychotherapy research as reported in several overviews (e.g., Bergin & Lambert, 1978; Luborsky, Singer, & Luborsky, 1975; Smith, Glass, & Miller, 1980). According to these overview studies no consistent differences in the effectiveness of different therapy forms have been shown. A possible explanation for this discrepancy is that the studies examined in these overviews usually compare the mean effectiveness of different therapy forms only by calculating analyses of variance for each single effect measure. If we had done the same we would also have found minimal differences, if any, among the different therapy forms.

The mean effectiveness in single variables is, however, only one aspect by which the effects of different therapy forms can be compared. Beyond mean effectiveness in single variables the therapies can differ in their effect spectrum; that is, one therapy could have comparatively more effects in one area and another therapy could produce more effects in other areas without the differences in the single variables being statistically significant. Moreover, psychotherapies can have differential effects, that is to say effects of varying strength with different types of patients. Furthermore, forms of psychotherapy can differ in that changes in different areas are related to each other in different ways in the different therapy forms (Grawe, 1981). They can also differ in the ways in which therapeutic outcomes dependent on different patient characteristics, therapist characteristics, and characteristics of the therapeutic interchange. All of these aspects of a differential analysis, which transcend mean effectiveness in single variables, have not been explicitly considered in previous reviews. The basic question that our research program has focused on is "which differential effects can be found in different therapy forms when all of these differential outcome aspects are explicitly taken into consideration?"

To answer this question, we began the following research program in 1980. We sought all comparative treatment studies in which a particular psychotherapy form was examined in a controlled research design. Our explicit goal was to assess all available studies. Five research assistants searched from 1980 to 1984 for all relevant publications with the assistance of computer searches and all available bibliographies. They found approximately 3,500 therapy studies published through the end of 1983 that met our criteria. This number, however, included many analog studies and studies that were clearly irrelevant to our interest in the differential effects of different psychotherapies. We limited our detailed analysis to those studies of a psychotherapy in which a controlled research design and a clinical population were used. In the final analysis, 897 studies were included.

As the studies were being collected, an extensive 63-page assessment catalog was developed and used to examine systematically every study with reference to 975 individual characteristics. Fourteen raters were intensively trained to evaluate the therapy studies with this assessment catalog. The assessment of a study by a trained rater took on the average 9 hours. The resulting data were entered into a computer file program, and this file contains our assessment of all controlled psychotherapy outcome studies with clinical populations published through 1983.

On the basis of this information, a standardized quality profile for each study was developed consisting of the following criteria: (a) clinical relevance; (b) internal validity; (c) quality of information (how well the study reports on the essential characteristics of the study; (d) caution in interpretation (severe methodological problems in the study that place in doubt the interpretability of the results); (e) breadth of measurement; (f) quality of the statistical analysis; (g) richness of results, and (h) relevance. In this way mean quality profiles for certain categories of studies can be calculated and compared with each other (e.g., the studies examining a particular therapy form or the studies conducted in different countries).

Some results of this research project have been reported (e.g., Grawe, 1988a; Grawe & Mezenen, 1985). Since 1987 the basis for our analysis has consisted of the computer data file, the completed assessment catalog for each study, and the original research report itself. The results of this project will be published in a monograph at the end of 1990. This monograph is intended to provide a comprehensive overview of all results reported up until 1983 on the absolute and comparative effects, mechanisms of change, and differential indication of individual therapy methods with different mental disorders. In contrast to previous reviews, this overview will include studies published in languages other than English. The results of this research program cannot be dealt with here in more detail, but it is not premature to say that this overview will shed light on several matters that have previously been unclear. Our findings from the detailed analysis of all relevant studies are quite clear but not necessarily in agreement with the opinions that prevail in the literature. It is planned that this book will be translated into English.

Psychotherapeutic Single-Case Research

Searching for methods of data analysis that are more suited to giving us a differentiated picture of what is really going on in different types of psychotherapy than the conventional methodology of group statistics, we became more and more interested in the analysis of single cases. Starting with the premise that one will hardly be able to understand the working mechanisms of different therapy forms before one has developed an adequate understanding of what is going on in the individual therapies, we started a research program aiming at the development of an adequate research methodology for the measurement and analysis of psychotherapeutic change processes on the level of the single case.

The first step toward this goal was a comparison and combination of group statistics and descriptive single-case analyses with the data from our comparative treatment study described above. The procedure and results of this first step were reported by Arnold and Grawe (in press). This first step could lead us only as far as the restrictions of the data set of our comparative treatment study allowed.

As a second and much more ambitious step, Dr. Kächele from the University of Ulm, Federal Republic of Germany, joined with Grawe to begin a collaborative research program called Psychotherapeutische Einzelfall-Prozessforschung (PEP; translation = Psychotherapeutic Single-Case Research). As the first project of this long-term program two therapies, a psychoanalytic time-limited therapy and a therapy conducted according to our schema-theory conceptualization (each consisting of 28 sessions), are being analyzed with diverse methods of process analysis. The therapies have been videotaped and transcribed and are available (in German) to all interested researchers and research groups.

In all, 25 research groups have joined our endeavor. This means that the therapies are being analyzed with almost 30 different methods of process analysis. The primary goal of this project is to compare the different methods of process analysis that are currently available with regard to the question, Which method, involving how much time, results in which findings in comparison with the other methods that have been used to analyze the same therapy segment? The group meets twice a year to present findings and to coordinate research activities. A large number of papers from this project was presented for the first time at the 1988 conference of the Society for Psychotherapy Research (SPR) in Santa Fe, New Mexico.

Programs Planned for the Future

During the next years, our research activities will involve continuing the four projects just described. The emphasis will be on the conceptual and methodological development of our schema-theory and heuristic psychotherapy approach. Evaluating the comparative treatment studies in the first project and carrying out further process analyses will take at least 2 years. An eight-member research team, which will remain together for at least two more years, is developing our therapeutic conceptualization and studying it empirically. The third project, the differential meta-analysis, will probably be completed and discontinued in 1990. The fourth project, PEP, will probably expand considerably during the next few years given that the PEP group, within 2 years, has become a central forum for almost all German-speaking psychotherapy process researchers.

Nature of the Research Organization

The research programs described above are being conducted in the Department of Clinical Psychology of the University of Bern. The department runs an outpatient clinic, in which psychotherapy is conducted on a regular basis for research and teaching purposes. The research assistants are employed by the Department of Clinical Psychology or the outpatient clinic or are funded by research grants from the Swiss National Research Foundation for limited periods of time. The four research programs are largely independent in terms of organization, but all are directed by Grawe. In all programs the contributions of graduate students, secretarial staff, and others were significant but must go without enumeration because of space limitations.

The research team for the comparative treatment study included psychologists Hans-Ruedi Ambühl, Hans-Peter Müller, Franz Caspar, Urs Mezenen, and research assistants Walter Kopp and Matthias Zingg. Most of the therapies were conducted by therapists who were paid on an hourly basis.

The project on schema theory and heuristic psychotherapy was conducted at the outpatient clinic by a team that included Ambühl, Wüthrich, Beatrice Amstutz, and research assistants Ruth Balmer, Günther Doblies, Barbara Heiniger, and Hansjörg Znoj. Thomas Nussbaum and Christian Hausammann wrote numerous ingenious computer programs for both the first and second projects.

The differential meta-analysis project involved psychologists Jürg Siegfried, Mezenen, and Cornelia Louis. Funded partially by the Swiss National Research Foundation and partially as permanent staff were Ruth Donati and Friederike Bernauer. In the concluding phase of the project, only Donati and Bernauer remain involved in the project as permanent staff.

The Bern group who contribute to the PEP project overlap with those contributing to the second project. In the starting phase of this project Eva Arnold played an important role, having written her doctoral thesis on the development of a new single-case research methodology (Arnold, 1987).

All four projects are supported by the infrastructure of the Department of Clinical Psychology and the affiliated outpatient clinic, both of which provide personnel, space, equipment, and finances supplemented according to the particular project by research grants. Since 1980 the described research projects have been supported by generous and continuous funding from the Swiss National Research Foundation.

Conducting such long-term, extensive projects would not be possible, however, with this funding alone. The projects are dependent on the personnel resources of the Department of Clinical Psychology. The hierarchical organization of Swiss universities in which a single professor is the head of a relatively large team has, along with some disadvantages, the advantage that all personnel over a long period of time can be concentrated on a clearly defined set of research goals. This creates the possibility of making long-term plans and also permits the conduct of a number of rather extensive research projects simultaneously.

Relation to Other Research Programs

Beginning with the founding of the group, intensive collaboration with other psychotherapy research groups in the German-speaking world has been taking place. At least in the area of single-case psychotherapy research there will be regular collaboration during the coming years, which we hope will result in new projects. The primary contribution that our research group can make to such projects is the application of the methods of process analysis that we have developed.

As far as the comparative treatment studies are concerned, we are collaborating with Dietmar Schulte of Bochum. His team has conducted in recent years an extensive comparative treatment study that has just been completed (Schulte, 1989). In this study with severely phobic patients, a standardized stimulus confrontation method is compared with a treatment form in which an individual treatment program is developed for each patient. An intensive data exchange is planned with this group to apply the methods of data analysis and process analysis developed by both research teams to both data sets.

Another data exchange has just been planned with David Shapiro from the Sheffield, England, group to apply the methods of data analysis that we have developed for the comparison of treatment effects in our own comparative treatment study to the Sheffield data. Furthermore, the data from our own comparative treatment study have been analyzed by Larry E. Beutler and his colleagues to test specific hypotheses about differential correlations between certain intake variables and therapy outcome.

In the analysis of the differential correlations between process factors and therapy outcome in our own comparative treatment study, we have used the generic model of psychotherapy of Orlinsky and Howard (1986) as a guideline. The results of these analyses that have been reported at the SPR conference in Toronto, Ontario, Canada (e.g., Ambühl, 1989b; Drew-Foppa, 1989) have an obvious relation to the research that is being done on the generic model at Northwestern University, Illinois.

Assessing the impact of our research on psychotherapy is not an easy task. The influence of the first and third research programs should be of a long-term nature. Because both projects have resulted in significant findings with reference to the clinical value and differential indication of different forms of therapy, one can expect that these results will have long-term influence.

The methods of plan analysis and schema analysis that we have developed have influenced previously behaviorally oriented psychotherapy in the German-speaking world; there is a great demand for workshops on the practical application of these methods. The most direct influence of our research activity during the past few years, however, has been on our own psychotherapeutic training and practice. The training of clinical psychology students in Bern takes place on the basis of our therapeutic conceptualization. Thus, at least in the case of psychotherapists trained at the University of Bern, our research results have a significant influence on future psychotherapeutic practice in Switzerland. To have a greater impact beyond our region would require increasing training opportunities for therapists from other regions. At present this would only be possible at the expense of our research work. Because we by no means view the development of our therapeutic conceptualization as complete, such a training program seems premature to us at present.

The international impact of our research is being restricted somewhat by our absence from English-speaking publications. Communicating our research results in the English-speaking world is difficult because researchers who are not native speakers of English have trouble producing an article in acceptable English. It is also due to the fact that papers by researchers who do not have an established name in the Anglo-American scientific community, and whose work reflects cultural value judgments that differ from those of this scientific community, are quickly rejected by editors of American journals. Thus, most readers of this chapter will probably not be familiar with our Bern research, although it is in its 10th year and has been documented in numerous publications. The publication of this book presents a welcome opportunity to familiarize our English-speaking colleagues with our research activities. We are interested in collaborating with other research groups dealing with the same questions we are, whatever language barriers we may have to overcome.

References

Ambühl, H. R. (1989a, September). *Schema-theoretic psychotherapy as subject and result of on-line-process-research: Current work of the Bern group. Change analysis with post-session questionnaires and heuristic rating scales.* Paper presented at the Third European Conference on Psychotherapy Research, Bern, Switzerland.

Ambühl, H. R. (1989b, June). *How general is Orlinsky and Howard's "generic model of psychotherapy"? Patient self-relatedness as a crucial link between therapeutic interventions and outcome.* Paper presented at the 20th Annual Meeting of the Society for Psychotherapy Research, Toronto, Ontario, Canada.

Ambühl, H. R., Grawe, K. (1989). Psychotherapeutisches Handeln als Verwirklichung therapeutischer Heuristiken: Ein Prozessvergleich dreier Therapieformen aus einer neuen Perspektive. *Zeitschrift für Psychotherapie, Psychosomatik und Medizinische Psychologie, 39*, 1–10.

Arnold, E. (1987). *Deskriptive einzelfallanalysen—Eine forschungsstrategie für die psychotherapieforschung.* Unpublished doctoral dissertation, University of Bern, Bern, Switzerland.

Arnold, E., & Grawe, K. (in press). Deskriptive Einzelfallanalysen—Eine Strategie zur Untersuchung von Wirkungszusammenhängen in der Psychotherapie. *Zeitschrift für Klinische Psychologie, Psychopathologie und Psychotherapie.*

Balmer, R., & Heiniger, B. (1989, September). *Schema-theoretic psychotherapy as subject and result of on-line-process-research: Current work of the Bern group. Schema analysis and schema analytic case formulation.* Paper presented at the Third European Conference on Psychotherapy Research, Bern, Switzerland.

Benjamin, L. S. (1974). Structural analysis of social behavior. *Psychological Review, 81*, 392–425.

Bergin, A. E., & Lambert, M. J. (1978). The evaluation of therapeutic outcomes. In S. L. Garfield & A. E. Bergin (Eds.), *Handbook of psychotherapy and behavior change* (2nd ed., pp. 139–189). New York: Wiley.

Caspar, F. M. (1988, June). *Schema theory, schema analysis and heuristic psychotherapy: A case conception in the view of the schema theory.* Paper presented at the 19th Annual Meeting of the Society for Psychotherapy Research, Santa Fe, NM.

Caspar, F. M. (in press). *Plananalyse.* Bern, Switzerland: Huber.

Caspar, F. M., & Grawe, K. (1982). *Vertikale verhaltensanalyse: Analyse des interaktionsverhaltens als grundlage für die problemdefinition und therapieplanung* (Forschungsbericht 5/1982). Bern, Switzerland: University of Bern, Psychological Institute.

Doblies, G. (1989, September). *Schema-theoretic psychotherapy as subject and result of on-line-process-research: Current work of the Bern group. Schema-analytic change analysis: A quantitative approach.* Paper presented at the Third European Conference on Psychotherapy Research, Bern, Switzerland.

Drew-Foppa, S. (1989, June). *How general is Orlinsky and Howard's "generic model of psychotherapy"? The empirical validity of the generic model on a single-case level: A longitudinal correlational analysis of 47 cases.* Paper presented at the 20th Annual Meeting of the Society for Psychotherapy Research, Toronto, Ontario, Canada.

Dziewas, H., Grawe, K., & Wedel, S. (1980). Anwendung und Wirkung des interaktionellen Problemlösungsvorgehens in Gruppen bei gehemmten Neurotikern. In K. Grawe (Ed.), *Verhaltenstherapie in gruppen.* Urban & Schwarzenberg: Munich, Federal Republic of Germany.

Grawe, K. (1976). *Differentielle psychotherapie: I. Indikation und spezifische wirkung von verhaltenstherapie und gesprächstherapie. Eine untersuchung an phobischen patienten.* Bern, Switzerland: Huber.

Grawe, K. (1981). Ueberlegungen zu möglichen Strategien der Indikationsforschung. In U. Baumann (Ed.), *Indikation zur psychotherapie* (pp. 221–236). Munich, Federal Republic of Germany: Urban & Schwarzenberg.

Grawe, K. (1986). *Schema-theorie und heuristische psychotherapie.* (Forschungsbericht 2/1986, 2. Auflage 1/1987). Bern, Switzerland: University of Bern, Psychological Institute.

Grawe, K. (1988a). Der Weg entsteht beim Gehen: Ein heuristisches Verständnis von Psychotherapie. *Verhaltenstherapie und Psychosoziale Praxis, 20*, 39–49.

Grawe, K. (1988b, June). *Schema theory, schema analysis and heuristic psychotherapy: Basic concepts of the schema approach to psychotherapy.* Paper presented at the 19th Annual Meeting of the Society for Psychotherapy Research, Santa Fe, NM.

Grawe, K. (1989). *Schema theory and heuristic psychotherapy.* Bern, Switzerland: University of Bern, Psychological Institute.

Grawe, K., & Dziewas, H. (1978). Interaktionelle Verhaltenstherapie: Sonderheft 1 der Mitteilungen der DGVT. *Auch Abgedruckt in Partnerberatung, 3*, 188–204.

Grawe, K., Dziewas, H., Brutscher, H., Schaper, P., & Steffani, K. (1978). Assertive Trainingsgruppen vs. interaktionelle Problemlösungsgruppen: Ein empirischer Vergleich. *Sonderheft 1 der Mittelungen der DGVT*, 63–85.

Grawe, H., Dziewas, H., & Wedel, S. (1980). Interaktionelle Problemlösungsgruppen. In K. Grawe (Ed.), *Verhaltenstherapie in gruppen.* Munich, Federal Republic of Germany: Urban & Schwarzenberg.

Grawe, K., & Mezenen, U. (1985). Therapeutische Misserfolge im Spiegel der empirischen Psychotherapieforschung. *Zeitschrift für Personenzentrierte Psychologie und Psychotherapie, 4*, 355–377.

Heiniger, B., & Jost, U. (1987). *Angst: Schematheoretische fallkonzeptionen von angstklientinnen.* Unpublished master's thesis, University of Bern, Bern, Switzerland.

Luborsky, L., Singer, B., & Luborsky, L. (1975). Comparative studies of psychotherapies: Is it true that "everyone has won and all must have prizes?" *Archives of General Psychiatry, 32*, 995–1008.

Orlinsky, D. E., & Howard, K. I. (1986). The relation of process to outcome in psychotherapy. In S. L. Garfield & A. E. Bergin (Eds.), *Handbook of psychotherapy and behavior change* (3rd ed., pp. 311–381). New York: Wiley.

Rice, L. N., & Greenberg, L. S. (1984). The new research paradigm. In L. N. Rice & L. S. Greenberg (Eds.), *Patterns of change* (pp. 7–25). New York: Guilford Press.

Schulte, D. (1989, September). *Tailor-made versus standardized therapy: Which is superior?* Paper presented at the Third European Conference on Psychotherapy Research, Bern, Switzerland.

Smith, M. L., Glass, G. V., & Miller, T. I. (1980). *The benefits of psychotherapy.* Baltimore: John Hopkins University Press.

Stiles, W. B., Shapiro, D. A., & Elliott, R. (1986). Are all psychotherapies equivalent? *American Psychologist, 41*, 165–180.

Thierstein, C. (1988). *33 Stunden im leben von Frau*

Galli: *Eine schematheoretische betrachtung des psychotherapeutischen veränderungsprozesses.* Unpublished master's thesis, University of Bern, Bern, Switzerland.

Thommen, M. (1988). *Schematheoretische analyse subjektiver krankheitstheorien: Zur beurteilung von erfolg und missserfolg in der psychotherapie.* Unpublished doctoral dissertation, University of Bern, Bern, Switzerland.

Wüthrich, U. (1987). *Ueber veränderungsprozesse in der psychotherapie: Eine konkretisierung des schemaansatzes.* Unpublished doctoral dissertation, University of Bern, Bern, Switzerland.

Zingg, M. (1988). *Schematheoretische sichtweise psychischer störungen.* Unpublished doctoral dissertation, University of Bern, Bern, Switzerland.

25

University of Hamburg: Hamburg Short-Term Psychotherapy Comparison Study

Ulrich Stuhr and Adolf-Ernst Meyer
University of Hamburg

Background and Aims

History

In the planning phase of our project (From 1969 to 1972), psychotherapy comparison studies were just starting to be developed. Sloane, Stables, Christel, Yorkson, and Whipple (1975) in Philadelphia had begun to compare psychodynamic therapy (PT) with behavior therapy, and Grawe (1976) in Hamburg also had started to compare behavioral therapy with client-centered therapy (CCT). We decided to fill in the remaining gap by comparing CCT with PT. As an example of the latter, we chose focal therapy as developed by Balint and Malan (Malan, 1963). Because randomization of patients was of paramount importance to us, our PT deviated from the Malan model. At the same time, we were aware that mere comparisons were no longer the optimal strategy in psychotherapy research. Hence, we planned our data collection in such a way (through audio recordings of interviews, therapy sessions, and follow-ups as well as repeated testing) that both process and outcome studies were equally feasible.

The actual realization of our project began in the spring of 1972. It was the first time in the history of the Psychosomatic Department of the Medical University Clinic of Hamburg that all of its members joined in the same research project, which they experienced as relevant. The planning of this project was connected with the aim (eventually attained) to establish an interdisciplinary center for research (Sonderforschungsbereich) on psychosomatic medicine, clinical psychology, and psychotherapy, integrating the research efforts of different departments of the university clinic. This center was to be supported financially by the German Research Foundation (Deutsche Forschungsgemeinschaft).

Overall Aims

The main aim of the study was to compare the efficacy of two forms of short-term psychotherapy. Such short-term procedures could be the cardinal solution to the well-known disparity between demand for and availability of psychotherapy in highly industrialized nations. This solution could prove to be illusory, however, if the efficacy of these short-term procedures is low or nil.

An additional motivation for our project stemmed from the fact that both CCT and PT were derived from psychoanalysis but that each capitalized on different aspects of it (Meyer &

Bolz, 1981). Only in retrospect did we discover (Meyer & Niemann, 1984) that CCT can be considered a focal therapy, albeit with an invariant focus identical for each and every patient. We suggest this focus to read as follows: Learn to perceive and express your emotional experiences (needs and reactions) and to accept your own self, and you will have learned how to live.

Subareas of Investigation

The following list outlines the areas of primary investigation in our studies:

• statistical comparison of outcome and clinical process variables of CCT and PT and two forms of waiting-list control groups (own control and reference control) along with a comparison of the two forms of therapy to evaluate the efficacy of short-term psychotherapy;

• taxometric procedures (e.g. cluster analyses) to find subgroups with similar therapy (and posttherapy) courses because there are strong arguments that overall sample analyses have grave disadvantages (in addition, they are alien to the practicing psychotherapist who is concerned with and responsible for individual patients);

• description of the covert selection factors operating from intake interview to initial psychotherapy session in our sample of outpatients;

• content analyses of focus formulations and the relation of these contents to outcome;

• factor analytic description of different clinical evaluation systems to determine the dimensions of clinical assessment used in our sample across several evaluations;

• intercorrelation of psychological test findings and clinical assessments to pinpoint convergence and divergence;

• description of CCT and PT according to frequencies of therapist interventions;

• factor analyses of therapist sessions questionnaires to identify different kinds of therapy hours (good hour or resistance hour);

• interactional analyses of therapist–patient communication by nonparametric time series;

• correlation of process variables in the form of intervention frequencies (psychoanalytic contents and Rogerian scales) with outcome variables;

• description of the posttherapy development of the patients after 12 years.

Method

Subjects and Selection

Beginning in 1972 and continuing over the next 1.5 years, all psychoneurotic and psychosomatic patients who applied for treatment intake at our outpatient department, who were between 20 and 40 years of age, and who reported receiving no previous psychotherapy were invited to undergo intake testing for our research program. Of 286 patients invited, 72 did not show up. The remaining 214 patients started intake assessments, but only 177 were entered into the study; the others either declined participation or were dropped because of contraindications (e.g., psychosis or absence of motivation).

The case histories of these 177 patients were presented by the intake interviewer to the focus formulation seminar. This seminar articulated a therapeutic focus and a psychotherapy prognosis (suitability). The prognosis for psychotherapy was considered good for 88 patients and these patients were then randomly assigned to PT or CCT conditions. Not all patients accepted our offer, but 34 of them started therapy in each therapy group.

Post hoc statistical examination indicated the success of the randomization procedure. The patients refusing therapy differed in only two respects from those accepting therapy: They were less sick and less sophisticated than their peers who accepted psychotherapy assignment. As is often the case, young, attractive, verbal, intelligent, and successful patients (Goldstein, 1971) were overrepresented in our sample. Even so, this was not caused by therapist selection factors because these characteristics also typified the intake sample (Kimm, Bolz, & Meyer, 1981).

Instruments

Psychotherapy outcome evaluation requires the measurement of a number of variables representing different levels. Therefore, we engaged as many evaluators as feasible, used a number of different measurement devices, and conducted repeated assessments (Bolz & Meyer, 1981; Burzig, Speidel, Bolz, & Meyer, 1981).

Subtests of a differential intelligence test; a

personality inventory for personality factors such as neuroticism, extraversion, and psychosomatic disturbances (the Freiburg Personality Inventory [FPI]; a personality questionnaire based on psychoanalytic theory; an anxiety questionnaire adapted from the Taylor Manifest Anxiety Scale; and a symptom checklist that contained 152 items incorporating neurotic and psychosomatic complaints were administered.

Clinical assessment scales and raters included the interviewer's assessment (symptom change, well-being, and insight); the patient's self-ratings (of symptom change, well-being, and interpersonal change); and blind ratings by a group of experts of the transcripts of the two follow-ups, which were permutated and censored for the identity of the patient, type of therapy, and length of follow-up (assessing symptom change, well-being, aspects of insight, etc.).

Process scales included the patient session questionnaire, the therapist session questionnaire, a content–analytic catalog for interventions and interaction, and Rogerian rating scales (of empathy, warmth, self-exploration, etc). Identification and rating were also carried out for crucial incidents (Rice & Greenberg, 1984).

Procedures

Comparison of the efficacy of short-term psychotherapy. All of the patient test variables were assessed five times: during the waiting period before assignment, immediately before therapy began, after therapy, at Follow-Up 1 (3 months), and at Follow-Up 2 (9 months). Thus, we were able to analyze the test results in two different ways. For the within-group or own-group comparison, we used 13 PT patients and 12 CCT patients whose treatment had been delayed. In this analysis, we compared the waiting period to the treatment period for each therapy by means of one-way analyses of variance (ANOVAs). For the between-groups, or reference group, comparison the two waiting groups were combined into one untreated control group ($n = 25$) and compared with 21 PT patients and 22 CCT patients who began their therapy immediately (bifactoral ANOVAs).

Clinical assessment. Each patient was assessed at 3 and 9 months during follow-up. These follow-up evaluations were performed by the clinician who had conducted the initial intake interview. Independent clinical experts were asked to make blind ratings of the transcribed interview.

In addition, we gathered patient self-ratings at these times.

Process research. Both randomly chosen therapy sessions and sessions selected on the questionnaire (e.g., "good hours") were subjected to a content analysis and associated ratings. These process data were used to assess differences between the two therapy groups and to investigate the interactions that occurred between patients and therapists in the sessions and were correlated with outcome variables.

Long-term follow-up. After 12 years the patients in this study were invited for another interview, which was conducted and coded by independent experts. The patient again answered the FPI, an anxiety questionnaire (SAL), and a social questionnaire concerning posttherapeutic developments (e.g., symptom change, further medical aid and psychotherapy, partnership, work, and sexuality).

Research Accomplishments

Findings

Psychological tests. To ensure a conservative interpretation of psychological test findings, we considered only those differences that were replicated in the own and reference control comparison and that were still observable at the 9-month follow-up. By using these rigorous criteria of change, we found significant gains in sociability and masculinity for patients in both types of therapy. Additionally, we observed significant reductions in psychosomatic disturbance, depressivity, and anxiety among patients in CCT.

In direct comparisons of psychological test scores between CCT and PT groups few significant differences emerged, and none of those that did were replicated in subsequent analyses. Thus, although more significant differences were observed for CCT than for PT, the advantage that this portends for CCT is apparently quite small.

Clinical ratings. When the dependent variables that relied on the blind ratings of clinicians were analyzed (Meyer, Bolz, Stuhr, & Burzig, 1981), a somewhat different pattern of between-treatment differences emerged. First, PT patients developed more insight as applied to the concepts described in and outside of the focus formulation than did CCT patients. Second, at Follow-Up 1, CCT patients showed a larger reduction of secondary symptoms than their PT counterparts. This difference vanished by Follow-Up 2, however, as a result of a slight additional reduction of symptoms in the PT patients and a slight symptom increase among those in the CCT sample. Third, in the general domain defined as personality and human relations variables patients in PT received higher ratings than those in CCT for introspection at Follow-Up 1, and patients in CCT received higher ratings for attitude toward self at Follow-Up 2. Fourth, there was a general indication that at Follow-Up 2, more CCT patients than PT patients felt that therapy had helped them.

Interactions among rating sources. When we undertook a factor analysis of the three different sources of ratings (blind clinical raters, intake interviewers, and self reports), four factors emerged:

1. All three groups of raters agreed that treated patients felt better, had fewer symptoms, and were better able to cope than they had been before treatment. We labeled this factor Gain in Subjective Symptom-Oriented Well-Being and in Coping Competence.

2. The ratings of independent (i.e., blind) clinicians emerged as a second factor reflecting a dimension of insight.

3. The intake interviewers' ratings also emerged as a separate factor unrelated to that defined by the independent clinicians but as one that appeared to reflect a dimension of insight.

4. The final factor describes the patient's belief that others act differently towards and see changes in him or her.

Process differences. The results of the content analyses of therapist interventions corresponded with the theoretical concepts of each therapy school. The strongest differences found in our study indicated that CCT therapists relied on verbal repetitions, emphasized the verbalization of emotions, and supported patient defenses, whereas PT therapists focused on working through, emphasized the importance of past experience, and used the focus formulation to direct their interventions.

Process–outcome relationships. The process–outcome analyses based on Rogerian rating scales (e.g., empathy, warmth, and self-exploration) were not as closely related to outcome in CCT as we had assumed. Nonetheless, the emotionally warm, concrete, and active CCT therapist induced positive changes in patients' extraversion. In contrast to these findings, we observed that the PT patient's process ratings (but not the PT therapist's ratings) of such dimensions as emotional involvement and acceptance of one's own feelings were positively related to reductions in neuroticism. An unusually active PT therapist, however, produced nonconstructive effects on aggression and self-confidence in interaction with highly resistant patients.

Patterns of change. A cluster–analytic investigation of different clinical assessments suggested that it is possible to identify patterns of outcome that distinguished between the treatments. For example, one cluster comprised CCT patients who had been successfully treated as judged by a reduction of symptoms and improved ratings but who did not show corresponding changes or increases in insight. On the other hand, another cluster comprised PT patients who gained insight but did not improve in symptom-oriented well-being. We found two clusters comprising patients from both therapy groups, one with nonresponders to therapy and the other with successful outcomes, as especially indexed by changes in variables related to introspection and attitudes toward themselves. Finally, two patients did not fit into any of the foregoing clusters, suggesting that there existed some highly specific outcome configurations.

Long-term follow-up. In our 12-year follow-up study, we were able to obtain relevant information from many patients. The patients who had been offered psychotherapy but did not accept it were used as a reference control group that showed small but at times significant gains (which can be interpreted as spontaneous remission). Compared with this control group, only changes indexed by the Extraversion scale were of sufficient magnitude to suggest the long-term advantages of both short-term psychotherapies. Additionally, long-term treatment advantages were observed on the Depression scale among patients in CCT. Among those in PT there was a tendency for changes to be observed somewhat later, during the follow-up period. PT patients also reported having more subsequent treatment during the follow-up period than those in CCT. This finding suggests that psychoanalytic short-term psychotherapy may be a more mobilizing experience than CCT.

Our global clinical results concerning symptomatic changes and coping skills showed no significant differences between the treatment groups and the nontreatment groups after 12 years.

Instruments Developed

We developed the following types of instruments during our investigations: (a) content-analytic catalog for interventions and interactions during therapy sessions; (b) therapy session questionnaires for therapists and patients; (c) clinical assessment scales for the therapist, the interviewer, and the blind rating experts at Follow-Up 1 (3 months), Follow-Up 2 (9 months), and the long-term follow-up (12 years); and (d) social questionnaires for the 12-year posttherapeutic period.

Research Programs in Progress

Hypotheses

A cluster-analytic investigation of therapy success could enable us to describe the movements of patients from one success subgroup to another over time (processive outcome). With such a procedure, it may also be possible to determine process–outcome types. Moreover, we are attempting to determine whether crucial events in the therapy process occurring during selected therapy hours are more closely related to therapy success than process ratings or content-analytic variables. Finally, our research is attempting to determine whether analysis of events during the long-term posttherapeutic period can help us to determine the differential effects of psychotherapies.

Tentative Findings

Our findings indicate that the timing of follow-up evaluations is an important factor in understanding differences among treatments. For example, we have found higher intercorrelations between posttherapy results with Follow-Up 2 (9 months) than with Follow-Up 1 (3 months). Thus, results of differential analyses may be dependent on when the analysis is undertaken. Concerning insight factors, we have discovered a clear "Rashomon" effect: Two groups of raters produced insight ratings that were statistically independent of each other. On our time-series interactional analysis, we found that only 15% of the whole interaction was explainable. The direct comparison of the two therapies did not yield enough findings for differential prognostic effects to be determined.

Programs Planned for the Future

New Directions and Hypotheses

In our future studies, we will use a combination of processive outcome research methods and analyses of crucial events during crucial therapy hours. The aim of this investigation is the development of a taxonomy of processive outcome types. The analyses of crucial events in therapy hours also may help explain outcome. The therapy hours are identified by P-technique factor analyses based on the therapist session report.

Significance

The analyses of processive outcome will yield a more time-dynamic and qualitative evaluation of therapy effects than is possible in conventional methods. This strategy is superior to static, quantitative, statistical comparisons of therapy groups against control groups.

Nature of the Research Organization

Team Members and Their Roles

The team members of the Hamburg Short-Term Psychotherapy Comparison Study as well as their roles are as follows:

A.-E. Meyer, M.D., PhD. (professor, research director; planning and scientific management, therapy, interviewing, and evaluation); U. Stuhr, Ph.D. (assistant professor; planning, evaluation, management of data, and interviewing); W. Bolz, Ph.D. (assistant professor; planning, evaluation, scientific management, management of data, and interviewing); F.-W. Deneke, M.D., B.A. (professor, assessment and partial evaluation); G. Burzig, M.D. (assessment and partial evaluation); U. Wirth, B.A. (organization of long-term follow-up and interviewing); and H. Speidel, M.D. (professor, planning, interviewing, and therapy).

Our project has used several (overlapping) teams. The CCT therapist team ($n = 72$) encountered no problems. They played on home ground because they were used to audio recording, filling out questionnaires and treating every patient assigned to them. Our maximum limit of 30 sessions was beyond their usual duration of therapy. They were members of the university's Department of Psychology or of the psychiatric clinic, or they were in private practice. One of these therapists (J. Eckert, Ph.D.) also performed half the CCT intake interviews. The therapists never met jointly.

The PT therapist team ($n = 13$) contained five members of Nuclear Team 1 plus eight analysts in private practice or from other institutions. They worked under novel and disconcerting conditions, accepting patients not seen before with a focus usually formulated by others (only the five nuclear analysts had participated in this seminar). They also were faced with a preannounced limit of 30 sessions, audio recording, and questionnaires. By the end of the therapy phase, the PT therapists outside of Nuclear Team 1 gave indications of feeling overtaxed and confined.

In Nuclear Team 1 (Boehncke, Bolz, Klug, Meyer, Speidel, and Scherf), Bolz and Meyer were responsible for the initial design. Thereafter, Bolz did half of the CCT interviews and the general organization, and Meyer and the others interviewed, treated, and did follow-up.

For the construction of the intervention catalog and for the focus formulation seminar Nuclear Team 1 was joined by two outside analysts (Muller-Proske and Renate Speidel) who were also members of Nuclear Team 2.

Nuclear Team 2 emerged because near the completion of Follow-Up 2 Boehncke, Scherf, and Speidel found other posts and left. They were replaced by Burzig, Deneke, and Haag. A little later, Klug left because he did not feel comfortable with the team and was replaced by Trentmann. This had the advantage that evaluation by the blind rating group and the formulation of initial results were performed by partially independent observers. Statistical analyses were done by Bolz and Stuhr.

When the first results were presented (and did not show a clear advantage for PT over CCT, the outside members of the PT therapy group protested. They claimed that the research team's selection of patients was too broad and that the experimental restrictions had prohibited real or true psychoanalytic therapy. In response to these protests, we offered the following: It is true that we accepted 50% of our outpatients, whereas Malan and Sifneos took only 5%–10% and Davanloo took only 35%. To be a relevant procedure in health care, however, a certain form of therapy should be applicable for a major portion of suitable patients. Furthermore, CCT would have accepted even a higher percentage of the patients (Kimm et al.,

1981). It is also true that our PT therapist team had to work under unfamiliar conditions. Nevertheless, the CCT group's performance showed that therapists can adapt to such restrictions. Finally, there is the argument that our PT therapists had insufficient experience with short-term psychotherapy. We think that this argument is justified.

Funding

Our research has been supported by several sources. The German Research Foundation (Deutsche Forschungsgemeinschaft) financed the project from 1972 to 1975 and also funded research at the Centre for Research on Psychosomatic Medicine (Sonderforschungsbereich 115) of the Hamburg University Clinic from 1975 to 1977 and again from 1985 to 1986. The Breuninger Foundation gave a Senior Scientist Grant to the research director.

Relation to Other Research Programs

Integration With Findings of Other Research

This study worked in cooperation with the Department of Psychotherapy at the University of Ulm (Thoma and Kachele) and the Centre for Psychotherapy Research in Stuttgart (Czogalik). The findings with the control group comparison are consistent with the findings of other investigators. Namely, there is an advantage for the treatment groups over the control group but no differential effects when the two treatment groups are compared. Only the standardized psychological test results, particularly those related to depression and extraversion, are really comparable to other German studies, however.

Impact on the Field of Psychotherapy

Our research has heightened acceptance of CCT therapy for outpatients in our department. It has also encouraged the staff in our department to adopt shorter psychoanalytic therapies. Our psychiatric clinic now uses more short-term psychotherapy accompanied by a scientific evaluation program. These advantages are incorporated into the training of students of medicine and psychology.

References

Bolz, W., & Meyer, A.-E. (1981). The general setting. *Psychotherapy and Psychosomatics, 35,* 85–95.

Burzig, G., Speidel, H., Bolz, W., & Meyer, A.-E. (1981). Our pluridimensional evaluation system for short psychotherapy outcome. *Psychotherapy and Psychosomatics, 35,* 134–137.

Goldstein, A. P. (1971). *Psychotherapeutic attraction.* New York: Pergamon Press.

Grawe, K. (1976). Bern, Switzerland: Huber.

Kimm, H. J., Bolz, W., & Meyer, A.-E. (1981). The patient sample: Overt and covert selection factors and prognostic predictions. *Psychotherapy and Psychosomatics, 35,* 96–109.

Malan, D. H. (1963). *A study of brief psychotherapy.* London: Tavistock.

Meyer A.-E., & Bolz, W. (1981). Foreword and introduction. *Psychotherapy and Psychosomatics, 35,* 81–84.

Meyer, A.-E., Bolz, W., Stuhr, U., & Burzig, G. (1981). Outcome results by clinical evaluation based on the blind group ratings. *Psychotherapy and Psychosomatics, 35,* 199–207.

Meyer, A.-E, & Niemann, I. (1984). Problemes lies a la limitation a un maximum de 30 seances, prealablement communique au patient, dans deux formes de psychotherapies breves. *Psychotherapies, 2,* 81–93.

Rice, L. N. & Greenberg, L. S. (1984). The new research paradigms. In L. N. Rice & L. S. Greenberg (Eds.), *Patterns of change.* New York: Guilford Press.

Sloane, R. B., Stables, F. R., Christel, A. H., Yorkston, N. J., & Whipple, K. (1975). *Psychotherapy versus behavior therapy.* Cambridge, MA: Harvard University Press.

26

University of Ulm: The Ulm Textbank Research Program

Erhard Mergenthaler and Horst Kächele
University of Ulm

Background and Aims

History

Since 1968 one of the major research efforts at the University of Ulm has been directed at establishing a methodology for performing psychoanalytic process research. The tape recording of long-term psychoanalytic treatments has been an essential component of this effort and has yielded the collection of a large number of verbatim transcripts. As our archives grew, we realized the need to establish a major computerized data bank for our research. With support from the German Research Foundation, the Ulm Textbank Management System (TMS) was begun in 1980 to serve this purpose.

In constructing TMS, we became aware that such a data bank would also serve other researchers involved in process research based on the analysis of verbatim material. The system was strongly influenced by our desire to serve various users and methodological approaches. Today, the now-completed TMS is available as a new versatile tool for psychotherapy research.

Overall Aims

One goal of the TMS is to make verbatim transcripts of psychotherapy sessions available to researchers in a way that is both efficient and cost-effective. Another goal is to give access to computer-aided analyses to those in the field who do not have their own computers. A third goal is to integrate the results of previous analyses of these data. Thus, the TMS has been designed to facilitate the following:

- input and editing of texts selected according to many different perspectives and criteria,

- management of an unlimited number of texts on the University of Ulm computer center's auxiliary storage center,

- management of an unlimited amount of information about the texts, their authors, and the related texts analyses,

- management of an open-ended variety of methods for editing and analyzing stored texts,

- interfaces between statistical and other user packages,

- simple, dialog-oriented communication.

In summary, the TMS is an information system that integrates techniques of linguistic data and text processing to make texts in the field of psychotherapy process research readily accessible to a wide range of users at relatively low cost. It features a uniform user interface that assists in the input, processing, output, and analysis of texts.

Documents stored in the TMS are primarily a collection of open-ended data bases that can be continually expanded. The degree of completeness of a data base influences strategies for handling the results of subsequent analyses of these texts. There are two main approaches: In the first approach, results of all the available analyses may be stored with the text or in direct relation to it. In the second approach, texts from the data base may be processed as needed according to the wishes of the researcher.

Subareas of Investigation

The TMS project attempts to use tools of computer science in psychotherapy research. One area of interest has been the performance and acceptability of this fairly new approach to psychotherapy investigation. In addition, while accumulating texts we have faced the challenge of convincing researchers to share primary data. One of the most gratifying aspects of this project has been recognition of the growing number of colleagues who understand our intention and are generously supporting it by sharing their data sources.

Method

Subjects and Selection

For optimal use of the TMS, the text data bases to be administered should answer the kinds of questions most likely to be posed. The definition of individual data bases in the TMS are especially significant. In this regard, two major areas of work at the TMS have involved longitudinal and cross-sectional studies.

Longitudinal studies concentrate on text from psychoanalytic cases; their goal is the study of the change process. Because of the length of a typical psychoanalysis, it is possible to prepare transcripts of only a small number of different cases. Thus, it is most important to obtain a wide variety of cases.

There are, of course, questions that go beyond variation in individual patients or therapists; these questions are examined by using the texts of initial interviews in cross-sectional studies. Focusing on the initial interview means that many different patients with only one interview can be examined, making it possible to study the effects of variables such as sex and diagnosis.

Maintained separately are the text data bases required for special investigations such as those of the Balint group research, verbal exchanges during doctors' visits, and verbal interactions during family consultations.

The data base of psychoanalysis texts now includes extensive excerpts from four psychoanalytic cases. Individual sessions from nine other psychoanalytic therapies are also included. The data base of initial interviews includes several hundred different interviews and is referenced according to the sex of the patient or therapist and whether the diagnosis is neurosis or pyschosomatic disturbance. This body of texts is being enlarged with special attention to the patient variables of sex, diagnosis, social class, and age and the therapist variables of experience and kind of pyschotherapy.

The kind of text included in the TMS is determined by the goals, questions, and scientific interests of the supporting and other institutions. For the Department of Psychotherapy at Ulm University, this means an emphasis on the establishment of an empirical basis for research in the field of psychotherapy and the enhancement of teaching. The latter takes the form of demonstration materials for the education of medical students and the use of verbatim transcripts in the clinical education and supervision of resident physicians and psychologists.

Two thirds of the material in the Ulm TMS has come from Ulm. The other third has been supplied as a result of scientific contacts and joint research projects with outside institutions. In most cases, these contributions were tied to actual uses of the TMS service. Although these donations were primarily from the narrow field of psychotherapy, the outside users were almost exclusively linguists who did not require the services of the TMS other than the provision of recording and transcripts along with word and line counts. At present, there are contacts with about 30 institutes in Germany, 4 in the United States, 2 in Sweden, 2 in Switzerland, and 1 in Austria. The electronically stored texts include a vocabulary of 155,000 German and 20,000 English words and a total of more than 10 million words of running text.

Questions as to the representativeness of the Ulm TMS are dependent upon the goals of research. Nevertheless, there are general practical limits, such as the large number of hours in each treatment.

In selecting the individual interviews to be stored in the TMS, a number of considerations are important. Several of these, in descending order of importance, are the numerical balance among the different therapists; diagnostic categories that are relevant to the central subject of research (e.g., anxiety); treatments lasting 300–500 hours; and the success of the treatment. Other criteria for selection that would be especially relevant for statistical evaluations, such as the sex distribution of patients and therapists and patients' social class, cannot be established because of the small number of cases. Thus, the data base of psychoanalytic texts at Ulm is representative only with respect to specific research goals.

Instruments and Procedures

Starting from a semiotic view of language, which goes back to Peirce, the founder of semiotics, and to its further development by Morris, language is understood as a system of symbols whose structure is determined according to rules based on the relation between form and content.

Accordingly, it is possible to distinguish among formal, grammatical, and substantive measurements. Each of these types of measurements can be further subdivided according to whether it can be applied to a speaker's text or to the entire speech activity in a conversation (the dialog). It is therefore possible to speak of monadic or dyadic values and to distinguish among these types of measurements according to the kind of data they use. Best known are simple frequencies of occurrence, which form the basis for ratios and distributions.

It should also be noted that some of the approaches for formal and grammatical measurements presume substantive knowledge of, for example, the denotative meaning of a word. The contrast with substantive measurements stems from the fact that the required knowledge does not come from the research field itself (namely psychoanalysis) but from the realm of methodologies (i.e., from linguistics or information science.

The formal measurements can generally be determined in a simple manner. In computer-aided approaches, only the capacity to segment a sequence of symbols (letters, numbers, and special symbols) into words and punctuation is necessary. The programming task is minimal; hardly any recording is necessary. Such formal measurements and indications of their applicability include text size (tokens), activity; vocabulary (types), diversity; type: token ratio, efficiency; redundancy, simplicity compared with complexity;

word distance, variability; word cluster, fixation or focus; and change of speaker, dynamics compared with rigidity.

The simplest and most elementary formal measurement is the number of words spoken by the analyst and patient. Kächele (1983) found that in a successful psychoanalytic treatment there was no correlation across 130 sessions in the number of words spoken by analyst and patient. In an unsuccessful treatment by the same analyst, these word counts were significantly (.30, N = 110) correlated. O'Dell and Winder (1975) also used text size as a measure of the therapist's activity to distinguish therapeutic techniques. They gave 7% as the proportion of the therapist's speech in analytic therapy and 31% in eclectic psychotherapy. Zimmer and Cowles (1972), in a study of one patient who visited three therapists with different orientations, also pointed out significant differences. With the same data, Pepinsky (1979) showed that the therapist's form of activity influences the patient to act in a similar way; that is, the speech activity of the patient conforms to that of the therapist as if there is "a convergence of the client toward the level of talk manifested by the therapist" (Pepinsky, 1979, p. 7).

The redundancy of a text is a measure adopted from information theory. Spence (1968) proposed some important ideas about psychodynamic redundancy without testing these ideas empirically. In addition, he formulated a series of hypotheses about the course that redundancy takes in psychoanalytic treatment. Kächele and Mergenthaler (1984) confirmed one of these hypotheses, namely that the repetitiousness of a patient's speech increases over the course of treatment. The therapist's values, in contrast, remain constant.

Grammatical measures address such features as interjections, word class (part of speech), and diminution and raising. The grammatical measures require the researcher to have linguistic knowledge about the language being studied (e.g., the grammar of German). The programming and precoding tasks in the computer-aided procedures are considerable. Moreover, many kinds of questions still cannot be correctly processed automatically. An example is lemmatization, which can assign 50%–90% of all word forms, depending on the kind of text, to the correct lemma. The psychoanalytic interview, a form of speech with the many syntactically deviant forms (such as incomplete words and sentences) that characterize spoken and spontaneous speech, pose unique challenges. Accordingly, there are hardly any computer-aided studies of psychoanalytic texts that use grammatical measures.

The distribution by word type was used by Lorenz and Cobb (1975) to differentiate patients with different psychotic illnesses. For example, they determined that neurotics used more verbs but fewer conjunctions than did the normal population. At least in German, other variables must to be taken into account, as Eisenmann (1973) demonstrated for conjunctions: "The use of particular conjunctions is determined first and foremost by locality, second by sex, third by age, and lastly by language class" (p. 407, translation from German by the authors).

The dependence of word choice on word type and semantic class was demonstrated by Busemann (1925) in investigations of children's speech. He spoke of an active and a qualitative style with regard to verbs and adjectives. He showed that these differences in style are only slightly dependent on the subject being discussed and stem from personality variables. With a computer-aided approach to the text of a psychoanalytic interview, Mergenthaler and Kächele (1985) showed that the realization of a word form in the text may (definitely) depend on the subject matter. Even so, this microanalytic view does not exclude the possibility that, viewed at the micro level, personality-dependent variables are effective, as described by Busemann (1925).

The verb–adjective quotient, introduced by Boder (1940) and analogous to Busemann's action quotients, was applied by Wirtz and Kächele (1983) to samples of first interviews of three different therapists. Wirtz and Kächele concluded that this quotient is a differential measure of the therapist's speech style as well as of differences associated with sex and diagnosis. The significance of personal pronouns for the structuring of object and self relations in language has been addressed a number of times. Several studies have investigated the speech material of psychoanalytically oriented group therapy (Cierpka, Ohlmeier, & Schaumburg, 1980, 1983).

Anxiety themes and regressive imagery may serve as samples of substantive measures. They require, in addition to the knowledge mentioned above, detailed expert knowledge of a theory and its area of application. Computer-aided procedures are only able to provide approximate results and are limited to narrowly defined constructions. New approaches in information science, especially in the field of artificial intelligence, could achieve a breakthrough by establishing data bases in conjunction with a system of rules. Two approaches that strongly emphasize the rule components are those of Clippinger (1977) and Teller and Dahl (1981).

The most important kind of quantitative method for substantive measurements has been content analysis. Gottschalk and Gleser (1969) and Gottschalk (1974) presented the scales most widely used in psychotherapy. Koch and Schöfer (1986) edited a survey of these methods, including a section by Grünzig and Mergenthaler (1986) on computer-aided approaches. Lolas, Mergenthaler, and von Rad (1982) provided a comparison of results by means of a computer-aided method, with results being derived from other methods.

In a pioneering study, Dahl (1972) was able to trace the downhill course of 363 hours during a 2.5-year segment of an unsuccessful psychoanalysis and to categorize convincingly 25 sessions as 10 extreme work hours, 10 extreme resistance hours, and 5 hours directly in the middle of the range. With single words derived from the *Harvard III Psychosociological Dictionary* categories, he was also able to demonstrate word clusters that manifestly appear to reflect oedipal and other unconscious conflicts (Dahl, 1974). This study convinced us to adopt the approach.

Using a German version of the *Harvard III Psychosociological Dictionary*, Kächele (1976) demonstrated that linear category combinations will predict highly inferential clinical concepts such as positive and negative transference constellations in conjunction with selected anxiety topics. His findings were based on a single case study of 55 sessions with correlations ranging from .77 to .91. In a similar vein, Grünzig and Kächele (1978) demonstrated the differentiation of anxiety concepts by automatic classification based on *Harvard III* content categories.

Reynes, Martindale, and Dahl (1984) used the *Regressive Imagery Dictionary* to compare this same patient's 10 working hours and 10 resistance hours. The working hours were characterized by increases in the dictionary categories that assessed primary process language, and the resistance hours were characterized by increases in the secondary process category scores. This agrees with Freud's earlier attribution of defensive functions to the secondary processes (Bucci, 1988).

Large continuous segments as well as selected sections of treatment transcripts may thus be examined using computer-aided text analysis as a tool in psychoanalytic process research (Kächele & Mergenthaler, 1984). Further progress requires that methods be developed more extensively, that basic research be conducted, and that techniques from related scientific disciplines such as information science and linguistics be integrated.

Privacy and Technical Aspects

When a text is entered into the TMS, all personal names, geographic references, and other personal characteristics are coded by means of a cryptographic procedure or are replaced by pseudonyms. Although the texts have been made virtually anonymous for processing at the university's computer center, the personal data remain in the microcomputers used exclusively by the Ulm TMS. This separate storage, as well as extensive controls on retrieval and manipulation, protect the Ulm TMS from misuse. Personnel working at the TMS are subject to professional discretion and are instructed as to the relevant regulation with regard to the protection of personal data. For more technical details concerning the structure, data, or usage of the Ulm TMS, see Mergenthaler (1985).

Research Accomplishments

Space limitations do not allow us to describe the many studies that have been performed with the help of the Ulm TMS methodology. The service has been used by researchers studying group dynamics, family interactions, individual psychotherapy process, Balint group dynamics, genetic counseling, sociological interviews, and psychiatric interviews. Our own work is focusing on psychoanalytic processes and has already been described briefly in the previous sections. One example of the international aspects of the TMS project is our study on Luborsky's 10 improved and unimproved cases from the Penn study, in which we analyzed the vocabulary for cues to the helping alliance.

Research Programs in Progress

Hypotheses

Speech is the most important tool in psychotherapy for both therapist and patient. At least two basic aspects of speech may be differentiated. First, speech is a medium to transfer information from one person to another. Second, it is a way of expressing a person's idiosyncratic characteristics. Use of language in the former sense seems to involve primarily conscious processes. The latter aspect, however, may be more related to the unconscious. Thus, language may be a good source to determine what constitutes therapeutic change in terms of both conscious and unconscious processes. Content-analytic or theme-oriented analyses reflect conscious activities. Linguistic variables are influenced by unconscious or inhibited phenomena. In contrast to the situation with content-related aspects of speech, clinicians are not used to considering linguistic variables while in dialog or while performing scientific analyses on transcripts. Thus, this area seems to be a good field for computer-aided techniques.

Tentative Findings

One study underway investigates vocabulary change in short-term therapy, focusing on emotion words. The construction of an emotion word dictionary in the framework of Dahl's emotion theory allows a description of the development of therapy in terms of specific changes in verbalized emotions.

Another investigation is analyzing the distribution of parts of speech: Nouns, verbs, and adjectives are the most prominent parts of speech. Each of them represents important underlying concepts such as states, activities, and properties. There is evidence that the distribution of these variables changes over time according to the therapeutic process and underlying emotions. In a pilot study, this measure was applied to patients' responses during a projective psychological test. Two groups of 30 neurotic and 30 borderline patients were clearly differentiated by the more frequent usage of verbs by the neurotic group.

A pilot study relating heart rate with various TMS measures in a single-case approach has shown promise. The findings were interpreted in terms of conflict-related and inhibited themes that have been evaluated by means of other methodological approaches and scholars in the same material. There is evidence of highly significant convergence of computer-assisted text analysis and other methodologies. This study is being done in collaboration with the Program for the Study of Conscious and Unconscious Mental Processes at the University of California, San Francisco (Horowitz and Stinson; see chapter 13), which is funded by the John D. and Catherine T. MacArthur Foundation.

An analysis of speaker sequences in family and group therapy as well as (mathematical models and procedures for the graphical representation of speaker sequences, has been developed and applied to a few family therapy sessions. The findings show clear differences among families. Concerning diagnostic aspects, however, this technique has not yet yielded systematic insights.

Initial steps toward the computerized measurement of Bucci's (1988) referential activity have been completed and appear to be promising. The project will be continued with attention to procedures applicable to both English and German text sources. This study is being done in collaboration with Wilma Bucci from the Derner Institute, Adelphi University and is funded by the Fund for Psychoanalytic Research of the American Psychoanalytic Association.

Programs Planned for the Future

Computer-aided text analysis has proven to be a valuable tool in psychoanalytic process research (Kächele & Mergenthaler, 1984). Further progress, however, requires the development of methods that can overcome the deficiencies of present techniques. This means that techniques from related scientific disciplines, such as information science and linguistics, have to become integrated more extensively. In fact, Teller (1988) has proposed artificial intelligence as a basic science for psychoanalytic research.

At the Ulm TMS project, we prefer the term *knowledge-based text analysis,* which taps insights from artificial intelligence as well as cognitive science. This approach integrates commonsense reasoning, theoretical and experienced-based knowledge provided by a therapist, and idiographic knowledge of a specific patient's idiosyncratic history. The first steps we have taken in this direction focus on childhood memories. Formal definitions of what constitute childhood memories have been developed using a first-order predicate logic calculus. Two early memories, each of them occurring twice in one patient's psychoanalytic treatment, have been entered into a computer-knowledge base with the PROLOGUE programming language. In the next step, we will attempt to input all 45 childhood memories from this patient. In a systematic approach, these early memories can undergo further analyses to reveal underlying general structures.

A more practical approach will involve the development of a psychotherapy researcher's "tool kit." With a hypertext approach, this tool kit will include tools for archiving, retrieving, analyzing, annotating, and editing textual sources with one application on a personal computer.

Sophisticated tools for text analysis, as outlined above, will provide better access to and important insights into the nature of therapeutic processes. The use of well-defined and clearly restricted domains as models of the real world will provide an opportunity to identify the salient features of clinical judgment.

Nature of the Research Organization

The TMS project began in 1980 in the Department of Psychotherapy (chaired by H. Thomä) as part of Collaborative Research Program 129 ("psychotherapeutic processes") of the German Research Foundation. After 9 years of funding, the Ulm TMS became a regular part of the University of Ulm within the structure of the newly established section on computer science in psychotherapy directed by Mergenthaler.

Relation to Other Research Programs

The services of the Ulm TMS are available essentially free of charge to scientific institutions. Charges are made only for the costs of labor-intensive tasks, such as the transcription of tape recordings, and for universities there are small charges for materials. In return, it is expected that once texts are added they will remain in the TMS and be accessible to other scientists. For text material lent by TMS, it is expected that a copy of the report of any work that uses this material will be supplied to the Ulm TMS. In this way, an increasing amount of knowledge about the texts from different disciplines can be stored in the TMS and made available to others. The Ulm TMS is open to all who wish to store their own texts there. The opportunity for routine or individually tailored text analyses, the convenience of text management, and the various options for different outputs make the TMS a unique resource in psychotherapy research.

In 9 years of TMS activities, it has become apparent that psychotherapy research can no longer be an isolated discipline relying only on clinicians' experience and expertise. An interdisciplinary approach involving medical doctors, psychologists, computer scientists, and linguists has proved to be a more successful one.

References

Boder, D. P. (1940). The adjective-verb-quotient: A contribution to the psychology of language. *Psychological Record, 3,* 310–343.

Bucci, W. (1988). Converging evidence for emotional structures: Theory and method. In H. Dahl, H. Kächele, & H. Thomä (Ed.), *Psychoanalytic process research strategies* (pp. 29–49). Berlin, Federal Republic of Germany: Springer-Verlag.

Busemann, A. (1925). *Die sprache der jugend als ausdruck der entwicklungsrhythmik.* Jena.

Cierpka, M., Ohlmeier, D., & Schaumburg, C. (1980). Personalpronomina als Indikatoren für interpersonale Beziehunger in einer psychoanalytischen Gruppentherapie. *Psychotherapy and Medical Psychology, 30,* 212–217.

Cierpka, M., Ohlmeier, D., & Schaumburg, C. (1983). Die Veränderungen im Gebrauch von Personalpronomina während einer psychoanalytischen Gruppentherapie. *Gruppensychotherapie Gruppendynamik, 18,* 205–216.

Clippinger, J. (1977). *Meaning and discourse: A computer model of psychoanalytic speech and cognition.* Baltimore: Johns Hopkins University Press.

Dahl, H. (1972). A quantitative study of psychoanalysis. In R. R. Holt & E. Peterfreund (Eds.), *Psychoanalysis and contemporary science* (pp. 237–257). New York: Macmillan.

Dahl, H. (1974). The measurement of meaning in psychoanalysis by computer analysis of verbal context. *Journal of the American Psychoanalytic Association, 22,* 37–57.

Eisenmann, F. (1973). *Die satzkonjunktionen in gesprochener sprache.* Tübingen: Niemeyer.

Gottschalk, L. A. (1974). Quantification and psychological indicators of emotions: The content analysis of speech and other objective measures of psychological states. *International Journal of Psychiatry in Medicine, 5,* 587–611.

Gottschalk, L., & Gleser, G. (1969). *The measurement of psychological states through the content analysis of verbal behavior.* Berkeley: University of California Press.

Grünzig, H., & Kächele, H. (1978). Zur Differenzierung psychoanalytischer Angstkonzepte: Ein empirischer Beitrag zur automatischen Klassifikation klinischen Materials. *Zeitschrift für Klinische Psychologie, 7,* 1–17.

Grünzig, H. J., & Mergenthaler, E. (1986). Computerunterstützte Ansätze. Empirische Untersuchungen am Beispiel der Angstthemen. In U. Koch & G. Schöfer (Eds.), *Sprachinhaltsanalyse in der psychosomatischen und psychiatrischen forschung: Grundlagen- und anwendungsstudien mit den affektskalen von Gottschalk and Gleser* (pp. 203–212).

Weinheim, Federal Republic of Germany: Psychologie-Verlags Union.

Kächele, H. (1976). *Maschinelle inhaltsanalyse in der psychoanalytischen prozessforschung.* University of Ulm: PSZ-Verlag.

Kächele, H. (1983). Verbal activity level of therapists in initial interviews and long-term psychoanalysis. In W. Minsel & W. Herff (Eds.), *Methodology in psychotherapy research* (pp. 125–129). Frankfurt, Federal Republic of Germany: Lang.

Kächele, H., & Mergenthaler, E. (1984). Auf dem Wege zur computerunterstützten Textanalyse in der psychotherapeutischen Prozeßforschung. In U. Baumann (Ed.), *Psychotherapie: Marko-/Mikroperspektive* (pp. 223–239). Göttingen, Federal Republic of Germany: Hogrefe.

Koch, U., & Schöfer, G. (1986). *Sprachinhaltsanalyse in der psychosomatischen und psychiatrischen forschung.* Weinheim, Federal Republic of Gemany: Psychologie-Verlags Union.

Lolas, F., Mergenthaler, E., & Von Rad, M. (1982). Content analysis of verbal behaviour in psychotherapy research: A comparison between two methods. *British Journal of Medical Psychology, 55,* 327–333.

Lorenz, M., & Cobbs, S. (1975). *Language and a woman's place.* New York: Harper & Row.

Mergenthaler, E. (1985). *Textbank systems: Computer science applied in the field of psychoanalysis.* Berlin, Federal Republic of Germany: Springer-Verlag.

Mergenthaler, E., & Kächele, H. (1985). Changes of latent meaning structures in psychoanalysis. *Sprache und Datenverarbeitung, 9,* 21–28.

O'Dell, J., & Winder, P. (1975). Evaluation of a content-analysis system for therapeutic interview. *Journal of Clinical Psychology, 31,* 737–744.

Pepinsky, H. B. (1979). *A computer-assisted language analysis system (CALAS) and its applications.* ERIC Document Reproduction Service.

Reynes, R., Martindale, C., & Dahl, H. (1984). Lexical differences between working and resistance sessions in psychoanalysis. *Journal of Clinical Psychology, 40,* 733–737.

Spence, D. P. (1968). The processing of meaning in psychotherapy: Some links with psycholinguistics and information theory. *Behavior Science, 13,* 349–361.

Teller, V. (1988). Artificial intelligence as a basic science for psychoanalytic research. In H. Dahl, H. Kächele, & H. Thomä (Eds.), *Psychoanalytic process research strategies* (pp. 163–177). Berlin, Federal Republic of Germany: Springer-Verlag.

Teller, V., & Dahl, H. (1981). The framework for a model of psychoanalytic inference. *Proceedings of IJCAI, 1,* 394–400.

Wirtz, E., & Kächele, H. (1983). Emotive aspects of therapeutic language: A pilot study on verb-adjective-ratio. In W. Minsel & W. Herff (Eds.), *Methodology and psychotherapy research* (pp. 130–135). Frankfurt, Federal Republic of Germany: Lang.

Zimmer, J., & Cowles, K. (1972). Content analysis using FORTRAN. *Journal of Counseling Psychology, 19,* 161–166.

27

University of Ulm: Interactional Processes in Psychotherapy

Dietmar Czogalik
Center for Psychotherapy Research
University of Ulm

Background and Aims

History

The Interactional Processes in Psychotherapy research program represents one research endeavor at the Center for Psychotherapy Research in Stuttgart, Federal Republic of Germany. The research program consists of three consecutive projects: stochastic models of structure and process in psychotherapeutic interaction, structure and process of psychotherapeutic interaction: single-case studies with a multiple-level approach, and patterns of regulation and control in psychotherapeutic interaction.

The research program was initiated by the doctoral dissertation of Czogalik (1979). In this work, Czogalik studied changes in the interactional system during the course of psychotherapy (e.g., phase phenomena). The interactional system was described by means of the sequential systematic of the verbalizations of therapist and patient and was analyzed with stochastic models. The project based on this work, stochastic models of structure and process in psychotherapeutic interaction, was conducted between 1983 and 1985 and financed by the German Research Foundation (Czogalik, 1983, 1989b).

Consequently, we started another project concerned with the structure and process of psychotherapeutic interaction that focused on single-

case studies with a multiple-level approach (Czogalik & Hettinger, 1987, 1988; Czogalik; Hettinger, Bechtinger-Czogalik, & Ehlers, 1990). Here, in addition to applying stochastic models, we used multivariate process procedures (e.g., P-technique factor analysis). This project also was supported by the German Research Foundation from 1986 to 1988. Both projects were organized under Special Collaborated Research Program 129 at Ulm University. This program is a conglomerate of research groups (Chair, Kächele) that deals empirically with behavioral, text-analytical, and psychophysiological procedures and approaches in the area of psychotherapeutic processes.

In 1989, we began a project that deals with clinical questions more directly than the preceding ones. In this project, we pursued and consolidated the interactional and process findings previously obtained. This project on patterns of regulation and control in the psychotherapeutic interaction of patients with eating disorders is supported by the Center for Psychotherapy Research and (potentially) by the German Research Foundation.

Overall Aims

The most basic objective of our research program is to contribute empirical data to investigations of psychotherapeutic processes. Psychotherapy process research deals with the conceptualization and exploration of change over time. Included under the heading of "process research" are studies that differ in objectives, methodology, and operationalization and that encompass a heterogeneous field. We have based our research on those approaches that are concerned with analyzing patterns of interaction and relationships among variables. The following questions are thus addressed in our studies: What are the basic processes of therapeutic change? What are the relevant units of process, change, or development? Which measurement instruments and methods can describe these units and their temporal interrelations? Which strategy best organizes the steps of analysis?

Within the overall objective of our studies there are three major subareas of investigation. First the search for the phases and segments in psychotherapy that might be described by specific interactions and functional interrelationships. Explicit assumptions about the existence of phases are of great importance in process research because they provide a counterpoint with respect to the implicit assumptions of uniformity.

Another related quest is to discover the variables, events, and characteristics of psychotherapeutic interaction that are especially process sensitive. We are searching for an economical and reliable system of classifying variables that reflects relevant changes in the course of therapy.

The categories and variables of nonverbal behavior are becoming increasingly important in our research project. The assumption that nonverbal behavior plays a great role in the regulation of interpersonal relationships has been repeatedly verified. Hence, the second subarea of our investigation will be to utilize nonverbal parameters for the longitudinal analysis of psychotherapeutic dialog.

Although the foregoing research objectives all focus on an academic understanding of psychotherapy, they are not specific to the clinical questions and specific problem areas that often are of importance to the clinician. Hence, the third subarea of study will guide our future research and deals with problems of direct clinical relevance, namely regulating interactional patterns in psychotherapy among anorexic patients. This investigation will be based on results obtained in earlier phases of our program, will use the measurement instruments we have developed, and will use time-tested methods of analysis.

In dealing with these issues, social psychological concepts of psychotherapy (e.g., Strong & Claiborn, 1982) serve as points of reference and as

a meta-theoretical integral. With this background, we have tried to formulate a social psychological-oriented process model for psychotherapeutic interaction (Czogalik, 1989b).

Method

A single-case approach to data gathering is the most appropriate for achieving the aims of this research program. Such an approach allows the elucidation of temporal and contextual aspects of psychotherapy. We assume that the structure and process of psychotherapeutic interaction are organized in a dyad-specific way. This does not preclude general or differential statements (e.g., with respect to functional components of the therapist–patient interaction). Indeed, a body of knowledge built up by the accumulation of results from comprehensive single-case studies may lend support to such statements.

The complexity of psychotherapeutic processes requires comprehensive analytical strategies, attention to a multitude of variables, assessment of the interaction among them, and the presence of time-dependent relationships. The intention of a multilevel approach is to obtain measures of mutually compensating, converging, or supplementing relationships. Every judgment system (e.g., self-report, external rating, clinical judgment) has its own strengths and weaknesses, and so they all become mutually enhancing. For example, sessions characterized by long intermissions lend themselves to equivocal interpretations; one may invoke concepts of either resistance or cognitive exposition. The presence of additional views of the process (e.g., evaluation of the session by the patient) may limit alternative explanations and highlight the most probable ones.

In our multilevel approach, we mainly use four rating sources and perspectives of the process that embody operational independence. These perspectives and rating sources include the perspective of interactional behavior judged by external raters, the perspective of session evaluation as judged by patient and therapist, the perspective of objective speech characteristics, and the perspective of clinical judgment.

Subjects and Selection

In our initial analysis of the psychotherapy process, we have used audiotaped dialogs from the following types of psychotherapy: 11 client-centered therapies (ranging from 4 to 28 sessions), 2 short-term insight therapies (29 and 30 sessions), 1 behavior therapy (29 sessions), and 3 psychodynamic-oriented therapies (ranging from 82 to 127 sessions). The selection of a specific therapy was not based on clinical criteria such as diagnosis, success, or therapist's experience. Our aim was to have a complete series of documented psychotherapeutic dialogs. The only criterion of selection was the willingness of both client (real client) and therapist (real therapist) to participate. In our most recent project, however, which started in 1989, we used a sample of therapists working with patients with eating disorders.

Instruments

The different therapies included in our initial project were evaluated with different measuring instruments. We emphasized procedures that could be used to represent the interactional verbal behavior. First, we used a categorization system similar to that used by Lichtenberg and Hummel (1976) because it allowed us to analyze the first 9 client-centered therapy cases with Markov models. For the remaining therapy cases we modified and amended this basic system, and it has since been incorporated as the Stuttgart Category Inventory for Interactional Analysis.

In addition to this inventory, which represents an external rating perspective of interactional behaviors, session evaluation questionnaires were filled out by therapist and client at the end of each session. These questionnaires represent the self-report perspective. In a few therapy cases represented in our early projects, we assessed additional variables such as affects of therapist and client, on–off patterns, therapeutic productivity, resistance of the client and others. In cases in which we were able to categorize and quantify the therapist's judgment, we included this variable as an additional perspective in the multilevel analysis.

Procedures

We have relied on two primary methodological strategies: the P-technique (Cattell, 1963) and Markov chain analysis (e.g., Hertel, 1972). These methods address different process concepts. The P-technique describes process as the quantitative variation of structural units. A structural unit or factor is formed by a specific set of variables, and the variables of this set stand in a constant, invariant relationship over time (we accepted only such units for which this condition is true). Thus, with the P-technique we attempt to show the quantitative change of qualitatively unchanging units over the course of therapy.

On the other hand, Markov analysis (as we use it) describes process primarily as a temporal sequence of qualitatively differing structural units (e.g., Anderson, 1955). A structural unit in the Markov model means that the interactional system (in terms of the sequential dependencies of verbal behavior of therapist and patient) remains stable for a specific time segment or episode (stationarity of the process). Thus, Markov analysis enables one to demonstrate the nature of qualitative changes in the interactional structure over the course of therapy.

These two analytical methods differ in that the P-technique concentrates on frequency, whereas the Markov model concentrates on the sequence of events (Russell & Czogalik, 1989). The aim of both methods is to discover meaningful episodes that occur over the course of therapy and that are governed by specific but distinct interactional systems.

Research Accomplishments

Findings

All 17 single-case studies were investigated by means of extensive process analyses among several levels. In all cases, every individual utterance issued by both patient and therapist was evaluated by means of the Stuttgart Category Inventory. Because we could not use all of the measuring instruments or measuring procedures available for every individual case, the data obtained were incomplete and could not be aggregated as complete sets to test each hypothesis. Because the single-case approach has limited generalizability of results, we have not relied heavily on single-case findings, and the aggregated findings can be understood best in terms of weighted casuistics.

The major accomplishments to date are now described.

We found that relationships exist between interaction patterns and the evaluations of those interactions. Clinically meaningful relationships were observed in all cases in which it was possible both to measure real interactional behavior and to obtain the evaluation of the interaction by the participants (12 cases). The nature of these relationships was dyad specific. For example, the more one therapist paraphrased or reflected, the less comfortable her client felt; the more another therapist referred to the client, the more the client became resistant. In still another example, the therapist's expressed contentment was positively related to the frequency with which the client addressed themes from her childhood. In general, the interactional variables with the strongest association to the therapist's and client's evaluations of the interaction were variables such as cognitive–affective involvement of the client and the type of therapeutic intervention (Czogalik, 1979; Czogalik & Hettinger, 1987).

When we evaluated psychotherapeutic interaction with a Markov model (11 cases), we found that for most of the cases there were therapy phases or segments in which different interactional structures (i.e., specific sequential patterns of verbal behavior) dominated. The therapy segments of phases that were revealed in this manner were not consistent enough to conclude that a generalized pattern of phases exist: Some therapies were very much segmented, and others were not. An exception to the idiosyncratic patterning of phases was found in the consistency with which the initial sessions of the therapies could be identified as a separate phase. We interpret this consistency as indicating the presence of an early orientation and adjustment period (Czogalik, 1983).

On the basis of our category system, it was shown that thematic reference (e.g., topic following, topic initiation, etc.) and mutual reference (e.g., asking questions, continuing the conversation, etc.) were sensitive indicators of psychologically meaningful phase or change phenomena. This means that the patterns of interaction revealed a serial dependency (from the client's utterance to the following utterance of the therapist, and vice versa) and that the structure of this dependency changed over the course of psychotherapy for most cases examined (Czogalik et al., 1990).

When we looked at the temporal development of the interactional patterns obtained with the P-technique, we also discovered significant and stable dyad-specific different patterns of interaction. For example, we found some segments that were dominated by therapist interventions, other segments that were characterized by client involvement and self-processing, still other segments representing external talk, and still other segments that contained a specific thematic focus

(such as the therapist–client relationship). Although these patterns were apparent, the nature and order of the sequences did not allow us to conclude that clear-cut, generalizable phases occur in psychotherapy (Czogalik & Hettinger, 1987; Czogalik, 1989a, 1989b).

The variables that were most likely to reflect process characteristics (i.e., followed temporal patterns) were self-reports of therapist–client interactions, external ratings of the therapist's interventions, and external ratings of client cognitive–affective involvement (Czogalik & Hettinger, 1988).

In most of the therapy cases that were analyzed, we discovered variables whose relationships with perceived interactions changed significantly during the course of treatment (e.g., from a positive to a negative correlation). These results suggest that interactional patterns change during the course of therapy and as a specific function of the patient–client dyad. Because they are so dependent on the particular client and therapist, these results not only contradict uniformity assumptions but also refute the belief that therapy follows a general and idealized sequence of phases (Czogalik & Hettinger, 1987, 1988).

It is our impression that the delineation of styles and patterns of interaction and analyses of their regulative and developmental characteristics offer a promising strategy for the study of psychotherapeutic processes (Czogalik, Bechtinger-Czogalik, & Hettinger, 1989; Czogalik & Russell, 1990). The extensive every session–every utterance strategy we used, however, does not seem necessary to obtain usable information from therapy sessions. Most of the information that this intensive analysis provides can be gained with a criterion-directed strategy (i.e., the criteria designate which sessions should be analyzed comprehensively). Appropriate criteria can be acquired by session-evaluation questionnaires.

Instruments Developed

Within the scope of our research program, we developed and tested a series of measurement instruments. Among them were scales for the assessment of events or characteristics such as self-disclosure of the therapist, interpretation by the therapist, client verbalization of symptoms, productivity of the session, client resistance, and interactional behaviors of therapists and clients. The variable that is most important to the understanding of treatment effect is the interactional behaviors that are observed. This class of variables was, and still is, the central focus of our research program. To describe reliably the interactional behavior of therapist and client, we developed the Stuttgart Categories Inventory (Stuttgarter Kategorien Inventar). With this instrument, more than 60,000 utterances have been assessed and evaluated by a number of raters (Czogalik, Hettinger, & Bechtinger-Czogalik, 1987; Czogalik et al., 1989). It is a multiple-level inventory; every utterance of the clinician and client is assessed simultaneously on different dimensions. Each statement is classified according to the following modes:

• mode of verbal representation of involvement (8 categories that allow ratings of utterance along such dimensions as their affective, cognitive, or evaluative nature);

• mode of mutual reference (8 categories that allow ratings of such behaviors as agreeing, disagreeing, inviting, or demanding continuation);

• intervention and processing mode (10 categories that allow rating of such characteristic behaviors as searching, exploring, confronting, directing, or indulging in fantasies);

• mode of thematic concern (13 categories reflecting such topical themes as the therapist–client relationship, therapeutic rules and goals, focus on primary persons of attachment, or focus on external events);

• mode of temporal reference (5 categories that identify statements that refer to childhood, the recent past, the present, or the future).

This system yields a voluminous amount of category combinations because every utterance is evaluated on several different levels. This method makes it possible to describe the interactional behavior of the therapist and client distinctly. An interpretation made by the therapist is not identified simply as an interpretation but is as an interpretation done with a certain type of reference to the patient, with concern to a specific topic, with a specific time reference, and directed to a specific mode of involvement. The levels (modes) of this observational procedure represent the essential dimensions of the psychotherapeutic interaction, such as the involvement of the client (Level 1), role participation of the client and the discourse partner (Level 2), the therapeutic intervention and self-processing of the client (Level 3), and as-

pects of the thematic temporal references (Levels 4 and 5).

Research Programs in Progress

Hypotheses

Our current research focuses on the conceptualization and measurement of nonverbal behavior as an additional level to the categories of verbal behavior just described. We are concerned primarily with body posture and gestures from longitudinal multiple-level perspectives. This means that nonverbal behavior is observed, classified, and quantified over relatively long time periods and then is analyzed on the basis of its time-specific covariance with other levels of measurement (e.g., verbal behavior).

For assessing body posture, we set forth the following hypotheses and presuppositions:

• The body posture of therapist and client reflects, among other things, moments of meta-communication that cannot be seized adequately on the verbal level alone.

• Interactive markers of body posture such as symmetry, complementarity, and synchrony represent aspects of the predominant relational status or changes in this status that occur during the course of psychotherapy.

• Markers such as redundancy and flexibility represent intraindividual aspects of behavior, such as rigidity and fluency, and the changes that might occur during the course of therapy.

• Nonverbal behavior covaries with verbal behavior, interactional evaluations of behavior, and so forth, to result in specific patterns of interaction behavior. Thus we expect that stable patterns comprising confrontation, cooperation, involvement, ambivalence, and participation of speaker and listener can be identified. Both therapy-specific and dyad-specific interactional rules may come into play in the course of psychotherapy.

Tentative Findings

At the time of this writing, our empirical data are based on 10 of 29 sessions of a short-term insight therapy. Therefore, the present findings are only suggestive. On the basis of impressions of raters,

32 body postures have been identified among the dyads studied. Seven body postures of the client and seven of the therapist constituted 91.8% and 85.8% of the client's and therapist's behavior repertoire, respectively. Ratings for this reduced set of body postures were reliable and relatively efficient.

We have also demonstrated that body postures are synchronous. In our studies, this synchrony was initiated by the client and was firmly established by the third therapeutic session. Thus, the client only exhibited body postures in the first two therapeutic sessions that were at significant variance from those of the therapist. After these early sessions, the client adopted the two basic postures of the therapist. Moreover, after initial contact the therapist began to react to the changes in the client's body posture by making accommodating changes in his or her own body posture. We interpret the client's initiation of synchrony as a reflection of a positive relationship and the therapist's response as an indication of an empathetic orientation toward the client.

To date, two meaningful patterns of interaction between verbal and nonverbal behavior have been identified. The first pattern is represented when the client leans backward with the legs crossed, head supported, and a diagonal frontal axis and is gesturing from time to time with the free hand. The dominant verbal material expressed in this posture is information, description, or (with less gesturing) reception. We describe this posture as the *relaxed reception* or *information* posture. It corresponded optically with the therapist's usual posture.

In the second pattern the client sits slightly erect with both elbows resting on the arms of the chair, gesturing with both hands; the head is bent forward, and there is a vertical frontal axis. The dominant verbal material expressed in this posture contains aspects of involvement and self-referential information. We describe this type of body language as *involved description* or *disclosing*.

Programs Planned for the Future

New Directions and Hypotheses

New research questions will be defined on the basis of proved instruments and strategies (Czogalik, 1989a; Czogalik & Russell, 1990) and will concern the dyads to be investigated. The focus will be an eating disorder, anorexia nervosa. Psychotherapy of anorexia nervosa is considered to be interactionally difficult for many reasons, including the patient's generally poor motivation, ambivalent goals, and powerful countermove strategies as well the therapist's affective countertransference moments. Frequently, the result is an interactional dyad consisting of an affectively directed helper reaction (supporting, overprotecting, manipulating, or punishing) by the therapist and a tactically directed complementary reaction by the client.

From this background, we hypothesize that effective therapeutic behavior with anorexic patients will differ significantly from ordinary therapeutic behavior because the different goals, strategies, and interactional demands that characterize treatment of these patients. To test this hypothesis, we plan to compare therapists' treatment of anorexic patients with their treatment of other patients. The interactional styles of clients and therapists will be delineated with multiple-level measuring instruments to facilitate the effort to describe the regulative characteristics or patterns that are present.

Significance

We are entering unexplored research territory, in which there is the possibility of making new and startling discoveries that could influence theories about therapist–client interactions and relationships. Furthermore, such studies can provide information that contributes to effective matching procedures. We also hope to gain additional information about anorexia nervosa, at least concerning interactive components and the corresponding system-maintaining strategies used.

Nature of the Research Organization

From 1983 to 1988, the two research projects then underway were funded entirely by the German Research Foundation with additional support from the Research Center for Psychotherapy. The research project beginning in 1989 is part of the regular program of the Research Center for Psychotherapy. Additional funding has been requested from the German Research Foundation.

Relation to Other Research Programs

Integration With Findings of Other Research

Our research program focuses on developing an understanding of psychotherapy processes. Our work has been influenced by the work of Kiesler (1973), Rice and Greenberg (1984), and Greenberg and Pinsof (1986). Our search is for the anatomy of change. Our research program includes metatheory and methodology. Over the years, our work has increasingly adopted a social-psychologic metatheory. The interactional paradigm underlying our work is reflective of the work of Strong (1982) and Strong and Claiborn (1982), and our system paradigm reflects the influence of Lennard and Bernstein (1960, 1969). Accordingly, our findings can easily be interpreted as supportive of the view of psychotherapy as a process of social influence, information exchange, or change through interaction.

In our work two methods have proved to be valuable: stochastic models and multiple-level analysis with the aid of P-technique. The use of stochastic models as process models of interaction items is based on the work of Raush (1965), Lichtenberg and Heck (1986), and others (see also Highlen, 1986). The temporal course of defined events is described by the specific system of sequential dependencies. From the beginning, our research has focused on the question of whether the system changes over the course of therapy and the characteristics of different therapeutic phases. The findings obtained from such a strategy lead (with limited generalizability) to a phase conception of the course of psychotherapeutic interaction as advocated by Tracey (1985) and Tracey and Ray (1985), for example.

P-technique was derived from Cattell (1963) and the empirical work of Luborsky (1953). The small amount of empirical literature available on the application of this method to psychotherapeutic research (e.g., Mook, 1982a, 1982b; Mintz, Luborsky, & Auerback, 1971) reports on structural characteristics that describe specific kinds of therapeutic behavior (e.g., interventions, minimal activity, confrontation, or support) and specific kinds of client behavior (e.g., self-exploration, information giving, or active resistance). The temporal course of these structural units emphasizes the developmental characteristic of psychotherapeutic interaction, which corresponds with our findings.

Impact on the Field of Psychotherapy

The road from research to clinical practice is long, arduous, intricate, and seldom traveled. With all modesty, we do not claim that our findings will directly influence clinical practice. On the other hand, we see our work as part of a research paradigm from which relevant application to clinical practice will evolve. Interactional process research can have clinical utility when it involves questions of client–therapist matching or prediction of outcome. The objective of interactional process research is to extract empirically the sequence of interactional patterns that are associated with constructive therapeutic processes and those patterns that are not. This type of research might shed some light on prognosis by means of the interactional fit of the participants.

More concrete, however, will be the gain in knowledge from our current project, for this will have a more direct impact on clinical practice. We hope to gain important knowledge by comparing interactionally difficult clients with ordinary clients. This will yield gains for the therapist with respect to treatment competence.

The road leading from scientific research to education, too, is a long one. We believe that additional information about the anatomy of change, in and through interaction will benefit travelers along this road. For example, findings in process research could provide clues for answering the question, what can one do, at what point in time, with which client? Clarifying this issue is as important for clinical training as it is for clinical practice.

References

Anderson, T. W. (1955). Probability models for analysing time changes in attitudes. In P. Lazarsfeld (Ed.), *Mathematical thinking in the social sciences*. New York: Plenum Press.

Cattell, R. B. (1963). The structuring of change by P-technique and incremental R-technique. In C. W. Harris (Ed.), *Problems in measuring change*. Madison: University of Wisconsin Press.

Czogalik, D. (1979). *Markoff-kette als prozeß-modell zur bescheibung der psychotherapeutischen interaktion*. Unpublished doctoral dissertation, University of Vienna, Vienna, Austria.

Czogalik, D. (1979). *Markoff-kette als prozeß-modell zur bescheibung der psychotherapeutischen interaktion.* Unpublished doctoral dissertation, University of Vienna, Vienna, Austria.

Czogalik, D. (1983). Markoff-Ketten als Prozeßmodelle zur Beschreibung der psychotherapeutischen Interaktion. In H. Enke, V. Tschuschke, & W. Volk (Eds.), *Psychotherapeutisches Handeln.* Stuttgart, Federal Republic of Germany: Kohlhammer.

Czogalik, D. (1989a, September). *Interactional change processes in psychotherapy: An empirical and conceptual approach.* Paper presented at the Third European Conference on Psychotherapy Research, Bern, Switzerland.

Czogalik, D. (1989b). *Psychotherapie als prozeß: Mehrebenenananlytische untersuchungen zu struktur und verlauf psychotherapeutischer interaktionen.* Unpublished manuscript, University of Ulm, Stuttgart, Federal Republic of Germany.

Czogalik, D., Bechtinger-Czogalik, S., & Hettinger, R. (1989, September). *Structures and processes in psychotherapeutic interaction: A conceptual and methodological approach using the Stuttgart-Categories-Inventory.* Paper presented at the Third European Conference on Psychotherapy Research, Bern, Switzerland.

Czogalik, D., & Hettinger, R. (1987). The process of psychotherapeutic interaction—A single case study. In W. Huber (Ed.), *Progress in psychotherapy research.* Louvain, Belgium: University of Louvain Press.

Czogalik, D., & Hettinger, R. (1988). Mehrebenenanalyse der psychotherapeutischen Interaktion: Eine Verlaufsstudie am Einzelfall. *Zietschrift für Klinische Psychologie, 17,* 31–45.

Czogalik, D., Hettinger, R., Bechtinger-Czogalik, D., & Ehlers, W. (1990). Strategien, Konzepte und Modelle für die Analyse psycho-therapeutischer Interaktionsprozesse. In H. Kachele, P. Novak, & H. C. Traue (Eds.), *Krankheit und psychotherapeutische prozesse—Interdisziplinre analysen.* Weinheim, Federal Republic of Germany: VCH Verlagsgesellschaft.

Czogalik, D., & Russell, R. L. (1990). *Analysis of structure and process of psychotherapeutic interaction.* Unpublished manuscript.

Greenberg, L. S., & Pinsof, W. (Eds.). (1986). *The psychotherapeutic process: A research handbook.* New York: Guilford Press.

Hertel, R. K. (1972). Application of stochastic process analyses to the study of psychotherapeutic process. *Psychological Bulletin, 77,* 421–430.

Highlen, P. S. (1986). Analyzing patterns and sequence in counseling: Reactions of a counseling process researcher. *Journal of Counseling Psychology, 33* 186–189.

Kiesler, D. J. (1973). *The process of psychotherapy.* Chicago: Aldine Publishing.

Lennard, H. L., & Bernstein, A. (1960). *The anatomy of psychotherapy.* New York: Columbia University Press.

Lennard, H. L., & Bernstein, A. (1969). *Patterns in human interaction.* San Francisco: Jossey-Bass.

Lichtenberg, J. W., & Heck, E. J. (1986). Analysis of sequence and pattern in process research. *Journal of Counseling Psychology, 33,* 170–189.

Lichtenberg, J. W., & Hummel, T. I. (1976). Counseling as stochastic process: Fitting Markov chain model to initial counseling interviews. *Journal of Counseling Psychology, 23,* 310–315.

Luborsky, L. (1953). Repeated intra-individual measurements (P-technique) in understanding symptom structure and psychotherapeutic change. In O. H. Mowrer (Ed.), *Psychotherapy: Theory and research.* New York: Ronald Press.

Mintz, J., Luborsky, L., & Auerbach, A. H. (1971). Dimensions of psychotherapy: A factor-analytic study of ratings of psychotherapy sessions. *Journal of Consulting and Clinical Psychology, 36,* 106–110.

Mook, B. (1982a). Analyses of therapist variables in a series of psychotherapy sessions with two child clients. *Journal of Clinical Psychology, 38,* 63–76.

Mook, B. (1982b). Analyses of client variables in a series of psychotherapy sessions with two child clients. *Journal of Clinical Psychology, 38,* 263–274.

Raush, H. L. (1965). Interaction sequences. *Journal of Personality and Social Psychology, 2,* 487–499.

Rice, L. N., & Greenberg, L. S. (Eds.). (1984). *Patterns of change.* New York: Guilford Press.

Russell, R. L., & Czogalik, D. (1989). Strategies for analyzing conversation: Frequencies, sequences, or rules. *Journal of Social Behavior and Personality, 4,* 221–236.

Strong, S. R. (1982). Emerging integrations of clinical and social psychology: A clinician's perspective. In G. Weary & H. L. Mirels (Eds.), *Integrations of clinical and social psychology.* Oxford, England: Oxford University Press.

Strong, S. R., & Claiborn, D. C. (1982). *Change through interaction.* New York: Wiley.

Tracey, T. J. (1985). Dominance and outcome: A sequential examination. *Journal of Counseling Psychology, 32,* 119–122.

Tracey, T. J., & Ray, P. B. (1985). The stages of successful counseling: An interactional examination. *Journal of Counseling Psychology, 31,* 13–27.

28

University of Sheffield Psychotherapy Research Program: Medical Research Council–Economic and Social Research Council Social and Applied Psychology Unit

**David A. Shapiro, Michael Barkham, Gillian E. Hardy, Leslie A. Morrison,
Shirley Reynolds, Mike Startup, and Heather Harper**
University of Sheffield

Background and Aims

The Psychotherapy Research Program of the University of Sheffield is founded on the assumption that the development of more effective forms of psychotherapy is most efficiently pursued by combining comparative outcome studies with the concurrent collection of data on the constituent processes in each treatment. To maximize the theoretical yield of this research, we focus on treatments with sharply differing theoretical rationales and procedures. The efficient development of any research program requires strategic decisions informed by careful and systematic consideration of the existing literature. The program described here is guided by six conclusions from our conceptual and quantitative reviews of the field.

Three considerations relate to outcome research. First, research attention has been disproportionately devoted to behavioral and cognitive methods to the neglect of psychodynamic, interpersonal, and experiential therapies (Shapiro &

Shapiro, 1977, 1982, 1983). Second, evidence that psychotherapies are in general effective in comparison with no treatment is sufficiently strong (Lambert, Shapiro, & Bergin, 1986; Shapiro & Shapiro, 1982) that the ethical and logistic costs of including no-treatment control groups are not warranted. Third, too much of the better designed research has been analogic in nature (Shapiro & Shapiro, 1983); there is a need for comparative outcome research that uses clinically realistic treatments with referred patients in clinically realistic settings. In addition, outcome research should pay attention to clinical as well as statistical significance in evaluating change and in presenting case outcomes.

Three further considerations bear on process–outcome research (i.e., studies that seek to describe the mechanisms whereby psychotherapies are effective by empirically relating processes in sessions to the outcome of treatment). First, we

We thank Robert Elliott and William B. Stiles for comments on a draft of this chapter.

have identified an equivalence paradox whereby evidence of broadly similar outcomes of disparate psychological treatments is hard to reconcile with their demonstrably dissimilar contents (Stiles, Shapiro, & Elliott, 1986). This may reflect insufficient precision in research methods or, alternatively, it could reflect the overriding importance of factors common across treatment methods in determining outcome. Our efforts to resolve the paradox involve detailed comparisons between treatments in both process and outcome, including process variables that are specific to each treatment as well as those reflecting factors that are common to all treatments.

Second, most studies seeking to link treatment process with outcome have been implicitly or explicitly guided by oversimplification and overextension of a drug metaphor, in which it is assumed that psychotherapy is usefully conceptualized in terms of effective ingredients delivered impersonally by the therapist to a passively recipient client (Stiles & Shapiro, in press); such research has been less productive than it appears (Shapiro, Harper, & Suokas, 1987). Process–outcome research therefore urgently requires theoretically grounded innovation in measurement, design, and data analysis.

Third, process research requires a distinction between the contents of treatment sessions and the immediate impact of these sessions on participants. This enables studies of session impact to afford valuable insight into the probable contributions of session-by-session occurrences to the eventual outcome of a case.

The Social and Applied Psychology Unit (SAPU) was founded by the U.K. Medical Research Council (MRC) in 1968 to increase understanding of occupational well-being and effectiveness and to identify factors leading to their enhancement. Commencing in 1977, SAPU began its psychotherapy program to complement ongoing stress research. The program's emphasis on substantial projects investigating both processes and outcomes combines a degree of continuity (deriving from the use of similar treatment and investigative methods) with continual evolution of its practical and theoretical concerns.

The program is funded from SAPU's core budget. The staffing and recurrent costs of the psychotherapy program total approximately £200,000 per annum. SAPU is jointly funded in the ratio 2:1 by MRC and the Economic and Social Research Council (ESRC). These are directly government-supported research agencies. SAPU's resource allocations are determined primarily through a review procedure undertaken five times each year, which also guides the unit director concerning the scale and objectives of specific programs in SAPU. The team leader is currently the only tenured scientist in the program; others are typically on 3-year contracts with a possible renewal for a further 3 years. In general, posts remain assigned to the program.

The aims of the program are (a) to develop cost-effective psychological treatments for adults presenting with depression, anxiety, and related disorders, with particular emphasis on the enhancement of clients' well-being and effectiveness at work; (b) to investigate and ameliorate the effects of job stress on clients' well-being and effectiveness; and (c) to advance theoretical understanding of the mechanisms of change in psychological treatments.

The program's studies fall into three interlinked areas: conceptual and quantitative reviews of existing literature to identify the most promising treatment techniques and investigative strategies, large-scale comparative outcome studies of theoretically important and clinically effective treatments, and empirical studies of change mechanisms relating the contents and impacts of therapy sessions to treatment outcomes.

Method

Empirical work is based in our clinic, which accepts referrals from occupational health and welfare services, general practitioners, and psychiatrists. Clients are also recruited through publicity materials distributed at workplaces and through trade unions. These materials describe our service for individuals with depression or anxiety that affects their work. Clients are screened with standard questionnaires such as the SCL-90 or the Beck Depression Inventory and must meet predefined severity levels at screening. Most of our investigations require additional interview and questionnaire measures at intake to ensure that clients meet research diagnostic criteria appropriate to the study in question. Additional exclusion criteria are set for each study. For example, we generally exclude those who have had psychological treatment within a defined period before screening. As in the U.K. National Health Service, our clients pay no fees for therapy.

We use an evolving set of instruments to measure the contents of treatment sessions, their immediate impacts on both clients and therapists, and the outcome of each treatment case. To ensure comparability with other programs, we use standard outcome instruments developed elsewhere.

Interviews are carried out by a trained graduate research assistant. Psychiatric symptomatology is assessed with the Present State Examination (Wing, Cooper, & Sartorius, 1974), which is the standard U.K. measure, with additional items from the Diagnostic Interview Schedule (Eaton & Kessler, 1985) as necessary to establish a diagnosis at intake based on the third edition of the *Diagnostic and Statistical Manual of Mental Disorders* (*DSM III*; American Psychiatric Association, 1980). This is accompanied by the SCL-90 (Derogatis, Lipman, & Covi, 1973) and more specific questionnaire measures of symptoms appropriate to a given study (e.g., the State-Trait Anxiety Inventory [Spielberger, 1983] or the Beck Depression Inventory [Beck, Ward, Mendelson, Mock, & Erbaugh, 1961]). We assess self-esteem with the O'Malley and Bachman (1979) scale. Social adjustment is measured with the Social Adjustment Scale (Weissman & Paykel, 1974) at interview or in its self-report form (Cooper, Osborn, Gath, & Fegetter, 1982). Interpersonal difficulties are assessed with the Inventory of Interpersonal Problems (Horowitz, Rosenberg, Baer, Ureno, & Villasenor, 1988).

Measures of session content have included an adaptation of Elliott's (1979) Helper Behavior Rating System (Shapiro, Barkham, & Irving, 1984) and Stiles's (1979) system of verbal response modes. The impact of treatment sessions is measured with Stiles's (1980) Session Evaluation Questionnaire and Wexler and Elliott's (1988) Session Impacts Questionnaire. In addition, impact over the days after a session is tapped by client-completed personal questionnaires (Barkham, Shapiro, & Firth-Cozens, 1989; Mulhall, 1976). Significant events during treatment sessions are described by clients with Llewelyn's (1985) helpful aspects of therapy form coded according to a taxonomy developed by Elliott, James, Reimschuessel, Cislo, and Sack (1985). Intensive study of significant events during selected sessions uses a version of interpersonal process recall (Elliott, 1986; Elliott & Shapiro, 1988).

Our procedures are designed to maximize the clinical realism of our investigations while retaining the degree of control over patient, therapist, and treatment variables required for informative research on the mechanisms of psychotherapeutic change.

After intake assessment, clients are assigned at random to the treatment conditions under comparison. The 1-hour sessions are recorded. Therapists are qualified clinical psychologists with prior training in the treatment methods under investigation, who are supported by tape-based supervision with both project peers and outside expert practitioners throughout each study. Therapist factors are controlled by having all project therapists deliver all treatments. Each treatment is defined by a manual outlining its principles and procedures. Therapist adherence is assessed with verbal response modes and our adaptation of the Collaborative Study Psychotherapy Rating Scale (Shapiro & Startup, 1988).

All studies compare two treatments chosen to represent the interpersonal–psychodynamic and cognitive–behavioral families of approaches. The interpersonal variant, *exploratory* therapy, is based on Hobson's (1985; Goldberg et al., 1984; Maguire, Hobson, Margison, Moss, & O'Dowd, 1984) conversational model. By means of psychodynamic and experiential concepts, it focuses on the therapist–client relationship as a vehicle for revealing and resolving interpersonal difficulties. The therapist's contributions include adopting a negotiating style, developing a language of mutuality, using metaphor to enhance the immediacy of experienced affect, focusing on here-and-now experiences, and offering hypotheses to express understanding of the client's experiences, linking these together and suggesting causes or reasons for behavior and experience. *Prescriptive* therapy, the cognitive–behavioral therapy, reflects an emphasis on the therapist's prescribing tasks for the client to undertake. It represents multimodal behavioral and cognitive treatments, incorporating anxiety control training (Snaith, 1974), self-management (Goldfried & Merbaum, 1973), cognitive restructuring (Beck, Rush, Shaw, & Emery, 1979; Meichenbaum, 1977), and a work-oriented package derived from management training (Ferner, 1980; Hackman & Suttle, 1977; Taylor, 1979).

Measures of treatment contents are obtained by using coders blind to the study design and hypotheses who are trained to acceptable reliability standards on the instrument in question. The professional level of coders varies with the measure, but all are social science graduates.

All assessment interviews and the completion of session impact measures take place in our clinic, which has an urban location close to the hospitals and university. Clients pass completed forms to the clinic secretary or research assistant and not to the therapist, who does not see any of these data until after the completion of treatment. Some longer questionnaires are completed by clients at home. On recruitment to the study, clients sign a consent form detailing all assignment, assessment, recording, and treatment procedures. This form details a contract between client and clinic in which treatment is offered in return for the client's participation in research procedures. At the end of therapy, clients sign a release form confirming their assent to the use of recordings for research purposes. The advantages offered by our clinic over National Health Service treatment usually include a shorter waiting time and our local reputation for providing specialist expertise in working with specific occupational groups.

Research Accomplishments

The first Sheffield Psychotherapy Project (SPP1; Shapiro & Firth, 1987) compared 8-session blocks of prescriptive and exploratory sessions in a crossover design in which each of 40 professional and managerial employees received both treatments with the same therapist throughout. Verbal response mode profiles of therapists' contributions to the two types of sessions showed large differences in accordance with the manuals' specifications (Hardy & Shapiro, 1985; Stiles, Shapiro, & Firth-Cozens, 1988b). Substantial and clinically significant improvement was shown by clients in the groups assigned to both treatment orders. Somewhat more improvement occurred during the first than during the second block of eight sessions and during prescriptive compared with exploratory therapy (Shapiro & Firth, 1987). In the first eight sessions young clients responded more favorably to prescriptive than to exploratory therapy (Barkham, Firth-Cozens, & Shapiro, in press). Further analysis revealed, however, that the differential effectiveness of the two treatments was confined to the clients of one of the two principal project therapists (Shapiro, Firth-Cozens, & Stiles, 1989) and was reversed among older compared with younger clients (Barkham, Firth-Cozens, & Shapiro, in press).

Analyses of the contents and impacts of the two types of treatment session exploited the crossover design's control for individual differences among clients and therapists. Some illustrative findings follow.

The immediate impacts of the two types of session differed in accordance with theoretical expectations (Stiles, Shapiro, & Firth-Cozens, 1988a). Exploratory sessions were rated as deeper and more powerful by therapists and external raters, whereas prescriptive sessions were rated as smoother and easier by therapists, clients, and external raters. After prescriptive sessions, clients' postsession mood was rated more positively by both external raters and the clients themselves. Significant therapy events reported by clients were more likely to give rise to problem solution and reassurance during prescriptive sessions and to awareness and personal contact with the therapist during exploratory sessions (Llewelyn, Elliott, Shapiro, Firth, & Hardy, 1988). A comprehensive process analysis of events giving rise to personal insight in the two treatments revealed clear differences in the therapist's contributions (Elliott, et al., in press).

Among the instruments developed for the SPP1 were the treatment manuals (Firth & Shapiro, 1985; Shapiro & Firth, 1985), an attributions questionnaire (Firth-Cozens & Brewin, 1988), and a more efficient method of interpersonal process recall for the identification and description of significantly helpful therapy events (Elliott & Shapiro, 1988).

Instruments developed subsequently have included a modified Present State Examination (Barkham & Shapiro, 1986) incorporating items from the Diagnostic Interview Schedule (Eaton & Kessler, 1985) required to establish relevant DSM-III diagnoses, a coding manual for the classification of clients' target complaints (Barkham, Morrison, & Shapiro, 1988; Barkham, Shapiro, & Morrison, 1988), a self-report measure of the client–therapist relationship that avoids confounding this with early indications of treatment outcome (Agnew & Shapiro, 1988), and manuals for the brief implementations of prescriptive and exploratory therapy to be described (Barkham & Shapiro, 1988b, 1988c). We have also developed the Sheffield Psychotherapy Rating Scale. This is an adaptation of the Collaborative Study Psychotherapy Rating Scale (Evans, Piasecki, Kriss, & Hollon, 1984) that includes new items to measure therapist contributions to exploratory therapy (Shapiro & Startup, 1988).

Research Programs in Progress

The second Sheffield Psychotherapy Project (SPP2; Shapiro, Barkham, Hardy, & Morrison, in press) examines the dose–effect relation by comparing 8- and 16-session treatments as well as replicating the comparison between prescriptive and exploratory therapy in a group comparative design to determine whether the slight advantage of prescriptive therapy is maintained when both treatments are extended to 16 sessions and when clients are followed over 1 year without receiving the alternate treatment. This study also examines therapist effects more thoroughly by assigning 24 clients to each of 5 therapists and examines client effects by testing theoretically grounded predictions that socially dependent clients will do well in exploratory therapy and autonomous clients in prescriptive therapy (Beck, 1983).

We are also developing brief forms of prescriptive and exploratory therapy, termed two-plus-one treatments, that comprise two sessions separated by 1 week with a review session 3 months later (Barkham, 1989a, 1989b; Barkham & Hobson, 1989; Barkham & Shapiro, 1988a). Process and outcome measures are drawn from those used in SPP2 to enable direct comparisons, although DSM-III Axes I and II diagnoses are assessed with the Millon Clinical Multiaxial Inventory (Millon, 1983). Such brief interventions are attractive to those designing cost-efficient treatment delivery systems and also lend themselves to implementation as stress-reduction services in employing organizations. They also offer opportunities for process–outcome analysis of entire therapies because the amount of material obtained on each case is relatively small; to that end, two-plus-one treatments are videotaped throughout. We are conducting a controlled evaluation of two-plus-one treatments, comparing prescriptive and exploratory treatments with a brief waiting period control to evaluate change over the first two sessions. Half the clients will report symptom levels at the low end of the clinical range, and the other half will be a mildly distressed, quasi-analog sample.

We are developing research in the events paradigm (cf., programs from York University and the University of Toledo). For example, a task analysis of therapists' efforts to resolve challenges to the therapeutic relationship examines the extent of their conformity to an idealized rational model of what is required and the relationship of this conformity to the therapist's apparent success in resolving the challenge (Harper & Shapiro, 1988). More generally, we are working in the events paradigm to refine and elaborate our treatment manuals by identifying helpful events in each treatment method. To assist in this, ratings of the therapist's contributions to sessions and to significant events in sessions will be made with the Sheffield Psychotherapy Rating Scale. Similarities and differences between the mechanisms of the two treatments are revealed by our analysis of 40 significant events identified and described by both client and therapist with brief structured recall (Morrison, Shapiro, & Elliott, 1988).

Early indications from SPP2 are that the effectiveness of the single-modality treatments is similar to that of the combined treatments offered by SPP1's cross-over design (Shapiro et al., in press). Quantitative case studies of two-plus-one therapies suggest that these are more effective than would be expected from the limited data on such brief treatments in the dose–effect literature (Howard, Kopta, Krause, & Orlinsky, 1986); assessing at an early stage of a longer treatment may underestimate benefits when therapist and client are committed to making maximum use of just three sessions.

Programs Planned for the Future

The primary focus of the program will continue to be on the comparative analysis of treatment outcomes and change mechanisms. Studies of change mechanisms will identify commonalities and divergences between the two treatments, blending qualitative and quantitative methods developed by ourselves and at other centers. Instruments under consideration include structural analysis of social behavior (Benjamin, 1986) and Goldfried, Newman, and Hayes' (1989) coding system of therapeutic feedback.

Theoretical models under development include one concerned with the process whereby clients assimilate problematic experiences in psychotherapy (Stiles et al., in press). Under this theory, changes during prescriptive therapy should typically be from understanding to problem solution and mastery, whereas during exploratory therapy changes should be from unassimilated or warded-off experience to problem clarification and understanding or insight.

In addition, the program incorporates a concurrent replication of SPP2 in the National Health Service (Shapiro, Barkham, & Halstead, 1988). Four clinical psychologists employed in nearby districts have received training and supervision in prescriptive and exploratory treatments; they will each treat 24 clients who meet our inclusion criteria (with the exception of white-collar job status, which was removed to increase generalizability), who will be drawn from the usual referral channels for mental health services and will be assigned at random to the four cells of a

2×2 design comparing treatment types and durations. This replication is designed to test the generalizability of our approach in service settings and to extend our collaboration with service providers.

In addition, we will be offering two-plus-one therapies in comparison with organizational interventions in geographically separate parts of a large employing organization that has approached the program team for help with work stress among its employees. This innovative experimental comparison of help for individuals with organizational interventions will also test the acceptability and effectiveness of the two-plus-one treatments in such an organization and will lead to the development of forms of intervention that combine both individual and organizational change.

The significance of these developments derives from the need for psychotherapy research to be more concerned with the organizational contexts in which treatment is offered and taken up. Particularly in the United Kingdom there are insufficient numbers of practitioners (and the clients in most need have insufficient resources) for large-scale delivery of psychotherapy on the traditional model of extended, consulting room–based, fee-paid treatment. Resource constraints on the National Health Service entail that psychotherapy services will be increasingly brief and may well be provided by other organizations, such as the client's employer.

Relation to Other Research Programs

We consider it more efficient, where possible, to make use of methods developed by others rather than to reinvent the wheel by devising new measures to suit our idiosyncratic preferences. This has the further advantage of increasing the utility of the program's results by other investigators. For example, our collaboration with William B. Stiles at Miami University originated from our use of his Session Evaluation Questionnaire (SEQ; Stiles, 1980) in SPP1; this enabled Stiles to use SPP1 materials for a study relating SEQ data to verbal response mode assessments of the same treatment sessions. Similarly, we have developed and applied methods of interpersonal process recall originated by Robert Elliott at the University of Toledo. Our outcome studies use clinical instru-

ments developed in other programs that have acquired the status of standard measures for the field, enabling direct comparisons in terms of the nature and severity of presenting problems, absolute amount of change, and extent of differences between treatments.

The treatments under study are well grounded in the literature: Prescriptive therapy combines elements from cognitive and multimodal therapies that yielded particularly promising outcomes in our meta-analysis (Shapiro & Shapiro, 1982); Exploratory therapy is based on the conversational model, which has been operationalized to an extent that is unusual for relationship-oriented treatments (Goldberg et al., 1984; Maguire et al., 1984).

The range of research methods employed and their convergence on the study of two readily learned methods of treatment representing contrasting and widely practiced theoretical approaches are features of our program designed to maximize its impact on clinical practice. For example, designers of treatment services pay particular attention to comparative outcome data and to treatment implementations that are relatively low cost. Thus, we are currently responding to demand from U.K. Health Service-based clinical psychologists for help in implementing our two-plus-one therapies (Riordan, Whitmore, & Barkham, 1989). Meanwhile, our events paradigm research (e.g., Elliott & Shapiro, 1988; Parry, Shapiro, & Firth, 1986) offers methods of investigation that address practitioners' theoretical concerns and can be applied by them in service settings, and this is reflected in requests received for help in carrying out such work. The team has been extensively involved in disseminating clinical research methods to practitioners at annual meetings of the U.K. chapter of the Society for Psychotherapy Research.

The program has also contributed to an increased coverage of psychodynamic and relationship-oriented therapies in U.K. clinical psychology training by demonstrating their compatibility with the scientist–practitioner model espoused in that training. Program staff are involved in training of clinical psychologists locally, receive frequent invitations to contribute as visiting lecturers to training programs nationally, and find that program publications are prominent in trainees' assigned readings. Visiting scientists from the United States have transmitted clinical and research skills to a wider United Kingdom audience by their involvement in training activities. Former members of the program are prominent in clinical teaching and research at other U.K. universities.

References

Agnew, R. M., & Shapiro, D. A. (1988). *Therapist-client relationships: The development of a measure* (SAPU Memo 765). Unpublished manuscript, University of Sheffield, Sheffield, England.

American Psychiatric Association. (1980). *Diagnostic and statistical manual of mental disorders* (3rd ed.). Washington, DC: Author.

Barkham, M. (1989a). Brief prescriptive therapy in two-plus-one sessions: I. Initial cases from the clinic. *Behavioural Psychotherapy, 17,* 161–175.

Barkham, M. (1989b). Exploratory therapy in two-plus-one sessions: I. Rationale for a brief psychotherapy model. *British Journal of Psychotherapy, 6,* 79–86.

Barkham, M., Firth-Cozens, J., & Shapiro, D. A. (in press). Change in prescriptive versus exploratory therapy: Older clients' responses to therapy. *Counselling Psychology Quarterly.*

Barkham, M., & Hobson, R. F. (1989). Exploratory therapy in two-plus-one sessions: II. A single case study. *British Journal of Psychotherapy, 6,* 87–98.

Barkham, M., Morrison, L. A., & Shapiro, D. A. (1988). *Reliability of the Sheffield Presenting Problems Classification System* (SAPU Memo 929). Unpublished manuscript, University of Sheffield, Sheffield, England.

Barkham, M., & Shapiro, D. A. (1986). *A modified and composite version of the Present State Examination and Diagnostic Interview Schedule for depression and anxiety* (SAPU Memo 968). Unpublished manuscript, University of Sheffield, Sheffield, England.

Barkham, M., & Shapiro, D. A. (1988a). *Brief psychotherapeutic interventions for job-related distress: A pilot study of prescriptive and exploratory therapy* (SAPU Memo 895). Unpublished manuscript, University of Sheffield, Sheffield, England.

Barkham, M., & Shapiro, D. A. (1988b). *Manual for brief exploratory therapy in two-plus-one sessions* (SAPU Memo 877). Unpublished manuscript, University of Sheffield, Sheffield, England.

Barkham, M., & Shapiro, D. A. (1988c). *Manual for brief prescriptive therapy in two-plus-one sessions* (SAPU Memo 1005). Unpublished manuscript, University of Sheffield, Sheffield, England.

Barkham, M., Shapiro, D. A., & Firth-Cozens, J. A. (1989). Personal questionnaire changes in prescriptive vs. exploratory psychotherapy. *British Journal of Clinical Psychology, 28,* 97–107.

Barkham, M., Shapiro, D. A., & Morrison, L. A. (1988). *The Sheffield Presenting Problems Classification System (SPPCS): A coding manual* (SAPU Memo 928). Unpublished manuscript, University of Sheffield, Sheffield, England.

Beck, A. T. (1983). Cognitive theory of depression: New perspectives. In P. Clayton (Ed.), *Treatment of depression: Old controversies and new approaches.* New York: Raven Press.

Beck, A. T., Rush, A. J., Shaw, B. F., & Emery, G. (1979). *Cognitive therapy of depression.* New York: Guilford Press.

Beck, A. T., Ward, C. H., Mendelson, M., Mock, J., & Erbaugh, J. (1961). An inventory for measuring depression. *Archives of General Psychiatry, 4,* 561–571.

Benjamin, L. S. (1986). Structural analysis of social behavior (SASB). In L. S. Greenberg & W. M. Pinsof (Eds.), *The psychotherapeutic process: A research handbook.* New York: Guildford Press.

Cooper, P., Osborn, M., Gath, D., & Fegetter, G. (1982). Evaluation of a modified self-report measure of social adjustment. *British Journal of Psychiatry, 141,* 68–75.

Derogatis, L. R., Lipman, R. S., & Covi, M. D. (1973). SCL-90: An outpatient rating scale: Preliminary report. *Psychopharmacology Bulletin, 9,* 13–20.

Eaton, W. W., & Kessler, L. G. (Eds.). (1985). *Epidemiologic field methods in psychiatry: The NIMH Epidemiologic Catchment Area Program.* New York: Academic Press.

Elliott, R. K. (1979). How clients perceive helper behaviors. *Journal of Counseling Psychology, 26,* 285–294.

Elliott, R. K. (1986). Interpersonal process recall (IPR) as a psychotherapy process research method. In L. S. Greenberg & W. M. Pinsof (Eds.), *The psychotherapeutic process: A research handbook* (pp. 503–527). New York: Guildford Press.

Elliott, R. K., & James, E., Reimschuessel, C., Cislo, D., & Sack, N. (1985). Significant events and the analysis of immediate therapeutic impacts. *Psychotherapy, 22,* 620–630.

Elliott, R. K., & Shapiro, D. A. (1988). Brief structured recall: A more efficient method of studying significant therapy events. *British Journal of Medical Psychology, 61,* 141–153.

Elliott, R. K., Shapiro, D. A., Firth, J. A., Stiles, W. B., Hardy, G. E., Llewelyn, S. P., & Margison, F. (in press). Insight events in prescriptive and exploratory therapies: A comprehensive process analysis. In R. K. Elliott (Ed.), *Comprehensive process analysis.*

Evans, D. M., Piasecki, J. M., Kriss, M. R., & Hollon, S. D. (1984). *Rater's manual for the Collaborative Study Psychotherapy Rating Scale.* Unpublished manuscript, University of Minnesota, Twin Cities, and St. Paul–Ramsey Medical Center.

Ferner, J. D. (1980). *Successful time management: A self-teaching guide.* New York: Wiley.

Firth, J. A., & Shapiro, D. A. (1985). *Prescriptive therapy manual for the Sheffield psychotherapy project* (SAPU Memo 734). Unpublished manuscript, University of Sheffield, Sheffield, England.

Firth-Cozens, J. A., & Brewin, C. R. (1988). Attributional change during psychotherapy. *British Journal of Clinical Psychology, 27,* 47–54.

Goldberg, D. P., Hobson, R. F., Maguire, G. P., Margison, F. R., O'Dowd, T., Osborn, M. S., & Moss, S. (1984). The clarification and assessment of a method of psychotherapy. *British Journal of Psychiatry, 144,* 567–575.

Goldfried, M. R., & Merbaum, M. (1973). *Behavior change through self-control.* New York: Holt, Rinenart & Winston.

Goldfried, M. R., Newman, C. F., & Hayes, A. M. (1989). *Coding system of therapeutic feedback.* Unpublished manuscript, State University of New York at Stony Brook.

Hackman, J. R., & Suttle, J. L. (1977). *Improving life at work: Behavioral science approaches to organizational change*. Santa Monica, CA: Goodyear.

Hardy, G. E., & Shapiro, D. A. (1985). Therapist verbal response modes in prescriptive vs. exploratory psychotherapy. *British Journal of Clinical Psychology*, *24*, 235–245.

Harper, H., & Shapiro, D. A. (1988). *Challenges to the alliance in exploratory therapy: Task analysis of resolution strategies* (SAPU Memo 907). Unpublished manuscript, University of Sheffield, Sheffield, England.

Hobson, R. F. (1985). *Forms of feeling: The heart of psychotherapy*. London: Tavistock.

Horowitz, L., Rosenberg, S., Baer, B., Ureno, G., & Villasenor, V.S. (1988). Inventory of Interpersonal Problems: Psychometric properties and clinical applications. *Journal of Consulting and Clinical Psychology*, *56*, 885–892.

Howard, K. I., Kopta, S. M., Krause, M. S., & Orlinsky, D. E. (1986). The dose–response relationship in psychotherapy. *American Psychologist*, *41*, 159–164.

Lambert, M. J., Shapiro, D. A., & Bergin, A. E. (1986). The effectiveness of psychotherapy. In S. L. Garfield & A. E. Bergin (Eds.), *Handbook of psychotherapy and behavior change* (3rd ed., pp. 157–211). New York: Wiley.

Llewelyn, S. P. (1985). *The experiences of patients and therapists in psychological therapy*. Unpublished doctoral dissertation, University of Sheffield, Sheffield, England.

Llewelyn, S. P., Elliott, R. K., Shapiro, D. A., Firth, J. A., & Hardy, G. E. (1988). Client perceptions of significant events in prescriptive and exploratory phases of individual therapy. *British Journal of Clinical Psychology*, *27*, 105–114.

Maguire, G. P., Hobson, R. F., Margison, F. R., Moss, S., & O'Dowd. (1984). Evaluating the teaching of a method of psychotherapy. *British Journal of Psychiatry*, *144*, 576–580.

Meichenbaum, D. (1977). *Cognitive-behavior modification: An integrative approach*. New York: Plenum Press.

Millon, T. (1983). *Millon Clinical Multiaxial Inventory manual*. Minneapolis, MN: Interpretive Scoring Systems.

Morrison, L. A., Shapiro, D. A., & Elliott, R. K. (1988). *Brief structured recall of significant events in prescriptive vs. exploratory psychotherapy* (SAPU Memo 930). Unpublished manuscript, University of Sheffield, Sheffield, England.

Mulhall, D. (1976). Systematic self-assessment by PQRST. *Psychological Medicine*, *6*, 591–597.

O'Malley, P. M., & Bachman, J. G. (1979). Self-esteem and education: Sex and cohort comparisons among high school seniors. *Journal of Personality and Social Psychology*, *37*, 1153–1159.

Parry, G., Shapiro, D. A., & Firth, J. A. (1986). The anxious executive: A case from the research clinic. *British Journal of Medical Psychology*, *59*, 221–233.

Riordan, J., Whitmore, R., & Barkham, M. (1989). Less talk: More action. *Health Service Journal*, *99*, 1164.

Shapiro, D. A., Barkham, M., & Halstead, J. (1988). *Comparative psychotherapy research in NHS settings: Concurrent replication of the second Sheffield Psychotherapy Project* (SAPU Memo 896). Unpublished manuscript, University of Sheffield, Sheffield, England.

Shapiro, D. A., Barkham, M., Hardy, G. E., & Morrison, L. A. (in press). The second Sheffield Psychotherapy Project: Rationale, design, and preliminary outcome data. *British Journal of Medical Psychology*.

Shapiro, D. A., Barkham, M., & Irving, D. L. (1984). The reliability of a modified helper behaviour rating system. *British Journal of Medical Psychology*, *57*, 45–48.

Shapiro, D. A., & Firth, J. A. (1985). *Exploratory therapy manual for the Sheffield Psychotherapy Project* (SAPU Memo 733). Unpublished manuscript, University of Sheffield, Sheffield, England.

Shapiro, D. A., & Firth, J. A. (1987). Prescriptive vs. exploratory psychotherapy: Outcomes of the Sheffield Psychotherapy Project. *British Journal of Psychiatry*, *151*, 790–799.

Shapiro, D. A., Firth-Cozens, J. A., & Stiles, W. B. (1989). The question of therapists' differential effectiveness: A Sheffield Psychotherapy Project addendum. *British Journal of Psychiatry*, *154*, 383–385.

Shapiro, D. A., Harper, H., & Suokas, A. (1987, June). *The high water mark of the drug metaphor*. Paper presented at the meeting of the Society for Psychotherapy Research, Ulm, Federal Republic of Germany.

Shapiro, D. A., & Shapiro, D. (1977). The "double standard" in the evaluation of psychotherapies. *Bulletin of the British Psychological Society*, *30*, 209–210.

Shapiro, D. A., & Shapiro, D. (1982). Meta-analysis of comparative therapy outcome research: A replication of refinement. *Psychological Bulletin*, *92*, 581–604.

Shapiro, D. A., & Shapiro, D. (1983). Comparative therapy outcome research: Methodological implications of meta-analysis. *Journal of Consulting and Clinical Psychology*, *51*, 42–53.

Shapiro, D. A., & Startup, M. (1988). *The Sheffield Psychotherapy Rating Scale*. Unpublished manuscript, University of Sheffield, Sheffield, England.

Spielberger, C. D. (1983). *Manual for the State-Trait Anxiety Inventory, STAI (Form Y)*. Palo Alto, CA: Consulting Psychologists Press.

Snaith, R. P. (1974). Psychotherapy based on relaxation techniques. *British Journal of Psychiatry*, *124*, 473–481.

Stiles, W. B. (1979). Verbal response modes and psychotherapeutic technique. *Psychiatry*, *42*, 49–62.

Stiles, W. B. (1980). Measurement of the impact of psychotherapy sessions. *Journal of Consulting and Clinical Psychology*, *48*, 176–185.

Stiles, W. B., Elliott, R. K., Llewelyn, S. P., Firth-Cozens, J. A., Margison, F., Shapiro, D. A., & Hardy, G. E. (in press). Assimilation of problematic experiences in psychotherapy. *Psychotherapy*.

Stiles, W. B., & Shapiro, D. A. (in press). Abuse of the drug metaphor in psychotherapy process–outcome research. *Clinical Psychology Review*.

Stiles, W. B., Shapiro, D. A., & Elliott, R. K. (1986). Are all psychotherapies equivalent? *American Psychologist*, *41*, 165–180.

Stiles, W. B., Shapiro, D. A., & Firth-Cozens, J. A. (1988a). Do sessions of different treatments have different impacts? *Journal of Counseling Psychology*, *35*, 391–396.

Stiles, W. B., Shapiro, D. A., & Firth-Cozens, J. A.

(1988b). Verbal response mode use in contrasting psychotherapies: A within-subjects comparison. *Journal of Consulting and Clinical Psychology, 56,* 727–733.

Taylor, M. (1979). *Coverdale on management.* London: Heinemann.

Weissman, M. M., & Paykel, E. S. (1974). *The depressed woman.* Chicago: University of Chicago Press.

Wexler, M. M., & Elliott, R. K. (1988, June). *Experiential therapy of depression: Initial psychometric analyses of session data.* Paper presented at the meeting of the Society for Psychotherapy Research, Santa Fe, NM.

Wing, J. K., Cooper, J. E., & Sartorius, N. (1974). *The measurement and classification of psychiatric symptoms.* Cambridge, England: Cambridge University Press.

29

University of Umeå: The Borderline Patient Project

Bengt-Åke Armelius
University of Umeå

Background and Aims

History

The Borderline Patient Project in Umeå, Sweden, began in 1982 as a collaborative project between a few researchers in the Department of Applied Psychology and a few clinicians at the psychiatric clinic at the University of Umeå in northern Sweden. A mutual dependency existed between these two organizations from the start. The researchers needed a clinic with patients, and the clinicians needed resources from outside to develop their skills and knowledge. The first year of the project featured a small study group that met every Friday to discuss literature and, eventually, to try diagnostic interviews and tests. The group consisted of one researcher (B.-Å. Armelius) and six clinicians (three psychiatrists, two psychologists, and one social worker) who participated in the study group as part of their clinical service. After the first year, we decided to implement an empirical investigation of the patients at the clinic. All inpatients at the clinic on a certain date (November 23, 1982) were to be included in the study. The objective was to determine how many borderline patients there were at the clinic and how the different borderline concepts were related to each other.

About a year later, we agreed to offer long-term psychodynamic psychotherapy to a number of borderline patients to determine whether this kind of treatment would be a possible alternative to ordinary psychiatric treatment. Our plan included a small treatment home with 6–8 patients who would be treated as intensively as possible. Inspired by the work of Grinker, Werble, and Drye (1968), the research would be integrated into the treatment in a form of action research design. An application for funds provided some money to start with as well as a psychoanalytically trained supervisor (Iréne Matthis). She gave a series of lectures for the whole clinic and supervised 10 therapists. Matthis was with the University of Umeå for at total of 4 1/2 years. During the past few years we have had regular seminars regarding the French psychoanalytic school, which has included a visit by Joyce McDougall.

In the beginning, the Borderline Patient Project was directed primarily toward the borderline concept and borderline patients. After a few years therapeutic interest also focused on the schizophrenic patient. There were two primary reasons for this expansion. One was the fact that the recruitment area for the patients was the inland of Lappland, so that patients had to travel at least 30 km (and sometimes as much as 400 km) to reach the clinic. The borderline patients we needed were not willing to leave their homes for a stay at the treatment home; most of them had jobs and families. There was, however, a relatively large group of young schizophrenic patients who were ill enough to require further care after the closing down of the mental hospitals. No one knew what to do with them, and there was no good treatment available besides the pharmacotherapy that most of them received.

There was pressure to invite a few of these schizophrenic patients to the treatment home and to test our therapeutic ideas on them instead of on the borderline patients. Our only hesitation was the fact that none of the therapists had treated any but neurotic patients in psychotherapy. Inspired by Matthis and the French psychoanalytic school of thought, we decided it was worth a try. In 1985 the first schizophrenic patients arrived at our treatment home, called Öbacka, where they received a room of their own and were expected to participate in daily activities with a staff of nine psychotherapeutically trained nurses. There was also an external individual psychotherapist available at the hospital for each of the patients.

Overall Aims

The major scientific aim of the Borderline Patient Project is to collect data that can answer certain questions. One such question is whether borderline patients constitute a separate clinical entity. To answer this question, it was necessary to define the concept and then to compare the borderline group with other diagnostic groups. We spent a lot of time translating and trying out methods that would be relevant for descriptive and diagnostic purposes. The project design allows for two types of comparisons. The first is a comparison between the borderline group and other clinical groups in terms of symptoms, social and family adjustment, psychological defenses, self-concept, and object representations as measured by our assessment battery. The second is a longitudinal comparison of course and outcome under different treatment conditions. A follow-up assessment of 5 years has been undertaken for the patients, who were initially assessed in 1982 to 1984.

In general it is required that a clinical entity show a homogeneous pattern of characteristics in a group that is distinct from the pattern in other clinical groups. At present, we use Kernberg's (1975, 1981) concept of personality organization (PO) as a basis for forming clinical groups. This means that most of the comparisons that have been carried out so far concern the difference between neurotic personality organization (NPO), borderline personality organization (BPO), and psychotic personality organization (PPO). Other comparisons based on, for example, the third edition of the *Diagnostic and Statistical Manual of Mental Disorders* (*DSM-III*; American Psychiatric Association, 1980) will be carried out later on.

Method

Subjects and Selection

The subjects in this program are psychiatric patients. In certain conditions there is a mixture of inpatients, but in most conditions the subjects are borderline and schizophrenic patients. Chronically disturbed patients or those with an organic or alcoholic diagnosis are excluded. Of primary interest are the severely disturbed cases with a hopeful prognosis.

Instruments

Much of our efforts have been devoted to defining the borderline concept. First, we had to translate and try some of the methods that others had developed for assessing borderline patients. We designed an assessment battery that has been used in several investigations since 1982. It consists of the following instruments.

Structural interview. The structural interview was designed by Kernberg (1981) as a technique for assessing the type of PO that a patient has. The NPO, BPO, and PPO are psychoanalytic concepts that must be assessed on the basis of information elicited from a special interview in which the psychological functions are observed and tested in the interaction with the patient. We trained ourselves to conduct these interviews and found that it is possible to get good reliability, and probably also good validity, for the PO concept (Kullgren, 1987).

Diagnostic Interview for Borderlines (DIB). The DIB, which was originally developed by Kolb and Gunderson (1980), has been translated into Swedish and is presently used widely in this country. Our results showed that it is relatively easy to get high reliability when the DIB is used as an interview and when it is used on hospital records (B.-Å. Armelius, Kullgren, & Renberg, 1985; Kullgren, 1987). The DIB has the advantage of discriminating a small and relatively homogeneous borderline group that correlates strongly with *DSM-III* criteria.

Defense Mechanism Test (DMT). The DMT is a subliminal test that was developed by Kragh

(1955) in Sweden. It has been used in various studies in Scandinavia and is closely related to the international tradition of subliminal perception. From a clinical point of view, it is interesting because it represents an alternative to the Rorschach test. The test usually consists of a Thematic Apperception Test-like picture with a hero to identify with and a threatening older person (the peripheral) in the background. The picture is presented tachistoscopically to the patient. The exposure times start at 5 ms and are increased in a geometrical series up to 2 s on the 22nd exposure. The task of the patient is to look into the tachistoscope and, immediately after the stimulus presentation, to draw a simple picture of what he or she saw while also giving a verbal account. This procedure is repeated for each of the 22 exposures in each of two series. The motif of the stimulus is changed in the second series.

The scoring of the test protocol follows a manual developed over a number of years (Kragh & Neumann, 1984). Each of the drawings is evaluated with respect to how it is different from the stimulus picture. The deviations, called *signs*, are interpreted as attempts by the person to manage the anxiety provoked by the pictures. In this respect, the deviations have the same function as the mechanisms of defense in psychoanalytic theory. The signs are grouped into 10 defense mechanisms such as repression, isolation, reaction formation, denial, regression, and introjection. The rationale for the grouping may be an obvious similarity to a certain defense mechanism or empirical results from studies of patients who typically show a certain defense mechanism. Each sign is given a specific code number. For example, *2.10* means that there is a sign of isolation because something, perhaps a line, is added to the picture to separate the hero from the threatening peripheral. Altogether there are more than 60 different signs specified in the manual. This is, of course, both an asset and a problem for the test. The advantage is that there is a rich source of information with which to work. The problem is that it requires a lot of inferential structure and competence to integrate all the signs into meaningful, synthetic interpretations.

Structural Analysis of Social Behavior (SASB). The SASB was developed by Benjamin (1974) and was translated into Swedish by B-Å. Armelius, Lindelöf, and Mårtensson (1983). It is a model for interpersonal diagnosis and gives a picture of a person's self-concept and view of his or her relations to other significant people. At this time, we have data from a number of different groups of people including students, women with premenstrual problems, personnel and patients in psychiatry, patients complaining of oral galvanism, and patients with psychosomatic complaints. Our results so far indicate that there are large differences among these groups. A consistent finding (K. Armelius & Stiwne, 1986) is that borderlines seem to have a negative or diffuse self-picture.

Other assessment methods. We also use the SCL-90 to assess the self-rated symptoms of patients. The patients are diagnosed according to the *DSM-III*. We also regularly use the Health–Sickness Rating Scale (HSRS) as described by Luborsky (1962, 1975). In fact, we have standardized the HSRS on a sample of 21 Swedish clinicians and found that the agreement of ratings on the 34 specimen cases is extremely good. A similar study was carried out in France, and in a joint paper (B.-Å. Armelius, Gerin, & Luborsky, 1985) we found that the average judgment of mental health is similar in Sweden, France, and the United States. A recent replication by Luborsky on judges in the United States verifies this impression. Therefore, the HSRS can be considered an international yardstick of mental health that can be used for comparisons between studies carried out in different countries.

Procedures

The design of the project is an open-ended design called an *ecological design* (B.-Å. Armelius, 1988). The purpose is to build a database consisting of a set of standardized instruments or assessment methods that can be applied to different problems and groups of patients. Two basic ideas underlie this design: a common set of instruments and a fixed time frame of 5 years between assessment periods. Everything else is allowed to vary. In fact, it is considered an advantage to have large variation, for example in terms of patient groups and treatment methods, as long as they are well described. The generalizability increases, as does the possibility of forming interesting comparison groups that are similar (in a randomized sense) in all other respects but the contrasting dimension. In reality, the number of conditions that can be included in the design is limited. However, in theory it is possible to reach an asymptotic value that gives the ecological design almost the same power as an experimental design to exclude alter-

Table 29.1
Patient and Treatment Conditions

Patient group	Treatment condition
50 Inpatients	Normal psychiatric care
10 Outpatients	Individual psychotherapy
14 Borderlines	Two-year group psychotherapy
6 Schizophrenics	Treatment home (Öbacka)
8 Borderlines	Treatment home (Vårgården)
8 Schizophrenics	Treatment home (Villan)
8 Schizophrenics and 4 borderlines	Treatment home (Regnbågen)
8 Schizophrenics	Treatment home (Mariagården)

Note. There were approximately 20 treatment homes.

native hypotheses. This is especially true in the area of long-term course and outcome of severely disturbed patients, where it is almost impossible to maintain strict control over the different design conditions. For example, some patients will not go to the therapy that they have been assigned to and will seek other treatment, as shown by the Boston study (Stanton et al., 1984).

Table 29.1 reveals the conditions that are included in the current design.

Normal psychiatric care. The Borderline Patient Project has been underway since 1982. In 1988 we asked the 48 patients in the normal psychiatric care condition to return to the clinic for reassessment. We have been able to see 38 patients, but it is too early to say how the patients in this group have changed. We have, however, examined hospital records to get an idea of how much treatment the patients have required, how much work they have been able to do, and how their family conditions have changed during the 5 years since their last assessment. In general, the NPO patients have needed little psychiatric care, whereas the BPO and PPO patients spend about one third of their time in hospital care each year. The BPO patients stay for shorter periods than do the PPO patients, but the total number of days is approximately the same. There is also a small but significant increase in the HSRS scores from the first to the fifth year for all patients taken together, which indicates that normal psychiatric care may be useful for NPO patients and perhaps a good maintenance strategy for BPO and PPO patients when they feel that they need help.

About 10 patients have been offered individual, long-term psychotherapy in our project as their principal treatment. The therapists are trained and supervised through our project, and the ther-

apies are recorded on videotape or audiotape. In a few more years, we hope to have a small but interesting library of recorded and completed therapies on which we can begin process research. Our contract with the patients and the therapists does not allow any research to be done until the therapies are completed and donated to the research project.

Group psychotherapy for borderline patients. Two groups of BPO patients with long psychiatric records have completed a 2-year, weekly outpatient course of group psychotherapy. Two different therapists, both with psychodynamic training in group therapy, individually led the groups. A total of 14 patients agreed to participate, and all were subjected to the diagnostic battery before treatment and 1 year after treatment. Each session was videotaped, and an interview or telephone contact was initiated after 4 or 5 years along with a careful reading of the patients' hospital records. Twelve patients came for therapy and stayed at least 3 months, 9 patients stayed at lease 75% of the time, and 5 patients remained in therapy for the whole 2-year period.

The results of this study have been summarized in a thesis (Stiwne, 1989). The process analysis shows that the patients who eventually drop out or have a poor outcome are sensitive to disturbances of any kind. Their process measures (ability to relate to others and to take an active part in the therapy) go down after each holiday or canceled session, and the therapist seems to leave them alone; the remainder continue to work and to receive attention from their therapist also on these occasions.

Treatment homes. Most of the old mental hospitals are being closed down in Sweden today, and the former patients are supposed to integrate into society and live as normal a life as possible. There is, however, a group of young schizophrenic patients who might benefit from intensive rehabilitation of a psychotherapeutic nature and who are too sick to live alone or without support. Since the middle of the 1980s, many hospitals have established small, intensive treatment homes for such patients. The therapeutic ambitions and contents may vary from site to site, but the format and package are the same.

Although most former inpatients have been seen in psychiatry for a few years, the aim is to get them into a treatment home as soon as possible. The nursing staff is well educated and usually trained in psychotherapy, which means that they view daily activities as an opportunity for psychotherapeutic experience.

We are running such a unit, the Öbacka, in our research project. The staff of the treatment home are responsible for the daily activities and the therapeutic interventions at the home. At the Öbacka, which is a villa in Umeå, the patients are assigned to an individual therapist outside the villa; at Mariagården, which is a similar home in another part of Sweden, the individual therapists share their experiences with the milieu therapists. In other treatment homes, on the other hand, there is no psychotherapy at all but only a social training program designed to help the patients live on their own in an apartment. This kind of variation is good for the design because it makes it possible to compare different treatment conditions as long as the same diagnostic battery and time frame are used in all places. Six patients can stay at the Öbacka at a time, and so far only two have left the home (one because he was too sick for this form of treatment and the other because he felt he no longer needed the treatment). Another four have lived there for 3–4 years, and a few of them are on their way out of the home. It is, however, still too early to evaluate the results.

We visit each site at least once a year to interview the patients and the staff. This is our way of assessing the treatment ideology, the treatment method, and the experiences of staff and patients.

The purpose of the ecological design of the project is to invite other treatment homes into the project. Each unit has too few patients for too long a time to facilitate good evaluations of the effectiveness of this form of treatment with severely disturbed patients. Together, however, the units include enough patients to draw conclusions and to make generalizations. At the present time, we have about 20 treatment homes in the design. They are located in various cities all over Sweden. We estimate the number of patients to be around 150, which is large enough to build a database that allows a careful analysis of important differences.

Research Accomplishments

Different Borderline Concepts

One of the main purposes of the project is to subject the borderline concept to strong empirical tests. Are borderline patients homogeneous enough to form a clinical entity of their own, or does the entity constitute a heterogeneous "waste basket" for the difficult clients who cannot be considered neurotic or psychotic? We have spent a lot of time defining the borderline concept in empirical terms. In one study (Kullgren, 1987), we found that the BPO criteria yielded almost twice as many borderline patients as the DIB or the *DSM-III* criteria in our sample of 50 psychiatric inpatients. We also have found that the BPO concept can be assessed reliably by both the structural interview and the DMT.

In a pilot study we also have presented a translated version of a BPO questionnaire developed by Kernberg's group (Oldham et al., 1985) to our 50 psychiatric inpatients. This instrument consists of 130 items keyed to the three criteria separating the PO groups: identity diffusion, level of defenses, and reality testing. We found (as did Kernberg's group) that the scales were consistent ($\alpha = .90$) and that the PO groups had averages on the scales that agreed with the theoretical distributions (Huff, 1988).

Linguistic Fingerprints

In a series of studies (Jeanneau & Armelius, 1987, 1988) we have examined what we call the *linguistic fingerprints* of the patients with different POs. The structural interviews are transcribed and converted to a computer format suited for a content analysis program developed in Germany. With this program it is possible to get frequency counts for single words, groups of words, or expressions from the transcribed interviews. These words form variables that are descriptive of the linguistic character of the interviews and are analyzed by means of principal-component models. In one such model, we have separated the NPO, BPO, and PPO groups almost perfectly by means of 40 linguistic variables.

Borderline Patients and Suicide

It is reasonable to assume that borderline patients are overrepresented among psychiatric patients who have attempted suicide because of their strong inclination toward suicide and other forms of self-destructive behavior. In two reports (Kullgren, Renberg, & Jacobsson, 1986; Kullgren, 1988) comparing over time, the borderline group with other groups of psychiatric patients who attempt suicide, it seems evident that the relative number of borderline patients among suicidal patients is increasing but is not higher than that found in the general psychiatric population.

Another question relating to borderline patients and suicide is whether there are psychological differences between living borderline patients and those who have committed suicide. Because we used the DIB and the HSRS on hospital records as diagnostic tools for our study of psychiatric patients who committed suicide, we were able to compare a group of 16 borderline patients who committed suicide with a group of 11 borderline patients who attempted suicide on all the DIB and HSRS variables (B.-Å. Armelius & Kullgren, 1986). By means of principal components models, we found that there is a different pattern of psychological characteristics in the two groups. The former group was characterized by lack of impulse control and strong affect, and the latter group was characterized by poor interpersonal relations with masochism, dependency, and manipulations. They also had more pronounced psychotic symptoms and were more socially isolated than were the former patients. In a case study, Kullgren (1985) interpreted many of the suicides as related to repressive countertransference reactions.

Nature of the Research Organization

Team Members

In addition to Bengt-Åke Armelius, PhD, who is the project leader and coordinator and an individual therapist, the project staff consists of the following individuals: Kerstin Armelius, PhD, who is responsible for SASB studies; Hans Fogelstam, psychologist, who is responsible for the ward climate studies and the interviews with patients every year; Rolf Holmqvist, psychologist, who is responsible for countertransference studies and implementation of a treatment home in Bollnäs; Lars Jacobsson, MD, professor of psychiatry, who is clinically and scientifically responsible for the project; Madeleine Jeanneau, psychologist and individual therapist, who is responsible for the linguistic studies on the structural interviews; Gunnar Kullgren, MD, psychiatrist and project therapist, who is responsible for *DSM-III* and DIB diagnosing and is involved in the suicide studies;

Iréne Matthis, psychiatrist and psychoanalyst, who is the supervisor for the therapists; Tomas Nilsson, psychologist, who is responsible for studies of defenses of process studies at the treatment homes; Anna-Maria Sandeberg, psychiatrist and individual therapist, who is responsible for the Öbacka and the process methods for the treatment homes; Dan Stiwne, PhD, who is responsible for the group psychotherapy study in Falun; Elisabet Sundbom, psychologist and individual therapist, who is responsible for the DMT studies; and Kari Öhman, psychologist, who has a special interest in SASB.

Funding

The program has been funded by the Swedish Medical Research Council (MFR) from 1982 through 1990. The amount granted is approximately $20,000 every year. In addition to this, the project leader has received a fellowship consisting of $25,000 a year for 3 years from MFR. Other grants from MFR have included funds for a study trip to the United States during the summer of 1986 ($10,000) and a contribution to a local Society for Psychotherapy Research conference with guests from the United States in the summer of 1987 ($8,500).

There also have been other funds for the project. Both Anna-Maria Sandeberg and Elisabet Sundbom have received grants of approximately $6,000 a year for 3 years from a local fund for clinical research in Umeå. Gunnar Kullgren and Lars Jacobsson have received funds from the Swedish Medical Doctors Society of approximately $7,000 each.

Finally, the University of Umeå and the psychiatric clinic have contributed by granting time for research to those employed there. B.-Å. Armelius has been an assistant professor at the Department of Applied Psychology during the whole period, and Kerstin Armelius has had 50% of her time available for research during the past 3 years. Kullgren has been able to do research in the Department of Psychiatry for about 40% of his time for a few years. A few of the research members (Dan Stiwne, Hans Fogelstam, and Madeleine Jeanneau) have received doctoral fellowships from the University of Umeå during the past 4 years. Rolf Holmqvist has been freed up from his other duties at a local hospital in Bollnäs for 3 months every year since 1985 to be able to participate in the project.

Relation to Other Research

The program has a firm basis in the clinical tradition and is closely dependent on the cooperation of clinicians. The ecological design is an attempt to make the most of this close link to the clinical situation. The disadvantage is that there is no control over the clinical situation by the researchers, thus requiring frequent negotiations and compromises. This cooperative research enterprise provides direct benefits to the clinicians. They are involved in a long-term systematic effort to gain knowledge, and their work is seen as an important contribution to that enterprise. By and large, they also get feedback relating their own work to that of others.

Although we have good relations with the clinical field, relations with the scientific community are less positive. There are important decision makers responsible for funds and power who find it difficult to adopt the long-term perspective and accept the lack of control over the important variables of the design. The usual academic training favors controlled experimental designs, and any deviation from this is regarded as unacceptable research. In this respect, we find the Society for Psychotherapy Research to be an important organization because it is a melting pot where people with different experiences can meet. Our international relations primarily are with Lester Luborsky, John Gunderson, Mardi Horowitz, Horst Kächele, and Lorna Smith-Benjamin, all of whom have been important in our thinking and work. In Sweden we have local psychotherapy research meeting every year, and there are quite a few groups sharing our interest in psychotherapy for the severely disturbed patient. We are also influenced by the work being done in Åbo, Finland, by Alanen and his colleagues and by some of the work being done in Oslo, Norway. We find the interest in psychotherapy and psychotherapy research for severely disturbed patients to be increasing in Scandinavia, in contrast to what seems to be the case in the United States, where the scene is characterized by pessimism.

References

American Psychiatric Association. (1980). *Diagnostic and statistical manual of mental disorders* (3rd ed.). Washington, DC: Author.

Armelius, B.-Å. (1988). *Ecological design as a solution to research on small treatment homes.* Paper presented at the Ninth International Symposium on the Psychotherapy of Schizophrenia, Turin, Italy.

Armelius, B.-Å., Gerin, P., & Luborsky, L. (1985). *Clinician's judgment of mental health: An international validation of HSRS.* (Research Rep. No. 13). Umeå, Sweden: University of Umeå, Department of Applied Psychology.

Armelius, B.-Å., & Kullgren, G. (1986). *Soft modelling of the psychological characteristics of suicided and non-suicided borderline patients* (Research Rep. No. 14). Umeå, Sweden: University of Umeå, Department of Applied Psychology.

Armelius, B.-Å. Kullgren, G., & Renberg, E. (1985). Borderline diagnosis from hospital records: Reliability and validity of Gunderson's Diagnostic Interview for Borderlines (DIB). *Journal of Nervous and Mental Disease, 173,* 32–34.

Armelius, K., Lindelöf, I.-S., & Mårtensson, B. (1983). *Structural Analysis of Social Behavior (SASB): En modell för analys av interaktioner* (TIPS Whole No. 5). Umeå, Sweden: University of Umeå.

Armelius, K., & Stiwne, D. (1986). *Borderlinepatienters skattning av sig själva och sin relation till en betydelsefull annan person med SASB* (TIPS Whole No. 18). Umeå, Sweden: University of Umeå.

Benjamin, L. S. (1974). Structural analysis of social behavior. *Psychological Review, 81,* 392–445.

Grinker, R., Werble, B., & Drye, R. (1968). *The borderline syndrome.* New York: Basic books.

Huff, D. (1988). *Validity and reliability of the borderline personality organization self-rating questionnaire: A replication study.* Unpublished manuscript, University of Umeå, Umeå, Sweden.

Jeanneau, M., & Armelius, B.-Å. (1988). *Linguistic characteristics of neurotic, borderline, and psychotic personality organization* (DAPS Whole No. 28). Umeå, Sweden: University of Umeå.

Jeanneau, M., & Armelius, B. (1987). *Lingvistiska strukturer som psykologiska fingeravtryck* (TIPS Whole No. 20). Umeå, Sweden: University of Umeå.

Kernberg, O. (1975). *Borderline states and pathological narcissism.* New York: Jason Aronson.

Kernberg, O. (1981). Structural interviewing. *Psychiatric Clinics of North America, 4,* 169–194.

Kolb, J., & Gunderson, J. (1980). Diagnosing borderline patients with a semistructured interview. *Archives of General Psychiatry, 37,* 41–46.

Kragh, U. (1955). *The actual-genetic model of perception-personality.* Lund, Sweden: Gleerups.

Kragh, U., & Neumann, T. (1984). *DMT manual.* Stockholm, Sweden: Swedish Psychology AB.

Kullgren, G. (1985). Borderline personality disorder and psychiatric suicides: An analysis of eleven consecutive cases. *Nordisk Psykiatrisk Tidskrift, 39,* 479–484.

Kullgren, G. (1987). An empirical comparison of three borderline concepts. *Acta Psychiatrica Scandinavia, 76,* 246–255.

Kullgren, G. (1988). Factors associated with completed suicide in borderline personality disorder. *Journal of Nervous and Mental Disease, 176,* 40–44.

Kullgren, G., Renberg, E., & Jacobsson, E. (1986). An empirical study of borderline personality disorder and psychiatric suicides. *Journal of Nervous and Mental Disease, 174,* 328–331.

Luborsky, L. (1962). Clinician's judgment of mental health: A proposed scale. *Archives of General Psychiatry, 7,* 407–417.

Luborsky, L. (1975). Clinician's judgment of mental health. Specimen case descriptions and forms for the Health–Sickness Rating Scale. *Bulletin of the Menninger Clinic, 39,* 448–480.

Oldham, J., et al. (1985). A self-report instrument for borderline personality organization. In McGlashan (Ed.), *The borderline: Current empirical research.* Washington, DC: American Psychiatric Press.

Stanton, A. H., Gunderson, J. G., Knapp, P. H., Frank, A. F., Vannicelli, M. L., Schnitzer, R. S., & Rosenthal, R. (1984). Effects of psychotherapy in schizophrenia: I. Design and implementation of a controlled study. *Schizophrenia Bulletin, 10,* 4.

Stiwne, D. (1989). *Borderline patients in group psychotherapy: Studies in process and outcome.* Unpublished doctoral dissertation, University of Umeå, Umeå, Sweden.

30

University of Groningen: Experimental Psychotherapy and Psychopathology

Paul M. G. Emmelkamp and Frans A. Albersnagel
Academic Hospital Groningen, the Netherlands

Background and Aims

History

From 1971 to 1974, Emmelkamp was involved in research at the University of Utrecht (the Netherlands) in the development of self-management programs for people with agoraphobic and obsessive–compulsive disorders. In 1974 this research program was continued at the Department of Clinical Psychology at the University of Groningen (the Netherlands). The research at Groningen focused on cognitive and behavioral processes in the treatment of agoraphobia and obsessive–compulsive disorders and on the etiology of these disorders. In 1978 Albersnagel, whose main area of research at that time was depression, joined the program. In 1979 Willem Boelens became a staff member for research in marital discord and marital therapy. One year later, joined by Dominique L. H. M. Debats, Boelens started a research program on the clinical effectiveness of cognitive and behavioral processes in depression. At the same time, the research on anxiety disorders was broadened to include research into social phobia.

In the early 1980s the department's research program was reorganized, and several clinical psychologists whose main interest was clinical assessment joined the program. From 1981 on, this research program was supported by the Dutch government for 5 years. This support was extended in 1987 for another 5 years.

Overall Aims

The aim of the research program on experimental psychotherapy and psychopathology is to study the process and effect of cognitive and behavioral therapies in relation to specific forms of psychopathology and distress. This research focuses on the study of abnormal behavior and on the study of treatment-induced changes. Results of studies in one domain influence the design of studies in the other domain. For example, the results of a therapy study may lead to hypotheses regarding the etiology and maintenance of a specific disorder; these hypotheses can be tested in either the laboratory or the clinic. Conversely, results of studies on abnormal psychology may lead to changes in treatment procedures that can be tested in clinical trials.

Because the Dutch have a (beautiful) language of their own, much of our research effort is devoted to constructing, translating, adapting, and psychometrically evaluating assessment instruments for use in therapy and more basic research studies. For this reason, many of our more ambitious plans cannot be carried out or must be delayed until appropriate assessment devices are made available.

Subareas of Investigation

The three major areas of our investigation are anxiety disorders (e.g., agoraphobia, obsessive–compulsive disorder, and social phobias), depression, and marital distress. In all three areas, research focuses on psychometrically evaluating assessment devices, basic processes, and cognitive–behavioral therapy.

Method

Anxiety Disorders

Subjects and selection. Treatment research in this area is conducted on individuals with agoraphobia, obsessive–compulsiveness, and social phobias who are referred to our department for treatment. Referrals come from general practitioners, psychiatrists, clinical psychologists, and mental health agencies. Basic research is also conducted on these patients and, depending on the hypotheses to be tested, may also involve patients from other institutions or volunteers in so-called analog studies. All patients in the clinical studies are seen by a clinical psychologist before entrance in the study, and all receive a diagnosis from the revised third edition of the *Diagnostic and Statistical Manual of Mental Disorders* (*DSM-III–R*; American Psychiatric Association, 1987).

Instruments. The instruments used in the project have varied from study to study, depending on the specific hypotheses to be tested. These instruments consist of self-report questionnaires for each specific disorder (the Fear Questionnaire [Arrindell, Emmelkamp, & Van der Ende, 1984] and the Maudsley Obsessive–Compulsive Inventory [Emmelkamp, 1988c]); psychopathology [the SCL-90; Arrindell & Ettema, 1986); and target ratings (Emmelkamp, 1982b). In the case of agoraphobia and social phobia, instruments also include behavioral assessment (Emmelkamp, 1988a). In treatment studies the effects are also evaluated by an independent assessor who is a clinical psychologist.

Procedures. We have evaluated a number of treatment procedures, including behavioral and cognitive procedures, exposure in vivo, exposure in imagination, self-management procedures, spouse-aided therapy, assertiveness training, self-instructional training, and rational-emotive therapy.

Depression

Subjects and selection. Several analog experiments have been conducted with hundreds of nondepressed students and scholars as subjects (Arrindell, Albersnagel, & Emmelkamp, 1978; Albersnagel, Arntz, & Gerlsma, 1986; Albersnagel, 1987, 1988; Gerlsma & Albersnagel, 1987). In clinical research projects, nonhospitalized patients are selected on the basis of Research Diagnostic Criteria (RDC) and DSM-III–R inclusion criteria for affective (mood) disorders (Boelens & Debats, 1983; Debats & Boelens, 1981). In all experiments, volunteer subjects are randomly assigned to experimental groups.

Instruments. In our analog research, induction procedures are used to produce behavioral changes by means of visual analog scales (repeated measures design). Several other instruments have been used, including the SCL-90 (Arrindell & Ettema, 1986) and the Attributional Style Questionnaire (ASQ; Arntz, Gerlsma, & Albersnagel, 1985). In clinical research, cognitive–behavioral interventions were applied according to procedures described in detail in treatment manuals developed at the department. Among the research tools used to evaluate process and outcome variables were the Beck Depression Inventory (BDI; e.g., Bouman, Luteijn, Albersnagel, & Van der Ploeg, 1985; Luteijn & Bouman, 1988a) the Pleasant Events Schedule (PES; Bouman, 1986; Bouman & Luteijn, 1986), the Scale for Interpersonal behavior (SIB; Arrindell, De Groot, & Walburg, 1980), the Irrational Belief Test (IBT), and the Rational Behavior Inventory (RBI; Sanderman, Mersch, Van der Sleen, Emmelkamp, & Ormel, 1987).

Procedures. Failure feedback procedures and Velten and musical mood induction procedures are independent variables in the analog studies. In clinical research, operant and cognitive intervention techniques are used in the experimental (treatment) designs.

Marital Distress

Subjects and selection. All patients treated in our marital therapy studies are referred by a community marital health center. Couples are accepted for the studies unless the main complaint involves a sexual dysfunction or one of the partners is psychotic or addicted to drugs. In addition, partners have to be living together for the time of treatment, although they need not necessarily be married.

Instruments. The main instruments used are as follows: (a) the Maudsley Marital Questionnaire, which is a 20-item questionnaire relating to marital, sexual, and general life adjustment; (b) the Marital Deprivation Scale, which is a version of the Marital Evaluation Scale adapted for use in the Netherlands; (c) the Relationship Beliefs Inventory, a 40-item questionnaire consisting of the subscales Disagreement Is Destructive, Mind reading Is Expected, Partners Cannot Change, Sexual perfectionism and the Sexes Are Different; and (d) the Communication Questionnaire, consisting of the subscales Intimate Communication, Destructive Communication, Discongruent Communication, and Avoidance of Communication.

In addition, couples have to score their main target problems. Furthermore, the communication between the partners is assessed on video (e.g., with the marital interaction coding system).

Procedures. The following treatment procedures have been evaluated:

• Reciprocity counseling involves contractual training, with partners establishing specific behavioral commitments for self and other and compromising with each other.

• Communication skills training focuses on ways to improve communication between spouses; partners are taught skills that enable them to talk with each other, listen, empathize, express feelings spontaneously, and be assertive.

• System-theoretic counseling is structured relationship therapy based on system-theoretic theories.

• Cognitive restructuring focuses on changing the causal attributions that partners give for events that take place in the marriage and on changing irrational beliefs and unrealistic expectations that couples often have.

Research Accomplishments

Findings

Agoraphobia. The main conclusions from our research program are the following:

• Exposure in vivo is superior to imaginal exposure (Emmelkamp & Wessels, 1975).

• Group exposure is about equally as effective as an individually conducted exposure program (Emmelkamp & Emmelkamp-Benner, 1975).

• Treatment can be conducted as a self-help program (Emmelkamp, 1974; Emmelkamp & Ultee, 1974).

• Effects of exposure programs are long lasting (Emmelkamp & Kuipers, 1979).

• Exposure in vivo is superior to cognitive therapy (Emmelkamp, Brilman, Kuipers, & Mersch, 1986; Emmelkamp, Kuipers, & Eggeraat, 1978; Emmelkamp & Mersch, 1982).

• Agoraphobics are often socially anxious (Arrindell & Emmelkamp, 1987). Assertiveness training improves assertiveness but does not lead to clinical improvement of phobias (Emmelkamp, Van der Hout, & De Vries, 1983).

• Parental rearing practices of people with agoraphobia are characterized by rejection and lack of emotional warmth (Arrindell, Emmelkamp, Brilman, & Monsma, 1983). Such parental attitudes are related to treatment failure (Emmelkamp & Van der Hout, 1983).

• The therapeutic relationship affects the outcome of exposure treatment (Emmelkamp & Van der Hout, 1983).

• The psychological profile of the partner of the agoraphobic individual is essentially normal (Arrindell & Emmelkamp, 1985). The marital relationships of couples with agoraphobia are more comparable to those of normal couples and nondistressed couples than to those of maritally distressed couples (Arrindell & Emmelkamp, 1986; Arrindell, 1987).

• The impact of relationship dysfunction on treatment outcome is small and does not account for much variance (Emmelkamp, 1980; Arrindell, Emmelkamp, & Sanderman, 1986).

• Spouse-aided therapy is no more effective than treatment of the patient alone (Emmelkamp, 1988b). For a more detailed discussion, refer to Emmelkamp (1979, 1982a, 1982b, 1989a) and Emmelkamp, Bouman, and Scholing (1989).

Obsessive–compulsive disorder. The results of our studies into obsessive–compulsive disorder can be summarized as follows (for more detailed review see Emmelkamp, 1987, 1989b):

• Modeling does not enhance the effects of exposure in vivo and response prevention (Boersma, Den Hengst, Dekker, & Emmelkamp, 1976).

• Exposure and response prevention can be conducted as a self-management program by patients themselves (Emmelkamp & Kraanen, 1977; Emmelkamp, Van Linden van den Heuvell, Rüphan, & Sanderman, 1989).

• Frequent practice is no more effective than spaced practice (Emmelkamp, Van Linden van den Heuvell, et al., 1989).

• Effects of exposure programs are long lasting (Emmelkamp & Rabbie, 1981; Visser, Hoekstra, & Emmelkamp, in press).

• Self-instructional training does not enhance the effects of exposure plus response prevention (Emmelkamp, Van der Helm, Van Zanten, & Plochg, 1980).

• Rational-emotive therapy is as effective as exposure plus response prevention (Emmelkamp, Visser, & Hoekstra, 1988).

• People with obsessive–compulsive disorder can be treated as outpatients rather than as inpatients (Van der Hout, Emmelkamp, Kraaykamp, & Griez, 1988).

• Imaginal exposure, thought stopping, and assertiveness training may be effective with patients with obsessions, but no one method has been found to be superior (Emmelkamp & Giesselbach, 1981; Emmelkamp & Kwee, 1977; Emmelkamp & Van der Heyden, 1980).

• People with obsessive–compulsive disorder evaluate their parents as being rejecting and lacking emotional warmth (Hoekstra, Visser, & Emmelkamp, 1989). Such parental characteristics were found to predict the response to treatment at 4-year follow-up (Visser et al., in press).

• The partners of obsessive–compulsive individuals are essentially normal. However, the marital relationship of obsessive–compulsive people can be characterized as being distressed (Emmelkamp, De Haan, & Hoogduin, in press).

• Relationship dysfunction does not affect treatment outcome (Emmelkamp et al., in press).

• Spouse-aided therapy with obsessive–compulsive patients is no more effective than treatment of the patient alone (Emmelkamp & De Lange, 1983; Emmelkamp, et al., in press).

Social phobias. Research has focused on comparative evaluations of cognitive therapies (rational-emotive therapy and self-instructional training) and behavioral therapies (exposure in vivo and assertiveness training) in both intergroup and intrasubject designs. For a detailed discussion, see Emmelkamp and Scholing (1989) and Scholing and Emmelkamp (1989a). The main conclusions are as follows:

• Cognitive therapies are equally as effective as exposure in vivo (Emmelkamp, Mersch, & Vissia,

1985; Emmelkamp, Mersch, Vissia, & Van der Helm, 1985).

• Scholing and Emmelkamp (1989b) evaluated the effects of exposure in vivo, cognitive therapy, and assertive training in intrasubject designs. No treatment appeared to be superior to the others, but each treatment enhanced the effect of the other treatments. This suggests that a combination of various techniques may be optimal.

• Cognitive therapy and assertiveness training were found to be effective regardless of the individual response pattern (Mersch, Emmelkamp, Bögels, & Van der Sleen, 1989).

Depression. Our evaluation of aspects of the (reformulated) learned helplessness model of depression and of the ASQ as an operationalization of this model did not give much support for the learned helplessness model. Mood-related influences on cognition (accessibility of cognitions hypothesis) could not be substantiated, possibly as a result of flaws in the materials used (thought associations). Biographical variables, particularly sex and academic level, showed some promise as contributors to depression, suggesting that learned helplessness and adjacent theorizing should incorporate such factors in theory and research (Albersnagel, 1988; Albersnagel, Arntz, et al., 1986; Arntz et al., 1985; Arrindell et al., 1978; Gerlsma & Albersnagel, 1987).

Clinical research focused on the comparison between cognitive and operant intervention methods in a crossover design with non-hospitalized depressed patients. Results indicated substantial treatment effects for both methods. After amelioration in both initial treatment phases, however, patients who had been treated operantly continued to make progress when being treated cognitively; in the other condition (operant treatment after initial cognitive treatment) no further amelioration took place (Boelens & Debats, 1983; Debats & Boelens, 1981). Furthermore, it was shown that the therapeutic relationship affected therapy outcome.

In addition to empirical research, several reviews have been published on the state of the art in depression theory, research, and therapy (Albersnagel, 1981, 1983, 1985; Albersnagel, Boelens, & Debats, 1986; Albersnagel, Emmelkamp, & Van den Hoofdakker, 1989; Albersnagel & Rouwendal, 1984; Boelens, 1986; 1990; Boelens & Emmelkamp, 1986; Emmelkamp & Albersnagel, 1979; Emmelkamp & Boelens, 1986).

Marital distress. Four comparative outcome

studies on distressed couples have now been conducted. The major conclusions of these studies are as follows:

1. Reciprocity counseling is as effective as system-theoretic counseling (Boelens, Emmelkamp, MacGillavry, & Markvoort, 1980).

2. The effects of reciprocity counseling and communication training are broadly comparable. There is no evidence to suggest that communication training should precede reciprocity counseling or vice versa (Emmelkamp, Van der Helm, MacGillavry, & Van Zanten, 1984).

3. Communication training in combination with system-theoretic counseling results in comparable effects; the sequence does not affect treatment outcome (Emmelkamp et al., 1984).

4. Cognitive restructuring leads to more improvement of the marriage than does communication training, although communication training does improve the communication (Emmelkamp, Van Linden van den Heuvell, Rüphan, Sanderman, Scholing, & Stroink, 1988).

Instruments Developed

Many instruments were adapted for use in the Netherlands or were developed by our research groups; only the major ones are discussed here. The Fear Questionnaire and the Fear Survey Schedule were psychometrically evaluated by Arrindell, Emmelkamp, et al. (1984). Both instruments were found to possess adequate internal structure and can be used as screening devices and assessment instruments in therapy outcome studies. The Maudsley Obsessive–Compulsive Inventory was studied in clinical samples (Kraaykamp, Emmelkamp, & Van den Hout, 1990). The internal consistency was high for the total score and moderate for the Checking and Cleaning subscales. The Slowness and doubting subscales appeared to be unreliable, whereas the Extrapunitive and Intrapunitive subscales were found to be highly reliable. To assess irrational ideas and negative thoughts of patients, we have evaluated the RBI, the IBT, and Self-Statement Questionnaires (Sanderman et al., 1987).

For a brief measure to assess the quality of the marital relationship, the Maudsley, Marital Questionnaire was adapted for use in the Netherlands and was psychometrically evaluated. This questionnaire was found to have high internal

consistency, good reliability, and high discriminant validity (Arrindell, Boelens, & Lambert, 1983; Arrindell, Emmelkamp, & Bast, 1983). To assess relationship beliefs of couples, the RBI was psychometrically evaluated. This questionnaire was found to have adequate internal consistency and reliability. Evidence was provided for its construct validity, but discriminant validity was found to be poor (Emmelkamp, Krol, Sanderman, & Rüphan, 1987).

A large-scale experimental study ($N = 278$) was conducted to test the psychometric qualities of the ASQ (Arntz et al., 1985). Results cast doubt on the attributional style concept and on the ASQ as a psychometrically sound operationalization of learned helplessness.

In addition, the attribution concept was examined by psychometric evaluation of the Causal Dimensions Scale in a longitudinal study on unemployment with 378 professional graduates. Results showed that contrary to expectation, subjects did not change their causal perceptions when they became unemployed (Schaufeli, 1988). Psychometric evaluation of the BDI (Albersnagel, 1986; Bouman, 1987; Bouman & Kok, 1987; Bouman et al., 1985; Luteijn, 1983, 1986; Luteijn and Bouman, 1988b) and the PES (Bouman, 1986; Bouman & Luteijn, 1986) found the psychometric qualities of these questionnaires to be satisfactory for use in the Netherlands. In addition, several other instruments were developed and psychometrically tested: the SCL-90 (Arrindell & Ettema, 1986); the Hopkins Symptom Check List (Luteijn, Hamel, Bouman, & Kok, 1984a, 1984b); the SIB (Arrindell, De Groot, & Walburg, 1980); the Dutch Personality Questionnaire (NPV; Luteijn, Starren, & Van Dijk, 1985; Luteijn & Van Dijk, 1982; Luteijn, Van Dijk, & Van der Ploeg, 1981); and the Dutch short-form of the Minnesota Multiphase Personality Inventory (Lambert & Luteijn, 1987; Luteijn & Kok, 1985). The psychometric qualities of these instruments, which are used in several research projects of the department, (especially for outcome evaluation), have shown to be satisfactory for use in the Netherlands (Ouborg, 1988).

Research Programs in Progress and Planned for the Future

We are currently studying which components of a comprehensive cognitive–behavioral package are responsible for the improvements achieved among agoraphobic individuals. Patients with agoraphobia are randomly assigned across four conditions: exposure in vivo, exposure in vivo plus breathing instructions and cognitive restructuring, breathing instructions and cognitive restructuring, and breathing instructions only. Initial results suggest that all four treatments cause a reduction of panic attacks. Given the small number of patients who have been treated in each condition, however, comments about the relative efficacy of the conditions are premature.

We are now investigating whether a combination of cognitive therapy and exposure in vivo is superior to each procedure on its own among individuals with social phobias. Half of the patients in each condition are treated in groups, and the other half are treated individually. It is too early to draw conclusions with respect to effectiveness of treatment condition or treatment format.

We are also investigating whether treatment based on a functional behavior analysis is superior to a standardized exposure in vivo plus a response prevention program among individuals with obsessive–compulsive disorder. A functional behavior analysis and a treatment plan based on this analysis are made for all patients. Half of the patients are then treated according to this plan, and the other half receive the standardized exposure program. Assignment of patients to conditions is made after the functional behavior analysis. Results are not yet available.

Recently, we began a study into the psychological effects of bank robberies on victims. We are in the process of designing a treatment study for these victims and for other persons with posttraumatic stress disorders. Whether this study will be carried out depends primarily on funding. Posttraumatic stress disorder appears to be prevalent and, apart from studies with Vietnam veterans, has hardly been studied. We hope that our projected research in this area will lead to a better understanding of the processes involved in this disorder, which in turn may result in new treatment approaches.

Another area of interest concerns the impact of the therapeutic relationship on the cognitive and behavioral treatment of anxious and depressed patients. In the area of depression, further studies are planned to investigate the relationship between mood and dysfunctional cognitions. Despite our successes with cognitive–behavioral therapy, a firm scientific basis for this approach is still lacking. We see a clear need for further fundamental theorizing and basic research in this area. Furthermore, the relationships of depressed patients with their partners will be studied, including the effects of marital therapy on depressed patients. In our marital therapy studies we often found that depression in one of the partners impeded progress in therapy.

Finally, we are currently psychometrically evaluating the Millon Clinical Multiaxial Inventory. When this measure proves to be reliable and to have adequate factorial validity in a Dutch population, we intend to use it to investigate whether personality disorders are related to treatment outcome. In previous research with the NPV, no such relationships were found (Ouborg, 1988).

Nature of the Research Organization

The research program is conducted at the Department of Clinical Psychology of the University of Groningen, the Netherlands. Most affiliated staff members also have teaching tasks outside the research program and are involved in clinical practice. All staff members work part-time conducting research apart from the researchers, who work full-time and are grant funded.

Since 1982 the faculty staff members have been funded by the Dutch government for the duration of their involvement in the research program. The University of Groningen supports the program by funding two junior research psychologists for two specific projects. The Dutch government supports the program by funding another junior psychologist. Smaller projects have been funded in the past by the Dutch Association for Pure Scientific Research and the Prevention Foundation.

The staff consists of the following persons: P. M. G. Emmelkamp, PhD, professor of clinical psychology and psychotherapy, head of the department, and director of the research program; F. A. Albersnagel, PhD, assistant professor and coordinator of experimental psychopathology; W. Boelens, assistant professor; T. K. Bouman, PhD, assistant professor; D. L. H. M. Debats, assistant professor; J. H. M. Ettema, assistant professor; and F. Luteijn, associate professor and coordinator. Externally funded investigators include H. A. Scholing, junior research psychologist; C. Gerlsma, junior research psychologist (funded by the Foundation for Medical and Health Research

[Medigon]); and two junior research psychologists (recent vacancies).

Relation to Other Research Programs

Integration With Findings of Other Research

Internationally, there is a close cooperation with the major research groups who work in this area. In the Netherlands cooperation exists with other researchers who work in the same field; these include researchers from both universities of Amsterdam, the University of Nijmegen, and the University of Maastricht. The Dutch government recently acknowledged this collaborative research program by giving extra financial support to doctoral training in our centers.

Impact on the Field of Psychotherapy

The major findings of our research program appear to have influenced clinical practice not only in the Netherlands but also in other parts of the world. For example, self-management treatment by means of gradual exposure in vivo is now used in many countries for people with phobias and obsessive–compulsive disorder. Our research program on the relationship problems of individuals with agoraphobia has shown that the relationship hypothesis of agoraphobia is a myth. This certainly will have a profound influence on marital therapists working with these patients. We expect that our recent positive findings concerning cognitive therapy with people with obsessive–compulsive disorder and with maritally distressed couples will also affect clinical practice.

Like clinical practice, clinical training is influenced by the findings of our research program. Because our staff members are involved not only in the research program but also in the training of clinical psychologists and psychotherapists, the findings of our research lead directly to changes in the content of courses given. For example, in behavior therapy courses there is now less emphasis on imagination-based procedures than in the past and more emphasis on self-controlled exposure in vivo programs. Similarly, in marital therapy courses the structured cognitive and behavioral programs developed and evaluated in

our research programs now form an essential element of the training that students receive.

References

Albersnagel, F. A. (1981). Leertheorie en depressie. Problemen in theorievorming en (poli)klinische bruikbaarheid. *Gedragstherapeutisch Bulletin, 14,* 57–64.

Albersnagel, F. A. (1983). Psychologische theorien over depressie en hun empirische fundering. In R. Beer & H. S. F. Mulders (Eds.), *Psychologische benaderingswijzen van depressie,* (pp. 1–21). Lisse, the Netherlands: Swets & Zeitlinger.

Albersnagel, F. A. (1985). Theorie, assessment en behandeling van depressie volgens Aron T. Beck: Overzicht en evaluatie. *Gedragstherapie, 18,* 207–223.

Albersnagel, F. A. (1986). Classificatie en meting van depressief gedrag. *Gedragstherapie, 19,* 171–194.

Albersnagel, F. A. (1987). *Cognition, emotion and depressive behavior: From learned helplessness theory to accessibility of cognitions theory.* Meppel: Krips.

Albersnagel, F. A. (1988). Velten and musical mood induction procedures: A comparison with accessibility of thought association. *Behaviour, Research and Therapy, 26,* 79–96.

Albersnagel, F. A., Arntz, A., & Gerlsma, C. (1986). Some limitations of the attributional learned helplessness model on understanding effects of (non-) contingency: A controlled study in Dutch adolescents. *Advances in Behaviour, Research and Therapy, 8,* 1–42.

Albersnagel, F. A., Boelens, W., & Debats, D. L. H. M. (1986). Depressief gedrag. In J. W. G. Orlemans, W. P. Haayman, & P. Eelen (Eds.), *Handboek gedragstherapie* (pp. C.2-1–C.2-50). Deventer: Van Loghum Slaterus.

Albersnagel, F. A., Emmelkamp, P. M. G., & Van den Hoofdakker, R. H. (1989). *Depressie: Diagnostiek en behandeling.* Deventer, the Netherlands: Van Loghum Slaterus.

Albersnagel,F. A., & Rouwendal, J. (1984). Cognitieve gedragstherapie van depressie: Overzicht en evaluatie van gecontroleerd outcome-onderzoek. *Gedragstherapie, 17,* 27–44.

American Psychiatric Association. (1987). *Diagnostic and statistical manual of mental disorders* (rev. 3rd ed.). Washington, DC: Author.

Arntz, A., Gerlsma, C., & Albersnagel, F. A. (1985). Attributional Style Questionnaire: Psychometric evaluation of the ASQ in Dutch adolescents. *Advances in Behavior, Research and Therapy, 7,* 55–89.

Arrindell, W. A. (1987). *Marital conflict and agoraphobia: Fact or fantasy?* Delft, the Netherlands: Eburon.

Arrindell, W. A., Albersnagel, F. A., & Emmelkamp, P. M. G. (1978). Learned helplessness inductie langs cognitieve weg: Een experimenteel onderzoek. *Nederlands Tijdschrift voor de Psychologie, 33,* 255–265.

Arrindell, W. A., Boelens, W., & Lambert, H. (1983). On

the psychometric properties of the Maudsley marital questionnaire (MMQ): Evaluation of self-ratings in distressed and "normal" volunteer couples based on the Dutch version. *Personality and Individual Differences, 4,* 293–306.

Arrindell, W. A., & Emmelkamp, P. M. G. (1986). Marital adjustment, intimacy and needs in female agoraphobics and their partners: A controlled study. *British Journal of Psychiatry, 149,* 592–602.

Arrindell, W. A., & Emmelkamp, P. M. G. (1985). Psychological profile of the spouse of the female agoraphobic patient: Personality and symptoms. *British Journal of Psychiatry, 146,* 405–414.

Arrindell, W. A., & Emmelkamp, P. M. G. (1987). Psychological states and traits in female agoraphobics: A controlled study. *Journal of Psychopathology and Behavioral Assessment, 9,* 237–253.

Arrindell, W. A., Emmelkamp, P. M. G., & Bast, S. (1983). The Maudsley Marital Questionnaire (MMQ): A further step towards its validation. *Journal of Personality and Individual Differences, 4,* 457–464.

Arrindell, W. A., Emmelkamp, P. M. G., Brilman, E., & Monsma, A. (1983). Psychometric evaluation of an inventory for assessment of parental rearing practices. A Dutch form of the EMBU. *Acta Psychiatrica Scandinavia,* 163–177.

Arrindell, W. A., Emmelkamp, P. M. G., & Sanderman, R. (1986). Marital quality and general life adjustment in relation to treatment outcome in agoraphobia. *Advances in Behaviour, Research and Therapy,* 139–185.

Arrindell, W. A., Emmelkamp, P. M. G., & Van der Ende, J. (1984). Phobic dimensions: Reliability and generalizability across samples, gender and nations. *Advances in Behaviour, Research and Therapy, 6,* 207–254.

Arrindell, W. A., & Ettema, J. H. M. (1986). *SCL-90: Handleiding bij een multidimensionele psychopathologie-indicator.* Lisse, the Netherlands: Swets & Zeitlinger.

Arrindell, W. A., De Groot, P. M., & Walburg, J. A. (1980). *De Schaal voor Interpersoonlijk Gedrag (SIG).* Lisse, the Netherlands: Swets & Zeitlinger.

Boelens, W. (1986). Cognitieve therapie bij depressie. *Directieve Therapie, 6,* 17–35.

Boelens, W. (1990). *Cognitive behavioral interventions in depression.* Unpublished doctoral dissertation.

Boelens, W., & Debats, D. (1983) Vergelijking van een puur gedragsmatige met een puur cognitieve behandeling voor depressieve patiënten. In R. Beer & H. Mulders (Eds.), *Psychologische benaderingen van depressie.* Lisse, the Netherlands: Swets & Zeitlinger.

Boelens, W., & Emmelkamp, P. M. G. (1986). Ontwikkelingen in de gedragstherapie. In B. G. Deelman, P. M. G. Emmelkamp, A. F. Kalverboer, & F. Luteijn (Eds.), *Ontwikkelingen in de klinische psychologie.* Deventer, the Netherlands: Van Loghum Slaterus.

Boelens, W., Emmelkamp, P. M. G., MacGillavry, D., & Markvoort, M. (1980). A clinical evaluation of marital treatment: Reciprocity counseling vs. system-theoretic counseling. *Behaviour Analysis and Modification, 4,* 85–96.

Boersma, K., Den Hengst, S., Dekker, J., & Emmelkamp, P. M. G. (1976). Exposure and response prevention in the natural environment: A comparison

with obsessive–compulsive patients. *Behaviour, Research and Therapy, 14,* 19–24.

Bouman, T. K. (1986). Een psychometrische evaluatie van de stemmingsschaal van de Pleasant Events Schedule (PES). *Gedragstherapie, 19,* 97–107.

Bouman, T. K., & Kok, A. R. (1987). Homogeneity of Beck's Depression Inventory: Applying Rasch analysis in conceptual exploration. *Acta Psychiatrica Scandinavia, 76,* 568–573.

Bouman, T. K., & Luteijn, F. (1986). Relations between the Pleasant Events Schedule, depression and other aspects of psychopathology. *Journal of Abnormal Psychology, 95,* 373–377.

Bouman, T. K., Luteijn, F., Albersnagel, F. A., & Van der Ploeg, F. A. E. (1985). Enige ervaringen met de Beck Depression Inventory (BDI). *Gedrag, Tijdschrift voor Psychologie, 13,* 13–24.

Debats, D., & Boelens, W. (1981). Depressieonderzoek: theorie en praktijk. *Gedragstherapie, 14,* 3–16.

Emmelkamp, P. M. G. (1974). Self-observation versus flooding in the treatment of agoraphobia. *Behaviour, Research and Therapy, 12,* 229–237.

Emmelkamp, P. M. G. (1979). The behavioral treatment of clinical phobias. In Hersen, Eisler, & Miller (Eds.), *Progress in behavior modification* (Vol. 8). New York: Academic Press.

Emmelkamp, P. M. G. (1980). Agoraphobics' interpersonal problems: Their role in the effects of exposure in vivo therapy. *Archives of General Psychiatry, 37,* 1303–1306.

Emmelkamp, P. M. G. (1982a). In vivo treatment of agoraphobia. In D. Chambless & A. Goldstein (Eds.), *Agoraphobia: Multiple perspectives on theory and treatment.* New York: Wiley.

Emmelkamp, P. M. G. (1982b). *Phobic and obsessive-compulsive disorders: Theory, research and practice.* New York: Plenum Press.

Emmelkamp, P. M. G. (1987). Obsessive–compulsive disorder. In L. Michelson & M. Ascher (Eds.), *Anxiety and stress.* New York: Guilford Press.

Emmelkamp, P. M. G. (1988a). In vivo measurement of agoraphobia. In M. Hersen & A. Bellack (Eds.), *Dictionary of behavioral assessment techniques.* New York: Pergamon Press.

Emmelkamp, P. M. G. (1988b). Marital quality and treatment outcome in anxiety disorders. In I. Hand & H. U. Wittchen (Eds.), *Panic and phobias II.* New York: Springer-Verlag.

Emmelkamp, P. M. G. (1988c). Maudsley obsessional-compulsive inventory. In M. Hersen & A. Bellack (Eds.), *Dictionary of behavioral assessment techniques.* New York: Pergamon Press.

Emmelkamp, P. M. G. (1989a). Anxiety disorders. In A. Bellack, M. Hersen, & A. Kazdin (Eds.), *The international handbook of behavior modification and therapy.*

Emmelkamp, P. M. G. (1989b). Obsessive–compulsive disorder in adulthood. In C. G. Last & M. Hersen (Eds.), *Handbook of child and adult psychopathology.* New York: Pergamon Press.

Emmelkamp, P. M. G., & Albersnagel, F. A. (1979). Depression: Une approche clinique et empirique. *Journal de Therapie Comportementale, 1,* 91–106.

Emmelkamp, P. M. G., & Boelens, W. (1986) Evaluatieonderzoek naar het effect van gedragstherapie en kognitieve therapie. In P. E. Boeke, A. P. Cassee, & C. van der Staak (Eds.), *Onderzoek naar effekten van psychotherapie*. Deventer, the Netherlands: Van Loghum Slaterus.

Emmelkamp, P. M. G., Bouman, T., & Scholing, H. A. (1989). *Angst, fobieën en dwang: Diagnostiek en behandeling*. Deventer, the Netherlands: Van Loghum Slaterus.

Emmelkamp, P. M. G., Brilman, E., Kuipers, H., & Mersch, P. P. A. (1986). Agoraphobia: A comparison of self-instructional training, rational emotive therapy and exposure in vivo. *Behavior Modification, 10*, 37–53.

Emmelkamp, P. M. G., & Emmelkamp-Benner, A. (1975). Effects of historically portrayed modeling and group treatment on self-observation: A comparison with agoraphobics. *Behaviour Research and Therapy, 13*, 135–139.

Emmelkamp, P. M. G., & Giesselbach, P. (1981). Treatment of obsessions: Relevant vs. irrelevant exposure. *Behavioural Psychotherapy, 9*, 322–329.

Emmelkamp, P. M. G., De Haan, E., & Hoogduin, C. A. L. (in press). Marital adjustment and obsessive–compulsive disorder. *British Journal of Psychiatry*.

Emmelkamp, P. M. G., Van der Helm, M., MacGillavry, D., & Van Zanten, B. (1984). Marital therapy with clinically distressed couples: A comparative evaluation of system-theoretic, contingency-contracting and communication skills approaches. In K. Hahlweg & N. Jacobson (Eds.), *Marital therapy and interaction*. New York: Guilford Press.

Emmelkamp, P. M. G., Van der Helm, M., Van Zanten, B., & Plochg, I. (1980). Contributions of self-instructional training to the effectiveness of exposure in vivo: A comparison with obsessive–compulsive patients. *Behaviour Research and Therapy, 18*, 61–66.

Emmelkamp, P. M. G., & Van der Heyden, H. (1980). Treatment of harming obsessions. *Behavioural Analysis and Modification, 4*, 28–35.

Emmelkamp, P. M. G., & Van der Hout, A. (1983). Failure in treating agoraphobia. In E. B. Foa & P. M. G. Emmelkamp (Eds.), *Failures in behavior therapy*. New York: Wiley.

Emmelkamp, P. M. G., Van der Hout, A., & De Vries, K. (1983). Assertive training for agoraphobics. *Behavior Research and Therapy, 21*, 63–68.

Emmelkamp, P. M. G., & Kraanen, J. (1977). Therapist controlled exposure in vivo versus self-controlled exposure in vivo: A comparison with obsessive–compulsive patients. *Behaviour Research and Therapy, 15*, 491–495.

Emmelkamp, P. M. G., Krol, B., Sanderman, R., & Rüphan, M. (1987). The assessment of relationship beliefs. *Journal of Personality and Individual Differences, 8*, 775–780.

Emmelkamp, P. M. G., & Kuipers, A. (1979). Agoraphobia: A four year follow-up. *British Journal of Psychiatry, 134*, 352–355.

Emmelkamp, P. M. G., Kuipers, A., & Eggeraat, J. (1978). Cognitive modification versus prolonged exposure in vivo: A comparison with agoraphobics. *Behaviour Research and Therapy, 16*, 33–41.

Emmelkamp, P. M. G., & Kwee, G. K. (1977). Obsessional ruminations: A comparison between thought-stopping and prolonged exposure in imagination. *Behaviour Research and Therapy, 15*, 441–444.

Emmelkamp, P. M. G., & De Lange, I. (1983). Spouse involvement in the treatment of obsessive–compulsive patients. *Behaviour Research and Therapy, 21*, 341–346.

Emmelkamp, P. M. G., Van Linden van den Heuvell, C., Rüphan, M., & Sanderman, R. (1989). Home-based treatment of obsessive-compulsive patients: Intersession interval and therapist involvement. *Behaviour Research and Therapy, 27*, 83–89.

Emmelkamp, P. M. G., Van Linden van den Heuvell, C., Rüphan, M., Sanderman, R., Scholing, A., & Stroink, F. (1988). Cognitive and behavioral interventions: A comparative evaluation with clinically distressed couples. *Journal of Family Psychology, 1*, 365–377.

Emmelkamp, P. M. G., & Mersch, P. P. A. (1982). Cognition and exposure in vivo in the treatment of agoraphobia: Short-term and delayed effects. *Cognitive Therapy and Research, 6*, 77–90.

Emmelkamp, P. M. G., Mersch, P. P. A., & Vissia, E. (1985). The external validity of analogue outcome research: Evaluation of cognitive and behavioural intervention. *Behaviour Research and Therapy, 23*, 83–86.

Emmelkamp, P. M. G., Mersch, P. P. A., Vissia, E., & Van der Helm, M. (1985). Social phobia: A comparative evaluation of cognitive and behavioral interventions. *Behaviour Research and Therapy, 23*, 365–369.

Emmelkamp, P. M. G., & Rabbie, D. M. (1981). Psychological treatment of obsessive-compulsive disorder: A follow-up four years after treatment. In Janson, Perris, & Struwe (Eds.), *Biological psychiatry*. Amsterdam, the Netherlands. Elsevier.

Emmelkamp, P. M. G., & Scholing, H. A. (1989). Behavioral treatment for simple and social phobics. In Roth & Noyes (Eds.), *Handbook of Anxiety*, (Vol. 4). Amsterdam, the Netherlands. Elsevier.

Emmelkamp, P. M. G., & Ultee, K. A. (1974). A comparison of successive approximation and self-observation in the treatment of agoraphobia. *Behavior Therapy, 5*, 605–613.

Emmelkamp, P. M. G., Visser, S., & Hoekstra, R. (1988). Cognitive therapy vs. exposure in the treatment of obsessive–compulsives. *Cognitive Therapy and Research, 12*, 103–114.

Emmelkamp, P. M. G., & Wessels, H. (1975). Flooding in imagination vs. flooding in vivo: A comparison with agoraphobics. *Behaviour Research and Therapy, 13*, 7–16.

Gerlsma, C., & Albersnagel, F. A. (1987). Effects of (non) contingency in a learned helplessness experiment: A re-analysis based on mood changes. *Behaviour, Research and Therapy, 25*, 329–340.

Hoekstra, R. J., Visser, S., & Emmelkamp, P. M. G. (1989). A social learning formulation of the etiology of obsessive–compulsive disorders. In P. M. G. Emmelkamp, W. T. A. M. Everaerd, F. Uraaimaat, & M. van Son (Eds.), *Annual series of European research in behavior therapy: Vol. 4. Fresh perspectives on anxiety disorders* (pp. 115–123). Amsterdam: Berwyn.

Hout, M. Van den, Emmelkamp, P. M. G., Kraaykamp, J., & Griez, E. (1988). Behavioural treatment of obsessive–compulsives: Inpatient versus outpatient. *Behaviour Research and Therapy, 26*, 331–332.

Kraaykamp, H. J. M., Emmelkamp, P. M. G., & Van den Hout, M. (1990). *The Maudsley Obsessive–Compulsive Inventory: Reliability and validity.* Manuscript submitted for publication.

Lambert, H., & Luteijn, F. (1987). De vergelijking van de NVM en de MMPI in de klinische praktijk. *Nederlands Tijdschrift voor de Psychologie, 42,* 81–85.

Luteijn, F. (1983). Diagnostiek van depressie. In R. Beer & H. S. F. Mulder (Eds.), *Psychologische benaderingen van depressie.* Lisse, the Netherlands: Swets & Zeitlinger.

Luteijn, F. (1986). Persoonlijkheidsvragenlijsten in de klinische psychologie. In B. G. Deelman, P. M. G. Emmelkamp, A. F. Kalverboer, & F. Luteijn (Eds.), *Ontwikkelingen in de klinische psychologie.* Deventer, the Netherlands: Van Loghum Slaterus.

Luteijn, F., & Bouman, T. K. (1988). The concepts of depression, anxiety and neuroticism in questionnaires. *European Journal of Personality, 2,* 113–120.

Luteijn, F., & Bouman, T. K. (1988) De validiteit van Beck's Depression Inventory. *Nederlands Tijdschrift voor de Psychologie, 43,* 340–343.

Luteijn, F., & Van Dijk, H. (1982). De validiteit van een nieuwe kinderpersoonlijkheidsvragenlijst: De NPV-J. *Nederlands Tijdschrift voor de Psychologie, 37,* 241–256.

Luteijn, F., Van Dijk, H., & Van der Ploeg, F. A. E. (1981). *Handleiding bij de NPV-J.* Lisse, the Netherlands: Swets & Zeitlinger.

Luteijn, F., Hamel, L. F., Bouman, T. K., & Kok, A. R. (1984). *Handleiding bij de HSCL.* Lisse, the Netherlands: Swets & Zeitlinger.

Luteijn, F., Hamel, L., Bouman, T. K., & Kok, A. R. (1984). *HSCL: Hopkins Symptom Check List.* Lisse, the Netherlands: Swets & Zeitlinger.

Luteijn, F., & Kok, A. R. (1985). *Herziene verantwoording en handleiding bij de NVM.* Lisse, the Netherlands: Swets & Zeitlinger.

Luteijn, F., Starren, J., & Van Dijk, H. (1985). *Herziene verantwoording en handleiding van de NPV.* Lisse, the Netherlands: Swets & Zeitlinger.

Mersch, P. P., Emmelkamp, P. M. G., Bögels, S., & Van der Sleen, J. (1989). Social phobia: Individual response patterns and the effects of behavioral and cognitive interventions. *Behaviour Research and Therapy, 27,* 421–434.

Ouborg, M. J. (1988). *Klinische psychodiagnostiek en psychotherapie.* Unpublished doctoral dissertation.

Sanderman, R., Mersch, P. P. A., Van der Sleen, J., Emmelkamp, P. M. G., & Ormel, J. (1987). The Rational Behavior Inventory (RBI): A psychometric evaluation. *Journal of Personality and Individual Differences, 8,* 561–569.

Schaufeli, W. B. (1988). Perceiving the causes of unemployment: An evaluation of the Causal Dimensions Scale in a real-life situation. *Journal of Personality and social Psychology, 54,* 347–356.

Scholing, H. A., & Emmelkamp, P. M. G. (1989a). Social phobia: Nature and treatment. In H. Leitenberg (Ed.), *Handbook of social anxiety.* New York: Plenum Press.

Scholing, H. A., & Emmelkamp, P. M. G. (1989b). Treatment of social phobia: Analyses in single cases. In P. M. G. Emmelkamp, W. T. A. M. Everaerd, F. Kraaimaat, & M. van Son (Eds.), *Annual series of European research in behavior therapy: Vol. 4. Fresh perspectives on anxiety disorders.* Amsterdam: Berwyn.

Visser, S., Hoekstra, R. J., & Emmelkamp, P. M. G. (in press). Follow up study on behavioural treatment of obsessive–compulsive disorders. In W. Fiegenbaum, A. Ehlers, J. Margraf, & I. Florin (Eds.), *Perspectives and promises of clinical psychology.*

Small-Scale and Developing Programs

31

George Washington University's International Data on Psychotherapy Delivery Systems: Modeling New Approaches to the Study of Therapy

E. Lakin Phillips
George Washington University

Background and Aims

Several years ago I began to study how the psychotherapy delivery system as a whole operated. This approach consisted of listing the patients who had one, two, three, or more sessions of treatment out to an asymptote. Once it was shown that a characteristic curve developed from analyzing data bases from a year or so, I began to extend my work nationally and internationally. Although all the people with whom I communicated had been aware of patients dropping out from treatment offered, accepted, or begun, none had actually described the attrition curve as such. Its properties proved to be those of a negatively accelerating, declining, attrition (noncompliance in medical terminology) "decay" curve with approximately equal mean and standard deviation values, with the median being smaller than the mean and the asymptote extending several standard deviations beyond the mean (Figure 1 in Rosenstein & Milazzo-Sayre, 1981).

After these observations were made, it became apparent that as many psychotherapy service delivery curves should be examined as possible. From the null hypothesis I conjectured that there would be no reliable differences between the standard American curves and those yet to be studied internationally, which would take into account ethnic, national, diagnostic, and possibly population differences. Styles of therapy and training of therapists also might be seen as possible contenders for differences in delivery curves.

The overall aim then became the corroboration, if possible, of the same or similar curves from as widely dispersed countries and conditions as possible. The rest of this chapter touches briefly on the pursuit of any corroborative or extenuating conditions that might affect the curves noted widely in the United States.

Method

Data bases were sought through personal contact from the Federal Republic of Germany, Japan, Poland, and Holland and more widely in the United States. These were generally already in existence in data files or computers. By starting at a place in the files where all previous cases had been closed and then counting backward for an appreciable number of cases (preferably in the hundreds) or over time (1 year or more), I was able to record the coded patients as to number of sessions, age, sex, presenting complaint (diagnosis), ethnic status, and any particular relevancies for the research at hand. The research was considered descriptive only at first; later, manipulations of the data base were considered, but these are too extensive to account for here. Subject selection was minimal: I simply took all applicants for psychotherapy in a given clinic and later disaggregated the total population for sex, age, diagnosis, and so on, to determine whether curve differences resulted. The procedures for collating and arranging attendance data at a clinic are so simple that any clerk can catch on to them in a few minutes. No psychometric instruments were used in most such studies, but their use was not precluded. Biographical items such as previous therapy, drug treatment, and so forth, could always become a topic for a subpopulation if such appeared useful.

The procedures undertaken after the collation of data were based on plotting in histogram from the number of sessions of therapy along the x-axis and the number of patients remaining in therapy after each session on the y-axis. The resulting curve was a negatively accelerated, declining, attrition (decay) curve. Data bases from any clinic whatsoever could readily be noted and statistical tests applied (chi-square, Lorenzo curve, inequality tests from economics). Tested differences between curves tended to be minor, but important data began to appear as to the length of the asymptote (what proportion of the clientele was being served by what percentage of professional time throughout the distribution) and how quickly after intake people left the service delivery system (possibly signaling policy considerations). Because selection of particular cases was left to the home-base clinic providing the data base, disaggregation of large samples was the method of examining particular problems of gender, diagnosis, and so forth. No attempts were made to select "ideal" patients insofar as I know, but such issues would fall out from the disaggregations carried out subsequently. Any personality tests or other measurements previously used by a particular clinic were left alone during the initial analysis and brought in later through the study of subgroups. The whole-cloth description of the entire service delivery system was first and foremost in our effort.

Research Accomplishments

Figures 31.1–31.7 summarize data across ethnic, national, gender, and diagnostic issues. This sampling purports to be broad based enough to give credence to the testing of the null hypothesis (i.e., that there are no differences to psychotherapy service delivery systems of a reliable nature) despite phenotypic differences such as the usual demographic variables, type of therapy, or the like. All data bases range in size from hundreds to more than a million cases and from 1 to 4 years or more of data collection.

Figure 31.1 (see also Table 11a, Rosenstein & Milazzo-Sayre, 1981, p. 104) summarizes the attrition curves for four subpopulations in the United States: White and non-White men and women. The compelling nature of the attrition curve is clearly present, although minor gender and ethnic differences exist. The overall median is about 4 sessions, the mean is in the 6–8-session range, and the asymptote extends more than 4 SDs. These outpatient cases set a baseline and standard for outpatient psychotherapy. We cannot reject the null hypothesis on the basis of these data as a whole or when disaggregated.

Data from a university outpatient mental health facility covering four consecutive years is shown in Figure 31.2 (Phillips, 1985, 1988a). The patients were 17–27 years old ($M = 23$ years, $SD = 6$ years); 60% were women; and all academic levels were represented, with heavier emphasis being placed on upper levels and graduate or professional school clientele. Mean number of sessions ranged between four and six, and standard deviations were comparably close. Satisfaction rating for these patients was about 90% (for self-improvement, willingness to return for future help if needed, and willingness to refer others for help).

Insofar as the mean number of outpatient sessions is concerned, these university data fit closely with national standards of about 5 sessions or more for 45–50 million cases (Phillips, 1985). Age and gender differences were minor, although they were not disaggregated here. This curve is typical of most in that the number returning for therapy (as agreed) after intake is about 50% and then the smaller incremental drop from session to session tends to follow a smooth curve. Although a nominal 10-session time limit was used, exceptions (accounting for more than 5% of the cases) took an average of about 15 sessions, a possibly disproportionate use of professional time for this number of patients. Such

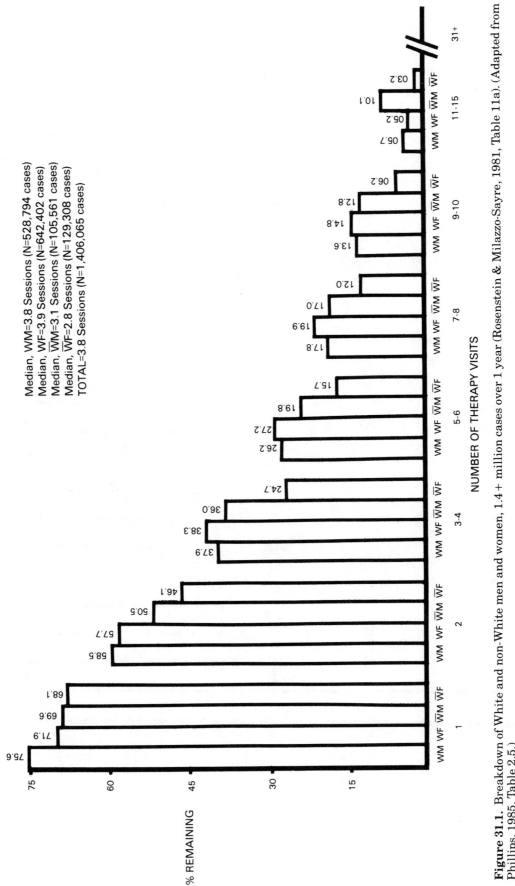

Median, WM=3.8 Sessions (N=528,794 cases)
Median, WF=3.9 Sessions (N=642,402 cases)
Median, W̄M=3.1 Sessions (N=105,561 cases)
Median, W̄F=2.8 Sessions (N=129,308 cases)
TOTAL=3.8 Sessions (N=1,406,065 cases)

Figure 31.1. Breakdown of White and non-White men and women, 1.4 + million cases over 1 year (Rosenstein & Milazzo-Sayre, 1981, Table 11a). (Adapted from Phillips, 1985, Table 2.5.)

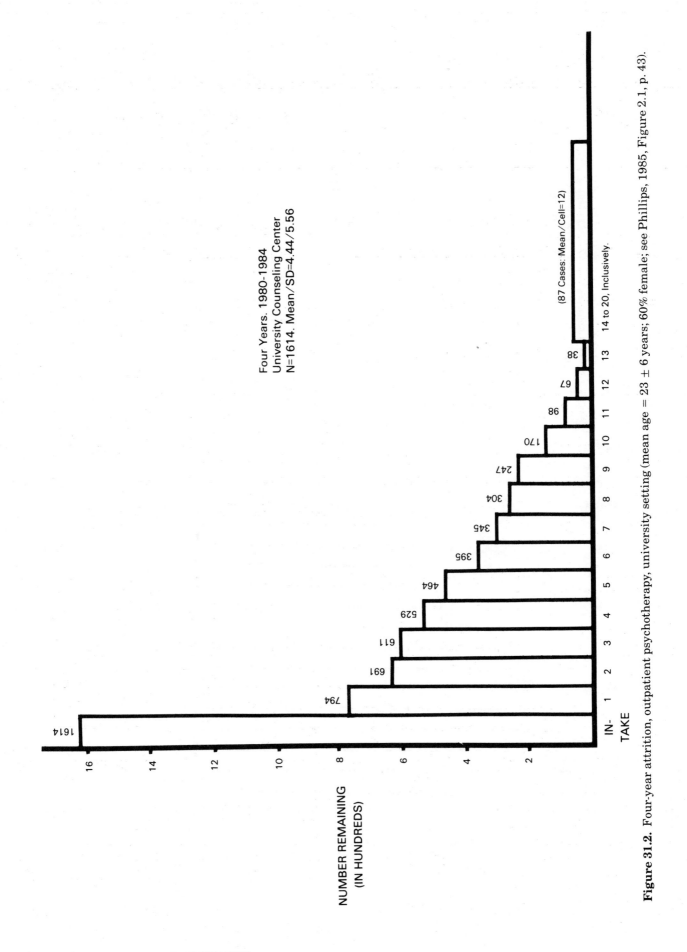

Figure 31.2. Four-year attrition, outpatient psychotherapy, university setting (mean age = 23 ± 6 years; 60% female; see Phillips, 1985, Figure 2.1, p. 43).

Four Years. 1980-1984
University Counseling Center
N=1614. Mean/SD=4.44/5.56

(87 Cases: Mean/Cell=12)

NUMBER REMAINING
(IN HUNDREDS)

comparisons are only likely to be made when the entire distribution is possible, as in Figure 31.2. Policy matters, better training of therapists, firmer limit setting, and so forth, may be indicated in these distributions.

Figure 31.3 shows a Dutch population of nearly 1,400 phobic cases; here the asymptote extends about 7–8 SDs beyond the mean to nearly 200 sessions. Peculiar to this curve is a 3-session assessment period that apparently had nothing to do with curtailing attrition but may have accelerated it. After about 15 sessions attrition appeared to accelerate somewhat; this was followed by a long asymptote that may have taken up an extraordinary amount of professional time compared with the rest of the distribution. The question is whether phobia cases command this much attention, whether "long-term therapists" may be operating on their own without due respect to the total clinic assignment of so many phobic cases, or whether system changes in treatment plans may have prevailed in part. Once the distribution is laid before one, a number of interesting theoretical and practical questions arise and suggest new research tactics that may affect the entire clinic's operation. There is probably no way to study this kind of problem other than through the whole-cloth service delivery system.

Highly similar to American university psychotherapy populations is the Japanese report of 1,281 cases over 5 years (see Figure 31.4). Despite obvious cultural differences and differences in therapy outlook and theory of treatment, this illustration could easily apply to almost any American university setting. Are all therapies the same if they end up the same in the form of highly similar distributions despite considerably different origins for the therapy practices as such? If all therapy distributions are essentially topologically similar, then the therapies must be likewise regarded, despite all the torturous theorizing about hypotheses concerning causality, process, outcome, and selection of cases. We may simply have a universal therapy in which all varieties and differences are tolerably small and the aggregate distributions are so similar that they can be almost completely interchanged.

With Figure 31.5 we note a decisively gradual service delivery attrition system from the Federal Republic of Germany. Although the mean and standard deviation values are larger than those of most American (and Japanese) outpatient populations, the slope of the curve is remarkably similar, and the asymptote extends out more than 3 SDs. By session 6 or 7, more than half of the patients

have left the system, and the last 10% of the cases extends 2 SDs. Thus, the final 32 cases (after the 24-session class interval) have a mean of about 34 sessions for a total of 1,000 sessions, compared with the first 232 cases being served in fewer than 4 sessions. How different are these subpopulations? Are they a function of some delivery system features not properly assessed or of some unilateral practices by a few therapists, or are they psychologically genuinely different? Attempts to spread out the whole distribution in this manner may help solve these and related cost problems.

Figure 31.6 switches focus to an inpatient childbirth population from Poland ($N = 100$) juxtaposed against an equal number of cases in the United States. Although the curves drop as expected, the slow drop at first (up to 4 days' length of stay for Poland) shows important cultural differences at least and possibly some other features not now recognized. The means represent almost a 4:1 ratio and the medians a 5:1 ratio, yet the asymptote for the Poland data is small (3 of 100 cases) and extends to nearly 1 month in the hospital. The American childbirth length of stay in the hospital is within the diagnosis-related group norms; evidently there are no such norms in Poland, so that the entire service delivery system is several times as expensive as the American system. Thus, not only do psychosocial treatments offer some differences among and between nations but medical treatments do as well, and we must look much further into this problem to understand its full implications.

Implications

These studies take a different look at psychotherapy than most comparative studies of psychotherapy between or among nations (Phillips, 1987, 1988b). The quest here is to discern the differences, if any, in how the service delivery system operates and how it appears topologically when plotted in the manner illustrated. If the curves are alike, then the therapies must be alike until shown to be different. Topography would seem to hold more sway than theories of therapy or hypotheses tested as to causal matters in personality disturbances and reasons for seeking help, if the present array of data (which is only a small sample of many other data bases that I have) can be interpreted as suggested (Phillips, 1986a, 1986b).

When we move from outpatients to length of

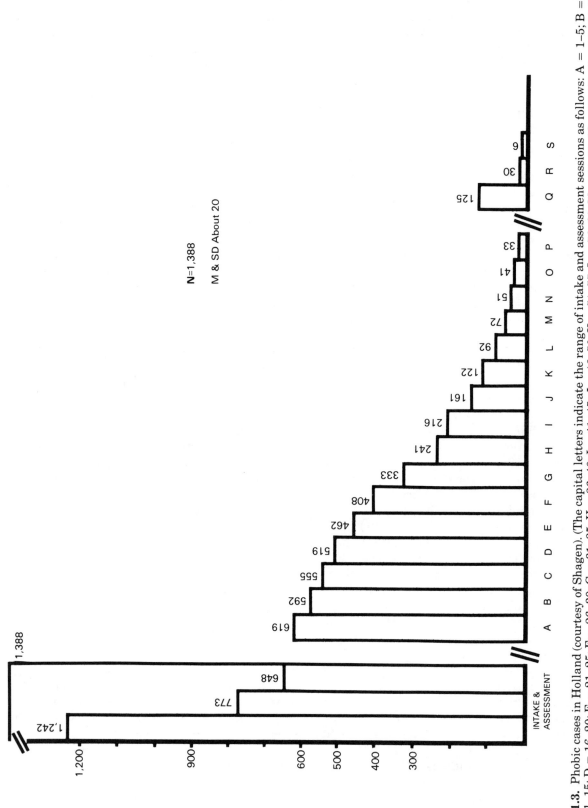

N=1,388

M & SD About 20

Figure 31.3. Phobic cases in Holland (courtesy of Shagen). (The capital letters indicate the range of intake and assessment sessions as follows: A = 1–5; B = 6–10; C = 11–15; D = 16–20; E = 21–25; F = 26–30; G = 31–35; H = 36–40; I = 41–45; J = 46–50; K = 51–55; L = 56–60; M = 61–65; N = 66–70; O = 71–75; P = 76–80; Q = 81–85; R = 111–140; and S = 141–195. Note 3 assessment sessions followed by therapy to 195 sessions.)

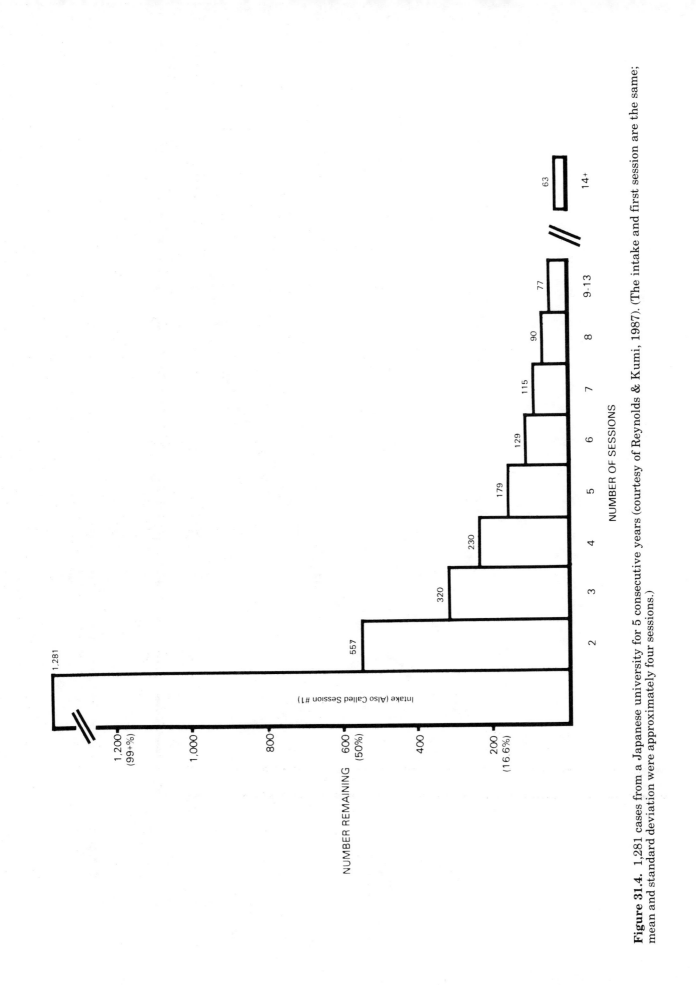

Figure 31.4. 1,281 cases from a Japanese university for 5 consecutive years (courtesy of Reynolds & Kumi, 1987). (The intake and first session are the same; mean and standard deviation were approximately four sessions.)

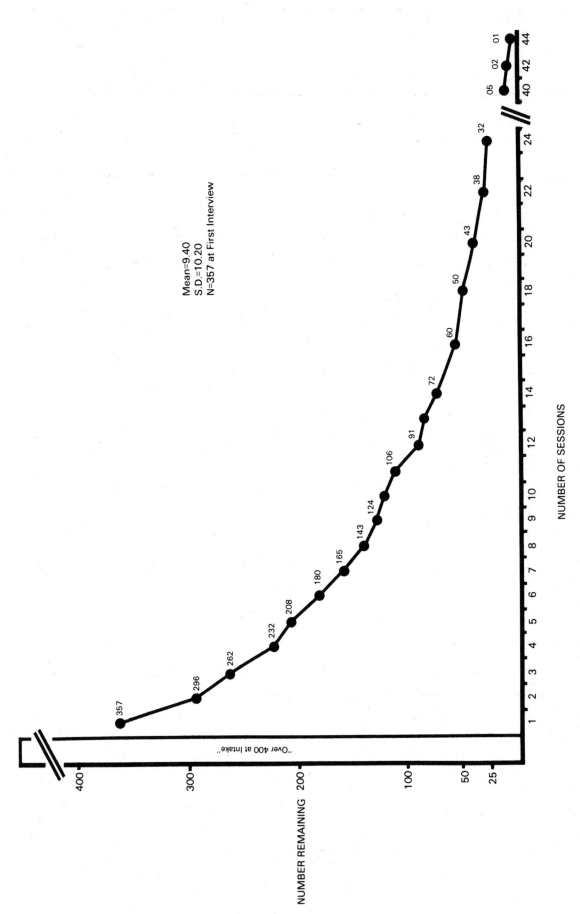

Figure 31.5. Outpatient psychotherapy in a Federal Republic of Germany community clinic (courtesy of Revensdorff, 1986).

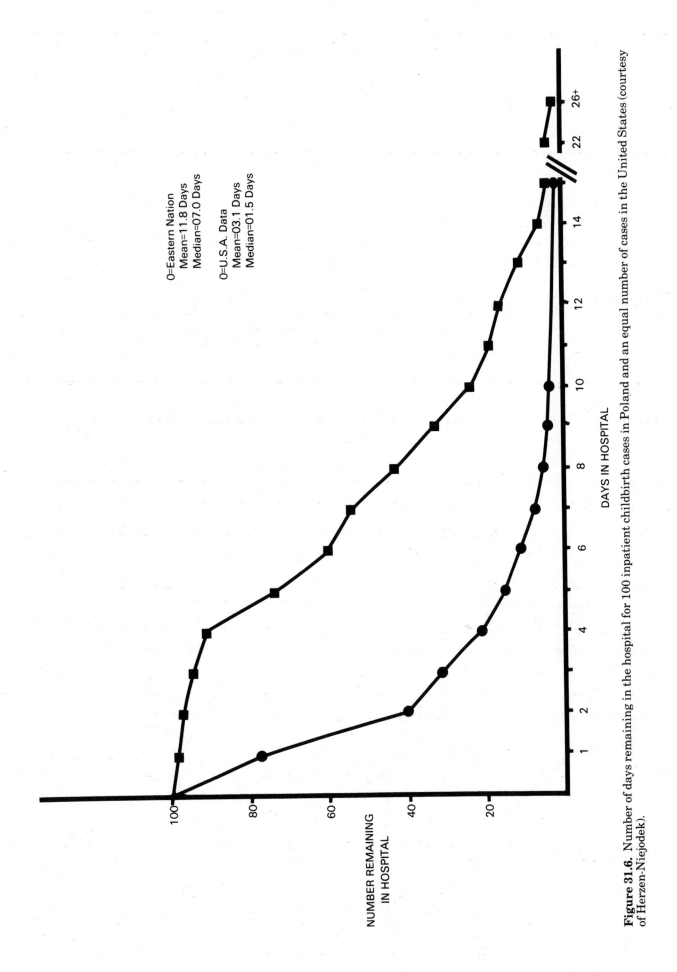

Figure 31.6. Number of days remaining in the hospital for 100 inpatient childbirth cases in Poland and an equal number of cases in the United States (courtesy of Herzen-Niejodek).

O=Eastern Nation
Mean=11.8 Days
Median=07.0 Days

O=U.S.A. Data
Mean=03.1 Days
Median=01.5 Days

NUMBER REMAINING
IN HOSPITAL

DAYS IN HOSPITAL

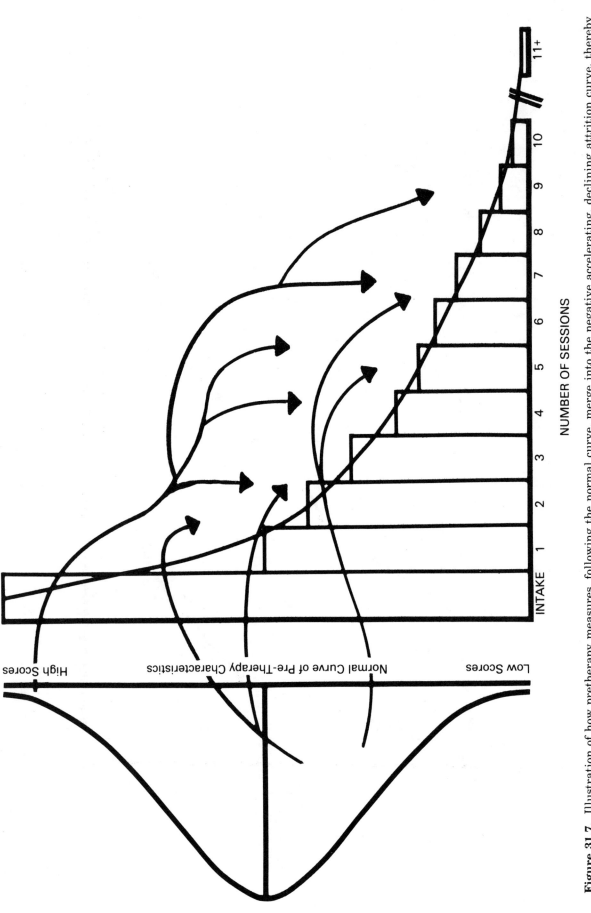

Figure 31.7. Illustration of how pretherapy measures, following the normal curve, merge into the negative accelerating, declining attrition curve, thereby largely precluding pre- and posttherapy relationships.

stay in inpatient treatment (childbirth in this case), we find larger differences than among psychosocial treatments. Are these biologically determined, more psychosocial in a policy way, or simply the result of systems of health care being run without regard to the nature of the problem of differences between delivery systems, even in medical treatment (although that is not our main concern here, it offers a contrasting role for the comparative psychotherapy study of delivery systems)?

The effort that we have spent trying to find who has the best psychotherapy should now be redirected toward the study of the entire delivery system (Beutler, Crago, & Arizmendi, 1986; Bloom, 1981). This offers a methodologically superior way to approach research on psychotherapy, offers a unifying basis for the many similarities among so-called different therapies, and helps set new research agendas that will presumably bring earlier, better, and more judicious services of a mental health nature to people of all countries (Kazdin, 1986; Koss & Butcher, 1986; Orlinsky & Howard, 1986).

As Figure 31.7 shows, the relation between pretherapy and posttherapy predictions has never been reliable (Phillips, 1986a, 1988b). This illustration shows that as patients move from a static description of their personality characteristics, areas of complaint, and so forth, their characteristics are transformed from a normal curve to a decay curve distribution with resultant poor correlation between the two time junctures. This changeover both illustrates and explains how and why there is a predictive failure when we rely solely on dyadic relationships and static measures of performance. The reply to this impasse—long with us—is not to continue to turn over every measurement stone we can but to set a new agenda through using the delivery system as the unit of study, which corrals, structures, and regulates the meaning and purpose of extant characteristics that interact with the delivery system itself.

In short, the delivery system controls most of the variance. Manipulation of individual and dyad variables is weak compared with the power of the delivery system. Moreover, the delivery system is far more apparent in its operation than are the many individual traits and characteristics associated with individual difference studies. Several basic features of the delivery system can be altered at will and the results studied, for example by revising intake procedures, setting variable time limits on the number of sessions, attenuating the length of the asymptote, spacing the time between sessions, and setting interim time limits on the number of sessions (e.g., by using blocks of three sessions or having short moratoriums after various numbers of sessions and disaggregating large populations to find valid subgroup differences).

A fully experimental approach to the delivery system, it would appear from many tentative but highly suggestive results, can turn up new ways to make possible more propitious and judicious treatments. We await only the courage and perseverance of researchers who are willing to strike out in new directions and leave aside the traditional problems about the fundamental nature of therapy and which are the best therapies.

References

Beutler, L. E., Crago, M., & Arizmendi, T. G. (1986). Research on therapist variables in psychotherapy. In S. L. Garfield & A. E. Bergin (Eds.), *Handbook of psychotherapy and behavior change* (3rd ed., pp. 285–310). New York: Wiley.

Bloom, B. L. (1981). Focused single-session therapy: Initial development and evaluation. In S. H. Budman (Ed.), *Forms of brief therapy* (pp. 167–216). New York: Guilford Press.

Kazdin, A. E. (1986). Editor's introduction to the special issue. *Journal of Consulting and Clinical Psychology, 54,* 3.

Koss, M. P., & Butcher, J. N. (1986). Research on brief psychotherapy. In S. L. Garfield & A. E. Bergin (Eds.), *Handbook of psychotherapy and behavior change.* (3rd ed., pp. 627–670). New York: Wiley.

Orlinsky, D. C., & Howard, K. I. (1986). Process and outcome in psychotherapy. In S. L. Garfield & A. E. Bergin (Eds.), *Handbook of psychotherapy and behavior change* (3rd ed., pp. 311–384). New York: Wiley.

Phillips, E. L. (1985). *Psychotherapy revised: New frontiers in research and practice.* Hillsdale, NJ: Erlbaum.

Phillips, E. L. (1986a, March). *Improving predictive value of health beliefs and medical/health compliance.* Paper presented at the meeting of the Southeastern Psychological Association, Atlanta, GA.

Phillips, E. L. (1986b, April). *A socio-behavioral approach to psychotherapy outcome evaluation.* Paper presented at the meeting of the Midwestern Psychological Association, Chicago.

Phillips, E. L. (1987). The ubiquitous decay curve: Service delivery similarities in psychotherapy, medicine, and addiction. *Professional Psychology: Theory, Research, Practice, Training, 18,* 650–652.

Phillips, E. L. (1988a). *Patient compliance: New light on health delivery systems in medicine and psychotherapy.* Bern, Switzerland: Hans Huber.

Phillips, E. L. (1988b, June). *Three basic patterns of psychotherapy delivery systems and what they mean.* Paper presented at the annual meeting of the Society for Psychotherapy Research, Sante Fe, NM.

Rosenstein, M. J., & Milazzo-Sayre, L. J. (1981). *Characteristics of admissions to selected mental health facilities: 1975.* Rockville, MD: Department of Health and Human Services.

32

Psychotherapy Research at the Institut National de la Santé et de la Recherche Médicale

Paul Gerin and Alice Dazord
Institut National de la Santé et de la Recherche Médicale

Background and Aims

In 1980 Gerin met with Professors Wildlöcher and Lazar, executive director of the Institut National de la Santé et de la Recherche Médicale (INSERM), who spoke on behalf of the institute's scientific committee. It was decided that Gerin would try to develop empirical psychotherapy research in France. In 1984 Gerin published a book summarizing the main findings on the subject in recent decades. He also met Lester Luborsky and developed some research on the core conflictual relationship theme and the Health–Sickness Rating Scale (HSRS, Baguet, Gerin, Sali, Marie-Cardine, 1984; Armelius, Gerin, Luborsky, 1984). In 1984 Dazord, another INSERM researcher joined Gerin.

Because French empirical research on psychotherapies is poorly developed, our major aim has been to popularize it among French clinicians, taking into account the specificity of the French context. We have focused on evaluation of therapeutic outcome in various psychiatric institutions of France and Geneva. The variables found to be related to outcome were as follows:

• patient variables (diagnosis, symptoms, and motivation);

• therapist variables (opinions about mental health, training, and expressed feeling toward the patient);

• patient–therapist interaction (therapeutic alliance and patient–therapist convergence concerning their opinions about the patient's difficulties);

• institutional variables (type of treatments, modalities of decisions, and informal psychotherapeutic situations).

Method

The treatments investigated were not restricted to well-defined psychotherapeutic approaches but addressed all interventions performed with a psychotherapeutic aim by professionals. Most of the instruments we have used are French translations of American scales that have been validated; these include the HSRS and the SCL-90. In most of our programs we used a naturalistic approach without any random distribution of patients between therapies and therapists.

Research Accomplishments

Nonspecific Factors of Change

The most important factors of change in psychiatric institutions are nonspecific. In several institutions (Gerin, Dazord, Sali, Guisti, & Marie-Cardine, 1987; Dazord, Gerin, Brochier, Guisti, &

Marie-Cardine, 1989), we correlated the changes presented by the patients with the therapeutic approaches. The therapeutic approaches considered were (a) well-defined and formalized psychotherapies (e.g., psychoanalysis or behavioral therapy); (b) nonformalized approaches (e.g., informal, irregularly schedules meetings with clinicians); and (c) institutional variables such as spontaneous interactions (e.g., meetings in a corridor) or special relationships between the patient and a member of the clinical team or another patient.

Each of these variables received two ratings to assess its presence or to evaluate the intensity of the patient's experience. The first rating was based on objective quantitative data such as the number of sessions or the presence or absence of a prescribed medication. The second was more subjective and based on the degree of the patient's involvement in the various therapeutic approaches. Measurements of the correlation between both ratings and outcome revealed the following:

• Ratings of nonformalized approaches and institutional variables correlated significantly with patients' changes. On the other hand, few correlations were found concerning formalized approaches; for some specific therapies (in French, *thérapies médiatisées* including somatic therapies or sociotherapies) negative correlations were found.

• Both subjective and objective ratings were involved in these correlations. Thus, concerning the *thérapies médiatisées* it is not the simple fact of undertaking such a therapy that correlates negatively with outcome but rather the degree of the patient's involvement in these approaches. This may suggest that a patient's strong involvement in such therapies might lead to a tendency to escape or disentangle himself or herself from more demanding but more efficient therapeutic situations.

• Nevertheless, the aforementioned correlations could be clearly observed only when different subgroups of patients (psychotic, depressed, or anxious) were differentiated. Nonformalized approaches were the most effective for psychotic patients.

Because Luborsky's (1976) helping alliance construct has previously been shown to correlate strongly with outpatients' outcome, we studied this parameter across institutions. Significant correlations were obtained, demonstrating that this factor is as important in the treatment of inpatients as in the treatment of outpatients.

Patient and Therapist Convergence

We used the comparison between patient and therapist opinions about the patient's difficulties as a new approach to investigate their interaction. With the instruments described later, we studied the correlation between this convergence and outcome in two different institutions (Reith, Andreoli, Gerin, & Dazord, 1988; Marie-Cardine, Gerin, Dazord, Guisti, & Terra, 1989).

Immediate outcome was evaluated at discharge time. For the first institution (a crisis intervention center in Geneva), we assessed the degree of success of the crisis intervention process; for the second (a psychiatric hospital in Lyon, France), we used a global rating of clinical change. In the first institution, the initial degree of congruence for any dimension was not found to correlate with outcome, whereas it did correlate at discharge time for the dimension *locus of causal attribution of the difficulty.* The degree of convergence still strongly correlated with outcome, and several other dimensions (locus of causal attribution, relationship, and treatment) were involved as well. Similar results were obtained in the psychiatric hospital.

For *late outcome*, clinical changes were assessed 1 or 2 years after discharge for patients in the crisis intervention center by means of a clinical change rating scale, which includes most of the additional variables of the HSRS. Only the convergence and congruence on the dimension *locus of causal attribution* correlated significantly at follow-up with the clinical changes.

It has been interesting to compare these correlations with the correlations obtained in the same study between outcome and other factors that can be considered to be possible factors of change. Although the initial seriousness of symptoms does not seem to have any predictive value, the quality of the patient's personal resources, as assessed by the quality of relationships developed, self-esteem, or motivations for treatment, is associated with strength of outcome. In terms of process, there was a stronger relationship between the instigation of crisis intervention and subsequent benefit than between outcome and the degree of adherence to a specific crisis intervention technique.

Professionals' Opinions About Mental Illness and Care

Another aspect of our research has focused on clinicians. The aim of this work (Dazord, Gerin,

Terra, Sali, & Hochmann, 1988) was to assess the relation between various opinions about mental illness and each of three clinician variables: occupational category personal experience with psychotherapy and institution of employment. Several questionnaires assessing opinions about mental illness were extracted from the literature and completed by 118 subjects from three different institutions. These questionnaires were designed to tap attitudes in the following domains: original, evolution, and nature of mental illness; care of mental illness; psychotherapy compared with pharmacotherapy; psychiatric institutions and mental illness; and care and relationships.

The first finding of interest was the degree of general agreement among professionals' opinions concerning (a) the patient's care (all professionals emphasized the importance of the relationship with patients and the importance of both the patient's and the clinician's understanding of the patient's mental functioning); and (b) the nature of the mental illness (all professionals tended to reject assertions implying some mechanistic explanation of the mental illness). In spite of their agreement, correspondence analysis showed that the opinions did differ on three dimensions:

1. *Personal psychotherapy and opinions about mental illness.* Subjects without a history of personal psychotherapy experience were more likely to refer to the institution and to the authority of the medical staff. In contrast, subjects who had undergone psychoanalysis expressed greater confidence about psychotherapy, their own reactions, and the reactions of their patients.

2. *Occupational category.* Among subjects who had undergone psychoanalysis, we looked at differences between psychiatrists and psychologists. Psychologists attributed less importance to the authority of the medical staff and referred less frequently to the institution or hierarchical organization than other groups. They spoke of mental illness from a theoretical point off view rather than an institutional one. Because these peculiarities of the psychologists distinguished them from most of the other subjects in the study, and because they were the only professionals with no medical training, it is possible that the observed differences were related to medical training.

3. *Institution.* The impact of the institution could be examined in therapists who had had the same experience of personal psychotherapy and the same professional training. We observed several significant differences relating to institution.

This is of particular interest in our country, where it is strongly recommended that therapists undergo psychoanalysis. This finding may favor a type of training: the everyday training by the institution team, which is less expensive than individual psychotherapy.

Instruments Developed

We have developed a specific instrument derived from previous work on target complaints (Dazord et al., 1988). Its raw material is derived form open-ended responses to the following questions: "What is the matter?" (asked to patients) and "What are the patient's problems?" (asked to clinicians). Data are extracted from this material by a specific method of content analysis. This analysis investigates several dimensions:

- the nature of the expressed difficulty (e.g., depressive state or social problem);

- the locus of causal attribution of the difficulty (e.g., completely outside and independent of the patient or part of the inner experience of the patient);

- the temporal attribution of the difficulty;

- the type of relationship difficulty (e.g., with relatives, co-workers, sexual partner).

Data were not analyzed and interpreted until the coding manual was unambiguous enough to allow different judges to reach a concordance level (Cohen's kappa) or at least .7. Analysis of these data allowed us to develop a measure of agreement between a patient's and therapist's opinion about a patient's problems. This agreement concerns either the focus or the range of the expressed difficulties. By *focus* we mean the expressed main difficulty, and by *range* we mean the extent of the whole set of difficulties. When studying agreement on focus we used Cohen's kappa coefficient of concordance. For studying range we built specific indexes. For each dimension, each subject mentioned a number of categories. This number indicated the range of expressed difficulties for this specific dimension. Thus, for any specific patient–therapist dyad, we got two ranges for each dimension and two additional ranges if we examined the same dyad's responses at a later time. For each dimension the number of categories mentioned simultaneously by both therapist and patient was the range of consensus, and the total number of different categories mentioned in these responses was the total range. Two normalized indexes extending from 0 to 1 were built: an index of *congruence* (i.e., the range of consensus divided by the total range) and an index of convergence between the patient and therapist from an initial questionnaire to a late questionnaire (i.e., the late congruence minus the initial one).

Research Programs in Progress

Now that our research has demonstrated the importance of some nonspecific factors of change, we are trying to extend these findings to different types of institutions and patients. To date, the results obtained have allowed us to give a description of the institutions involved in these projects as far as patients, therapists, and institutional factors are concerned. For instance, in a project concerning child psychiatry, we have been able to describe the population (900 children) attending consultation centers in the Lyon area for three years. Among the most important findings are the importance of the school in sending children to consultation centers and the fact that, although the social conditions of these children were fairly good, the family environment was frequently disturbed. Regarding convergence and congruence between children (or family members) and clinicians we have found, as expected, that the initial discourse of the clinicians was different from both the parents' and the children's discourses. More interesting was that after a few weeks this point of view converged, primarily because of a change in the clinician's view. In a family systems perspective, this might suggest that such a clinician is becoming a part of the patient's system rather than helping the patient get out of this system. We are investigating this process to see how outcome is related to the initial difficulties of the children, the family context, the type of treatment, and a varied set of nonspecific factors such as convergence and congruence.

Programs Planned for the Future

Besides extending the aforementioned studies to various clinical contexts, we intend to develop an assessment of quality of life among psychiatric patients. We have developed some tools used in cardiovascular therapies (Gerin, Dazord, Boissel, & Hanauer, 1988). This part of our research is not summarized here because it departs from the domain of psychotherapy research, but we plan to adapt our findings to the psychiatric context.

Nature of the Research Organization

We are both members of the INSERM, which is a national public research institute. The other members of our research team are located in the hospital St. Jean de Dieu in Lyon and are also members of a university research team directed by Professor Boissel. This team is involved in therapeutic evaluations. Part of our financial support has come from INSERM grants, part from the university, and part from the resources of the clinical teams with which we are working.

Relation to Other Research Programs

Our aim is to develop process–outcome research (as described by Luborsky, Orlinsky, Greenberg, and others; see chapters 9, 16, and 21) in France. It is probably premature to discuss the impact of our research on clinical practice at this time.

In achieving our goals, we are currently faced with two kinds of problems: (a) Our research institute, which is the major one in France in the clinical field, is mostly oriented toward biology research; and (b) as far as clinical research in psychiatry is concerned, French clinicians are used to a speculative approach (as illustrated by the past influence of Lacan). Nonetheless, more and more French clinicians are interested in this type of approach. After working with our team they clearly start to reconsider the field of psychotherapy research. With this goal in mind, we have begun translating a number of English publications in this field for a French psychiatric journal (*Psychologie Médicale*), and we plan to have the 1991 Society for Psychotherapy Research meeting in Lyon.

References

Armelius, B-Å., Gerin, P., Luborsky, L. (1985). Clinician's judgments of mental health: Specimen case descriptions and forms for the Health–Sickness Rating Scale. *DAPS Report, 13*, 1–10.

Baguet, J., Gerin, P., Sali, M., & Marie-Cardine, M. (1984). Evolution des thèmes transférentiels dans une psychothérapie de groupe. *Psychothérapies, 1*, 43–49.

Dazord, A., Gerin, P., Brochier, C., Guisti, P., & Marie-Cardine, M. (1989). Evaluation des facteurs non spécifiques de changement en milieu psychiatrique. *Actualités Psychiatriques, 4,* 79–87.

Dazord, A., Gerin, P., Sali, A., Guisti, P., Guillaud-Bataille, J. M., Marie-Cardine, M., Chenet, J. P., & Brochier, C. (1988). Le questionnaire "Difficultés et changements exprérimés (DCE): intérét dans l'évaluation des psychothérapies. *Psychologie Médicale, 8,* 1233–1235.

Dazord, A., Gerin, P., Terra, J. L., Sali, A., & Hochmann, J. (1988, October). *Influence des formations des soignants sur leur représentation de la maladie mentale.* Paper presented at the Congrés International de Psychothérapie Médicale, Lausanne, Switzerland.

Gerin, P., Dazord, A., Boissel, J. P., & Hanauer, M. T. (1988, September). *L'évaluation de la qualité de la vie dans les essais thérapeutiques.* Paper presented at the Fifth Recontres Nationales de Pharmacologies Clinique, Editions de l'INSERM, Giens.

Gerin, P. (1984). *L'évaluation des Psychothérapies.* Paris: Presses Universitaires de France.

Gerin, P., Dazord, A., Sali, A., Guisti, P., & Marie-Cardine, M. (1987). Psychotherapeutic factors within psychiatric institutions. In W. Huber (Ed.), *Progress in psychotherapy research* (pp. 694–711). Louvain, Belgium: University of Louvain.

Luborsky, L. (1976). Helping alliances in psychotherapy: The groundwork for a study of their relationship to its outcome. In J. L. Claghorn (Ed.), *Successful psychotherapy* (pp. 92–116). New York: Brunner/Mazel.

Marie-Cardine, M., Gerin, P., Dazord, A., Guisti, P., & Terra, J. L. (1989). Etude de la relation médecin-malade á travers un questionnaire de plaintes. *Psychologie Medicale, 21,* 320–324.

Reith, B., Andreoli, A., Gerin, P., & Dazord, A. (1988). Orientations possibles d'une recherche scientifique en intervention de crise. *Accueils, 30*–38.

33

Illinois School of Professional Psychology: Brief Psychotherapy Research Project

B. Rudolph, R. Cardella, H. Datz, J. Jochem,
M. Kadlec, G. Mann, E. Somberg, and M. Stone
Illinois School of Professional Psychology

Background and Aims

The Brief Psychotherapy Research Project (BPRP) is a pilot program that investigates the ways in which some women negatively react to elective abortion and how they use brief stress-response psychotherapy. The project was designed to duplicate closely the clinical practice of brief psychotherapy in fee for service outpatient settings.

Elective abortion is unusual among stress events in that it is not simply imposed but involves an element of choice. Abortion has become a common event in our society, with 1.5 million abortions being performed annually. Reviews of the literature indicate that as many as 10% of women who elect to abort may experience adverse reactions. It is important, then, to identify women who need help and who may seek psychotherapy in response to this event and to investigate whether brief stress-response therapy is a useful treatment for them.

The project is designed to be a two-pronged exploratory study. Our first purpose is to study the event of elective abortion and its attendant personal meanings and to identify characteristics of women who experience troubling reactions to it and seek psychotherapy. Second, in providing services to women who are experiencing difficulty

dealing with this stress event we investigate closely many process and outcome variables of stress-response psychotherapy, a model of brief dynamic psychotherapy described by Horowitz (1986). In so doing we contribute to the research already compiled on stress-response syndromes and their treatment by investigating elective abortion, a little studied stress event.

Figure 33.1 provides a schematic outline of the project design, and Table 33.1 lists the specific instruments used. Measures from various schools of psychotherapy and research are used. Three kinds of variables are investigated: input, process, and output.

Most research in brief dynamic therapies has focused on outcome variables. The BPRP addresses the much written about but less thoroughly investigated input and process variables by means of exploratory methods. A broad research question of the project is, Which women from our sample benefit from this modified form of stress-response psychotherapy under which circumstances? Within each variable category (input, process, and output), more specific research questions are posed. The BPRP has also selected the initial assessment interview as a target of detailed investigation. In particular, we are investigating what consequences occur when the therapist structures and focuses this interview with

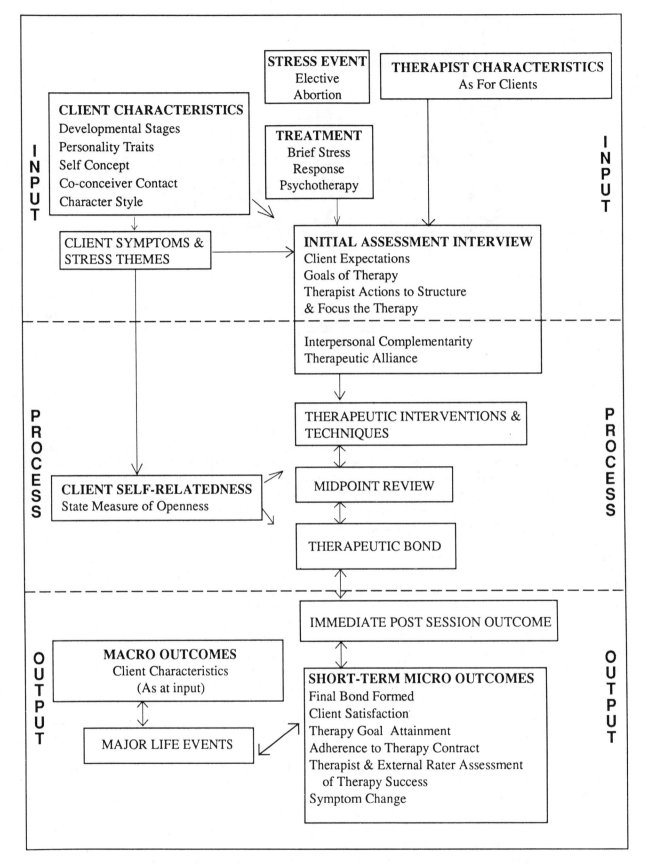

Figure 33.1. Input, process, and output variables in the Brief Psychotherapy Research Project (adapted from Orlinsky & Howard, 1986).

Table 33.1
Multifaceted Assessment in the Brief Psychotherapy Research Project

Variable	Instrument	Perspective
Input variables measurement		
Client and therapist personality	NEO Personality Inventory (Costa & McCrae, 1985)	Self-report
Client and therapist psychosocial developmental level	Inventory of Psychosocial Development (Constantinople, 1969)	Self-report
Client and therapist self-concept	Tennessee Self-Concept Scale (Fitts, 1965)	Self-report
Stress response syndrome	Stress Response Rating Scale	Therapist report
Stress themes	Impact of Event Scale	Client report
Psychiatric symptomology	Stress Theme Checklist (Jochem, 1988)	External raters
	Brief Psychiatric Rating Scale	Therapist report
	SCL-90	Client report
Initial therapist actions to facilitate alliance and focus treatment	Structure and Focus Scale (Datz & Rudolph, 1987)	External raters
Initial therapeutic alliance	Therapeutic Alliance Rating Scale (Marziali, Marmar, & Krupnick 1982)	External raters
Process variables measurement		
State openness	Vocal Quality (Rice et al., 1979)	External rater
Interpersonal complementarity	Structural Analysis of Social Behavior (Benjamin, 1981)[a]	External rater
Therapeutic interventions	Therapist Action Scale (Hoyt et al., 1981)[a]	External rater
	Therapy Process Q Set (Jones, 1985)[a]	External rater
Midpoint review	Midpoint Review Scale (Rudolph & Pettorini, 1988)[a]	External rater
Therapeutic alliance	Therapeutic Alliance Rating Scale (Marziali, et al., 1981)[a]	All three perspectives
	Therapy Session Report Form (Orlinsky & Howard, 1975)[a]	Client report
Therapist liking for client	Liking Scale (Rudolph & Jochem, 1986)[a]	Therapist report
Output variables measurement		
Immediate post	Therapy Session Report Form[a]	Client report
Session outcome	Therapeutic Alliance Rating Scale[a]	All three perspectives
	Therapist Liking Scale[a]	Therapist report
Short-term micro outcomes	Instrument	Perspective
Final alliance formed	Therapeutic Alliance Rating System	All three perspectives
Client satisfaction	Client Satisfaction Questionnaire (Rudolph, 1982)	Client report
Goal attainment	Therapy Assessment Questionnaire (Rudolph, 1982)	All three perspectives
Adherence to prescription contract		All three perspectives
Success of therapy	SCL-90	All three perspectives
Symptom change	IES, SRRS, BPRS	All three perspectives
Major life events	Schedule of Recent Experience (Holmes & Rahe, 1967)	Client report
Macro outcomes	Measure	Perspective
Client characteristics as at input	As at input	Client report
Therapist characteristics as at input	As at input	Therapist report

[a]Repeated measure.

patients of different personality styles and what the therapist's contributions are to rapid development of the working alliance in the initial assessment interview. The initial assessment interview has been all but ignored by researchers even though most brief therapy writers emphasize careful screening at the initiation of treatment. Our study investigates the initial assessment interview and relates patient characteristics to both process and outcome variables. The BPRP also measures such hallmark brief therapy process features as maintaining a focus, high therapist activity; and encouragement of affective ventilation. Eventually these variables will be related to outcome variables identified in Figure 33.1. In terms of output variables, a major research question is, do women in our sample experience improvement beyond symptom change and, if so, under which circumstances? Likewise, which women worsen under which circumstances?

Method

The project was first funded in June of 1986, and recruitment of subjects began the following fall. Women contacted the BPRP in response to media announcements, referrals by friends, and local service agencies. To date our sample consists of 20 nulliparous women ranging in age from 21 to 36 years; 18 are single, 1 is married, and 1 is divorced. Nineteen are White, and one is Black. All have some college education, and 75% possess an undergraduate or graduate degree. Half of our sample had had more than one abortion, and all underwent the dilation–extraction type of procedure. Most were in their 20s at the time of the first abortion. Time elapsed since last abortion ranged from 2 weeks to 12 years.

Appropriateness for inclusion of subjects in the BPRP was assessed in a telephone interview, which was followed by a 90-minute individual evaluation. Before the interview the women completed a demographic face sheet, written consent form, and various research instruments. Treatment consisted of 12 60-minute, audiotaped, individual sessions. A model of stress-response psychotherapy (Horowitz, 1986) was modified to highlight goals and to include midpoint progress reviews. Only 1 of 20 women chose to work with a male therapist. Therapists were licensed clinical psychologists experienced in brief psychotherapy. Patients, therapists, and external raters completed various instruments on a repeated basis throughout treatment.

Research Accomplishments

The initial findings of the BPRP were presented at the 1988 and 1989 annual meetings of the Society for Psychotherapy Research. Seven patient variables and two therapist variables were investigated from the initial assessment interview in a comparison of a successful and an unsuccessful case. A key question of the input portion of the BPRP was, Did our sample experience stress responses?

Results indicate that our sample did show signs and symptoms of stress-response syndrome. All items on the Impact of Event Scale (IES) were frequently endorsed (range = 42%–100%). IES scores of our sample were comparable to those reported by Zilberg, Weiss, and Horowitz (1982) with bereaved patients. The project also developed a methodology for external raters' assessment of stress themes, and in a pilot study of 12 patients a specific cluster of stress themes was identified. The most frequently reported themes were guilt over responsibility, sadness over the loss, and rage at the source. An important finding not previously reported as a sequel of elective abortion is the predominance of rage.

In this same pilot sample we identified some other characteristics of women who want and need brief pyschotherapy after elective abortion. In terms of self-esteem, 75% of the women scored below the mean on the Moral–Ethical subscale of the Tennessee Self-Concept Scale, which measures the client's own sense or moral goodness. Eriksonian psychosocial developmental level was also measured with the Inventory of Psychosocial Development (IPD), which had not been used previously in psychotherapy research. On the IPD one third of the women reported unsuccessful resolutions. Personality traits were also assessed with the NEO Personality Inventory. This instrument revealed that the women's scores were elevated on the Neuroticism dimension, and they scored at the upper border of the normal range on Extraversion and well above the median on Openness. In spite of our small sample, correlations of the scores on the patient characteristics instruments were computed to investigate initially whether these scales might merely assess symptoms from different perspectives. Few significant correlations were found.

A key component under investigation in our initial assessment interview is therapist activity. The Structure and Focus Scale (SFS) was developed to measure empirically therapist actions to foster rapid development of a therapeutic alliance and to focus the subsequent brief treatment. Raters identifying specific therapist interventions achieved interrater agreement ranging from .81 to .88. For the first time the Therapeutic Alliance Rating Scale (TARS) was used to assess the alliance in the initial evaluation interview. The TARS separately taps patient and therapist contributions, both positive and negative. Pearson correlation of the SFS with the TARS Client Negative Contribution scale was .67 ($p < .05$). This suggests that therapeutic activity increased with increased negative contribution from the patient. The SFS, the Mid-point Review Scale, and the TARS can be used to teach tasks in the initial evaluation interview and subsequent brief therapy. Pilot use of these instruments as training aids at the Illinois School of Professional Psychology has been promising.

Research Programs in Progress and Planned for the Future

The patient characteristics and the therapist structuring and focusing variables just discussed continue to be investigated in the project at the initial evaluation and as variables that influence the psychotherapy process. Therapist activity and therapeutic alliance are pivotal process variables investigated in the BPRP. The Therapist Action Scale measures both prescribed and contraindicated techniques of stress-response psychotherapy. We hypothesize that there will be a number of relationships among the therapist actions and various patient input and process measures. Comparison of patient and therapist therapeutic alliance assessments throughout therapy with the TARS is in progress. Bordin's concepts of tasks, goals, and bond are also being used to study the relationship between alliance and therapist and patient actions throughout treatment.

Single-case process studies are investigating patient anger and other "negative" patient factors leading to an abbreviated, unsuccessful therapy. This case is being contrasted with a successful case through investigation of patient and therapist actions. Figure 33.1 indicates output variables currently under investigation. These variables will be studied in relation to the input and process variables.

For the future, we plan to apply two process measures not previously used in stress-response psychotherapy research. The system developed by Rice, Koke, Greenberg, and Wagstaff (1979) for describing vocal quality will be used to assess the impact of therapist interventions and to measure patient openness as a state. The structural analysis of social behavior system (Benjamin, 1981) will be used to evaluate interpersonal complementarity and its relationship to therapeutic alliance.

A unique feature of the psychotherapy provided in this project is the use of a midpoint review. This structured intervention involves deliberate assessment of treatment progress and therapeutic relationship by both patient and therapist midway through the brief treatment. A scale to measure therapist actions at the midpoint session is underway. The relationship between this assessment and the patient's eventual response to therapy at termination will be investigated.

Nature of the Research Organization

The director of the BPRP is Bonnie A. Rudolph, PhD, core faculty member, Illinois School of Professional Psychology (ISPP). She oversees the overall operation of the project and reports annually to the ISPP Dean of Faculty, Marc Lubin and ISPP's president, James McHolland. She is responsible for planning the broad research program and relates project developments to training needs for faculty and administration.

The director supervises a research assistant and administrative fellows who coordinate data collection, data analysis, and referral development. Three additional ISPP faculty are involved in the project presently. Eliezer Schwartz, PhD, provides input on methodology and implementation and is investigating patient cognitive development. Helen Evans, PhD, provides consultation on research design, ethnic and minority issues, and referral development. Judith Flaxman, PhD, chairs the ISPP Ethics Committee and reviews all project proposals to ensure compliance with the American Psychological Association's regulations concerning human subjects.

Three consultants advise the project director: Ariadne Beck, MA, chair of the American Group Psychotherapy Society Research Committee; Kenneth Howard, PhD, past executive officer of the Society for Psychotherapy Research and professor at Northwestern University; and Marc Stone, PhD, dean of faculty at the Alfred Adler Institute of Chicago. These consultants provide additional expertise on design methodology, research theory and practice, instrument development, and test construction.

Students are involved in the creation of new measures and the development of psychotherapy process rating systems that use audiotapes and transcripts. Senior project students coteach a one-credit introduction to psychotherapy research course with Rudolph.

Funding for the project thus far has come from faculty research grants at ISPP and grants from The Chicago Stress Center, Ltd., a private brief psychotherapy center. The direct service costs of the project have been paid by patient fees.

Relation to Other Research Programs

The BPRP uses a modified form of Horowitz's (1986) model of stress-response psychotherapy. Horowitz identified a cluster of specific symptoms and stress themes that constitute a recognizable syndrome. Cohen and Roth (1984) took this one step farther and looked at women who had the stress event of an elective abortion. Their results provided evidence for stress-response syndrome among this population. Our research supports their findings in that our sample manifested similar scores on the IES. A further contribution from our study is the identification of a specific cluster of stress themes relevant to the abortion stress event: sadness over loss, guilt over responsibility, and rage at the source. The TARS external raters version (Marmar, Horowitz, Weiss, & Marziali, 1986) was used for the first time in the initial evaluation interview and was correlated with the SFS (Datz & Rudolph, 1987), which measures therapist actions to foster an alliance and to focus and structure the subsequent treatment. Correlations of scores on the SFS and the TARS suggest that therapist activity increased with negative contributions from the patient.

Our initial findings suggest that brief stress-response psychotherapy is an effective treatment for some women who experience distress after elective abortion. Our findings also suggest that the initial evaluation interview is crucial to development of the alliance and that greater therapist activity to structure and focus the goals and tasks of brief therapy may be needed with more difficult patients.

References

Benjamin, L. S. (1981). *Manual for coding social interactions in terms of structural analysis of social behavior (SASP).* Madison: University of Wisconsin Press.

Cohen, L., & Roth, S. (1984). Coping with abortion. *Journal of Human Stress, 10,* 140–145.

Constantinople, A. (1969). An Eriksonian measure personality development in college students. *Developmental Psychology, 1,* 357–372.

Costa, P. T., & McCrae, R. R. (1985). *NEO Personality Inventory manual.* Odessa, FL: Psychological Assessment Resources.

Datz, H., & Rudolph, B. (1988, June). *Structure and Focus Scale: Initial findings.* Paper presented at the Society for Psychotherapy Research, Santa Fe, NM.

Fitts, W. H. (1965). *Tennessee Self-Concept Scale manual.* Nashville, TN: Counselor of Recordings Test.

Holmes, T. H., & Rahe, R. H. (1967). The Social Readjustment Rating Scale. *Journal of Psychosomatic Research, 11,* 213–218.

Horowitz, M. J. (1986). *Stress response syndromes* (2nd ed.). Northvale, NJ: Jason Aronson.

Hoyt, M. F., Marmar, C. R., Horowitz, M. J., & Alvarez, W. (1981). The Therapist Action Scale and Patient Action Scale: Instruments for the assessment of behavior during therapy session. *Psychotherapy: Theory, Research, and Practice, 18,* 109–116.

Jochem, J. (1988). *Brief psychotherapy following elective induced abortion: Pilot study of thematic content.* Unpublished manuscript, Illinois School of Professional Psychology, Chicago.

Jones, E. E. (1985). *Manual for the Psychotherapy Process Q-Sort.* Unpublished manuscript, University of California, Berkeley.

Marmar, C., Horowitz, M. J., Weiss, D., & Marziali, E. (1986). The development of the Therapeutic Alliance Rating Scale. In L. S. Greenberg and W. M. Pinsof (Eds.), *The psychotherapeutic process: A research handbook* (pp. 367–390). New York: Guilford Press.

Marziali, N. E., Marmar, C., & Krupnick, J. (1981). Therapeutic Alliance Scales: Development and outcome. *American Journal of Psychiatry, 138,* 361–364.

Orlinksy, D., & Howard, K. I. (1975). *Varieties of psychotherapeutic experience.* New York: Teachers College Press.

Orlinsky, D., & Howard, K. I. (1986). Process and outcome in psychotherapy. In S. L. Garfield & A. E. Bergin (Eds.), *Handbook of psychotherapy and behavior change.* New York: Wiley.

Rice, L., Koke, C., Greenberg, L. S., & Wagstaff, A. (1979). *Manual for client voice quality.* Toronto, Ontario, Canada: University Counseling and Development Center.

Rudolph, B. (1982). *Client satisfaction questionnaires with collaborative brief therapy.* Unpublished manuscript, Chicage Stress Center, Chicago.

Rudolph, B. (1988). *Therapy assessment: Multiple perspectives.* Unpublished manuscript, Illinois School of Professional Psychology, Chicago.

Rudolph, B., & Jochem, J. (1986). *Development of the Liking Scale: Client and therapist versions.* Unpublished manuscript, Illinois School of Professional Psychology, Chicago.

Rudolph, B., & Pettorini, P. (1988). *Development of a Midpoint Review Scale.* Unpublished manuscript, Illinois School of Professional Psychology, Chicago.

Zilberg, N. J., Weiss, D. S., & Horowitz, M. J. (1982). Impact of Event Scale: A cross-validation study and some empirical evidence supporting a conceptual model of stress response syndromes. *Journal of Consulting and Clinical Psychology, 50,* 407–414.

The Psychotherapy Research Program at Memphis State University

Jeffrey S. Berman, Robert A. Neimeyer, Arthur C. Houts, William R. Shadish, Jr., Andrew W. Meyers, and James P. Whelan
Memphis State University

Background and Aims

In the past 5 years, the Department of Psychology at Memphis State University has developed an active and growing program of psychotherapy research. This research represents an important component of the department's Center for Applied Psychological Research, an established Center of Excellence given special financial support by the state of Tennessee. The department's designation as a Center of Excellence has provided it with substantial funding and resources, permitting the creation of a first-rate collaborative research environment.

Participants in this ongoing psychotherapy research program include six members of the psychology department faculty. Instead of a single team effort on one large project, the research program is based on a more loosely structured collaborative model. Each investigator on the research team pursues specific psychotherapy research topics, and this effort is then accompanied by various levels of collaboration with other members of the program. This approach has permitted the research team to examine a wide array of issues concerning psychological interventions and the evaluation of their efficacy.

Research Accomplishments

Treatment of Adult Victims of Incest

This research, coordinated by Neimeyer and Pamela C. Alexander (who is now at the University of Maryland), has examined the treatment of adult victims of childhood incest and the prediction of response to treatment. In light of evidence that incest survivors experience long-term problems with social isolation and social adjustment (Harter, Alexander, & Neimeyer, 1988), two alternative forms of group therapy have been compared that focus on interpersonal difficulties. These include an unstructured process-oriented group and a semistructured interpersonal transaction group format. In the interpersonal transaction group, members spend a portion of each session engaging in dyadic self-disclosure exercises that encourage progressively deeper sharing about their reactions to the incest experience (Neimeyer, 1988). A controlled outcome study of these two group formats funded by the National Institute of Mental Health has provided the first empirical evidence for the efficacy of these or any other treatments for incest survivors, with group members showing reductions in depression, fearfulness, and general distress relative to delayed-treatment controls (Alexander, Neimeyer, Follette, Moore, & Harter, 1989). Research is currently being conducted on those dimensions of group process that are associated with favorable outcome across conditions.

Quantitative Summaries of Psychotherapy Outcome Research

This research, led by Berman in collaboration with other members of the research program, involves the use of quantitative review techniques, often referred to as meta-analysis, to examine various facets of the psychotherapy outcome literature. Recognizing the difficulties in summarizing the burgeoning outcome literature in a purely narrative fashion, these researchers have addressed issues concerning the effectiveness of treatment by using quantitative procedures to combine the results of large numbers of individual studies. This quantitative review strategy has been used to examine the effectiveness of cognitive and behavioral interventions (Berman, Miller, & Massman, 1985; Miller & Berman, 1983), the relative efficacy of professional and paraprofessional therapists (Berman & Norton, 1985), the effectiveness of psychotherapy for children (Casey & Berman, 1985), and the degree to which gains achieved during psychotherapy are maintained once treatment has ended (Nicholson & Berman, 1983). More recently, these investigators have used the available outcome literature to provide comprehensive summaries of the effectiveness of psychological interventions for the treatment of depression (Robinson, Berman, & Neimeyer, 1990), anorexia nervosa (Qualls & Berman, 1988), and childhood enuresis.

One intriguing issue that has emerged from these quantitative reviews is the importance of considering the theoretical allegiance of researchers who conduct psychotherapy research (Berman, 1989). A consistent finding in studies comparing different forms of treatment is that the treatment found to be most effective also tends to be the intervention that was favored by the investigator who conducted the study. Furthermore, after an adjustment is made for the investigator's allegiance, apparent differences in the relative efficacy of psychotherapies typically disappear. This pattern has been observed in a review of studies that compared behavioral psychotherapies with more traditional verbal therapies (Berman & Camp, 1989) as well as in reviews of

studies comparing the effectiveness of cognitive and behavioral interventions (Berman et al., 1985) and psychotherapies used in the treatment of depression (Robinson et al., 1990). Such findings suggest that empirical claims concerning the superiority of particular forms of treatments must be judged only after controlling for the allegiance of the investigators who conduct the research. Future work in this area is therefore focusing on systematic techniques for adjusting for researcher allegiance when reviewing evidence concerning treatment efficacy.

Treatments for Childhood Elimination Disorders

This research, led by Houts, examines the efficacy of treatments for childhood enuresis and encopresis. The overall aim of the research is to assess whether nonmedical interventions based on conditioning principles are more effective than traditional medical interventions for the treatment of these pediatric problems. Early work by the research group focused on developing effective behavioral treatments for enuresis that could be delivered with maximum cost efficiency (Houts, Liebert, & Padawer, 1983; Houts, Whelan, & Peterson, 1987). In recent years, the research team has also begun to investigate behavioral and medical treatments for the related problem of childhood encopresis (Houts, Mellon, & Whelan, 1988).

The primary investigation currently underway is funded by a major grant from the National Institute of Child Health and Human Development. This research involves an extensive randomized trials study comparing outcomes and long-term psychosocial consequences of pharmacological and behavioral treatments for nocturnal enuresis. Initial results from the project indicate that commonly used drug treatments are not as effective as behavioral treatment in terms of either immediate gains or long-term maintenance.

Additional studies being conducted by the research group include a quantitative review of the outcome literature on the treatment of enuresis and an investigation of the generalizability of standard behavioral treatment approaches for the treatment of secondary enuresis. Findings from this range of treatment studies should allow the research team to develop sound empirical recommendations for physicians and psychologists who treat these pediatric problems.

Research on Cognitive and Constructivist Psychotherapy

This research, conducted jointly by Neimeyer and collaborators at other universities, examines the efficacy of cognitive and behavioral treatments for depression conducted in both individual and group formats. For example, one series of studies compared the efficacy of exercise treatments involving group therapy with no-treatment controls, yielding evidence for the superiority of active treatments that use relaxation, running, or cognitive and group process interventions (Klein et al., 1985). More recent studies in this program demonstrate that alternative behavioral exercise interventions (running and weightlifting) are comparable in their effects on both depression (Doyne et al., 1987) and self-concept (Ossip-Klein et al., 1989) and that both clearly outperform a delayed-treatment control. Together, these studies demonstrate that fairly global and enduring improvement can result from these treatments and that such changes cannot simply be attributed to a cardiovascular training effect.

A second line of research in this general program concerns the efficacy of group cognitive therapy for mood disorder patients. The first study in this series documented the substantial improvement shown in cognitive therapy patients relative to waiting-list controls, which was reflected in both symptomatic measures and indices of cognitive structure derived from repertory grid assessments (Neimeyer, Heath, & Strauss, 1985). A recent quantitative review of the growing literature on cognitive and alternative group therapies for depression indicated that such treatments not only outperform no-treatment controls but actually equal individual psychotherapy in overall outcome (Neimeyer, Robinson, Berman, & Haykal, 1989). Finally, in light of the promise of group approaches, research has been conducted to identify cognitive predictors of treatment response that can permit the assignment of patients to group treatments on a rational rather than a random basis (Neimeyer & Weiss, 1990).

Evaluation of Exercise and Interventions to Enhance Athletic Performance

This research, directed by Meyers and Whelan, has examined two issues: the potential impact of exercise on psychological well-being and the use of cognitive–behavioral interventions for the enhancement of athletic performance.

Efforts to evaluate the relationship between exercise and mental health have focused on exercise as a viable treatment alternative for depression (Mulling, Meyers, Summerville, & Neimeyer, 1986; Weinstein & Meyers, 1983). One current project has been designed to identify the mechanisms by which exercise produces antidepressive effects in clinically depressed adults. The initial findings suggest that although exercise promotes a decrease in self-reported depression, the mechanism responsible for this change may not be a characteristic of the exercise but rather a result of the sense of increased competence that accompanies involvement in such activities. Future research will be directed at the identification of the possible mechanisms by which physical activity and improvements in fitness affect the individual's sense of competence.

The centerpiece of the investigation of cognitive–behavioral interventions for the enhancement of athletic performance is a recently completed quantitative review (Whelan, Meyers, & Berman, 1989) that has supported the efficacy of these treatment strategies for improving sport performance. The findings of this meta-analysis highlight the value of using athletic and sport performance measures as contexts for examining the utility of cognitive–behavioral interventions. Although past efforts by the research group have focused on athletic performance enhancement through the use of multicomponent interventions (Meyers, 1980; Meyers & Schleser, 1980; Meyers, Schleser, & Okwumabua, 1982), the aims of current work are to identify psychological variables that influence athletic performance (e.g., Whelan, Epkins, Meyers, Shermer, Klesges, & Meyers, 1989; Whelan et al., 1987) and to evaluate the effectiveness of more specific intervention strategies such as arousal management (Mahoney & Meyers, 1989; Whelan, Epkins, & Meyers, 1990), goal setting, or concentration strategies.

Efficacy of Marital and Family Therapies

This research project, led by Shadish, involves an extensive meta-analytic review of the effectiveness of marital and family therapies. First funded by a grant from the National Institute of Mental Health, the project has assessed more than 160 randomized controlled outcome studies of marital and family interventions. The aim of the research is not only to provide a comprehensive summary of the findings bearing on the efficacy of marital and family therapies but also to examine how methodological issues can affect the results of individual studies and the results of a meta-analysis. Initial findings from this work (Shadish, 1989; Shadish, Montgomery, et al., 1989) suggest effects similar to those reported in other psychotherapy meta-analyses. For example, distressed clients undergoing treatment improved far more than those in control groups, and no particular form of therapy proved to be systematically better than any other.

Perhaps the most striking finding, however, was methodological rather than substantive: This project located many more randomized experiments than previous reviews. Such a finding indicates that psychotherapy researchers may well be overlooking a large number of high-quality studies in the published and unpublished literature. In fact, a random sample survey of the marital and family treatment literature (Shadish, Doherty, & Montgomery, 1989) suggest that there may be as many unpublished randomized experiments as there are published sources and dissertations. More sophisticated analysis of this marital and family research literature is currently continuing with additional funding from the Russell Sage Foundation.

Nature of the Research Organization

In addition to the convergence of interests on the part of core faculty, the general research environment in the Department of Psychology encourages the development and continuation of psychotherapy investigations. For example, two additional faculty members in the department (Robert C. Klesges and Kenneth L. Lichstein) conduct treatment research in the area of behavioral medicine, contributing methodological and substantive competence to faculty involved more specifically in psychotherapy process and outcome investigations. The department also supports a number of postdoctoral fellows and awards competitive stipends to doctoral students in the clinical psychology training program, and these postdoctoral fellows and doctoral trainees often work closely with psychotherapy research faculty on joint projects. Finally, cooperative arrangements with psychiatric facilities in the Memphis area give students a faculty access to specific inpatient populations, offering further research opportunities. This combination of academic, financial, and institutional support ensures the continuation of a strong psychotherapy research program at Memphis State University.

References

Alexander, P. C., Neimeyer, R. A., Follette, V. M., Moore, M. K., & Harter, S. (1989). A comparison of group treatments of women sexually abused as children. *Journal of Consulting and Clinical Psychology*, *57*, 479–483.

Berman, J. S. (1989, June). Investigator allegiance and the findings from comparative outcome research. In V. Shoham-Salomon (Chair), *Beyond the competition: Are some therapies better for some clients?* Symposium conducted at the meeting of the Society for Psychotherapy Research, Toronto, Ontario, Canada.

Berman, J. S., & Camp, D. (1989, June). *Are behavioral therapies really better than verbal therapies?* Paper presented at the meeting of the Society for Psychotherapy Research, Toronto, Ontario, Canada.

Berman, J. S., Miller, R. C., & Massman, P. J. (1985). Cognitive therapy versus systematic desensitization: Is one treatment superior? *Psychological Bulletin*, *97*, 451–461.

Berman, J. S., & Norton, N. C. (1985). Does professional training make a therapist more effective? *Psychological Bulletin*, *98*, 401–407.

Casey, R. J., & Berman, J. S. (1985). The outcome of psychotherapy with children. *Psychological Bulletin*, *98*, 388–400.

Doyne, E. J., Ossip-Klein, D. J., Bowman, E. D., Osborn, K. M., McDougall-Wilson, I. B., & Neimeyer, R. A. (1987). Running versus weight-lifting in the treatment of depression. *Journal of Consulting and Clinical Psychology*, *55*, 748–754.

Harter, S., Alexander, P. C., & Neimeyer, R. A. (1988). Long-term effects of incestuous child abuse in college women. *Journal of Consulting and Clinical Psychology*, *56*, 5–8.

Houts, A. C., Liebert, R. M., & Padawer, W. (1983). A delivery system for the treatment of primary enuresis. *Journal of Abnormal Child Psychology*, *11*, 513–519.

Houts, A. C., Mellon, M. W., & Whelan, J. P. (1988). Use of dietary fiber and stimulus control to treat retentive encopresis: A multiple baseline investigation. *Pediatric Psychology*, *13*, 435–445.

Houts, A. C., Whelan, J. P., & Peterson, J. K. (1987). Filmed vs. live delivery of full-spectrum home training for primary enuresis: Presenting the information is not enough. *Journal of Consulting and Clinical Psychology*, *55*, 902–906.

Klein, M. J., Greist, J. H., Gurman, A. S., Neimeyer, R. A., Lesser, D. P., Bushnell, N. J., & Smith, R. E. (1985). A comparative outcome study of psychotherapy versus exercise treatments for depression. *International Journal of Mental Health*, *13*, 148–176.

Mahoney, M. J., & Meyers, A. W. (1989). Anxiety and athletic performance: Traditional and cognitive developmental perspectives. In C. Spielberger & D. Hackfort (Eds.), *Anxiety and sports* (pp. 77–94). Washington, DC: Hemisphere.

Meyers, A. W. (1980). Cognitive-behavior therapy and athletic performance. In C. H. Garcia Cadena (Ed.), *Proceedings of the First International Sports Psychology Symposium*. Monterrey, Mexico: Editorial Trillas.

Meyers, A. W., & Schleser, R. (1980). A cognitive behavioral intervention for improving basketball performance. *Journal of Sports Psychology, 2*, 69–73.

Meyers, A. W., Schleser, R., & Okwumabua, T. M. (1982). A cognitive behavioral intervention for improving basketball performance. *Research Quarterly for Exercise and Sport, 53*, 344–347.

Miller, R. C., & Berman, J. S. (1983). The efficacy of cognitive behavior therapies: A quantitative review of the research evidence. *Psychological Bulletin, 94*, 39–53.

Mulling, C., Meyers, A. W., Summerville, M., & Neimeyer, R. A. (1986, October). *Aerobic exercise and depression: Is it worth the effort?* Paper presented at the Association for the Advancement of Applied Sport Psychology, Jekyll Island, GA.

Neimeyer, R. A. (1988). Clinical guidelines for conducting interpersonal transaction groups. *International Journal of Personal Construct Therapy, 1*, 181–190.

Neimeyer, R. A., Heath, A., & Strauss, J. (1985). Personal reconstruction during group cognitive therapy for depression. In F. Epting & A. W. Landfield (Eds.), *Anticipating personal construct psychology* (pp. 180–197). Lincoln: University of Nebraska Press.

Neimeyer, R. A., Robinson, L. A., Berman, J. S., & Haykal, R. F. (1989). Clinical outcome of group psychotherapies for depression. *Group Analysis, 22*, 73–86.

Neimeyer, R. A., & Weiss, M. E. (1990). Cognitive and symptomatic predictors of outcome of group therapies for depression. *Journal of Cognitive Psychotherapy, 4*, 23–32.

Nicholson, R. A., & Berman, J. S. (1983). Is follow-up necessary in evaluating psychotherapy? *Psychological Bulletin, 93*, 261–278.

Ossip-Klein, D. J., Doyne, E. J., Bowman, E. D., Osborn, K. M., McDougall-Wilson, I. B., & Neimeyer, R. A. (1989). Effects of running and weight lifting on self-concept in clinically depressed women. *Journal of Consulting and Clinical Psychology, 57*, 158–161.

Qualls, R. C., & Berman, J. S. (1988, August). Anorexia nervosa: A quantitative review of the treatment outcome literature. In J. S. Berman (Chair), *Psychotherapy for specific disorders: Depression, agoraphobia, and anorexia nervosa*. Symposium conducted at the meeting of the American Psychological Association, Atlanta, GA.

Robinson, L. A., Berman, J. S., & Neimeyer, R. A. (1990). Psychotherapy for the treatment of depression: A comprehensive review of controlled outcome research. *Psychological Bulletin, 108*, 30–49.

Shadish, W. R. (1989, October). *Methodological findings from a family/marital therapy meta-analysis*. Paper presented at the meeting of the American Evaluation Association, San Francisco.

Shadish, W. R., Doherty, M., & Montgomery, L. M. (1989). How many studies are in the file drawer? An estimate from the family/marital psychotherapy literature. *Clinical Psychology Review, 9*, 589–603.

Shadish, W. R., Montgomery, L. M., Wilson, P., Wilson, M. R., Bright, I., & Okwumabua, T. M. (1989, August). *Marital/family therapy effectiveness: Meta-analysis of 163 randomized trials*. Paper presented at the meeting of the American Psychological Association, New Orleans, LA.

Weinstein, W. S., & Meyers, A. W. (1983). Running as a treatment for depression: Is it worth it? *Journal of Sports Psychology, 5*, 288–301.

Whelan, J. P., Epkins, C. C., & Meyers, A. W. (1990). Arousal interventions for athletic performance: Influence of mental preparation and competitive experience. *Anxiety Research, 2*, 293–307.

Whelan, J. P., Epkins, C. C., Meyers, A. W., Shermer, M., Klesges, R. C., & Meyers, A. W., Shermer, M., Klesges, R. C., & Meyers, L. D. (1989, September). *Ultra-endurance cyclists: A profile of participants in the Race Across America*. Paper presented at the meeting of the Association for the Advancement of Applied Sport Psychology, Seattle, WA.

Whelan, J. P., Meyers, A. W., & Berman, J. S. (1989, August). Cognitive-behavioral interventions for athletic performance enhancement. In M. Greenspan (chair), *Sport psychology intervention research: Reviews and issues*. Symposium conducted at the meeting of the American Psychological Association, New Orleans, LA.

Whelan, J., Meyers, A. W., O'Toole, M., Hiller, D., Stephens, M., Bryant, F. V., & Mellon, M. (1987, September). *Psychological contributions to triathlon performance: An exploratory investigation*. Paper presented at the meeting of the Association for the Advancement of Applied Sport Psychology, Newport Beach, CA.

Taking a Closer Look: Psychotherapy Research at Miami University

William B. Stiles, William W. Sloan, Jr., Christopher M. Meshot, and Timothy M. Anderson
Miami University

Background and Aims

Reflecting the position that smaller units of analysis often lead to a more thorough understanding (Stiles, Shapiro, & Elliott, 1986), the psychotherapy research program at Miami University has focused on details of the psychotherapy process. We have paid particular attention to the verbal behavior (speech acts) of therapists and patients; the impact of sessions as evaluated by participants; logical and methodological problems that arise in establishing the value of process components; and patients' assimilation of problematic experiences across sessions.

Methods and Research Accomplishments

Date for some of this program's research have been collected in the Miami University Psychology Clinic, a small outpatient facility that serves university students and community residents in Oxford, Ohio. Clinic staff are doctoral students in clinical psychology at Miami University who are supervised by faculty members. Additional studies have used data collected by other investigators (see the section, Relation to Other Research).

Much of our work has involved systematic ob-

servation or coding of tape recordings or verbatim session transcripts. In the session impact work, patients and therapists have completed self-report forms immediately after sessions. Measurement instruments developed in this program include a taxonomy of verbal response modes (VRMs; Stiles, 1978, 1979b, 1981, 1986a, 1987c), the Session Evaluating Questionnaire (SEQ; Stiles, 1980; Stiles & Snow, 1984b), the Assimilation of Problematic Experiences Scale (APES; Stiles, Meshot, Anderson, & Sloan, 1990; Stiles, Morrison, Haw, Harper, Shapiro & Firth-Cozens, in press), and the relational immediacy coding system (RICS; Sloan, 1988; Sloan & Stiles, 1990).

The VRM taxonomy is a conceptually based, mutually exclusive, exhaustive classification of utterances. Although it is directly comparable to response mode coding systems developed specifically for psychotherapy research (Elliott, Hill, Stiles, Friedlander, Mahrer, & Margison, 1987), this is a general purpose system and has been used successfully to study such related areas as general medical interviews (Stiles, Orth, Scherwitz, Hennrikus, & Vallbona, 1984), conversations of depressed university students with their roommates (Burchill & Stiles, 1988), the effect of patient gender on psychotherapy process (Knight & Stiles, 1987), and radio call-in programs

(Henricks & Stiles, 1989) as well as other areas of applied and experimental social psychology.

VRM coding of psychotherapy has shown, among other things, that therapists taking different theoretical approaches (e.g., client-centered, interpersonal, psychoanalytic, gestalt, cognitive–behavioral) use systematically different verbal techniques (e.g., different proportions of questions, reflections, interpretations, and advisements [Stiles, 1979b; Stiles, Shapiro, & Firth-Cozens, 1988b]). In contrast to therapists' technical diversity, however, psychotherapy patients' use similar VRM profiles regardless of which approach their therapist takes (McDaniel, Stiles, & McGaughey, 1981; Stiles et al., 1988b; Stiles & Sultan, 1979). This patient VRM profile, in which self-disclosure features prominently, may be considered to be a common core component of psychotherapy process across the varied schools (Stiles, 1982, 1984, 1987a; Stiles, McDaniel, & McGaughey, 1979).

The session impact work has included development of the SEQ, an easy-to-administer bipolar adjective checklist that assesses respondents' evaluations of sessions and their postsession moods. Factor analytic studies have shown that participants' evaluative judgments contain two independent dimensions: a task-oriented dimension called *depth*, which reflects the session's perceived power and value; and a socioemotionally oriented dimension called *smoothness*, which reflects the session's perceived comfort, ease, and safety (Stiles, 1980; Stiles & Snow, 1984b). Although these dimensions are internally consistent in each perspective, comparison between therapist and patient perspectives shows only moderate consensus on session smoothness and little or no consensus on session depth (Dill-Standiford, Stiles, & Rorer, 1988; Stiles, Shapiro, & Firth-Cozens, 1988a; Stiles & Snow, 1984a). Despite this lack of consensus about particular sessions, there is convergence across perspectives (external raters as well as therapists and patients) regarding some process–impact relationships. For example, cognitive–behavioral sessions tend to be more smooth but less deep than interpersonal–psychodynamic sessions (Stiles et al., 1988a), and sessions high in patient VRM disclosure are relatively low in smoothness (Stiles, 1984). Individual differences can also affect participants' experience: Sessions are rated as relatively uncomfortable (lower in smoothness) by introverted patients compared with extraverted patients (Nocita & Stiles, 1986) and by novice

male therapists compared with novice female therapists (Nocita & Stiles, 1987).

Part of this program's effort has gone toward logical and methodological consideration of issues involved in taking a closer look. This has included reviewing alternative therapy coding systems (Russell & Stiles, 1979) and assessing these in relation to philosophical and linguistic topics such as speech act theory (Stiles, 1981) and on-record and off-record levels of meaning (Stiles, 1986b, 1987b). It has also included a broader evaluation of conceptual and methodological difficulties that have prevented investigators from identifying links between psychotherapy processes and outcomes (Stiles, 1982, 1983, 1987a, 1988; Stiles & Shapiro, 1989; Stiles et al., 1986). For example, a reconsideration indicates that a common interpretation of process–outcome correlations is flawed by failure to acknowledge differences in client requirements and therapist responsiveness to these differences (Stiles, 1988). Any appropriate therapist responsiveness to the patient's momentary requirements specifically defeats the process-outcome correlations, so that vitally important process components may show null or negative correlations with outcomes. In response to such limitations on linear approaches, we have moved toward more developmental conceptualizations of the therapist–patient relationship (Stiles, 1979a) and the therapeutic process (Stiles, Morrison, et al., in press).

Research in Progress and Planned for the Future

Our current research continues the relatively molecular, descriptive interest in verbal processes and change mechanisms. Even though our previous verbal coding and session impact work tended to be extensive, involving correlations and comparisons of group means, our current and planned research takes an intensive and developmental approach, including in-depth qualitative and quantitative study of single-therapy cases. Our unit of analysis in this work is not the patient but particular topics or themes within patients examined longitudinally.

We are developing and testing a theory about how problematic experiences are assimilated during therapy (Stiles, Elliott, et al., 1990; Stiles, Meshot, et al., 1990; Stiles, Morrison, et al., in press). Briefly, the theory proposes that problematic experiences are gradually assimilated into a schema (frame of reference, narrative, metaphor) that is developed during therapy and follows a predictable sequence. Across sessions, the problematic experience is transformed from initially warded-off content, to unwanted thoughts that enter awareness, to a recognized problem, to a concern that attracts insight and understanding, to an understanding that contributes to adaptive changes, and finally to an area of mastery that is integrated and used in everyday life. Associated with these cognitive changes is a corresponding process of emotional change. From a communication perspective, problematic experiences appear in the patient's discourse as initially vague themes whose structure and meaning become clearer as therapy progresses.

To measure the evolution of themes during therapy, we are developing and validating two verbal process instruments. The APES is an 8-point Likert-type scale used for rating the degree to which a particular problematic experience has been assimilated. It is applied to segments of patient discourse on a particular topic that are selected on the basis of a systematic, intensive review of tapes or transcripts. The RICS (Sloan, 1988), which scores individual utterances on a 0–10 scale, is based on the assumption that disowned problematic experiences are communicated distantly, as if they are unrelated to the patient. Theoretically, as an experience is assimilated its association with the patient's current feelings is gradually recognized and expressed more directly. Thus, high relational immediacy involves recognizing and discussing experiential content in the here-and-now therapeutic interaction. For example, "It rained last weekend" is a relationally distant utterance, whereas "I'm feeling upset with you right now" illustrates relational immediacy.

Nature of the Research Organization

Stiles is a professor in the Department of Psychology at Miami University. Other team members have been graduate students in clinical psychology at Miami; they include Timothy M. Anderson, Sue Ann Ludwig Burchill, Teresa J. Dill-Standiford, William H. Henricks, David P. Knight, Christopher M. Meshot, Andrew Nocita, James E. Orth, Roberta Rigsby, William W. Sloan, Jr. and James Steven Snow.

This program has received funding from the

Miami University Faculty Research Committee and the National Institute of Mental Health.

Relation to Other Research

This program has benefited greatly from collaboration with other programs. An early study used data from the Vanderbilt program for VRM coding of patient utterances (McDaniel et al., 1979). The Miami program participated in a multicenter comparison of therapist response mode coding systems (Elliott et al., 1987). Current work includes the use of data from the Mount Zion program in developing the APES and RICS measures of assimilation. A particularly fruitful continuing collaboration with the Sheffield (UK) program has led to a series of empirical studies, reviews, and theoretical articles (e.g., Barkham et al., 1990; Shapiro, Firth-Cozens, & Stiles, 1989; Stiles et al., 1986; Stiles, Elliott, et al., 1990; Stiles, Morrison, et al., in press; Stiles & Shapiro, 1989; Stiles, Shapiro, & Firth-Cozens, 1988a, 1988b, 1989, 1990).

References

Barkham, M., Stiles, W. B., & Shapiro, D. A. (1990). *The shape of change in psychotherapy: Longitudinal assessment of personal problems.* Manuscript submitted for publication.

Burchill, S. A. L., & Stiles, W. B. (1988). Interactions of depressed college students with their roommates: Not necessarily negative. *Journal of Personality and Social Psychology, 55,* 410–419.

Dill-Standiford, T. J., Stiles, W. B., & Rorer, L. G. (1988). Counselor-client agreement on session impact. *Journal of Counseling Psychology, 35,* 47–55.

Elliott, R., Hill, C. E., Stiles, W. B., Friedlander, M. L., Mahrer, A. R., & Margison, F. R. (1987). Primary therapist response modes: Comparison of six rating systems. *Journal of Consulting and Clinical Psychology, 55,* 218–223.

Henricks, W. H., & Stiles, W. B. (1989). Verbal processes on psychological radio call-in programs: Comparison with other help-intended interactions. *Professional Psychology: Research and Practice, 20,* 315–321.

Knight, D. P., & Stiles, W. B. (1987, June). *Gender and verbal interaction in therapy.* Paper presented at the Society for Psychotherapy Research meeting, Ulm, Federal Republic of Germany.

McDaniel, S. H., Stiles, W. B., & McGaughey, K. J. (1981). Correlates of male college students' verbal response mode use in psychotherapy with measures of psychological disturbance and psychotherapy outcome. *Journal of Consulting and Clinical Psychology, 49,* 571–582.

Nocita, A., & Stiles, W. B. (1987, June). *Some effects of*

gender upon psychotherapy impact ratings. Paper presented at the Society for Psychotherapy Research meeting, Ulm, Federal Republic of Germany.

Nocita, A., & Stiles, W. B. (1986). Client introversion and counseling session impact. *Journal of Counseling Psychology, 33,* 235–241.

Russell, R. L., & Stiles, W. B. (1979). Categories for classifying language in psychotherapy. *Psychological Bulletin, 86,* 404–419.

Shapiro, D. A., Firth-Cozens, J., & Stiles, W. B. (1989). The question of therapists' differential effectiveness: A Sheffield Psychotherapy Project addendum. *British Journal of Psychiatry, 154,* 383–385.

Sloan, W. W., Jr. (1988). *Revised draft of the relational immediacy coding manual.* Unpublished manuscript, Miami University, Oxford, OH.

Sloan, W. W., Jr., & Stiles, W. B. (1990, June). *Development of the Relational Immediacy Coding System: Correlations with the Experiencing Scale.* Paper presented at the meeting of the Society for Psychotherapy Research, Wintergreen, VA.

Stiles, W. B. (1978). Verbal response modes and dimensions of interpersonal roles: A method of discourse analysis. *Journal of Personality and Social Psychology, 36,* 693–703.

Stiles, W. B. (1979a). Psychotherapy recapitulates ontogeny: The epigenesis of intensive interpersonal relationships. *Psychotherapy: Theory, Research, and Practice, 16,* 391–404.

Stiles, W. B. (1979b). Verbal response modes and psychotherapeutic technique. *Psychiatry, 42,* 49–62.

Stiles, W. B. (1980). Measurement of the impact of psychotherapy sessions. *Journal of Consulting and Clinical Psychology, 48,* 176–185.

Stiles, W. B. (1981). Classification of intersubjective illocutionary acts. *Language in Society, 10,* 227–249.

Stiles, W. B. (1982). Psychotherapeutic process: Is there a common core? In L. E. Abt & I. R. Stuart (Eds.), *The newer therapies: A sourcebook* (pp. 4–17). New York: Van Nostrand.

Stiles, W. B. (1983). Normality, diversity, and psychotherapy. *Psychotherapy: Theory, Research, and Practice, 20,* 183–189.

Stiles, W. B. (1984). Client disclosure and psychotherapy session evaluation. *British Journal of Clinical Psychology, 23,* 311–312.

Stiles, W. B. (1986a). Development of taxonomy of verbal response modes. In L. S. Greenberg & W. M. Pinsof (Eds.), *The psychotherapeutic process: A research handbook* (pp. 161–199). New York: Guilford Press.

Stiles, W. B. (1986b). Levels of intended meaning of utterances. *British Journal of Clinical Psychology, 25,* 213–222.

Stiles, W. B. (1987a). "I have to talk to somebody." A fever model of disclosure. In V. J. Derlega & J. H. Berg (Eds.), *Self-disclosure: Theory, research, and therapy* (pp. 257–282). New York: Plenum Press.

Stiles, W. B. (1987b). Some intentions are observable. *Journal of Counseling Psychology, 34,* 236–239.

Stiles, W. B. (1987c). Verbal response modes as inter-

subjective categories. In R. L. Russell (Ed.), *Language in psychotherapy: Strategies of discovery* (pp. 131–170). New York: Plenum Press.

Stiles, W. B. (1988). Psychotherapy process–outcome correlations may be misleading. *Psychotherapy, 25,* 27–35.

Stiles, W. B., Elliott, R., Llewelyn, S. P., Firth-Cozens, J. A., Margison, F. R., Shapiro, D. A., & Hardy, G. (1990). Assimilation of problematic experiences by clients in psychotherapy. *Psychotherapy, 27,* 411–420.

Stiles, W. B., McDaniel, S. H., & McGaughey, K. (1979). Verbal response mode correlates of experiencing. *Journal of Consulting and Clinical Psychology, 47,* 795–797.

Stiles, W. B., Meshot, C. M., Anderson, T. M., & Sloan, W. W., Jr. (1990). *Assimilation of problematic experiences: The case of John Jones.* Manuscript submitted for publication.

Stiles, W. B., Morrison, L. A., Haw, S. K., Harper, H., Shapiro, D. A., & Firth-Cozens, J. A. (in press). A longitudinal study of assimilation of in exploratory psychotherapy, *Psychotherapy.*

Stiles, W. B., Orth, J. E., Scherwitz, L., Hennrikus, D., & Vallbona, C. (1984). Role behavior in routine medical interviews with hypertensive patients: A repertoire of verbal exchanges. *Social Psychology Quarterly, 47,* 244–254.

Stiles, W. B., & Shapiro, D. A. (1989). Abuse of the drug metaphor in psychotherapy process–outcome research. *Clinical Psychology Review, 9,* 521–543.

Stiles, W. B., Shapiro, D. A., & Elliott, R. (1986). Are all psychotherapies equivalent? *American Psychologist, 41,* 165–180.

Stiles, W. B., Shapiro, D. A., & Firth-Cozens, J. A. (1988a). Do sessions of different treatments have different impacts? *Journal of Counseling Psychology, 35,* 391–396.

Stiles, W. B., Shapiro, D. A., & Firth-Cozens, J. A. (1988b). Verbal response mode use in contrasting psychotherapies: A within-subjects comparison. *Journal of Consulting and Clinical Psychology, 56,* 727–733.

Stiles, W. B., Shapiro, D. A., & Firth-Cozens, J. A. (1989). Therapist differences in the use of verbal response mode forms and intents. *Psychotherapy, 26,* 314–322.

Stiles, W. B., Shapiro, D. A., & Firth-Cozens, J. A. (1990). Correlations of session evaluations with treatment outcome. *British Journal of Clinical Psychology, 29,* 13–21.

Stiles, W. B., & Snow, J. S. (1984a). Counseling session impact as viewed by novice counselors and their clients. *Journal of Counseling Psychology, 31,* 3–12.

Stiles, W. B., & Snow, J. S. (1984b). Dimensions of psychotherapy session impact across sessions and across clients. *British Journal of Clinical Psychology, 23,* 59–63.

Stiles, W. B., & Sultan, F. E. (1979). Verbal response mode use by clients in psychotherapy. *Journal of Consulting and Clinical Psychology, 47,* 611–613.

36

Nathan S. Kline Institute for Psychiatric Research: Quantitative Studies of the Therapeutic Interaction Guided by Consideration of Unconscious Communication

Robert Langs and Anthony Badalamenti
Nathan S. Kline Institute for Psychiatric Research

Background and Aims

The research described in this chapter arose from 20 years of clinical study in which a pivotal role was played by consideration of unconsious communications from both patients and therapists. The key to this work entails decoding the patient's material in light of the manifest and implied meanings of the therapist's interventions. This specific decoding technique has been seen by mathematician Ralph Abraham as the creation of a psychoscope; it provides a deep view of the underlying structure of the therapy experience and its frame. The overall method is termed *the communicative approach to psychoanalysis and psychoanlytic psychotherapy.*

The theory that has been derived from psychoscopic studies and that informs this research posits two systems of the mind (Langs, 1988b). The first is a conscious system, which has its own superficial unconscious storage system of memories available to direct recall. The second is deeply unconscious and accessible only through encoded expressions (images previously subjected to displacement and disguise). A decoding procedure that accepts the therapist's interventions as the organizing stimuli for these transformed narratives and images is essential to their dynamic comprehension.

A major clinical finding is the extent to which the boundary conditions of therapy—its ground rules and frame—are central to the deep unconscious concerns of the patient (and therapist), to the therapeutic process, and to sound cure. Overall, this approach uniquely defines psychoanalysis as the investigation of how we communicate and process emotionally charged meaning and information (Langs, 1988a, 1988c, 1989).

The resultant research program is, at this writing, but 3 years old. Its goals are to examine therapeutic interactions of all kinds on a moment-to-moment basis, to create a reliable and valid means of quantitatively scoring the contents and framework of these interactions, to define in detail the basic phenomenology of therapeutic exchanges, to generate nontrivial mathematic models of these interactions to define the basic laws and structures of human emotional communication and the therapeutic process, and to place psychoanalysis squarely among the family of sciences.

Method

The research is now studying 10 psychiatric consultations carried out by six psychoanalysts and recorded for presentation at seminars. Five female patients in ongoing therapy participated; 2 patients were seen by three different analysts, 1 was seen by two analysts, and 2 were seen by single analysts. Of the six analysts, one of whom was a woman, four saw 2 patients each, and two saw 1 patient each. Thus comparative study is feasible; this is a unique feature of the research.

A second study involves a patient who is seropositive for the human immunodeficiency virus (HIV). The first 3 sessions between this male patient and his male therapist are under study. An eclectic approach to the therapy was used.

The scoring manual, which contains 23 categories of items (many quantitatively scaled), is applied comparably to patient and therapist for every one to two lines of dialog (every 5–10 seconds). Included are items related to people referred to, time frame, type of comment made, allusions to symptoms and affects, and other items described later. To date, all but three items (frames, rectifications, and themes) have been scored by two scorers with significant reliability coefficients. All disagreements between scorers have been resolved through discussion; consensus scores are used throughout. One study, noted later, has shown the validity of two hypothesized measures of unconscious communication.

At present, the entire set of scores is available for only 1 of the 10 consultation sessions. Six items have been scored for 6 consultations, however: three between a single patient and three male analysts, and three between a different patient and one female and two male analysts. These items are duration in speaker role (an item now scored for all of the sessions under study), newness of themes, narrative and images compared with intellectualizations, positive tone, negative tone, and continuity of dialog.

Initially, correlation and statistical studies were carried out among the last 5 items. In addition, stochastic mathematic techniques developed mainly by Box and Jenkins (1976) have been applied to the speaker duration data. The five item vectors have also been studied for degree of entropy (i.e., complexity) over the course of these six

sessions. We have also examined power spectra and harmonics (cyclicity) for these particular items. Still other investigations (carried out by M. King and R. Abraham) are using superscores that combine items in keeping with selected dynamic principles. The resultant superscores are used to generate topological mathematical models and phase-space studies that include the search for system attractors, chaotic and otherwise. A basic model of the mind and its information and meaning-processing systems has also been created and is being subjected to computer simulation. Planned, too, are studies of entire psychotherapies and of couple and family therapy situations.

Research Accomplishments

Our first completed study (carried out with assistance of M. Kessler, R. Bryant, and R. Ferguson) involved a depressed woman who saw three consultants, one of whom was a woman. Quantitative scores of the degree of narration and presence of new themes, theorized (as noted) to be a measure of depth and intensity of unconscious expressions, were made by two scorers at a significantly high level of interrater reliability. Three findings emerged: Analyst B intervened significantly more often than Analysts A and C; with Analyst A, the patient produced significantly more narrative images and new themes than with the other two analysts; and there was a significant correlation between these scores and a set of scores for referential activity (Bucci, 1984), the latter of which is also theorized to be a measure of unconscious activation (Langs, Bucci, Bryant, Ferguson, & Thomson, 1990). It appears that unconscious activation can be reliably and validly measured quantitatively and that relative silence in a therapist fosters such expressions, whereas active intervention reduces them.

A second correlation study (Langs, Rapp, Thomson, & Pinto, 1990) involved the interaction between the three male analysts and another female patient. This investigation explored the gender and identity themes of the dialog. The analyses showed, first that the gender and identity material is significantly different in each interview. The first consultation is relatively devoid of such themes, the second is concentrated on family issues, and the third centers on problems of sexuality. Second, we found that the degree of information complexity, a measure used for the first time with psychotherapy data, also differed.

The second interview, with its massive concentration on family gender themes, showed comparatively simple informational patterns; the third was most complex, and the second was intermediate. It seems, then, that analysts significantly influence the nature of the material produced by a patient. Furthermore, analysts vary in the degree of informational complexity (and instability) that they develop in interacting with their patients.

An unexpected finding appeared in the analysis of informational complexity for the third interaction. Because the patient tended to speak often and for long periods in all three consultations, the expectation was that she would show greater informational complexity with respect to the pattern of gender themes alluded to and their positive or negative tone. This was borne out in the first two protocols but not in the third. There, the level of complexity was comparable for patient and therapist. This finding is of special interest in that other measures indicate that this analyst was by far the most unstable therapist in our sample; he obtained instability scores on other measures that were significantly higher than those of the other therapists measured and of the patient sample as well. Indeed, this therapist was the only one in this sample who showed greater complexity than the patient toward the end of the consultation on a time sequence study of cumulative entropy. For the therapist, at least, complex patterns of informational sequences may well be a sign of notable instability (and perhaps pathology).

Time-series analysis of the speaker role has shown a powerfully significant fit with the Box–Jenkins models, indicating strong predictive power in the models. The consultation sessions all showed order one (direct scores) autoregressive fits, indicating high prior state sensitivity and considerable inertia to the unfolding scores. This indicates that these consultations showed considerable resistance to change, a finding that was borne out with other measures.

Histograms of the frequency with which utterances of various durations appeared showed a descending exponential curve for both patient and therapist in all 10 cases, with the greatest frequency being in the shorter durations of speech. These curves significantly fit the Poisson family of curves, which model aspects of nature such as the rate of radioactive decay. A rate constant, endogenous to the Poisson model, was estimated to measure the tendency of each speaker to hold forth or to interrupt the other party in the therapeutic consultation. With these measures it was possible to identify blindly three of the four therapist pairs ($p < .001$, two-tailed t test) but only one of the several patient match-ups (a significantly poor result; $p < .01$, two-tailed t test).

These findings indicate the presence of deep structures in the therapeutic dialog. They also suggest that the therapist dominates or powers the dialog, at least along two dimensions (the appearance of theses of gender and identity and duration in speaker role). A similar analysis of the three sessions held with the HIV-positive patient showed considerably more disorder in the speaker duration sequence and both autoregressive and moving average (the influence of unidentified shocks to the system) effects at the level of the first difference in the data (a level that reflects the velocity or rate of change of the speaker). There, too, the therapist appeared to be the stronger influence on the trajectories of the interview.

Although these time domain studies showed identifiable features for these therapists with respect to speaker duration, the frequency domain investigations carried out through estimations of the power spectra showed no consistency in the therapists with respect to their harmonics (their cyclical activity). Other studies in this domain that used the five dimensional vectors alluded to above revealed strong power over cycles of low frequency with little strength at high frequencies. High-power items also tended to show the strongest cross-correlations between patient and therapist, as revealed in another study in which a 10-minute window was used to investigate the interplay of the five vectors in the course of six of the consultation sessions. The main findings in this latter study indicated that three of these consultation interactions showed little in the way of cross-correlations of any type; two showed moderate amounts, and one showed a significantly large measure of correlation across most of the items investigated. This finding suggests that linear influence varies greatly among patient–therapist interactions; we are now investigating nonlinear influences in these protocols.

Much work is being done to develop new types of features and profiles of these patients and therapists, and their interacting systems. The data indicate that the fundamental entity in psychotherapy is the patient–therapist system, of which the two participants are the key subsystems and for which the ground rules are the boundary conditions. Entropy and complexity measures developed for these patient–therapist systems indicate that these time series are also autoregressive and therefore prior state dependent. A counterintuitive finding indicates that, in each of the six consultations studied, entropy increased over the course of these sessions; this suggests that these patient–therapist systems do not settle into attractors of favored states or configurations but instead wander about and do so even more extensively toward the end of these hours. Another finding in our analysis of the entropy data indicates strong cyclical patterning; in all but one case, patient and therapist were "in sync" (with one and then the other leading the way). In the one case with the most linear influence, the therapist consistently led the patient by a half-cycle in the complexity domain.

Initial profiles indicate that therapists, more powerfully than patients, determine much of the trajectory of the patient–therapist systems over the course of a session. With a newly created "index of linear influence," we have found that therapists fall along a continuum, with highly ordered interactions and influence at one end and highly disordered effects at the other. We are at present attempting to characterize these systems and subsystems in terms of the domains of time sequence, frequency or harmonics, and complexity. Other dimensions will be added (e.g., favored states, attractors, phase-space behaviors, etc.) as they are developed.

Research Programs in Process and Planned for the Future

At present, we are attempting to absorb and interpret our many unprecedented findings in domains not previously applied to psychotherapy data. As our data base expands, we will develop new measures of entropy and complexity. We plan to shift into topological models and to use three-dimensional phase spaces to trace trajectories over time. The search for nonlinear relationships and attractors has already begun. We are also developing power scores that combine items along dimensions such as conscious compared with unconscious expression and psychodynamic compared with systems dynamic realms. Although factor analytic techniques will also be applied to our complex data base, we plan to concentrate initially on intuitively derived power scores. Our overall goals include the development of entirely new ways of configuring and conceptualizing the patient–therapist interaction and its two partici-

pants and the study of individual psychotherapies to generate entirely new and more effective treatments. Along the way, we expect to realize as well the goal of identifying fundamental laws, structures, and rules of interaction and with these to forge a new psychodynamic and systems dynamic theory applicable to the therapeutic interaction and to the processing of emotionally charged information and meaning in both therapy and everyday life.

Each of the 23 items in our scoring system is being scored for all protocols, and the results will be analyzed in various new ways. As specific patterns emerge, we will study the factors that best account for their properties. To cite several initial leads, a study of allusions to symptoms reveals cyclical trends in both patient and therapist. A sudden shift from psychological to physical symptoms has been noticed in certain protocols. A key factor in this shift, now being explored, appears to be certain types of disturbing therapist interventions.

In another current study, a cyclic pattern has been noted in the patient's expression of images that are likely to be laden with unconscious meaning. Here, too, therapist intervention seems to be a major determinant. One study suggests that system instability occurs when there is a build-up in the material from the patient of negative unconscious perceptions of the clinician. When these encoded images become unconsciously unbearable for the therapist he or she intervenes in an evidently disruptive manner, and the patient–therapist system destabilizes. In time, a restabilizing process is set in motion. We are attempting now to operationalize the quantitative measures through which these impressions can be investigated systematically.

Another study of the first 100 lines (10 minutes) of the 10 consultations has revealed a related trend in all protocols: When patients' unconscious expressions become strong, therapists intervene in various ways that reduce the intensity and frequency of these unconscious vehicles. That is, all types of interventions as now practiced (questions, confrontations, so-called transference interpretations, genetic interpretations, etc.) reduce a patient's level of unconscious communication. Communicative theory predicts such a result, whereas current psychoanalytic thinking does not.

Another study (being carried out by R. Albanese) involves the investigation of decoding procedures used in cryptography as a means of formalizing the clinical rules of decoding and interpreting developed by various schools of therapy, including the communicative approach. Still another investigation entails using a mathematical model designed in terms of a closed-loop signal flow system and fitting the scored data to the computer model developed in this manner; the fit proved to be significant with frame management scores. This study also indicates that there are conditions under which it is impossible to determine meaningfully how the patient is responding to the therapist. Findings such as these challenge our usual ways of thinking about the therapeutic interaction.

At present, there are plans to expand these studies toward the investigation of therapy sessions with schizophrenic patients. This work will provide an opportunity to include neurophysiological and biochemical correlates for these communicative scores. We are hoping also to do a study of a therapy consultation in which both participants are being monitored with electroencephalographic tracings and other physiological measures. Another contemplated study involves the factors related to the emergence of violent imagery and behavior during psychotherapy with violence-prone patients.

The history of science indicates that meaningful quantification and the judicious use of pertinent mathematical techniques consistently revolutionize and transform the field to which they are applied. The most far-reaching goal of this research program is nothing less than such a transformation of the fields of psychoanalysis and psychotherapy.

Relation to Other Research Programs

Other researchers with whom we have collaborated include Wilma Bucci of Adelphi University, who is scoring her measure of unconscious expression for our sessions. Robert Russell, PhD, a psycholinguist of the New School for Social Research, is also scoring several of our sessions on his measures of linguistic structure.

References

Box, E., & Jenkins, G. (1976). *Time series analysis: Forecasting and control.* San Francisco: Holden-Day.

Bucci, W. (1984). Linking words and things: Basic processes and individual variation. *Cognition, 17,* 137–153.

Langs, R. (1988a). Perspectives on psychoanalysis as a late arrival to the family of sciences. *Contemporary Psychoanalysis, 24,* 397–419.

Langs, R. (1988b). *A primer of psychotherapy.* New York: Gardner Press.

Langs, R. (1988c). Psychotherapy systems and science. *Reality Club, 1,* 175–192.

Langs, R. (1989). Models, theory, and research strategies: Toward the evolution of new paradigms. *Psychoanalytic Inquiry, 9,* 305–331.

Langs, R., Bucci, W., Bryant, R., Ferguson, R., & Thomson, L. (1990). *Two methods of quantitatively assessing unconscious communication in psychotherapy.* Manuscript submitted for publication.

Langs, R., Rapp, P. E., Thomson, L., & Pinto, A. (1990). *A method for quantifying the therapeutic process: Themes of gender and identity.* Manuscript submitted for publication.

CHAPTER

37

Stanford University Collaborative: Assessing Interpersonal Problems in Psychodynamic Treatment

Leonard M. Horowitz
Stanford University

Saul E. Rosenberg
University of California, San Francisco

Background and Aims

History

This research program concerns interpersonal problems, their relationship to other manifestations of psychopathology, and their amenability to change through psychotherapy. Although patients describe a large number of interpersonal problems in the first clinical interview (Horowitz, 1979), the field has lacked an easily administered self-report inventory that describes specific types of interpersonal problems.

An inventory of interpersonal problems was needed for at least three reasons. First, interpersonal problems are related to the work of psychotherapy, but no norms have existed to show the relative frequency of different types of problems. A standardized inventory would help us identify systematically the most common types of problems that people bring to treatment. Second, an inventory would help to specify what has been achieved through treatment. If an inventory cataloged typical interpersonal problems a patient and therapist could note independently which interpersonal problems had been discussed, and problems that had been discussed could be examined more closely to determine which had shown improvement. We could then identify interventions associated with improvement on particular problems. Third, a measure of interpersonal distress would help us differentiate between distress due to interpersonal problems and distress due to noninterpersonal problems (e.g., unwanted thoughts, overeating). Interpersonal and noninterpersonal problems may show different courses of change in treatment, and this difference may be related to prognosis and outcome.

The impetus for developing an inventory of interpersonal problems was a case study of a woman in psychoanalysis who complained of being sexually unresponsive (Horowitz, Sampson, Siegelmen, Weiss, & Goodfriend, 1978). As part of that study, we recorded every interpersonal complaint that began "I can't (do something)" or "I can't stop (doing something)." Many of the complaints reflected difficulties with intimacy and

This research was supported by Grant R01-MH-40417 of the National Institute of Mental Health and by Grant BRSG2-S07-RR0552124 of the Biomedical Research Support Grant Program, Division of Research Resources, National Institutes of Health. Much of the work reported in this chapter was done when Saul E. Rosenberg was on the staff of Kaiser Permanente Medical Center, South San Francisco.

other interpersonal problems, and it became apparent to us that an inventory listing common interpersonal problems related to the woman's sexual difficulty could be a valuable assessment tool.

Later, we studied the intake interviews of a large sample of patients and identified their self-reported interpersonal problems. The problematic behaviors were subjected to scaling methods to determine underlying dimensions and major themes. Then a preliminary version of an inventory was developed in a student population that showed internal consistency (Horowitz, French, Gani, & Lapid, 1980; Horowitz, Weckler, & Doren, 1983). We found that people who reported one problem of socializing (e.g., participating in groups) tended to report other problems of socializing (e.g., making new friends); similarly, people who reported one problem of assertiveness (e.g., making demands of other people) tended to report other problems of assertiveness (e.g., criticizing other people). In our most recent work we developed the Inventory of Interpersonal Problems (IIP), (Horowitz, Rosenberg, Baer, Ureño, & Villaseñor, 1988) and standardized it on an outpatient psychiatric population.

Overall Aims

The general purpose of our research has been to clarify the role of interpersonal problems in assessing and treating problems that patients bring to psychotherapy. We have been interested in comparing the treatment outcomes of patients whose primary distress is interpersonal with those of patients whose primary distress is noninterpersonal (e.g., somatic complaints). We have also been interested in comparing the treatment outcomes of patients with different kinds of interpersonal problems (e.g., intimacy problems and assertiveness problems) and examining how these problems relate to specific disorders such as depression.

A separate aim of our research has been to develop a procedure for generating a narrative type of dynamic formulation that is standardized, reliable, and valid. Dynamic formulations identify specific interpersonal and intrapsychic issues that serve as the focus of treatment interventions and provide implicit guidelines for the therapeutic relationship. Because psychodynamic formulations usually mention interpersonal problems and often organize inferences about etiology and treatment around interpersonal issues, the problems that are identified should be consistent with those identified on the IIP. We wanted to formalize the way in which a dynamic formulation is generated and to use one method to cross-validate the other. The development of a new procedure to construct a reliable formulation, called the *consensual response method,* is described in greater detail later.

Subareas of Investigation

We have been interested in using the IIP to predict which patients are most likely to remain in and benefit from psychodynamic psychotherapy. We are also interested in determining which types of interpersonal problems are most responsive to different kinds of treatment.

Method

Subjects

Subjects for developing the IIP were recruited from the Department of Psychiatry of the Kaiser Permanente Medical Center, South San Francisco (a health maintenance organization). Patients were entitled to receive up to 20 outpatient visits as part of their health plan coverage. The patients in the study consisted of 103 individuals, including 14 men and 89 women between 20 and 64 years of age; 29 were single, 48 were married, 24 were divorced or separated, and 2 were widowed; 5 were Black, 6 were Asian, and 8 were Hispanic. The mean amount of schooling was 13.8 years. Patients met the usual selection criteria for brief dynamic psychotherapy (not psychotic, not acutely suicidal, etc.) and had no complicating medical conditions.

Instruments

IIP. The IIP is a self-report measure that asks patients to rate the amount of distress that they have experienced from each of 127 interpersonal problems. The items are organized into two sections corresponding to the most common ways in which patients express complaints during an intake interview (Horowitz, 1979). Seventy-eight items in the first section begin with the phrase "It is hard for me to (e.g., "trust other people" or "say 'no' to other people"), and 49 items in the second section begin with the phrase "These are things I do too much" (e.g., "please other people" or "avoid other people"). The instructions ask each respondent to consider each problem and to rate how distressing that problem has been on a scale ranging from 0 (*not at all*) to 4 (*extremely*).

The IIP has high test–retest reliability and high internal consistency and is sensitive to clinical change (Horowitz et al., 1988). A special form of the IIP, called *Progress in Interpersonal Problems,* lists the interpersonal problems from the IIP and asks the patient and the therapist separately to indicate which problems had been discussed during the treatment and which had shown improvement.

The consensual response method. This method provides a procedure for generating a narrative type of dynamic formulation that is standardized, reliable, and valid (Horowitz, Rosenberg, Ureño, Kalehzan, & O'Halloran, 1989). First, a videotape of an evaluation interview is shown to a group of clinicians, who write individual formulations of the case. Every sentence of each formulation is divided into elementary ideas called *thought units.* Thought units that occur most frequently across the formulations of a given case (consensual responses) are then identified, and those responses are combined into a final formulation, which constitutes a prototypic description of that patient's problem. We call the final formulation the *consensual formulation.*

Procedures

The IIP lends itself to repeated administration in the assessment of interpersonal problems before, during, and after psychotherapy. In our study, patients completed the IIP at four points: when they requested treatment, just before they began treatment, after 10 sessions of brief therapy, and after 20 sessions (termination). After the 10th and 20th sessions, patients also rated which interpersonal problems had been discussed in the treatment and which had shown improvement.

The procedure for the consensual response method was the following: A panel of eight clinical formulators watched each videotaped initial interview and then independently wrote their individual formulations. They were instructed to include the kinds of observations that they typically mention in their own dynamic formulations, such as the patient's reasons for wanting treatment, historical material, the patient's presenting problems, nature of conflicts and defenses, and so on.

After writing their initial formulation they spent 30 minutes discussing the case, and finally they spent 15 minutes writing their individual formulations again, being free to use observations or hypotheses that had arisen during the discussion.

The eight prediscussion formulations (and, separately, the eight postdiscussion formulations) for each patient were treated as follows: Two editors checked each formulation to make sure that it contained complete sentences. Each sentence was then typed in a standard format and presented to a group of four judges, who divided each sentence into elementary thought units. We then examined the thought units that were mentioned by more than one formulator. A panel of five judges examined the thought units in the eight formulations of a set, looking for thought units with the same or similar meaning that occurred in different formulations. Consensual responses were defined as thought units that were mentioned by three or more of the eight formulators. The final listing showed the most commonly cited thought units and their relative frequency of occurrence across the eight formulations. These frequent thought units were then integrated into a single text that constituted the final composite formulation.

Research Accomplishments

Findings Based on the IIP

We have found that patients beginning psychotherapy generally complain of more distress arising from interpersonal problems than from noninterpersonal sources (e.g., somatic). Second, noninterpersonal distress showed the greatest improvement during the first 10 sessions of treatment and then leveled off, whereas interpersonal distress showed improvement during early and later phases of a 20-session psychotherapy. Third, patients who expressed more somatic distress than interpersonal distress were more likely to terminate treatment prematurely and less likely to benefit from their therapeutic experience.

We also found that particular types of interpersonal problems improved more than others (i.e., problems of assertiveness improved more than problems of intimacy). In addition to highlighting a patient's characteristic type of interpersonal problem, the IIP allowed us to compare the relative emphasis that a patient placed on interpersonal compared with symptomatic (primarily somatic) sources of distress. We computed a score, which we call the *I–S difference score,* by subtracting the patient's average symptomatic distress (*S*), measured by the mean response to the SCL 90–R, from the patient's average interpersonal distress (*I*), measured by the mean response to the IIP. The I–S difference score reflects the degree to which interpersonal distress is relatively more salient than noninterpersonal distress. We tentatively regard the difference as a measure of the patient's psychological mindedness. Our results (Horowitz et al., 1988) showed that the I–S difference score successfully discriminated patients who subsequently completed a 20-session treatment from patients who did not. Patients who completed the treatment had significantly higher I–S difference scores. In addition, for patients who did complete the treatment, those with high I–S difference scores generally showed more favorable treatment outcomes.

By using the criterion of a circumplex, a two-dimensional interpersonal space that is composed of an affiliation dimension (friendly to hostile behavior) and a power dimension (submissive to dominating behavior; Wiggins, 1979), eight subscales of the IIP have been devised to occupy different octants of the space. A person's characteristic interpersonal problems can then be located in this space. Our results showed that problematic behaviors reflecting oversubmissiveness are changed more easily than problematic behaviors reflecting hostile dominance.

Findings Based on the Consensual Response Method

We have found that formulations based on the consensual response method are substantially shorter than the original individual formulations. Few thought units in a given consensual formulation were cited by all or even most of the eight formulators, but the resulting formulation tended to be highly stable across replications.

We hypothesized that a consensual formulation helps a clinician anticipate which interpersonal problems are likely to be discussed in treatment. Ten clinical raters were asked to read a formulation and to judge, for each of the interpersonal problems listed on the IIP, whether that problem was apt to be a distressing problem for that patient. Then we determined whether each problem had in fact been discussed in that patient's treatment. We counted the number of times that each problem was said to have been discussed by the

patient and the therapist. Raters showed substantial ability to anticipate, from the formulation alone, which interpersonal problems would be discussed in the treatment. We also found that the greater the proportion of interpersonal content in the formulations, the more easily raters could anticipate correctly which interpersonal problems would subsequently be discussed in the treatment.

Finally, we hypothesized that a formulation with a high proportion of interpersonal content would characterize patients with a more favorable treatment outcome. One reason for this hypothesis is that formulations that describe interpersonal processes should help a therapist to identify appropriate foci for the treatment; a second reason is that patients who do not describe interpersonal processes may have poor conceptions of people and may be more severely disturbed. Therefore, we hypothesized that the higher the proportion of thought units with interpersonal content, the greater the probability of a successful treatment outcome. To test this hypothesis, we evaluated each patient's improvement during treatment. Patients with high interpersonal content had positive improvement scores, and those with low interpersonal content mainly had negative improvement scores. This finding suggests that formulations with a high proportion of interpersonal content are associated with greater improvement. This result confirms our finding from the IIP that patients whose problems are primarily interpersonal tend to be better candidates for brief dynamic psychotherapy than those whose problems are apparently noninterpersonal.

Programs Planned for the Future

We intend to investigate three areas in future research. First, we wish to examine the generality of the above findings. We hope to demonstrate that the IIP continues to be sensitive to change 2 years after patients have completed their treatment. Second, we are interested in evaluating whether the I–S difference score predicts outcome in other patient populations and whether patients with low I–S difference scores might benefit from other therapeutic approaches (e.g., pharmacotherapy or cognitive therapy). Third, we are examining other characteristics of people with low I–S difference scores. Such people may have a poor capacity to form internal representations of others; in that case their descriptions of significant people would be vague, hard to paraphrase, and hard to remember.

Nature of the Research Organization

The research program has been directed by Horowitz, Department of Psychology, Stanford University for the last 10 years. The associate director of the study conducted at Kaiser was Rosenberg. Sources of funding have been grants from the National Institute of Mental Health and the Biomedical Research Support Grant Program, Division of Research Resources, National Institutes of Health.

Relation to Other Research Programs

Integration With Findings of Other Research

Many other researchers have been interested in measuring interpersonal behaviors, traits, and styles (e.g., Benjamin, 1974, 1986; Kiesler, 1983; Strupp & Binder, 1984; Wiggins, 1979). Our work has focused specifically on interpersonal problems; the relationship between interpersonal problems and styles awaits further study.

In the last decade a number of researchers have developed methods for formulating a patient's psychodynamics (Luborsky, 1984; Horowitz, 1987; Strupp & Binder, 1984; Weiss & Sampson, 1986). A review and comparison of these methods can be found in Miller, Luborsky, and Docherty (1990).

Impact on the Field of Psychotherapy

Clinical practice. Our work enables a clinician to identify a patient's specific interpersonal problems and to distinguish quantitatively and qualitatively between a patient's interpersonal and noninterpersonal distress. By examining the relative salience of interpersonal and noninterpersonal sources of distress, the therapist can determine a patient's therapeutic potential in brief dynamic psychotherapy. Our method also enhances a therapist's ability to anticipate the fate of different types of interpersonal problems during treatment.

The consensual response method provides a procedure for constructing a reliable and valid dynamic case formulation. Dynamic formulations are useful for identifying specific issues that serve as the focus of treatment interventions and for judging their impact. A formulation describes the source of a patient's distress, so that it implicitly states the conditions that need to be addressed and modified if the treatment is to be considered successful.

Clinical training. Our methods provide students in clinical training with two assessment tools for measuring the kinds of problems that are salient for patients beginning psychotherapy. They help students to identify important interpersonal problems, focus on the value of predicting treatment outcome, and judge their own dynamic formulations against a standard that is objectively derived from a panel of experienced therapists.

References

Benjamin, L. (1974) Structural analysis of social behavior. *Psychological Review, 81,* 392–425.

Benjamin, L. (1986). Adding social and intrapsychic descriptors to Axis I of DSM-III. In T. Millon & G. Klerman (Eds.), *Contemporary issues in psychopathology* (pp. 599–638). New York: Guilford Press.

Horowitz, L. M. (1979). On the cognitive structure of interpersonal problems treated in psychotherapy. *Journal of Consulting and Clinical Psychology, 47,* 5–15.

Horowitz, M. J. (1987). *States of mind: Configurational analysis* (2nd ed.). New York: Plenum Press.

Horowitz, L. M., French, R. de S., Gani, M., & Lapid, J. S. (1980). The occurrence of semantically similar interpersonal problems. *Journal of Consulting and Clinical Psychology, 48,* 413–415.

Horowitz, L. M., Rosenberg, S. E., Baer, B., Ureño, G., & Villaseñor, V. (1988). Inventory of Interpersonal Problems: Psychometric properties and clinical application. *Journal of Consulting and Clinical Psychology, 56,* 885–892.

Horowitz, L. M., Rosenberg, S. E., Ureño, G., Kalehzan, M., & O'Halloran, P. (1989). Psychodynamic formulation, consensual response method, and interpersonal problems. *Journal of Consulting and Clinical Psychology, 57,* 599–606.

Horowitz, L. M., Sampson, H., Siegelman, E. Y., Weiss, J., & Goodfriend, S. (1978). Cohesive and dispersal behaviors: Two classes of concomitant change in psychotherapy. *Journal of Consulting and Clinical Psychology, 46,* 556–564.

Horowitz, L. M., Weckler, D. A., & Doren, R. (1983). Interpersonal problems and symptoms: A cognitive approach. In P. Kendall (Ed.), *Advances in cognitive-behavior research and therapy* (pp. 81–125). London: Academic Press.

Kiesler, D. J. (1983). The 1982 interpersonal circle: A taxonomy for complementarity in human transactions. *Psychological Review, 90,* 185–215.

Luborsky, L. (1984). *Principles of psychoanalytic psychotherapy: A manual for supportive-expressive (SE) treatment.* New York: Basic Books.

Miller, N. E., Luborsky, L., & Docherty, J. (Eds.) (1990). *Psychodynamic treatment research.* New York: Guilford Press.

Strupp, H., & Binder, J. (1984). *Psychotherapy in a new key: Time-limited dynamic psychotherapy.* New York: Basic Books.

Weiss, J., & Sampson, H. (1986). *The psychoanalytic process.* New York: Plenum Press.

Wiggins, J. (1979). A psychological taxonomy of trait-descriptive terms: The interpersonal domain. *Journal of Personality and Social Psychology, 37,* 395–412.

38

University of California, San Francisco: Group Therapy Research Program

Nick Kanas
Veterans Administration Medical Center

Background and Aims

This program of group therapy research has been in existence since 1978. The aim of the program has been to study the process, content, and outcome of individuals interacting in therapy groups, support groups, and other small group settings. Most of the work was conducted at the San Francisco Veterans Administration Medical Center (SFVAMC), although projects also took place in the psychiatric outpatient clinics at the University of California, San Francisco (UCSF) and at the Tenderloin Clinic, a community mental health center in downtown San Francisco.

The major focus dealt with therapy groups composed of schizophrenic patients. The program began in 1978 with pilot work involving a group of schizophrenics on an acute inpatient psychiatric unit. As clinical techniques were refined, process, content, and outcome studies were performed on this group. The model was extrapolated to the outpatient setting, and most recently it was used to establish short-term outpatient therapy groups for schizophrenics. A second focus was the study of both inpatient and outpatient groups for alcoholics, with the goal of establishing an approach that would fit into a phasic model of treatment for these patients. A third activity was the study of support groups for medical residents, with the goal of evaluating a short-term, time-limited approach that takes into account the vicissitudes of

medical training. A fourth focus consisted of delineating psychological and interpersonal issues involving small groups of astronauts and cosmonauts working in space for long periods of time. Most of this effort stemmed from a review of the literature, although a research proposal is being planned to study astronauts interacting on board a space station. Finally, a group therapy approach of treating patients with posttraumatic stress disorder (PTSD) is being piloted, with formal study being planned for the future.

Method

For the studies involving specialized psychiatric populations, patients have been recruited from the following sites:

• Schizophrenic group studies: SFVAMC, UCSF, and the Tenderloin Clinic;

• Alcoholic group studies: SFVAMC;

• Studies involving support groups for medical and psychiatric residents: SFVAMC;

• Literature review involving astronauts and cosmonauts interacting in space: SFVAMC and UCSF (although earlier work in this area was done at the National Aeronautics and Space Administration, Johnson Spacecraft Center, Houston, Texas);

• PTSD group studies: SFVAMC (in collaboration with Charles Marmar, MD, PTSD program director).

Process instruments for those studies included the Group Climate Questionnaire and the Hill Interaction Matrix. Discussion topics were evaluated by means of content analysis procedures based on data supplied by therapists or raters who used one-way mirrors. Outcome studies included questionnaires, attitude measures (e.g., the Social Avoidance and Distress Scale), symptom measures (e.g., the Brief Psychiatric Rating Scale, the SCL-90, the Psychiatric Evaluation Form, and the Psychiatric Status Scale), and follow-up interviews assessing behavioral improvement and psychiatric status. Basic procedures included literature reviews, uncontrolled pilot work, controlled studies, and studies comparing results with other published normative data.

Research Accomplishments

Schizophrenic Group Studies

In 1977, we (Kanas, Rogers, Kreth, Patterson, & Campbell, 1980) completed a study of 86 acutely hospitalized psychiatric patients who were randomly assigned to participate in one of three conditions: insight-oriented therapy group, activity-oriented task group, or unstructured ward activity. After 20 days of hospitalization, the group therapy and task group patients did not improve more than the control patients. Even so, significantly more schizophrenics in the group therapy condition scored worse on the Overall Severity of Illness measure of the Psychiatric Evaluation Form as well as on a behavioral indicator of clinical status. This suggested that insight-oriented heterogeneous group therapy was not only ineffective but also harmful for some acutely psychotic inpatients.

In response to these findings, we developed a homogeneous group therapy approach for schizophrenics at SFVAMC. The approach was supportive and discussion oriented, and topics focused on ways of improving relationships and strategies of coping with psychotic experiences. Several clinical studies to evaluate this approach were conducted on the psychiatric inpatient unit. In a questionnaire evaluation of 22 patients participating in the group for an average of nine sessions, 95% stated that the group was helpful

(Kanas & Barr, 1982b). Significantly more nonparanoid schizophrenics and significantly more patients younger than the median age found the group to be helpful. In a rank ordering of 13 questionnaire statements reflecting important group therapy curative factors, the patients especially valued the group as a place to talk about emotions and to learn ways to interact better with others.

In a second study (Kanas, Barr, & Dossick, 1985), group process was evaluated with the Hill interaction matrix. The group scored above the 95th percentile of a normative sample of therapy groups in its use of general topics or personal problems to confront patients with aspects of their behavior in a realistic manner. The group environment supported mutual interactions and trust, and it resulted in little total group resistance. Recently, this work was replicated (Kanas & Smith, in press), with the rank order of matrix cells correlating significantly between the original and repeat studies.

In another study (Kanas & Barr, 1986), process and content issues were evaluated during 34 consecutive group sessions with the Group Climate Questionnaire. Compared with a normative sample of outpatient neurotic therapy groups, the schizophrenic group scored significantly lower in the "engaged" and "conflict" dimensions. In a content analysis of important discussion topics, interpersonal issues were brought up most frequently; these were followed by topics involving the expression of emotions, reality testing, and advice giving.

Extrapolating our approach to the outpatient setting, we studied a long-term schizophrenic group (Kanas, DiLella, & Jones, 1984) over the first 6 months of its existence at UCSF. On the Group Climate Questionnaire, this group scored higher in the "avoiding" dimension than the normative sample. The group was found to be as cohesive as the normative sample, and there was more cohesion and less interpersonal conflict as time progressed. A content analysis revealed that issues involved with improving relationships and testing reality were discussed most frequently.

Encouraged by these findings as well as by the recent popularity of short-term, time-limited therapy groups for nonpsychotic outpatients, we modified our approach with a format that allowed schizophrenics to be treated in outpatient groups for 12 weekly 1-hour sessions. In an uncontrolled study (Kanas, Stewart, & Haney, 1988) of a group at UCSF, the patients experienced a significant drop on the Social Avoidance and Distress Scale from beginning to end of the group treatment. Issues aimed at improving and encouraging contact with others were discussed most frequently; these were followed by topics related to reality-testing. In a structured telephone interview conducted 4 months after the group ended, all but one of the patients noted positive gains in ability to relate to others or ability to cope with psychotic experiences (or both).

In a second study of this group therapy format taking place at SFVAMC, 12 schizophrenic patients completing one of two short-term therapy groups were compared with 9 similar waiting-list control patients (Kanas, Deri, Ketter, & Fein, 1989). The attendance rate was 88.9%. On the SCL-90 the group patient scores decreased on all nine symptom dimensions from before to after group therapy, with several of these drops being significant when compared with the controls by means of analysis of variance. In a 4-month follow-up interview, significantly more group patients than controls reported improvement in their ability to relate to others and to cope with psychotic experiences as judged from the Fisher exact test.

In a third study (Kanas, Stewart, Deri, Ketter, & Haney, 1989), the Group Climate Questionnaire was used to evaluate process in the above three groups. The short-term schizophrenic groups scored significantly lower on the avoiding and conflict dimensions compared with the normative sample of outpatient neurotic groups and our long-term outpatient schizophrenic group. There was a tendency for the engaged scores to increase and for the avoiding and conflict scores to decrease over time. Further work is being planned to evaluate this promising approach.

Alcoholic Group Studies

Alcoholic patients participating in group therapy were studied in both inpatient and outpatient settings. On the basis of this work, we proposed a phasic model of treating alcoholics (Kanas, 1982). In Phase 1, issues involving the newly abstinent state and denial were discussed. In Phase 2, the major concern was dealing with the sequelae of alcoholism. In Phase 3, the primary issue was dealing with the predisposing causes of alcoholism. On a 28-day inpatient rehabilitation unit for postdetoxification alcoholics at SFVAMC, Phases 1 and 2 issues were addressed during the group therapy sessions. In a program evaluation survey of 152 patients discharged from this unit over 17 months, 71% rated the therapy group as excellent or good, 23% rated it as satisfactory, and 6% rated it as fair or poor (Kanas, 1982). In the outpatient alcoholic groups, Phases 2 and 3 issues predominated.

In a study of outpatient alcoholics whose major treatment activity was semiweekly group therapy, the patients rank ordered the following 5 items from a 13-item curative factor questionnaire as most helpful: instillation of hope, altruism, group cohesiveness, interpersonal output, and universality (Kanas & Barr, 1982a).

Support Group Studies

At the SFVAMC, a support group was set up for first-year residents rotating on the inpatient medical wards. Content and process were studied in this group over the first 2 years of its existence. A frequency count of important topics discussed in the group identified three important issue clusters: high self-expectations, feelings of lack of control, and topics related to dependence and independence (Ziegler, Kanas, Strull, & Bennet, 1984). By using the Group Climate Questionnaire to study process, this support group was found to be different from a normative sample of outpatient therapy groups in that they scored significantly higher in the engaged dimension and lower in the avoiding and conflict dimensions (Kanas & Ziegler, 1984). Thus these first-year residents were open and cohesive but respectful of each other's privacy, and they avoided interpersonal conflicts.

Work Involving Space Missions

A review was made of more than 60 American and Soviet simulation and space flight studies and reports, with the goal of isolating important psychological and interpersonal factors affecting people interacting in space over long periods of time. Although the missions accomplished most of their goals, psychological and social stresses were present and tended to relate to mission length (Kanas, 1985). On the basis of this review, nine important psychological issues and seven important interpersonal issues were isolated that ranged from psychosomatic symptoms and transcendent experiences to interpersonal tensions and displacement of anger to ground personnel (Kanas, 1987).

Research Programs in Progress and Planned for the Future

At present, we are engaged in a controlled study at the Tenderloin Clinic to evaluate further the effectiveness of time-limited short-term group therapy on outpatient schizophrenics. We hypothesize that schizophrenic patients participating in these groups will show more improvement on measures of social attitude and behavior, symptom-coping, and outpatient adjustment than similar patients who are randomly assigned to a no-group condition or to an activities group that controls for attention and social interaction. This study is supported by the Group Psychotherapy Foundation with funds donated by the Brown Foundation of Houston, Texas.

At SFVAMC, a pilot study is underway evaluating process, content, and outcome in short-term therapy groups for patients with PTSD. Patients are treated in sequential time-limited groups, and we believe that this approach will prove to be helpful and cost-effective.

We hope to use the findings from these two studies to justify further support for larger, better controlled studies in the future. In addition, we are planning a proposal to study the interactions of astronauts in space by using voice analysis and sociometric techniques.

References

Kanas, N. (1982). Multi-factor group therapy for alcoholics. *Current Psychiatric Therapies, 21,* 149–154.

Kanas, N. (1985). Psychosocial factors affecting simulated and actual space missions. *Aviation, Space and Environmental Medicine, 56,* 806–811.

Kanas, N. (1987). Psychological and interpersonal issues in space. *American Journal of Psychiatry, 144,* 703–709.

Kanas, N., & Barr, M. A. (1982a). Outpatient alcoholics view group therapy. *Group, 6*(1), 17–20.

Kanas, N., & Barr, M. A. (1982b). Short-term homogeneous group therapy for schizophrenic inpatients: A questionnaire evaluation. *Group, 6*(4), 2–38.

Kanas, N., & Barr, M. A. (1986). Process and content in a short-term inpatient schizophrenic group. *Small Group Behavior, 17,* 355–363.

Kanas, N., Barr, M. A., & Dossick, S. (1985). The homogeneous schizophrenic inpatient group: An evaluation using the Hill Interaction Matrix. *Small Group Behavior, 16,* 397–409.

Kanas, N., Deri, J., Ketter, T., & Fein, G. (1989). Short-term outpatient therapy groups for schizophrenics. *International Journal of Group Psychotherapy, 39,* 4.

Kanas, N., DiLella, V. J., & Jones, J. (1984). Process and content in an outpatient schizophrenic group. *Group, 8*(2), 13–20.

Kanas, N., Rogers, M., Kreth, E., Patterson, L., & Campbell, R. (1980) The effectiveness of group psychotherapy during the first three weeks of hospitalization: A controlled study. *Journal of Nervous and Mental Disease, 168,* 487–492.

Kanas, N., & Smith, A. J. (in press). Schizophrenic group process: A comparison and replication using the HIM-G. *Group.*

Kanas, N., Stewart, P., Deri, J., Ketter, T., & Haney, K. (1989). Group process in short-term outpatient therapy groups for schizophrenics. *Group, 13*(2), 67–73.

Kanas, N., Stewart, P., & Haney, K. (1988). Content and outcome in a short-term therapy group for schizophrenic outpatients. *Hospital and Community Psychiatry, 39,* 437–439.

Kanas, N., & Ziegler, J. (1984). Group climate in a stress discussion group for medical interns. *Group, 8*(1), 35–38.

Ziegler, J. L., Kanas, N., Strull, W. M., & Bennet, N. E. (1984). A stress discussion group for medical interns. *Journal of Medical Education, 59,* 205–207.

39

Universität Hamburg: Imperative-Centered Focusing as a Method of Psychotherapy and Research

**A. C. Wagner, B. Berckhan, C. Krause,
U. Röder, B. Schenk, and U. Schütze**
Universität Hamburg

Background and Aims

Our theory on self-commanding thought processes and their effects on behavior has been developed under a 6-year research project funded by the Deutsche Forschungsgesellschaft (Wagner, Barz, Maier-Störmer, Uttendorfer-Marek, & Weidle, 1984).

On the basis of the cognitive theory of Miller, Galanter, and Pribram (1960), this research project investigated the behavioral strategies and subjective theories of teachers and pupils in the classroom. In-depth interviews of teachers and pupils were conducted by means of the method of retrospective thinking aloud (Wagner, Uttendorfer-Marek, & Weidle, 1977), a method of stimulated recall that uses videotapes of classroom behavior. The teachers and pupils were asked to recall what they had been thinking in various class situations. The results of those interviews showed that one third (30%) of all interview statements by teachers and pupils contained conflicts of consciousness, the so-called *knots*.

We developed an extensive theoretical model to explain how these knots arise and how they impair the ability for action. The model is based on the assumption that knots are a result of self-commanding thought processes (I must–I must not).

In other words, violation of these self-commanded cognitions leads to inner conflicts (imperative violation conflict). These inner conflicts are associated with different emotions, inner tension, anxiety, anger, and multiple somatic manifestations.

The retrospective thinking aloud interviews were analyzed for their content and the cognitions involved by means of a system of analysis developed for this purpose (Uttendorfer-Marek et al., 1982). The question of how these knots can be resolved is one with great significance for psychotherapy.

Research Accomplishments and Research Programs in Progress

Over a period of several years an approach for resolving these knots was developed and tested, first informally and later more formally.

The first project dealt specifically with the fear of speaking in public. The hypothesis was that conscious conflict could be dissolved by means of a conflict-centered focusing (Gendlin, 1981). The experimental group undergoing this treatment showed significant positive changes compared with the two control groups.

Our current research focuses on enhancement

and extension of the theoretical model for the dissolution of conflicts, further testing of the model in counseling practice, and an interview method that enables the interviewer better to recognize and come to terms with self-commanding processes. We also are trying to develop an approach for teaching patients how to dissolve knots on their own. Much of our work to date has addressed the analysis of imperatives in counseling situations, and we are exploring the possibility of using computer programs to analyze and evaluate the verbal data. We are pursuing these goals in several research projects and in a doctoral thesis. These projects are now described.

Pilot Study on Reducing Fear of Public Speaking in Women

This project was undertaken from 1986 to 1987 and investigated the validity of the theoretical approach of imperative centered focusing. It was also intended as an extensive examination of the effects of the focusing method when used on the core of the various anxieties. The project was designed as a pre–post study with two control groups: placebo treatment and no treatment. Particular attention was paid to behavioral changes and to the results on fear questionnaires and subjective evaluation of assertiveness by the patient. The statistical data show the positive effects of the focusing treatment. The focusing group showed significant behavioral changes as well as a reduction in speech anxiety. A qualitative analysis of the videotaped treatment and counseling sessions indicates that the core anxieties were probably resolved in 7 of 13 cases. Moreover, the data show that the emotional core of the commanding process is often quite deeply seated, in some cases being closely aligned with the fear of death (Wagner, 1987c).

Process of Self-Commanding

Subsequent to and in connection with the project outlined in the foregoing section, another investigation (January 1988 to November 1989) began analyzing the videotaped focusing sessions to track the process of self-commanding. Also investigated in this project was the role that self-commanding processes play in anxieties (angst). Future research will include the definition of a theory of angst based on the imperative theory and its theoretical delineation from other theories of angst. This project is conducted by two part-time staff members, Schenk and Schütze.

Role of Self-Commanding Processes in Public Speaking

In her doctoral thesis, Schenk is investigating what role self-commanding processes play in the self-experience of women speaking in public. Her hypothesis is that self-commanding processes lead to negating parts of the self-experience and therefore will have negative impacts on the development of personal identity, particularly in the process of self-idealism (Horney, 1950).

Apart from laying an extensive theoretical foundation, her thesis will include a qualitative analysis of protocols of psychotherapy sessions. The overall aims of the project are to develop the theoretical approach and to integrate the findings into the treatment of conflict-centered focusing and the therapeutical work with self-concepts.

Manual for Counseling Women With Test and Public Speaking Anxiety

This project was funded by the German government and was conducted by Krause and Röder (March 1988 to February 1990). It aims to develop a counseling manual for women with fears of examination situations and fear of talking in public (or in large groups). Treatment and counseling sessions are offered to students as part of this project. The therapy sessions rely on the theory of imperatives (Wagner et al., 1984; Wagner, 1987a, 1987b), client-centered psychotherapy (Rogers, 1973a, 1973b), and the focusing method (Gendlin, 1981; Wild-Missong 1983). The project itself is designed to test the therapeutic procedures in practice and attempts to incorporate practical experiences into the theoretical framework under study.

Unlike many rhetorical classes, this project does not aim to train the recipient's verbal behavior (in the sense of teaching certain behavior patterns as being appropriate for certain situations). Rather, it focuses on helping the recipient to (re)gain inner calmness and outer composure.

Analysis of Subjective Imperatives

This project is under the direction of Berckhan and aims to develop a computer-based analysis of subjective imperatives in different kinds of texts (e.g., records and transcripts of therapy and counseling sessions, speeches of politicians, and newspaper and magazine articles). In the future, computer-supported textual analysis should enable us quickly to analyze extensive transcripts of therapy sessions with regard to subjective imperatives.

References

Gendlin, E. T. (1981). *Focusing: Technik der selbsthilfe bei der Lösung persönlicher Probleme.* Salzburg, Austria: Otto Müller Verlag.

Horney, K. (1950). *Neurosis and human growth.* New York: Norton.

Miller, G. A., Galanter, E., & Primbram, K. H. (1960). *Plans and structure of behavior.* New York: Holt, Rinehart & Winston.

Rogers, C. R. (1973a). *Entwicklung der Persönlichkeit.* Stuttgart, Federal Republic of Germany: Klett.

Rogers, C. R. (1973b). *Die klient-bezogene Gesprächstherapie.* Munich, Federal Republic of Germany: Kindler.

Uttendorfer-Marek, I., Wagner, A. C., et al. (1982). *Das Handlungs-interaktions-knoten-auswertungssystem (HIK) auswertungsmanual.* Paper presented to the DFG-Projekt Unterrichtsstrategien, Pädagogische Hochschule Reutlingen.

Wagner, A. C. (1987a). Gelassenheit und Handlungsfähigkeit: Über das Aufhören der Imperative als Essenz feministischer Therapie. In B. Rommelspacher (Ed.), *Weibliche Beziehungsmuster: Psychologie und Therapie von Frauen* (pp. 157–184). Frankfurt, Federal Republic of Germany: Campus.

Wagner, A. C. (1987b). "Ich kann mich nicht wehren." Das Aufhören von Imperativen in der Therapiepraxis—Ein Fallbeispiel. In B. Rommelspacher (Ed.), *Weibliche Beziehungsmuster: Psychologie und Therapie von Frauen* (pp. 185–208). Frankfurt, Federal Republic of Germany: Campus.

Wagner, A. C. (1987c). *Todesangst.* Paper presented to the Pädagogischen Psychologie am Fachbereich Erziehungswissenschaft der Universität Hamburg, Hamburg, Federal Republic of Germany.

Wagner, A. C., Barz, M., Maier-Störmer, S., Uttendorfer-Marek, I., & Weidle, R. (1984). *Bewußtseinskonflikte im schulalltag-Denkknoten bei Lehrern und Schlern erkennen und lösen.* Weinheim: Beltz.

Wagner, A. C., Uttendorfer-Marek, I., & Weidle, R. (1977). Die Analyse von Unterrichtsstrategien mit der Methode des "Nachträglichen Lauten Denkens" von Lehrern und Schülern zu ihrem unterrichtlichen Handeln. *Unterrichtswissenschaft, 5,* 244–250.

Wild-Missong, A. (1983). *Neuer Weg zum Unbewußten: Focusing als Methode klientenzentrierter Psychoanalyse.* Salzburg, Austria: Otto Müller Verlag.

40

University of Maryland, College Park: Studying the Effects of Therapist Techniques in a Psychotherapy Process Model

Clara E. Hill
University of Maryland, College Park

Background and Aims

The aim of the University of Maryland psycho-therapy research program has been to investigate the effects of therapist techniques on the process and outcome of therapy. This project is organized around the belief that although a good therapeu-tic relationship, a competent therapist, a good pa-tient for the type of therapy provided, and a lack of interfering external factors are all necessary as a foundation for effective therapy, these factors are not sufficient to cause change. The therapist must deliver specific techniques that are most suited to the particular patient to help him or her change.

To understand the role that therapist tech-niques play in the therapy process, we developed a process model (Hill & O'Grady, 1985) that de-scribes the interaction between the therapist and patient. At any given moment in a session, the therapist draws from his or her theory, diagnostic formulations of the patient, and clinical observa-tions of the patient's behavior to develop an inten-tion for the impact that he or she wants to have on the patient. To implement the intention the thera-pist chooses among several possible verbal inter-ventions, such as reflection, self-disclosure, or

guided imagery. The patient has specific reactions to the therapist's interventions, which determine how he or she responds overtly to the therapist. On the basis of the therapist's perception of the patient's reaction and overt response, the thera-pist formulates the next intention and interven-tion to meet the altered needs of the patient. The process continually evolves as each participant reacts verbally and nonverbally to the other.

This process model is atheoretical, at least in terms of adhering to any of the current psycho-therapy theories. We believe that the change pro-cesses are similar across all theoretical ap-proaches and that we can advance our knowledge most through observation of what occurs in therapy.

Method

To test this psychotherapy process model, we first developed measures of the various components.

Therapist Response Modes

The first instrument that we developed was for therapist verbal response modes (Hill, 1978, 1985,

1986), which tap the grammatical construction of the therapist's intervention (e.g., approval, direct guidance, open question, and interpretation). Hill, Thames, and Rardin (1979) found that Rogers, Perls, and Ellis differed in the response modes that they used. Elliott, Hill, Stiles, Friedlander, Mahrer, and Margison (1987) found evidence for convergent and discriminant validity of the Hill counselor verbal response category system.

Therapist Intentions

Hill and O'Grady (1985) developed a list of 19 therapist intentions, which were defined as a therapist's rationale for selecting a specific intervention to use with a patient at a given moment in the sessions. In a case study, we found that intentions changed systematically both within and across sessions. In a cross-sectional study, we found that intentions were related to theoretical orientation for experienced therapists and that intentions changed systematically within sessions. We also found (Hill & O'Grady, 1985; Hill, Helms, Tichenor, Spiegel, O'Grady, & Perry, 1988) that therapist intentions were closely associated with therapist response modes (e.g., the intention of promoting feelings was typically implemented through either open question or reflection). There was not a one-to-one correspondence, however, suggesting that the best definition of therapist techniques may be the combination of response modes and intentions.

Patient Reactions

Hill, Helms, Spiegel, and Tichenor (1988) developed a measure to tap patients' covert reactions to the therapist's interventions. We found that patient pretreatment symptomatology was strongly related to which reactions patients reported, such that more disturbed patients reported more negative reactions (e.g., they felt worse, confused, or misunderstood).

Patient State

Hill, Greenwald, Reed, Charles, O'Farrell, and Carter (1981) described a patient response modes system that was used by Hill, Carter, and O'Farrell (1983) in a case study. Although we obtained fairly good agreement between judges ($\kappa = .92$), we were somewhat dissatisfied with this measure

because it did not provide a differentiated picture of patient behavior. We will be revising this system in the near future.

Research Accomplishments

The first major tests of therapist techniques took place in two case studies (Hill et al., 1983; O'Farrell, Hill, & Patton, 1986). Therapist interpretation and exploration of feelings were found to be helpful in both cases. Additionally, direct feedback about behavior, gestalt exercises, and discussion of the relationship were helpful in one case, whereas confrontation, permission for the patient to be herself, analogies, and direct guidance were helpful in the second case.

Improving on the methodology of the first two cases, we examined a series of eight cases with experienced therapists and anxious, depressed patients (Hill, Helms, Tichenor, et al., 1988). Results indicated that therapist response modes had a significant effect on immediate outcome (patient and therapist helpfulness ratings, patient reactions, and patient experiencing), with self-disclosure, interpretation, approval, and paraphrase being the most helpful response modes. Response modes accounted for about 1% of the variance, however, and individual differences among patients accounted for about 40%, indicating that patients responded differently to therapist techniques.

In the next set of analyses, we added therapist intentions and patient experiencing in the turn before the therapist intervention to the prediction model. We found that both therapist intentions and previous patient experiencing added significantly more to the variance than response modes. Even more of the variance, however, was accounted for by the interactions among the variables, suggesting the importance of all the variables in combination. Regarding the results for previous patient experiencing, we found that at low levels of patient experiencing therapist exploration of feelings, efforts to change, education, use of open question, and giving of information through direct guidance were most helpful. At higher levels of experiencing, type of therapist intervention was not important. Thus, when patients were experiencing at a high level, they could productively use most therapist interventions. As in the first analysis, individual differences among patients accounted for most of the variance in immediate outcome ratings.

To follow up on the results of Hill, Helms, Tichenor, et al. (1988) regarding individual differences among patients, we performed separate analyses for each case (Hill, 1989). These analyses include not only the data on immediate outcome mentioned earlier but also information collected from questionnaires and interviews regarding the most and least helpful events in the therapies. These two sources of information (quantitative data on immediate outcome and qualitative data from interviews) were collated with information about the moderating effects of patient pretreatment variables, therapist orientation, the therapeutic relationship, and external factors to arrive at some conclusions about what variables were effective in each case. In all eight cases, therapist approval and interpretation were effective interventions. Other techniques were effective for some patients but not others. Regarding patient variables, dependent patients seemed to like direct guidance and information but not confrontation; vulnerable, fearful patients found open question and confrontation helpful but threatening; and insight-oriented patients received more interpretation. Regarding therapist variables, therapist orientation seemed to determine which techniques were used in that psychodynamic therapists used more interpretation but less self-disclosure than behavioral therapists. Furthermore, therapists who were able to be flexible and to negotiate the treatment approach with the patient seemed to have the best outcomes. Regarding the therapeutic relationship, a minimally acceptable relationship was necessary for therapist techniques to be heard and used by patients. Regarding external events, hindering external influences on the patient during therapy (e.g., lack of extratherapy involvement, lack of a support network, and negative external events) made it difficult for some patients to incorporate changes begun in therapy.

In a series of studies, our research team examined the effects of specific response modes in these eight cases of therapy. Hill, Mahalik, and Thompson (1989) found that reassuring disclosures were more helpful than challenging disclosures across all eight cases. An examination of two cases (Hill, 1989), however, revealed that the two therapists involved used disclosures differently, although both were effective. One therapist used mostly immediate (here and now) disclosures with an introspective patient. The other therapist used mostly disclosing (there and then) disclosures with a dependent client.

Hill, Thompson, and Mahalik (1989) traced the effective interpretations in a single case. They found that effective interpretations were offered in the context of approval and support and were interwoven with questions and paraphrases aimed at catharsis and followed by direct guidance. The interpretations were of moderate depth, were presented mostly in the second half of treatment, were repeated many times, and seemed to be accurate. The patient not only accepted the interpretations but slowly began to incorporate them into her own cognitive framework.

In another test of the process model, Fuller and Hill (1985) examined whether patients could perceive therapist intentions. Patients were most able to perceive the intentions of getting information, setting limits, and clarifying. Match rate, however, was not related to session outcome, indicating that patients did not need to know exactly what their therapists meant to do to evaluate the session positively.

Thompson and Hill (in press) examined whether therapists could perceive patient reactions. They found that therapists were able to perceive patient reactions of engaging in therapeutic work 62% of the time and of feeling supported 54% of the time. They were able to perceive the lack of reaction 46% of the time but were able to perceive negative reactions only 27% of the time and challenge reactions about 14% of the time. Thus, they could perceive positive but not negative reactions. Furthermore, when therapists matched on therapeutic work the helpfulness ratings in the subsequent turn were higher than when they did not match. In contrast, when therapists matched on negative reactions or no reaction subsequent helpfulness ratings were lower than when they did not match. This suggests that when therapists think patients are responding well to their interventions they can plan helpful interventions, but when they think patients are reacting negatively they produce less effective interventions.

With the same data as in the Thompson and Hill (in press) study, Hill and Stephany (1990) examined whether patients exhibited nonverbal behaviors that, in concert with their negative reactions, would provide clues for therapists who had trouble recognizing these reactions. We found that negative and positive head nods by patients were associated with supported and therapeutic work reactions but that none of the patients' nonverbal behaviors was associated with negative work.

In sum, we have done several studies examining the effects of therapist techniques. Therapist techniques, in and of themselves, seem to have a small but detectable effect on immediate outcome, particularly when other variables in the process (e.g., therapist orientation, therapist intentions, patient type, patient state, therapeutic relationship, and external factors) are examined simultaneously.

Research Programs in Progress and Planned for the Future

Continuing the study of specific therapeutic interventions, Lee Edward is studying therapist confrontation. Dana Falk is studying whether patient laughter is a productive patient behavior in therapy. We are also studying the effects of therapist and patient metaphors (Hill & Regan, in press).

One research team (Barbara Thompson, Jim Mahalik, Roberta Diemer, and Anne Regan) is currently engaged in the project to determine whether we can train graduate student therapists to be more aware of patients' reactions. We are also interested in determining whether greater awareness of patients' reactions results in more effective therapy.

Our next study (by Hill and Kevin O'Grady) will be to follow up on the findings of individual differences in patient reactions to therapist interventions. We hope to find out more about which therapist techniques are most helpful for different types of patients and for patients when they are in different states.

Relation to Other Research Programs

Elliott (e.g., Elliott, Barker, Caskey, & Pistrang, 1982; Elliott, 1985) has been examining the impact of therapist interventions for several years and has developed a measure of patient impact that preceded the Hill patient reactions system. Martin (e.g., Martin, 1984; Martin, Martin, & Slemon, 1987, 1989; Martin, Martin, Meyer, & Slemon, 1986) has developed a process model similar to ours, which he calls a *cognitive mediational model*. He has also been studying the linkages among the various components of his model. These three research programs have been developing in parallel during the last few years. Given that we all come from different theoretical perspectives and work with different research teams, the amount of convergence in findings among the research programs is encouraging.

References

Elliott, R. (1985). Helpful and nonhelpful events in brief counseling interview: An empirical taxonomy. *Journal of Counseling Psychology, 32,* 307–322.

Elliott, R., Barker, C. B., Caskey, N., & Pistrang, N. (1982). Differential helpfulness of counselor verbal response modes. *Journal of Counseling Psychology, 29,* 354–361.

Elliott, R., Hill, C. E., Stiles, W. B., Friedlander, M. L., Mahrer, A. R., & Margison, F. R. (1987). Primary therapist response modes: Comparison of six rating systems. *Journal of Consulting and Clinical Psychology, 55,* 218–223.

Fuller, F., & Hill, C. E. (1985). Counselor and client perceptions of counselor intentions in relationship to outcome in a single counseling session. *Journal of Counseling Psychology, 32,* 329–338.

Hill, C. E. (1978). Development of a counselor verbal response category system. *Journal of Counseling Psychology, 25,* 461–468.

Hill, C. E. (1985). *Manual for the Hill counselor verbal response modes category system* (rev. ed.). Unpublished manuscript, University of Maryland, College Park.

Hill, C. E. (1986). An overview of the Hill counselor and client verbal response modes category systems. In L. Greenberg & W. Pinsof (Eds.), *The psychotherapeutic process: A research handbook* (pp. 131–160). New York: Guilford Press.

Hill, C. E. (Ed.). (1989). *Therapist techniques and client outcomes: Eight cases of brief psychotherapy.* Newbury Park, CA: Sage.

Hill, C. E., Carter, J. A., & O'Farrell, M. K. (1983). A case study of the process and outcome of time-limited counseling. *Journal of Counseling Psychology, 30,* 3–18.

Hill, C. E., Greenwald, C., Reed, K. G., Charles, D., O'Farrell, M., & Carter, J. (1981). *Manual for counselor and client verbal response modes category systems.* Columbus, OH: Marathon Consulting Press.

Hill, C. E., Helms, J., Spiegel, S. B., & Tichenor, V. (1988). Development of a system for assessing client reactions to therapist interventions. *Journal of Counseling Psychology, 34,* 27–36.

Hill, C. E., Helms, J. E., Tichenor, V., Spiegel, S. B., O'Grady, K. E., & Perry, E. (1988). The effects of therapist response modes in brief psychotherapy. *Journal of Counseling Psychology, 35,* 222–233.

Hill, C. E., Mahalik, J. R., & Thompson, B. J. (1989). Therapist self-disclosure. *Psychotherapy, 26,* 290–295.

Hill, C. E., & O'Grady, K. E. (1985). List of therapist intentions illustrated in a case study and with therapists of varying theoretical orientations. *Journal of Counseling Psychology, 32,* 3–22.

Hill, C. E., & Regan, A. (in press). Therapist use of metaphors in a case of brief psychotherapy. *Journal of Integrative and Eclectic Psychotherapy.*

Hill, C. E., & Stephany, A. (1990). The relationship of nonverbal behaviors to client reactions. *Journal of Counseling Psychology, 37,* 22–26.

Hill, C. E., Thames, T. B., & Rardin, D. (1979). A comparison of Rogers, Perls, and Ellis on the Hill counselor verbal response category system. *Journal of Counseling Psychology, 26,* 198–203.

Hill, C. E., Thompson, B. J., & Mahalik, J. R. (1989). Therapist interpretation. In C. E. Hill (Ed.), *Therapist techniques and client outcomes: Eight cases of brief psychotherapy* (pp. 284–310). Newbury Park, CA: Sage.

Martin, J. (1984). The cognitive mediational paradigm for research in counseling. *Journal of Counseling Psychology, 31*, 559–572.

Martin, J., Martin, W., Meyer, M., & Slemon, A. G. (1986). Empirical investigation of the cognitive mediational paradigm for research on counseling. *Journal of Counseling Psychology, 33*, 115–123.

Martin, J., Martin, W., & Slemon, A. G. (1987). Cognitive mediational paradigm in person-centered and ra-tional-emotive therapy. *Journal of Counseling Psychology, 34*, 251–260.

Martin, J., Martin, W., & Slemon, A. G. (1989). Cognitive-mediational models of action-act sequences in counseling. *Journal of Counseling Psychology, 36*, 8–16.

O'Farrell, M. K., Hill, C. E., & Patton, S. (1986). Comparison of two cases of counseling with the same counselor. *Journal of Counseling and Development, 65*, 141–145.

Thompson, B., & Hill, C. E. (in press). Therapist perceptions of client reactions. *Journal of Counseling and Development*.

41

University of Toledo: Investigating Significant Therapy Events

Robert Elliott
University of Toledo

Background and Aims

The psychotherapy research program at the University of Toledo began in 1978 and has produced more than 60 publications, conference presentations, and measurement procedures and instruments. It has served as a source of new ideas and methods in psychotherapy research and has coordinated studies with a number of prominent therapy process researchers elsewhere.

A common set of core interests or aims has characterized the research conducted throughout this period, including (a) measurement of patient in-therapy experiences and interest in patient phenomenology, generally utilizing the tape-assisted recall procedure (see Elliott, 1986); (b) close analysis of therapy process, especially as this relates to patient experiences; (c) search for effective ingredients in therapy and testing the limits of what is assumed to be effective; (d) developing results of relevance to clinical practice and training; and (e) development and testing of new measures and research approaches for capturing psychotherapeutic change processes.

Method and Research Accomplishments

The most straightforward way to summarize this research program is by tracing its evolution, including the methods and accomplishments of each phase of its development.

Phase 1: Collecting Significant Events (1978–1983)

The research program originated in two studies carried out at the University of California, Los Angeles by fellow graduate students Chris Barker, Nancy Pistrang, Nick Caskey, and myself. These studies were the first to adapt Kagan's (1975) interpersonal process recall method to a systematic research procedure for obtaining patient and therapist ratings of the experiences associated with particular moments in therapy. These initial studies (e.g., Elliott, Barker, Caskey, & Pistrang, 1982) focused on the perceived helpfulness of therapist response modes; although relationships were discovered, they were too small to be clinically useful.

These studies, however, produced one important serendipitous finding: the existence of occasional helpful or significant therapist interventions. This discovery led to an analog study in which volunteer patients identified and described the impact of the most and least helpful therapist responses in brief counseling sessions. These patient descriptions were later cluster analyzed, leading to the discovery of a taxonomy of immediate therapeutic impacts (Elliott, 1985), one of the most important findings to date from this research program.

Fueled by growing interest in what we came to call *significant therapy events*, a team of graduate students (especially John Cline and Elisabeth James) and I then carried out a series of systematic case studies. In these studies, patients and therapists underwent the arduous process of reviewing each session in its entirety and providing detailed information about the most helpful and hindering therapist responses.

We eventually carried out four of these case studies. In our enthusiasm to get our hands on what was important in these therapies, we amassed a large number of quantitative and qualitative date (including several hundred hours of untranscribed recall interviews) but were not yet certain about what to do without "treasure." We next carried out a series of analyses of one or more of the case studies, using a wide variety of quantitative research methods (e.g., Elliott, James, Reimschuessel, Cislo, & Sack, 1985). This work culminated in an exhaustive attempt to apply a battery of 42 patient and therapist process variables to the significant events identified in the first of the case studies (Elliott, Cline, & Shulman, 1983). When this attempt failed to produce clinically meaningful results, we became disillusioned with attempts to study therapeutic change in quantitative terms and began to search for alternatives.

Phase 2: Development of Comprehensive Process Analysis (1983–1985)

In parallel with the analyses just described, my students and I had already begun doing in-depth demonstration analyses of individual significant therapy events. These analyses relied heavily on the idea of applying a standard, complete set of quantitative therapy process measures (a process battery). This early work forced us to begin developing a comprehensive framework for understanding significant events and to start working directly with patients' and therapists' descriptions of their experiences. We coined the term *comprehensive process analysis* to describe this emerging approach. The first such study (Elliott, 1983) was an analysis of a single striking therapy event. The second of these quantitative comprehensive process analysis studies involved four insight events (Elliott, 1984).

When we became disillusioned with the quantitative battery approach, we began exploring qualitative research methods (e.g., Glaser & Strauss, 1967) and sociolinguistics (e.g., Labov & Fanshel, 1977). My students and I came to three conclusions: First, for psychotherapy research to produce clinically meaningful results, it must be based on open-ended description rather than confirmatory quantification. Second, little progress can be made toward unlocking therapeutic change processes without first understanding what brings about change in individual significant events. Third, following Rice and Greenberg (1984), we decided to abandon the systematic case study approach in favor of focusing on common factors in collections of similar significant events (e.g., insight events). The result of such analyses would be a model or microtheory of one kind of therapeutic change process, a kind of road map for therapists.

In 1983, we began carrying out qualitative analyses of significant therapy events. After a pilot study, we developed the current, qualitative version of comprehensive process analysis (Elliott, 1989). In it, multiple qualitative observers analyze a series of similar events, describing each along the lines suggested by an exhaustive framework of types of factors that might contribute to significant events. The method also includes procedures for controlling for observer bias and for evaluating the clinical significance of events.

We applied the new method to a collection of significant events in which patients reported arriving at a greater degree of self-awareness (Elliott, 1989). Then, in 1984 and 1985, I spent a sabbatical year at the University of Sheffield; while I was there, David Shapiro, members of his research team, Bill Stiles, and I carried out a comprehensive process analysis study comparing insight events in exploratory and prescriptive therapies (Elliott et al., 1987). Although the method is time consuming and unconventional, we are enthusiastic about its potential for capturing and integrating the clinical richness of significant events and for discovering unexpected features of events (e.g., patients change the subject after awareness events, but they are still helped).

Once we had finally developed a satisfactory method for analyzing therapy events, we found that it was possible to design a more efficient data collection procedure tailored to the new method of analysis. This method, called *brief structured recall*, was developed in collaboration with Shapiro (Elliott & Shapiro, 1988).

Phase 3: Experiential Therapy of Depression (1985 to the Present)

At this point, we had a set of data collection and analysis procedures for understanding significant therapy events. The next step was choosing a disorder and treatment model with which to work. Depression seemed a logical choice for two reasons: (a) the extensive research literature on treatments of depression and (b) our experience with studying the treatment of depression in the earlier systematic case studies.

This left us with the decision about the treatment on which to focus. Cognitive–behavioral and interpersonal–dynamic therapies had been studied extensively and were being investigated with our methods in the second Sheffield Psychotherapy Project. In contrast, there was comparatively little recent work on humanistic or experiential therapies in spite of recent developments (e.g., Greenberg & Safran, 1987). Thus, my students (Claudia Clark, John Brinkerhoff, Carol Mack, and Vivian Kemeny) and I decided to study an integrative experiential therapy based on the task-analytic approach (Rice & Greenberg, 1984). Additional considerations included our personal therapeutic predilections, the need to broaden the range of treatments available for treating depression, and earlier indirect evidence in the literature indicating the effectiveness of experiential therapies with depression.

The Experiential Therapy of Depression Project (conducted with colleague Sue Labott, postdoctoral fellow Lorraine Jackson, and students Cheryl Anderson, Ken Davis, and Claudia Clark) is an investigation of change processes in an integrative, experiential treatment with clinically depressed patients. A treatment manual has been drafted in collaboration with Les Greenberg and Laura Rice at York University in Toronto (Elliott, Greenberg, Rice, & Clark, 1988). The study has been designed to parallel many of the design features of the Sheffield Psychotherapy Projects I and II (Shapiro & Firth, 1987), including population, change measures, and recall procedure.

The main research questions in this study center on change processes, in particular identifying types of significant event and the factors that contribute to them and assessing the effects and effective ingredients in the treatment.

To date, we have completed treatment for 75% of the projected 20 cases. Some tentative findings based on the available data, which we have presented in a series of papers (e.g., Elliott, Clark,

Wexler, Kemeny, Brinkerhoff, & Mack, 1990), are as follows:

• Experiential therapy seems to be effective in treating clinical depression. Pre–post change data so far are equivalent to meta-analytic data in the literature and in the first Sheffield Psychotherapy Project (Shapiro & Firth, 1987).

• Brief structured recall, the new recall method geared toward comprehensive process analysis, has proven feasible and has good reliability and validity.

• A central issue with many of our depressed patients is unfinished business with significant others, which is generally treated with the empty-chair method from Gestalt therapy.

• Consistent with the treatment model, patients in experiential therapy report experiencing high levels of increased awareness of avoided aspects of self and of feeling understood and supported by the therapist.

When data collection for the current project is complete, we will have an archive of significant therapy events and related materials (session ratings and change data) documenting the change process in the experiential therapy of depression. From this archive, we will be able to draw collections of similar significant events for a series of comprehensive process analysis studies. For example, work has begun on a study of significant events involving the use of Gendlin's (1978) experiential focusing technique. Beyond this, work comparing similar events from different therapies is envisioned with the use of parallel data being collected in the second Sheffield Psychotherapy Project. Finally, a study comparing experiential and cognitive therapies with depressed patients is currently envisioned, which will allow the comparison of change processes in therapies that alternatively emphasize evoking or containing emotion.

Nature of the Research Organization

The Toledo Psychotherapy Research Program has been supported by five faculty research fellowships and grants from the University of Toledo Graduate School, a National Institute of Mental Health small grant, and a State of Ohio Academic

Challenge Grant to the graduate clinical psychology program. Two regular faculty members (Sue Labott and I) are currently involved. Continuing institutional support consists of faculty course reductions, graduate assistants, research equipment and space, secretarial support and additional space in the Psychology Clinic and Training Center, and undergraduate college work-study assistants. The research program has benefited particularly from the support of Fred Kitterle, the current department chair, and Kay Schaffer, director of clinical training. The graduate clinical psychology program attracts talented practice-oriented students, many of whom have had previous clinical experience. Many of the brightest and most skilled of these students have contributed to the psychotherapy research program.

Relation to Other Research Programs

Integration With Findings of Other Research

The Toledo Psychotherapy Research Program often acts as a source of measures, research materials (e.g., transcripts or tapes), consultation, and occasionally training for psychotherapy researchers in North America and Europe. A number of more elaborate collaborations have been undertaken with researchers elsewhere. The most developed of these is the collaboration with David Shapiro's research program at the University of Sheffield. This has included coordination of study methods and comparison of results, measure development, data analysis, and training of Sheffield team members in the recall procedure.

Another set of links exists between Toledo and York University, where Leslie Greenberg and Laura Rice are located. In addition to sharing of research methods and data, they have provided invaluable consultation on the experiential therapy model. The collaboration also includes theoretical work on an experiential theory of depression (Greenberg, Elliott, & Foerster, 1990).

Impact on the Field of Psychotherapy

Most of the accomplishments of the Toledo Psychotherapy Research Program have so far been methodological. First, we have helped to open up new areas for therapy research by pointing to new subject matter (e.g., significant events) or by providing new measures. These areas and measures have been taken up by other researchers (e.g., Hill, Helms, Spiegel, & Tichenor, 1988). Second, we have demonstrated the limits of traditional therapy process research, thus supporting the paradigm shift advocated by Rice and Greenberg (1984) and others (e.g., Stiles et al., 1986).

The research program has also produced a number of clinically relevant findings in addition to those cited already. For one, patient and therapist perspectives on therapy often differ markedly (Caskey, Barker, & Elliott, 1984); therefore, therapists should not assume that they know their patients' experience but should routinely inquire about it. For another, therapist advice-giving often stimulates increased patient awareness of uncomfortable aspects of self (Elliott, 1989); the immediate aftermath of advice is a good time to help patients explore emerging awareness.

To conclude, the psychotherapy research program at the University of Toledo is small but has a number of strengths, including its comparative longevity and methodological continuity, its stable institutional supports, and its close links to other important therapy research programs. Paradoxically, its limited size and lack of large grant funding have forced it to act as a model of small-scale "cottage industry" psychotherapy research and have allowed it to function freely outside the mainstream as a source of methodological innovation.

References

Caskey, N., Barker, C., & Elliott, R. (1984). Dual perspectives: Clients' and therapists' perceptions of therapist responses. *British Journal of Clinical Psychology, 23,* 281–290.

Elliott, R. (1983). "That in your hands...": A comprehensive process analysis of a significant event in psychotherapy. *Psychiatry, 46,* 113–129.

Elliott, R. (1984). A discovery-oriented approach to significant change events in psychotherapy: Interpersonal process recall and comprehensive process analysis. In L. N. Rice & L. Greenberg (Eds.), *Patterns of change,* (pp. 249–286). New York: Guilford Press.

Elliott, R. (1985). Helpful and nonhelpful events in brief counseling interviews: An empirical taxonomy. *Journal of Counseling Psychology, 32,* 307–322.

Elliott, R. (1986). Interpersonal process recall (IPR) for psychotherapy process research. In L. Greenberg & W. Pinsof (Eds.), *Handbook of psychotherapy process research* (pp. 503–527). New York: Guilford Press.

Elliott, R. (1989). Comprehensive process analysis: Understanding the change process in significant therapy events. In M. Packer & R. B. Addison (Eds.), *Entering the circle: Hermeneutic investigation in psy-*

chology (pp. 165–184). Albany: State University of New York Press.

Elliott, R., Barker, C. B., Caskey, N., & Pistrang, N. (1982). Differential helpfulness of counselor verbal response modes. *Journal of Counseling Psychology, 29,* 379–387.

Elliott, R., Clark, C., Wexler, M., Kemeny, V., Brinkerhoff, J., & Mack, C. (1990). The impact of experiential therapy of depression: Initial results. In G. Lietaer, J. Rombauts, & R. Van Balen (Eds.), *Client-centered and experiential psychotherapy towards the nineties* (pp. 549–577). Leuven, Belgium: Leuven University Press.

Elliott, R., Cline, J., & Shulman, R. (1983, July). *Effective processes in psychotherapy: A single case study using four evaluative paradigms.* Paper presented at the meeting of the Society for Psychotherapy Research, Sheffield, England.

Elliott, R., Greenberg, L. S., Rice, L. N., & Clark, C. (1988). *Draft manual for experiential therapy of depression.* Unpublished manuscript, University of Toledo, Ontario, Canada.

Elliott, R., James, E. Reimschuessel, C., Cislo, D., & Sack, N. (1985). Significant events and the analysis of immediate therapeutic impacts. *Psychotherapy, 22,* 620–630.

Elliott, R., & Shapiro, D. A. (1988). Brief structured recall: A more efficient method for identifying and describing significant therapy events. *British Journal of Medical Psychology, 61,* 141–153.

Elliott, R., Shapiro, D. A., Firth, J., Stiles, W. B., Llewelyn, S. P., Hardy, G., & Margison, F. (1987). *Insight events in prescriptive and exploratory therapies: A comprehensive process analysis.* Unpublished manuscript, University of Toledo, Ontario, Canada.

Gendlin, E. T. (1978). *Focusing.* New York: Everest House.

Glaser, B. G., & Strauss, A. (1967). *The discovery of grounded theory: Strategies for qualitative research.* Chicago: Aldine.

Greenberg, L. S., Elliott, R., & Foerster, F. (1990). Experiential processes in the psychotherapeutic treatment of depression. In N. Endler & D. C. McCann (Eds.), Depression: New directions in theory, research, and perspectives practice (pp. 157–185). Toronto, Ontario, Canada: Wall & Emerson.

Greenberg, L. S., & Safran, J. D. (1987). *Emotion in psychotherapy.* New York: Guilford Press.

Hill, C. E., Helms, J. E., Spiegel, S. B., & Tichenor, V. (1988). Development of a system for assessing client reactions to therapist interventions. *Journal of Counseling Psychology, 35,* 27–36.

Kagan, N. (1975). *Interpersonal process recall: A method of influencing human interaction.* (Available from N. Kagan, Educational Psychology Department, University of Houston—University Park, Houston, TX 77004).

Labov, W., & Fanshel, D. (1977). *Therapeutic discourse.* New York: Academic Press.

Rice, L. N., & Greenberg, L. (Eds.). (1984). *Patterns of change.* New York: Guilford Press.

Shapiro, D. A., & Firth, J. (1987). Prescriptive vs. exploratory psychotherapy: Outcomes of the Sheffield psychotherapy project. *British Journal of Psychiatry, 151,* 790–799.

Stiles, W. B., Shapiro, D. A., & Elliott, R. (1986). Are all psychotherapies equivalent? *American Psychologist, 41,* 165–180.

Summary Issues

The Status of Programmatic Research

Larry E. Beutler
University of California, Santa Barbara

Marjorie Crago
University of Arizona

Paulo P. P. Machado
University of California, Santa Barbara

The chapters in this book represent 40 different programs from different countries. *Diversity* is an accurate but inadequate descriptor for the variation that exists among the foci, the types of psychotherapies and modalities studied, and the methods explored. Given the tremendous productivity of these programs, this diversity must be taken as a sign of health in the field of psychotherapy research. It is a vital field in which much creative effort is being directed toward an understanding of how people grow and change.

Another sign of this vitality is the gradual increase of research reports from countries that are not traditionally known to support psychotherapy research. Research on psychotherapy recently has been reported from Italy (e.g., Guidano, 1987, in press), Portugal (Goncalves, 1990), and Spain (e.g., Feixas i Viaplana & Villegas i Besora, 1990). The emergence of research from regions that heretofore have made relatively little contribution to the world literature in this area of study suggests an expanding interest among behavioral scientists worldwide in psychotherapy process and outcome.

In spite of the great diversity among programs worldwide, one must be impressed that there are also commonalities. Indeed, from reading the chapters in this book one may get a general sense that investigators are making systematic efforts to apply some common methods of measurement and to impose some common standards on data collection. These efforts may well be enhanced through improved international communication linkages (e.g., Bitnet, INet, international journals, etc.), visits among investigators at different sites, and the opportunities for sharing ideas and for developing collaborative research projects that is afforded by such organizations as the Society for Psychotherapy Research. As a result of this sharing, perhaps some common conclusions about the nature of psychotherapy processes and outcomes are being reached and common methods evolving.

However, the diversity that exists among programs should not be dismissed too quickly. Variations among methodologies and targets of investigation seem to characterize, in a differential way, geographic identities, but even this statement is too simplistic in view of the wide diversity that also exists within major geographical regions. The differences rather than the similarities among programs and regions may mark the vitality of the field. In view of this diversity, it may be useful to highlight some of the differences that appear to index the value systems that characterize different geographic regions and that suggest a still-emerging and diversifying field. Regional as well as programmatic diversities emerge in at least four domains: (a) process versus outcome focus, (b) the theoretical models of psychotherapy considered for investigation, (c) the modality of service delivery studied, and (d) the methodologies preferred.

Process Versus Outcome Focus

Research programs are still classifiable generally on the basis of whether they focus principally on psychotherapy processes or outcomes. Some programs (e.g., see chapters 3, 6, 7, 13, 22, 23, 26, 27, 35, 36, and 39) emphasize the importance of understanding treatment processes and entail little formal assessment of outcomes, whereas others relegate interactional processes and change mechanisms to a secondary role in favor of assessing clinical effectiveness (e.g., see chapters 4, 9, 15, 17, 19, 30, and 33). Yet, overall, there appears to be a consistent movement by many, if not most, programs toward combining the two domains of focus in order to emphasize specifically the relation between process and outcome. Indeed, several programs report either a longstanding and primary emphasis on process–outcome relationships (e.g., see chapters 5, 8, 10, 12, 14, 16, 18, 20, 24, 32, 37, 38, 40, and 41) or a recent shift of focus toward merging these two general areas of research (e.g., see chapters 11, 21, 25, 28, and 29).

Although there is a good deal of intraregional variation, a review of the clustering of programs in each of these interest areas suggests the presence of geographical differences in the degree to which process and outcome research is valued. In Northern Europe, especially in the Federal Republic of Germany, and in the coastal regions of North America there seems to be much focus on the assessment of processes that characterize psychotherapy. On the other hand, the preponderance of outcome-focused programs derives from either North America or Scandinavia. Support for the conclusion that there is an escalating interest in merging process and outcome interests may be indicated by the observation that the programs claiming increasing interest in the combination of process and outcome emphases represent all regions covered in this volume in similar proportions.

Theoretical Models of Psychotherapy

The type or model of psychotherapy explored is closely related to whether a program values processes or outcomes. Characteristically, the programs that have emphasized process research over outcome research have almost uniformly targeted either psychodynamic or psychoanalytic treatments for study. Outcome researchers, on the other hand, have tended to favor interpersonal (see chapters 4 and 15), behavioral (see chapters 19 and 30), and cognitive (see chapters 9 and 17) therapies. Those who are systematically focused on assessing process and outcome linkages are even more diverse, targeting unstructured or naturally occurring therapies (see chapters 8, 18, 32, 38, 40, and 41); cognitive or behavioral interventions (see chapters 11 and 24); experiential and humanistic models (see chapters 11, 21, 24, and 25); interpersonal therapies (see chapters 14 and 28); integrative approaches (see chapters 11, 15, 24, and 28), and psychodynamic approaches (see chapters 5, 10, 12, 16, 20, 25, 29, and 37).

The geographical distributions of studies with varying commitments to psychodynamic methods reveal again the psychodynamic leanings of Germany and the coastal regions of North America. However, there is also some clear indications of European interest in client-centered therapy, and this interest contrasts with the strong disposition toward cognitive therapies in North America. An emerging interest appears also to be present for both experiential therapies and integrative therapies, although geographical distributions of these interests are not obvious.

Mode of Delivery

Although most research represented in this book is of individually administered treatment, there are some notable exceptions. Several programs have systematically investigated group therapies (see chapters 5, 10, 11, and 38) as well as marital (see chapters 4, 9, 19, 21, and 34) and family (see chapters 15 and 34) therapies. A few studies have also included drug therapies (see chapters 4, 11, 12, and 17). However, only a surprisingly small number of programs report research on the prevention of emotional problems (see chapters 14 and 17).

The investigation of short-term and time-limited treatments also characterizes North American research programs (see chapters 2, 4, 5, 9, 10, 11, 13, 14, 17, 19, 20, and 31). This focus contrasts with the attention given to research on long-term psychotherapies and psychoanalysis in continental Europe (see chapters 22, 23, 24, 26, 27, 29, and 32). Provocatively, the health care delivery system and research funding priorities of Germany appear to encourage the use and investigation of these long-term treatments, especially psychoanalysis (see chapters 22, 26, and 27). It will be interesting to see if these interests can be maintained in Germany with the inevitable homogenizing effects of the reunification of Germany and the extension of the European common market.

Although some research on psychoanalysis has been conducted in North America (see chapters 3, 7, and 36), it is less often supported by federal money than in Germany. More often in North America, long-term research is an open-ended psychotherapy (see chapters 6, 8, 12, 16, 18, 31, 33, 38, 40, and 41), but even in the United States federal money does not appear to be a frequent means of support.

Preferred Methodologies

Research programs tend to rely on combinations of four basic methods: (a) randomized clinical trials, (b) comparisons (usually post hoc) of nonrandomized groups, (c) intensive case (or $n = 1$) studies, and (d) mathematical analyses or modeling of psychotherapy data.

As suggested by the extent and variety of their use (see chapters 4, 5, 9, 10, 11, 12, 13, 14, 15, 16, 17, 18, 34, 38, and 41), the methodologies preferred among programs based in North America embody three central qualities: (a) random assignment of subjects to treatments, (b) the use of manual-driven therapies, and (c) the selection of diagnostically homogeneous samples. Although there are a few programs outside of North America that incorporate all three of these elements (see chapters 28, 30, and 39), they are exceptions to the more frequently used naturalistic methods. To the degree that randomized clinical trial studies are conducted in Europe, the preferred methodology excludes the criteria of selecting diagnostically homogeneous samples, instead favoring the use of diverse samples (see chapters 24 and 25). Although this methodological variation is also applied in North American research, it occurs at a proportionately lower rate than in Europe (see chapters 5, 10, 18, and 20).

In both Europe and North America, by far the largest number of studies that do not routinely restrict entry to a specific set of diagnostic groups have used a naturalistic rather than a randomized clinical trials design. In a naturalistic study, correlations are sought between predictor and dependent variables (see chapters 6, 11, 32, 33, 37, 38, and 40), sometimes with the variation of comparing naturally occurring contrast groups (see chapters 2, 8, 12, 16, 18, 21, 22, 23, 29, and 37).

A large variety of patients has been studied in controlled trials and post hoc comparison studies. Investigators have reported results on disparate groups such as those with personality disorders (see chapters 2 and 29), psychotic conditions (see chapters 3, 29, and 38), psychosomatic complaints (see chapters 11, 17, and 27), neurotic conflicts (see chapters 20 and 29), disorders of childhood and adolescence (see chapters 3, 15, 17, and 34), anxiety disorders (see chapters 9, 13, and 30), substance abuse (see chapters 15, 16, and 38), and depression (see chapters 4, 11, 17, 19, 28, and 34) among others.

Intensive case study methodologies have been used most often as the primary method for assessing psychoanalytic treatments (see chapters 3, 6, 7, 12, 26, 27, and 36), but they are also increasingly used as secondary analyses for a variety of psychotherapies (see chapters 16, 19, 20, 21, 38, and 41). In these case study methodologies, it is more difficult than in controlled comparison and clinical trials studies to tease out the type of patients to which the results can be applied.

Variations in the breadth of the dependent measure selected is a natural offshoot of the selection of either naturalistic or randomized-trials designs. Most programs that target diagnostically homogeneous samples rely on similarly focused outcome measures, whereas the programs that use naturalistic designs tend to rely more heavily on general measures of outcome. Especially in North America, however, there seems to be some movement toward incorporating psychophysiological measures as both predictor and dependent variables in psychotherapy research in controlled trials and naturalistic studies (see chapters 11, 16, 17, and 18).

Finally, a number of studies have used statistical procedures as a primary method in psychotherapy research. These approaches have included meta-analysis (see chapters 28 and 34), mathematical modeling of therapeutic interactions and outcomes (see chapters 31, 36, and 39), and textual analysis of process data (see chapter

26). These innovations may mark the evolution of new means for compiling psychotherapy data with the development of computer technology. The applications are varied but are too infrequent to detect regional differences in their use.

Collectively, the pattern of regional differences suggests that North American research programs tend to value randomized clinical-trials methods, as applied within diagnostically homogeneous samples, process and process–outcome patterns, the use of manualized therapies, and an exploration of diverse therapies. In contrast, researchers in continental Europe appear to value naturalistic studies of psychoanalytic processes occurring in unmanualized treatments among heterogeneous samples. Some movement toward randomized clinical trials and manualized treatments is noted in Europe but largely without restriction of samples to diagnostic groupings.

It should again be emphasized that Europe is more diverse in its interests and values than this summary would indicate, with considerable variation being seen among countries. Variations range from the biological focus of France to the strongly behavioral focus of the Netherlands.

It is difficult to determine the preferences of either Scandinavian investigators or those from the United Kingdom because of low levels of representations among research programs. However, if one were to guess, one might conclude that at least the United Kingdom holds values that are similar to those represented in North America. Namely, there is a preference for randomized clinical-trial designs, a focus on process–outcome relationships, and structured short-term therapies.

Conclusion

A summary of the findings from the many programs reported here is beyond the limits of available space. The findings have been diverse and clearly suggest that psychotherapy research is productive and vital. At the beginning of this book, Lambert (see chapter 1) outlined six conclusions, none of which are disputed significantly by the findings reported here. Namely, he concluded that (a) psychotherapy is effective, (b) it is more effective than placebo interventions, (c) clients who improve in therapy maintain that improvement for extended periods, (d) some treatments have a negative effect on some clients, (e) common factors and specific therapy interventions affect client posttreatment status, and (f) the client is a principal determiner of how effective treatment will be.

Although these conclusions still seem safe, it should be pointed out that considerable controversy still exists regarding some aspects of both methodology and conclusions. For example, there is still some disagreement about the relative efficacy of specific psychotherapy models, although the current movement toward an inspection of therapy and patient-type interactions suggests that researchers may yet discover that different models are effective for different client groups.

Likewise, controversy still exists around the importance of understanding psychotherapy processes in the absence of specific outcome data. Many programs still emphasize the importance of discovering principles of change from individual samples, even in the absence of a clear demonstration of efficacy. Generally, however, the field seems to be moving toward an integration of these process focused studies and research on outcome efficacy.

Investigators also differ in the relative value placed on studying diagnostically homogeneous groups. Although some investigators and programs have found value in developing treatments for specific diagnostic conditions, others have emphasized the cross-cutting nature of psychotherapy and have suggested that variables yet undisclosed in diagnosis may be more important to understanding psychotherapy efficacy.

Finally, there continues to be disagreement about the relative value of different methods of delivering psychotherapy. Group, family, and individual delivery systems are being developed and compared. It is likely once again that all will win and all will have prizes as researchers discover the limitations and indicators for each of these delivery mechanisms.

The foregoing concerns raise the need to consider and revisit the goals and methods of programmatic research. It is to this task that we now turn with the last chapter of this book.

References

Feixas i Viaplana, G., & Villegas i Besora, M. (1990). *Constructivismo y psicoterapia* [Constructivism and psychotherapy]. Barcelona, Spain: PPU.

Goncalves, O. F. (1990). Psicologia clinica: Estado actual e perspectivas de futuro. [Clinical psychology: Current state and future trends]. *Jornal de Psicologia, 9,* 8–13.

Guidano, V. F. (1987). *Complexity of the self: A developmental approach to psychopathology and therapy.* New York: Guilford Press.

Guidano, V. F. (in press). *The self in process: Toward a post-rationalist cognitive therapy.* New York: Guilford Press.

43

Future Research Directions

Larry E. Beutler
University of California, Santa Barbara

John Clarkin
New York Hospital, Cornell Medical Center

This final chapter reaffirms the need for programmatic research and provides some guidelines for its implementation. We have seen that research programs differ in many ways, whether they seek simply to gain a heuristic understanding of psychotherapeutic change processes or to develop new or refined psychotherapeutic practices. Programs also differ, both across and within countries, in the amount of institutional and governmental support they enjoy and in the degree to which individual studies are integrated and organized around pragmatic or theoretically derived objectives. In spite of these wide ranging differences, the programs we have reviewed have been unified by a consistent emphasis on and appreciation for the importance of translating research knowledge into clinical practice.

Thus, it is striking that most observers believe that clinical research has added little to clinical practice to date (e.g., Barlow, 1981; Garfield, 1981). There are many reasons for this gap between knowledge and practice. We focus on some of the factors that we believe are central to the problem, evaluate the methods and means that will most constructively close this gap, and direct clinical researchers to the information that will be both acceptable and valuable for practitioners.

Translating Research Knowledge Into Clinical Practice

Psychotherapy research has not been helpful for the clinician, first, because of the low believability of the research yield. Despite numerous psychotherapy studies and numerous reviews of these studies, including meta-analytic reviews,

the consensus is that widely diverse therapies and procedures produce equivalent outcomes. This result is quite disappointing and may seem counterintuitive to the clinician. If clinicians accept the conclusion that all interventions are equivalent, it will be relatively easy for them to ignore the research and simply to do what they judge is best.

For those of us who are concerned about the development of fruitful research programs, the clinical utilization of research results, and the fine points of clinical practice, however, the verdict that all psychotherapies are equally effective for most conditions and patients demands further inspection. Reasons and arguments exist to suggest that the conclusion of equivalence may be erroneous (e.g., Beutler, Crago, & Arizmendi, 1986; Grawe, 1989; Stiles, Shapiro, & Elliott, 1986). For example, current research may have failed to reveal specific and differential therapeutic effects because we still lack sound measurement methods. Our instruments for measuring symptom change are reasonably good, but we have only a few (recent) instruments for assessing changes in interpersonal behavior and hardly any instruments at all for measuring the characterological or structural changes that may occur in psychotherapy (e.g., Lambert, Christensen, & DeJulio, 1983).

Still another difficulty of existing research is the problem of assessing the statistical compared with the clinical significance of outcomes. Traditionally the researcher has been most interested in statistical differences between group means, whereas the clinician has been most interested in the individual patient. Each patient will have similarities to and differences from the researchers' modal patient, and herein lies a major obstacle to the clinical utilization of research. As Jacobson, Follette, and Revenstorf (1984) pointed out, the usual research design utilizes an average improvement score for all subjects and thus gives no information about the effects of treatment for the individuals studied. Furthermore, although two treatments may reveal statistically significant differences because of a large sample size, the actual magnitude of differences between treatments may appear to be quite trivial to a clinician.

Jacobson et al. (1984) proposed conventions for assessing the clinical significance of outcome and suggested various ways to measure it. This work is in its early phases, but it does raise the hope that research designs that measure clinical significance will be of more value to the practicing clinician than current designs that report only statistical significance.

A third impediment to the easy translation of research findings resides in the researcher's penchant for seeking differential treatment effects on the basis of patient differences that are often considered to be of minor importance to the psychotherapist. Clinical diagnosis (e.g., endogenous compared with exogenous depression), for example, is the most frequently explored variable in research that seeks differential rates of response, but the dimensions of diagnosis seldom have relevance for the specific, moment-to-moment decisions made by the practicing therapist (Beutler, 1989). On the other hand, the theories that guide practitioners are diverse and propose a nearly endless variety of patient variables that may predict differential responses. Many of these variable cannot be researched and few are suitable for comparing different psychotherapy schools. The absence of a consensually accepted theoretical model of change processes may prevent us from narrowing the range of variables to those that may be most fruitfully targeted for investigation (cf. Beutler, 1989; Stiles et al., 1986).

We believe that research must proceed by following theory. In this case, we refer not to the need for another theoretical model of psychopathology but to the need for a theory of treatment selection. Although the usual theories that guide the clinician are based on the etiology of behavior, systematic theories of clinical decision making and change give greater weight to factors that maintain behavior and that set the stage for future behavior than they do to the unchangeable past. Only by implementing a systematic program of research that is based on a rational set of dimensions and principles of influence, however, can we hope to sort out the processes that make our treatments maximally successful.

Several programs in North America (e.g., Elliott, Howard, Beutler, and others in this book), the United Kingdom (Shapiro, this book), and continental Europe (e.g., Grawe and Meyer, this book) have attempted specifically to look at Therapy × Therapist × Patient × Setting interactions. Most of these efforts have been hampered by their post hoc methods, but their cumulative data may suggest general principles of treatment planning. From these principles, perhaps a treatment selection model for directing research efforts could be developed. All process and outcome research on psychotherapy and all studies of psychoactive medication used alone or in combination with psychotherapy contribute to a body of information that can be used to develop such a differential therapeutic system. Recently, Beutler and Clarkin (1990) reviewed a number of contemporary systems of clinical decision making (cf., Norcross, 1986) and attempted to utilize the best of these to arrive at a superordinate system for directing research efforts on treatment specificity.

The argument both for and against embarking on a detailed program of research examining the interactions (treatment by therapist by patient by problem area by setting) that would be relevant to the clinician is the staggering matrix of cells and subjects that must be used. Needless to say, the systematic exploration of all of these combinations would take several lifetimes if it were conducted in the form of isolated studies. This explains our belief that specific integrative models of treatment planning will guide the development of specific hypotheses and narrow our search for variables in which differences may be revealed.

The lack of resources is another important reason for the researcher's failure to provide answers to the clinician's questions. For a single outcome study to achieve maximum usefulness, it must investigate interactions among specific treatments, therapist qualities, patient factors, problem areas, and setting characteristics. This is a difficult task, and one that requires larger samples and more personnel than are usually available. In a typical study, for example, a group of individuals who are homogeneous only on one or two dimensions, some of which may represent relatively meaningless qualities for psychotherapy studies (cf., Beutler, 1989), may be provided with one of two packaged treatments that each include diverse elements, and the researchers may measure outcome with instruments that reflect only symptomatic change.

Such studies could be corrected with additional resources or with planning that is guided by clinical theories. The ability of such studies to address the specific effects of treatments is limited by the following:

• Patients are often selected for a specific diagnosis (e.g., schizophrenia) or a specific symptom (e.g., depression, phobia) because of availability rather than theoretical relevance.

• The specificity with which treatments are defined has improved with the construction of treatment manuals. Nevertheless, treatment manuals do not eliminate the differential outcome rates that are related to those therapist variables that are not controlled by the manual. The identification of such therapist contributors would help to clarify the role of manualized interventions.

• Most treatment studies concentrate on short-term individual treatment formats that are applied in 10 to 25 sessions. Thus, an indeterminant amount of relevant information is available for the clinician who utilizes group, family, and individual treatments over long periods of time.

• The outcome measures used in most isolated studies are in general quite disappointing to clinicians. Often these measures are not designed to pick up the differential effects of contrasting treatments. For example, although patients in cognitive treatment and interpersonal therapy may earn lower depression scores on a global clinical rating of depression at the end of treatment compared with scores at intake, individual research programs seldom allow a clear determination of the different mechanisms by which this change occurs.

• Because of limited resources and samples, it is difficult for isolated studies to assess other important areas of the individual's life that might contribute to changes. Such studies must always weigh the danger of overinterpretation and redundant analysis against the relevance of the questions asked.

Given the diversity of variables to be studied, the absence of a consensually accepted model for prioritizing targets of study, and the limited resources available to any study, it should not be surprising that few differences are found in isolated research projects. The diversity of samples, the breadth of measurement, and the variety of therapists and treatments needed to obtain the answers to our questions can best be obtained in longitudinally integrated programs. Even a cursory comparison of the foregoing proposal to the usual method of research demonstrates the advantages of programmatic research. Research occurring in the absence of a programmatic focus usually begins with a sample of patients defined mainly or entirely by diagnosis and then implements some control over only one component of a comprehensive treatment package, such as individual psychotherapy or a specific psychoactive drug. With no prior demonstration that the total package of treatment has any particular benefit, whatever effects are found may actually be the result of some other aspect of the formal or informal treatment being received by patients that is not being monitored and controlled by the research protocol. Under these circumstances, it is not surprising that results of similar studies on similar populations and similar treatments but different settings often produce different results.

Overall, the validity of conclusions may be greater if they are derived from a series of studies that are sequentially linked rather than from a collection of loosely related, individual projects. With this understanding, we can now turn to a consideration of the characteristics of sound research programs.

Developing a Program of Research

For psychotherapy research to be productive, it must have an established focus and a set of defined directions. Research plans can include both programmatic and methodological guidelines for individual studies. Programmatic guidelines set the long-term objectives, outline a coordinated plan of attack on these objectives, and prioritize the questions to be addressed by specific research projects. In contrast, methodological guidelines define the common and unique characteristics of the specific studies conducted within the long-term plan to preserve uniform quality and to maximize interstudy generalization.

Without attending both to programmatic objectives and to specific methodologies, research may be fragmented, methods may be inconsistent across studies, and findings may fail to advance the field in a focused direction. Numerous methodologically sound and interesting studies, each separately conducted but without a unifying set of objectives, do not lend themselves to the systematic, step-by-step accumulation of information from which new knowledge is best derived. Overarching programmatic objectives allow investigators to design specific studies in ways that minimize redundancies, allow for systematic cross-validation of findings, capitalize on comparable measures, and persistently move the research in maximally productive directions.

Programmatic research is particularly helpful for selecting and prioritizing researchable problems. Programmatic guidelines ensure that research on the myriad of variables that contribute to psychotherapeutic changes will emphasize certain properties:

• It will be both socially and politically relevant and will address questions that can be answered.

• It will sequentially address problems in an order of priority designed to maximize the accumulation of knowledge toward a focused set of objectives.

• It will develop hypotheses that, through sequential studies, will be disprovable as well as provable, thus allowing theory to evolve as an open rather than a closed system.

• It will be integrative in the sense that, rather than pitting one theory against another in a "dogma eat dogma" struggle, research will explore the ways in which different approaches, procedures, and viewpoints add to rather than subtract from one another.

• It will allow for the complexity of relationships among treatments, contexts, patients, and outcomes, avoiding the tendency to seek linear relationships between outcomes and single techniques or isolated patient and therapist variables.

Several writers (e.g., Klerman, 1983; Parloff, 1979; Strupp, 1986) have attempted to outline some of the limitations of treatment research, which will help other investigators define politically responsible directions while avoiding dead ends. The consensual opinion of these writers seems to be that treatment research has often failed to communicate its intentions and limitations to the public and to the policy maker. Few attempts have been made to control quality or to reconcile what is relevant with what is reachable. Strupp (1986) emphasized that relevant and

reachable goals can be defined by a clear understanding of the limitations of research, a concerted effort to avoid research models that are based on single techniques and single outcomes, a perspective of treatment that does not draw hard lines between specific and nonspecific therapeutic properties, and an awareness that mental health treatment is based on a specialized human relationship. These principles, incorporated into our theoretical definition of what is relevant and meaningful, will help to focus and strengthen our programmatic goals.

Kazdin (1983, 1986) has suggested that various psychotherapy research strategies can and perhaps should be ordered in particular patterns in a program of research to maximize efficiency. He suggested that research programs should integrate eight types of research strategies. These strategies include those that (a) develop internally consistent manuals (i.e., treatment package strategies); (b) assess the impact of isolated techniques from these packages (i.e., dismantling strategies); (c) explore the most effective or optimal method of administering specific procedures (i.e., parametric strategies); (d) assess the effects of combining specific procedures (i.e., constructive strategies); (e) determine the mechanisms through which specific procedures work (i.e., process strategies); (f) evaluate the impact of patient and therapist interaction (i.e., client–therapist variation strategies); (g) compare different treatment packages (i.e., comparative strategies); and (h) explore how manualized systems might best be combined (i.e., combined strategies).

The research strategies described by Kazdin (1986) can be combined in different ways, and not all may be incorporated in any given program of research. Nevertheless, there are some logical sequences that can best be incorporated into a broad research program. For example, it is logical first to develop packages of treatments that can be applied in reliable and competent ways and then to validate the efficacy of these programs or manuals. Only when comprehensive treatment packages and their constituent procedures have been tested for efficacy can one make meaningful statements abut why the procedures are important (rather than just different) and how they produce change.

Once the efficacy of these broad-band interventions has been established, then constructive and dismantling strategies designed to explore the effects of adding and subtracting specific procedures as well as parametric studies to refine the administration of these procedures will have more meaning. When the effects of specific procedures are then established, process research findings can be usefully applied to understand the mechanisms of change and the differences that exist among the procedures. The final step might explore variations in specific patient and therapist variables and attempt to integrate selected treatment manuals.

Some investigators have traditionally studied the specific processes or additive components of a treatment package with relatively little regard for establishing beforehand the efficacy of the treatment package itself. Demonstrations of differences between treatments at this level of process without efficacy data only have as much meaning as logic, rather than good science, will allow. Although process research is helpful in describing the differences among treatments, findings from such research say little about the mechanisms of therapeutic change and provide little information by which to increase treatment effectiveness. A long history of often unproductive research that has not been planned to proceed logically has led recent investigators (cf. Greenberg & Pinsoff, 1986) to argue for a closer tie between outcome and process data and to emphasize the need for a clear demonstration of clinical efficacy to precede pure process studies. Their arguments emphasize the advantages of establishing the process-to-outcome linkages from which the benefits of treatment derive. They also emphasize the importance of conceptually linked and sequentially constructed studies in a program of research.

Conclusion

To address the complexity of our clinical methods, programmatic rather than study-oriented research is needed. Only through planned programmatic efforts will we be able to tease apart the various components and interactions that contribute to treatment efficacy. Moreover, programmatically derived sequences of studies, such as those described in this book, offer the greatest hope for defining the variables that are important to therapeutic efforts and for providing the large samples of patients that are needed to assess statistically the relevance of our postulations.

Because it focuses on the task of developing and assessing models of prescriptive and differential treatment planning, this book may aid in establishing a third order of investigation. Just as individual research studies have their limitations, so

do programs such as those described here. Programs are necessarily limited by their guiding philosophies and available samples. Hence, there is some advantage in acknowledging some common principles around which collaborative research among major research centers might be developed. By accommodating the differences that characterize different programs and settings and by assimilating the common features, concerted efforts could be made to compare and contrast a wide variety of treatment packages, therapists, conditions, and outcome variables. Questions remain about the similarities among components of treatment packages; the effects of variations in setting, format, and duration of treatments; indicators for the combining of treatment components; methods for preparing the patient for treatment; methods for selecting compatible patients and enhancing treatment relationships; and methods for selecting psychotherapeutic menus and strategies (Beutler & Clarkin, 1990). These questions could be addressed by combining resources and opening the data banks of individual programs to other researchers across cultural boundaries.

Systematic demonstrations of efficacy and process conducted in some settings might be complemented by the naturalistic designs conducted in other settings. The limits to which efficacy could be generalized could be defined by the use of available meta-analytic procedures and several comparisons as well as by the use of different subsamples of patients, settings, therapists, and theoretical constructs. Then, the specific components in a comprehensive treatment package might be dismantled by using the collective resources of several programs and might be investigated by utilizing homogeneous patient samples and by systematically varying (adding or subtracting select elements) key treatment components (e.g., the modality or frequency of treatment). This procedure would eventually allow the various treatment domains (i.e., treatment contexts, relationship variables, and specific psychotherapeutic procedures) to be ordered by their contribution to benefit. Such a demonstration also would provide the rationale for looking at the specific components in each of these larger treatment domains, such as comparing methods of relationship enhancement for different patient types, exploring the distinguishing processes of psychotherapy among different patients, and studying the effects of varying specific therapeutic foci, levels of interventions, amounts of directiveness, and other aspects of psychotherapy procedures.

References

Barlow, D. H. (1981). On the relation of clinical research to clinical practice: Current issues, new directions. *Journal of Consulting and Clinical Psychology, 49*, 147–155.

Beutler, L. E. (1989). Differential treatment selection: The role of diagnosis in psychotherapy. *Psychotherapy, 26*, 271–281.

Beutler, L. E., & Clarkin, J. (1990). *Differential treatment selection: Toward prescriptive psychological treatments.* New York: Brunner/Mazel.

Beutler, L. E., Crago, M., & Arizmendi, T. G. (1986). Therapist variables in psychotherapy process and outcome. In S. L. Garfield & A. E. Bergin (Eds.), *Handbook of psychotherapy and behavior change* (3rd ed., pp. 257–310). New York: Wiley.

Garfield, S. L. (1981). Evaluating the psychotherapies. *Behavior Therapy, 12*, 295–307.

Grawe, K. (1989, September). *Differential effects of psychotherapies.* Paper presented at the Third European Conference on Psychotherapy Research, Berne, Switzerland.

Greenberg, L. S., & Pinsoff, W. M. (Eds.). (1986). *The psychotherapeutic process: A research handbook.* New York: Guilford Press.

Jacobson, N. S., Follette, W. C., & Revenstorf, D. (1984). Psychotherapy outcome research: Methods for reporting variability and evaluating clinical significance. *Behavior Therapy, 15*, 335–352.

Kazdin, A. E. (1983). Treatment research: The investigation and evaluation of psychotherapy. In M. Hersen, A. E. Kazdin, & A. S. Bellack (Eds.), *The clinical psychology handbook* (pp. 265–284). New York: Pergamon Press.

Kazdin, A. E. (1986). The evaluation of psychotherapy: Research design and methodology. In S. L. Garfield & A. E. Bergin (Eds.), *Handbook of psychotherapy and behavior change* (3rd ed., pp. 23–68). New York: Wiley.

Klerman, G. L. (1983). The efficacy of psychotherapy as the basis for public policy. *American Psychologist, 38*, 929–934.

Lambert, M. J., Christensen, E. R., & DeJulio, S. S. (Eds.). (1983). *The assessment of psychotherapy outcome.* New York: Wiley.

Norcross, J. C. (Eds.). (1986). *Handbook of eclectic psychotherapy.* New York: Brunner/Mazel.

Parloff, M. B. (1979). Can psychotherapy research guide the policymaker? A little knowledge may be a dangerous thing. *American Psychologist, 34*, 296–306.

Stiles, W. B., Shapiro, D. A., & Elliott, R. (1986). Are all psychotherapies equivalent? *American Psychologist, 41*, 165–180.

Strupp, H. H. (1986). Psychotherapy: Research, practice, and public policy (how to avoid dead ends). *American Psychologist, 41*, 120–130.